Medieval Answers

TO
MODERN PROBLEMS

Second Edition

EDITED BY

ALBRECHT CLASSEN

UNIVERSITY OF ARIZONA

cognella® | ACADEMIC PUBLISHING

Bassim Hamadeh, CEO and Publisher
Kassie Graves, Director of Acquisitions
Jamie Giganti, Senior Managing Editor
Jess Estrella, Senior Graphic Designer
David Miano, Senior Specialist Acquisitions Editor
Claire Benson, Project Editor
Elizabeth Rowe, Licensing Coordinator
Chelsey Schmid, Associate Editor

Cover Image   Copyright © Depositphotos/davidschrader.
               Copyright © Depositphotos/SWEvil.

Printed in the United States of America

ISBN: 978-1-5165-1091-7 (pbk) / 978-1-5165-1092-4 (br)

CONTENTS

DATELINE FOR THE MIDDLE AGES
By Albrecht Classen   1

INTRODUCTION TO THE MIDDLE AGES   5
By Emilie Amt and Albrecht Classen

THE CONSOLATION OF PHILOSOPHY   17
By Boethius

BOOK II (SELECTION)   29
By Boethius

BOOK III   37
By Boethius

THE SONG OF HILDEBRAND   51
By Anonymous

THE NIBELUNGENLIED   55
By Anonymous (circa. 1200)

OUR LADY'S TUMBLER   101
By Gautier de Coinci (1177–1236, Prior of Vic-sur-Aisne, France)

SIR LANVAL   107
By Marie de France

THE LAY OF THE TWO LOVERS   115
By Marie de France

BISCLAVRET   119
By Marie de France

THE LAY OF ELIDUC   123
By Marie de France

POEMS BY WALTHER VON DER VOGELWEIDE   135
By Walther von der Vogelweide

UNDER THE LINDEN   141
By Walther von der Vogelweide

THE UNFORTUNATE LORD HEINRICH   143
By Hartmann von Aue

DIVINA COMMEDIA: HELL   157
By Dante Alighieri

THE NATURE OF A TRUE PRINCE   173
By John of Salisbury

THE PROBLEMS OF A CHRISTIAN HUMANIST   179
By John of Salisbury

A PHILOSOPHY OF HISTORY   183
By Otto of Freising

THE VISION OF GOD   187
By Nicholas of Cusa

THE LIFE OF CHARLEMAGNE   191
By Einhard

CHARLEMAGNE'S INCOME FROM HIS FARMS   197
By Charlemagne

ENGLAND IN THE MIDDLE AGES   199
By King Alfred, his Introduction to the Pastoral Charge by Gregory the Great

BRUNO, THE IDEAL OF A SCHOLAR IN THE TENTH CENTURY   201
By Ruotger

TALES ILLUSTRATING THE MIRACULOUS POWER OF THE SACRAMENTS   203
By Caesarius of Heisterbach, Jacques de Vitry, Stephen of Bourbon

TALES ILLUSTRATING THE MEDIEVAL ATTITUDE TOWARD HERETICS   207
By Caesarius of Heisterbach

THE EUCHARIST AS A CHARM   211
By Caesarius of Heisterbach

CONFESSION, ORDEAL AND MIRACLE   215
By Caesarius of Heisterbach

ADMONITIONS OF THE BLESSED FATHER ST. FRANCIS TO HIS BRETHREN   217
By St. Francis of Assisi

ATTITUDE OF THE CIVIL GOVERNMENT TOWARD HERETICS   239
Law Issued by Emperor Frederick II (for Sicily, ca. 1235)

MEDIEVAL IDEAS OF THE EARTH AND STARS   243
By Anonymous

QUESTIONS IN ABELARD'S *YEA AND NAY*   247
By Peter Abelard

PROLOGUE TO *SIC ET NON*   249
By Peter Abelard

ON THE FAME OF ABELARD   253
By Heloise

ROGER BACON AND THE BEGINNING OF MODERN EXPERIMENTAL
SCIENCE   257
By Roger Bacon

EXPERIMENTAL SCIENCE CONT.   259
By Roger Bacon

MARSIGLIO OF PADUA AND HIS "DEFENDER OF PEACE"   265
By Marsiglio of Padua

THE DECAMERON   269
By Giovanni Boccaccio

SIR GAWAIN AND THE GREEN KNIGHT   293
By Anonymous

SOME LYRIC POEMS OF CHRISTINE DE PIZAN   319
By Christine de Pizan

MUTACION DE FORTUNE (BOOK OF FORTUNE'S TRANSFORMATION)   329
By Christine de Pizan

ON THE PEACE OF FAITH   335
By Nicholas of Cusa

THE PLOWMAN AND DEATH   365
By Johann Tepl

Dateline for the Middle Ages

By Albrecht Classen

Ca. 750	B.C.E. Foundation of Rome
Ca. 3rd–5th c.	C.E. Age of Migration
313	Edict of Milan: Toleration of Christians
324–337	Emperor Constantine
476	Romulus Augustulus (last Roman Emperor) forced to abdicate by Odoacer
772–814	Charlemagne rules the Carolingian Empire; beginning of the Middle Ages
8th–10th c.	Christianization of Europe
8th–10th c.	Attacks by Arabs and Vikings
9th and 10th c.	Establishment of England, France, and Germany, along with smaller states on the Iberian Peninsula
10th c.	Development of the Empire of Kiev
1066	William the Conqueror defeats the English King Harold, controls all of England
8th–12th c.	Romanesque art and architecture

8th–9th c.	Carolingian Renaissance
9th c.	*Beowulf*
ca. 1071–ca. 1141	Judah Halevi, *Book of the Kuzari*
1096–1099	First Crusade
1291	Last Christian fortress, Acre, falls against the Muslims
10th and 11th c.	Scandinavian countries, Poland, and other kingdoms in the east form
1179–1241	Snorri Sturluson, *Edda*
12th–14th c.	Beginning of the colonization of central and eastern Europe from the west
12th–15th c.	Gothic art and architecture
12th c.	Twelfth-Century Renaissance
12th–13th c.	High point of courtly literature: Chrétien de Troyes, *troubadour* poets, Marie de France, Hartmann von Aue, Walther von der Vogelweide, Wolfram von Eschenbach (ca. 1205), Gottfried von Strassburg (ca. 1210), German *minnesinger*, and Italian poets of the *stil dolce nuovo*
ca. 1220–1240	Guillaume de Lorris, *Roman de la rose*
ca. 1235/40–1305	Jean de Meun, continuator of the *Roman de la rose*
1265–1321	Dante Alighieri, *Divina Commedia*
13th c.	Attack by Mongols (death of Dschinghis Khan in 1241)
12th–15th c.	Evolution of the trade organization *Hanse*/Hanseatic League
1304–1374	Francesco Petrarca
1313–1375	Giovanni Boccaccio
11th–15th c.	Reconquista on the Iberian Peninsula (last Arabic fortress, Granada, falls in 1492)

1339–1453	Hundred Years' War between England and France
1347–1351	Black Death
ca. 1343–1400	Geoffrey Chaucer, *Canterbury Tales*
14th–15th c.	Rise of national states in Europe (Switzerland, Bohemia, England, France, Spain, Denmark, Lithuania, Poland, Russia, etc.)
ca. 1364–1430	Christine de Pizan, feminist writer, prolific author
14th–15th c.	Growth of cities all over Europe
14th–15th c.	Italian Renaissance, which then spreads to other parts of Europe
1453	Mohammed II conquers Constantinople—the end of the Eastern Roman Empire
ca. 1450	Johannes Gutenberg invents the moveable type/printing press
1492	Christopher Columbus discovers America

INTRODUCTION TO THE MIDDLE AGES

By Emilie Amt and Albrecht Classen

INTRODUCTION BY EMILIE AMT FROM *WOMEN'S LIVES IN MEDIEVAL EUROPE. A SOURCEBOOK*

Until the fifth century A.D., much of **western Europe** lay within the **Roman Empire**, a vast collection of territories including parts of the Middle East and North Africa. In Europe itself during the centuries of Roman rule, much of the native Celtic population had become highly Romanized in its culture, political allegiance, and legal practices. In the last few centuries of the Roman Empire, the Germanic tribes that had long lived on the eastern fringes of the European provinces moved into the Romanized lands in large numbers. This wave of "**barbarian**" **invasions**, along with severe political and economic problems, gradually killed off the Roman Empire, which was replaced by a number of **Germanic successor kingdoms**, including those of the Franks in Gaul (modern France), the Visigoths in Spain, the Ostrogoths in Italy, the Burgundians in and around what is now Switzerland, and the Anglo-Saxons in England.

The Germanic tribes brought with them a very different society from that of Rome. Whereas Roman civilization was highly **urbanized**, for example, the Germans had until then seldom settled even in **villages**. The Romans had a long history of **written legislation**; the Germans used a system of **customary law** that had not yet been written down. Different practices regarding marriage and family can be seen in the extracts from Roman and Germanic law in this book. Centuries of contact between the Germans and the empire, however, had wrought changes on both sides, and now, as the Germans settled in what had long been Roman territory, further mingling of the two cultures occurred. The Germanic kingdoms that were established inside the old boundaries of the now defunct empire were by no means entirely Germanic in their ethnic makeup or their culture.

Even more influential than Roman tradition in this process of change was the religion of the late Roman Empire. Christianity had originated in Palestine, where a small group of **Jews** believed that the Jewish carpenter Jesus, who had been executed by the Roman authorities early in the first century A.D., was the "Christ," the son of God and savior of humanity. Although Christians were persecuted at first by both the Jewish religious authorities and the Roman government, their religion survived and spread. In the year 313 it achieved official sanction from the Roman emperor Constantine, and in the late fourth century it became the official religion of the empire. The cultural initiative of the late Roman Empire passed from pagan writers to Christian theologians such as **St. Jerome and St. Augustine of Hippo**, who explored the details of Christian belief and laid the foundation for church law. It was the Christian church, too, which filled the vacuum in leadership during the fifth century, as the Roman world faced widespread military, political, and economic crises and the Roman government crumbled. Bishops began to provide the services for which the government had once been responsible; in particular, the bishop of Rome came to assume a prominent role in Italy, so much so that as the **pope** he was eventually recognized as the leader of the church throughout the western Mediterranean regions. Clergymen and monks also preserved what ancient learning survived the fall of the Roman Empire in the west, and throughout most of the Middle Ages the church maintained a near monopoly on literacy and education.

The church was eager to **convert** the **pagan** Germans to Christianity. It accomplished this through intensive mission work and through alliances with Germanic kings, queens, and nobles, who saw advantages to themselves in allying with the existing authority in their new territories. Christian beliefs, including ideas about women, marriage, and family, had already mingled with Roman traditions. Now Christian views were adopted by the Germanic settlers as well. Thus the three main ingredients of medieval European civilization had come together: **the Roman, the Germanic, and the Christian**.

The period from the fifth century to the eleventh is often designated the "**Early Middle Ages**." This is the time sometimes known as the "**Dark Ages**" in part because of the collapse of Roman civilization, with the loss of much classical knowledge, but also because relatively few historical sources remain to tell us of the events of these years. The documents that do survive include the laws which the Germanic kings were by now having written down and the works of historians such as **Gregory of Tours**. Much of the essential character of medieval Europe was already apparent in this early period, especially in religious matters. **Monasteries** and **convents**, for example, came to play a key role in economic and cultural life, and many noble families dedicated sons and daughters to the religious life, in which they lived according to a monastic "rule," such as that of **Benedict of Nursia** and **Caesarius of Arles**. Women were encouraged to be nuns, but their other options in the church—serving as deaconesses or in partnership with husbands who were priests—were closed off by the decisions of church councils. These councils established "canon law" or church law, which regulated the lives of members of the clergy and many aspects of private life for lay people. For most of the laity, canon law was enforced by the local priest, who heard one's confession regularly and assigned penance for one's sins. Thus the church gradually succeeded in imposing on secular society its standards of behavior in areas such as marriage.

The political face of early medieval Europe was dominated by the **Franks**, and in the eighth century the Frankish kingdom under **Charlemagne** (768–814 A.D.) and his descendants conquered and ruled many neighboring kingdoms. The resulting **Carolingian Empire** included much of what is now France, Germany, and Italy. Among their other activities, the emperors promulgated new rules for the administration of the empire and their own estates, some of which survive to inform us about everyday life in Carolingian Europe. In this new realm, cultural energy reached a height unknown since the days of Roman power. The rich intellectual life of the royal court produced many of the written works of the period, but relatively isolated individuals, such as the noblewoman **Dhuoda**, who lived in the pre-Carolingian time of the Merovingians, could also be well educated.

While the Carolingian Empire flourished, however, the west was beginning to suffer **invasions** by three new groups: the Scandinavian **Vikings**, the North African Muslim **Saracens**, and the Asian **Magyars**. Under these onslaughts and other stresses in the ninth and tenth centuries, imperial government once again collapsed, and

Europe entered another period of political fragmentation. This time, the surviving political units were small kingdoms, duchies, and counties, ruled by local nobles who could offer some degree of protection to their followers. The bond between a lord and each his followers, or vassals, became an important one in many parts of western Europe during these years. Noblemen put themselves under the lordship of more powerful men who could grant them estates called "**fiefs**" (from the Latin feud um) in return for loyalty and military service. Such **feudal** relationships dominated many aspects of life for the ruling classes in the centuries to follow.

The period from the eleventh century through the thirteenth is often called the "**High Middle Ages**." Underlying much of the history of these years was a widespread **economic revival** in Europe, which had begun long before the eleventh century in some parts of the continent and continued throughout the High Middle Ages in others. New **technology** (new plow, field rotation, water mill, etc.), a slightly improved **climate** and expanding **frontiers** gradually raised the standard of living and produced surpluses which formed the basis for a commercial boom. **Towns** flourished as centers of trade, and the town-dwelling population, which made its living in trade and industry, grew. The use of **money** as a medium of exchange increased, along with **banking** and written record-keeping. Townspeople organized themselves into guilds: the merchant **guild**, which often served as a sort of town government, included only the wealthiest citizens, while each industry had its own craft guild, which set standards and regulated the industry and to which all practitioners of that trade belonged. Towns were often able to use their wealth to buy a certain amount of independence from their lords.

Christianity in the High Middle Ages was characterized by an increasing variety of activities and outlooks. In the eleventh century the church struggled overtly with **secular authorities for ecclesiastical power** and independence, and in the twelfth century **canon lawyers** like **Gratian** codified church policy and reasserted its pre-eminence in many areas of life. In 1095, the increasingly militant church launched the first of the **Crusades**, papally **sanctioned holy wars** against the Muslims of the **Holy Land** and Spain and against **heretics** in Europe. The **Crusades** would last through the thirteenth century (1291), and one of their unintended effects was the widespread persecution of the **Jewish minority** in Europe. Another characteristic of high medieval religion was dissatisfaction with the wealth, worldliness, and soft living that critics perceived in many monasteries and convents. New "reform" orders of monks—and less often of nuns—were founded in the late eleventh century, only to become so worldly themselves that a new wave of reform was called for in the early thirteenth century. From this second wave came the **Dominican and Franciscan** orders, including the Poor Clares. Large numbers of Christians also turned to less formal religious movements, such as that of the **Beguines** and their male counterparts, the **Beghards**. **Mysticism**, the direct communication of the soul with God, was practiced by such respected individuals as **Hildegard of Bingen** and **St. Bernard of Clairvaux**. Some groups, such as the **Waldensians**, found that their spiritual enthusiasm led them into beliefs and practices condemned by the church; and this upsurge in heresy in the twelfth and thirteenth centuries caused the church to found the Inquisition to deal with Christians who had strayed from the fold.

Many of these religious developments centered on towns and cities, and so too did the new forms of higher education. The **cathedral schools** of the twelfth century and the **universities** of the thirteenth century were urban institutions. While women participated fully in the religious revival of these years, they were excluded from formal higher education once the university became the standard seat of learning. The **universities** also guarded their monopoly on certain fields, such as medicine, carefully. In other spheres of culture, however, noblewomen played a prominent role, serving as patrons and producers of music and poetry and shaping the codes of chivalry and courtly love, which softened the hard-working and unromantic lives of the nobility.

Medieval writers commonly divided the members of society into **three estates** or "orders": those who fought, those who prayed, and those who worked. While the estates were often described in terms of men only, in reality women belonged to or were attached to each of them.

The "fighters" were the knights or noblemen, whose wealth, power, and status derived from their lands; for this reason, they were willing to swear allegiance to the lords who gave them fiefs and let their heirs inherit these. The women of this estate did not normally fight, but they shared in the other jobs of the nobility, running households and estates; and the concern with land shaped every noblewoman's life in fundamental ways, such as the choice of a husband.

The praying estate consisted of the clergy and the monastic community, and while women were excluded from the former, they made up a sizeable and often active portion of the latter. The third estate, the workers, did not mean everyone who worked—for virtually everyone, including nobles, monks, and nuns, did work in medieval society—but those whose position in society was defined by their **manual labor**: **artisans, servants**, and the **peasantry**. Artisans might work for themselves or as employees; servants worked for employers or their lords. **Peasants** worked the land, raising their own food and supporting their lords. There were many degrees of social status within the working estate, even among the peasantry. Some peasants were free, but most were serfs or villeins, who were not slaves but were legally bound to the land and required to perform certain work for their lords. Serfs might hope to achieve freedom through manumission or by running away to a town, where the law often granted them freedom if they remained for a set length of time, often a year and a day. Women participated fully in the working life in industry, domestic service, and agriculture.

Many aspects of life, culture, and institutions were similar across medieval Europe, but there were also important differences from region to region, in agricultural and industrial products, in political and social organization, and in the ethnic and religious makeup of the population. The **towns of Italy**, for example, tended to be freer of outside control than were most European towns, and some of them specialized in Mediterranean trade, which brought eastern luxury goods to the west. The **Iberian Peninsula** comprised Muslim territories in the south along with a number of small Christian principalities in the north, and the warfare between them was a major factor in shaping Spanish society. At the same time, Germans were pushing eastward into the lands of the pagan Slavs, bringing new lands into cultivation, on which grain was grown for much of Europe and which drew surplus peasants eastward as settlers. The German king also claimed the prestigious title of **Holy Roman Emperor** and lands stretching as far south as central Italy; yet the real power in Germany usually lay with the territorial princes and the bishops, and few emperors were able to assert control in Italy. The **kings of France**, on the other hand, steadily enlarged their territories and their control over their vassals, forming alliances with rich towns and with the church. **Wine** was already one of the major products of the thriving French economy, and a new market for French wine was one of the results when a Norman French duke, **William the Conqueror**, conquered the **Anglo-Saxon** kingdom of England in **1066** and replaced the old Anglo-Saxon nobility there with French noble families. England's greatest export was raw wool, large amounts of which were sold to the towns of **Flanders**, a particularly important center for cloth making on the northern French coast. Medieval merchants visited **fairs** across the continent, and while the vast majority of Europeans probably never traveled far from the place of their birth, pilgrims, scholars, and soldiers also helped to spread goods, news, and ideas.

The fourteenth and fifteenth centuries, known as the **Later Middle Ages**, are best known for the **traumas** they brought. Population growth had already begun to slow in the early fourteenth century, before the **Black Death**, or bubonic plague, killed between a quarter and a third of the entire population of Europe in 1347–49 or even 1351. For the next few centuries, this terrifying disease would continue to break out periodically. The initial plague left behind a land surplus and a severe labor shortage, which enabled peasants and workers to win improved legal status, pay, and conditions; their lords and employers then attempted to limit such gains through laws controlling wages and prices. Meanwhile, England and France engaged in a long series of wars known collectively as the **Hundred Years' War** (1337–1453), which battered the French countryside and left England in political disarray. Yet this period of upheaval was also the backdrop to a great deal of cultural activity, such as the period in which **Christine de Pizan** participated at the French royal court and the literary and artistic developments in fourteenth- and fifteenth-century Italy, which are known today as the **Renaissance** (**Petrarch** and **Boccaccio**).

The modern reader may encounter certain difficulties in reading medieval texts. For example, there are strong religious elements and ecclesiastical biases in many of the documents here, which may be alien or frustrating to the reader familiar with a more secular society. This is in part because medieval Europe was indeed a highly religious civilization, and the modern reader must therefore resist the urge to dismiss the true religious feelings and important religious motivations of the men and women who appear in these sources. **Miracles and religious visions** were accepted as real by many or most people. The church itself was an integral part of the power structure, controlling vast wealth and wielding great political influence and judicial power. Religious differences even defined marginal and persecuted groups within society (Jews, Muslims, and heretics). The church's views played a large part in shaping secular laws and social norms, and sex roles and gender constructs are perhaps the areas in which this is most obvious. On the other hand, the religious viewpoint of the sources can sometimes distort our view of even religious subjects. Much of the written material that survives from the Middle Ages was written by churchmen, but this does not mean that churchmen spoke for everyone.

Similarly, the reader should be aware that medieval standards of truth, originality, and accuracy were not the same as ours. Supernatural explanations of events were more widely accepted than they are today. Authors of literature and history borrowed freely from other works, and the boundaries between myth, story, and history were not clear ones. But medieval thinkers were also keenly aware of mathematical precision, arithmetic, medical research, geometry, philosophical logic, etc. They were different from us, but in many ways still the same. We encounter the phenomenon of **alterity**—difference within the framework of similarity.

INTRODUCTION TO THIS TEXT, BY ALBRECHT CLASSEN

Considering the **end of the Middle Ages**, we face similarly difficult issues with identifying a clear historical limit, since the transition from one period to another cannot be easily determined. Whereas older research tended to conceive of a sharp divide between the Middle Ages and the (Italian) Renaissance, most modern scholars assume that we are dealing with a long transitional period which ultimately led to the establishment of the early modern world. There are many ways to identify the beginning of the Renaissance, whether with the discovery of the individual (Jules **Michelet**, *Renaissance*, 1855; Jacob **Burckhardt**, *The Civilization of the Renaissance in Italy*, 1860), or with the emergence of a new style of painting, based on the principle of the central perspective and realism, or with the rediscovery of the classical world of antiquity, or with the development of Neoplatonism. Our critical examination of fourteenth- and fifteenth-century arts, literature, philosophy, music, religion, and architecture has, however, shattered this conviction of an absolutely innovative **paradigm shift**. Certainly, the Gothic style was replaced by the Renaissance style, and scholars and poets such as Petrarch, Boccaccio, and

Poggio Bracciolini rediscovered the language and literature of ancient Rome once again, but they were not the first ones to do so, and they were also not necessarily embracing an entirely different intellectual approach. In fact, both in the eighth and in the twelfth century a renewed interest in the philosophers and poets from antiquity had already triggered strong revivalism in the schools, in the administrations, at the courts, and within the Church. In other words, Petrarch and Boccaccio had significant forerunners, such as Alcuin at the court of Charlemagne (eighth century), and, about three hundred fifty years later, Peter Abelard, John of Salisbury, and Bernard of Clairvaux (twelfth century). It makes perfect sense to talk about the "Eighth-Century Renaissance" and the "Twelfth-Century Renaissance" as equally powerful periods of innovation and invigoration compared with the "Italian Renaissance."

Scholars have often referred to the emergence of the early-modern **city life** with its money-based economy as a significant indication of the end of the Middle Age, but the ancient Roman cities had never fully ceased to exist throughout the centuries, and many of the major urban centers that dominated the fifteenth and sixteenth centuries had been founded between the tenth and the twelfth century by the Vikings in the West, by French, Dutch, German, and Italian lords in the western and southern parts of the continent, and by the Slavic lords in the eastern parts. The rise of the class of burghers throughout the thirteenth and fourteenth centuries did not necessarily imply a decline of the aristocracy, rather required them to adapt to a new way of life for their own survival. By the same token, we know of many **wealthy bankers** who quickly tried to imitate aristocracy, purchasing castles and adopting courtly manners. Many late-medieval cities organized knightly tournaments for their own entertainment, and the early-modern book market saw a strong interest in chapbooks with chivalric themes and heroes. Inversely, the development of a strongly capitalistic society can be traced back at least to the twelfth and thirteenth century when the Anglo-Norman poet Marie de France and the German poets Walther von der Vogelweide and Boppe clearly addressed the relevance of money as the foundation of a comfortable lifestyle irrespective of the personal standing within one specific class. We ought not to forget that even in military, or technological, terms, knighthood increasingly faced severe challenges, first by the establishment of English and Swiss armies of foot soldiers equipped with the longbow, the Swiss pike, the crossbow, and eventually, by the end of the fourteenth century, with early types of firearms. **Gunpowder**, allegedly invented around 1300 by the German monk Berthold Schwarz of Freiberg, or by the English scholar and scientist Francis Bacon (1214–1292)—if it was not imported by traders from China or Persia—ultimately doomed medieval knighthood, though the ideals of chivalry and the strict separation of estates—clergy, aristocracy, and common people—did not disappear until the nineteenth century. This also led to the rise of the early **modern nation**, or statehood, especially England, Spain, and France.

Several other monumental events lend themselves for the identification of the end of the Middle Ages. In **1453** the ancient city **Constantinople** was conquered by the Ottoman Turks, and with the fall of this city the end of the Eastern Roman Empire had arrived. Large numbers of Greek scholars, poets, and other intellectuals sought refuge in the West, primarily in Italy, where they introduced the knowledge of Greek. At first, the fall of Constantinople did not effect a tremendous change, but militarily the Turks had breached the final defense barrier against Europe and soon after began their constant onslaught against the Balkans, Hungary, and eventually Austria. This was to put the European powers, including Venice and Genoa, under tremendous pressure until they finally gained the upper hand in the early seventeenth century. On a different level, the introduction of Greek in Europe made it possible for many intellectuals to gain personal knowledge of the ancient sources of philosophy and religion in their original language. The refugees from Constantinople, however, were not the first Greek teachers in Europe. The conquest of Constantinople in 1204 in the course of the Fourth Crusade had destroyed the old power structures there and opened, despite the cruel destruction of the city, the contacts between the Latin West and the Greek East. Many Greek manuscripts arrived in the West, along with such magnificent teachers as Manuel Chrysoloras, who assumed his assignment in Florence in 1397, and George of Trebizond, who began teaching Greek in Mantua in 1420.

The development of **humanism**, supported by intellectuals such as **Erasmus of Rotterdam** (1465–1536), made available the world of ancient Greek antiquity and slowly transformed the entire medieval world view. **Martin Luther**, for example, learned Greek and was thus able to translate the New Testament from the sources (*ad fontes*) in 1522, laying the textual foundation for the Protestant Reformation. Nevertheless, we should not forget that during the early twelfth century many texts by ancient Greek philosophers, medical experts, and scientists, which had been only preserved in Arabic translations, became known in Europe first through Hebrew then through Latin translations, most of them produced at the universities of Salerno (near Naples) and Toledo (Spain).

When **Johann Gutenberg** invented the **printing press** (movable type) in Mainz, Germany, ca. 1450, this did not immediately lead to a profound paradigm shift. In fact, for decades the traditional manuscript culture continued to dominate the book markets, whereas the early prints—incunabula (until ca. 1500)—remained very expensive and were used to reproduce the biblical texts. Beginning with the early sixteenth century, however, the print media gained the upper hand and ushered in a revolution in public communication, information transfer, data storage, and intellectual discourse. Nevertheless, it would be erroneous to identify this transformation as a quick and absolute victory. On the contrary, the manuscript remained a strong element far into the sixteenth century, whereas the print culture did not replace the medieval tradition until the 1520s and 1530s.

Even the **Protestant Reformation** was not the absolute death knell to the Middle Ages. Martin Luther did not intend at all to destroy the Catholic Church when he allegedly nailed his ninety-five theses on the church door at Wittenberg on October 31, 1517. On the contrary, the Church had been severely criticized by clerics such as the British **John Wyclif** (1328–1384) and the Czech **John Hus** (1369–1415), not to mention scores of other theologians throughout the fourteenth and fifteenth centuries. Before that, the **Albigensians**, or **Cathars**, in Southern France and elsewhere, who were crushed in two crusades in 1209 and 1213, and the **Waldensians** in Eastern France, Southern Germany, and Western Switzerland, who were excommunicated in 1184 but later readmitted into the Church under strict regulations, had radically criticized the Catholic theology and Church practice. Luther in turn attempted to introduce reforms of a church that suffered from serious moral and ethical decline. Anti-clericalism had been rampant throughout the late Middle Ages, especially since the French Pope Clement V (1305–1314) had established himself in **Avignon** in 1309, the beginning of the so-called "**Babylonian Captivity**." The subsequent six popes also stayed there because of political unrest in Italy and because they yielded to the pressure of the French kings. The time of Avignon came to an end in 1377 when Pope Gregory XI (1370–1378) finally returned the Holy See to Rome. **Simony**, a common practice in the late-medieval church to sell offices to the highest bidder, was furiously criticized, but mostly without any effect. Moreover, by the end of the Middle Ages the strict rule of **celibacy** for clerics, enforced since the early Middle Ages (eleventh century, above all, as part of the **Gregorian Reform**), was often broken and disregarded. Not surprisingly, late-medieval and early Renaissance literature is filled with satires and bitter attacks against lecherous priests and other clerics. Between 1387 and 1415, several popes competed against each other, each of them claiming to be the only representative of Saint Peter here on earth, until finally the German Emperor Sigismund dethroned all three and nominated Pope Martin V (1417–1431) as the true successor, thus ending the highly destructive **schism** within the Catholic Church. Finally, throughout the fifteenth century the common practice of selling indulgence letters all over Europe for the redemption of one's sins and even those of deceased family members led to excessive abuse and strongly contributed to the genesis of the Protestant Reformation. The latter seems to have been revolutionary because of its sudden and forceful development, but the general decline of the Catholic Church throughout the entire late Middle Ages led to this final point, which then rang in a new era in which at first just two, but soon many other, Christian churches emerged, all competing against each other for recognition, power, and influence. This eventually led to disastrous religious wars throughout the sixteenth and seventeenth centuries.

We also must not forget the enormous widening of the geological perspective, begun with the **(re-)discovery of America** through Columbus in 1492. Soon, **Vasco da Gama** discovered the route around South Africa to reach India (1497–1499). The Bible had never even mentioned the New World, so this was a profound paradigm shift for the Europeans.

The Literary History

The literary history of medieval Europe can be generally divided into three major periods: the **early Middle Ages**, the **high Middle Ages**, and the **late Middle Ages** (the same applies to the history of arts and philosophy). Before courtly culture emerged in western and central Europe, Old English, Old High German, Old French, and Old Spanish poets produced predominantly **heroic epics** such as *Beowulf* (OE), the *Hildebrandslied* (OHG), the *Waltharilied* (medieval Latin), *El poema di mio Cid* (OS), the *Chanson de Roland* (OF), and, as a very late representative, the *Nibelungenlied* (Middle High German), which was followed by many Old Norse and Icelandic sagas and epics collected in the *Edda*. The common elements to them all are the heroic ideal, the fatalistic approach to life, the existential experience of the protagonists, and almost always the absence of religious concerns. **Beowulf**, for instance, confronts the monster Grendel and kills it. Subsequently, Grendel's mother attacks Beowulf, but he manages to overcome her as well and kills her. At the end, probably in his old age, Beowulf fights against a dragon and slays it, but he as well succumbs in this struggle. In the **Hildebrandslied**, the old but war-experienced father Hildebrand is challenged by his son Hadubrand, who does not want to believe that Hildebrand is his father and who believes himself to be a Hun because of his appearance. The ensuing battle dooms them to their heroic destiny, though we are missing the conclusion because of text loss. Tragedy strikes them at any case, whether the father kills his son, or the son his father, or whether both die. Both in the **Poema de Mio Cid** and in the **Chanson de Roland**—the German poet Pfaffe Konrad (Cleric Konrad) translated this as *Rolandslied*—the protagonists struggle primarily against Muslims (medieval sources: Saracens) and also traitors within the Christian camp. In the **Njal's Saga**, the hero faces many opponents within his own community and eventually succumbs to its evil mindset, though he dies a heroic death and is glorified by the survivors. Remarkably, he struggles for a long time to avoid bloody conflicts and resorts to legal means, and yet his enemies eventually overpower him and burn him and his wife to death, along with other mighty family members. Heroic poetry, however, does not simply glorify the gory details and the existential struggle. In fact, most of the poems offer powerful messages about the consequences of failed human communication, the breakdown of a community, the loss of justice, ethical principles, and individual honor.

Mystical Literature

The high and late Middle Ages also witnessed the emergence of highly unusual but most powerful mystical literature in which religious visionaries related their spiritual experiences with the Godhead both in Latin and in the vernacular. Among the women mystics we find regular members of convents and abbesses, many beguines, and also religious individuals living in the world outside of the Church. The most important mystics were **Hildegard of Bingen** (1098–1179), Elisabeth of Schönau (1129–1165), Marie d'Oignies (1177–1213), Hadewijch of Brabant (early thirteenth century), **Mechthild of Magdeburg** (1207–1282), St. Gertrude the Great (1241–1298), St. Clare of Assisi (1196–1253), Angela of Foligno (1248–1309), **St. Bridget of Sweden** (1302/03–1373), **St. Catherine of Siena** (1347–1380), **Marguerite Porete** (d. 1310), Julian of Norwich (1343–1413), **Margery Kempe** (1373–1439). St. Bernard of Clairvaux (1090–1153), Hugh (1096/1100–1141), Richard of St. Victor (d. 1173), Meister Eckhart (1260–1328), Heinrich Seuse (Henry Suso) (1295–1366), and Johannes Tauler (1300–1361). Not all of them had really mystical visions. Many worked more as intellectuals/theologians, enjoying the highest respect and influence among the male mystics, but they also deeply influenced some of the women mystics. In a way, we also would have to count **St. Francis of Assisi** (1182–1226), the founder of the Franciscans, who only wrote few texts (mostly rules for his order, *Opuscula*), but spurred a huge flood of Franciscan spiritual literature, and the Italian poet Jacopone da Todi (ca. 1236–1306) among the most significant mystical authors, though this stretches the definition of mysticism. There were also many Muslim and Jewish mystics in the wider sense of the word.

Religious literature also enjoyed tremendous popularity, both in Latin and in the various vernaculars, such as **Iacobus de Voragine's** *Legenda Aurea*, or *Golden Legend* (1258–1270), consisting of 180 short lives of the saints. Many Latin authors wrote beast epics and bestiaries, hymns, biographies, hagiographies, pastoralia, debate poems, travel literature, dramas, exempla, proverbs and epigrams, and satires.

Literature of the High Middle Ages

In the wake of the crusades, and also as a consequence of the cultural contacts with the Arabic world—highly refined and sophisticated in its living conditions, scholarship, architecture, and philosophy at that time—European knighthood was familiarized with a much more advanced culture and quickly copied many of its features. At the same time, originating in the Provence, the ideas of **courtly love** emerged, expressed in courtly love poetry by the *troubadours*, who soon inspired the *trouvères* in northern France, and the *minnesingers* in Germany, finally followed by the Italian (and Sicilian) poets of the *dolce stil nuovo*.

From ca. 1165 onward the French poet **Chrétien de Troyes**, drawing from Geoffrey of Monmouth's *Histories of the Kings of Britain* (ca. 1137) and Robert Wace's *Roman de Brut* (ca. 1155), introduced the idea of King Arthur through his various courtly romances (*Erec et Enide*, *Cligès*, *Lancelot*, *Yvain*, and *Les Contes de Graal ou Perceval li Galois*). The Swabian poet **Hartmann von Aue** translated the first two romances into Middle High German, along with love poetry, a religious tale, *Gregorius*, and a love tale, *Poor Henry*, and the Bavarian poet **Wolfram von Eschenbach** adapted Chrétien's *Perceval* as *Parzival*. The latter also composed the crusade epic *Willehalm*, beautiful dawn songs, and the fragmentary piece *Titurel*. **Gottfried von Strassburg** composed one of the most famous versions of the rich, European-wide tradition of the *Tristan* romance in ca. 1210, and this was followed by many other courtly romances and verse narratives written by other German, French, Italian, Spanish, and English poets.

In England, **Marie de France**, apart from her *fables* and a visionary text (*Saint Patrick's Purgatory*) produced her famous amatory narratives, her *lais* (ca. 1170–1200). The French court chaplain **Andreas Capellanus**, on the basis of the classical source by Ovid, *Ars amatoria*, composed his highly influential treatise on love, *De amore* (ca. 1190). In France, at about the same time when Chrétien composed his earliest texts (ca. 1170), an anonymous poet wrote the highly influential romance *Partonopeus de Blois*, which was subsequently translated into many European languages, such as by **Konrad von Würzburg** (*Partonopier und Meliur*, ca. 1280).

Together, Latin and vernacular authors contributed to courtly literature all over Europe, perhaps best represented by the famous collection of religious and erotic love poems in the collections *Cambridge Songs* (eleventh century) and *Carmina Burana* (early thirteenth century). Concurrently, many poets explored the literary myth of King Alexander, and wrote monumental epics about the ancient conflict between the Saracens and Emperor Charlemagne and his Paladins, especially Roland (*Chansons de gestes*). Whole cycles of epic poetry were dedicated to Count William of Orange in his desperate struggles against the Saracens. Both an anonymous French author and the German poet Heinrich von Veldeke introduced the ancient topic of the Trojan Aeneas's foundation of Rome to their audiences (*Roman d'Eneas, Eneit*).

Literature of the Late Middle Ages

This cannot be covered here well because of the enormous spread of new writers from that period. But we need to keep in mind, above all, Geoffrey Chaucer (d. ca. 1400), in England, Boccaccio, and Petrarch (d. 1374 and 1375 respectively) in Italy, Christine de Pizan (d. 1430) in France, Juan Ruiz (fourteenth century) in Spain, Johannes von Tepl (d. ca. 1430) in Bohemia/Germany.

Jewish History and Literature

Whereas in the early Middle Ages Jews experienced a remarkable degree of tolerance in most parts of Europe, beginning with the crusades in 1096 they increasingly faced anti-Jewish hostility, eventually leading to horrible pogroms, which finally resulted in their expulsion from England in 1291, from France in 1306, from Spain in 1492, and from Portugal in 1497. A majority of the Jews who did not accept forced conversion moved to Poland, Hungary, and the Ottoman Empire, but numerous Jewish communities remained in Germany, Italy, and neighboring territories.

Anti-Judaism grew significantly throughout the late Middle Ages because the Christians depended on Jewish financial loans and often accused their bankers of heavy usury. Religious-ideological aggression, strongly influenced by the fabricated accusations of ritual murder, provided additional ammunition against the Jews and inspired the mob.

Despite this tremendous hostility and excessive pressure exerted against the Jews, many of their Rabbis, such as **Rashi** in Tours (1040–1105) and **Nahmanides** (1194–ca. 1270), philosophers such as **Ibn Gabirol** (1021–1058) and **Maimonides** (1135–1204), exegetes, grammarians, translators, and teachers such as Joseph **Kimhi** (ca. 1105–ca. 1170), scholars and scientists such as Abraham bar Hija (1065–1135), travelers such as **Benjamin of Tudela**—who explored southern Europe, the Middle East, and China between 1153 and 1173—and lyric poets such as Jehuda Halevi (1086–1141) demonstrated that Jewish culture was a considerable force in medieval Europe. Joseph Ibn Zabara (ca. 1140–ca. 1200), for instance, composed a most remarkable collection of tales, fables, and proverbs in his *Sefer Shashuim* (*The Book of Delight*) which shares many elements with ancient Roman and Greek and also with medieval Latin and vernacular exempla, anecdotes, and moral tales.

Although the heyday of medieval Jewish literature seems to have been the twelfth century, many other names of famous didactic, lyric, religious, and philosophical poets, and Kabbalists would have to be mentioned here, such as Shem Tob ben Joseph Ibn Falaquera (1225–1290), Yehiel of Eisenach (fl. 1235), Abraham Abulafia (1241–ca. 1292), Asher ben Yehiel (1250–1327), Immanuel ha-Romi (1265–1330), Solomon ben Meshul-Iam da Piera (1340–1417), and Solomon ben Reuben Bonfed (1380–1450). Surprisingly, in the sixteenth and seventeenth centuries many Jewish authors, particularly in the German-speaking lands, recreated medieval courtly themes and retold or recreated Arthurian romances, such as *Gabain, Paris and Vienna, Tristan und Isolde,* and *Sigemunt und Magdalina.*

REFERENCES

Clifford R. Backman. 2003. *The Worlds of Medieval Europe.* New York: Oxford University Press.

Janetta Rebold Benton. 2002. *Art of the Middle Ages.* New York: Thames & Hudson.

Joachim Bumke. 1986; 1991. *Courtly Culture: Literature and Society in the High Middle Ages* Berkeley: University of California Press.

Marcia Collish. 1997. *Medieval Foundations of the Western Intellectual Tradition, 400–1400.* New Yaven and London: Yale University Press.

Giles Constable. 1996. *The Reformation of the Twelfth Century.* Cambridge: Cambridge University Press.

Richard C. Dales. 1992. *The Intellectual Life of Western Europe in the Middle Ages.* Sec. rev. ed. Leiden, New York, and Cologne: Brill.

G. R. Evans. 2002. *Fifty Key Medieval Thinkers.* London and New York: Routledge, 2002.

Heinrich Fichtenau. 1992; 1998. *Heretics and Scholars in the High Middle Ages, 1000–1200.* University Park: The Pennsylvania State University Press.

Paul H. Freedman. 2000. *Images of the Medieval Peasant.* Stanford: Stanford University Press.

Albrecht Classen, ed. 2010. *Handbook of Medieval Studies: Terms – Methods – Trends.* 3 vols. Berlin and New York: Walter de Gruyter.

Albrecht Classen, ed. 2015. *Medieval Culture: A Handbook. Fundamental Aspects and Conditions of the European Middle Ages.* 3 vols. Berlin and Boston: Walter de Gruyter.

Friedrich Heer. 1961; 1962. *The Medieval World.* Toronto and New York: The New American Library.

C. Stephen Jaeger. 1985. *The Origins of Courtliness. Civilizing Trends and the Formation of Courtly Ideals, 939–1210.* Philadelphia: University of Pennsylvania Press.

Roberta L Krueger. 2000. *The Cambridge Companion to Medieval Romance.* Cambridge and New York: Cambridge University Press.

Lexikon des Mittelalters. 1977–1999. 10- vols. Munich and Zürich: Artemis.

Keith D. Lilley 2002. *Urban Life in the Middle Ages, 1000–1450.* Houndsmills, Basingstoke, and New York: Palgrave.

Paul B Newman. 2001. *Daily Life in the Middle Ages.* Jefferson, N.C.: McFarland.

Elizabeth Alvilda Petroff, ed. 1986. *Medieval Women's Visionary Literature.* New York and Oxford: Oxford University Press.

Barbara H. Rosenwein. 2002. *A Short History of the Middle Age.* Peterborough, Ontario: Broadview Press.

Joseph R. Strayer, ed. 1982–1989. *Dictionary of the Middle Ages*. 13 vols. New York: Scribner, 1982–1989.

James Trager. 1992. *The People's Chronology. A Year-by-Year Record of Human Events from Prehistory to the Present*. Rev. and updated edition. New York: Henry Holt.

André Vauchez, R. B. Dobson, Michael Lapidge, eds. 2000. *Encyclopedia of the Middle Ages*, 2 vols. Paris, Cambridge, and Rome: Cerf, J. Clarke, Città Nuova.

Meyer Waxman, *A History of Jewish Literature*. 1930; 1960. 5 vols. New York and London: Thomas Yoseloff.

THE CONSOLATION OF PHILOSOPHY

By Boethius

Often, and rightly so, called the "father of western education," Boethius (ca. 480–ca. 524 or 525) was one of the most influential philosophers in late antiquity and has had a tremendous impact on the entire intellectual and cultural world of the West since then, powerfully straddling the divide between antiquity and the Middle Ages. Most famously, he composed a treatise shortly before his death, De consolatione philosophiae (On the Consolation of Philosophy), which promises to answer many of the fundamental questions humans face when they are treated unjustly, are afraid of dying, and have to deal with the quintessential unfairness of life in which the good seem to suffer and the bad seem to triumph. But Boethius also wrote many treatises on a wide range of scholarly subject matters through which he became, so to speak, the schoolmaster of the West. He laid the foundation for the artes liberales (liberal arts) through his studies of philosophy, science, music, and religion, and invented the term of quadrivium for the four-part study area comprising arithmetic, geometry, astronomy, and music. He heavily relied on ancient Greek philosophy (Isocrates and Plato), and in his Principles of Arithmetic he drew much from Nicomachus of Gerasa's Introduction to Arithmetic (early 2nd century C.E.). In his De institutione musica (Principles of Music, ca. 503), in part based on a treatise by Cassiodorus (ca. 490–ca. 590), on some thoughts by Vitruvius (1st c. B.C.E.) on architectural patterns and designs, and on Saint Augustine (354–430), he explored in great detail this subtle subject matter as well, providing guidelines for music that were to be followed for the next thousand years to come by theoreticians and practitioners.

In 524 Boethius was suddenly accused of state treason, and thrown into prison in Pavia (northern Italy). As far as we can tell today, his accusers had no solid ground, and only tried to undermine the political influence of this upright and sincerely concerned philosopher and advisor to the Ostrogothic King Theoderic (the Great; 454–526). Facing certain death by stoning, Boethius composed this famous treatise, De consolatione philosophiae, in order to sort his own thoughts, to regain his philosophical composure, and to provide fundamental answers to one of the most challenging questions in all of human life, why the innocent and "good" have to suffer and die an unjust and early death, while the guilty and "bad" ones triumph and live a long and seemingly good life. Very much being a Neo-Platonist, Boethius successfully developed one of the most powerful and insightful philosophical treatises ever written, which speaks to us as much as to all other medieval and early-modern readers who have consistently praised Boethius for his supreme accomplishments as a scholar and thinker.

Translated into English Prose and Verse by
H. R. James, M.A., CH. CH. Oxford.
London: Elliot Stock, 62, Paternoster Row. 1897.

PREFACE

The book called 'The Consolation of Philosophy' was throughout the Middle Ages, and down to the beginnings of the modern epoch in the sixteenth century, the scholar's familiar companion. Few books have exercised a wider influence in their time. It has been translated into every European tongue, and into English nearly a dozen times, from King Alfred's paraphrase to the translations of Lord Preston, Causton, Ridpath, and Duncan, in the eighteenth century. The belief that what once pleased so widely must still have some charm is my excuse for attempting the present translation. The great work of Boethius, with its alternate prose and verse, skillfully fitted together like dialogue and chorus in a Greek play, is unique in literature, and has a pathetic interest from the time and circumstances of its composition. It ought not to be forgotten.

BOOK I

SONG I

Boethius's Complaint

Who wrought my studious numbers Smoothly once in happier days, Now perforce in tears and sadness Learn a mournful strain to raise. Lo, the **Muses**, grief-dishevelled, Guide my pen and voice my woe; Down their cheeks unfeigned the tear drops To my sad complainings flow! These alone in danger's hour Faithful found, have dared attend On the footsteps of the exile To his lonely journey's end. These that were the pride and pleasure Of my youth and high estate Still remain the only solace Of the old man's **mournful fate**. Old? Ah yes; swift, ere I knew it, By these sorrows on me pressed Age hath come; lo, Grief hath bid me Wear the garb that fits her best. O'er my head untimely sprinkled These white hairs my woes proclaim, And the skin hangs loose and shrivelled On this sorrow-shrunken frame. Blest is **death** that intervenes not In the sweet, sweet years of peace, But unto the broken-hearted, When they call him, brings release! Yet Death passes by the wretched, Shuts his ear and slumbers deep; Will not heed the cry of anguish, Will not close the eyes that weep. For, while yet inconstant Fortune Poured her gifts and all was bright, Death's dark hour had all but whelmed me In the gloom of endless night. Now, because misfortune's shadow Hath o'erclouded that false face, **Cruel Life** still halts and lingers, Though I loathe his weary race. Friends, why did ye once so lightly Vaunt me happy among men? Surely he who so hath fallen Was not firmly founded then.

I.

While I was thus mutely pondering within myself, and recording my sorrowful complainings with my pen, it seemed to me that there appeared above my head a **woman of a countenance exceeding venerable.** Her eyes were bright as fire, and of a more than human keenness; her complexion was lively, her vigour showed no trace of enfeeblement; and yet her years were right full, and she plainly seemed not of our age and time. Her stature was difficult to judge. At one moment it exceeded not the common height, at another her forehead seemed to strike the sky; and whenever she raised her head higher, she began to pierce within the very heavens, and to baffle the eyes of them that looked upon her. Her garments were of an imperishable fabric, wrought with the finest threads and of the most delicate workmanship; and these, as her own lips afterwards assured me, she had herself woven with her own hands. The beauty of this vesture had been somewhat tarnished by age and neglect, and wore that dingy look which marble contracts from exposure. On the lower-most edge was inwoven the Greek letter? [Greek: P], on the topmost the letter? [Greek: Th],[A] and between the two were to be seen steps, like a staircase, from the lower to the upper letter. This robe, moreover, had been torn by the hands of violent persons, who had each snatched away what he could clutch.[B] Her right hand held a note-book; in her left she bore a staff. And when she saw the **Muses of Poesie** standing by my bedside, dictating the words of my lamentations, she was moved awhile to wrath, and her eyes flashed sternly. 'Who,' said she, 'has allowed yon play-acting wantons to approach this sick man—these who, so far from giving medicine to heal his malady, even feed it with sweet poison? These it is who kill the rich crop of reason with the barren thorns of passion, who accustom men's minds to disease, instead of setting them free. Now, were it some common man whom your allurements were seducing, as is usually your way, I should be less indignant. On such a one I should not have spent my pains for naught. But this is one nurtured in the Eleatic and Academic **philosophies**. Nay, get ye gone, ye sirens, whose sweetness lasts not; leave him for my muses to tend and heal!' At these words of upbraiding, the whole band, in deepened sadness, with downcast eyes, and blushes that confessed their shame, dolefully left the chamber.

But I, because my sight was dimmed with much weeping, and I could not tell who was this woman of authority so commanding—I was **dumfounded**, and, with my gaze fastened on the earth, continued silently to await what she might do next. Then she drew near me and sat on the edge of my couch, and, looking into my face all heavy with grief and fixed in sadness on the ground, she bewailed in these words the disorder of my mind:

SONG II

His Despondency

Alas! in what abyss his mind Is plunged, how wildly tossed! Still, still towards the outer night She sinks, her true light lost, As oft as, lashed tumultuously By earth-born blasts, care's waves rise high.

Yet once he ranged the open heavens, The sun's bright pathway tracked; Watched how the cold moon waxed and waned; Nor rested, till there lacked To his wide ken no star that steers Amid the maze of circling spheres.

The causes why the blusterous winds Vex ocean's tranquil face, Whose hand doth turn the stable globe, Or why his even race From out the ruddy east the sun Unto the western waves doth run:

What is it tempers cunningly The placid hours of spring, So that it blossoms with the rose For earth's engarlanding: Who loads the year's maturer prime With clustered grapes in autumn time:

All this he knew—thus ever strove Deep Nature's lore to guess. Now, reft of reason's light, he lies, And bonds his neck oppress; While by the heavy load constrained, His eyes to this dull earth are chained.

II.

'But the time,' said she, 'calls rather for healing than for lamentation.' Then, with her eyes bent full upon me, 'Art thou that man,' she cries, 'who, erstwhile fed with the milk and reared upon the nourishment which is mine to give, had grown up to the full vigor of a manly spirit? And yet I had bestowed such armor on thee as would have proved an invincible defense, had thou not first cast it away. Does thou know me? Why art thou silent? Is it shame or amazement that hath struck thee dumb? Would it were shame; but, as I see, a stupor hath seized upon thee.' Then, when she saw me not only answering nothing, but mute and utterly incapable of speech, she gently touched my breast with her hand, and said: 'There is no danger; these are the symptoms of lethargy, the usual sickness of deluded minds. For awhile he has forgotten himself; he will easily recover his memory, if only he first recognizes me. And that he may do so, let me now wipe his eyes that are clouded with a mist of mortal things.' Thereat, with a fold of her robe, she dried my eyes all swimming with tears.

SONG III

The Mists dispelled

Then the gloom of night was scattered, Sight returned unto mine eyes. So, when haply rainy Caurus Rolls the storm-clouds through the skies, Hidden is the sun; all heaven Is obscured in starless night. But if, in wild onset sweeping, Boreas frees day's prisoned light, All suddenly the radiant god outstreams, And strikes our dazzled eyesight with his beams.

III.

Even so the clouds of my melancholy were broken up. I saw the clear sky, and regained the power to recognize the face of my physician. Accordingly, when I had lifted my eyes and fixed my gaze upon her, I beheld **my nurse, Philosophy**, whose halls I had frequented from my youth up.

'Ah! why,' I cried, 'mistress of all excellence, have thou come down from on high, and entered the solitude of this my exile? Is it that thou, too, even as I, mayst be persecuted with false accusations?'

'Could I desert thee, child,' said she, 'and not lighten the burden which thou have taken upon thee through the hatred of my name, by sharing this trouble? Even forgetting that it were not lawful for Philosophy to leave companionless the way of the innocent, should I, do you really think, fear to incur reproach, or shrink from it, as though some strange new thing had befallen? Do you think that now, for the first time in an evil age, **Wisdom** hath been assailed by peril? Did I not often in days of old, before my servant Plato lived, wage stern warfare with the rashness of folly? In his lifetime, too, Socrates, his master, won with my aid the victory of an unjust death. And when, one after the other, the Epicurean herd, the Stoic, and the rest, each of them as far as in them lay, went about to seize the heritage he left, and were dragging me off protesting and resisting, as their booty, they tore in pieces the garment which I had woven with my own hands, and, clutching the torn pieces, went off, believing that the whole of me had passed into their possession. And some of them, because some traces of my vesture were seen upon them, were destroyed through the mistake of the lewd multitude, who falsely deemed them to be my disciples. It may be that you do not know of the banishment of Anaxagoras, of the poison drought of Socrates, nor of Zeno's torturing, because these things happened in a distant country; yet you might have learnt the fate of Arrius, of Seneca, of Soranus, whose stories are neither old nor unknown to fame. These men were brought to destruction for no other reason than that, settled as they were in my principles, their lives were a **manifest contrast to the ways of the wicked**. So there is nothing you should wonder at, if on the seas of this life we are tossed by storm-blasts, seeing that we have made it our loftiest aim to refuse compliance with evil-doers. And though, maybe, the host of the wicked is many in number, yet is it contemptible, since it is under no leadership, but is hurried hither and thither at the blind driving of mad error. And if at times and seasons they set in array against us, and fall on in overwhelming strength, our leader draws off her forces into the citadel while they are busy plundering the useless baggage. But we from our vantage ground, safe from all this wild work, laugh to see them making prize of the most valueless of things, protected by a bulwark which aggressive folly may not aspire to reach.'

SONG IV

Nothing can subdue Virtue

Whoso calm, serene, sedate, Sets his foot on haughty fate; Firm and steadfast, come what will, Keeps his mien unconquered still; Him the rage of furious seas, Tossing high wild menaces, Nor the flames from smoky forges That Vesuvius disgorges, Nor the bolt that from the sky Smites the tower, can terrify. Why, then, should thou feel affright At the tyrant's weakling might? Dread him not, nor fear no harm, And thou shall his rage disarm; But who to hope or fear gives way—Lost his bosom's rightful sway—He hath cast away his shield, Like a coward fled the field; He hath forged all unaware Fetters his own neck must bear!

IV.

'Do you understand?' she asks. Do my words sink into thy mind? Or art thou dull "as the ass to the sound of the lyre"? Why do you weep? Why do tears stream from thy eyes?

'"Speak out, hide it not in thy heart."

If you look for the physician's help, thou must disclose thy wound.'

Then I, gathering together what strength I could, began: 'Is there still need of telling? Is not the **cruelty of fortune** against me plain enough? Doth not the very aspect of this place move thee? Is this the library, the room which you had chosen as thy constant resort in my home, the place where we so often sat together and held discourse of all things in heaven and earth? Was my garb and mien like this when I explored with thee nature's hid secrets, and you traced for me with thy wand the courses of the stars, molding the while my character and the whole conduct of my life after the pattern of the celestial order? Is this the recompense of my obedience? Yet thou have enjoined by Plato's mouth the maxim, "that states would be happy, either if philosophers ruled them, or if it should so befall that their rulers would turn philosophers." By his mouth likewise you did point out this imperative reason **why philosophers should enter public life**, to wit, lest, if the reins of government be left to unprincipled and profligate citizens, trouble and destruction should come upon the good. Following these precepts, I have tried to apply in the business of public administration the principles which I learnt from thee in leisured seclusion. Thou art my witness and that divinity who hath implanted thee in the hearts of the wise, that I brought to my duties no aim but zeal for the public good. For this cause I have become involved in bitter and irreconcilable feuds, and, as happens inevitably, if a man holds fast to the independence of conscience, I have had to think nothing of giving offence to the powerful in the cause of **justice**.

How often have I encountered and balked Conigastus in his assaults on the fortunes of the weak? How often have I thwarted Trigguilla, steward of the king's household, even when his villainous schemes were as good as accomplished? How often have I risked my position and influence to protect poor wretches from the false charges innumerable with which they were for ever being harassed by the greed and license of the barbarians? No one has ever drawn me aside from justice to oppression. When ruin was overtaking the fortunes of the provincials through the combined pressure of private rapine and public taxation, I grieved no less than the sufferers. When at a season of grievous scarcity a forced sale, disastrous as it was unjustifiable, was proclaimed, and threatened to overwhelm Campania with starvation, I embarked on a struggle with the prætorian prefect in the public interest, I fought the case at the king's judgment-seat, and succeeded in preventing the enforcement of the sale. I rescued the consular Paulinus from the gaping jaws of the court bloodhounds, who in their covetous hopes had already made short work of his wealth. To save Albinus, who was of the same exalted rank, from the penalties of a prejudged charge, I exposed myself to the hatred of Cyprian, the informer.

'Do you think I had laid up for myself store of enmities enough? Well, with the rest of my countrymen, at any rate, my safety should have been assured, since my love of justice had left me no hope of security at court. Yet who was it brought the charges by which I have been struck down? Why, one of my accusers is Basil, who, after being dismissed from the king's household, was driven by his debts to lodge an information against my name. There is Opilio, there is Gaudentius, men who for many and various offences the king's sentence had condemned to banishment; and when they declined to obey, and sought to save themselves by taking sanctuary, the king, as soon as he heard of it, decreed that, if they did not depart from the city of Ravenna within a prescribed time, they should be branded on the forehead and expelled. What would exceed the rigor of this severity? And yet on that same day these very men **lodged an information against me**, and the information was admitted. Just Heaven! had I deserved this by my way of life? Did it make them fit accusers that my condemnation was a foregone conclusion? Has **fortune** no shame—if not at the accusation of the innocent, at least for the vileness of the accusers? Perhaps you wondered what is the sum of the charges laid against me? I wished, they say, to save the senate. But how? I am accused of hindering an informer from producing evidence to prove the senate guilty of treason. Tell me, then, what is thy counsel, O my mistress. Shall I deny the charge, lest I bring shame on thee? But I did wish it, and I shall never cease to wish it. Shall I admit it? Then the work of thwarting the informer will come to an end. Shall I call the wish for the preservation of that illustrious house a crime? Of a truth the senate, by its decrees concerning me, has made it such! But blind folly, though it deceive itself with false names, cannot alter the true merits of things, and, mindful of the precept of Socrates, I do not think it right either to keep the truth concealed or allow falsehood to pass. But this, however it may be, I leave to thy judgment and to the verdict of the discerning. Moreover, lest the course of events and the true facts should be hidden from posterity, I have myself committed to writing an account of the transaction.

'What need to speak of the **forged letters** by which an attempt is made to prove that I hoped for the freedom of Rome? Their falsity would have been manifest, if I had been allowed to use the confession of the informers themselves, evidence which has in all matters the most convincing force. Why, what hope of freedom is left to us? Would there were any! I should have answered with the epigram of Canius when Caligula declared him to have been cognizant of a conspiracy against him. "If I had known," said he, "you should never have known." Grief has not so blunted my perceptions in this matter that I should complain because impious wretches contrive their villainies against the virtuous, but at their achievement of their hopes I do exceedingly marvel. For evil purposes are, perchance, due to the **imperfection of human nature**; that it should be possible for scoundrels to carry out their worst schemes against the **innocent**, while God beholds, is verily monstrous. For this cause, not without reason, one of thy disciples asked, "**If God exists, whence comes evil?** Yet whence comes good, if He exists not?" However, it might well be that wretches who seek the blood of all honest men and of the whole senate should wish to destroy me also, whom they saw to be a bulwark of the senate and all honest men.

But did I deserve such a fate from the Fathers also? You remember, methinks—since you did ever stand by my side to direct what I should do or say—you remember, I say, how at Verona, when the king, eager for the general destruction, was bent on implicating the whole senatorial order in the charge of treason brought against Albinus, with what indifference to my own peril I maintained the innocence of its members, one and all. You know that what I say is the truth, and that I have never boasted of my good deeds in a spirit of self-praise. For whenever a man by proclaiming his good deeds receives the recompense of fame, he diminishes in a measure the secret reward of a good conscience. What issues have overtaken my innocency you sees. Instead of reaping the rewards of true virtue, I undergo the penalties of a guilt falsely laid to my charge—nay, more than this; never did an open confession of guilt cause such unanimous severity among the assessors, but that some consideration, either of the mere frailty of human nature, or of fortune's universal instability, availed to soften the verdict of some few. Had I been accused of a design to fire the temples, to slaughter the priests with impious sword, of plotting the massacre of all honest men, I should yet have been produced in court, and only punished on due confession or conviction. Now for my too great zeal towards the senate I have been **condemned to outlawry and death**, unheard and undefended, at a distance of near five hundred miles away. Oh, my judges, well do ye deserve that no one should hereafter be convicted of a fault like mine!

'Yet even my very accusers saw how honorable was the charge they brought against me, and, in order to overlay it with some shadow of guilt, they falsely asserted that in the pursuit of my ambition I had stained my conscience with sacrilegious acts. And yet thy spirit, indwelling in me, had driven from the chamber of my soul all lust of earthly success, and with thine eye ever upon me, there could be no place left for sacrilege. For you did daily repeat in my ear and instill into my mind the Pythagorean maxim, "**Follow after God.**" It was not likely, then, that I should covet the assistance of the vilest spirits, when you wert molding me to such an excellence as should conform me to the likeness of God. Again, the innocency of the inner sanctuary of my home, the company of friends of the highest probity, a father-in-law revered at once for his pure character and his active beneficence, shield me from the very suspicion of sacrilege. Yet—atrocious as it is—they even draw credence for this charge from thee; I am like to be thought implicated in wickedness on this very account, that I am imbued with thy teachings and established in thy ways. So it is not enough that my devotion to thee should profit me nothing, but thou also must be assailed by reason of the odium which I have incurred. Verily this is the very crown of my misfortunes, that men's opinions for the most part look not to real merit, but to the event;

and only recognize foresight where Fortune has crowned the issue with her approval. Whereby it comes to pass that **reputation** is the first of all things to abandon the unfortunate. I remember with chagrin how perverse is popular report, how various and discordant men's judgments. This only will I say, that the most crushing of misfortune's burdens is, that as soon as a charge is fastened upon the unhappy, they are believed to have deserved their sufferings. I, for my part, who have been banished from all life's blessings, stripped of my honors, stained in repute, am punished for well-doing.

'And now methinks I see the villainous dens of the wicked surging with joy and gladness, all the most recklessly unscrupulous threatening a new crop of lying informations, the good prostrate with terror at my danger, every ruffian incited by impunity to new daring and to success by the profits of audacity, the guiltless not only robbed of their peace of mind, but even of all means of defence. Wherefore I would fain cry out:

SONG V

Boethius's Prayer

'Builder of yon starry dome, You that whirl, throned eternal, Heaven's swift globe, and, as they roam, Guid the stars by laws supernal: So in full-sphered splendor dight Cynthia dims the lamps of night, But unto the orb fraternal Closer drawn,[D] doth lose her light.

'Who at fall of eventide, Hesper, his cold radiance shows, Lucifer his beams doth hide, Paling as the sun's light grows, Brief, while winter's frost holds sway, By thy will the space of day; Swift, when summer's fervor glows, Speed the hours of night away.

'You do **rule the changing year**: When rude Boreas oppresses, Fall the leaves; they reappear, Wooed by Zephyr's soft caresses. Fields that Sirius burns deep grown By Arcturus' watch were sown: Each the reign of law confesses, Keeps the place that is his own.

'Sovereign Ruler, Lord of all! Can it be that You disdain Only man? 'Against him, poor thrall, Wanton Fortune plays her vainest. Guilt's deserved punishment Falls on the innocent; High uplifted, the most profane On the just their malice vent.

'Virtue cowers in dark retreats, Crime's foul stain the righteous bears, Perjury and false deceits Hurt not him the wrong who dares; But whene'er the wicked trust In ill strength to work their lust, Kings, whom nations' awe declares Mighty, grovel in the dust.

'Look, oh look upon this earth, You who on law's sure foundation Framed all! Have we no worth, We poor men, of all creation? Sore we toss on fortune's tide; Master, bid the waves subside! And earth's ways with consummation Of Thy heaven's order guide!'

V.

When I had poured out my **griefs** in this long and unbroken strain of lamentation, she, with calm countenance, and in no wise disturbed at my complainings, thus spake:

'When I saw thee sorrowful, in tears, I straightway knew thee wretched and an **exile**. But how far distant that exile I should not know, had not thine own speech revealed it. Yet how far indeed from thy country have you, not been banished, but rather have strayed; or, if you wilt have it banishment, have banished thyself! For no one else could ever lawfully have had this power over thee. Now, if you will call to mind from what **country you art sprung**, it is not ruled, as once was the Athenian polity, by the sovereignty of the multitude, but "one is its Ruler, one its King," who takes delight in the number of His citizens, not in their banishment; to submit to whose governance and to obey whose ordinances is perfect freedom. Art you ignorant of that most ancient law of this thy country, whereby it is decreed that no one whatsoever, who hath chosen to fix there his dwelling, may be sent into exile? For truly there is no fear that one who is encompassed by its ramparts and defenses should deserve to be exiled. But he who has ceased to wish to dwell therein, he likewise ceases to deserve to do so.

And so it is not so much the aspect of this place which moves me, as thy aspect; not so much the library walls set off with glass and ivory which I miss, as the chamber of thy mind, wherein I once placed, not books, but that which gives books their value, the doctrines which my books contain. Now, what you have said of thy services to the **commonweal** is true, only too little compared with the greatness of thy deservings. The things laid to thy charge whereof you have spoken, whether such as redound to thy credit, or mere false accusations, are publicly known. As for the crimes and deceits of the informers, you have rightly deemed it fitting to pass them over lightly, because the popular voice hath better and more fully pronounced upon them. You have bitterly complained of the injustice of the senate. You have grieved over my calumniation, and likewise have lamented the damage to my good name. Finally, thine indignation blazed forth against fortune; you have complained of the unfairness with which thy merits have been recompensed. Last of all thy frantic muse framed a prayer that the peace which reigns in heaven might rule earth also. But since a throng of tumultuous passions hath assailed thy soul, since you art distraught with anger, pain, and grief, strong remedies are not proper for thee in this thy present mood. And so for a time I will use milder methods, that the tumors which have grown hard through the influx of disturbing passion may be softened by gentle treatment, till they can bear the force of sharper remedies.'

SONG VI

All Things have their Needful Order

He who to th' unwilling furrows Gives the generous grain, When the Crab with baleful fervours Scorches all the plain; He shall find his garner bare, Acorns for his scanty fare.

Go not forth to cull sweet violets From the purpled steep, While the furious blasts of winter Through the valleys sweep; Nor the grape overhavey bring to the press in days of spring.

For to each thing God hath given Its appointed time; No perplexing change permits He In His plan sublime. So who quits the order due Shall a luckless issue rue.

VI.

'First, then, wilt you suffer me by a few questions to make some attempt to test the state of thy mind, that I may learn in what way to set about thy cure?'

'Ask what you will,' said I, 'for I will answer whatever questions you choosest to put.'

Then said she: 'This world of ours—do you think it is governed haphazard and fortuitously, or do you believe you that there is in it any **rational guidance**?'

'Nay,' said I, 'in no wise may I deem that such fixed motions can be determined by random hazard, but I know that God, the Creator, presides over His work, nor will the day ever come that shall drive me from holding fast the truth of this belief.'

'Yes,' said she; 'you did even but now affirm it in song, lamenting that men alone had no portion in the divine care. As to the rest, you wert unshaken in the belief that they were ruled by reason. Yet I marvel exceedingly how, in spite of thy firm hold on this opinion, you art fallen into **sickness**. But let us probe more deeply: something or other is missing, I think. Now, tell me, since you doubt not that God governs the world, do you perceive by what means **He rules it**?'

'I scarcely understand what you meanest,' I said, 'much less can I answer thy question.'

'Did I not say truly that something is missing, whereby, as through a breach in the ramparts, disease hath crept in to disturb thy mind? But, tell me, do you remember the **universal end towards which the aim of all nature is directed**?'

'I once heard,' said I, 'but sorrow hath dulled my recollection.'

'And yet you know whence all things have proceeded.'

'Yes, that I know,' said I, 'and have answered that it is from **God**.'

'Yet how is it possible that you know not what is the **end of existence**, when you do understand its source and origin? However, these disturbances of mind have force to shake a man's position, but cannot pluck him up and root him altogether out of himself. But answer this also, I pray thee: do you remember that you are a **man**?'

'How should I not?' said I.

'Then, can you say what man is?'

'Is this thy question: Whether I know myself for a being endowed with **reason and subject to death**? Surely I do acknowledge myself such.'

Then she: 'Do you know nothing else that you art?'

'Nothing.'

'Now,' said she, 'I know another cause of thy disease, one, too, of grave moment. You have ceased to know **thy own nature**. So, then, I have made full discovery both of the causes of thy sickness and the means of restoring thy health. It is because **forgetfulness** of thyself hath bewildered thy mind that you have bewailed thee as an exile, as one stripped of the blessings that were his; it is because you know not the end of existence that you deem abominable and **wicked men to be happy and powerful**; while, because you have forgotten by what means the earth is governed, you deem that fortune's changes ebb and flow without the restraint of a guiding hand. These are serious enough to cause not sickness only, but even death; but, thanks be to the Author of our health, the light of nature hath not yet left thee utterly. In thy true judgment concerning the world's government, in that you believe it subject, not to the random drift of chance, but to divine reason, we have the divine spark from which thy recovery may be hoped. Have, then, no fear; from these weak embers the vital heat shall once more be kindled within thee. But seeing that it is **not yet time** for **strong remedies**, and that the mind is manifestly so constituted that when it casts off true opinions it straightway puts on false, wherefrom arises a cloud of confusion that disturbs its true vision, I will now try and disperse these mists by **mild and soothing application**, that so the darkness of misleading passion may be scattered, and you may come to discern the splendor of the true light.'

SONG VII

The Perturbations of Passion

Stars shed no light Through the black night, When the clouds hide; And the lashed wave, If the winds rave O'er ocean's tide,—

Though once serene As day's fair sheen,— Soon fouled and spoiled By the storm's spite, Shows to the sight Turbid and soiled.

Oft the fair rill, Down the steep hill Seaward that strays, Some tumbled block Of fallen rock Hinders and stays.

Then art you fain Clear and most plain Truth to discern, In the right way Firmly to stay, Nor from it turn?

Joy, hope and fear Suffer not near, Drive grief away: Shackled and blind And lost is the mind Where these have sway.

Book II (selection)

By Boethius

'Now I would fain also reason with thee a little in Fortune's own words. Do thou observe whether her contentions be just. "Man," she might say, "why dost thou pursue me with thy daily complainings? What wrong have I done thee? What goods of thine have I taken from thee? Choose an thou wilt a judge, and let us dispute before him concerning the rightful ownership of wealth and rank. If thou succeedest in showing that any one of these things is the true property of mortal man, I freely grant those things to be thine which thou claimest. When nature brought thee forth out of thy mother's womb, I took thee, naked and destitute as thou wast, I cherished thee with my substance, and, in the partiality of my favour for thee, I brought thee up somewhat too indulgently, and this it is which now makes thee rebellious against me. I surrounded thee with a royal abundance of all those things that are in my power. Now it is my pleasure to draw back my hand. Thou hast reason to thank me for the use of what was not thine own; thou hast no right to complain, as if thou hadst lost what was wholly thine. Why, then, dost bemoan thyself? I have done thee no violence. Wealth, honour, and all such things are placed under my control. My handmaidens know their mistress; with me they come, and at my going they depart. I might boldly affirm that if those things the loss of which thou lamentest had been thine, thou couldst never have lost them.

Am I alone to be forbidden to do what I will with my own? Unrebuked, the skies now reveal the brightness of day, now shroud the daylight in the darkness of night; the year may now engarland the face of the earth with flowers and fruits, now disfigure it with storms and cold. The sea is permitted to invite with smooth and tranquil surface to-day, to-morrow to roughen with wave and storm. Shall man's insatiate greed bind me to a constancy foreign to my character? This is my art, this the game I never cease to play. I turn the wheel that spins. I delight to see the high come down and the low ascend. Mount up, if thou wilt, but only on condition that thou wilt not think it a hardship to come down when the rules of my game require it. Wert thou ignorant of my character? Didst not know how Crresus, King of the Lydians, erstwhile the dreaded rival of Cyrus, was afterwards pitiably consigned to the flame of the pyre, and only saved by a shower sent from heaven? Has it 'scaped thee how

Paullus paid a meed of pious tears to the misfortunes of King Perseus, his prisoner? What else do tragedies make such woeful outcry over save the overthrow of kingdoms by the indiscriminate strokes of Fortune? Didst thou not learn in thy childhood how there stand at the threshold of Zeus 'two jars,' 'the one full of blessings, the other of calamities'? How if thou hast drawn over-liberally from the good jar? What if not even now have I departed wholly from thee? What if this very mutability of mine is a just ground for hoping better things? But listen now, and cease to let thy heart consume away with fretfulness, nor expect to live on thine own terms in a realm that is common to all.'

III.

'If Fortune should plead thus against thee, assuredly thou wouldst not have one word to offer in reply; or, if thou canst find any justification of thy complainings, thou must show what it is. I will give thee space to speak.'

Then said I: 'Verily, thy pleas are plausible—yea, steeped in the honeyed sweetness of music and rhetoric. But their charm lasts only while they are sounding in the ear; the sense of his misfortunes lies deeper in the heart of the wretched. So, when the sound ceases to vibrate upon the air, the heart's indwelling sorrow is felt with renewed bitterness.'

Then said she: 'It is indeed as thou sayest, for we have not yet come to the curing of thy sickness; as yet these are but lenitives conducing to the treatment of a malady hitherto obstinate. The remedies which go deep I will apply in due season. Nevertheless, to deprecate thy determination to be thought wretched, I ask thee, Hast thou forgotten the extent and bounds of thy felicity? I say nothing of how, when orphaned and desolate, thou wast taken into the care of illustrious men; how thou wast chosen for alliance with the highest in the state—and even before thou wert bound to their house by marriage, wert already dear to their love—which is the most precious of all ties. Did not all pronounce thee most happy in the virtues of thy wife, the splendid honours of her father, and the blessing of male issue?

I pass over—for I care not to speak of blessings in which others also have shared—the distinctions often denied to age which thou enjoyedst in thy youth. I choose rather to come to the unparalleled culmination of thy good fortune. If the fruition of any earthly success has weight in the scale of happiness, can the memory of that splendour be swept away by any rising flood of troubles? That day when thou didst see thy two sons ride forth from home joint consuls, followed by a train of senators, and welcomed by the good-will of the people; when these two sat in curule chairs in the Senate-house, and thou by thy panegyric on the king didst earn the fame of eloquence and ability; when in the Circus, seated between the two consuls, thou didst glut the multitude thronging around with the triumphal largesses for which they looked—methinks thou didst cozen Fortune while she caressed thee, and made thee her darling. Thou didst bear off a boon which she had never before granted to any private person. Art thou, then, minded to cast up a reckoning with Fortune? Now for the first time she has turned a jealous glance upon thee. If thou compare the extent and bounds of thy blessings and misfortunes, thou canst not deny that thou art still fortunate. Or if thou esteem not thyself favoured by Fortune in that thy then seeming prosperity hath departed, deem not thyself wretched, since what thou now believest to be calamitous passeth also. What! art thou but now come suddenly and a stranger to the scene of this life? Thinkest thou there is any stability in human affairs, when man himself vanishes away in the swift course of time? It is true that there is little trust that the gifts of chance will abide; yet the last day of life is in a manner the death of all remaining Fortune. What difference, then, thinkest thou, is there, whether thou leavest her by dying, or she leave thee by fleeing away?'

IV.

Then said I: 'True are thine admonishings, thou nurse of all excellence; nor can I deny the wonder of my fortune's swift career. Yet it is this which chafes me the more cruelly in the recalling. For truly in adverse fortune the worst sting of misery is to have been happy.'

'Well,' said she, 'if thou art paying the penalty of a mistaken belief, thou canst not rightly impute the fault to circumstances. If it is the felicity which Fortune gives that moves thee—mere name though it be—come reckon up with me how rich thou art in the number and weightiness of thy blessings. Then if, by the blessing of Providence, thou hast still preserved unto thee safe and inviolate that which, howsoever thou mightest reckon thy fortune, thou wouldst have thought thy most precious possession, what right hast thou to talk of ill-fortune whilst keeping all Fortune's better gifts? Yet Symmachus, thy wife's father—a man whose splendid character does honour to the human race—is safe and unharmed; and while he bewails thy wrongs, this rare nature, in whom wisdom and virtue are so nobly blended, is himself out of danger—a boon thou wouldst have been quick to purchase at the price of life itself. Thy wife yet lives, with her gentle disposition, her peerless modesty and virtue—this the epitome of all her graces, that she is the true daughter of her sire—she lives, I say, and for thy sake only preserves the breath of life, though she loathes it, and pines away in grief and tears for thy absence, wherein, if in naught else, I would allow some marring of thy felicity. What shall I say of thy sons and their consular dignity—how in them, so far as may be in youths of their age, the example of their father's and grandfather's character shines out? Since, then, the chief care of mortal man is to preserve his life, how happy art thou, couldst thou but recognise thy blessings, who possessest even now what no one doubts to be dearer than life! Wherefore, now dry thy tears. Fortune's hate hath not involved all thy dear ones; the stress of the storm that has assailed thee is not beyond measure intolerable, since there are anchors still holding firm which suffer thee not to lack either consolation in the present or hope for the future.'

'I pray that they still may hold. For while they still remain, however things may go, I shall ride out the storm. Yet thou seest how much is shorn of the splendour of my fortunes.'

'We are gaining a little ground,' said she, 'if there is something in thy lot wherewith thou art not yet altogether discontented. But I cannot stomach thy daintiness when thou complainest with such violence of grief and anxiety because thy happiness falls short of completeness. Why, who enjoys such settled felicity as not to have some quarrel with the circumstances of his lot? A troublous matter are the conditions of human bliss; either they are never realized in full, or never stay permanently. One has abundant riches, but is shamed by his ignoble birth. Another is conspicuous for his nobility, but through the embarrassments of poverty would prefer to be obscure. A third, richly endowed with both, laments the loneliness of an unwedded life. Another, though happily married, is doomed to childlessness, and nurses his wealth for a stranger to inherit. Yet another, blest with children, mournfully bewails the misdeeds of son or daughter. Wherefore, it is not easy for anyone to be at perfect peace with the circumstances of his lot.

There lurks in each several portion something which they who experience it not know nothing of, but which makes the sufferer wince. Besides, the more favoured a man is by Fortune, the more fastidiously sensitive is he; and, unless all things answer to his whim, he is overwhelmed by the most trifling misfortunes, because utterly unschooled in adversity. So petty are the trifles which rob the most fortunate of perfect happiness! How many are there, dost thou imagine, who would think themselves nigh heaven, if but a small portion from the wreck of thy fortune should fall to them? This very place which thou callest exile is to them that dwell therein their native land. So true is it that nothing is wretched, but thinking makes it so, and conversely every lot is happy if borne with equanimity. Who is so blest by Fortune as not to wish to change his state, if once he gives rein to a rebellious spirit? With how many bitternesses is the sweetness of human felicity blent! And even if that sweetness seem to him to bring delight in the enjoying, yet he cannot keep it from departing when it will. How manifestly wretched, then, is the bliss of earthly fortune, which lasts not for ever with those whose temper is equable, and can give no perfect satisfaction to the anxious-minded!

'Why, then, ye children of mortality, seek ye from without that happiness whose seat is only within us? Error and ignorance bewilder you. I will show thee, in brief, the hinge on which perfect happiness turns. Is there anything more precious to thee than thyself? Nothing, thou wilt say. If, then, thou art master of thyself, thou wilt possess that which thou wilt never be willing to lose, and which Fortune cannot take from thee. And that thou mayst see that happiness cannot possibly consist in these things which are the sport of chance, reflect that, if happiness is the highest good of a creature living in accordance with reason, and if a thing which can in any wise be reft away is not the highest good, since that which cannot be taken away is better than it, it is plain that Fortune cannot aspire to bestow happiness by reason of its instability. And, besides, a man borne along by this transitory felicity must either know or not know its unstability. If he knows not, how poor is a happiness which depends on the blindness of ignorance! If he knows it, he needs must fear to lose a happiness whose loss he believes to be possible. Wherefore, a never-ceasing fear suffers him not to be happy. Or does he count the possibility of this loss a trifling matter? Insignificant, then, must be the good whose loss can be borne so equably. And, further, I know thee to be one settled in the belief that the souls of men certainly die not with them, and convinced thereof by numerous proofs; it is clear also that the felicity which Fortune bestows is brought to an end with the death of the body: therefore, it cannot be doubted but that, if happiness is conferred in this way, the whole human race sinks into misery when death brings the close of all. But if we know that many have sought the joy of happiness not through death only, but also through pain and suffering, how can life make men happy by its presence when it makes them not wretched by its loss?'

V.

'But since my reasonings begin to work a soothing effect within thy mind, methinks I may resort to remedies somewhat stronger. Come, suppose, now, the gifts of Fortune were not fleeting and transitory, what is there in them capable of ever becoming truly thine, or which does not lose value when looked at steadily and fairly weighed in the balance? Are riches, I pray thee, precious either through thy nature or in their own? What are they but mere gold and heaps of money? Yet these fine things show their quality better in the spending than in the hoarding; for I suppose 'tis plain that greed Alva's makes men hateful, while liberality brings fame. But that which is transferred to another cannot remain in one's own possession; and if that be so, then money is only precious when it is given away, and, by being transferred to others, ceases to be one's own. Again, if all the money in the world were heaped up in one man's possession, all others would be made poor. Sound fills the ears of many at the same time without being broken into parts, but your riches cannot pass to many without being lessened in the process. And when this happens, they must needs impoverish those whom they leave. How poor and cramped a thing, then, is riches, which more than one cannot possess as an unbroken whole, which falls not to any one man's lot without the impoverishment of everyone else! Or is it the glitter of gems that allures the eye? Yet, how rarely excellent soever may be their splendour, remember the flashing light is in the jewels, not in the man. Indeed, I greatly marvel at men's admiration of them; for what can rightly seem beautiful to a being endowed with life and reason, if it lack the movement and structure of life? And although such things do in the end take on them more beauty from their Maker's care and their own brilliancy, still they in no wise merit your admiration since their excellence is set at a lower grade than your own.

'Does the beauty of the fields delight you? Surely, yes; it is a beautiful part of a right beautiful whole. Fitly indeed do we at times enjoy the serene calm of the sea, admire the sky, the stars, the moon, the sun. Yet is any of these thy concern? Dost thou venture to boast thyself of the beauty of any one of them? Art thou decked with spring's flowers? is it thy fertility that swelleth in the fruits of autumn? Why art thou moved with empty transports? why embracest thou an alien excellence as thine own? Never will fortune make thine that which the nature of things has excluded from thy ownership. Doubtless the fruits of the earth are given for the sustenance of living creatures. But if thou art content to supply thy wants so far as suffices nature, there is no need to resort to fortune's bounty. Nature is content with few things, and with a very little of these. If thou art minded to force superfluities upon her when she is satisfied, that which thou addest will prove either unpleasant or harmful. But, now, thou thinkest it fine to shine in raiment of divers colours; yet—if, indeed, there is any pleasure in the sight of such things—it is the texture or the artist's skill which I shall admire.

'Or perhaps it is a long train of servants that makes thee happy? Why, if they behave viciously, they are a ruinous burden to thy house, and exceeding dangerous to their own master; while if they are honest, how canst thou count other men's virtue in the sum of thy possessions? From all which 'tis plainly proved that not one of these things which thou reckonest in the number of thy possessions is really thine. And if there is in them no beauty to be desired, why shouldst thou either grieve for their loss or find joy in their continued possession? While if they are beautiful in their own nature, what is that to thee? They would have been not less pleasing in themselves, though never included among thy possessions. For they derive not their preciousness from being counted in thy riches, but rather thou hast chosen to count them in thy riches because they seemed to thee precious.

'Then, what seek ye by all this noisy outcry about fortune? To chase away poverty, I ween, by means of abundance. And yet ye find the result just contrary. Why, this varied array of precious furniture needs more accessories for its protection; it is a true saying that they want most who possess most, and, conversely, they want very little who measure their abundance by nature's requirements, not by the superfluity of vain display. Have ye no good of your own implanted within you, that ye seek your good in things external and separate? Is the nature of things so reversed that a creature divine by right of reason can in no other way be splendid in his own eyes save by the possession of lifeless chattels? Yet, while other things are content with their own, ye who in your intellect are God-like seek from the lowest of things adornment for a nature of supreme excellence, and perceive not how great a wrong ye do your Maker. His will was that mankind should excel all things on earth. Ye thrust down your worth beneath the lowest of things. For if that in which each thing finds its good is plainly more precious than that whose good it is, by your own estimation ye put yourselves below the vilest of things, when ye deem these vile things to be your good: nor does this fall out undeservedly. Indeed, man is so constituted that he then only excels other things when he knows himself; but he is brought lower than the beasts if he lose this self-knowledge. For that other creatures should be ignorant of themselves is natural; in man it shows as a defect. How extravagant, then, is this error of yours, in thinking that anything can be embellished by adornments not its own. It cannot be. For if such accessories add any lustre, it is the accessories that get the praise, while that which they veil and cover remains in its pristine ugliness. And again I say, That is no good, which injures its possessor. Is this untrue? No, quite true, thou sayest. And yet riches have often hurt those that possessed them, since the worst of men, who are all the more covetous by reason of their wickedness, think none but themselves worthy to possess all the gold and gems the world contains. So thou, who now dreadest pike and sword, mightest have trolled a carol "in the robber's face," hadst thou entered the road of life with empty pockets. Oh, wondrous blessedness of perishable wealth, whose acquisition robs thee of security!'

VI.

'What now shall I say of rank and power, whereby, because ye know not true power and dignity, ye hope to reach the sky? Yet, when rank and power have fallen to the worst of men, did ever an Etna, belching forth flame and fiery deluge, work such mischief? Verily, as I think, thou dost remember how thine ancestors sought to abolish the consular power, which had been the foundation of their liberties, on account of the overweening pride of the consuls, and how for that self-same pride they had already abolished the kingly title! And if, as happens but rarely, these prerogatives are conferred on virtuous men, it is only the virtue of those who exercise them that pleases. So it appears that honour cometh not to virtue from rank, but to rank from virtue. Look, too, at the nature of that power which ye find so attractive and glorious! Do ye never consider, ye creatures of earth, what ye are, and over whom ye exercise your fancied lordship? Suppose, now, that in the mouse tribe there should rise up one claiming rights and powers for himself above the rest, would ye not laugh consumedly? Yet if thou lookest to his body alone, what creature canst thou find more feeble than man, who oftentimes is killed by the bite of a fly, or by some insect creeping into the inner passage of his system! Yet what rights can one exercise over another, save only as regards the body, and that which is lower than the body—I mean fortune? What! wilt thou bind with thy mandates the free spirit? Canst thou force from its due tranquillity the mind that is firmly composed by reason? A tyrant thought to drive a man of free birth to reveal his accomplices in a conspiracy, but the prisoner bit off his tongue and threw it into the furious tyrant's face; thus, the tortures which the tyrant thought the instrument of his cruelty the sage made an opportunity for heroism. Moreover, what is there that one man can do to another which he himself may not have to undergo in his turn? We are told that Busiris, who used to kill his guests, was himself slain by his guest, Hercules. Regulus had thrown into bonds many of the Carthaginians whom he had taken in war; soon after he himself submitted his hands to the chains of the vanquished. Then, thinkest thou that man hath any power who cannot prevent another's being able to do to him what he himself can do to others?

'Besides, if there were any element of natural and proper good in rank and power, they would never come to the utterly bad, since opposites are not wont to be associated. Nature brooks not the union of contraries. So, seeing there is no doubt that wicked wretches are oftentimes set in high places, it is also clear that things which suffer association with the worst of men cannot be good in their own nature. Indeed, this judgment may with some reason be passed concerning all the gifts of fortune which fall so plentifully to all the most wicked. This ought also to be considered here, I think: No one doubts a man to be brave in whom he has observed a brave spirit residing. It is plain that one who is endowed with speed is swift-footed. So also music makes men musical, the healing art physicians, rhetoric public speakers. For each of these has naturally its own proper working; there is no confusion with the effects of contrary things—nay, even of itself it rejects what is incompatible. And yet wealth cannot extinguish insatiable greed, nor has power ever made him master of himself whom vicious lusts kept bound in indissoluble fetters; dignity conferred on the wicked not only fails to make them worthy, but contrarily reveals and displays their unworthiness. Why does it so happen? Because ye take pleasure in calling by false names things whose nature is quite incongruous thereto—by names which are easily proved false by the very effects of the things themselves; even so it is; these riches, that power, this dignity, are none of them rightly so called. Finally, we may draw the same conclusion concerning the whole sphere of Fortune, within which there is plainly nothing to be truly desired, nothing of intrinsic excellence; for she neither always joins herself to the good, nor does she make good men of those to whom she is united.'

VII.

Then said I: 'Thou knowest thyself that ambition for worldly success hath but little swayed me. Yet I have desired opportunity for action, lest virtue, in default of exercise, should languish away.'

Then she: 'This is that "last infirmity" which is able to allure minds which, though of noble quality, have not yet been moulded to any exquisite refinement by the perfecting of the virtues—I mean, the love of glory—and fame for high services rendered to the commonweal. And yet consider with me how poor and unsubstantial a thing this glory is! The whole of this earth's globe, as thou hast learnt from the demonstration of astronomy, compared with the expanse of heaven, is found no bigger than a point; that is to say, if measured by the vastness of heaven's sphere, it is held to occupy absolutely no space at all. Now, of this so insignificant portion of the universe, it is about a fourth part, as Ptolemy's proofs have taught us, which is inhabited by living creatures known to us. If from this fourth part you take away in thought all that is usurped by seas and marshes, or lies a vast waste of waterless desert, barely is an exceeding narrow area left for human habitation. You, then, who are shut in and prisoned in this merest fraction of a point's space, do ye take thought for the blazoning of your fame, for the spreading abroad of your renown? Why, what amplitude or magnificence has glory when confined to such narrow and petty limits?

'Besides, the straitened bounds of this scant dwelling-place are inhabited by many nations differing widely in speech, in usages, in mode of life; to many of these, from the difficulty of travel, from diversities of speech, from want of commercial intercourse, the fame not only of individual men, but even of cities, is unable to reach. Why, in Cicero's days, as he himself somewhere points out, the fame of the Roman Republic had not yet crossed the Caucasus, and yet by that time her name had grown formidable to the Parthians and other nations of those parts. Seest thou, then, how narrow, how confined, is the glory ye take pains to spread abroad and extend! Can the fame of a single Roman penetrate where the glory of the Roman name fails to pass? Moreover, the customs and institutions of different races agree not together, so that what is deemed praise worthy in one country is thought punishable in another. Wherefore, if any love the applause of fame, it shall not profit him to publish his name among many peoples. Then, each must be content to have the range of his glory limited to his own people; the splendid immortality of fame must be confined within the bounds of a single race.

'Once more, how many of high renown in their own times have been lost in oblivion for want of a record! Indeed, of what avail are written records even, which, with their authors, are overtaken by the dimness of age after a somewhat longer time? But ye, when ye think on future fame, fancy it an immortality that ye are begetting for yourselves. Why, if thou scannest the infinite spaces of eternity, what room hast thou left for rejoicing in the durability of thy name? Verily, if a single moment's space be compared with ten thousand years, it has a certain relative duration, however little, since each period is definite. But this same number of years—ay, and a number many times as great—cannot even be compared with endless duration; for, indeed, finite periods may in a sort be compared one with another, but a finite and an infinite never. So it comes to pass that fame, though it extend to ever so wide a space of years, if it be compared to never-lessening eternity, seems not short-lived merely, but altogether nothing. But as for you, ye know not how to act aright, unless it be to court the popular breeze, and win the empty applause of the multitude—nay, ye abandon the superlative worth of conscience and virtue, and ask a recompense from the poor words of others. Let me tell thee how wittily one did mock the shallowness of this sort of arrogance. A certain man assailed one who had put on the name of philosopher as a cloak to pride and vain-glory, not for the practice of real virtue, and added: "Now shall I know if thou art a philosopher if thou bearest reproaches calmly and patiently." The other for awhile affected to be patient, and, having endured to be abused, cried out derisively: "Now, do you see that I am a philosopher?" The other, with biting sarcasm, retorted: "I should have hadst thou held thy peace." Moreover, what concern have choice spirits—for it is of such men we speak, men who seek glory by virtue—what concern, I say, have these with fame after the dissolution of the body in death's last hour? For if men die wholly—which our reasonings forbid us to believe—there is no such thing as glory at all, since he to whom the glory is said to belong is altogether non-existent. But if the mind, conscious of its own rectitude, is released from its earthly prison, and seeks heaven in free flight, doth it not despise all earthly things when it rejoices in its deliverance from earthly bonds, and enters upon the joys of heaven?'

VIII.

'But that thou mayst not think that I wage implacable warfare against Fortune, I own there is a time when the deceitful goddess serves men well—I mean when she reveals herself, uncovers her face, and confesses her true character. Perhaps thou dost not yet grasp my meaning. Strange is the thing I am trying to express, and for this cause I can scarce find words to make clear my thought. For truly I believe that Ill Fortune is of more use to men than Good Fortune. For Good Fortune, when she wears the guise of happiness, and most seems to caress, is always lying; Ill Fortune is always truthful, since, in changing, she shows her inconstancy. The one deceives, the other teaches; the one enchains the minds of those who enjoy her favour by the semblance of delusive good, the other delivers them by the knowledge of the frail nature of happiness. Accordingly, thou mayst see the one fickle, shifting as the breeze, and ever self-deceived; the other sober-minded, alert, and wary, by reason of the very discipline of adversity. Finally, Good Fortune, by her allurements, draws men far from the true good; Ill Fortune ofttimes draws men back to true good with grappling-irons. Again, should it be esteemed a trifling boon, thinkest thou, that this cruel, this odious Fortune hath discovered to thee the hearts of thy faithful friends—that other hid from thee alike the faces of the true friends and of the false, but in departing she hath taken away her friends, and left thee thine? What price wouldst thou not have given for this service in the fulness of thy prosperity when thou seemedst to thyself fortunate? Cease, then, to seek the wealth thou hast lost, since in true friends thou hast found the most precious of all riches.'

Book III

By Boethius

She ceased, but I stood fixed by the sweetness of the song in wonderment and eager expectation, my ears still strained to listen. And then after a little I said: 'Thou sovereign solace of the stricken soul, what **refreshment** hast thou brought me, no less by the sweetness of thy singing than by the weightiness of thy discourse! Verily, I think not that I shall hereafter be unequal to the blows of Fortune. Wherefore, **I no longer dread the remedies** which thou saidst were something too severe for my strength; nay, rather, I am eager to hear of them and call for them with all vehemence.'

Then said she: 'I marked thee fastening upon my words silently and intently, and I expected, or—to speak more truly—I myself brought about in thee, this state of mind. What now remains is of such sort that to the taste indeed it is biting, but when received within it turns to sweetness. But whereas thou dost profess thyself desirous of hearing, with what ardour wouldst thou not burn didst thou but perceive whither it is my task to lead thee!'

'Whither?' said I.

'To **true felicity,**' said she, 'which even now thy spirit sees in dreams, but cannot behold in very truth, while thine eyes are engrossed with semblances.'

Then said I: 'I beseech thee, do thou show to me her true shape without a moment's loss.'

'Gladly will I, for thy sake,' said she. 'But first I will try to sketch in words, and describe a cause which is more familiar to thee, that, when thou hast viewed this carefully, thou mayst turn thy eyes the other way, and recognise the **beauty of true happiness.'**

For a little space she remained in a fixed gaze, withdrawn, as it were, into the august chamber of her mind; then she thus began:

'All mortal creatures in those anxious aims which find employment in so many varied pursuits, though they take many paths, yet strive to reach one goal—the **goal of happiness.** Now, the good is that which, when a man hath got, he can lack nothing further. This it is which is **the supreme good** of all, containing within itself all particular good; so that if anything is still wanting thereto, this cannot be the supreme good, since something would be left outside which might be desired. 'Tis clear, then, that **happiness is a state perfected by the assembling together of all good things.** To this state, as we have said, **all men try to attain,** but by different paths. For the desire of the true good is **naturally implanted** in the minds of men; only **error** leads them aside out of the way in pursuit of the false. Some, deeming it the highest good to want for nothing, spare no pains to attain **affluence;** others, judging the good to be that to which respect is most worthily paid, strive to win the **reverence** of their fellow-citizens by the attainment of official **dignity.** Some there are who fix the chief good in supreme power; these either wish themselves to enjoy **sovereignty,** or try to attach themselves to those who have it. Those, again, who think **renown** to be something of supreme excellence are in haste to spread abroad the glory of their name either through the arts of war or of peace. A great many measure the attainment of good by **joy and gladness of heart;** these think it the height of happiness to give themselves over to **pleasure.** Others there are, again, who interchange the ends and means one with the other in their aims; for instance, some want riches for the sake of pleasure and power, some covet power either for the sake of money or in order to bring renown to their name. So it is on these ends, then, that the aim of human acts and wishes is centred, and on others like to these—for instance, **noble birth** and **popularity,** which seem to compass a certain renown; **wife and children,** which are sought for the sweetness of their possession; while as for **friendship,** the most sacred kind indeed is counted in the category of virtue, not of fortune; but other kinds are entered upon for the sake of power or of enjoyment. And as for **bodily excellences,** it is obvious that they are to be ranged with the above. For strength and stature surely manifest power; beauty and fleetness of foot bring celebrity; health brings pleasure. It is plain, then, that the only object sought for in all these ways is happiness. For that which each seeks in preference to all else, that is in his judgment the supreme good. And we have defined the supreme good to be happiness. Therefore, that state which each wishes in preference to all others is in his judgment happy.

'Thou hast, then, set before thine eyes something like a scheme of **human happiness—wealth, rank, power, glory, pleasure.** Now Epicurus, from a sole regard to these considerations, with some consistency concluded the highest good to be pleasure, because all the other objects seem to bring some delight to the soul. But to return to human pursuits and aims: man's mind seeks to recover its **proper good,** in spite of the mistiness of its recollection, but, like a drunken man, knows not by what path to return home. Think you they are wrong who strive to escape want? Nay, truly there is nothing which can so well complete happiness as a state abounding in all good things, needing nothing from outside, but wholly **self-sufficing.** Do they fall into error who deem that which is best to be also best deserving to receive the homage of reverence? Not at all. That cannot possibly be vile and contemptible, to attain which the endeavours of nearly all mankind are directed. Then, is power not to be reckoned in the category of good? Why, can that which is plainly more efficacious than anything else be esteemed a thing feeble and void of strength? Or is **renown** to be thought of no account? Nay, it cannot be ignored that the highest renown is constantly associated with the highest excellence. And what need is there to say that **happiness is not haunted by care and gloom, nor exposed to trouble and vexation,** since that is a condition we ask of the very least of things, from the possession and enjoyment of which we expect delight? So, then, these are the blessings men wish to win; they want riches, rank, sovereignty, glory, pleasure, because they believe that by these means they will secure independence, reverence, power, renown, and joy of heart. Therefore, it is the good which men seek by such divers courses; and herein is easily shown the might of Nature's power, since, although opinions are so various and discordant, yet they agree in cherishing good as the end.' [**summary of wrong path toward happiness!**]

'Ye, too, creatures of earth, have some glimmering of your **origin,** however faint, and though in a vision dim and clouded, yet in some wise, notwithstanding, ye discern the true end of happiness, and so the aim of nature leads you thither—to that true good—while error in many forms leads you astray therefrom. For reflect whether men are able to win happiness by those means through which they think to reach the proposed end. Truly, if either wealth, rank, or any of the rest, bring with them anything of such sort as seems to have nothing wanting to it that is good, we, too, acknowledge that some are made happy by the acquisition of these things. But if they are not able to fulfil their promises, and, moreover, lack many good things, is not the happiness men seek in them clearly discovered to be a false show? Therefore do I first ask thee thyself, who but lately were living in affluence, amid all that abundance of wealth, was thy mind never troubled in consequence of some wrong done to thee?'

'Nay,' said I, 'I cannot ever remember a time when **my mind was so completely at peace** as not to feel the **pang of some uneasiness.**'

'Was it not because either something was **absent** which thou wouldst not have absent, or present which thou wouldst have away?'

'Yes,' said I.

'Then, thou didst want the presence of the one, the absence of the other?'

'Admitted.'

'But a man lacks that of which he is in want?' 'He does.'

'And he who lacks something is not in all **points self-sufficing?**'

'No; certainly not,' said I.

'So were thou, then, in the plenitude of thy wealth, supporting this insufficiency?' 'I must have been.'

'Wealth, then, cannot make its possessor independent and free from all want, yet this was what it seemed to promise. Moreover, I think this also well deserves to be considered—that there is nothing in the special nature of **money** to hinder its being **taken away from** those who possess it against their will.'

'I admit it.'

'Why, of course, when every day the stronger wrests it from the weaker without his consent. Else, whence come lawsuits, except in seeking to recover moneys which have been taken away against their owner's will by force or fraud?'

'True,' said I.

'Then, everyone will need some extraneous means of protection to keep his money safe.'

'Who can venture to deny it?'

'Yet he would not, unless he possessed the money which it is possible to lose.'

'No; he certainly would not.'

'Then, we have worked round to an opposite conclusion: the **wealth** which was thought to make a man independent rather puts him in need of further **protection.** How in the world, then, can want be driven away by riches? Cannot the rich feel hunger? Cannot they thirst? Are not the limbs of the wealthy sensitive to the winter's cold? "But," thou wilt say, "the rich have the wherewithal to sate their hunger, the means to get rid of thirst and cold." True enough; want can thus be soothed by riches, **wholly removed** it cannot be. For if this ever-gaping, ever-craving want is glutted by wealth, it needs must be that the want itself which can be so glutted still remains. I do not speak of how very little suffices for nature, and how for avarice nothing is enough. Wherefore, if **wealth cannot get rid of want,** and **makes new wants of its own,** how can ye believe that it bestows independence?' [**true happiness rests in independence**]

'Well, but official dignity clothes him to whom it comes with honour and reverence! Have, then, offices of state such power as to plant virtue in the minds of their possessors, and drive out vice? Nay, they are rather wont to signalize iniquity than to chase it away, and hence arises our indignation that honours so often fall to the most iniquitous of men. Accordingly, Catullus calls Nonius an "ulcer-spot," though "sitting in the curule chair." Dost not see what infamy high position brings upon the bad? Surely their unworthiness will be less conspicuous if their rank does not draw upon them the public notice! In thy own case, wouldst thou ever have been induced by all these perils to think of sharing office with Decoratus, since thou hast discerned in him the spirit of a rascally parasite and informer? No; we cannot deem men worthy of reverence on account of their office, whom we deem unworthy of the office itself. But didst thou see a man endued with wisdom, couldst thou suppose him not worthy of reverence, nor of that wisdom with which he was endued?'

'No; certainly not.'

'There is in Virtue a dignity of her own which she forthwith passes over to those to whom she is united. And since **public honours** cannot do this, it is clear that they **do not possess** the true beauty of dignity. And here this well deserves to be noticed—that if a man is the more scorned in proportion as he is despised by a greater number, high position not only fails to win reverence for the wicked, but even loads them the more with contempt by drawing more attention to them. But not without retribution; for the wicked pay back a return in kind to the dignities they put on by the pollution of their touch. Perhaps, too, another consideration may teach thee to confess that true reverence cannot come through these counterfeit dignities. It is this: If one who had been many times consul chanced to visit barbaric lands, would his office win him the reverence of the barbarians? And yet if reverence were the natural effect of dignities, they would not forego their proper function in any part of the world, even as fire never anywhere fails to give forth heat. But since this **effect is not due to their own efficacy, but is attached to them by the mistaken opinion of mankind,** they disappear straightway when they are set before those who do not esteem them dignities. Thus the case stands with foreign peoples. But does their repute last for ever, even in the land of their origin? Why, the prefecture, which was once a great power, is now an empty name—a burden merely on the senator's fortune; the commissioner of the public corn supply was once a personage—now what is more contemptible than this office? For, as we said just now, that which hath no true comeliness of its own now receives, now loses, lustre at the caprice of those who have to do with it. So, then, if **dignities cannot win men reverence,** if they are actually sullied by the contamination of the wicked, if they lose their splendour through time's changes, if they come into contempt merely for lack of public estimation, what precious beauty have they in themselves, much less to give to others?' [**does office give people inherent dignity, or the other way around?**]

'Well, then, does **sovereignty and the intimacy of kings prove able to confer power?** Why, surely does not the happiness of kings endure for ever? And yet antiquity is full of examples, and these days also, of kings whose happiness has turned into calamity. How glorious a power, which is not even found effectual for its own preservation! But if happiness has its source in sovereign power, is not happiness diminished, and misery inflicted in its stead, in so far as that power falls short of completeness? [**so, what is true happiness, if not political power?**] Yet, however widely human sovereignty be extended, there must still be more peoples left, over whom each several king holds no sway. Now, at whatever point the power on which happiness depends ceases, here powerlessness steals in and makes wretchedness; so, by this way of reckoning, there must needs be a balance of wretchedness in the lot of the king. The **tyrant** who had made trial of the perils of his condition figured the fears that haunt a throne under the image of a sword hanging over a man's head.[G] What sort of power, then, is this which cannot drive away the gnawings of **anxiety,** or shun the stings of terror? Fain would they themselves have lived secure, but they cannot; then they boast about their power! Dost thou count him to possess power whom thou seest to wish what he cannot bring to pass? Dost thou count him to possess power who encompasses himself with a **body-guard,** who fears those he terrifies more than they fear him, who, to keep up the semblance of power, is himself at the mercy of his slaves? Need I say anything of the **friends of kings,** when I show royal dominion itself so utterly and miserably weak—why ofttimes the royal power in its plenitude brings them low, ofttimes involves them in its fall? Nero drove his friend and preceptor, Seneca, to the choice of the manner of his death. Antoninus exposed Papinianus, who was long powerful at court, to the swords of the soldiery. Yet each of these was willing to renounce his power. Seneca tried to surrender his wealth also to Nero, and go into retirement; but neither achieved his purpose. When they tottered, their very greatness dragged them down. What manner of thing, then, is this power which keeps men in fear while they possess it—which when thou art fain to keep, thou art not safe, and when thou desirest to lay it aside thou canst not rid thyself of? Are friends any protection who have been attached by fortune, not by virtue? Nay; him whom good fortune has made a friend, ill fortune will make an enemy. And what plague is more effectual to do hurt than a foe of one's own household?' [**temporary happiness through power**]

VI.

For many have won a great name through the mistaken beliefs of the multitude—and what can be imagined more shameful than that? Nay, they who are praised falsely must needs themselves blush at their own praises! And even when praise is won by merit, still, how does it add to the good conscience of the wise man who measures his good not by popular repute, but by the truth of inner conviction? And if at all it does seem a fair thing to get this same **renown** spread abroad, it follows that any failure so to spread it is held foul. But if, as I set forth but now, there must needs be many tribes and peoples whom the fame of any single man cannot reach, it follows that he whom thou esteemest glorious seems all inglorious in a neighbouring quarter of the globe. As to **popular favour,** I do not think it even worthy of mention in this place, since it never cometh of judgment, and never lasteth steadily.

'Then, again, who does not see how empty, how foolish, is the **fame of noble birth?** Why, if the nobility is based on renown, the renown is another's! For, truly, nobility seems to be a sort of reputation coming from the **merits of ancestors.** But if it is the praise which brings renown, of necessity it is they who are praised that are famous. Wherefore, the fame of another clothes thee not with splendour if thou hast none of thine own. So, if there is any excellence in nobility of birth, methinks it is this alone—that it would seem to impose upon the nobly born the obligation not to degenerate from the virtue of their ancestors.'

'Then, what shall I say of the **pleasures of the body?** The lust thereof is full of uneasiness; the sating, of repentance. What sicknesses, what intolerable pains, are they wont to bring on the bodies of those who enjoy them—the fruits of iniquity, as it were! Now, what sweetness the stimulus of pleasure may have I do not know. But that the issues of pleasure are painful everyone may understand who chooses to recall the memory of his own fleshly lusts. Nay, if these can make happiness, there is no reason why the beasts also should not be happy, since all their efforts are eagerly set upon satisfying the bodily wants. I know, indeed, that the sweetness of **wife and children** should be right comely, yet only too true to nature is what was said of one—that he found in **his sons his tormentors.** And how galling such a **contingency** would be, I must needs put thee in mind, since thou hast never in any wise suffered such experiences, nor art thou now under any uneasiness. In such a case, I agree with my servant Euripides, who said that a man without children was fortunate in his misfortune.'[H]

VIII. [**this is a kind of summary**]

'It is beyond doubt, then, that these paths do not lead to happiness; they cannot guide anyone to the promised goal. Now, I will very briefly show what serious evils are involved in following them. Just consider. Is it thy endeavour to heap up money? Why, thou must wrest it from its present possessor! Art thou minded to put on the splendour of official dignity? Thou must beg from those who have the giving of it; thou who covetest to outvie others in honour must lower thyself to the humble posture of petition. Dost thou long for power? Thou must face perils, for thou wilt be at the mercy of thy subjects' plots. Is glory thy aim? Thou art lured on through all manner of hardships, and there is an end to thy peace of mind. Art fain to lead a life of pleasure? Yet who does not scorn and contemn one who is the slave of the weakest and vilest of things—the body? Again, on how slight and perishable a possession do they rely who set before themselves bodily excellences! Can ye ever surpass the elephant in bulk or the bull in strength? Can ye excel the tiger in swiftness? Look upon the infinitude, the solidity, the swift motion, of the heavens, and for once cease to admire things mean and worthless. And yet the heavens are not so much to be admired on this account as for the reason which guides them. Then, how transient is the lustre of beauty! how soon gone!—more fleeting than the fading bloom of spring flowers. And yet if, as Aristotle says, men should see with the eyes of Lynceus, so that their sight might pierce through obstructions, would not that body of Alcibiades, so gloriously fair in outward seeming, appear altogether loathsome when all its inward parts lay open to the view? Therefore, it is not thy own nature that makes thee seem beautiful, but the weakness of the eyes that see thee. Yet prize as unduly as ye will that body's excellences; so long as ye know that this that ye admire, whatever its worth, can be dissolved away by the feeble flame of a three days' fever. From all which considerations we may conclude as a whole, that these things which cannot make good the advantages they promise, which are never made perfect by the assemblage of all good things—these neither lead as by-ways to happiness, nor themselves make men completely happy.'

IX.

This much may well suffice to set forth the form of false happiness; if this is now clear to thine eyes, the next step is to show what true happiness is.'

'Indeed,' said I, 'I see clearly enough that neither is independence to be found in wealth, nor power in sovereignty, nor reverence in dignities, nor fame in glory, nor true joy in pleasures.'

'Hast thou discerned also the causes why this is so?'

'I seem to have some inkling, but I should like to learn more at large from thee.'

'Why, truly the reason is hard at hand. That which is simple and indivisible by nature human error separates, and transforms from the true and perfect to the false and imperfect. Dost thou imagine that which lacketh nothing can want power?'

'Certainly not.'

'Right; for if there is any feebleness of strength in anything, in this there must necessarily be need of external protection.'

'That is so.'

'Accordingly, the nature of independence and power is one and the same.'

'It seems so.'

'Well, but dost think that anything of such a nature as this can be looked upon with contempt, or is it rather of all things most worthy of veneration?'

'Nay; there can be no doubt as to that.'

'Let us, then, **add reverence to independence and power, and conclude these three to be one**.'

'We must if we will acknowledge the truth.'

'Thinkest thou, then, this combination of qualities to be obscure and without distinction, or rather famous in all renown? Just consider: can that want renown which has been agreed to be lacking in nothing, to be supreme in power, and right worthy of honour, for the reason that it cannot bestow this upon itself, and so comes to appear somewhat poor in esteem?'

'I cannot but acknowledge that, being what it is, this union of qualities is also right famous.' 'It follows, then, that we must admit that renown is not different from the other three.' 'It does,' said I.

'That, then, which needs nothing outside itself, which can accomplish all things in its own strength, which enjoys fame and compels reverence, must not this evidently be also fully crowned with joy?'

'In sooth, I cannot conceive,' said I, 'how any sadness can find entrance into such a state; wherefore I must needs acknowledge it full of joy—at least, if our former conclusions are to hold.'

'Then, for the same reasons, this also is necessary—that independence, power, renown, reverence, and sweetness of delight, are different only in name, but in substance differ no wise one from the other.'

'It is,' said I.

'This, then, which is one, and simple by nature, human perversity separates, and, in trying to win a part of that which has no parts, fails to attain not only that portion (since there are no portions), but also the whole, to which it does not dream of aspiring.'

'How so?' said I.

'He who, to escape want, seeks riches, gives himself no concern about power; he prefers a mean and low estate, and also denies himself many pleasures dear to nature to avoid losing the money which he has gained. But at this rate he does not even attain to independence—a weakling void of strength, vexed by distresses, mean and despised, and buried in obscurity. He, again, who thirsts alone for power squanders his wealth, despises pleasure, and thinks fame and rank alike worthless without power. But thou seest in how many ways his state also is defective. Sometimes it happens that he lacks necessaries, that he is gnawed by anxieties, and, since he cannot rid himself of these inconveniences, even ceases to have that power which was his whole end and aim. In like manner may we cast up the reckoning in case of rank, of glory, or of pleasure. For since each one of these severally is identical with the rest, whosoever seeks any one of them without the others does not even lay hold of that one which he makes his aim.'

'Well,' said I, 'what then?'

'Suppose anyone desire to obtain them together, he does indeed wish for happiness as a whole; but will he find it in these things which, as we have proved, are unable to bestow what they promise?'

'Nay; by no means,' said I.

'Then, happiness must certainly not be sought in these things which severally are believed to afford some one of the blessings most to be desired.'

'They must not, I admit. No conclusion could be more true.'

'So, then, the form and the causes of false happiness are set before thine eyes. Now turn thy gaze to the other side; there thou wilt straightway see the **true happiness** I promised.'

'Yea, indeed, 'tis plain to the blind.' said I. 'Thou didst point it out even now in seeking to unfold the causes of the false. For, unless I am mistaken, that is true and perfect happiness which crowns one with the union of independence, power, reverence, renown, and joy. And to prove to thee with how deep an insight I have listened—since all these are the **same—that which can truly bestow one of them I know to be without doubt full and complete happiness.'**

'Happy art thou, my scholar, in this thy conviction; only one thing shouldst thou add.'

'What is that?' said I.

'Is there aught, thinkest thou, amid these mortal and perishable things which can produce a state such as this?' [**mortals cannot achieve this goal**]

'Nay, surely not; and this thou hast so amply demonstrated that no word more is needed.'

'Well, then, these things seem to give to mortals shadows of the true good, or some kind of imperfect good; but the true and perfect good they cannot bestow.'

'Even so,' said I.

'Since, then, thou hast learnt what that true happiness is, and what men falsely call happiness, it now remains that thou shouldst learn from what source to seek this.'

'Yes; to this I have long been eagerly looking forward.'

'Well, since, as Plato maintains in the "Timæus," we ought even in the most trivial matters to implore the Divine protection, what thinkest thou should we now do in order to deserve to find the seat of that highest good?'

'We must invoke the Father of all things,' said I; 'for without this no enterprise sets out from a right beginning.'

'Thou sayest well,' said she; and forthwith lifted up her voice and sang:

X.

'Since now thou hast seen what is the form of the imperfect good, and what the form of the perfect also, me-thinks I should next show in what manner this perfection of felicity is built up. And here I conceive it proper to inquire, first, whether any excellence, such as thou hast lately defined, can exist in the nature of things, lest we be deceived by an empty fiction of thought to which no true reality answers. But it cannot be denied that such does exist, and is, as it were, the source of all things good. For everything which is called **imperfect** is spoken of as imperfect by reason of the privation of some perfection; so it comes to pass that, whenever imperfection is found in any particular, there must necessarily be a perfection in respect of that particular also. For were there no such perfection, it is utterly inconceivable how that so-called imperfection should come into existence. **Nature does not make a beginning with things mutilated and imperfect; she starts with what is whole and perfect, and falls away later to these feeble and inferior productions.** So if there is, as we showed before, a happiness of a frail and imperfect kind, it cannot be doubted but there is also a happiness substantial and perfect.'

'Most true is thy conclusion, and most sure,' said I.

'Next to consider where the dwelling-place of this happiness may be. The common belief of all mankind agrees that **God, the supreme of all things, is good.** For since nothing can be imagined better than God, how can we doubt Him to be good than whom there is nothing better? Now, reason shows God to be good in such wise as to prove that in Him is **perfect good.** For were it not so, He would not be supreme of all things; for there would be something else more excellent, possessed of perfect good, which would seem to have the advantage in priority and dignity, since it has clearly appeared that all perfect things are prior to those less complete. Wherefore, lest we fall into an infinite regression, we must acknowledge the **supreme God to be full**

of supreme and perfect good. But we have determined that true happiness is the perfect good; therefore true happiness must dwell in the supreme Deity.'

'I accept thy reasonings,' said I; 'they cannot in any wise be disputed.'

'But, come, see how strictly and incontrovertibly thou mayst prove this our assertion that the supreme **Godhead hath fullest possession of the highest good.**'

'In what way, pray?' said I.

'Do not rashly suppose that He who is the Father of all things hath received that highest good of which He is said to be possessed either from some external source, or hath it as a natural endowment in such sort that thou mightest consider the essence of the happiness possessed, and of the God who possesses it, distinct and different. For if thou deemest it received from without, thou mayst esteem that which gives more excellent than that which has received. But Him we most worthily acknowledge to be the most supremely excellent of all things. If, however, it is in Him by nature, yet is logically distinct, the thought is inconceivable, since we are speaking of God, who is supreme of all things. Who was there to join these distinct essences? Finally, when one thing is different from another, the things so conceived as distinct cannot be identical. Therefore that which of its own nature is distinct from the highest good is not itself the highest good—an impious thought of Him than whom, 'tis plain, nothing can be more excellent. For **universally nothing can be better in nature than the source from which it has come;** therefore on most true grounds of reason would I conclude that which is the **source of all things** to be in its own essence the highest good.'

'And most justly,' said I.

'But the highest good has been admitted to be happiness.'

'Yes.'

'Then,' said she, 'it is necessary to acknowledge that **God is very happiness.**'

'Yes,' said I; 'I cannot gainsay my former admissions, and I see clearly that this is a necessary inference therefrom.'

'Reflect, also,' said she, 'whether the same conclusion is not further confirmed by considering that there cannot be two supreme goods distinct one from the other. For the goods which are different clearly cannot be severally each what the other is: wherefore neither of the two can be perfect, since to either the other is wanting; but since it is not perfect, it cannot manifestly be the supreme good. By no means, then, can goods which are supreme be different one from the other. But we have concluded that both **happiness and God are the supreme good;** wherefore that which is highest Divinity must also itself necessarily be supreme happiness.'

'No conclusion,' said I, 'could be truer to fact, nor more soundly reasoned out, nor more worthy of God.'

'Then, further,' said she, 'just as geometricians are wont to draw inferences from their demonstrations to which they give the name "deductions," so will I add here a sort of corollary. For since men become happy by the acquisition of happiness, while happiness is very Godship, it is manifest that they **become happy by the acquisition of Godship.** But as by the acquisition of justice men become just, and wise by the acquisition of wisdom, so by parity of reasoning by acquiring Godship they must of necessity become gods. So **every man who is happy is a god; and though in nature God** is One only, yet there is nothing to hinder that very many should be gods by participation in that nature.' [**happiness rests in God, in goodness, in unity, in harmony, in the origin of all things**]

'A fair conclusion, and a precious,' said I, 'deduction or corollary, by whichever name thou wilt call it.'

'And yet,' said she, 'not one whit fairer than this which reason persuades us to add.'

'Why, what?' said I.

'Why, seeing happiness has many particulars included under it, should all these be regarded as forming one body of happiness, as it were, made up of various parts, or is there some one of them which forms the full essence of happiness, while all the rest are relative to this?'

'I would thou wouldst unfold the whole matter to me at large.'

'We judge happiness to be good, do we not?'

'Yea, the supreme good.'

'And this superlative applies to all; for this same happiness is adjudged to be the completest independence, the highest power, reverence, renown, and pleasure.'

'What then?'

'Are all these goods—independence, power, and the rest—to be deemed members of happiness, as it were, or are they all relative to good as to their summit and crown?'

'I understand the problem, but I desire to hear how thou wouldst solve it.'

'Well, then, listen to the determination of the matter. Were all these members composing happiness, they would differ severally one from the other. For this is the nature of parts—that by their difference they compose one body. All these, however, have been **proved to be the same;** therefore they cannot possibly be members, otherwise happiness will seem to be built up out of one member, which cannot be.'

'There can be no doubt as to that,' said I; 'but I am impatient to hear what remains.'

'Why, it is manifest that all the others are relative to the good. For the very reason why independence is sought is that it is judged good, and so power also, because it is believed to be good. The same, too, may be supposed of reverence, of renown, and of pleasant delight. **Good, then, is the sum and source of all desirable things.** That which has not in itself any good, either in reality or in semblance, can in no wise be desired. Contrariwise, even things which by nature are not good are desired as if they were truly good, if they seem to be so. Whereby it comes to pass that **goodness is rightly believed to be the sum and hinge and cause of all things desirable.** Now, that for the sake of which anything is desired itself seems to be most wished for. For instance, if anyone wishes to ride for the sake of health, he does not so much wish for the exercise of riding as the benefit of his health. Since, then, all things are sought for the sake of the good, it is not these so much as good itself that is sought by all. But that on account of which all other things are wished for was, we agreed, **happiness;** wherefore thus also it appears that it is happiness alone which is sought. From all which it is transparently clear that the essence of absolute good and of happiness is one and the same.' [**we all aim for happiness, hence goodness, hence unity, hence oneness with God**]

'I cannot see how anyone can dissent from these conclusions.'

'But we have also proved that God and true happiness are one and the same.'

'Yes,' said I.

'Then we can safely conclude, also, that God's essence is seated in absolute good, and nowhere else.'

'I quite agree,' said I, 'truly all thy reasonings hold admirably together.'

XII.

Then said she: 'What value wouldst thou put upon the boon shouldst thou come to the knowledge of the **absolute good?**'

'Oh, an infinite,' said I, 'if only I were so blest as to learn to know God also who is the good.'

'Yet this will I make clear to thee on truest grounds of reason, if only our recent conclusions stand fast.'

'They will.'

'Have we not shown that those things which most men desire are not true and perfect good precisely for this cause—that they differ severally one from another, and, seeing that one is wanting to another, they cannot bestow full and absolute good; but that they become the true good when they are gathered, as it were, into one form and agency, so that that which is independence is likewise power, reverence, renown, and pleasant delight, and unless they are all one and the same, they have no claim to be counted among things desirable?'

'Yes; this was clearly proved, and cannot in any wise be doubted.'

'Now, when things are far from being good while they are different, but become good as soon as they are one, is it not true that these become good by acquiring unity?'

'It seems so,' said I.

'But dost not thou allow that all which is good is good by participation in goodness?'

'It is.'

'Then, thou must on similar grounds admit that unity and goodness are the same; for when the effects of things in their natural working differ not, their essence is one and the same.'

'There is no denying it.'

'Now, dost thou know,' said she, 'that all which is abides and subsists so long as it continues one, but so soon as it ceases to be one it perishes and falls to pieces?' [**loss of unity means loss of happiness**]

'In what way?'

'Why, take **animals,** for example. When soul and body come together, and continue in one, this is, we say, a living creature; but when this unity is broken by the separation of these two, the creature dies, and is clearly no longer living. The body also, while it remains in one form by the joining together of its members, presents a human appearance; but if the separation and dispersal of the parts break up the body's unity, it ceases to be what it was. And if we extend our survey to all other things, without doubt it will manifestly appear that each several thing subsists while it is one, but when it ceases to be one perishes.'

'Yes; when I consider further, I see it to be even as thou sayest.'

'Well, is there aught,' said she, 'which, in so far as it acts conformably to nature, **abandons the wish for life, and desires to come to death and corruption?**'

'Looking to living creatures, which have some faults of choice, I find none that, without external compulsion, forego the will to live, and of their own accord hasten to destruction. For every creature diligently pursues the end of self-preservation, and shuns death and destruction! As to herbs and trees, and inanimate things generally, I am altogether in doubt what to think.' [**we all want to live**]

'And yet there is no possibility of question about this either, since thou seest how **herbs and trees** grow in places suitable for them, where, as far as their nature admits, they cannot quickly wither and die. Some spring up in the plains, others in the mountains; some grow in marshes, others cling to rocks; and others, again, find a fertile soil in the barren sands; and if you try to transplant these elsewhere, they wither away. **Nature gives to each the soil that suits** it, and uses her diligence to prevent any of them dying, so long as it is possible for them to continue alive. Why do they all draw their nourishment from roots as from a mouth dipped into the earth, and distribute the strong bark over the pith? Why are all the softer parts like the pith deeply encased within, while the external parts have the strong texture of wood, and outside of all is the bark to resist the weather's inclemency, like a champion stout in endurance? Again, how great is nature's diligence to secure universal propagation by multiplying seed! Who does not know all these to be contrivances, not only for the present maintenance of a species, but for its lasting continuance, generation after generation, for ever? And do not also the things believed inanimate on like grounds of reason seek each what is proper to itself? Why do the flames shoot lightly upward, while the earth presses downward with its weight, if it is not that these motions and situations are suitable to their respective natures? Moreover, each several thing is preserved by that which is agreeable to its nature, even as it is destroyed by things inimical. Things solid like stones resist disintegration by the close adhesion of their parts. Things fluid like air and water yield easily to what divides them, but swiftly flow back and mingle with those parts from which they have been severed, while fire, again, refuses to be cut at all. And we are not now treating of the voluntary motions of an intelligent soul, but of the drift of nature. Even so is it that we digest our food without thinking about it, and draw our breath unconsciously in sleep; nay, even in living creatures the love of life cometh not of conscious will, but from the principles of nature. For oftentimes in the stress of circumstances will chooses the death which nature shrinks from; and contrarily, in spite of natural appetite, will restrains that work of reproduction by which alone the persistence of perishable creatures is maintained. So entirely does this **love of self** come from drift of nature, not from animal impulse. **Providence** has furnished things with this most cogent reason for continuance: they must desire life, so long as it is naturally possible for them to continue living. Wherefore in no way mayst thou doubt but that **things naturally aim at continuance of existence, and shun destruction.'**

'I confess,' said I, 'that what I lately thought uncertain, I now perceive to be indubitably clear.'

'Now, that which seeks to subsist and continue desires to be one; for if its oneness be gone, its very existence cannot continue.' [**what do we all desire and need to be happy, or good?**]

'True,' said I.

'All things, then, desire to be one.'

'I agree.'

'But we have proved that one is the very same thing as good.'

'We have.'

'All things, then, seek the good; indeed, you may express the fact by defining good as that which all desire.'

'Nothing could be more truly thought out. Either there is no single end to which all things are relative, or else the end to which all things universally hasten must be the highest good of all.'

Then she: 'Exceedingly do I rejoice, dear pupil; thine eye is now fixed on the very central mark of truth. Moreover, herein is revealed that of which thou didst erstwhile profess thyself ignorant.'

'What is that?' said I.

'**The end and aim of the whole universe.** Surely it is that which is desired of all; and, since we have concluded the good to be such, we ought to acknowledge the end and aim of the whole universe to be "the good."' [**this is the key message**]

XII.

Then said I: 'With all my heart I agree with Plato; indeed, this is now the second time that these things have been brought back to my mind—first I lost them through the clogging contact of the body; then after through the stress of heavy grief.'

Then she continued: 'If thou wilt reflect upon thy former admissions, it will not be long before thou dost also recollect that of which erstwhile thou didst confess thyself ignorant.'

'What is that?' said I.

'The principles of the world's government,' said she.

'Yes; I remember my confession, and, although I now anticipate what thou intendest, I have a desire to hear the argument plainly set forth.'

'Awhile ago thou deemedst it beyond all doubt that God doth govern the world.'

'I do not think it doubtful now, nor shall I ever; and by what reasons I am brought to this assurance I will briefly set forth. This world could never have taken shape as a single system out of parts so diverse and opposite were it not that there is One who joins together these so diverse things. And when it had once come together, the very diversity of natures would have dissevered it and torn it asunder in universal discord were there not One who keeps together what He has joined. Nor would the order of nature proceed so regularly, nor could its course exhibit motions so fixed in respect of position, time, range, efficacy, and character, unless there were One who, Himself abiding, disposed these various vicissitudes of change. This power, whatsoever it be, whereby they remain as they were created, and are kept in motion, I call by the name which all **recognise—God.**'

Then said she: 'Seeing that such is thy belief, it will cost me little trouble, I think, to enable thee to **win happiness, and return in safety to thy own country.** But let us give our attention to the task that we have set before ourselves. Have we not counted independence in the category of happiness, and agreed that God is absolute happiness?'

'Truly, we have.'

'Then, He will need no external assistance for the ruling of the world. Otherwise, if He stands in need of aught, He will not possess complete independence.'

'That is necessarily so,' said I.

'Then, by His own power alone He disposes all things.'

'It cannot be denied.'

'Now, God was proved to be absolute good.' 'Yes; I remember.'

'Then, He disposes all things by the agency of good, if it be true that He rules all things by His own power whom we have agreed to be good; and He is, as it were, the rudder and helm by which the world's mechanism is kept steady and in order.'

'Heartily do I agree; and, indeed, I anticipated what thou wouldst say, though it may be in feeble surmise only.'

'I well believe it,' said she; 'for, as I think, thou now bringest to the search eyes quicker in discerning truth; but what I shall say next is no less plain and easy to see.'

'What is it?' said I.

'Why,' said she, 'since God is rightly believed to govern all things with the rudder of goodness, and since all things do likewise, as I have taught, haste towards good by the very aim of nature, can it be doubted that His governance is willingly accepted, and that all submit themselves to the sway of the Disposer as conformed and attempered to His rule?' [**the natural drive goes toward the good, or God**]

'Necessarily so,' said I; 'no rule would seem happy if it were a yoke imposed on reluctant wills, and not the safe-keeping of obedient subjects.'

'There is **nothing, then, which, while it follows nature, endeavours to resist good.**'

'No; nothing.'

'But if anything should, will it have the least success against Him whom we rightly agreed to be supreme Lord of happiness?'

'It would be utterly impotent.'

'**There is nothing, then, which has either the will or the power to oppose this supreme good.**'

'No; I think not.'

'So, then,' said she, 'it is the supreme good which rules in strength, and graciously disposes all things.'

Then said I: 'How delighted am I at thy reasonings, and the conclusion to which thou hast brought them, but most of all at these very words which thou usest! I am now at last ashamed of the folly that so sorely vexed me.'

'Thou hast heard the story of the giants assailing heaven; but a beneficent strength disposed of them also, as they deserved. But shall we submit our arguments to the shock of mutual collision?—it may be from the impact some fair spark of truth may be struck out.'

'If it be thy good pleasure,' said I.

'No one can doubt that God is all-powerful.'

'No one at all can question it who thinks consistently.'

'Now, there is nothing which One who is all-powerful cannot do.'

'Nothing.'

'But can **God do evil, then?**'

'Nay; by no means.'

'Then, **evil is nothing,**' said she, 'since He to whom nothing is impossible is unable to do evil.'

'Art thou mocking me,' said I, 'weaving a labyrinth of tangled arguments, now seeming to begin where thou didst end, and now to end where thou didst begin, or dost thou build up some wondrous circle of Divine simplicity? For, truly, a little before thou didst begin with happiness, and say it was the supreme good, and didst declare it to be seated in the supreme Godhead. God Himself, too, thou didst affirm to be supreme good and all-complete happiness; and from this thou didst go on to add, as by the way, the proof that no one would be happy unless he were likewise God. Again, thou didst say that the very form of good was the essence both of God and of happiness, and didst teach that the absolute One was the absolute good which was sought by universal nature. Thou didst maintain, also, that God rules the universe by the governance of goodness, that all things obey Him willingly, and that evil has no existence in nature. And all this thou didst unfold without the help of assumptions from without, but by inherent and proper proofs, drawing credence one from the other.'

Then answered she: 'Far is it from me to mock thee; nay, by the blessing of God, whom we lately addressed in prayer, we have achieved the most important of all objects. For such is the form of the Divine essence, that neither can it pass into things external, nor take up anything external into itself; but, as Parmenides says of it, '"In body like to a sphere on all sides perfectly rounded,"

… it rolls the restless orb of the universe, keeping itself motionless the while. And if I have also employed reasonings not drawn from without, but lying within the compass of our subject, there is no cause for thee to marvel, since thou hast learnt on Plato's authority that words ought to be akin to the matter of which they treat.'

[He concludes by saying in Book IV that the evil ones in life, who truly exist, really do not exist because they move deliberately away from good, hence destroy themselves, since they turn against their own instinct, and so deserve only pity!]

THE SONG OF HILDEBRAND

By Anonymous

This is the oldest medieval German literary text, and the first heroic poem, copied down in a liturgical manuscript sometime during the early ninth century in the famous Benedictine monastery of Fulda, today northeast of Frankfurt and south of Kassel. We do not know why this fragmentary text was even written down in the first place in a liturgical manuscript (first and last page), but we can be certain that the monks considered it an important text, perhaps building intriguing bridges to the pagan cultures that they tried to convert to Christianity. The tragic development between father and son, both leaders of hostile armies, strongly suggests that the poem reflects on the collapse of ancient tribal values among the Germanic people, on the devastating consequences of failed communication between close family members, and on the desperate need to abandon traditional heroic values and to subscribe to new, perhaps Christian, ideals and principles of personal exchanges. The two pages of this epic were stored in presumably safe salt mines at the end of the Second World War, but were nevertheless stolen by some American soldier. The first leaf reappeared in the USA during the 1950s and was returned to Kassel in 1955, the second one was restored to Germany in 1972.

The first part of this heroic poem might be hard to understand because the poet manipulated the historical account, turning everything on its head. Theoderic, here Dietrich, had actually conquered Italy with the silent approval of the Eastern Roman emperor Zeno in Constantinople, and in that process had defeated the general-king Odoacer, whom he personally murdered in 493. This Theoderic was also the Ostrogothic ruler in whose service we find Boethius (see above). Later poets and chroniclers changed all those events, and made Theoderic/Dietrich to Odoacer's victim who had to flee and to go into exile with the Hunnish ruler Attila/Etzel. Hildebrand is described as one of Dietrich's liege men who had to follow his lord into exile.

Ik gihorta ðat seggen,
ðat sih urhettun aenon muotin,
Hiltibrant enti Hadubrant untar heriun tuem.

I heard this tale   [of hap and harm],
That two warriors wielded   their weapons against each other,
Hildebrand and Hadubrand,   between two hosts.
The father and son   fastened their armor,
Buckled their harness,   belted their swords on
Over coat of mail   as to combat they rode.
Hildebrand spoke then,   the hoary-hair'd warrior,
More wise in life's wisdom: he warily asked,
And few were his words,   who his father was
In the folk of the foemen.   "[Thy friends would I know,
And kindly tell me]   what kin thou dost claim.
If thou namest but one,   I shall know then the others:
The kin of this kingdom   are couth to me all."
Hadubrand answer'd,   Hildebrand's son:
"This lore I learned   from long ago,
From the wise and old   who were of yore,
That Hildebrand hight my father: my name is Hadubrand.
Off to the east he wander'd,   the anger of Ottokar fleeing,
Marching away with Dietrich,   and many a man went with him.
He left in the land   a little one lorn,
A babe at the breast   in the bower of the bride,
Bereft of his rights: thus he rode to the east.
But later Dietrich   lost my father
And lived henceforth   a lonely man.
For the foe of Ottokar,   so fierce and keen,
Was the dearest of thanes   to Dietrich his lord.
He was fain to fight   where the fray was thick:
Known was his bravery   among bold warriors.
I can not believe   that he lives longer.
"I swear by the God   who sways the heavens
That the bonds of blood   forbid our strife."
Then he unclaspt from his arm   the clinging gold,
Which was wrought of coin   that the king had given.
The lord of the Huns: "With love I give it."
But Hadubrand answer'd,   Hildebrand's son:

"With the tip of the spear   one takes the gift
From the sharpened edge   of the foeman's shaft.
Thou thinkest, old Hun,   thy thoughts are deep,
Thou speakest alluring words   with the spear it would like thee
    to wound me.
With untruth art thou come to old age   for trickery clings to thee
    ever.
It was said to me   by seafarers
Coming west over the wave   that war slew him.
Dead is Hildebrand,   Heribrand's son."
"Great Weirdwielder,   woe worth the day!
For sixty winters   and summers I wander'd,
Battling with foemen   where blows keen fell.
From the scarped wall   unscathed I came.
Now the son of my loins   with the sword will hew me;
He will deal me death   or I dash him to earth.
But now canst thou strike,   if strong be thine arm,
Canst win the harness   from so hoary a man.
And strip the spoils   from the stricken foe.
Hadubrand answer'd,   Hildebrand's son:
"Full well I hold,   from thy harness rich.
That thou comest hither   from a kindly lord,
In whose kingdom thou wast not   a wandering wretch."
"The heart of a coward   would the Hun now have
Who would shrink from a foe   so fain to fight.
To struggle together.   Let each now strive
To see whether today   he must bite the dust
Or may bear from the field   the byrnies of both.[35]
Then first they hurled   the hurtling spears
In sharpest showers   that shook the shields.
Then they clasht with their brands,   the battle-boards bursting
And hewed with might   the white linden
Till they shivered the shields   with shattering strokes,
As they wielded their weapons. …

[trans. Francis A. Wood]

THE NIBELUNGENLIED

By Anonymous (circa. 1200)

T he anonymous Nibelungenlied *was composed around 1200 at the court of Bishop Wolfger von Erlau in Passau, today at the border of Germany and Austria, northwest of Salzburg. Although surviving as a written heroic epic in numerous manuscripts, the anonymous poet drew on a variety of oral sources dating back to the fifth and sixth centuries. In fact, the appearance of the Hunnish King Etzel/Attila who marries the Burgundian princess Kriemhild proves to be a strangely modified historical reference to the highly feared Hunnish ruler Attila (d. 453) who had tried to attack Rome but was defeated in 451 in the area of modern-day northeastern France. The Middle High German poet might have been a scribe in the service of Bishop Wolfger, and he managed to preserve, or create once again, one of the most important heroic epics from the entire Middle Ages with this work. Although there are two distinct parts, the first taking us to the death of the hero Siegfried, the second one to the total annihilation of all Burgundians (by then mysteriously called "Nibelungen") and the death of the entire dynasty of King Gunther, including his own sister Kriemhild, the scribe managed to merge both parts, and others, and created a most ominous heroic poem, which enjoyed great popularity far into the sixteenth century. Its rediscovery began in the middle of the eighteenth century, and the* Nibelungenlied *has been regarded one of the greatest German heroic epics ever since.*

(1) In old tales they tell us many wonders of heroes and of high courage, of glad feasting, of weeping and of mourning; herein ye shall read of the marvellous deeds and of the strife of brave men.

There grew up in Burgundy a noble maiden; in no land was a fairer. Kriemhild was her name. Well favoured was the damsel, and by reason of her died many warriors. Doughty knights in plenty wooed her, as was meet, for of her body she was exceeding comely, and her virtues were an adornment to all women.

Three kings noble and rich guarded her, Gunther and Gernot, warriors of fame, and Giselher the youth, a chosen knight. The damsel was their sister, and the care of her fell on them. These lords were courteous and of high lineage, bold and very strong, each of them the pick of knights. The name of their country was Burgundy, and they did great deeds, after, in Etzel's land. At Worms, by the Rhine, they dwelled in might with many a proud lord for vassal.

Their mother was a rich queen and hight Uta, and the name of their father was Dankrat, who, when his life was ended, left them his lands. A strong man was he in his time, and one that in his youth won great worship.

Now it so fell that Kriemhild, the pure maid, dreamed a dream that she fondled a wild falcon, and eagles wrested it from her; the which to see grieved her more than any ill that had happened to her heretofore.

This dream she told to Uta, her mother, who interpreted it on this wise. "The falcon that thou sawest is a noble man; yet if God keep him not, he is a lost man to thee."

"What speakest thou to me of a man, mother mine? Without their love would I still abide, that I may remain fair till my death, nor suffer dole from any man's love."

Said her mother then, "Be not so sure; for wouldst thou ever on this earth have heart's gladness, it cometh from the love of a man. And a fair wife wilt thou be, if God but lead hither to thee a true and trusty knight."

"Say not so, mother mine," answered the maiden, "for on many a woman and oft hath it been proven that the meed of love is sorrow. From both I will keep me, that evil betide not."

Long in such wise abode the high, pure maiden, nor thought to love any. Nevertheless, at the last, she wedded a brave man; that was the falcon she dreamed of erstwhile, as her mother foretold it. Yea, bitter was her vengeance on her kinsmen that slew him, and by reason of his death died many a mother's son.

(2) There grew up in the Netherland a rich king's child, whose father was called Siegmund and his mother Sieglind, in a castle high and famous called Xanten, down by the Rhine's side. Goodly was this knight, by my troth, his body without blemish, a strong and valiant man of great worship; abroad, through the whole earth, went his fame. The hero hight Siegfried, and he rode boldly into many lands. Ha! in Burgundy, I trow, he found warriors to his liking. Or he was a man grown he had done marvels with his hand, as is said and sung, albeit now there is no time for more word thereof.

(3) No love pangs ever entered the heart of the hero Siegfried until one day he received news that there was a fair maid in Burgundy of utmost beauty. Because of her he was later to experience many joys and also many troubles.

Her beauty was rumoured far and wide, and the fame of her virtues, joined thereto, brought many strangers into Gunther's land. Yet, though many wooed her, Kriemhild was firm-minded to wed none. The man that was to win her was yet a stranger.

Thereupon Siegmund's son yearned to her with true love. Weighed with him all other suitors were as wind, for he was meet to be chosen of fair women; and, or long, Kriemhild the high maiden was bold Sir Siegfried's bride.

The tidings came to Siegmund's ear. His knight told him Siegfried's intent, and it irked him that his son should woo the royal maiden. To Sieglind, the king's wife, they told it also, and she feared for his life, for she knew Gunther and his men.

They would have turned him from his quest.

Spoke bold Siegfried then, "Dearest father mine, either I will think no more on women at all, or I will woo where my heart's desire is." And for all they could say, he changed not his purpose.

Then said the king, "If thou wilt not yield in this, by my faith, I approve thy choice, and will further thee therein as I best can. Nevertheless, Gunther hath many mighty men, were it none other than Hagen, an arrogant and overweening knight. I fear both thou and I must rue that thou goest after this king's daughter."

Siegfried answered, "I will not ride with an army of warriors to the Rhine; it would shame me so to win the maiden by force. I would win her with mine own hand. One of twelve I will forth to Gunther's land, and to this shalt thou help me, my father Siegmund."

They gave to his knights cloaks of fur, some grey and some striped.

Now the time was come to ride forth, and all the folk, men and women, made dole, lest they should return never more.

The knights were downcast, and the maidens wept. Their hearts told them, I ween, that by reason of this day's doings, many a dear one would lie dead. Needs made they dole, for they were sorrowful.

On the seventh morning after this, the fearless band drew toward Worms on the Rhine.

They told the king that a valiant knight, fair equipped and apparelled, that knew none in Burgundy, was come thither. And the king marvelled where these proud knights in shining harness, with their shields new and massy, might hie from. It irked him that none knew it.

Ortwin of Metz, a goodly man of high courage, spoke to the king then, "Since we know nothing thereof, bid to thee Hagen mine uncle, and show them to him. For he hath knowledge of the mighty men of all lands; and what he knoweth he will tell us."

The king summoned Hagen with his vassals, and he drew nigh with proud step, and asked the king his will.

"Strange knights are come to my court that none knoweth. If thou hast ever seen them afore, tell me thereof truly."

"That will I," spoke Hagen, and went to the window, and looked down on the strangers below. The show of them and their equipment pleased him, but he had not seen them afore in Burgundy. And he said, "From wheresoever they be come, they must be princes, or princes' envoys. Their horses are good, and wonderly rich their vesture. From whatso quarter they hie, they be seemly men. But for this I vouch, that, though I never saw Siegfried, yonder knight that goeth so proud is, of a surety, none but he. New adventures he bringeth hither. By this hero's hand fell the brave Nibelungen, Shilbung and Nibelung, the high princes. Wonders hath he wrought by his prowess. I have heard tell that on a day when he rode alone, he came to a mountain, and chanced on a company of brave men that guarded the Nibelungen hoard, whereof he knew nothing. The Nibelung men had, at that moment, made an end of bringing it forth from a hole in the hill, and oddly enow, they were about to share it. Siegfried saw them and marvelled thereat. He drew so close that they were ware of him and he of them. Whereupon one said, 'Here cometh Siegfried, the hero of the Netherland!' Strange adventure met he amidst of them. Shilbung and Nibelung welcomed him, and with one accord the princely youths asked him to divide the treasure atween them, and begged this so eagerly that he could not say them nay. The tale goeth that he saw there more precious stones than an hundred double waggons had sufficed to carry, and of the red Nibelung gold yet more. This must bold Siegfried divide. In guerdon therefor they gave him the sword of the Nibelungen, and were ill paid by Siegfried for the service. He strove vainly to end the task, whereat they were wroth. And when he could not bear it through, the kings, with their men, fell upon him. But with their father's sword that hight Balmung, he wrested from both hoard and land. The princes had twelve champions—strong giants, yet little it bested them. Siegfried slew them wrathfully with his hand, and, with Balmung, vanquished seven hundred knights; and many youths there, afraid of the man and his sword, did homage for castles and land. He smote the two kings dead. Then he, himself, came in scathe by Alberic, that would have avenged the death of his masters then and there, till that he felt Siegfried's exceeding might. When the dwarf could not overcome him, they ran like lions to the mountain, where Siegfried won from Alberic the cloud-cloak that hight *Tarnkappe*. Then was Siegfried, the terrible man, master of the hoard. They that had dared the combat lay slain; and he bade carry the treasure back whence the Nibelungen had brought it forth; and he made Alberic the keeper thereof, after that he had sworn an oath to serve him as his man, and to do all that he commanded him.

"These are his deeds," said Hagen; "bolder knight there never was. Yet more I might tell of him. With his hand he slew a dragon, and bathed him in its blood, that his skin is as horn, and no weapon can cut him, as hath been proven on him ofttimes.

"Let us welcome the young lord, that we come not in his hate. So fair is he of his body that one may not look unfriendly thereon; with his strength he hath done great deeds."

"Thou art welcome," said Uta's son; "thou and thy comrades that are with thee. We will serve thee gladly, I and my kinsmen."

They let pour for them Gunther's wine, and the host of the land, even Gunther the king, said, "All that is ours, and whatsoever thou mayest with honour desire, is thine to share with us, body and goods."

The king and his men busied them with sports, and in each undertaking Siegfried still approved him the best. Whether they threw the stone or shot with the shaft, none came near him by reason of his great strength. Held the doughty warriors tourney before the women, then looked these all with favour on the knight of the Netherland. But, as for him, he thought only on his high love. The fair women of the court demanded who the proud stranger was. "He is so goodly," they said, "and so rich his apparel."

And there answered them folk enow, "It is the king of the Netherland." Whatsoever sport they followed, he was ready. In his heart he bare the beautiful maiden that as yet he had not seen: the which spoke in secret kind words also of him. When the youths tilted in the courtyard, Kriemhild, the high princess, looked down at them from her window; nor, at that time, desired she better pastime. Neither had he asked better, had he known that his heart's dear one gazed upon him.

When the rich kings rode abroad, it behoved the knights to go with them, wherefore Siegfried also rode forth, the which irked the damsel sore; and likewise, for love of her, he was heavy enow of his cheer.

So a year (I say honestly) he abode by these princes, nor in all that time had once seen his dear one, that afterward brought him much gladness and dole.

(5) On Whitsun morning there drew toward the hightide a goodly company of brave men, fairly clad: five thousand or more, and they made merry far and wide, and strove with one another in friendly combat.

Now Gunther knew well how, truly and from his heart, the hero of the Netherland loved his sister whom he had not yet seen, and whose beauty the people praised before that of all other maidens.

And he said, "Now counsel me, my kinsmen and my lieges, how we may order this hightide, that none may blame us in anything; for only unto such deeds as are good, pertaineth lasting fame."

Then answered Ortwin, the knight, to the king, "If thou wilt win for thyself glory from the hightide, let now the maidens that dwell with honour in our midst appear before us. For what shall pleasure or glad a man more than to behold beautiful damsels and fair women? Bid thy sister come forth and show herself to thy guests."

And this word pleased the knights.

"That will I gladly do," said the king; and they that heard him rejoiced. He sent a messenger to Queen Uta, and besought her that she would come to the court with her daughter and her womenfolk.

And these took from the presses rich apparel, and what lay therein in wrapping-cloths; they took also brooches, and their silken girdles worked with gold, and attired themselves in haste. Many a noble maiden adorned herself with care, and the youths longed exceedingly to find favour in their eyes, and had not taken a rich king's land in lieu thereof. And they that knew not one another before looked each upon each right gladly.

The rich king commanded an hundred men of his household, his kinsmen and hers, to escort his sister, their swords in their hand. Uta, with an hundred and more of her women, gorgeously attired, came forth from the female apartments, and many noble damsels followed after her daughter. The knights pressed in upon them, thinking thereby to behold the beautiful maiden.

And lo! the fair one appeared, like the dawn from out the dark clouds. And he that had borne her so long in his heart was no more aweary, for the beloved one, his sweet lady, stood before him in her beauty. Bright jewels sparkled on her garments, and bright was the rose-red of her hue, and all they that saw her proclaimed her peerless among maidens.

As the moon excelleth in light the stars shining clear from the clouds, so stood she, fair before the other women, and the hearts of the warriors were uplifted. The chamberlains made way for her through them that pressed in to behold her. And Siegfried joyed, and sorrowed likewise, for he said in his heart, "How should I woo such as thee? Surely it was a vain dream; yet I were liefer dead than a stranger to thee."

Thinking thus he waxed oft white and red; yea, graceful and proud stood the son Sieglind, goodliest of heroes to behold, as he were drawn on parchment by the skill of a cunning master. And the knights fell back as the escort commanded, and made way for the high-hearted women, and gazed on them with glad eyes. Many a dame of high degree was there.

She greeted him mild and maidenly, and her colour was kindled when she saw before her the high-minded man, and she said, "Welcome, Sir Siegfried, noble knight and good." His courage rose at her words, and graceful, as beseemed a knight, he bowed himself before her and thanked her. And love that is mighty constrained them, and they yearned with their eyes in secret. I know not whether, from his great love, the youth pressed her white hand, but two love-desirous hearts, I trow, had else done amiss.

Nevermore, in summer or in May, bore Siegfried in his heart such high joy, as when he went by the side of her whom he coveted for his dear one. And many a knight, thought, "Had it been my hap to walk with her, as I have seen him do, or to lie by her side, certes, I had suffered it gladly! Yet never, truly, hath warrior served better to win a queen." From what land soever the guests came, they were ware only of these two. And she was bidden kiss the hero. He had never had like joy before in this world.

(6) A fresh rumour from Iceland spread down to the Rhine. It was reported that many maidens dwelt there; and Gunther was minded to woo one of them, whereat his knights and his liegeman were well pleased.

There was a queen high throned across the sea, that had not her like, beyond measure fair and of mickle strength, and her love was for that knight only that could pass her at the spear. She hurled the stone and leapt after it to the mark. Any that desired the noble damsel's love must first win boldly in these three games. If he failed but in one, he lost his head.

On a day that the king sat with his men, and they cast to and fro whom their prince might best take to wife for his own comfort and the good of his land, the lord of Rhineland said, "I will hence across the sea to Brunhild, let what will betide. For her sake I will peril my body, for I lose it if I win her not to wife."

"Do not so," said Siegfried. "Cruel is the queen, and he that would woo her playeth too high a stake. Make not this journey."

But King Gunther answered, "Never yet was woman born so strong and bold, that, with this single hand, I could not vanquish her in strife."

"Then I counsel thee," said Hagen, "to ask Siegfried to share with thee this hard emprise. It were well, since he knoweth so much of Brunhild."

So the king spoke, "Wilt thou help me, most noble Siegfried, to woo the damsel? Grant me this, and if I win the royal maiden for my dear one, I will adventure honour and life for thy sake."

Siegfried, the son of Siegmund, made answer, "Give me thy sister Kriemhild, the high princess, and I will do it. Other meed I ask not."

Said Gunther, "I swear it, Siegfried, on thy hand. If Brunhild come hither, I will give thee my sister to wife; and mayest thou live joyfully with her to thy life's end."

The noble warriors sware an oath; and travail enow they endured, or they led back the fair one to the Rhine; yea, ofttimes they were straightened sore.

I have heard tell of wild dwarfs: how that they dwell in hollow mountains, and wear wonderful cloaks called *Tarnkappes*. And whoso hath this on his body cometh not in scathe by blows or spear-thrusts; nor is he seen of any man so long as he weareth it, but may spy and hearken at his will. His strength also waxeth thereby; so runneth the tale.

Siegfried took the *Tarnkappe* with him that he had wrested from Alberic the dwarf. And these high and noble knights made ready for the journey. When strong Siegfried did on the *Tarnkappe,* he was strong with the strength of twelve men, and with these cunning devices he won the royal maiden; for the cloak of cloud was fashioned on such wise, that whoso wore it did what him listed, none seeing; and he won Brunhild thereby, that after brought him dole.

Kriemhild said, "Dear brother, thou didst better to stay here and woo other women without risk to thy body. It were easy to find, nigh at hand, a wife of as high lineage."

I ween her heart told her the dole that was to come.

She spoke further, "Sir Siegfried, to thy care and good faith I commend my dear brother, that no evil betide him in Brunhild's land." The knight gave his hand thereon, and promised it. He said, "Fear not, lady; if I live, I will bring him back safe to the Rhine. I swear it by mine own body."

And the fair maiden thanked him.

They say that by the twelfth morning the wind had blown them afar to Isenstein in Brunhild's land, the which none had seen before that, save Siegfried. When King Gunther beheld so many towers and broad marches, he cried out, "Now say, friend Siegfried; knowest thou whose are these castles and these fair lands? By my troth, I have never in my life seen castles so many and so goodly as stand there before us. A mighty man he must be that hath builded them."

Whereto Siegfried made answer, "Yea, I know well. They are all Brunhild's—towers and lands, and the castle of Isenstein. I say honestly; and many fair women shall ye behold this day. Now I counsel you, O knights, for so it seemeth good to me, that ye be all of one mind and one word; we must stand warily before Brunhild the queen. And when we see the fair one amidst of her folk, be sure ye tell all the same story: that Gunther is my lord and I his liegeman. So shall he win to his desire. Yet this I do less for love of thee than for the fair maid, thy sister, that is to me as my soul and mine own body, and for whom I gladly serve, that I may win her to wife."

They promised with one accord, and none gainsayed him through pride, the which stood them in good stead when the king came to stand before Brunhild.

(7) They left the vessel unguarded on the beach, and rode up to the castle. There they saw eighty and six towers, three great palaces, and a stately hall of costly marble, green like grass, wherein the queen sat with her courtiers.

Brunhild's men unlocked the castle gate and threw it wide, and ran toward them, and welcomed the guests to their queen's land. They bade hold the horses, and take the shields from their hands. And the chamberlain said, "Do off your swords now, and your bright armour." "Not so," answered Hagen of Troneck; "we will bear these ourselves."

But Siegfried told them the custom of the court. "It is the law here that no guest shall bear arms. Wherefore ye did well to give them up."

Gunther's man obeyed, much loth. They bade pour out the wine for the guests, and see that they were well lodged. Willing knights in princely attire ran to and fro to serve them, spying with many glances at the strangers.

They brought word to Brunhild that unknown warriors in rich apparel were come thither, sailing on the sea, and the beautiful maiden questioned them. "Tell me," said the queen, "who these strangers be that stand yonder so proudly, and for whose sake they be come." And one of the courtiers made answer. "In honesty, Lady, albeit I never set eyes on them, one among them much resembleth Siegfried, and him I counsel thee to welcome. The second of the company hath so lofty a mien that, if his power be equal thereto, he might well be a great king and a ruler of wide lands, for he standeth right proudly before the others. The third, O Queen, is grim, yet a goodly man withal. His glance is swift and dark; he is fierce-tempered, I ween. The youngest pleaseth me well. Maidenly and modest he standeth, yet it went hard, methinketh, with any that angered him. For all that he seemeth gentle, and is fashioned daintily, if his wrath were once kindled, many a woman might weep, for he is a bold and virtuous knight, and right worshipful."

The queen said, "Bring me my robe. If strong Siegfried be come into my land to woo me, he shall pay for it with his life. I fear him not so greatly that I should yield me to be his wife."

Then Brunhild attired her in haste. An hundred or more of her damsels went with her, richly adorned, whom the guests beheld gladly. Brunhild's knights of Issland gave them escort, to the number of five hundred or thereabout, their swords in their hands, the which irked the bold strangers. They stood up from their seats; and the queen spoke courteously to them when she saw Siegfried, "Thou art welcome, Siegfried, to this land. To what end art thou come? I prithee tell me."

"I thank thee, O Brunhild, fair daughter of a king, that thou greetest me before this worshipful knight. Thou showest Siegfried too much honour, for he is my lord, and the king of Rhineland."

She answered, "If he be thy lord, and thou be his man, let him withstand me at the games. If he have the mastery, then am I his wife, but let him fail in one of them, and ye be all dead men."

Then said Hagen of Troneck, "Lady, show us the games that thou proposest. It will go hard with Gunther or he yield thee the mastery, for he troweth well to win so fair a maiden."

"He must put the stone, and leap after it, and throw the spear with me. Ye may easily forfeit honour and life; wherefore be not so confident, but bethink you well."

Then bold Siegfried went to the king, and bade him fear nothing, but speak freely to the queen. "For," said he, "I will aid thee with cunning devices."

And King Gunther said, "Command me, great queen, and were it more yet, I would risk it for thy sake. I will lose my head, or win thee to wife."

When the queen heard this word, she bade haste to the sports, as was meet, and let them bring her harness, a golden buckler and a goodly shield. She did on a surcoat of silk from Libya, that had never been pierced in combat, cunningly fashioned and embroidered, and shining with precious stones. Her pride greatly angered the knights, and Dankwart and Hagen were downcast, for they feared for their lord, and thought, "Ill-starred was this journey."

Meanwhile, Siegfried, the cunning man, went, when none spied him, to the ship, where he found the *Tarnkappe,* and he did it on swiftly, that none knew. Then he hasted back to the crowd of knights, where the queen gave order for the sports, and, by his magic, he stole in among them, that no man was ware of him. The ring was marked out in the presence of armed knights to the number of seven hundred. These were the umpires, that should tell truly who won in the sports.

Then came Brunhild. She stood armed, as she had meant to do battle with all the kings of all the world. The silk was covered with gold spangles that showed her white skin. Her attendants brought her, for the strife, a shield of ruddy gold with iron studs, mickle and broad. The maid's thong was an embroidered band, whereon lay stones green like grass, that sparkled among the gold. The knight must, certes, be bold that won such a lady. They say the shield the maiden bore was three spans thick under the folds, rich with steel and gold, that four of her chamberlains scarce could carry it.

When strong Hagen saw them drag the shield forward, the hero of Troneck was wroth, and cried, "How now, King Gunther? We be dead men, for thou wooest the Devil's wife!"

Yet more must ye hear of her vesture. Her coat of mail was covered with silk from Azagouc, costly and rich, and the stones thereof sparkled on the queen's body. They brought her the spear, heavy and big and sharp, that she was wont to throw. Strong and huge it was, mickle and broad, and made grim wounds with its edges. And hear, now, the marvel of its heaviness. Three weights and a half of iron were welded for it. Three of. Brunhild's lords scarce carried it. A woeful man was King Gunther, and he thought, "Lo! now, not the Devil in Hell could escape her. Were I in Burgundy with my life, she might wait long enough for my wooing." He stood dismayed. Then they brought him his armour, and he did it on.

Brunhild's great strength appeared. They brought her a stone into the circle, heavy and huge, round also, and broad. Twelve strong knights scarce sufficed thereto. And this she threw when she had hurled the spear. Whereat the Burgundians were sore troubled, and Hagen cried, "Who is this that Gunther wooeth? Would she were the Devil's bride in Hell!"

Then she turned back the sleeves from her white arms, and seized the shield, and brandished the spear above her head, and the contest began. Gunther was sore dismayed. If Siegfried had not helped him, certes he had lost his life; but Siegfried went up to him secretly, and touched his hand. Gunther fell in fear by reason of his magic, and he thought, "Who touched me?" He looked round and saw no man. But Siegfried said, "It is I, Siegfried, thy friend. Fear nothing from the queen. Give me the shield from thy hands, and let me carry it, and give heed to what I say. Make thou the gestures, and I will do the work." And Gunther was glad when he knew him. "Guard well the secret of my magic, for all our sakes, lest the queen slay thee. See how boldly she challengeth thee."

Thereupon the royal maiden hurled her spear against the mickle and broad shield of Sieglind's child, that sparks flew from it, as before a wind. The strong spear pierced through the shield, and struck fire from the coat of mail below. And the mighty man fell, and had perished but for the *Tarnkappe*. The blood gushed from Siegfried's mouth. But he sprang up swiftly, and took the spear that she had shot through his buckler, and threw it back again with great force. He thought, "I will not slay so fair a maiden," and he turned the spear, and hurled it with the haft loud against her harness. From her mail, also, the sparks flew as on the wind, for Siegmund's child threw mightily; and her strength failed before the blow. King Gunther, I ween, had never done it alone.

Brunhild sprang to her feet again, and cried, "I thank thee, Gunther, for that blow." For she thought he had done it with his own strength, nor guessed that a far mightier man had felled her.

Then, greatly wroth, she hasted and lifted the stone on high; she flung it far from her, and leaped after it with loud-ringing armour. The stone landed twenty and four paces off; but the maid sprang further. Then Siegfried went swiftly where the stone lay. Gunther lifted it, but it was the man they saw not that threw it. Siegfried was mighty, bold and big. He hurled the stone further, and he leaped further; moreover, through his magic, he had strength enow to bear King Gunther with him. The spring was made, the stone lay on the ground, and none was seen there but Gunther, the knight. Fair Brunhild was red with anger.

So Siegfried saved Gunther from death.

Then Brunhild said aloud to her folk, when she saw the hero at the far end of the ring unhurt, "Gome hither at once, my kinsmen and my lieges. Ye are subject henceforth to King Gunther."

The bold men laid the weapons from their hands at the feet of great Gunther of Burgundy. For they deemed he had won the game by his own strength.

He greeted them fair, for he was a courteous man, and he took the beautiful maiden by the hand. She gave him power in her kingdom, whereat bold Hagen rejoiced.

(8) She chose from among her knights two thousand men to follow her to the Rhine, and the thousand Nibelung warriors. Then she made ready for the journey, and rode down to the shore. She took with her six and eighty women, and an hundred fair damsels, and they tarried not longer, but set out. They that were left behind wept sore! Graciously and sweetly the lady quitted her land. She kissed her nearest of kin that stood round. With loving farewells they reached the sea. To the land of her fathers the maiden returned nevermore.

(10) On the far bank of the Rhine appeared a mighty host—the king with his guests—and they drew nigh to the strand, where damsels, led by the bridle, stood ready with welcome.

Gunther, with his friends, went down from the ships; he led Brunhild by the hand; garments and precious stones shone bright and sparkled. And Kriemhild went eagerly toward them and greeted Brunhild and her following. They drew back their, headbands with white fingers, and kissed one another through love. Then Kriemhild the maid spoke courteously, "Thou are right welcome in this land, to me and to my mother, and to our friends." And they courtsied and embraced. Never, I ween, was any greeted fairer than the bride by Uta and her daughter, for they ceased not to kiss her sweet mouth.

When Brunhild's women were all gotten to land, the knights led them before the queen, where welcome was not stinted them and where many a red mouth was kissed. The rich kings' daughters stood long side by side, and the warriors gazed on them. What these had heard tell they saw with their eyes, that none surpassed those two women in beauty, neither was any blemish found in them. They that esteem women for the comeliness of the body and what the eye beholdeth, extolled King Gunther's wife, but the wise that look deeper said, "Praised shall Kriemhild be before Brunhild." And the bright-attired women drew together where the silken canopies were spread, and the goodly tents, in the field before Worms.

The chairs were set, for the king was ready to go to table with his guests, and beautiful Brunhild stood by him and wore her crown in Gunther's land. Certes, she was proud enough.

Many were the seats, they say, and the tables goodly and broad and laden with food. Little, I trow, was lacking! And many a noble guest sat there with the king. Gunther's chamberlains carried round water in golden ewers. If any tell you of a prince's table better served, believe it not.

Or Gunther took the water, Siegfried, as was meet, minded him of his oath that he had sworn or ever he saw Brunhild in Issland.

He said, "Forget not the vow thou swarest with thy hand that, if Brunhild came into Burgundy, thou wouldst give me thy sister. Where is thine oath now? Mickle toil was mine on the journey."

The king answered his guest, "Thou hast done well to remind me. I go not back from the oath of my hand. What I can do therein I will do."

They bade Kriemhild to the court before the king. She went up to the hall with her maidens, but Giselher sprang down the stair and cried, "Send back these maidens. My sister goeth alone to the king."

They brought Kriemhild before Gunther, where he stood amidst of knights from many lands. And they bade her stand in the middle of the hall. Brunhild, by this time, was come to the table, and knew nothing of what was toward. Then said Dankrat's son to his kinsmen, "Help me now, that my sister take Siegfried to her husband."

And they answered with one accord, "That may she do with honour."

Gunther said, "Dear sister, I prithee of thy goodness, loose me from mine oath. I promised thee to a knight; and truly thou wilt do my will, if thou take him to husband."

The maiden answered, "Dear brother mine, thou needest not to entreat. Command and I will obey. Him that thou givest me to husband I will gladly wed."

Siegfried grew red for love and joy, and vowed his service to Kriemhild. And they bade them stand together in a circle, and asked her if she would take the knight.

On maidenly wise she was shamefast at the first, yet so great was Siegfried's good fortune and his grace that she refused not his hand; and the king of the Netherland, from his side also, plighted his troth to Kriemhild.

When their word was given, Siegfried took his queen in his arms straightway, and kissed her before the warriors.

The circle brake up when this was ended, and Siegfried took the seat of honour with Kriemhild. The vassals served before them, and his Nibelung knights stood nigh.

The king and Brunhild were seated and Brunhild saw Kriemhild sitting by Siegfried, the which irked her sore; she fell to weeping, and the hot tears ran down her bright cheeks.

Whereupon the host said, "What aileth thee sweet Lady, that the light of thine eyes is dim? Rejoice shouldst thou rather, for my land and rich castles and true liegeman are all subject to thee."

"I have cause to weep," said the maiden. "I grieve from my heart for thy sister, that she sitteth there by thy vassal. I must ever weep to see her so shamed."

But King Gunther answered, "I prithee, silence! Another time I will tell thee why I gave my sister to Siegfried. May she live happily with the knight."

But she said, "I must grieve for her beauty and her birth. If I knew whither I might flee, I would not suffer thee by me, till that thou hadst told me how Siegfried hath gotten Kriemhild."

Gunther answered then, "Hearken, and I will tell thee. Know that he hath lands and castles even as I, and is a rich king; wherefore I give him my beautiful sister gladly to wife." Yet, for all the king could say to her, she was downcast.

The knights rose from the table, and the tourney waxed so fierce that the castle rang with the noise. But the king wearied amidst of his guests. He thought, "It were softer alone with my wife." And his heart dwelled on the mickle joy her love must bring him, and he looked at her sweetly.

Then they stopped the tourney, that the king might retire with his wife.

At the foot of the stair that led forth from the hall, Kriemhild and Brunhild came face to face. They were not foes yet. Their attendants followed them, and longer they tarried not. The chamberlains brought candles, and the knights of the two kings parted in two companies, and many followed Siegfried.

Then came the heroes where they were to lie, and each thought to win his wife's favour, whereat their hearts melted.

With Siegfried all went well. He caressed the maiden lovingly, and she was as his life. He had not given her alone for a thousand other women.

Of them I will tell no further. Hear now how it fared with Gunther. Better had been his case with any but Brunhild.

The folk had departed, dames and knights. The door was made fast. He thought to win her love, but it was long yet or she became his wife. He lay down in a white garment and thought, "Now have I my heart's desire." The king's hand hid the light. He went to Brunhild and embraced her with his arm. He was greatly glad. He would have caressed her sweetly if she had let him. But she was so wroth that he was dismayed. He thought to find joy, but found deep hate.

She said, "Noble knight, let me alone, for it shall not be as thou desirest. Mark well that I will have nothing to do with thee, till that thou hast answered me concerning Kriemhild."

Then Gunther began to be angry with her, and fought with her, and tore her raiment. And the royal maiden seized a girdle, a strong embroidered silk cord that she wore round her waist, and did hurt enow to the knight. She bound his hands and his feet, and carried him to a nail, and hung him on the wall. She forbade him to touch her because he disturbed her sleep. He almost perished from her strength.

Then he that should have been master began to pray, "Now loose my bands, most noble queen. I promise never to touch thee, or even to come nigh thee."

She asked not how he fared while she lay soft. There must he hang the long night through till the day, when the bright morning-shone through the window. If he had ever had strength, he had little in his body now.

"Tell me, Sir Gunther," said the beautiful maiden, "doth it not irk thee that thy chamberlains find thee bound by the hand of a woman."

The noble knight answered, "It were the worse for thee. Also little were my honour therein. Of thy charity allow me to lie down. Seeing thou hatest my love, I will not so much as touch thy garment with my hand."

Then she loosed his bands, and let him go, and he laid him down, but so far from her that he ruffled not her beautiful gown. Even that she had gladly foregone.

Thereupon their attendants came and brought them new apparel, as much as they could wear, that had been made ready against the wedding morn. But, amidst of them that rejoiced, the king was heavy of his cheer beneath his crown that day.

According to the good custom of the land, Gunther and Brunhild tarried not longer, but went to the minster to hear mass. Thither also went Siegfried and there was great press of people.

He and Siegfried were different in their moods. The hero guessed what ailed him, and went to him and asked him, "Tell me how it hath fared with thee."

Then said the host to his guest, "Shame and hurt have I suffered from my wife in my house. When I would have caressed her, she bound me tight, and took me to a nail, and hung me up on the wall. There I dangled in fear the night through till the day, or she loosed me. How soft she lay there! I tell thee this in secret."

And strong Siegfried said, "I grieve for thee. I will tell thee a remedy if thou keep it from her. I will so contrive it that this night she will defy thee no longer." The word was welcome to Gunther after his pain.

"Now see my hands, how they are swollen. She overmastered me, as I had been a child, that the blood spurted all over me from my nails. I thought not to come off with my life."

Said Siegfried, "It will yet be well. Unequal was our fortune last night. Thy sister Kriemhild is dearer to me than mine own body. This day must Brunhild be thy wife. I will come to-night to thy room secretly in my *Tarnkappe,* that none may guess the trick. Send the chamberlains to their beds. I will put out the lights in the hands of the pages, and by this sign thou shalt know that I am nigh. I will win thy wife for thee or perish."

"If only thou winnest her not for thy self. She is my dear wife. Otherwise I rejoice. Do to her what thou wilt. If thou tookest her life, I would bear it. She is a terrible woman."

"I vow to thee on mine honour that I will have nothing to do with her. Thy dear sister is more to me than any I have ever seen." And Gunther believed Siegfried's word.

Fair Kriemhild and also Brunhild were led to their chambers. Ha! what bold knights went before the queens!

Joyful and without hate Siegfried the knight sat sweetly beside his beautiful wife. With her white hand she caressed his, till, she knew now how, he vanished from before her eyes. When she played with him and saw him no longer, she said to her maidens, "I marvel much where the king is gone. Who took his hands out of mine?" And so the matter dropped.

He had gone where he found the chamberlains with the lights, which he began to put out. By this sign Gunther perceived that it was Siegfried. He knew well what he wanted, and he sent away the women and maidens. When that was done, the king himself locked the door, and shot two strong bolts before it. He hid the light quickly behind the bed curtain, and the struggle that had to come began between strong Siegfried and the beautiful maiden, King Gunther was both glad and sorry.

Siegfried lay down by the queen, but she said "Stop, Gunther, lest thou suffer as afore. Thou mayest again receive a hurt at my hand."

Siegfried concealed his voice and spoke not. Gunther heard well all that passed, albeit he saw nothing. There was little ease for the two. Siegfried feigned that he was Gunther and put his arm round the valiant maiden. She threw him on to a bench, that his head rang loud against a foot-stool.

The bold man sprang up undaunted, but evil befell him. Such defence from a woman I ween the world will never see more. Because he would not let her be, Brunhild rose up.

"It is unseemly of thee," said the brave maiden. "Thou wilt tear my beautiful gown. Thou art churlish and must suffer for it. Thou shalt see!"

She caught the good knight in her arms, and would have bound him as she had done to the king, that she might have peace. Grimly she avenged her torn raiment.

What availed him then his strength and his prowess? She proved to him the mastery of her body, and carried him by force, since there was no other way, and squeezed him hard against a press that stood by the bed.

"Alas!" thought the knight, "if I lose my life by the hand of a woman, all wives evermore will make light of their husbands, that, without this, would not dare."

The king heard it well. He feared for the man. Then Siegfried was ashamed and waxed furious. He grappled fiercely with her, and, in terror of his life, strove to overcome Brunhild. When she squeezed him down, he got up again in spite of her, by dint of his anger and his mickle strength. He came in great scathe. In the chamber there was smiting with many blows. King Gunther, likewise, stood in peril. He danced to and fro quickly before them. So mightily they strove, it was a wonder they came off with their lives. The trouble of the king was twofold, yet most he feared Siegfried's death. For she had almost killed the knight. Had he dared, he had gone to his help.

The strife endured long atwixt them. Then Siegfried got hold of Brunhild., Albeit she fought valiantly, her defence was grown weak. It seemed long to the king, that stood there, till Siegfried had won. She squeezed his hands till, by her strength, the blood spurted out from his nails. Then he brake the strong will that she had shown at the first. The king heard it all, but he spoke no word. Siegfried pressed her down till she cried aloud, for his might hurt her greatly. She clutched at her side, where she found her girdle, and sought to tie his hands. But he gripped her till the joints of her body cracked. So the strife was ended.

She said, "Noble king, let me live. I will make good to thee what I have done, and strive no more; truly I have found thee to be my master."

Siegfried rose up then and left her, as though he would throw off his clothes. He drew from her hand a gold ring, without that she was ware of it. He took her girdle also, a good silken band. I know not if he did it from pride. He gave them to his wife, and suffered for it after.

The king and the fair maiden were left together, and, for that she was grown weak, she hid her anger, for it availed her nothing. So they abode there till the bright day.

Meanwhile Siegfried went back to his sweet love, that received him kindly. He turned the questions aside that she asked him, and hid from her for long what he had brought with him, till at the last, when they were gotten home to the Netherland, he gave her the jewel; the which brought him and many knights to their graves.

Much merrier was Gunther of his cheer the next morning than before. Throughout his lands many a noble knight rejoiced, and the guests that he had bidden to the hightide were well feasted and served.

(14) One day, before vespers, there arose in the court of the castle a mighty din of knights that tilted for pastime, and the folk ran to see them.

The queens sat together there, thinking each on a doughty warrior. Then said fair Kriemhild, "I have a husband of such might that all these lands might well be his."

But Brunhild answered, "How so? If there lived none other save thou and he, our kingdom might haply be his, but while Gunther is alive it could never be."

But Kriemhild said, "See him there. How he surpasseth the other knights, as the bright moon the stars! My heart is uplifted with cause."

Whereupon Brunhild answered, "Howso valiant thy husband, comely and fair, thy brother Gunther excelleth him, for know that he is the first among kings."

But Kriemhild said, "My praise was not idle; for worshipful is my husband in many things. Trow it, Brunhild. He is, at the least, thy husband's equal."

"Mistake me not in thine anger, Kriemhild. Neither is my word idle; for they both said, when I saw them first, and the king vanquished me in the sports, and on knightly wise won my love, that Siegfried was his man. Wherefore I hold him for a vassal, since I heard him say it."

Then Kriemhild cried, "Evil were my lot if that were true. How had my brothers given me to a vassal to wife? Prithee, of thy courtesy, cease from such discourse."

"That will I not," answered Brunhild. "Thereby should I lose many knights that, with him, owe us homage."

Whereat fair Kriemhild waxed very wroth. "Lose them thou must, then, for any service he will do thee. He is nobler even than Gunther, my noble brother. Wherefore, spare me thy foolish words. I wonder, since he is thy vassal, and thou art so much mightier than we, that for so long time he hath failed to pay tribute. Of a truth thine arrogancy irketh me."

"Thou vauntest thyself too high," cried the queen; "I would see now whether thy body be holden in like honour with mine."

Both the women were angry.

Kriemhild answered, "That shalt thou see straightway. Since thou hast called Siegfried thy vassal, the knights of both kings shall see this day whether I dare enter the minster before thee, the queen. For I would have thee know that I am noble and free, and that my husband is of more worship than thine. Nor will I be chidden by thee. To-day thou shalt see thy vassals go at court before the Bur-gundian knights, and me more honoured than any queen that ever wore a crown." Fierce was the wrath of the women.

"If thou art no vassal," said Brunhild, "thou and thy women shall walk separate from my train when we go to the minster." And Kriemhild answered, "Be it so."

"Now adorn ye, my maidens," said Siegfried's wife, "that I be not shamed. If ye have rich apparel, show it this day. She shall take back what her mouth hath spoken."

She needed not to bid twice; they sought out their richest vesture, and dames and damsels were soon arrayed.

Then the wife of the royal host went forth with her attendants. Fair to heart's desire were clad Kriemhild and the forty and three maidens that she had brought with her to the Rhine. Bright shone the stuffs, woven in Araby, whereof their robes were fashioned. And they came to the minster, where Siegfried's knights waited for them.

The folk marvelled much to see the queens apart, and going not together as afore. Many a warrior was to rue it.

Gunther's wife stood before the minster, and the knights dallied in converse with the women, till that Kriemhild came up with her company. All that noble maidens had ever worn was but as a wind to what these had on. So rich was Kriemhild that thirty king's wives together had not been as gorgeous as she was. None could deny, though they had wished it, that the apparel Kriemhild's maidens wore that day was the richest they had ever seen. Kriemhild did this on purpose to anger Brunhild.

So they met before the minster. And Brunhild, with deadly spite, cried out to Kriemhild to stand still. "Before the queen shall no vassal go."

Out then spoke Kriemhild, for she was wroth. "Better hadst thou held thy peace. Thou hast shamed thine own body. How should the leman of a vassal become a king's wife?"

"Whom namest thou leman?" cried the queen.

"Even thee," answered Kriemhild. "For it was Siegfried my husband, and not my brother, that won thee first. Where were thy senses? It was surely ill done to favour a vassal so. Reproaches from thee are much amiss."

"Verily," cried Brunhild, "Gunther shall hear of it."

"What is that to me? Thine arrogancy hath deceived thee. Thou hast called me thy vassal. Know now of a truth it hath irked me, and I am thine enemy evermore."

Then Brunhild began to weep, and Kriemhild tarried not longer, but went with her attendants into the minster before the king's wife. There was deadly hate, and bright eyes grew wet and dim.

Whether they prayed or sang, the service seemed too long to Brunhild, for her heart and her mind were troubled, the which many a bold and good man paid for afterward.

Brunhild stopped before the minster with her women, for she thought, "Kriemhild, the foul-mouthed woman, shall tell me further whereof she so loud accuseth me. If he hath boasted of this thing, he shall answer for it with his life."

Then Kriemhild with her knights came forth, and Brunhild began, "Stop! thou hast called me a wanton and shalt prove it, for know that thy words irk me sore."

Said Kriemhild, "Let me pass. With this gold that I have on my hand I can prove it. Siegfried brought it when he came from thee."

It was a heavy day for Brunhild. She said, "That gold so precious was stolen from me, and hath been hidden these many years. Now I know who hath taken it." Both the women were furious.

"I am no thief," cried Kriemhild. "Hadst thou prized thine honour thou hadst held thy peace, for, with this girdle round my waist, I can prove my word, and that Siegfried was verily thy leman." She wore a girdle of silk of Nineveh, goodly enow, and worked with precious stones.

When Brunhild saw it she started to weep. And soon Gunther knew it, and all his men, for the queen cried, "Bring hither the King of Rhineland; I would tell him how his sister hath mocked me, and sayeth openly that I be Siegfried's leman."

The king came with his warriors, and, when he saw that his dear one wept, he spoke kindly, "What aileth thee, dear wife?"

She answered, "Shamed must I stand, for thy sister would part me from mine honour? I make my plaint to thee. She proclaimeth aloud that Siegfried hath had me to his leman."

Gunther answered, "Evilly hath she done."

"She weareth here a girdle that I have long lost, and my red gold. Woe is me that ever I was born! If thou clearest me not from this shame, I will never love thee more."

Said Gunther, "Bid him hither, that he confess whether he hath boasted of this, or no."

They summoned Siegfried, who, when he saw their anger and knew not the cause, spoke quickly, "Why weep these women? Tell me straight; and wherefore am I summoned?"

Whereto Gunther answered, "Right vexed am I. Brunhild, my wife, telleth me here that thou hast boasted thou wert her leman. Kriemhild declareth this. Hast thou done it, O knight?"

Siegfried answered, "Not I. If she hath said so, I will rest not till she repent it. I swear with a high oath in the presence of all thy knights, that I said not this one thing."

The king of the Rhine made answer, "So be it. If thou swear the oath here, I will acquit thee of the falsehood." Then the Burgundians stood round in a ring, and Siegfried swore it with his hand; whereupon the great king said, "Verily, I hold thee guiltless, nor lay to thy charge the word my sister imputeth to thee."

Said Siegfried further, "If she rejoiceth to have troubled thy fair wife, I am grieved beyond measure." The knights glanced at each other.

"Women must be taught to bridle their tongues. Forbid proud speech to thy wife: I will do the like to mine. Such bitterness and pride are a shame."

Angry words have divided many women. Brunhild made such dole, that Gunther's men had pity on her. And Hagen of Troneck went to her and asked what ailed her, for he found her weeping. She told him the tale, and he sware straightway that Kriemhild's husband should pay for it, or never would Hagen be glad again.

While they talked together, Ortwin and Gernot came up, and the warriors counselled Siegfried's death. But when Giselher, Uta's fair child, drew nigh and heard them, he spoke out with true heart, "Alas, good knights, what would ye do? How hath Siegfried deserved such hate that he should lose his life? A woman is lightly angered."

"Shall we rear fools?" cried Hagen. "That were small honour to good knights. I will avenge on him the boast that he hath made, or I will die."

But the king himself said, "Good, and not evil, hath he done to us. Let him live. Wherefore should I hate the knight? He hath ever been true to me."

"Not so," said Hagen. "Assure thee on that score. For I will contrive secretly that he pay for Brunhild's weeping. Hagen is his foe evermore."

(15) Then went Hagen of Troneck to Kriemhild.

"Well for me," said Kriemhild, "that ever I won to husband a man that standeth so true by his friends, as doth Siegfried by my kinsmen. Right proud am I. Bethink thee now, Hagen, dear friend, how that in all things I am at thy service, and have ever willed thee well. Requite me through my husband, that I love, and avenge not on him what I did to Brunhild. Already it repenteth me sore. My body hath smarted for it, that ever I troubled her with my words. Siegfried, the good knight, hath seen to that."

Whereto Hagen answered, "Ye will shortly be at one again. But Kriemhild, prithee tell me wherein I can serve thee with Siegfried, thy husband, and I will do it, for I love none better."

"I should fear nothing for his life in battle, but that he is foolhardy, and of too proud a courage. Save for that, he were safe enow."

Then said Hagen, "Lady, if thou fearest hurt for him in battle, tell me now by what device I may hinder it, and I will guard him afoot and on horse."

She answered, "Thou art my cousin, and I thine. To thy faith I commend my dear husband, that thou mayst watch and keep him."

Then she told him what she had better have left unsaid.

"My husband is strong and bold. When that he slew the dragon on the mountain, he bathed him in its blood; wherefore no weapon can pierce him. Nevertheless, when he rideth in battle, and spears fly from the hands of heroes, I tremble lest I lose him. Alas! for Siegfried's sake how oft have I been heavy of my cheer! And now, dear cousin, I will trust thee with the secret, and tell thee, that thou mayst prove thy faith, where my husband may be wounded. For that I know thee honourable, I do this. When the hot blood flowed from the wound of the dragon, and Siegfried bathed therein, there fell atween his shoulders the broad leaf of a lime tree. There one might stab him, and thence is my care and dole."

Then answered Hagen of Troneck, "Sew, with thine own hand, a small sign upon his outer garment, that I may know where to defend him when we stand in battle."

She did it to profit the knight, and worked his doom thereby. She said, "I will sew secretly, with fine silk, a little cross upon his garment, and there, O knight, shalt thou guard to me my husband when ye ride in the thick of the strife, and he withstandeth his foemen in the fierce onset."

"That will I do, dear lady," answered Hagen.

Kriemhild thought to serve Siegfried; so was the hero betrayed.

Then Hagen took his leave and went forth glad; and his king bade him say what he had learned.

"Let us go hunting; for I have learned the secret, and have him in my hand. Wilt thou contrive this?"

"That will I," said the king.

The next morning Siegfried rode to the king, that thanked him. "I hold thee trustiest of all my friends. Seeing we be quit of war, let us ride a hunting to the Odenwald after the bear and the boar, as I have often done." Hagen, the false man, had counselled this.

"Let it be told to my guests straightway that I will ride early. Whoso would hunt with me, let him be ready betimes. But if any would tarry behind for pastime with the women, he shall do it, and please me thereby."

Siegfried answered on courtly wise, "I will hunt with thee gladly, and will ride to the forest, if thou lend me a huntsman and some brachs."

(16) But or he set out, and when the hunting-gear was laid ready on the sumpters that they were to take across the Rhine, he went to Kriemhild, and that was right doleful of her cheer. He kissed his lady on the mouth. "God grant I may see thee safe and well again, and thou me. Bide here merry among thy kinsfolk, for I must forth."

Then she thought on the secret she had betrayed to Hagen, but durst not tell him. The queen wept sore that ever she was born, and made measureless dole.

She said, "Go not hunting. Last night I dreamed an evil dream: how that two wild boars chased thee over the heath; and the flowers were red with blood. Have pity on my tears, for I fear some treachery. There be haply some offended, that pursue us with deadly hate. Go not, dear lord; in good faith I counsel it."

But he answered, "Dear love, I go but for a few days. I know not any that beareth me hate. Thy kinsmen will me well, nor have I deserved otherwise at their hand."

"Nay, Siegfried, I fear some mischance. Last night I dreamed an evil dream: how that two mountains fell on thee, and I saw thee no more. If thou goest, thou wilt grieve me bitterly."

But he caught his dear one in his arms and kissed her close; then he took leave of her and rode off.

She never saw him alive again.

Siegfried's horse bare him smoothly, and the others pricked fast behind. The noise roused a grim bear, whereat the knight cried to them that came after him, "Now for sport! Slip the dog, for I see a bear that shall with us to the tryst-fire. He cannot escape us, if he ran ever so fast."

They slipped the limehound; off rushed the bear. Siegfried thought to run him down, but he came to a ravine and could not get to him; then the bear deemed him safe. But the proud knight sprang from his horse, and pursued him. The beast had no shelter. It could not escape from him, and was caught by his hand, and, or it could wound him, he had bound it, that it could neither scratch nor bite. Then he tied it to his saddle, and, when he had mounted up himself, he brought it to the tryst-fire for pastime.

When he had alighted, he loosed the band from the paws and from the mouth of the bear that he had bound to his saddle.

So soon as they saw the bear, the dogs began to bark. The animal tried to win back to the wood, and all the folk fell in great fear. Affrighted by the noise, it ran through the kitchen. Nimbly started the scullions from their place by the fire. Pots were upset and the brands strewed over all. Alas! the good meats that tumbled into the ashes!

Then up sprang the princes and their men. The bear began to growl, and the king gave order to slip the hounds that were on leash. I' faith, it had been a merry day if it had ended so.

Hastily, with their bows and spears, the warriors, swift of foot, chased the bear, but there were so many dogs that none durst shoot among them, and the forest rang with the din. Then the bear fled before the dogs, and none could keep pace with him save Kriemhild's husband, that ran up to him and pierced him dead with his sword, and carried the carcase back with him to the fire. They that saw it said he was a mighty man.

Then they bade the sportsmen to the table, and they sat down a goodly company enow, on a fair meadow. Ha! what dishes, meet for heroes, were set before them. But the cup-bearers were tardy, that should have brought the wine. Save for that, knights were never better served. If there had not been false-hearted men among them, they had been without reproach. The doomed man had no suspicion that might have warned him, for his own heart was pure of all deceit. Many that his death profited not at all had to pay for it bitterly.

Then said Sir Siegfried, "I marvel, since they bring us so much from the kitchen, that they bring not the wine. If good hunters be entreated so, I will hunt no more. Certes, I have deserved better at your hands."

Whereto the king at the table answered falsely, "What lacketh to-day we will make good another time. The blame is Hagen's, that would have us perish of thirst."

Then said Hagen of Troneck, "Dear master, methought we were to hunt to-day at Spessart, and I sent the wine thither. For the present we must go thirsty; another time I will take better care."

But Siegfried cried, "Small thank to him. Seven sumpters with meat and spiced wines should he have sent here at the least, or, if that might not be, we should have gone nigher to the Rhine."

Hagen of Troneck answered, "I know of a cool spring close at hand. Be not wroth with me, but take my counsel, and go thither." The which was done, to the hurt of many warriors. Siegfried was sore athirst and bade push back the table, that he might go to the spring at the foot of the mountain. Falsely had the knights contrived it. The wild beasts that Siegfried's hand had slain they let pile on a waggon and take home, and all they that saw it praised him.

Foully did Hagen break faith with Siegfried. He said, when they were starting for the broad lime tree, "I hear from all sides that none can keep pace with Kriemhild's husband when he runneth. Let us see now."

Bold Siegfried of the Netherland answered, "Thou mayst easily prove it, if thou wilt run with me to the brook for a wager. The praise shall be to him that winneth there first."

"Let us see then," said Hagen the knight.

And strong Siegfried answered, "If I lose, I will lay me at thy feet in the grass."

A glad man was King Gunther when he heard that!

Said Siegfried further, "Nay, I will undertake more. I will carry on me all that I wear—spear, shield, and hunting gear." Whereupon he girded on his sword and his quiver in haste. Then the others did off their clothes, till they stood in their white shirts, and they ran through the clover like two wild panthers; but bold Siegfried was seen there the first. Before all men he won the prize in everything. He loosed his sword straightway, and laid down his quiver. His good spear he leaned against the lime tree; then the noble guest stood and waited, for his courtesy was great. He laid down his shield by the stream. Albeit he was sore athirst, he drank not till that the king had finished, who gave him evil thanks.

The stream was cool, pure, and good. Gunther bent down to the water, and rose again when he had drunk. Siegfried had gladly done the like, but he suffered for his courtesy. Hagen carried his bow and his sword out of his reach, and sprang back and gripped the spear. Then he spied for the secret mark on his vesture; and while Siegfried drank from the stream, Hagen stabbed him where the cross was, that his heart's blood spurted out on the traitor's clothes. Never since hath knight done so wickedly. He left the spear sticking deep in his heart, and fled in grimmer haste than ever he had done from any man on this earth afore.

When strong Siegfried felt the deep wound, he sprang up maddened from the water, for the long boar spear stuck out from his heart. He thought to find bow or sword; if he had, Hagen had got his due. But the sore-wounded man saw no sword, and had nothing save his shield. He picked it up from the water's edge and ran at Hagen. King Gunther's man could not escape him. For all that he was wounded to the death, he smote mightily that the shield well-nigh brake, and the precious stones flew out. The noble guest had fain taken vengeance.

Hagen fell beneath his stroke. The meadow rang loud with the noise of the blow. If he had had his sword to hand, Hagen had been a dead man. But the anguish of his wound constrained him. His colour was wan; he could not stand upright; and the strength of his body failed him, for he bare death's mark on his white cheek. Fair women enow made dole for him.

Then Kriemhild's husband fell among the flowers. The blood flowed fast from his wound, and in his great anguish he began to upbraid them that had falsely contrived his death. "False cowards!" cried the dying knight. "What availeth all my service to you, since ye have slain me? I was true to you, and pay the price for it. Ye have done ill by your friends. Cursed by this deed are your sons yet unborn. Ye have avenged your spite on my body all too bitterly. For your crime ye shall be shunned by good knights."

All the warriors ran where he lay stabbed. To many among them it was a woeful day. They that were true mourned for him, the which the hero had well deserved of all men.

The King of Burgundy also wept for his death, but the dying man said, "He needeth not to weep for the evil, by whom the evil cometh. Better had he left it undone, for mickle is his blame."

Then said grim Hagen, "I know not what ye rue. All is ended for us—care and trouble. Few are they now that will withstand us. Glad am I that, through me, his might is fallen."

"Lightly mayst thou boast now," said Siegfried; "if I had known thy murderous hate, it had been an easy thing to guard my body from thee. My bitterest dole is for Kriemhild, my wife. God pity me that ever I had a son. For all men will reproach him that he hath murderers to his kinsmen. I would grieve for that, had I the time."

He said to the king, "Never in this world was so foul a murder as thou hast done on me. In thy sore need I saved thy life and thine honour. Dear have I paid for that I did well by thee." With a groan the wounded man said further, "Yet if thou canst show truth to any on this earth, O King, show it to my dear wife, that I commend to thee. Let it advantage her to be thy sister. By all princely honour stand by her. Long must my father and my knights wait for my coming. Never hath woman won such woe through a dear one."

He writhed in his bitter anguish, and spoke painfully, "Ye shall rue this foul deed in the days to come. Know this of a truth, that in slaying me ye have slain yourselves."

The flowers were all wet with blood. He strove with death, but not for long, for the weapon of death cut too deep. And the bold knight and good spoke no more.

When the warriors saw that the hero was dead, they laid him on a shield of ruddy gold, and took counsel how they should conceal that Hagen had done it. Many of them said, "Evil hath befallen us. Ye shall all hide it, and hold to one tale—when Kriemhild's husband was riding alone in the forest, robbers slew him."

But Hagen of Troneck said, "I will take him back to Burgundy. If she that hath troubled Brunhild know it, I care not. It concerneth me little if she weep."

Of that very brook where Siegfried was slain ye shall hear the truth from me. In the Odenwald is a village that hight Odenheim, and there the stream runneth still; beyond doubt it is the same.

(17) They tarried there that night, and then crossed the Rhine. Heroes never went to so woeful a hunt. For one thing that they slew, many women wept, and many a good knight's body paid for it. Of overweening pride ye shall hear now, and grim vengeance.

Hagen bade them bear dead Siegfried of the Nibelung land before the chamber where Kriemhild was, and charged them to lay him secretly outside the door, that she might find him there when she went forth to mass or it was day, the which she was wont to do.

The minster bell was rung as the custom was. Fair Kriemhild waked her maidens, and bade them bring her a light and her vesture.

Then a chamberlain came and found Siegfried. He saw him red with blood, and his garment all wet, but he knew not yet that he was his king. He carried the light into the room in his hand, and from him Kriemhild heard evil tidings.

When she would have gone with her women to the minster, the chamberlain said, "Lady, stop! A murdered knight lieth on the threshold."

"Woe is me!" cried Kriemhild. "What meanest thou by such news?"

Or she knew for certain that it was her husband, she began to think on Hagen's question, how he might guard him. From that moment her dole began; for, with his death, she took leave of all joy. She sank on the floor speechless; they saw the miserable woman lying there. Kriemhild's woe was great beyond measure, and after her swoon she cried out, that all the chamber rang.

Then said her attendants, "What if it be a stranger?"

But the blood burst from her mouth by reason of her heart's anguish, and she said, "Nay, it is Siegfried, my dear husband. Brunhild hath counselled it, and Hagen hath done it."

Gunther said, "Dear sister, woe is me for this grief of thine, and that this great misadventure hath befallen us. We must ever mourn Siegfried's death."

"Ye do wrongly," said the wailing queen. "If it grieved thee, it had never happed. I was clean forgotten by thee when thou didst part me from my dear husband. Would to God thou hadst done it to me instead!"

But they held to their lie, and Kriemhild went on, "Let him that is guiltless prove it. Let him go up to the bier before all the folk, and soon we shall know the truth."

It is a great marvel, and ofttimes seen even now, how that, when the murderer standeth by the dead, the wounds bleed again. And so it fell then, and Hagen's guilt was plain to all.

The wounds burst open and bled as they had done afore; and they that had wept already wept now much more. King Gunther said, "Hear the truth. He was slain by robbers. Hagen did it not."

"These robbers," she answered, "I know well. God grant that his kinsmen's hands may avenge it. By you, Gunther and Hagen, was it done."

(19) When noble Kriemhild was widowed, Count Eckewart stayed by her in Burgundy with his men, as honour bade him, and served his mistress with goodwill till his death.

At Worms, by the minster, they gave her a room, wide and high, rich and spacious, where she sat joyless with her attendants. To church she went often and gladly. Since her dear one was buried, how seldom she failed there! She went thither sorrowfully every day, and prayed to great God for his soul. Faithfully and without stint the knight was mourned.

Soon after, they contrived that Kriemhild won the great hoard from the land of the Nibelungen, and brought it to the Rhine. It was her marriage-morning gift, and rightly hers. Giselher and Gemot went for it. Kriemhild sent eighty hundred men to fetch it from where it lay hid, and where Alberic with his nearest kinsmen guarded it.

When they saw the men of the Rhine come for the treasure, bold Alberic spoke to his friends, "We dare not refuse her the treasure, for it is the noble queen's wedding gift. Yet we had never parted with it, if we had not lost with Siegfried the good *Tarnkappe*. At all times it was worn by fair Kriemhild's husband. A woeful thing hath it proved for Siegfried that he took from us the *Tarnkappe,* and won all this land to his service."

Then the chamberlain went and got the keys. Kriemhild's men and some of her kinsmen stood before the mountain. They carried the hoard to the sea, on to the ships, and bare it across the waves from the mountain to the Rhine.

Now hear the marvels of this treasure. Twelve waggons scarce carried it thence in four days and four nights, albeit each of them made the journey three times. It was all precious stones and gold, and had the whole world been bought therewith, there had not been one coin the less. Certes, Hagen did not covet it without cause.

The wishing-rod lay among it, the which, if any discovered it, made him master over every man in all the world.

Many of Alberic's kinsmen went with Gernot. When Gernot and Giselher the youth got possession of the hoard, there came into their power lands, and castles, also, and many a good warrior, that served them through fear of their might.

When the hoard came into Gunther's land, and the queen got it in her keeping, chambers and towers were filled full therewith. One never heard tell of so marvelous a treasure. But if it had been a thousand times more, but to have Siegfried alive again, Kriemhild had gladly stood bare by his side. Never had hero truer wife.

Now that she had the hoard, it brought into the land many stranger knights; for the lady's hand gave more freely than any had ever seen. She was kind and good; that must one say of her.

To poor and rich she began to give, till Hagen said that if she lived but a while longer, she would win so many knights to her service that it must go hard with the others.

But King Gunther said, "It is her own. It concerneth me not how she useth it. Scarcely did I win her pardon. And now I ask not who she divideth her jewels and her red gold."

But Hagen said to the king, "A wise man would leave such a treasure to no woman. By reason of her largess, a day will come that the bold Burgundians may rue."

Then King Gunther said, "I sware an oath to her that I would do her no more hurt, nor will I do it. She is my sister."

But Hagen said, "Let me be the guilty one."

And so they brake their oath and took from the widow her rich hoard. Hagen got hold of all the keys.

Gemot was wroth when he heard thereof, and Giselher said, "Hagen hath greatly wronged Kriemhild. I should have withstood him. Were he not my kinsman, he should answer for it with his life."

Then Siegfried's wife began to weep anew.

And Gemot said, "Sooner than be troubled with this gold, let us sink it in the Rhine. Then it were no man's."

She went wailing to Giselher, and said, "Dear brother, forsake me not, but be my kind and good steward."

He answered her, "I will, when we win home again. For the present we ride on a journey."

The king and his kinsmen left the land. He took the best he had with him. Only Hagen tarried behind through the hate he bare Kriemhild, and that he might work her ill.

Or the great king came back, Hagen had seized all the treasure and sunk it in the Rhine at Lochheim. He thought to profit thereby, but did not.

Or Hagen hid the treasure, they had sworn a mighty oath that it should remain a secret so long as they lived. Neither could they take it themselves nor give it to another.

(20) It was in the days when Queen Helche died, and King Etzel wooed other women, that his friends commended to him a proud widow in the land of Burgundy, that hight Queen Kriemhild.

Seeing fair Helche was dead, they said, "If thou wouldst win a noble wife, the highest and the best that ever a king won, take this woman. Strong Siegfried was her husband."

The great king answered, "How could that be, since I am a heathen, and have not received baptism? The woman is a Christian—she will not consent. It were a wonder, truly, if it came to pass."

But the good knights said, "What if she do it gladly, for thy high name's sake, and thy great possessions? One can ask her at the least; she were a fitting and comely mate for thee."

Then the noble king answered, "Which among ye knoweth the folk by the Rhine, and their land?"

Said good Rudeger of Bechlaren, "From a child I have known the high and noble kings, Gunther and Gernot, good knights both. The third hight Giselher; each of these doeth whatso goeth best with honour and virtue. The like did their fathers,"

He said, "Then woo her, Rudeger, in my name and for my sake. And come I ever to wed Kriemhild, I will reward thee as I best can. Thereto, thou wilt have done my will faithfully. From my store I will bid them give thee what thou requirest of horses and apparel, that thou and thy fellows may live merrily. They shall give thee therefrom without stint for thine embassy."

Within twelve days they came to the Rhine. The news was not slow to spread. They told the king and his men that stranger guests had arrived. Then the king began to ask that, if any knew them, he might declare it. They perceived that their sumpters were heavy laden, and saw that they were rich; and they gave them lodging in the wide city straightway.

When the strangers arrived, the folk spied at them curiously. They wondered whence they had journeyed to the Rhine.

The king asked Hagen who the knights were, and the hero of Troneck answered, "So far as I know, for it is long since I saw the knights, they ride like the men of Rudeger, a bold warrior from the land of the Huns."

Then said the faithful envoy, "My great lord commendeth his true service to thee at the Rhine, and to all the friends thou hast. This he doth with true heart. The noble king biddeth thee mourn for his loss. His people are joyless, for my mistress, great Helche, my lord's wife is dead; whereby many high-born maidens, children of great princes, that she hath reared, are orphaned. By reason thereof the land is full of sorrow, for these, alas! have none now to care for them. The king also ceaseth not to make dole."

Then said Gernot of Burgundy, "The world may well rue beautiful Helche's death, for the sake of her many virtues."

Hagen and many another knight said the same.

But Rudeger, the noble envoy, went on: "If thou allow it, O king, I will tell thee further what my dear master hath charged me with. Dolefully hath he lived since Helche's death. And it hath been told him that Kriemhild is without a husband, for that Siegfried is dead. If that be so, and thou grant it, she shall wear the crown before Etzel's knights. This hath my lord bidden me say."

Then the great king spoke courteously, "If she be willing, she followeth my desire therein. In three days I will let thee know. If she say not nay to Etzel, wherefore should I?"

Meanwhile they gave the guests good lodging. On such wise were they entreated that Rudeger was fain to confess he had friends among Gunther's men. Hagen served him gladly, the which Rudeger had done to Hagen aforetime.

So Rudeger tarried there till the third day. The king did prudently, and called a counsel, to ask his friends whether it seemed good to them that Kriemhild should take King Etzel to husband.

And they all counselled it save Hagen, that said to Gunther, the bold knight, "If thou be wise, thou wilt see to it that she do it not, even if she desire it."

"Why should I hinder it?" said Gunther. "If any good fall to the queen, I may well grant it. She is my sister. If it be to her honour, we ourselves should seek the alliance."

But Hagen answered, "Say not so. Didst thou know Etzel as I do, thou wouldst see that thou, first of all, must suffer if she wedded him as thou counsellest."

"How so?" answered Gunther. "Were she his wife, I need not come so nigh him that I must feel his hate."

But Hagen said, "I will never approve it."

They summoned Gemot and Giselher, and asked whether it seemed good to them that Kriemhild should take the great king. And none save Hagen was against it.

Gemot and Giselher, the proud knights and good, and Gunther, the great king, agreed in the end, that they would allow it gladly, if Kriemhild were so minded.

They brought Rudeger to Kriemhild. And the knight asked the queen gently to let him bear the message she sent to Etzel. He won nothing from her but denial, for never could she love another man.

Then said the Margrave, "That were ill done. Wherefore ruin so fair a body? Still mayest thou with honour become a good man's wife." Yet all their entreaty availed not, till that Rudeger said secretly to the queen that he would make good to her any hurt that might befall her. At that, her grief abated somewhat.

He said to the queen, "Weep no more. If thou hadst none among the Huns save me, by faithful kinsmen, and my men, sore must he pay for it that did thee wrong."

Much milder was the lady's mood, and she said, "Swear me an oath that, should any do anything against me, thou wilt be the first to avenge it."

The Margrave answered, "I will swear."

So Rudeger swore with all his men alway to serve her truly, and to deny her nothing in Etzel's land that her honour called for, and he confirmed it with his hand.

Then thought the faithful woman, "Since I, a forlorn woman, can win so many friends, I will let the folk say what they please. Haply I may yet avenge my dear husband's death. Etzel hath so many knights, that, were they mine to command, I could do what I would. Thereto, he is so wealthy that I shall have wherewith to bestow gifts. Cruel Hagen hath taken my treasure from me."

She said to Rudeger, "Had I not heard he was a heathen, I would go gladly at his bidding, and take him to husband."

The Margrave answered, "Say no more of that, Lady. He is not quite a heathen, be assured, for my dear master hath been christened; albeit he hath turned again. Haply he will think better of it shouldst thou wed him. He hath so many Christian knights that no ill could betide thee. And thou mightst easily win back the good prince, heart and soul, to God."

Her brothers said, "Promise it, sister, and give over grieving."

They begged it so long that at the last the sorrowful woman promised, before the warriors, to become Etzel's wife.

She said, "Poor queen that I am, I will follow you! I will go to the Huns, if I find friends to lead me thither." Fair Kriemhild gave her hand on it before the knights.

(22) Etzel's household, that Helche had aforetime ruled, passed many a happy day with Kriemhild. Noble maidens stood waiting, that since Helche's death had suffered heart's dole. Kriemhild found there seven kings' daughters that were an adornment to Etzel's whole land. The charge of the damsels was with Herrat, Helche's sister's daughter, famed for virtue, and the betrothed of Dietrich, a noble king's child, the daughter of Nentwine; the which afterward had much worship. Glad of her cheer was she at the coming of the guests, and many a goodly thing was made ready. What tongue might tell how merrily King Etzel dwelled there? Never under any queen fared the Huns better.

When the king rode up with his wife from the strand, Kriemhild was told the name of them that led forward the maidens, that she might greet them the more fitly. Ha! how mightily she ruled in Helche's stead! She had true servants in plenty. The queen gave gold and vesture, silver and precious stones. All that she had brought with her from over the Rhine to the Huns, she divided among them. All the king's kinsmen and liegemen vowed their service to her, and were subject to her, so that Helche herself had never ruled so mightily as Kriemhild, that they had all to serve till her death.

So famous was the court and the country, that each found there, at all times, the pastime he desired; so kind was the king and so good the queen.

(23) So in high honour (I say honestly), they dwelled together till the seventh year. Meanwhile Kriemhild had borne a son. Nothing could have rejoiced Etzel more. She set her heart on it that he should receive Christian baptism. He was named Ortlieb, and glad was all Etzel's land.

When now she saw that none withstood her (the which a king's knights will sometimes do to their prince's wife), and that twelve kings stood ever before her, she thought on the grievous wrongs that had befallen her in her home. She remembered also the honour that was hers among the Nibelungen, and that Hagen's hand had robbed her of by Siegfried's death, and she pondered how she might work him woe.

One night, when she lay by the king, and he held her in his arms, as was his wont, for she was to him as his life, the royal woman thought on her foes, and said to him, "My dearest lord, I would fain beg a boon of thee. I would have thee show, if I have deserved it at thy hand, that my kinsmen have found favour in thy sight."

The great king answered with true heart, "That will I readily prove to thee. All that profiteth and doth honour to the knights rejoiceth me, for through no woman's love have I won better friends."

Then said the queen, "Thou knowest well that I have noble kinsmen. It irketh me that they visit me so seldom. The folk here deem me kinless."

Whereto King Etzel answered, "If it seem good to thee, dearest wife, I will send my minstrels as envoys to thy friends in Burgundy."

He bade summon the good fiddlers straightway, that hasted to where he sat by the queen, and he told them both to go as envoys to Burgundy.

Then said the great king, "I will tell ye what ye shall do. I send to my friends love and every good wish, and pray them to ride hither to my land. I know few other guests so dear. And if Kriemhild's kinsmen be minded to do my will, bid them fail not to come, for love of me, to my hightide, for my heart yearneth toward the brethren of my wife."

Whereto Schwemmel, the proud minstrel, answered, "When shall thy hightide fall, that we may tell thy friends yonder?"

King Etzel said, "Next midsummer."

"Thy command shall be obeyed," answered Werbel.

The queen bade summon the envoys secretly to her chamber, and spoke with them. Little good came thereof. She said to the two envoys, "Ye shall deserve great reward if ye do my bidding well, and deliver the message wherewith I charge you, at home, in my land. I will make you rich in goods, and give you sumptuous apparel. See that ye say not to any of my friends at Worms, by the Rhine, that ye have ever seen me sad of my cheer, and commend my service to the heroes bold and good. Beg them to grant the king's prayer and end all my sorrow. The Huns deem me without kin. Were I a knight, I would go to them myself. Say to Gernot, my noble brother, that none is better minded to him in the world than I.

Bid him bring here our best friends, that we win honour. And tell Giselher to remember that never, through his fault, did ill betide me; for which reason mine eyes are fain to behold him. Evermore I would serve him. Tell my mother, also, what worship is mine. And if Hagen of Troneck tarry behind who shall lead them through the land? From a child up he hath known the roads hither to the Huns."

The envoys guessed not why she could not leave Hagen of Troneck at the Rhine. They knew it afterward to their cost, for, through him, many a knight was brought face to face with grim death.

Letters and greetings were given to them. They rode forth rich in goods, that they might live merrily by the way. They took leave of Etzel and his fair wife. Their bodies were adorned with goodly vesture.

(24) Within twelve days Werbel and Schwemmel reached Worms on the Rhine. And the kings and their men were told the news, that foreign envoys were come.

The gracious prince greeted them, and said, "Ye are both welcome, Etzel's minstrels, ye and your followers. Wherefore hath the mighty Etzel sent you into Burgundy?"

They bowed before him, and Werbel answered, "First of all, we are sent to the king, to invite you to ride into Etzel's land, and Sir Gernot with you. Mighty Etzel commanded me to say to you all that, even if ye desire not to see your sister, he would fain learn what wrong he hath done you, that ye are such strangers to him and his court. Had ye never known the queen, he deserveth no less of you than that ye come to see him. If ye consent to this, ye shall please him well."

And Gunther answered, "A sennight from now I will let thee know what I and my friends have determined on. Go meanwhile to thy lodging and rest."

The Huns went to their lodging. Meanwhile, the great king had sent for his friends, and noble Gunther asked his men how the message pleased them. And many of them began to say that he might well ride into Etzel's land. The best among them counselled him thereto—all save Hagen. Him it irked exceedingly. He said to the king apart, "Ye strike at your own life. Surely ye know what we have done. Evermore we stand in danger from Kriemhild. I smote her husband dead with my hand. How dare we ride into Etzel's land?"

But the great king answered, "My sister forgot her anger. With a loving kiss she forgave us for all we had done to her or she rode away. Hath she anything against any, it is against thee alone, Hagen."

"Be not deceived," said Hagen, "by the words of the Hunnish envoys. If thou goest to see Kriemhild, thou mayst lose thine honour and thy life. The wife of King Etzel hath a long memory."

Then Gernot spoke out before the assembly, "Because thou fearest death with reason among the Huns, it were ill done on our part to keep away from our sister."

And Sir Giselher said to the knight, "Since thou knowest thyself guilty, friend Hagen, stay thou at home, and guard thyself well, and let them that dare, journey with us to the Huns."

Then the knight of Troneck fell in a passion. "None that ye take with you will be readier to ride to the court than I. And well I will prove it, since ye will not be turned."

But knight Rumolt, the cook, said, "Strangers and friends ye can entertain at home, at your pleasure. For here is abundance. Hagen, I trow, hath never held you back afore. If ye will not follow him in this, be counselled by Rumolt (for your true and loving servant am I) and tarry here as I would have ye do, and leave King Etzel yonder by Kriemhild. Where in the wide world could ye be better? Here ye are safe from your enemies. Ye can adorn your bodies with goodly vesture, drink the best wine, and woo fair women. Thereto, ye are given meats, the best on earth that ever king ate. The land is prosperous. Ye may give up Etzel's hightide with honour, and live merrily at home with your friends. Even had ye nothing else to feast on here, I could always give you your fill of one dish—cutlets fried in oil. This is Rumolt's advice, my masters, since there is danger among the Huns."

And there were many that would not go, and said, "God guard you among the Huns."

The king was wroth when he saw they desired to take their ease at home. "We will go none the less. The prudent are safe in the midst of danger."

Hagen answered, "Be not wroth at my word. Whatever betide, I counsel thee in good faith to ride strongly armed to the Huns, Since thou wilt not be turned, summon the best men thou canst find, or knowest of, among thy vassals, and from among them I will choose a thousand good knights, that thou come not in scathe by Kriemhild's anger."

Kriemhild's envoys were bidden to Gunther's presence. When they appeared, Gemot said, "The king will obey Etzel's wish. We go gladly to his hightide to see our sister. She may count on us."

Gunther asked, "Can ye tell us when the hightide falleth, or when we must set forth?"

And Schwemmel answered, "Next midsummer, without fail."

The king gave them leave, for the first time, to visit Brunhild, but Volker, to please her, said them nay.

(25) Hagen counselled them now to the journey, but he rued it later. He had withstood them, but that Gemot had mocked him. He minded him on Siegfried, Kriemhild's husband, and said, "It is for that, that Hagen durst not go."

But Hagen said, "I hold not back from fear. If ye will have it so, heroes, go forward. I am ready to ride with you to Etzel's land." Soon many a helmet and shield were pierced by him.

The Christian faith was still weak in those days. Nevertheless they had a chaplain with them to say mass. He returned alive, escaped from much peril. The rest tarried dead among the Huns.

Gunther's men shaped their course toward the Main, up through East Frankland. Hagen led them, that knew the way well. Their marshal was Dankwart, the knight of Burgundy. As they rode from East Frankland to Schwanfeld, the princes and their kinsmen, knights of worship, were known by their stately mien.

On the twelfth morning the king reached the Danube. Hagen of Troneck rode in front of the rest. He was the helper and comforter of the Nibelungen. The bold knight alighted there on the bank, and tied his horse to a tree. The river was swoln, there was no boat, and the knights were troubled how to win across. The water was too wide. Many a bold knight sprang to the ground.

"Mischief might easily befall thee here, King of Rhineland," said Hagen; "thou canst see for thyself that the river is swoln, and the current very strong. I fear me we shall lose here to-day not a few good knights."

Then he sought the ferrymen up and down. He heard the splash of water and began to listen. It came from mermaidens that bathed their bodies in a clear brook to cool them.

Hagen spied them, and stole up secretly. When they were ware of him, they fled. Well pleased were they to escape him. The hero took their garments, but did them no further annoy.

Then one of the mermaids (she hight Hadburg) said, "We will tell thee, noble Hagen, if thou give us our clothes again, how ye shall all fare on this journey among the Huns."

They swayed like birds in the water before him. He deemed them wise and worthy of belief, so that he trusted the more what they told him. They informed him concerning all he asked them. Hadburg said, "Ye may ride safely into Etzel's land; I pledge my faith thereon, that never yet heroes journeyed to any court to win more worship. I say honestly."

Hagen's heart was uplifted at her word; he gave them back their clothes and stayed no longer. When they had put on their wonderful raiment, they told him the truth about the journey.

The other mermaid, that hight Sieglind, said, "Be warned, Hagen, son of Aldrian. My aunt hath lied to thee because of her clothes. If ye go to the Huns, ye are ill-advised. Turn while there is time, for ye bold knights have been bidden that ye may die in Etzel's land. Who rideth thither hath death at his hand."

But Hagen said, "Your deceit is vain. How should we all tarry there, dead, through the hate of one woman?"

Then they began to foretell it plainer, and Hadburg said also, "Ye are doomed. Not one of you shall escape, save the king's chaplain: this we know for a truth. He, only, shall return alive into Gunther's land."

Grimly wroth spoke bold Hagen then. "It were a pleasant thing to tell my masters that we must all perish among the Huns! Show us a way across the water, thou wisest of womankind."

She answered, "Since thou wilt not be turned from the journey, up yonder by the river standeth an inn. Within it is a boatman; there is none beside."

He betook him thither to ask further. But the mermaiden cried after the wrothful knight, "Stay, Sir Hagen. Thou art too hasty. Hearken first concerning the way. The lord of this march hight Elsy. The name of his brother is Gelfrat, a prince in Bavaria. It might go hard with thee if thou wentest through his march. Look well to thyself, and proceed warily with the boatman. He is so grim of his mood that he will kill thee, if thou speak him not fair. If thou wouldst have him ferry thee across, give him hire. He guardeth this land, and is Gelfrat's friend. If he come not straight way, cry across the river to him that thou art Amelrich; he was a good knight, that a feud drove from this land. The boatman will come when he heareth that name."

Proud Hagen thanked the women for their warning and their counsel, and said no more. He went up the river's bank, till he came to an inn that stood on the far side. He began to shout across the water, "Boatman, row me over, and I will give thee, for thy meed, an armlet of red gold. I must across."

The boatman was so rich that he needed not to serve for hire, and seldom took reward from any. His men also were overweening, and Hagen was left standing on the bank of the river.

Thereupon he shouted so loud that all the shore rang with it. He was a strong man. "Row across for Amelrich, I am Elsy's liegeman, that, for a feud, fled the country." He swung the armlet aloft on his sword—it was of red gold, bright and shining—that they might ferry him over to Gelfrat's march. At this the haughty boatman himself took the oar, for he was greedy and covetous of gain, the which bringeth oft to a bad end. He thought to win Hagen's red gold, but won, in lieu thereof, a grim death by his sword.

He rowed over to the shore with mighty strokes. When he found not him that had been named, he fell in a fury; he saw Hagen, and spoke wrothfully to the hero, "Thy name may be Amelrich, but, or I greatly err, thy face is none of his. By one father and one mother he was my brother. Since thou hast deceived me, thou canst stay where thou art."

"Nay, for the love of God," said Hagen. "I am a stranger knight that have the charge of other warriors. Take thy fee and row me over, for I am a friend."

But the boatman answered, "I will not. My dear masters have foemen, wherefore I must bring no stranger across. If thou lovest thy life, step out on to the shore again."

"Nay now," said Hagen, "I am sore bested. Take, as a keepsake, this goodly gold, and ferry us over with our thousand horses and our many men."

But the grim boatman answered, "Never!" He seized an oar, mickle and broad, and smote Hagen (soon he rued it), that he staggered and fell on his knees. Seldom had he of Troneck encountered so grim a ferryman. Further, to anger the bold stranger, he brake a boat-pole over his head, for he was a strong man. But he did it to his own hurt.

Grimly wroth, Hagen drew a weapon from the sheath, and cut off his head, and threw it on the ground. The Burgundians were soon ware of the tidings.

In the same moment that he slew the ferryman, the boat was caught by the current, which irked him no little, for he was weary or he could bring her head round, albeit Gunther's man rowed stoutly. With swift strokes he sought to turn it, till the oar brake in his hand. He strove to reach the knights on the strand, but had no other oar. Ha! how nimbly he bound it together with the thong of his shield, a narrow broidered band, and rowed to a wood down the river.

There he found his masters waiting on the beach. Many a valiant knight ran to meet him, and greeted him joyfully. But when they saw the boat full of blood from the grim wound he had given the ferryman, they began to question him.

When Gunther saw the hot blood heaving in the boat, he said quickly, "Tell me what thou hast done with the ferryman. I ween he hath fallen by thy strength."

But he answered with a lie, "I found the boat by a waste meadow, and loosed it. I have seen no ferryman this day, nor hath any suffered hurt at my hand."

Then said Sir Gernot of Burgundy, "I am heavy of my cheer because of the dear friends that must die or night, for boatmen we have none. Sorrowfully I stand, nor know how we shall win over."

But Hagen cried, "Lay down your burdens on the grass, ye squires. I was the best boatman by the Rhine, and safe, I trow, I shall bring you into Gelfrat's land."

That they might cross the quicker, they drave in the horses. These swam so well that none were drowned, albeit a few, grown weary, were borne down some length by the tide. Then they carried their gold and harness on board, since they must needs make the passage. Hagen was the helmsman, and steered many a gallant knight to the unknown land. First he took over a thousand, and thereto his own band of warriors. Then followed more: nine thousand squires. The knight of Troneck was not idle that day. The ship was huge, strongly built and wide enow. Five hundred of their folk and more, with their meats and weapons, it carried easily at a time. Many a good warrior that day pulled sturdily at the oar.

When he had brought them safe across the water, the bold knight and good thought on the strange prophecy of the wild mermaids. Through this the king's chaplain came nigh to lose his life. He found the priest beside the sacred vessels, leaning with his hand upon the holy relics. This helped him not. When Hagen saw him, it went hard with the poor servant of God. He threw him out of the ship on the instant. Many cried, "Stop, Hagen, stop!" Giselher, the youth, was very wroth, but Hagen ceased not, till he had done him a hurt.

Then strong Gemot of Burgundy said, "What profiteth thee the chaplain's death, Hagen? Had another done this, he had paid dear for it. What hast thou against the priest?"

The chaplain swam with all his might. He had gotten on board again had any helped him. But none could do it, for strong Hagen pushed him fiercely under. None approved his deed.

When the poor man saw that they would not aid him, he turned and made for the shore. He was in sore peril. But, albeit he could not swim, the hand of God upbore him, that he won safe to the dry land again. There he stood, and shook his clothes,

By this sign Hagen knew there was no escape from what the wild women of the sea had foretold. He thought, "These knights be all dead men."

When they had unloaded the ship, and brought all across that belonged to the three kings, Hagen brake it in pieces and threw these on the water. Much the bold knights marvelled thereat.

"Wherefore dost thou so, brother?" said Dankwart. "How shall we get over when we ride home from the Huns to the Rhine?"

Hagen told him, after, that that would never be, but for the meantime he said, "I did it a-purpose. If we have any coward with us on this journey, that would forsake us in our need, he shall die a shameful death in these waves."

(26) Then they rode into Rudeger's country. When Rudeger had heard the news, he was glad.

(27) The Margrave went to find his wife and daughter, and told them the good news that he had heard, how that their queen's brethren were coming to the house.

"Dear love," said Rudeger, "receive the high and noble kings well when they come here with their followers. Hagen, Gunther's man, thou shalt also greet fair. There is one with them that hight Dank-wart; another hight Volker, a man of much worship. These six thou shalt kiss—thou and my daughter. Entreat the warriors courteously."

The women promised it, nothing loath. They took goodly apparel from their chests, wherein to meet the knights. The fair women made haste enow. Their cheeks needed little false colour. They wore fillets of bright gold on their heads, fashioned like rich wreaths, that the wind might not ruffle their beautiful hair. They were dainty and fresh.

The noble Margravine came out before the castle with her beautiful daughter. Lovely women and fair maids not a few stood beside her, adorned with bracelets and fine apparel. Precious stones sparked bright on their rich vesture. Goodly was their raiment.

The guests rode up and sprang to the ground. Ha! courteous men all were they of Burgundy! Six and thirty maidens and many women beside, fair to heart's desire, came forth to meet them, with bold men in plenty. The noble women welcomed them sweetly. The Margravine kissed the kings all three. Her daughter did the like. Hagen stood by. Him also her father bade her kiss. She looked up at him, and he was so grim that she had gladly let it be. Yet must she do as the host bade her. Her colour came and went, white and red. She kissed Dankwart, too, and, after him, the fiddler. By reason of his body's strength he won this greeting. Then the young Margravine took Giselher, the youth of Burgundy, by the hand. Her mother did the same to Gunther, and they went in merrily with the heroes.

The host led Gernot into a wide hall. There knights and ladies sat down, and good wine was poured out for the guests. Never were warriors better entreated.

Rudeger's daughter was looked at with loving eyes, she was so fair; and many a good knight loved her in his heart. And well they might, for she was an high-hearted maiden. But their thoughts were vain: it could not be.

Women and knights were parted then, as was the custom, and went into separate rooms. The table was made ready in the great hall, and willing service was done to the strangers.

To show love to the guests, the Margravine went to table with them. She left her daughter with the damsels, as was seemly, albeit it irked the guests to see her no longer.

When they had all drunk and eaten, they brought the fair ones into the hall again, and there was no lack of sweet words. Volker, a knight bold and good, spoke plenty of them. This same fiddler said openly, "Great Margrave, God hath done well by thee, for he hath given thee a right beautiful wife, and happy days. Were I a king," said the minstrel, "and wore a crown, I would choose thy sweet daughter for my queen. She would be the choice of my heart, for she is fair to look upon, and thereto, noble and good."

The Margrave answered, "How should a king covet my dear daughter? My wife and I are both strangers here, and have nothing to give. What availeth then her beauty?"

But said Gernot, the courteous man, "Might I choose where I would, such a wife were my heart's desire."

Then said Hagen graciously, "It is time Giselher wedded. Of such high lineage is the noble Margravine, that we would gladly serve her, I and his men, if she wore the crown in Burgundy."

The word pleased both Rudeger and Gotelind greatly. Their hearts were uplifted. So it was agreed among the heroes that noble Giselher should take her to wife; the which a king might well do without shame.

If a thing be right, who can withstand it? They bade the maiden before them, and they swore to give her to him, whereupon he vowed to cherish her. They gave her castles and lands for her share. The king and Gernot sware with the hand that it should be even as they had promised.

Then said the Margrave, "Since I have no castles, I can only prove me your true friend evermore. I will give my daughter as much silver and gold as an hundred sumpters may carry, that ye warriors may, with honour, be content."

Then the two were put in a circle, as the custom was. Many a young knight stood opposite in merry mood, and thought in his heart as young folk will. They asked the lovely maiden if she would have the hero. She was half sorry, yet her heart inclined to the goodly man. She was shamefast at the question, as many a maid hath been.

Rudeger her father counselled her to say "yes," and to take him gladly. Giselher, the youth, was not slow to clasp her to him with his white hands. Yet how little while she had him!

Then said the Margrave, "Great and noble kings, I will give you my child to take with you, for this were fittest, when ye ride home again into your land." And it was so agreed.

The din of tourney was bidden cease. The damsels were sent to their chambers, and the guests to sleep and to take their rest till the day. Then meats were made ready, for their host saw well to their comfort.

When they had eaten, they would have set out again for the country of the Huns, but Rudeger said, "Go not, I pray you. Tarry here yet a while, for I had never dearer guests."

Dankwart answered, "It may not be. Where couldst thou find the meat, the bread and the wine, for so many knights?"

But when the host heard him, he said, "Speak not of that. Deny me not, my dear lords. I can give you and all them that are with you, meat for fourteen days. Little hath King Etzel ever taken of my substance."

Albeit they made excuse, they had to tarry till the fourth morning. He gave both horses and apparel so freely that the fame of it spread abroad.

But longer than this it could not last, for they must needs forth. Rudeger was not sparing of his goods. If any craved for anything, none denied him. Each got his desire.

The attendants brought the saddled horses to the door. There many stranger knights joined them, shield in hand, to ride with them to Etzel's court. To each of the noble guests Rudeger offered a gift, or he left the hall. He had wherewithal to live in honour and give freely. Upon Giselher he had bestowed his fair daughter. He gave to

Gernot a goodly weapon enow, that he wielded well afterward in strife. The Margrave's wife grudged him not the gift, yet Rudeger, or long, was slain thereby.

To Gunther, the valiant knight, he gave a coat of mail, that did the rich king honour, albeit he seldom took gifts. He bowed before Rudeger and thanked him.

Gotelind offered Hagen a fair gift, as was fitting, since the king had taken one, that he might not fare to the hightide without a keepsake from her, but he refused.

"Nothing that I ever saw would I so fain bear away with me as yonder shield on the wall. I would gladly carry it into Etzel's land."

When the Margravine heard Hagen's word, it reminded her of her sorrow, and she fell to weeping. She thought sadly on the death of Nudung, that Wittich had slain; and her heart was heavy.

She said to the knight, "I will give thee the shield. Would to God he yet lived that once bore it! He died in battle. I must ever weep when I think on him, for my woman's heart is sore."

The noble Margravine rose from her seat, and took down the shield with her white hands and carried it to Hagen, that used it as a hero should. A covering of bright stuff lay over its device. The light never shone on better shield. It was so rich with precious stones that had any wanted to buy it it had cost him at the least a thousand marks.

The knight bade his attendants bear it away. Then came his brother Dankwart, to whom the Margrave's daughter gave richly broidered apparel, that afterward he wore merrily among the Huns.

None had touched any of these things but for love of the host that offered them so kindly. Yet, or long, they bare him such hate that they slew him.

Bold Volker then stepped forth with knightly bearing and stood before Gotelind with his viol. He played a sweet tune and sang her his song. Then he took his leave and left Bechlaren. But first the Margravine bade them bring a drawer nearer. Of loving gifts now hear the tale. She took therefrom twelve armlets, and drew them over his hand, saying, "These shalt thou take with thee and wear for my sake at Etzel's court. When thou comest again, I will hear how thou hast served me at the hightide." Well he did her behest.

The host said to the guest, "That ye may journey the safer, I will myself escort you, and see that none fall on you by the way." And forthwith they loaded his sumpter. He stood ready for the road with five hundred men, mounted and equipped. These he led merrily to the hightide. Not one of them came back alive to Bechlaren.

The swift envoys pressed down through Austria, and soon the folk knew, far and near, that the heroes were on their way from Worms beyond the Rhine. It was welcome news to the king's vassals. The envoys spurred forward with the tidings that the Nibelungen were come to the Huns.

"Receive them well, Kriemhild, my wife. Thy brethren are come to show thee great honour."

Kriemhild stood at a window and looked out as a friend might for friends. Many drew thither from her father's land. The king was joyful when he heard the news.

"Glad am I," said Kriemhild, "my kinsmen come with many new shields and shining bucklers. I will ever be his friend that taketh my gold and remembereth my wrong."

She thought in her heart, "Now for the reckoning! If I can contrive it, it will go hard at this hightide with him that killed all my happiness. Fain would I work his doom. I care not what may come of it: my vengeance shall fall on the hateful body of him that stole my joy from me. He shall pay dear for my sorrow."

(28) King Etzel saw them, and asked, "I would know who yonder knight is that Dietrich welcometh so lovingly. He beareth him proudly. Howso is his father hight, he is, certes, a goodly warrior."

One of Kriemhild's men answered the king, "He was born at Troneck. The name of his father was Aldrian. Albeit now he goeth gently, he is a grim man. I will prove to thee yet that I lie not."

"How shall I find him so grim?" He knew nothing, as yet, of all that the queen contrived against her kinsmen by reason whereof not one of them escaped alive from the Huns.

"I know Hagen well. He was my vassal. Praise and mickle honour he won here by me. I made him a knight, and gave him my gold. For that he proved him faithful, I was ever kind to him. Wherefore I may well know all about him. I brought two noble children captive to this land—him and Walter of Spain. Here they grew to manhood. Hagen I sent home again. Walter fled with Hildegund."

So he mused on the good old days, and what had happed long ago, for he had seen Hagen, that did him strong service in his youth. Yet now that he was old, he lost by him many a dear friend.

(29) The Huns gaped at the proud heroes as they had been wild beasts, and Etzel's wife saw them through a window and was troubled anew. She thought on her old wrong and began to weep. Etzel's men marvelled much what had grieved her so sore. She said, "Good knights, it is Hagen that hath done it."

Then said they to the queen, "How came it to pass? A moment ago we saw thee of good cheer. There is no man so bold, had he done thee a hurt and thou badest us avenge thee, but he should answer for it with his life."

"Him that avenged my wrong I would thank evermore. All that he asked I would give him. I fall at your feet; only avenge me on Hagen, that he lose his life."

Thereupon sixty bold men armed them swiftly, and would have gone out with one accord to slay Hagen, the bold knight, and the fiddler, for Kriemhild's sake.

But when the queen saw so small a number, she spoke wrothfully to the heroes, "Think not to withstand Hagen with so few. Strong and bold as is Hagen of Troneck, much stronger is he that sitteth by him, Volker the fiddler by name, a wicked man. Ye shall not so lightly overcome them."

(30) They led the guests to a spacious hall, where they found beds, big and costly, standing ready. Gladly had the queen worked their doom. Coverlets of bright stuffs from Arras were there, and testers of silk of Araby, the goodliest that could be, broidered and shining with gold. The bed-clothes were of ermine and black sable, for them to rest under, the night through, till the day. In such state never king lay before with his men.

"Woe is me for our lodging!" said Giselher the youth, "and for my friends that came hither with us. My sister sent us fair words, but I fear we must all soon lie dead through her."

"Grieve not," said Hagen the knight. "I will myself keep watch, and will guard thee well, I trow, till the day. Fear nothing till then. After that, each shall look to himself."

They bowed to him and thanked him. They went to their beds, and, or long, the valiant men were lying soft. Then bold Hagen began to arm him.

Volker the fiddler said, "If thou scorn not my help, Hagen, I would keep watch with thee till the morning."

The hero thanked Volker, "God in Heaven quit you, dear Volker. In all my troubles and my straits I desire thee only and no other. I will do as much for thee, if death hinder it not."

They both did on their shining harness. Each took his shield in his hand, and went out before the door to keep watch over the strangers. They did it faithfully.

Brave Volker leaned his good shield against the wall, and went back and took his fiddle, and did fair and seemly service to his friends. He sat down under the lintel upon the stone. There never was a bolder minstrel. When the sweet tones sounded from his strings, the proud homeless ones all thanked him. He struck so loud that the house echoed. Great were his skill and strength both. Then he played sweeter and softer, till he had lulled many a careworn man to sleep. When Volker found they were all asleep, he took his shield in his hand again, and went out and stood before the door, to guard his friends from Kriemhild's men.

About the middle of the night, or sooner, bold Volker saw a helmet in the distance, shining in the dark. Kriemhild's vassals were fain to do them a hurt. Or she sent them forth, she said, "For God's sake, if ye win at them, slay none save the one man, false Hagen; let the others live."

Then spoke the fiddler, "Friend Hagen, we must bear this matter through together. I see armed folk before the house. I ween they come against us."

"Hold thy peace," answered Hagen. "Let them come nigher. Or they are ware of us, there will be helmets cloven by the swords in our two hands. They shall be sent back to Kriemhild in sorry plight."

One of the Hunnish knights saw that the door was guarded, and said hastily, "We cannot carry this thing through. I see the fiddler standing guard. He hath on his head a shining helmet, bright and goodly, with no dint therein, and strong thereto. The rings of his harness glow like fire. Hagen standeth by him. The strangers are well watched."

They turned without more ado. When Volker saw this, he spoke angrily to his comrade, "Let me go out to these knights. I would ask Kriemhild's men a question."

"Nay, as thou lovest me," said Hagen. "If thou wentest to them, thou wouldst fall in such strait by their swords that I must help thee, though all my kinsmen perished thereby. If both the two of us fell to fighting, two or three of them might easily spring into the house, and do such hurt to the sleepers as we could never mourn enow."

But Volker said, "Let us tell them that we have seen them, that they deny not their treachery." Then Volker called out to them, "Why go ye there armed, valiant knights? Is it murder ye are after, ye men of Kriemhild? Take me and my comrade to help you."

None answered him. Right wroth was he.

"Shame on you, cowards! Would ye have slain us sleeping? Seldom afore hath so foul a deed been done on good knights."

The queen was heavy of her cheer when they told her that her messengers had failed. She began to contrive it otherwise, for grim was her mood, and by reason thereof many a good knight and bold soon perished.

(31) "My harness is grown so cold," said Volker, "that I ween the night is far spent. I feel, by the air, that it will soon be day."

Then they waked the knights that still slept.

The bright morning shone in on the warriors in the hall, and Hagen began to ask them if they would go to the minster to hear mass. The bells were ringing according to Christian custom.

The folk sang out of tune: it was not mickle wonder, when Christian and heathen sang together. Gunther's men were minded to go to church, and rose from their beds. They did on their fine apparel—never knights brought goodlier weed into any king's land. But Hagen was wroth, and said, "Ye did better to wear other raiment. Ye know how it standeth with us here. Instead of roses, bear weapons in your hands, and instead of jewelled caps, bright-helmets. Of wicked Kriemhild's mood we are well aware. I tell you there will be fighting this day. For your silken tunics wear your hauberks, and good broad shields for rich mantles, that, if any fall on you, ye may be ready. My masters dear, my kinsmen, and my men, go to the church and bewail your sorrow and your need before great God, for know, of a surety, that death draweth nigh. Forget not wherein ye have sinned, and stand humbly before your Maker. Be warned, most noble knights. If God in heaven help you not, ye will hear mass no more."

So the kings and their men went to the minster. Hagen bade them pause in the churchyard, that they might not be parted. He said, "None knoweth yet what the Huns may attempt on us. Lay your shields at your feet, my friends, and if any give you hostile greeting, answer him with deep wounds and deadly. That is Hagen's counsel, that ye may be found ready, as beseemeth you."

Volker and Hagen went and stood before the great minster. They did this that the queen might be forced to push past them. Right grim was their mood.

Then came the king and his beautiful wife. Her body was adorned with rich apparel, and the knights in her train were featly clad. The dust rose high before the queen's attendants.

When the rich king saw the princes and their followers armed, he said hastily, "Why go my friends armed? By my troth it would grieve me if any had done anything to them. I will make it good to them on any wise they ask it. Hath any troubled their hearts, he shall feel my displeasure. Whatso they demand of me I will do."

Hagen answered, "None hath wrought us annoy. It is the custom of my masters to go armed at all hightides for full three days. If any did us a mischief, Etzel should hear thereof."

Right well Kriemhild heard Hagen's word. She looked at him from under her eyelids with bitter hate. Yet she told not the custom of her land, albeit she knew it well from aforetime. Howso grim and deadly the queen's anger was, none had told Etzel how it stood, else he had hindered what afterward befell They scorned, through pride, to tell their wrong.

The queen advanced with a great crowd of folk, but the two moved not two hands' breadth, whereat the Huns were wroth, for they had to press past the heroes. This pleased not Etzel's chamberlains, and they had gladly quarrelled with them, had they dared before the king. There was much jostling, and nothing more.

When mass was over, many a Hun sprang to horse.

The host went with his guests into the palace, and bade the anger cease. They set the table, and brought water. The knights of the Rhine had strong foemen enow. Though it irked Etzel, many armed knights pressed in after the kings, when they went to table, by reason of their hate. They waited a chance to avenge their kinsman.

"Ye be too unmannerly," said the host, "to sit down armed to eat. Whoso among you toucheth my guests shall pay for it with his head. I have spoken, O Huns."

It was long or the knights were all seated. Bitter was Kriemhild's wrath. She said, "Prince of Bern, I seek thy counsel and thy kind help in my sore need."

But Hildebrand, the good knight, answered, "Who slayeth the Nibelungen shall do it without me; I care not what price thou offerest. None shall essay it but he shall rue it, for never yet have these doughty knights been vanquished."

"I ask the death of none save Hagen, that hath wronged me. He slew Siegfried, my dear husband. He that chose him from among the others for vengeance should have my gold without stint. I were inly grieved did any suffer save Hagen."

But Hildebrand answered, "How could one slay him alone? Thou canst see for thyself, that if he be set upon, they will all to battle, and poor and rich alike must perish."

Said Dietrich also, courteously, "Great queen, say no more. Thy kinsmen have done nothing to me that I should defy them to the death. It is little to thine honour that thou wouldst compass the doom of thy kinsmen. They came hither under safe conduct, and not by the hand of Dietrich shall Siegfried be avenged."

When she found no treachery in the knight of Bern, she tempted Bloedel with the promise of a goodly estate that had been Nudung's. Dankwart slew him after, that he clean forgot the gift.

She said, "Help me, Sir Bloedel. In this house are the foes that slew Siegfried, my dear husband. If any avenge me, I will ever serve him."

Bloedel, that sat by her, answered, "I dare not show thy kinsmen such hate, so long as my brother showeth them favour. The king would not forgive me if I defied them."

"Nay now, Sir Bloedel, I will stand by thee, and give thee silver and gold for meed, and, thereto, a beautiful woman, the widow of Nudung, that thou mayest have her to thy dear one. I will give thee all, land and castles, and thou shalt live joyfully with her on the march that was Nudung's. In good honesty I will do what I promise."

When Bloedel heard the fee, and because the woman pleased him for her fairness, he resolved to win her by battle. So came he to lose his life.

He said to the queen, "Go back into the hall. Or any is ware thereof, I will raise a great tumult. Hagen shall pay for what he hath done. I will bring thee King Gunther's man bound."

"Now arm ye, my men," cried Bloedel, "and let us fall on the foemen in their lodging. King Etzel's wife giveth me no peace, and at her bidding we must risk our lives."

When the queen had left Bloedel to begin the strife, she went in to table with King Etzel and his men. She had woven an evil snare against the guests.

I will tell you now how they went into the hall. Crowned kings went before her; many high princes and knights of worship attended the queen. Etzel assigned to all the guests their places, the highest and the best in the hall. Christians and heathens had their different meats, whereof they ate to the full; for so the wise king ordered it. The yeomen feasted in their own quarters, where sewers served them, that had been charged with the care of their food. But revel and merriment were soon turned to weeping.

Kriemhild's old wrong lay buried in her heart, and when the strife could not be kindled otherwise, she bade them bring Etzel's son to table. Did ever any woman so fearful a thing for vengeance?

Four of Etzel's men went straightway and brought in Ortlieb, the young king, to the princes' table, where Hagen also sat. Through his murderous hate the child perished.

When Etzel saw his son, he spoke kindly to his wife's brethren, "See now, my friends, that is my only son, and your sister's child. Some day he will serve you well. If he take after his kin, he will be a valiant man, rich and right noble, strong and comely. If I live, I will give him the lordship of twelve countries. Fair service ye may yet have from young Ortlieb's hand. Wherefore I pray ye, my dear friends, that, when ye ride back to the Rhine, ye take with you your sister's son, and do well by the child. Rear him in honour till he be a man, and when he is full grown, if any harry your land, he will help you to avenge it." Kriemhild, the wife of Etzel, heard all that the king said.

Hagen answered, "If he grow to be a man, he may well help these knights. But he hath a weakly look. Methinketh I shall seldom go to Ortlieb's court."

The king eyed Hagen sternly, for his word irked him. Albeit he answered not again, he was troubled, and heavy of his cheer. Hagen was no friend to merriment.

The king and his liegemen misliked sore what Hagen had said of the child, and were wroth that they must bear it. They knew not yet what the warrior was to do after. Not a few that heard it, and that bare him hate, had gladly fallen upon him: the king also, had not honour forbidden him. Ill had Hagen sped. Yet soon he did worse: he slew his child before his eyes.

(32) Bloedel's knights all stood ready. With a thousand hauberks they went where Dankwart sat at table with the yeomen. Grim was soon the hate between the heroes.

When Sir Bloedel strode up to the table, Dankwart the marshal greeted him fair. "Welcome to this house, Sir Bloedel. What news dost thou bring?"

"Greet me not," said Bloedel. "My coming meaneth thy death, because of Hagen, thy brother, that slew Siegfried. Thou and many another knight shall pay for it."

"Nay now, Sir Bloedel," said Dankwart. "So might we well rue this hightide. I was a little child when Siegfried lost his life. I know not what King Etzel's wife hath against me."

"I can tell thee nothing, save that thy kinsmen, Gunther and Hagen, did it. Now stand on your defense, ye homeless ones. Ye must die, for your lives are forfeit to Kriemhild."

"Dost thou persist?" said Dankwart. "Then it irketh me that I asked it. I had better have spared my words."

The good knight and bold sprang up from the table, and drew a sharp weapon that was mickle and long, and smote Bloedel a swift blow therewith, that his head, in its helmet, fell at their feet.

"That be thy wedding-gift to Nudung's bride, that thou though test to win!" he cried. "Let them mate her to-morrow with another man; if he ask the dowry, he can have the like." A faithful Hun had told him that morning, secretly, that the queen plotted their doom.

When Bloedel's men saw their master lying slain, they endured it no longer, but fell with drawn swords in grim wrath on the youths.

The homeless youths made grim defence. They drave the armed men from the house. Yet five hundred and more lay therein dead. They were red and wet with blood.

He fought his way through his foemen like a wild boar in the forest through the hounds—bolder he could not have been. His path was ever wet anew with hot blood. When did single knight withstand foemen better? Proudly Hagen's brother went to court.

(33) Bold Dankwart strode in through the door, and bade Etzel's followers void the way; all his harness was covered with blood. It was at the time they were carrying Ortlieb to and fro from table to table among the princes, and through the terrible news the child perished.

Dankwart cried aloud to one of the knights, "Thou sittest here too long, brother Hagen. To thee, and God in Heaven, I bewail our wrong. Knights and squires lie dead in our hall."

Hagen called back to him, "Who hath done it?"

"Sir Bloedel and his men. He paid for it bitterly, I can tell thee. I smote off his head with my hands."

"He hath paid too little," said Hagen, "since it can be said of him that he hath died by the hand of a hero. His womenfolk have the less cause to weep. Now tell me, dear brother; wherefore art thou so red? I ween thy wounds are deep. If he be anywhere near that hath done it, and the devil help him not, he is a dead man."

"Unwounded I stand. My harness is wet with the blood of other men, whereof I have today slain so many, that I cannot swear to the number."

Hagen said, "Brother Dankwart, keep the door, and let not a single Hun out; I will speak with the knights as our wrong constraineth me. Guiltless, our followers lie dead."

"To such great kings will I gladly be chamberlain," said the bold man; "I will guard the stairs faithfully."

Kriemhild's men were sore dismayed.

"I marvel much," said Hagen, "what the Hunnish knights whisper in each other's ears. I ween they could well spare him that standeth at the door, and hath brought this court news to the Burgundians. I have long heard

Kriemhild say that she could not bear her heart's dole. Now drink we to Love, and taste the king's wine. The young prince of the Huns shall be the first."

With that, Hagen slew the child Ortlieb, that the blood gushed down on his hand from his sword, and the head flew up into the queen's lap. Then a slaughter grim and great arose among the knights. He slew the child's guardian with a sword stroke from both his hands, that the head fell down before the table. It was sorry pay he gave the tutor. He saw a minstrel sitting at Etzel's table, and sprang at him in wrath, and lopped off his right hand on his viol: "Take that for the message thou broughtest to the Burgundians."

"Woe is me for my hand!" cried Werbel. "Sir Hagen of Troneck, what have I done to thee? I rode with true heart to thy master's land. How shall I make my music now?"

Little recked Hagen if he never fiddled more. He quenched on Etzel's knights, in the house there, his grim lust for blood, and smote to death not a few.

Swift Volker sprang from the table; his fiddle-bow rang loud. Harsh were the tunes of Gunther's minstrel. Ha! many a foe he made among the Huns!

The three kings, too, rose hastily. They would have parted them or more harm was done. But they could not, for Volker and Hagen were beside themselves with rage.

When the King of Rhineland could not stint the strife, he, also, smote many a deep wound through the shining harness of his foemen. Well he showed his hardihood.

Then strong Gernot came into the battle, and slew many Huns with the sharp sword that Rudeger had given him. He brought many of Etzel's knights to their graves therewith.

Uta's youngest son sprang into the fray, and pierced the helmets of Etzel's knights valiantly with his weapon. Bold Giselher's hand did wonderly.

But howso valiant all the others were, the kings and their men, Volker stood up bolder than any against the foes. He was a hero; he wounded many, that they fell down in their blood.

Etzel's liegemen warded them well, but the guests hewed their way with their bright swords up and down the hall. From all sides came the sound of wailing. They that were without would gladly have won in to their friends, but could not; and they that were within would have won out, but Dankwart let none of them up the stair or down.

The host and his wife fell in great fear. Many a dear friend was slain before their eyes. Etzel himself scarce escaped from his foemen. He sat there affrighted. What did it profit him that he was a king?

Proud Kriemhild cried to Dietrich, "Help me, noble knight, by the princely charity of an Amelung king, to come hence alive. If Hagen reach me, death standeth by my side."

"How can I help thee, noble queen? I cannot help myself. Gunther's men are so grimly wroth that I can win grace for none."

"Nay now, good Sir Dietrich, show thy mercy, and help me hence or I die. Save me and the king from this great peril."

"I will try. Albeit, for long, I have not seen good knights in such a fury. The blood gusheth from the helmets at their sword-strokes."

The chosen knight shouted with a loud voice that rang out like the blast of a buffalo horn, so that all the castle echoed with its strength, for strong and of mickle might was Dietrich.

King Gunther heard his cry above the din of strife, and hearkened. He said, "The voice of Dietrich hath reached me. I ween our knights have slain some of his men. I see him on the table, beckoning with his hand. Friends and kinsmen of Burgundy, hold, that we may learn what we have done to Dietrich's hurt."

When King Gunther had begged and prayed them, they lowered their swords. Thereby Gunther showed his might, that they smote no blow. Then he asked the Prince of Bern what he wanted. He said, "Most noble Dietrich, what hurt have my friends done thee? I will make it good. Sore grieved were I, had any done thee scathe."

But Sir Dietrich answered, "Nothing hath been done against me. With thy safe-conduct let me quit this hall, and the bitter strife, with my men. For this I will ever serve thee."

"Why ask this grace?" said Wolfhart. "The fiddler hath not barred the door so fast that we cannot set it wide, and go forth."

"Hold thy peace," cried Dietrich. "Thou hast played the devil."

Then Gunther answered, "I give thee leave. Lead forth few or many, so they be not my foemen. These shall tarry within, for great wrong have I suffered from the Huns."

When the knight of Bern heard that, he put one arm round the queen, for she was greatly affrighted, and with the other he led out Etzel. Six hundred good knights followed Dietrich.

Then said noble Rudeger, the Margrave, "If any more of them that love and would serve thee may win from this hall, let us hear it; that peace may endure, as is seemly, betwixt faithful friends."

Straightway Giselher answered his father-in-law. "Peace and love be betwixt us. Thou and thy liegemen have been ever true to us, wherefore depart with thy friends, fearing nothing."

When Sir Rudeger left the hall, five hundred or more went out with him. The Burgundian knights did honourably therein, but King Gunther suffered scathe for it after.

One of the Huns would have saved himself when he saw King Etzel go out with Dietrich, but the fiddler smote him such a blow that his head fell down at Etzel's feet.

All that they would let go were gone. Then arose a mighty din. The guests avenged them bitterly. Ha! many a helmet did Volker break!

Of the Huns that had been in the hall, not one was left alive. The tumult fell, for there was none to fight, and the bold warriors laid down their swords.

(34) The knights sat down through weariness. Volker and Hagen went out before the hall. There the overweening men leaned on their shields and spoke together.

Then said Giselher of Burgundy, "Rest not yet, dear friends. Ye must carry the dead out of the house. We shall be set upon again; trow my word. These cannot lie longer among our feet. Or the Huns overcome us, we will hew many wounds; to the which I am nothing loth."

"Well for me that I have such a lord," answered Hagen. "This counsel suiteth well such a knight as our young master hath approved him this day. Ye Burgundians have cause to rejoice."

They did as he commanded, and bare the seven thousand dead bodies to the door, and threw them out. They fell down at the foot of the stair, Then arose a great wail from their kinsmen. Some of them were so little wounded that, with softer nursing, they had come to. Now, from the fall, these died also. Their friends' wept and made bitter dole.

Then said bold Volker the fiddler, "Now I perceive they spoke the truth that told me the Huns were cowards. They weep like women, when they might tend these wounded bodies."

A Margrave that was there deemed he meant this truly. He saw one of his kinsmen lying in his blood, and put his arms round him to bear him away. Him the minstrel shot dead.

(35) When the Thuringians and Danes saw their masters slain, they rushed yet fiercer against the house, and grisly was the strife or they won to the door. Many a helmet and buckler were hewn in pieces.

"Give way," cried Volker, "and let them in. They shall not have their will, but, in lieu thereof, shall perish. They will earn the queen's gift with their death."

The proud warriors thronged into the hall, but many an one bowed his head, slain by swift blows. Well fought bold Gernot; the like did Giselher.

A thousand and four came in. Keen and bright flashed the swords; but all the knights died. Great wonders might be told of the Burgundians.

When the tumult fell, there was silence. Over all the blood of the dead men trickled through the crannies into the gutters below. They of the Rhine had done this by their prowess.

Then the Burgundians sat and rested, and laid down their weapons and their shields.

(36) Before nightfall the king and queen had prevailed on the men of Hungary to dare the combat anew. Twenty thousand or more stood before them ready for battle. These hasted to fall on the strangers.

The day was done; they were in sore straits. They deemed a quick death had been better than long anguish. The proud knights would fain have had a truce. They asked that the king might be brought to them.

The heroes, red with blood, and blackened with the soil of their harness, stepped out of the hall with the three kings. They knew not whom to bewail their bitter woe to.

Both Etzel and Kriemhild came.

Then said young Giselher, "Fairest sister mine, right evil I deem it that thou badest me across the Rhine to this bitter woe. How have I deserved death from the Huns? I was ever true to thee, nor did thee any hurt. I rode hither, dearest sister, for that I trusted to thy love. Needs must thou show mercy."

"I will show no mercy, for I got none. Bitter wrong did Hagen of Troneck to me in my home yonder, and here he hath slain my child. They that came with him must pay for it. Yet, if ye will deliver Hagen captive, I will grant your prayer, and let you live; for ye are my brothers, and the children of one mother. I will prevail upon my knights here to grant a truce."

"God in heaven forbid!" cried Gernot. "Though we were a thousand, liefer would we all die by thy kinsmen, then give one single man for our ransom. That we will never do."

"We must perish then," said Giselher; "but we will fall as good knights. We are still here; would any fight with us? I will never do falsely by my friend."

Cried bold Dankwart too (he had done ill to hold his peace), "My brother Hagen standeth not alone. They that have denied us quarter may rue it yet. By my troth, ye will find it to your cost."

Then said the queen, "Ye heroes undismayed, go forward to the steps and avenge our wrong. I will thank you forever, and with cause. I will requite Hagen's insolence to the full. Let not one of them forth at any point, and I will let kindle the hall at its four sides. So will my heart's dole be avenged."

Etzel's knights were not loth. With darts and with blows they drave back into the house them that stood without. Loud was the din; but the princes and their men were not parted, nor failed they in faith to one another.

Etzel's wife bade the hall be kindled, and they tormented the bodies of the heroes with fire. The wind blew, and the house was soon all aflame. Folk never suffered worse, I ween. There were many that cried, "Woe is me for this pain! Liefer had we died in battle. God pity us, for we are all lost. The queen taketh bitter vengeance."

One among them wailed, "We perish by the smoke and the fire. Grim is our torment. The strong heat maketh me so athirst, that I die."

Said Hagen of Troneck, "Ye noble knights and good, let any that are athirst drink the blood. In this heat it is better than wine, and there is nothing sweeter here."

Then went one where he found a dead body. He knelt by the wounds, and did off his helmet, and began to drink the streaming blood. Albeit he was little used thereto, he deemed it right good. "God quit thee, Sir Hagen!" said the weary man, "I have learned a good drink. Never did I taste better wine. If I live, I will thank thee."

When the others heard his praise, many more of them drank the blood, and their bodies were strengthened, for the which many a noble woman paid through her dear ones.

The fire-flakes fell down on them in the hall, but they warded them off with their shields. Both the smoke and the fire tormented them. Never before suffered heroes such sore pain.

Then said Hagen of Troneck, "Stand fast by the wall. Let not the brands fall on your helmets. Trample them with your feet deeper in the blood. A woeful hightide is the queen's."

The night ended at last. The bold gleeman, and Hagen, his comrade, stood before the house and leaned upon their shields. They waited for further hurt from Etzel's knights. It advantaged the strangers much that the roof was vaulted. By reason thereof more were left alive.

Etzel deemed the guests were all dead of their travail and the stress of the fire. But six hundred bold men yet lived. Never king had better knights. They that kept ward over the strangers had seen that some were left, albeit the princes and their men had suffered loss and dole. They saw many that walked up and down in the house.

They told Kriemhild that many were left alive, but the queen answered, "It cannot be. None could live in that fire. I trow they all lie dead."

The kings and their men had still gladly asked for mercy, had there been any to show it. But there was none in the whole country of the Huns. Wherefore they avenged their death with willing hand.

They were greeted early in the morning with a fierce onslaught, and came in great scathe. Strong spears were hurled at them. Well the knights within stood on their defence.

Etzel's men were the bolder, that they might win Kriemhild's fee. Thereto, they obeyed the king gladly; but soon they looked on death.

One might tell marvels of her gifts and promises. She bade them bear forth red gold upon shields, and gave thereof to all that desired it, or would take it. So great treasure was never given against foemen.

Twelve hundred warriors strove once and again to win entrance. The guests cooled their hardihood with wounds. None could part the strife. The blood flowed from death-deep wounds. Many were slain. Each bewailed some friend. All Etzel's worthy knights perished. Their kinsmen sorrowed bitterly.

(37) The strangers did valiantly that morning. Gotelind's husband came into the courtyard and saw the heavy loss on both sides, whereat the true man wept inly.

"Woe is me," said the knight, "that ever I was born, since none can stop this strife! Fain would I have them at one again, but the king holdeth back, for he seeth alway more done to his hurt."

Good Rudeger sent to Dietrich, that they might seek to move the great king. But the knight of Bern sent back answer, "Who can hinder it? King Etzel letteth none intercede."

A knight of the Huns, that had oft seen Rudeger standing with wet eyes, said to the queen, "Look how he standeth yonder, that Etzel hath raised above all others, and that hath land and folk at his service. Why hath Rudeger so many castles from the king? He hath struck no blow in this battle. I ween he careth little for our scathe, so long as he has enow for himself. They say he is bolder than any other. Ill hath he shown it in our need."

The faithful man, when he heard that word, looked angrily at the knight. He thought, "Thou shalt pay for this. Thou callest me a coward. Thou hast told thy tale too loud at court."

He clenched his fist, and ran at him, and smote the Hun so fiercely that he fell down at his feet, dead. Whereat Etzel's grief waxed anew.

"Away with thee, false babbler!" cried Rudeger. "I had trouble and sorrow enow. What was it to thee that I fought not? Good cause have I also to hate the strangers, and had done what I could against them, but that I brought them hither. I was their escort into my master's land, and may not lift my wretched hand against them."

Then said Etzel, the great king, to the Margrave, "How hast thou helped us, most noble Rudeger? We had dead men enow in the land, and needed no more. Evilly hast thou done."

But the knight answered, "He angered me, and twitted me with the honour and the wealth thou hath bestowed on me so plenteously. It hath cost the liar dear."

Then came the queen, that had seen the Hun perish by Rudeger's wrath. She mourned for him with wet eyes, and said to Rudeger, "What have we ever done to thee that thou shouldst add to our sorrow? Thou hast oft times promised, noble Rudeger, that thou wouldst risk, for our sake, both honour and life, and I have heard many warriors praise thee for thy valour. Hast thou forgotten the oath thou swearest to me with thy hand, good knight, when thou didst woo me for King Etzel—how that thou wouldst serve me till my life's end, or till thine? Never was my need greater than now."

"It is true, noble lady. I promised to risk for thee honour and life, but I sware not to lose my soul. I brought the princes to this hightide."

She said, "Remember, Rudeger, thy faith, and thine oath to avenge all my hurt and my woe."

The Margrave answered, "I have never said thee nay."

Etzel began to entreat likewise. They fell at his feet. Sore troubled was the good Margrave. Full of grief, he cried, "Woe is me that ever I saw this hour, for God hath forsaken me. All my duty to heaven, mine honour, my good faith, my knightliness, I must forego. God above have pity, and let me die! Whether I do this thing, or do it not, I sin. And if I take the part of neither, all the world will blame me. Let Him that made me guide me."

Then the bold man said to the king, "Take back what thou hast given me—castles and land. Leave me nothing at all. I will go forth afoot into exile. I will take my wife and my daughter by the hand, and I will quit thy country empty, rather than I will die dishonoured. I took thy red gold to my hurt."

King Etzel answered, "Who will help me then? Land and folk I gave to thee, Rudeger, that thou mightest avenge me on my foes. Thou shalt rule with Etzel as a great king."

But Rudeger said, "How can I do it? I bade them to my house and home; I set meat and drink before them, and gave them my gifts. Shall I also smite them dead? The folk may deem me a coward. But I have always served them well. Should I fight with them now, it were ill done. Deep must I rue past friendship. I gave my daughter to Giselher. None better in this world had she found, of so great lineage and honour, and faith, and wealth. Never saw I young king so virtuous."

But Kriemhild answered, "Most noble Rudeger, take pity on us both. Bethink thee that never host had guests like these."

Then said the Margrave, "What thou and my master have given me I must pay for, this day, with my life. I shall die, and that quickly. Well I know that, or nightfall, my lands and castles will return to your keeping. To your grace I commend my wife and my child, and the homeless ones that are at Bechlaren."

"God reward thee, Rudeger," cried the king. He and the queen were both glad. "Thy folk shall be well seen to; but thou thyself, I trow, will come off scatheless."

So he put his soul and body on the hazard. Etzel's wife began to weep. He said, "I must keep my vow to thee. Woe is me for my friends, that I must fall upon in mine own despite!"

They saw him turn heavily from the king. To his knights that stood close by, he said, "Arm ye, my men all. For I must fight the Burgundians, to my sorrow."

The heroes called for their harness, and the attendants brought helm and buckler. Soon the proud strangers heard the sad news.

Rudeger stood armed with five hundred men, and twelve knights that went with him, to win worship in the fray. They knew not that death was so near.

Rudeger went forth with his helmet on; his men carried sharp swords, and, thereto, broad shields and bright. The fiddler saw this, and was dismayed. But when Giselher beheld his father-in-law with his helmet on, he weened that he meant them well. The noble king was right glad. "Well for me that I have such friends," cried Giselher, "as these we won by the way! For my wife's sake he will save us. By my faith, I am glad to be wed."

"Thy trust is vain," said the fiddler. "When ever did ye see so many knights come in peace, with helmets laced on, and with swords? Rudeger cometh to serve for his castles and his lands."

Or the fiddler had made an end of speaking, Rudeger, the noble man, stood before the house. He laid his good shield before his feet. He must needs deny greeting to his friends.

Then the Margrave shouted into the hall, "Stand on your defence, ye bold Nibelungen. I would have helped you, but must slay you. Once we were friends, but I cannot keep my faith."

The sore-tried men were dismayed at this word. Their comfort was gone, for he that they loved was come against them. From their foemen they had suffered enow.

"God in Heaven forbid," said Gunther the knight, "that thou shouldst be false to the friendship and the faith wherein we trusted. It cannot be."

"I cannot help it," said Rudeger. "I must fight with you, for I have vowed it. As ye love your lives, bold warriors, ward you well. King Etzel's wife will have it so."

Then said the youngest of fair Uta's sons, "How canst thou do this thing, Sir Rudeger? All that came hither with me are thy friends. A vile deed is this. Thou makest thy daughter too soon a widow. If thou and thy knights defy us, ill am I apayed, that I trusted thee before all other men, when I won thy daughter for my wife."

"Forget not thy troth, noble king, if God send thee hence," answered Rudeger. "Let not the maiden suffer for my sin. By thine own princely virtue, withdraw not thy favour from her."

"Fain would I promise it," said Giselher the youth. "Yet if my high-born kinsmen perish here by thy hand, my love for thee and thy daughter must perish also."

"Then God have mercy!" cried the brave man; whereat he lifted his shield, and would have fallen upon the guests in Kriemhild's hall.

But Hagen called out to him from the stairhead, "Tarry awhile, noble Rudeger. Let me and my masters speak with thee yet awhile in our need. What shall it profit Etzel if we knights die in a strange land? I am in evil case," said Hagen. "The shield that Gotelind gave me to carry, the Huns have hewn from my hand. In good faith I bore it hither. Would to God I had such a shield as thou hast, noble Rudeger! A better I would not ask for in the battle."

"I would gladly give thee my shield, durst I offer it before Kriemhild. Yet take it, Hagen, and wear it. Ha! mightst thou but win with it to Burgundy!"

When they saw him give the shield so readily, there were eyes enow red with hot tears. It was the last gift that Rudeger of Bechlaren ever gave.

Then the Margrave's men ran at their foemen, and followed their master like good knights. They carried sharp weapons, wherewith they clove many a helmet and buckler. The weary ones answered the men of Bechlaren with swift blows that pierced deep and straight through their harness to their life's blood. They did wonderly in the battle.

Gernot cried out to the Margrave, "Noble Rudeger, thou leavest none of my men alive. It irketh me sore; I will bear it no longer. I will turn thy gift against thee, for thou hast taken many friends from me. Come hither, thou bold man. What thou gavest me I will earn to the uttermost."

Or the Margrave had fought his way to him, bright bucklers grew dim with blood. Then, greedy of fame, the men ran at each other, and began to ward off the deadly wounds. But their swords were so sharp that nothing could withstand them. Rudeger the knight smote Gernot through his flint-hard helmet, that the blood brake out. Soon the good warrior was avenged. He swung Rudeger's gift on high, and, albeit he was wounded to the death, he smote him through his good shield and his helmet, that Gotelind's husband died. So rich a gift was never worse requited. So they fell in the strife—Gernot and Rudeger—slain by each other's hand.

(38) So loud they wept on all sides, that palace and towers echoed with the sound. One of Dietrich's men of Bern heard it, and hasted with the news.

The prince of Amelung bade them inquire further. He sat down at a window sore troubled, and bade Hildebrand go to the guests, and ask them what had happened.

Master Hildebrand, bold in strife, took with him neither shield nor sword, and would have gone to them on peaceful wise. But his sister's child chid him. Grim Wolfhart cried, "Why goest thou naked? If they revile thee, thou wilt have the worst of the quarrel, and return shamed. If thou goest armed, none will withstand thee."

The old man armed him as the youth had counselled. Or he had ended, all Dietrich's knights stood in their harness, sword in hand.

Hildebrand laid his shield at his feet, and said to Gunther's men, "Alas! ye good knights! What have ye done to Rudeger? Dietrich, my master, sent me hither to ask if any here slew the good Margrave, as they tell us. We could ill endure such loss."

Hagen of Troneck answered, "The news is true. Glad were I had the messenger lied to thee, for Rudeger's sake, and that he lived still. Both men and women must evermore bewail him."

Hildebrand could ask no more for grief. He said, "Grant now, ye warriors, that for which my master sent me. Give us dead Rudeger from out the hall, with whom all our joy hath perished, and let us requite him for all the kindness he hath shown to us and many another. Like him we are homeless. Why tarry ye? Let us bear him hence, and serve him dead, as we had gladly served him living."

But Volker answered, "Ye shall get him from none here. Come and take him out of the house, where he lieth with his death-wounds in the blood. So shall ye serve Rudeger truly."

Then Dietrich's men rushed in from all sides. They smote till the links of their foemen's mail whistled asunder, and their broken sword-points flew on high. They struck hot-flowing streams from the helmets.

When Hagen of Troneck saw Volker dead, he grieved more bitterly than he had done yet, all the hightide, for kinsmen or vassal. Alas! how grimly he began to avenge him!

"Old Hildebrand shall not go scatheless, for his hand hath slain my friend, the best comrade I ever had."

Hagen thought on the fiddler that old Hildebrand had slain, and he said to the knight, "Thou shalt pay for my teen. Thou hast robbed us of many a good warrior." He smote Hildebrand, that Balmung, the sword he had taken from Siegfried when he slew him, rang loud. But the old man stood boldly on his defence. He brought his sharp-edged sword down on Hagen, but could not wound him. Then Hagen pierced him through his good harness.

When Master Hildebrand felt the wound, he feared more scathe from Hagen, so he threw his shield over his back and fled.

Now, of all the knights, none were left alive save two, Gunther and Hagen.

Old Hildebrand, covered with blood, ran with the news to Dietrich, that he saw sitting sadly where he had left him. Soon the prince had more cause for woe. When he saw Hildebrand in his bloody harness, he asked fearfully for his tale. "Now tell me. Master Hildebrand, why thou art so wet with thy life's blood? Who did it? I ween thou hast fought with the guests in the hall, albeit I so sternly forbade it. Thou hast better have forborne."

Hildebrand answered his master, "Hagen did it. He gave me this wound in the hall when I turned to flee from him. I scarce escaped the devil with my life."

Said the prince of Bern, "Thou art rightly served. Thou heardest me vow friendship to the knights, and thou hast broken the peace I gave them. Were it not that I shame me to slay thee, thy life were forfeit."

"Be not so wroth, my lord Dietrich. Enough woe hath befallen me and mine. We would have borne away Rudeger's body, but Gunther's men denied it."

"Woe is me for this wrong! Is Rudeger then dead? That is the bitterest of my dole. Noble Gotelind is my cousin's child. Alas! The poor orphans of Bechlaren!" With ruth and sorrow he wept for Rudeger. "Woe is me for the true comrade I have lost. I must mourn Etzel's liegeman forever. Canst thou tell me, Master Hildebrand, who slew him?"

Hildebrand answered, "It was strong Gernot, but the hero fell by Rudeger's hand."

Said Dietrich, "Bid my men arm them, for I will thither straight-way. Send me my shining harness. I, myself, will question the knights of Burgundy."

But Master Hildebrand answered, "Who is there to call? Thy sole living liegeman standeth here. I am the only one. The rest are dead."

Dietrich trembled at the news, and was passing doleful, for never in this world had he known such woe. He cried, "Are all my men slain? Then God hath forgotten poor Dietrich! I was a great king, rich and proud. Yet how could they all die, these valiant heroes, by foemen so battle-weary and sore beset? Death had spared them, but that I am doomed to sorrow. Since this hard fate is needs mine, tell me if any of the guests be left alive."

Hildebrand answered, "None save Hagen, and Gunther, the king. God knoweth I say honestly."

(39) Dietrich came where both the knights stood outside the house, leaning against the wall. Good Dietrich laid down his shield, and, moved with deep woe, he said, "There is nothing for it. Of thy knightliness, atone to me for the wrong thou hast done me, and I will avenge it no further. Yield thee captive, thee and thy man, and I will defend thee to the uttermost against the wrath of the Huns. Thou wilt find me faithful and true."

"God in Heaven forbid," cried Hagen, "that two knights, armed as we are for battle, should yield them to thee! I would hold it a great shame, and ill done."

"Deny me not," said Dietrich. "Ye have made me heavy-hearted enow, O Gunther and Hagen; and it is no more than just, that ye make it good. I swear to you, and give you my hand thereon, that I will ride back with you to your own country. I will bring you safely thither, or die with you, and forget my great wrong for your sakes."

"Ask us no more," said Hagen. "It were a shameful tale to tell of us, that two such bold men yielded them captive. I see none save Hildebrand by thy side."

When Dietrich heard grim Hagen's mind, he caught up his shield, and sprang up the steps. The Nibelung sword rang loud on his mail. Sir Dietrich knew well that the bold man was fierce. The prince of Bern warded off the strokes. He needed not to learn that Hagen was a valiant knight. Thereto, he feared strong Balmung. But ever and anon he struck out warily, till he had overcome Hagen in the strife. He gave him a wound that was deep and wide. Then thought Sir Dietrich, "Thy long travail hath made thee weak. I had little honour in thy death. Liefer will I take thee captive." Not lightly did he prevail. He threw down his shield. He was strong and bold, and he caught Hagen of Troneck in his arms. So the valiant man was vanquished. King Gunther grieved sore.

Dietrich bound Hagen, and led him to the queen, and delivered into her hand the boldest knight that ever bare a sword. After her bitter dole, she was glad enow. She bowed before the knight for joy. "Blest be thou in soul and body. Thou hast made good to me all my woe. I will thank thee till my dying day."

Then said Dietrich, "Let him live, noble queen. His service may yet atone to thee for what he hath done to thy hurt. Take not vengeance on him for that he is bound."

She bade them lead Hagen to a dungeon. There he lay locked up, and none saw him.

Then King Gunther called aloud, "Where is the hero of Bern? He hath done me a grievous wrong."

Sir Dietrich went to meet him. Gunther was a man of might. He tarried not, but ran toward him from the hall. Loud was the din of their swords.

Howso famed Dietrich was from aforetime, Gunther was so wroth and so fell, and so bitterly his foeman, by reason of the wrong he had endured, that it was a marvel Sir Dietrich came off alive. They were strong and mighty men both. Palace and towers echoed with their blows, as their swift swords hewed their good helmets. A high-hearted king was Gunther.

But the knight of Bern overcame him, as he had done Hagen. His blood gushed from his harness by reason of the good sword that Dietrich carried. Yet Gunther had defended him well, for all he was so weary.

The knight was bound by Dietrich's hand, albeit a king should never wear such bonds. Dietrich deemed, if he left Gunther and his man free, they would kill all they met.

He took him by the hand, and led him before Kriemhild. Her sorrow was lighter when she saw him. She said, "Thou art welcome, King Gunther."

He answered, "I would thank thee, dear sister, if thy greeting were in love. But I know thy fierce mind, and that thou mockest me and Hagen."

Then said the prince of Bern, "Most high queen, there were never nobler captives than these I have delivered here into thy hands. Let the homeless knights live for my sake."

She promised him she would do it gladly, and good Dietrich went forth weeping. Yet soon Etzel's wife took grim vengeance, by reason whereof both the valiant men perished. She kept them in dungeons, apart, that neither saw the other again, till she bore her brother's head to Hagen. Certes, Kriemhild's vengeance was bitter.

The queen went to Hagen, and spoke angrily to the knight. "Give me back what thou hast taken from me, and ye may both win back alive to Burgundy."

But grim Hagen answered, "Thy words are wasted, noble queen. I have sworn to show the hoard to none. While one of my masters liveth, none other shall have it."

"I will end the matter," said the queen. Then she bade them slay her brother, and they smote off his head. She carried it by the hair to the knight of Troneck. He was grieved enow.

When the sorrowful man saw his master's head, he cried to Kriemhild, "Thou hast wrought all thy will. It hath fallen out as I deemed it must. The noble King of Burgundy is dead, and Giselher the youth, and eke Gernot. None knoweth of the treasure now save God and me. Thou shalt never see it, devil that thou art."

She said, "I come off ill in the reckoning. I will keep Siegfried's sword at the least. My true love wore it when I saw him last. My bitterest heart's dole was for him."

She drew it from the sheath. He could not hinder it. She purposed to slay the knight. She lifted it high with both hands, and smote off his head.

King Etzel saw it, and sorrowed. "Alas!" cried the king, "The best warrior that ever rode to battle, or bore a shield, hath fallen by the hand of a woman! Albeit I was his foeman, I must grieve."

Then said Master Hildebrand, "His death shall not profit her. I care not what come of it. Though I came in scathe by him myself, I will avenge the death of the bold knight of Troneck."

Hildebrand sprang fiercely at Kriemhild, and slew her with his sword. She suffered sore by his anger. Her loud cry helped her not.

Dead bodies lay stretched over all. The queen was hewn in pieces. Etzel and Dietrich began to weep. They wailed piteously for kinsmen and vassals. Mickle valour lay there slain. The folk were doleful and dreary.

The end of the king's hightide was woe, even as, at the last all joy turneth to sorrow.

I know not what fell after. Christian and heathen, wife, man, and maid, were seen weeping and mourning for their friends.

I will tell you no more. Let the dead lie.
However it fared after with the Huns,
my tale is ended. This is the fall of the
Nibelungen.

[trans. Margaret Armour]

OUR LADY'S TUMBLER

By Gautier de Coinci (1177–1236, Prior of Vic-sur-Aisne, France)

T his charming religious narrative dates from the end of the twelfth or early thirteenth century and was created
somewhere in northern France. It is a powerful and also delightful tale about the result of deep personal devotion, irrespective of any formal training as a member of the clergy. The author reflects on the world of the Cistercian
Order with its harsh ascetic rules, but he also allows glimpses of the activities on the ordinary city market or any other
stage where performers tried to gain money by means of their athletic or dance acts and performances. Essentially,
however, here we can observe the profound cult of the Virgin Mary prevalent since the twelfth century.

In the "Lives of the Fathers," the matter of which is of profit, a story is told, which I dare say none more pleasing
has been heard, but this one is not so without worth that it may not well be told. Now will I tell and rehearse
unto you of that which happened to a minstrel.

So much had he journeyed to and fro in so many places, and so prodigal had he been, that he became a monk
of a holy Order, for that he was weary of the world. Therefore he entered this holy profession at Clairvaux.

And when that this tumbler, who was so graceful, and fair, and comely, and well formed, became a monk,
he knew not how to perform any office that fell to be done there. Of a truth, he had lived only to tumble, to
turn somersaults, to spring, and to dance. To leap and to jump, this he knew, but nothing else, and truly no
other learning had he, neither the "Paternoster," nor the "Canticles," nor the "Credo," nor the "Ave Maria," nor
anything that could make for his salvation. He was sore affrighted in their midst, for he knew not what to say, or
what to do of all that fell to be done there. And because of this, he was very sad and pensive. And everywhere he
saw the monks and the novices each one serving God in such office as he held. He saw the priests at the altars,
for such was their office, the deacons at the Gospels, and the subdeacons at the epistles. And at the proper time,
the acolytes straightway rang the bell at the vigils. One recited a verse, and another a lesson, and the young
priests were at the psalter, and the novices at the misereres, and the least experienced were at the paternosters,
for in suchwise was their work ordered. And he looked everywhere throughout the offices and the cloisters, and
saw hidden in the corners here four, here three, here two, here one. And he observed each one as closely as he
was able. One made lamentation, another wept, and another groaned and sighed. And much did he marvel what
ailed them.

Of the Tumbler of Our Lady and Other Miracles, trans. Alice Kemp-Welch. Chatto & Windus Ltd., 1903. Copyright in the Public Domain.

And at length he said, "Holy Mary, what ails these folk that they deport themselves thus, and make show in this manner of such grief? Much disquieted must they be, it seems to me, when they all with one accord make such great dolour!" And then he said, "Ah, miserable being! By the Holy Mary, what have I said? I trow that they pray God's grace. But, unhappy being that I am, what do I here, when that he who, in his calling, serves God with all his might, is thus enslaved? Never shall I render any service here, for nothing can I do or say. Very hapless was I when that I became a monk, for I know not how even to pray aright. I look hither and thither, and nothing do I, save to waste time and to eat bread to no purpose. If in this I am found out, I shall be utterly undone. I am a lusty villain, and if I do nothing here but eat, I shall be turned out into the fields. Very miserable am I in this high office!"

Then he wept to allay his grief, and truly did he desire to be dead. "Holy Mother Mary" said he, "beseech your sovereign Father of His grace to guide me, and to bestow upon me such wisdom that I may be able to serve both Him and you in suchwise as to be worthy of the food which I eat here, for well know I that now I do wrong."

And when he had thus made lament, he went prying about the Church until that he entered a crypt, and he crouched down nigh unto an altar, and hid himself there as best he could. And above the altar was the image of Our Lady, the Holy Mary. And in nowise did it surprise him that he felt in safety there, and he perceived not that it was God, who well knows how to guide His own, who had led him there.

And when he had heard the bell ring for the Mass, he rushed forth from the crypt all trembling. "Ah!" said he, "I am like unto a traitor! Even now each one is saying his response, and here am I a tethered ox, and I do nothing here but browse, and waste food in vain. Shall I therefore neither speak nor act? By the Mother of God, this will I do, and never shall I be blamed for it. I will do that which I have learnt, and thus, after mine own manner, will I serve the Mother of God in her Church. The others do service with song, and I will do service with tumbling."

And he took off his habit, and then stripped himself, and laid his garments beside the altar, but so that his body should not be uncovered, he kept on a tunic, the which was very clinging and close fitting. Little better was it than a shift; nevertheless was his body wholly covered. And thus was he fitly clad and equipped, and he girded his tunic, and duly prepared him, and he turned him to the image, and gazed on it very humbly. "Lady," said he, "to your keeping I commend my body and my soul. Gentle Queen and Lady, despise not that which I am acquainted with, for, without ado, I will essay me to serve you in good faith, if so be that God will aid me."

Then he began to turn somersaults, now high, now low, first forwards, then backwards, and then he fell on his knees before the image, and bowed his head. "Ah, very gentle Queen!" said he, "of your pity, and of your generosity, despise not my service." Then he tumbled, and leaped, and turned gaily the somersault of Metz. And he bowed to the image, and worshipped it, for he paid homage to it as much as he was able. And anon he turned the French somersault, and then the somersault of Champagne, and after that, those of Spain and of Brittany, and then that of Lorraine. And he laboured to the utmost of his power.

And after that, he did the Roman somersault, and then he put his hand before his face, and turned him with great grace, and looked very humbly at the image of the Mother of God. "Lady," said he, "I do homage to you with my heart, and my body, and my feet, and my hands, for nothing beside this do I understand. Now would I be your gleeman. Yonder they are singing, but I am come here to divert you. Lady, you who can protect me, for God's sake do not despise me." Then he beat his breast, and sighed, and mourned very grievously that he knew not how to do service in other manner. And then he turned a somersault backwards. "Lady," said he, "so help me God, never before have I done this. Lady! How that one would have his utmost desire, who could dwell with you in your right glorious mansion! For God's sake, Lady, receive me there. I do this for your sake, and in nowise for mine own." Then he again turned the somersault of Metz, and tumbled and capered full many a time.

And when he heard the monks celebrating, he began to exert himself, and so long as the Mass dured, he ceased not to dance, and to jump, and to leap, until that he was on the point to faint, and he could not stand up, and thus he fell to the ground, and dropped from sheer fatigue. And like as the grease issues from the spitted meat, so the sweat issued from him all over, from head to foot. "Lady," said he, "no more can I do now, but of a surety I shall come back again."

And he was quite overcome of heat. And he took up his clothing, and when that he was dressed, he took his leave, and he bowed to the image, and went his way. "Farewell, very gentle friend," said he. "For God's sake, grieve not at all, for if that I am able, and it is permitted unto me, I will come back, for each hour would I serve you to the utmost of my power, so gracious are you."

And longwhiles he led this life, and, at each hour precisely he repaired to the image, to render service and homage. Certes, so greatly did it please him, and with such right good will did he do this, that never a day was he so tired that he could not do his very utmost to delight the Mother of God, and never did he desire to do other service.

Well known was it that he went each day into the crypt, but no one, save God, knew what he did there, nor would he, for all the riches of the whole world, that any, save the supreme God alone, should know of his doings.

Think you now that God would have prized his service if that he had not loved Him? By no means, however much he tumbled. But He prized it because of his love. Much labour and fatigue, many fasts and vigils, many tears and sighs and groans and prayers, much diligence in discipline, both at Mass and at matins, the bestowal of all that you have and the payment of whatsoever you owe, if you love not God with all your heart, all these are wholly thrown away in such manner, understand well, that they avail nothing for true salvation. Of a truth, without love and without pity, before God all counts for nothing. God asks not for gold or for silver, but only for true love in the hearts of men, and this one loved God truly. And because of this, God prized his service.

Longwhiles did the good man live thus, but for how long time he so lived contented, I cannot tell unto you, but in the course of time sore trouble came to him, for one of the monks, who in his heart greatly blamed him that he came not to matins, kept watch on him. And he much marvelled what happened, and said that never would he desist until that he knew who he was, and for what he was worth, and in what manner he earned his bread. And so closely did the monk pursue him, and follow him, and keep watch on him, that he distinctly saw him perform his service in a simple manner, even as I have told it unto you. "By my faith," said he, "he has a good time of it, and much greater diversion, it seemeth to me, than we have all together. Whiles that the others are at prayer, and at work in the house, this one dances with as much vigour as if he had an hundred silver marks. Right well does he perform his service, and in this manner he pays for us that which is his due. A goodly proceeding, this, forsooth! We sing for him, and he tumbles for us! We pray for him, and he plays for us! If we weep, he soothes us! I would that all the convent could see him at this very moment just as I do, even if I had to fast for it till dusk! Not one would there be, me-thinks, who would be able to restrain his laughter if that he witnessed the tumbling of this fellow, who thus kills himself, and who so excites him by tumbling, that he has no pity on himself. God counts it unto him for penance, for he does it without evil intent, and, certes, I hold it not to be ill, for, as I believe, he does it, according to his lights, in good faith, for he wishes not to be idle."

And the monk saw how that he laboured without ceasing all the day long. And he laughed much, and made merry over the matter, but it caused him sorrow as well as merriment. And he went to the abbot, and rehearsed unto him, from beginning to end, all that he had learnt, even as you have heard it.

And the abbot arose, and said to the monk, "On your vow of obedience, I command that you keep silence, and noise this not abroad, and that you so well observe this command, that you speak not of this matter save to me alone, and we will both go thither, and we shall see if this can be, and we will beseech the heavenly King, and His very gentle and dear Mother, who is so precious, and of so great renown, that she, of her sweetness, will go pray of her Son, her Father, and her Lord, that if it so pleases Him, He will this day suffer me to witness this service in such sort that God may be the more loved on account of this, and that, if thus it pleases Him, the good man may not be found worthy of blame for it."

And then they went thither quite quietly, and without delay they hid themselves in a covert nook nigh unto the altar, so that he saw them not. And the abbot, watching there, observed all the service of the novice, and the divers somersaults the which he turned, and how that he capered, and danced, and bowed before the image, and jumped, and leaped, until that he was nigh fainting. And so greatly was he overcome of fatigue, that he fell heavily to the ground, and so exhausted was he, that he sweated all over from his efforts, so that the sweat ran all down the middle of the crypt. But in a little, the Mother of God, whom he served all without guile, came to his succour, and well knew she how to aid him.

And anon the abbot looked, and he saw descend from the vaulting so glorious a lady, that never had he seen one so fair or so richly crowned, and never had another so beautiful been created. Her vesture was all wrought with gold and precious stones, and with her were the angels and the archangels from the heavens above, who came around the tumbler, and solaced and sustained him. And when that they were ranged around him, he was wholly comforted, and they made ready to tend him, for they desired to make recompense unto him for the services the which he had rendered unto their Lady, who is so precious a gem. And the sweet and noble Queen took a white cloth, and with it she very gently fanned her minstrel before the altar. And the noble and gracious Lady fanned his neck and body and face to cool him, and greatly did she concern herself to aid him, and gave herself up to the care of him; but of this the good man took no heed, for he neither perceived, nor did he know, that he was in such fair company.

And the holy angels who remained with him, paid him much honour, but the Lady no longer sojourned there, and she made the sign of the cross as she turned away, and the holy angels, who greatly rejoiced to keep watch over their companion, took charge over him, and they did but await the hour when God would take him from this life, and they might bear away his soul.

And full four times did the abbot and the monk witness, without hindrance, how that each hour he went there, and how that the Mother of God came there to aid and succour her liegeman, for well knows she how to protect her own. And the abbot had much joy of it, for very desirous had he been to know the truth concerning it. Now had God verily shown unto him that the services the which this poor man rendered were pleasing unto Him. And the monk was quite bewildered by it, and from anguish he glowed like fire. "Your mercy, Sire!" said he to the abbot, "this is a holy man whom I see here. If that I have said anything concerning him that is evil, it is right that my body should make amends for it. Therefore ordain me a penance, for without doubt he is altogether an upright man. Verily have we seen all, and no longer can we be mistaken."

And the abbot said, "You speak truly. God has indeed made us to know that He loves him with a very great love. And now I straightway give command unto you that, in virtue of obedience, and so that you fall not under condemnation, you speak to no one of that which you have seen, save to God or to me."

"Sire," said he, "to this do I assent."

And at these words they departed, and no longer did they stay in the crypt, and the good man did not remain, but when that he had done all his service, he clothed himself again in his garments, and went to divert himself in the monastery.

And thus passed the time, until that, a little while after, it came to pass that the abbot sent for him who was so good. And when he heard that he was sent for, and that it was the abbot who made enquiry for him, so greatly was he troubled, that he knew not what he should say. "Alas," said he, "I am found out. Never a day passes without distress, or without toil or disgrace, for my service counts for nothing. Methinks it is not pleasing unto God. Gentle Lady, Holy Mary, how troubled is my mind! I know not, Lady, from whom to get counsel, so come now to mine aid. And at the first word, anon will they say, 'Away with you!' Woe is me! How shall I be able to make answer when I know not one single word with the which to make explanation? But what avails this? It behoves me to go."

And weeping, so that his face was all wet, he came before the abbot, and he knelt before him in tears. "Sire," said he, "for God's sake, have mercy! Would you drive me hence? Tell me all your behests, and all your bidding will I do."

Then said the abbot, "This would I know, and I would that you answer me truly. Longwhiles have you been here, both winter and summer, and I would know by what services, and in what manner, you earn your bread."

"Alas," said he, "well knew I that all would become known, and that when all my doings were known, no longer would any one have to do with me. Sire," said he, "now will I depart hence. Miserable am I, and miserable shall I be, for I never do anything that is right."

Then the abbot made answer, "Never have I said this, but I pray and demand of you, and further I command you, that, in virtue of obedience, you wholly reveal unto me your thoughts, and tell unto me in what manner you serve us in our monastery."

"Sire," said he, "this will be my death! This command will kill me."

Then he straightway unfolded unto him, howsoever grievous it was, his whole life, from beginning to end, in such sort that he left nothing unsaid, just as I have told it unto you. And with clasped hands, and weeping, he told and rehearsed unto him everything, and, sighing, he kissed his feet.

And the holy abbot turned to him, and, all weeping, raised him up. And he kissed both his eyes. "Brother," said he, "be silent now, for truly do I promise unto you that you shall be at peace with us. God grant that we may have your fellowship so long as we are deserving of it. Good friends shall we be. Fair, gentle brother, pray for me and I will pray in return for you. And so I beseech and command of you, my sweet friend, that you forthwith render this service openly, just as you have done it, and still better even, if that you know how."

"Sire," said he, "are you in good earnest?"

"Yea, truly," said the abbot, "and I charge you, on pain of penance, that you no longer doubt it."

Then was the good man so very joyous, so the story relates, that he scarce knew what he did. But despite himself, he was constrained to rest, for he had become all pale. And when that he was come to himself again, he was so overcome of joy, that he was seized with a sickness, of the which in a short space he died. But very cheerfully did he perform his service without ceasing, morning and evening, by night and by day, so that not an hour did he miss, until that he fell ill. Then verily such great sickness laid hold upon him, that he could riot move from his bed. But that which distressed him the most, since never did he make complaint of his sufferings, was that he could not pay tor his sustenance, for the which he was much troubled in mind, and moreover he feared that his penance would be in vain, for that he did not busy himself with such service as was his wont, and very deserving of blame did he seem unto himself to be.

And the good man, who was so filled with anguish, besought of God that He would receive him before that more shame came unto him. For so much grieved was he that his doings were become known, that he could not endure it. And he was constrained to lie down forthwith.

And greatly did the holy abbot hold him in honour, and he and his monks went each hour to chant beside his bed, and such great delight had he in that which was sung to him of God, that in nowise did he long for Poitou, so much did it pleasure him to learn that all would be pardoned unto him. And he made a good confession and repentance, but nevertheless he was fearful. And, as I have told unto you, at last it came to pass that he died.

And the abbot was there, and all his monks, and the novices and good folk, who kept watch over him very humbly, and quite clearly did they see a right wondrous miracle. Of a truth they saw how that, at his death, the angels, and the Mother of God, and the archangels, were ranged around him. And there, also, were the very evil and cruel and violent devils, for to possess them of his soul, and no fancy is this. But to no purpose had they so long lain in wait for him, and striven so earnestly for him and pursued him, for now no power had they over his soul. And forthwith his soul quitted his body, but in nowise was it lost, for the Mother of God received it. And the holy angels who were there, sang for joy, and then they departed, and bare it to heaven, and this was seen of all the monks, and of all the others who were there.

Now they wholly knew and perceived that God willed it that the love of His good servant should no longer be hid, and that all should know and perceive his goodness, and they had great joy and great wonderment of it, and much honour did they pay to his body, and they carried it into the Church, and heartily did they celebrate the service of God. And they buried him with honour in the choir of the mother-church.

With great honour did they bury him, and then, like some saintly body, they kept watch over him. And anon, without concealing anything, the abbot told unto them all his doings, and his whole life, and all that he had seen in the crypt, even as you have heard it. And eagerly did the monks listen unto him. "Certes," said they, "well may it be believed. It cannot be misdoubted, for the truth bears witness to it. Fully is the matter proven, and certain is it that he has done his penance." And greatly did they rejoice together there.

Thus died the minstrel. Cheerfully did he tumble, and cheerfully did he serve, for the which he merited great honour, and none was there to compare unto him.

And the holy Fathers have related unto us that it thus befell this minstrel. Now let us pray God, without ceasing, that He may grant unto us so worthily to serve Him, that we may be deserving of His love. The story of the Tumbler is set forth.

[trans. Alice Kemp-Welch]

SIR LANVAL

By Marie de France

Marie de France, whose identity has not yet been determined, lived at the end of the twelfth century either at the English royal court (perhaps she was the sister of King Henry II) or in a monastery (Reading). We know of three major works by her, the Lais *(verse narratives), the* Fables *(animal fables; here often with strong political and social criticism), and the religious, hagiographical work of* Saint Patrick's Purgatory *(L'Espurgatoire de Saint Patrice). She also might have composed another religious work,* La vie Seinte Audree, *but full evidence escapes us. In the* Lais *she regularly outlines most centrally ponderous problems between man and woman, the ideal of love (within and outside of marriage), and the basics of courtly values. Often we come across a discussion of marital issues, intimately connected with love, but then we also hear of considerable social criticism against the king and the court, as in* Lanval. *Marie de France ranks among the best twelfth-century European authors. Not only did she compose some of the most intriguing erotic tales, her* lais, *but she also proved to be an expert in writing of fables, based ultimately on the ancient Aesop.*

This is the adventure of the rich and noble night Sir Lanval, even as the Breton lay recounts it

The valiant and courteous King Arthur was sojourning at Carduel, because of the Picts and the Scots who had greatly destroyed the land, for they were in the kingdom of Logres and often wrought mischief therein.

In Carduel, at Pentecost, the king held his summer court, and gave rich gifts to the counts, the barons, and all the knights of the Round Table. Never before in all the world were such gifts given. Honours and lands he shared forth to all, save to one alone, of those who served him.

This was Sir Lanval; of him and his the king thought not. And yet all men loved him, for worthy he was, free of hand, very valiant, and fair to look upon. Had any ill happened to this knight, his fellows would have been but ill-pleased.

Lanval was son to a king of high descent, but his heritage was far hence in a distant land; he was of the household of King Arthur, but all his money was spent, for the king gave him nothing, and nothing would Lanval ask from him. But now Sir Lanval was much perplexed, very sorrowful, and heavy of heart. Nor need ye wonder at it, for one who is a stranger and without counsel is but sorrowful in a foreign land when he knows not where to seek for aid.

This knight of whom I tell ye, who had served the king so well, one day mounted his horse and rode forth for diversion. He left the city behind him, and came all alone into a fair meadow through which ran a swift water. As he rode downwards to the stream, his horse shivered beneath him. Then the knight dismounted, and loosening the girth let the steed go free to feed at its will on the grass of the meadow. Then folding his mantle beneath his head he laid himself down; but his thoughts were troubled by his ill fortune, and as he lay on the grass he knew nothing that might pleasure him.

Suddenly, as he looked downward toward the bank of the river, he saw two maidens coming toward him; never before had he seen maidens so fair. They were richly clad in robes of purple grey, and their faces were wondrous beautiful. The elder bore in her hands a basin of gold finely wrought (indeed it is but truth I tell you); the other held a snow-white towel.

They came straight to where the knight was lying, and Lanval, who was well taught in courteous ways, sprang to his feet in their presence. Then they saluted him, and delivered to him their message. "Sir Lanval," said the elder, "my lady, who is most fair and courteous, has sent us to you, for she wills that you shall return with us. See, her pavilion is near at hand. We will lead you thither in all safety."

Then Lanval went with them, taking no thought for his steed, which was grazing beside him in the meadow. The maidens led him to the tent; rich it was and well placed. Not even the Queen Semiramis in the days of her greatest wealth and power and wisdom, nor the Emperor Octavian, could have equalled from their treasures the drapery alone.

Above the tent was an eagle of gold, its worth I know not how to tell you; neither can I tell that of the silken cords and shining lances which upheld the tent; there is no king under heaven who could purchase its equal, let him offer what he would for it.

Within this pavilion was a maiden, of beauty surpassing even that of the lily and the new-blown rose, when they flower in the fair summer-tide. She lay upon a rich couch, the covering of which was worth the price of a castle, her fair and gracious body clothed only in a simple vest. Her costly mantle of white ermine, covered with purple of Alexandria, had she cast from her for the heat, and face and throat and neck were whiter than flower of the thorn. Then the maiden called the knight to her, and he came near and seated himself beside the couch.

"Lanval," she said, "fair friend, for you have I come forth from my own land; even from Lains have I come to seek you. If you be of very truth valiant and courteous then neither emperor, count, nor king have known such joy as shall be yours, for I love you above all things."

Then Love smote him swiftly, and seized and kindled his heart, and he answered:

"Fair lady, if it so please you, and such joy may be my portion that you deign to love me, then be the thing folly or wisdom you can command nothing that I will not do to the utmost of my power. All your wishes will I fulfil. For you I will renounce folk and my land. Nor will I ever ask to leave you, if that be what you most desire of me."

When the maiden heard him whom she could love well speak thus, she granted him all her heart and her love.

And now was Lanval in the way to good fortune. A gift the lady bestowed upon him: there should be nothing so costly but that it might be his if he so willed it. Let him give or spend as freely as he would he should always have enough for his need. Happy indeed was Lanval, for the more largely he spent the more gold and silver should he have.

"Friend," said the maiden, "of one thing must I now warn you, nay more, I command and pray you, reveal this your adventure to no man. The reason will I tell you; if this our love be known you would lose me for ever, never again might you look upon me, never again embrace me."

Then he answered that he would keep faithfully all that she should command him.

Thus were the two together even till the vesper-tide, and if his lady would have consented fain would Lanval have remained longer.

"Friend," said she, "rise up, no longer may you linger here, you must go and I must remain. But one thing will I tell you: When you wish to speak with me (and I would that may ever be when a knight may meet his lady without shame and without reproach) I shall be ever there at your will, but no man save you shall see me or hear me speak."

When the knight heard that, he was joyful; and he kissed his lady and rose up and the maidens who led him to the tent brought him new and rich garments, and when he was clad in them there was no fairer knight under heaven. Then they brought him water for his hands, and a towel whereon to dry them, and laid food before him, and he supped with his lady. Courteously were they served, and great was the joy of Sir Lanval, for ever and again his love kissed him and he embraced her tenderly.

When they were risen from supper his horse was brought to him, saddled and bridled; right well had they tended it. Then the knight took leave of his lady, and mounted and rode toward the city; but often he looked behind him, for he marvelled greatly at all that had befallen him, and he rode ever thinking of his adventure, amazed and half-doubting, for he scarcely knew what the end thereof should be.

Then he entered his hostel and found all his men well clad, and he held great state but knew not whence the money came to him. In all the city there was no knight that had need of lodging but Lanval made him come unto him and gave him rich service. Lanval gave costly gifts; Lanval ransomed prisoners; Lanval clothed the minstrels; Lanval lavished wealth and honours; there was neither friend nor stranger to whom he gave not gifts. Great were his joy and gladness, for whether by day or by night he might full often look upon his lady, and all things were at his commandment.

Now in the self-same year, after the feast of St. John, thirty of the knights went forth to disport themselves in a meadow below the tower wherein the queen had her lodging. With them went Sir Gawain and his cousin, the gallant Iwein. Then said Gawain, the fair and courteous, who was loved of all: "Pardieu, my lords, we do ill in that we have not brought with us our companion, Sir Lanval, who is so free-handed and courteous, and son to so rich a king." Then they turned back to his hostelry, and by their prayers persuaded Lanval to come with them.

It so chanced that the queen leant forth from an open casement, and three of her chosen ladies with her. She looked upon Sir Lanval and knew him. Then she called one of her ladies, and bade her command the fairest and most graceful of her maidens to make ready and come forth with her to the meadow. Thirty or more she took with her, and descended the stairway of the tower. The knights were joyful at their coming, and hastened to meet them, and took them by the hand with all courtesy. But Sir Lanval went apart from the others, for the time seemed long to him ere he could see his lady, kiss her, and hold her in his arms. All other joys were but small to him if he had not that one delight of his heart.

When the queen saw him alone she went straight toward him, and seated herself beside him; then, calling him by his name, she opened her heart to him.

"Lanval," she said, "greatly have I honoured, cherished, and loved you. All my love is yours if you will have it, and if I thus grant you my favour, then ought you to be joyful indeed."

"Lady," said the knight, "let me be; I have small desire of your love. Long have I served King Arthur; I will not now deny my faith. Neither for you nor for your love will I betray my liege lord."

The queen was angry, and in her wrath she spoke scoffingly. "They but spoke the truth," she said, "who told me that you knew not how to love: that you do not like women. You prefer handsome young men, and you take your pleasure with them. Coward and traitor, false knight, my lord has done ill to suffer you so long about him; he loses much by it, to my thinking."

When Sir Lanval heard that, he was wroth and answered her swiftly, and by misfortune he said that of which he afterwards repented sorely. "Lady," he said, "you have been ill-advised. I love and I am loved by one who deserves the prize of beauty above all whom I know. One thing I will tell you, hear and mark it well; one of her serving maidens, even the meanest among them, is worth more than you. my lady queen, in face and figure, in beauty, wisdom, and goodness."

Then the queen rose up and went weeping to her chamber, shamed and angered that Lanval should have thus insulted her. She laid herself down on her bed as if sick; never, she said, would she arise off it till the king did justice on the plaint she would lay before him.

King Arthur came back from the woods after a fair day's hunting and sought the queen's chamber. When she saw him she cried out, and fell at his feet, beseeching his favour, and saying that Sir Lanval had shamed her, for he had asked her love, and when she refused him had mocked and insulted her, for he had boasted of his lady that she was so fair, so noble, and so proud that even the lowest of her waiting women was worth more than the queen.

At this King Arthur fell into a rage, and swore a solemn oath that unless the knight could defend himself well and fully in open court, he should be hanged or burnt.

Forth from the chamber went the king and called three of his barons to him, and bade them fetch Sir Lanval, who indeed was sad and sorry enough. He had returned to his hostelry, but alas! he learnt all too soon that he had lost his lady, since he had revealed the secret of their love. He was all alone in his chamber, full of anguish. Again and again he called upon his love, but it availed him nothing. He wept and sighed, and once and again fell on the ground in his despair. A hundred times he besought her to have mercy on him, and to speak once more to her true knight. He cursed his heart and his mouth that had betrayed him; 'twas a marvel he did not slay himself. But neither cries nor blows nor lamentations sufficed to awaken her pity and make her show herself to his eyes.

Alas, what comfort might there be for the unhappy knight who had thus made an enemy of his king? The barons came and bade him follow them to court without delay, for the queen had accused him, and the king, by their mouth, commanded his presence. Lanval followed them, sorrowing greatly; had they slain him it would have pleased him well. He stood before the king, mute and speechless, his countenance changed for sorrow.

The king spoke in anger: "Vassal," he said, "you have greatly wronged me; and evil excuse have you found to shame and injure me and insult the queen. Foolish was your boast, and foolish must be your lady to hold that her maid-servant is fairer than my queen."

Sir Lanval denied that he had dishonoured himself or insulted his liege lord. Word by word he repeated what the queen had said to him; but of the words he himself had spoken, and the boast he had made concerning his love, he owned the truth; sorrowful enough he was, since by so doing he had lost her. And for this speech he would make amends, as the court might require.

The king was sorely enraged against him, and conjured his knights to say what might rightfully be done in such a case, and how Lanval should be punished. And the knights did as he bade them, and some spoke fair, and some spoke ill. Then they all took counsel together and decreed that judgment should be given on a fixed day; and that Sir Lanval should give pledges to his lord that he would return to his hostelry and await the verdict. Otherwise, he should be held a prisoner till the day came. The barons returned to the king, and told him what they had agreed upon; and King Arthur demanded pledges, but Lanval was alone, a stranger in a strange land, without friend or kindred.

Then Sir Gawain came near, with all his companions, and said to the king: "I offer to give bail," and all his companions did the same. And when they had thus given bail for him who had nothing of his own, he was free to go to his hostelry. The knights bore Sir Lanval company, chiding him as they went for his grief, and cursing the mad love that had brought him to this pass. Every day they visited him that they might see if he ate and drank, for they feared much that he would go mad for sorrow.

At the day they had named the barons were all assembled, the king was there, and the queen, and sureties delivered up Lanval. Very sorrowful they were for him. I think there were even three hundred of them who had done all in their power without being able to deliver him from peril. Of a great offence did they accuse him, and the king demanded that sentence should be given according to the accusation and the defence.

Then the barons went forth to consider their judgment, heavy at heart, many of them, for the gallant stranger who was in such stress among them. Others, indeed, were ready to sacrifice Lanval to the will of their seigneur.

Then spoke the Duke of Cornwall, for the right was his. Whoever might weep or rage, to him it pertained to have the first word, and he said:

"The king lays his plea against a vassal, Lanval ye call him, of felony and misdeed he accuses him in the matter of a love of which he boasted himself, thus making my lady, the queen, wrathful. None save the king, has anything against him; therefore do ye as I say, for he who would speak the truth must have respect unto no man, save only such honour as shall be due to his liege lord. Let Lanval be put upon his oath (the king will surely have nothing against it) and if he can prove his words, and bring forward his lady, and that which he said and which so angered the queen be true, then he shall be pardoned; 'twas no villainy that he spoke. But if he cannot bring proof of his word, then shall we make him to know that the king no longer desires his service and gives him dismissal from his court."

Then they sent messengers to the knight, and spoke, and made clear to him that he must bring forth his lady that his word might be proved, and he held guiltless. But he told them that was beyond his power, never through her might succour come to him. Then the messengers returned to the judges, who saw there was no chance of aid, for the king pressed them hard, urged thereto by the queen, who was weary of awaiting their judgment.

But as they arose to seek the king they saw two maidens come riding on white palfreys. Very fair they were to look upon, clad in green sendal over their white skin. The knights beheld them gladly, and Gawain, with three others, hastened to Sir Lanval and told him what had chanced, and bade him look upon the maidens; and they prayed him eagerly to say whether one of the two were his lady, but he answered them nay.

The two, so fair to look upon, had gone forward to the palace, and dismounted before the dais whereon King Arthur was seated. If their beauty was great, so also was their speech courteous.

"King," they said, "command that chambers be assigned to us, fair with silken hangings, wherein our mistress can fitly lodge, for with you will she sojourn awhile."

They said no more, and the king called two knights, and bade them lead the maidens to the upper chambers.

Then the king demanded from his barons their judgment and their verdict, and said he was greatly wroth with them for their long delay.

"Sire" they answered, "we were stayed by the coming of the damsels. Our decision is not yet made, we go but now to take counsel together." Then they reassembled, sad and thoughtful, and great was the clamour and strife among them.

While they were yet in perplexity, they saw, descending the street, two maidens of noble aspect, clad in robes broidered with gold, and mounted on Spanish mules. Then all the knights were very joyful, and said each to the other: "Surely now shall Sir Lanval, the valiant and courteous, be safe."

Gawain and six companions went to seek the knight. "Sir," they said, "be of good courage, for the love of God speak to us. Hither come two damsels, most beautiful, and richly clad, one of them must of a truth be your lady!" But Lanval answered simply: "Never before today have I looked upon, or known, or loved them."

Meantime, the maidens had come to the palace and stood before the king. Many praised them for their beauty and bright colour, and some deemed them fairer even than the queen.

The elder was wise and courteous, and she delivered her message gracefully. "King," she said, "bid your folk give us chambers wherein we may lodge with our lady; she comes hither to speak with you."

Then the king commanded that they should be led to their companions who had come before them. Nor as yet was the judgment spoken. So when the maidens had left the hall, he commanded his barons to deliver their verdict, their judgment already tarried too long, and the queen waxed wrathful for their delay.

But even as they sought the king, through the city came riding a maiden, in all the world was none so fair. She rode a white palfrey, that bore her well and easily. Well shaped were its head and neck, no better trained steed was there in all the world. Costly were the trappings of that palfrey, under heaven was there no king rich enough to purchase the like, save that he sold or pledged his land.

And thus was the lady clad: her raiment was all of white, laced on either side. Slender was her shape, and her neck whiter than snow on the bough. Her eyes were blue, her skin fair. Straight was her nose, and lovely her mouth. Her eyebrows were brown, her forehead white, and her hair fair and curling. Her mantle was of purple, and the skirts were folded about her; on her hand she bare a hawk, and a hound followed behind her.

In all the burg there was no one, small nor great, young nor old, but was eager to look upon her as she passed. She came riding swiftly, and her beauty was no mere empty boast, but all men who looked upon her held her for a marvel, and not one of those who beheld her but felt his heart verily kindled with love.

Then those who loved Sir Lanval went to him, and told him of the maiden who came, if by the will of heaven she might deliver him. "Sir knight and comrade, hither comes one, no nutbrown maid is she, but the fairest of all fair women in this world." And Lanval heard, and sighed, for well he knew her. He raised his head and the blood flew to his cheek as he made swift answer: "Of a faith," he said, *"this* is my lady! Now let them slay me if they will and she has no mercy on me. I am whole if I do but see her."

The maiden reached the palace; fairer was she than any who had entered there. She dismounted before the king that all might behold her; she had let her mantle fall that they might the better see her beauty. King Arthur, in his courtesy, had risen to meet her, and all around him sprang to their feet and were eager to offer their service. When they had looked well upon her and praised her beauty, she spoke in these words, for no will had she to delay:

"King Arthur, I have loved one of your knights, behold him there, seigneur. Sir Lanval. He hath been accused at your court, but it is not my will that harm shall befall him. Concerning that which he said, know that the queen was in the wrong; never on any day did he pray her for her love. Of the boast that he hath made, if he may by me be acquitted, then shall your barons speak him free, as they have rightfully engaged to do."

The king granted that so it might be nor was there a single voice but declared that Lanval was guiltless of wrong, for their own eyes had acquitted him.

And the maiden departed; in vain did the king pray her to remain; and many there were who would fain have served her. Without the hall was there a great block of grey marble, from which the chief knights of the kings court were wont to mount their steeds; on this Lanval took his stand, and when the maiden rode forth from the palace he sprang swiftly upon the palfrey behind her. Thus, as the Bretons tell us, he departed with her for that most fair island, Avalon; thither the fairy maiden had carried her knight, and none hath heard man speak further of Sir Lanval. Nor know I more of his story.

trans. Jessie L. Weston

THE LAY OF THE TWO LOVERS

By Marie de France

VII

Once upon a time there lived in Normandy two lovers, who were passing fond, and were brought by Love to Death. The story of their love was bruited so abroad, that the Bretons made a song in their own tongue, and named this song the Lay of the Two Lovers.

In Neustria—that men call Normandy—there is verily a high and marvellously great mountain, where lie the relics of the Two Children. Near this high place the King of those parts caused to be built a certain fair and cunning city, and since he was lord of the Pistrians, it was known as Pistres. The town yet endures, with its towers and houses, to bear witness to the truth; moreover the country thereabouts is known to us all as the Valley of Pistres.

This King had one fair daughter, a damsel sweet of face and gracious of manner, very near to her father's heart, since he had lost his Queen. The maiden increased in years and favour, but he took no heed to her trothing, so that men—yea, even his own people—blamed him greatly for this thing. When the King heard thereof he was passing heavy and dolent, and considered within himself how he might be delivered from this grief. So then, that none should carry off his child, he caused it to be proclaimed, both far and near, by script and trumpet, that he alone should wed the maid, who would bear her in his arms to the pinnacle of the great and perilous mountain, and that without rest or stay. When this news was noised about the country, many came upon the quest. But strive as they would they might not enforce themselves more than they were able. However mighty they were of body, at the last they failed upon the mountain, and fell with their burthen to the ground. Thus, for a while, was none so bold as to seek the high Princess.

Now in this country lived a squire, son to a certain count of that realm, seemly of semblance and courteous, and right desirous to win that prize, which was so coveted of all. He was a welcome guest at the Court, and the King talked with him very willingly. This squire had set his heart upon the daughter of the King, and many a time spoke in her ear, praying her to give him again the love he had bestowed upon her. So seeing him brave and courteous, she esteemed him for the gifts which gained him the favour of the King, and they loved together in their youth. But they hid this matter from all about the Court. This thing was very grievous to them, but the damoiseau thought within himself that it were good to bear the pains he knew, rather than to seek out others that might prove sharper still. Yet in the end, altogether distraught by love, this prudent varlet sought his friend, and showed her his case, saying that he urgently required of her that she would flee with him, for no longer could he endure the weariness of his days. Should he ask her of the King, well he knew that by reason of his love he would refuse the gift, save he bore her in his arms up the steep mount. Then the maiden made answer to her lover, and said,

"Fair friend, well I know you may not carry me to that high place. Moreover should we take to flight, my father would suffer wrath and sorrow beyond measure, and go heavily all his days. Certainly my love is too fond to plague him thus, and we must seek another counsel, for this is not to my heart. Hearken well. I have kindred in Salerno, of rich estate. For more than thirty years my aunt has studied there the art of medicine, and knows the secret gift of every root and herb. If you hasten to her, bearing letters from me, and show her your adventure, certainly she will find counsel and cure. Doubt not that she will discover some cunning simple, that will strengthen your body, as well as comfort your heart. Then return to this realm with your potion, and ask me at my father's hand. He will deem you but a stripling, and set forth the terms of his bargain, that to him alone shall I be given who knows how to climb the perilous mountain, without pause or rest, bearing his lady between his arms.'

When the varlet heard this cunning counsel of the maiden, he rejoiced greatly, and thanking her sweetly for her rede, craved permission to depart. He returned to his own home, and gathering together a goodly store of silken cloths most precious, he bestowed his gear upon the pack horses, and made him ready for the road. So with a little company of men, mounted on swift palfreys, and most privy to his mind, he arrived at Salerno. Now the squire made no long stay at his lodging, but as soon as he might, went to the damsel's kindred to open out his mind. He delivered to the aunt the letters he carried from his friend, and bewailed their evil case. When the dame had read these letters with him, line by line, she charged him to lodge with her awhile, till she might do according to his wish. So by her sorceries, and for the love of her maid, she brewed such a potion that no man, however weaned and outworn, but by drinking this philtre, would not be refreshed in heart and blood and bones. Such virtue had this medicine, directly it were drunken. This simple she poured within a little flacket, and gave it to the varlet, who received the gift with great joy and delight, and returned swiftly to his own land.

The varlet made no long sojourn in his home. He repaired straightway to the Court, and, seeking out the King, required of him his fair daughter in marriage, promising, for his part, that were she given him, he would bear her in his arms to the summit of the mount. The King was no wise wrath at his presumption. He smiled rather at his folly, for how should one so young and slender succeed in a business wherein so many mighty men had failed. Therefore he appointed a certain day for this judgment. Moreover he caused letters to be written to his vassals and his friends—passing none by—bidding them to see the end of this adventure. Yea, with public cry and sound of trumpet he bade all who would, come to behold the stripling carry his fair daughter to the pinnacle of the mountain. And from every region round about men came to learn the issue of this thing. But for her part the fair maiden did all that she was able to bring her love to a good end. Ever was it fast day and fleshless day with her, so that by any means she might lighten the burthen that her friend must carry in his arms.

Now on the appointed day this young dansellon came very early to the appointed place, bringing the flacket with him. When the great company were fully met together, the King led forth his daughter before them; and all might see that she was arrayed in nothing but her smock. The varlet took the maiden in his arms, but first he gave her the flask with the precious brewage to carry, since for pride he might not endure to drink therefrom, save at utmost peril. The squire set forth at a great pace, and climbed briskly till he was halfway up the mount.

Because of the joy he had in clasping his burthen, he gave no thought to the potion. But she—she knew the strength was failing in his heart.

"Fair friend," said she, "well I know that you tire: drink now, I pray you, of the flacket, and so shall your manhood come again at need."

But the varlet answered,

"Fair love, my heart is full of courage; nor for any reason will I pause, so long as I can hold upon my way. It is the noise of all this folk—the tumult and the shouting—that makes my steps uncertain. Their cries distress me, I do not dare to stand."

But when two thirds of the course was won, the grasshopper would have tripped him off his feet. Urgently and often the maiden prayed him, saying,

"Fair friend, drink now of thy cordial."

But he would neither hear, nor give credence to her words. A mighty anguish filled his bosom. He climbed upon the summit of the mountain, and pained himself grievously to bring his journey to an end. This he might not do. He reeled and fell, nor could he rise again, for the heart had burst within his breast.

When the maiden saw her lover's piteous plight, she deemed that he had swooned by reason of his pain. She kneeled hastily at his side, and put the enchanted brewage to his lips, but he could neither drink nor speak, for he was dead, as I have told you. She bewailed his evil lot, with many shrill cries, and flung the useless flacket far away. The precious potion bestrewed the ground, making a garden of that desolate place. For many saving herbs have been found there since that day by the simple folk of that country, which from the magic philtre derived all their virtue.

But when the maiden knew that her lover was dead, she made such wondrous sorrow, as no man had ever seen. She kissed his eyes and mouth, and falling upon his body, took him in her arms, and pressed him closely to her breast. There was no heart so hard as not to be touched by her sorrow; for in this fashion died a dame, who was fair and sweet and gracious, beyond the wont of the daughters of men.

Now the King and his company, since these two lovers came not again, presently climbed the mountain to learn their end. But when the King came upon them lifeless, and fast in that embrace, incontinent he fell to the ground, bereft of sense. After his speech had returned to him, he was passing heavy, and lamented their doleful case, and thus did all his people with him.

Three days they kept the bodies of these two fair children from earth, with uncovered face. On the third day they sealed them fast in a goodly coffin of marble, and by the counsel of all men, laid them softly to rest on that mountain where they died. Then they departed from them, and left them together, alone.

Since this adventure of the Two Children this hill is known as the Mountain of the Two Lovers, and their story being bruited abroad, the Breton folk have made a Lay thereof, even as I have rehearsed before you.

BISCLAVRET

By Marie de France

VIII

Amongst the tales I tell you once again, I would not forget the Lay of the Were-Wolf. Such beasts as he are known in every land. Bisclavret he is named in Brittany; whilst the Norman calls him Garwal.

It is a certain thing, and within the knowledge of all, that many a christened man has suffered this change, and ran wild in woods, as a Were-Wolf. The Were-Wolf is a fearsome beast. He lurks within the thick forest, mad and horrible to see. All the evil that he may, he does. He goeth to and fro, about the solitary place, seeking man, in order to devour him. Hearken, now, to the adventure of the Were-Wolf, that I have to tell.

In Brittany there dwelt a baron who was marvellously esteemed of all his fellows. He was a stout knight, and a comely, and a man of office and repute. Right private was he to the mind of his lord, and dear to the counsel of his neighbours. This baron was wedded to a very worthy dame, right fair to see, and sweet of semblance. All his love was set on her, and all her love was given again to him. One only grief had this lady. For three whole days in every week her lord was absent from her side. She knew not where he went, nor on what errand. Neither did any of his house know the business which called him forth.

On a day when this lord was come again to his house, altogether joyous and content, the lady took him to task, right sweetly, in this fashion,

"Husband," said she, "and fair, sweet friend, I have a certain thing to pray of you. Right willingly would I receive this gift, but I fear to anger you in the asking. It is better for me to have an empty hand, than to gain hard words."

When the lord heard this matter, he took the lady in his arms, very tenderly, and kissed her.

"Wife," he answered, "ask what you will. What would you have, for it is yours already?"

"By my faith," said the lady, "soon shall I be whole. Husband, right long and wearisome are the days that you spend away from your home. I rise from my bed in the morning, sick at heart, I know not why. So fearful am I, lest you do aught to your loss, that I may not find any comfort. Very quickly shall I die for reason of my dread. Tell me now, where you go, and on what business! How may the knowledge of one who loves so closely, bring you to harm?"

"Wife," made answer the lord, "nothing but evil can come if I tell you this secret. For the mercy of God do not require it of me. If you but knew, you would withdraw yourself from my love, and I should be lost indeed."

When the lady heard this, she was persuaded that her baron sought to put her by with jesting words. Therefore she prayed and required him the more urgently, with tender looks and speech, till he was overborne, and told her all the story, hiding naught.

"Wife, I become Bisclavaret. I enter in the forest, and live on prey and roots, within the thickest of the wood."

After she had learned his secret, she prayed and entreated the more as to whether he ran in his raiment, or went spoiled of vesture.

"Wife," said he, "I go naked as a beast."

"Tell me, for hope of grace, what you do with your clothing?"

"Fair wife, that will I never. If I should lose my raiment, or even be marked as I quit my vesture, then a Were-Wolf I must go for all the days of my life. Never again should I become man, save in that hour my clothing were given back to me. For this reason never will I show my lair."

"Husband," replied the lady to him, " love you better than all the world. The less cause have you for doubting my faith, or hiding any tittle from me. What savour is here of friendship? How have I made forfeit of your love; for what sin do you mistrust my honour? Open now your heart, and tell what is good to be known."

So at the end, outwearied and overborne by her importunity, he could no longer refrain, but told her all.

"Wife," said he, "within this wood, a little from the path, there is a hidden way, and at the end thereof an ancient chapel, where oftentimes I have bewailed my lot. Near by is a great hollow stone, concealed by a bush, and there is the secret place where I hide my raiment, till I would return to my own home."

On hearing this marvel the lady became sanguine of visage, because of her exceeding fear. She dared no longer to lie at his side, and turned over in her mind, this way and that, how best she could get her from him. Now there was a certain knight of those parts, who, for a great while, had sought and required this lady for her love. This knight had spent long years in her service, but little enough had he got thereby, not even fair words, or a promise. To him the dame wrote a letter, and meeting, made her purpose plain.

"Fair friend," said she, "be happy. That which you have coveted so long a time, I will grant without delay. Never again will I deny your suit. My heart, and all I have to give, are yours, so take me now as love and dame."

Right sweetly the knight thanked her for her grace, and pledged her faith and fealty. When she had confirmed him by an oath, then she told him all this business of her lord—why he went, and what he became, and of his ravening within the wood. So she showed him of the chapel, and of the hollow stone, and of how to spoil the Were-Wolf of his vesture. Thus, by the kiss of his wife, was Bisclavaret betrayed. Often enough had he ravished his prey in desolate places, but from this journey he never returned. His kinsfolk and acquaintance came together to ask of his tidings, when this absence was noised abroad. Many a man, on many a day, searched the woodland, but none might find him, nor learn where Bisclavaret was gone.

The lady was wedded to the knight who had cherished her for so long a space. More than a year had passed since Bisclavaret disappeared. Then it chanced that the King would hunt in that self-same wood where the Were-Wolf lurked. When the hounds were unleashed they ran this way and that, and swiftly came upon his scent. At the view the huntsman winded on his horn, and the whole pack were at his heels. They followed him from morn to eve, till he was torn and bleeding, and was all adread lest they should pull him down. Now the King was very close to the quarry, and when Bisclavaret looked upon his master, he ran to him for pity and for grace. He took the stirrup within his paws, and fawned upon the prince's foot. The King was very fearful at this sight, but presently he called his courtiers to his aid.

"Lords," cried he, "hasten hither, and see this marvellous thing. Here is a beast who has the sense of man. He abases himself before his foe, and cries for mercy, although he cannot speak. Beat off the hounds, and let no man do him harm. We will hunt no more to-day, but return to our own place, with the wonderful quarry we have taken."

The King turned him about, and rode to his hall, Bisclavaret following at his side. Very near to his master the Were-Wolf went, like any dog, and had no care to seek again the wood. When the King had brought him safely to his own castle, he rejoiced greatly, for the beast was fair and strong, no mightier had any man seen. Much pride had the King in his marvellous beast. He held him so dear, that he bade all those who wished for his love, to cross the Wolf in naught, neither to strike him with a rod, but ever to see that he was richly fed and kennelled warm. This commandment the Court observed willingly. So all the day the Wolf sported with the lords, and at night he lay within the chamber of the King. There was not a man who did not make much of the beast, so frank was he and debonair. None had reason to do him wrong, for ever was he about his master, and for his part did evil to none. Every day were these two companions together, and all perceived that the King loved him as his friend.

Hearken now to that which chanced.

The King held a high Court, and bade his great vassals and barons, and all the lords of his venery to the feast. Never was there a goodlier feast, nor one set forth with sweeter show and pomp. Amongst those who were bidden, came that same knight who had the wife of Bisclavaret for dame. He came to the castle, richly gowned, with a fair company, but little he deemed whom he would find so near. Bisclavaret marked his foe the moment he stood within the hall. He ran towards him, and seized him with his fangs, in the King's very presence, and to the view of all. Doubtless he would have done him much mischief, had not the King called and chidden him, and threatened him with a rod. Once, and twice, again, the Wolf set upon the knight in the very light of day. All men marvelled at his malice, for sweet and serviceable was the beast, and to that hour had shown hatred of none. With one consent the household deemed that this deed was done with full reason, and that the Wolf had suffered at the knight's hand some bitter wrong. Right wary of his foe was the knight until the feast had ended, and all the barons had taken farewell of their lord, and departed, each to his own house. With these, amongst the very first, went that lord whom Bisclavaret so fiercely had assailed. Small was the wonder that he was glad to go.

No long while after this adventure it came to pass that the courteous King would hunt in that forest where Bisclavaret was found. With the prince came his wolf, and a fair company. Now at nightfall the King abode within a certain lodge of that country, and this was known of that dame who before was the wife of Bisclavaret. In the morning the lady clothed her in her most dainty apparel, and hastened to the lodge, since she desired to speak with the King, and to offer him a rich present. When the lady entered in the chamber, neither man nor leash might restrain the fury of the Wolf. He became as a mad dog in his hatred and malice. Breaking from his bonds he sprang at the lady's face, and bit the nose from her visage. From every side men ran to the succour of the dame. They beat off the wolf from his prey, and for a little would have cut him in pieces with their swords. But a certain wise counsellor said to the King,

"Sire, hearken now to me. This beast is always with you, and there is not one of us all who has not known him for long. He goes in and out amongst us, nor has molested any man, neither done wrong or felony to any, save only to this dame, one only time as we have seen. He has done evil to this lady, and to that knight, who is now the husband of the dame. Sire, she was once the wife of that lord who was so close and private to your heart, but who went, and none might find where he had gone. Now, therefore, put the dame in a sure place, and question her straitly, so that she may tell—if perchance she knows thereof—for what reason this Beast holds her in such mortal hate. For many a strange deed has chanced, as well we know, in this marvellous land of Brittany."

The King listened to these words, and deemed the counsel good. He laid hands upon the knight, and put the dame in surety in another place. He caused them to be questioned right straitly, so that their torment was very grievous. At the end, partly because of her distress, and partly by reason of her exceeding fear, the lady's lips were loosed, and she told her tale. She showed them of the betrayal of her lord, and how his raiment was stolen from the hollow stone. Since then she knew not where he went, nor what had befallen him, for he had never come again to his own land. Only, in her heart, well she deemed and was persuaded, that Bisclavaret was he.

Straightway the King demanded the vesture of his baron, whether this were to the wish of the lady, or whether it were against her wish. When the raiment was brought him, he caused it to be spread before Bisclavaret, but the Wolf made as though he had not seen. Then that cunning and crafty counsellor took the King apart, that he might give him a fresh rede.

"Sire," said he, "you do not wisely, nor well, to set this raiment before Bisclavaret, in the sight of all. In shame and much tribulation must he lay aside the beast, and again become man. Carry your wolf within your most secret chamber, and put his vestment therein. Then close the door upon him, and leave him alone for a space. So we shall see presently whether the ravening beast may indeed return to human shape."

The King carried the Wolf to his chamber, and shut the doors upon him fast. He delayed for a brief while, and taking two lords of his fellowship with him, came again to the room. Entering therein, all three, softly together, they found the knight sleeping in the King's bed, like a little child. The King ran swiftly to the bed and taking his friend in his arms, embraced and kissed him fondly, above a hundred times. When man's speech returned once more, he told him of his adventure. Then the King restored to his friend the fief that was stolen from him, and gave such rich gifts, moreover, as I cannot tell. As for the wife who had betrayed Bisclavaret, he bade her avoid his country, and chased her from the realm. So she went forth, she and her second lord together, to seek a more abiding city, and were no more seen.

The adventure that you have heard is no vain fable. Verily and indeed it chanced as I have said. The Lay of the Were-Wolf, truly, was written that it should ever be borne in mind.

THE LAY OF ELIDUC

By Marie de France

IV

Now will I rehearse before you a very ancient Breton Lay. As the tale was told to me, so, in turn, will I tell it over again, to the best of my art and knowledge. Hearken now to my story, its why and its reason.

In Brittany there lived a knight, so courteous and so brave, that in all the realm there was no worthier lord than he. This knight was named Eliduc. He had wedded in his youth a noble lady of proud race and name. They had long dwelt together in peace and content, for their hearts were fixed on one another in faith and loyalty. Now it chanced that Eliduc sought his fortune in a far land, where there was a great war. There he loved a Princess, the daughter of the King and Queen of those parts. Guillardun was the maiden's name, and in all the realm was none more fair. The wife of Eliduc had to name, Guildeluec, in her own country. By reason of these two ladies their story is known as the Lay of Guildeluec and Guillardun, but at first it was rightly called the Lay of Eliduc. The name is a little matter; but if you hearken to me you shall learn the story of these three lovers, in its pity and its truth.

Eliduc had as lord and suzerain, the King of Brittany over Sea. The knight was greatly loved and cherished of his prince, by reason of his long and loyal service. When the King's business took him from his realm, Eliduc was his master's Justice and Seneschal. He governed the country well and wisely, and held it from the foe with a strong hand. Nevertheless, in spite of all, much evil was appointed unto him. Eliduc was a mighty hunter, and by the King's grace, he would chase the stag within the woods. He was cunning and fair as Tristan, and so wise in venery, that the oldest forester might not gainsay him in aught concerning the shaw. But by reason of malice and envy, certain men accused him to the King that he had meddled with the royal pleasaunce. The King bade Eliduc to avoid his Court. He gave no reason for his commandment, and the knight might learn nothing of the cause. Often he prayed the King that he might know whereof he was accused. Often he begged his lord not to heed the specious and crafty words of his foes. He called to mind the wounds he had gained in his master's wars, but was answered never a word. When Eliduc found that he might get no speech with his lord, it became his honour to depart. He returned to his house, and calling his friends around him, opened out to them this business of the King's wrath, in recompense for his faithful service.

"I did not reckon on a King's gratitude; but as the proverb says, it is useless for a farmer to dispute with the horse in his plough. The wise and virtuous man keeps faith to his lord, and bears goodwill to his neighbour, not for what he may receive in return."

Then the knight told his friends that since he might no longer stay in his own country, he should cross the sea to the realm of Logres, and sojourn there awhile, for his solace. His fief he placed in the hands of his wife, and he required of his men, and of all who held him dear, that they would serve her loyally. Having given good counsel to the utmost of his power, the knight prepared him for the road. Right heavy were his friends and kin, that he must go forth from amongst them. Eliduc took with him ten knights of his household, and set out on his journey. His dame came with him so far as she was able, wringing her hands, and making much sorrow, at the departure of her husband. At the end he pledged good faith to her, as she to him, and so she returned to her own home. Eliduc went his way, till he came to a haven on the sea. He took ship, and sailed to the realm of Totenois, for many kings dwell in that country, and ever there were strife and war. Now, near to Exeter, in this land, there dwelt a King, right rich and strong, but old and very full of years. He had no son of his body, but one maid only, young, and of an age to wed. Since he would not bestow this damsel on a certain prince of his neighbours, this lord made mortal war upon his fellow, spoiling and wasting all his land. The ancient King, for surety, had set his daughter within a castle, fair and very strong. He had charged the sergeants not to issue forth from the gates, and for the rest there was none so bold as to seek to storm the keep, or even to joust about the barriers. When Eliduc was told of this quarrel, he needed to go no farther, and sojourned for awhile in the land. He turned over in his mind which of these princes dealt unjustly with his neighbour. Since he deemed that the aged king was the more vexed and sorely pressed in the matter, he resolved to aid him to the best of his might, and to take arms in his service. Eliduc, therefore, wrote letters to the King, telling him that he had quitted his own country, and sought refuge in the King's realm. For his part he was willing to fight as a mercenary in the King's quarrel, and if a safe conduct were given him, he and the knights of his company would ride, forthwith, to their master's aid. This letter, Eliduc sent by the hands of his squires to the King. When the ancient lord had read the letter, he rejoiced greatly, and made much of the messengers. He summoned his constable, and commanded him swiftly to write out the safe conduct, that would bring the baron to his side. For the rest he bade that the messengers meetly should be lodged and apparelled, and that such money should be given them as would be sufficient to their needs. Then he sealed the safe conduct with his royal seal, and sent it to Eliduc, straightway, by a sure hand.

When Eliduc came in answer to the summons, he was received with great honour by the King. His lodging was appointed in the house of a grave and courteous burgess of the city, who bestowed the fairest chamber on his guest. Eliduc fared softly, both at bed and board. He called to his table such good knights as were in misease, by reason of prison or of war. He charged his men that none should be so bold as to take pelf or penny from the citizens of the town, during the first forty days of their sojourn. But on the third day, it was bruited about the streets, that the enemy were near at hand. The country folk deemed that they approached to invest the city, and to take the gates by storm. When the noise and clamour of the fearful burgesses came to the ears of Eliduc, he and his company donned their harness, and got to horse, as quickly as they might. Forty horsemen mounted with him; as to the rest, many lay sick or hurt within the city, and others were captives in the hands of the foe. These forty stout sergeants waited for no sounding of trumpets; they hastened to seek their captain at his lodging, and rode at his back through the city gate.

"Sir," said they, "where you go, there we will follow, and what you bid us, that shall we do."

"Friends," made answer the knight, "I thank you for your fellowship. There is no man amongst us but who wishes to molest the foe, and do them all the mischief that he is able. If we await them in the town, we defend ourselves with the shield, and not with the sword. To my mind it is better to fall in the field than to hide behind walls; but if any of you have a wiser counsel to offer, now let him speak."

"Sir," replied a soldier of the company, "through the wood, in good faith, there runs a path, right strict and narrow. It is the wont of the enemy to approach our city by this track. After their deeds of arms before the walls, it is their custom to return by the way they came, helmet on saddle bow, and hauberk unbraced. If we might catch them, unready in the path, we could trouble them very grievously, even though it be at the peril of our lives."

"Friends," answered Eliduc, "you are all the King's men, and are bound to serve him faithfully, even to the death. Come, now, with me where I will go, and do that thing which you shall see me do. I give you my word as a loyal gentleman, that no harm shall hap to any. If we gain spoil and riches from the foe, each shall have his lot in the ransom. At the least we may do them much hurt and mischief in this quarrel."

Eliduc set his men in ambush, near by that path, within the wood. He told over to them, like a cunning captain, the crafty plan he had devised, and taught them how to play their parts, and to call upon his name. When the foe had entered on that perilous path, and were altogether taken in the snare, Eliduc cried his name, and summoned his companions to bear themselves like men. This they did stoutly, and assailed their enemy so fiercely that he was dismayed beyond measure, and his line being broken, fled to the forest. In this fight was the constable taken, together with fifty and five other lords, who owned themselves prisoners, and were given to the keeping of the squires. Great was the spoil in horse and harness, and marvellous was the wealth they gained in gold and ransom. So having done such great deeds in so short a space, they returned to the city, joyous and content.

The King looked forth from a tower. He feared grievously for his men, and made his complaint of Eliduc, who—he deemed—had betrayed him in his need. Upon the road he saw a great company, charged and laden with spoil. Since the number of those who returned was more than those who went forth, the king knew not again his own. He came down from the tower, in doubt and sore trouble, bidding that the gates should be made fast, and that men should mount upon the walls. For such coil as this, there was slender warrant. A squire who was sent out, came back with all speed, and showed him of this adventure. He told over the story of the ambush, and the tale of the prisoners. He rehearsed how the constable was taken, and that many a knight was wounded, and many a brave man slain. When the King might give credence thereto, he had more joy than ever king before. He got him from his tower, and going before Eliduc, he praised him to his face, and rendered him the captives as a gift. Eliduc gave the King's bounty to his men. He bestowed on them besides, all the harness and the spoil; keeping, for his part, but three knights, who had won much honour in the battle. From this day the King loved and cherished Eliduc very dearly. He held the knight, and his company, for a full year in his service, and at the end of the year, such faith had he in the knight's loyalty, that he appointed him Seneschal and Constable of his realm.

Eliduc was not only a brave and wary captain; he was also a courteous gentleman, right goodly to behold.

That fair maiden, the daughter of the King, heard tell of his deeds, and desired to see his face, because of the good men spake of him. She sent her privy chamberlain to the knight, praying him to come to her house, that she might solace herself with the story of his deeds, for greatly she wondered that he had no care for her friendship. Eliduc gave answer to the chamberlain that he would ride forthwith, since much he desired to meet so high a dame. He bade his squire to saddle his destrier, and rode to the palace, to have speech with the lady. Eliduc stood without the lady's chamber, and prayed the chamberlain to tell the dame that he had come, according to her wish. The chamberlain came forth with a smiling face, and straightway led him in the chamber.

When the princess saw the knight, she cherished him very sweetly, and welcomed him in the most honourable fashion. The knight gazed upon the lady, who was passing fair to see. He thanked her courteously, that she was pleased to permit him to have speech with so high a princess. Guillardun took Eliduc by the hand, and seated him upon the bed, near her side. They spake together of many things, for each found much to say. The maiden looked closely upon the knight, his face and semblance; to her heart she said that never before had she beheld so comely a man. Her eyes might find no blemish in his person, and Love knocked upon her heart, requiring her to love, since her time had come. She sighed, and her face lost its fair colour; but she cared only to hide her trouble from the knight, lest he should think her the less maidenly therefore. When they had talked together for a great space, Eliduc took his leave, and went his way. The lady would have kept him longer gladly, but since she did not dare, she allowed him to depart. Eliduc returned to his lodging, very pensive and deep in thought. He called to mind that fair maiden, the daughter of his King, who so sweetly had bidden him to her side, and had kissed him farewell, with sighs that were sweeter still. He repented him right earnestly that he had lived so long a while in the land without seeking her face, but promised that often he would enter her palace now. Then he remembered the wife whom he had left in his own house. He recalled the parting between them, and the covenant he made, that good faith and stainless honour should be ever betwixt the twain. But the maiden, from whom he came, was willing to take him as her knight! If such was her will, might any pluck him from her hand?

All night long, that fair maiden, the daughter of the King, had neither rest nor sleep. She rose up, very early in the morning, and commanding her chamberlain, opened out to him all that was in her heart. She leaned her brow against the casement.

"By my faith," she said, "I am fallen into a deep ditch, and sorrow has come upon me. I love Eliduc, the good knight, whom my father made his Seneschal. I love him so dearly that I turn the whole night upon my bed, and cannot close my eyes, nor sleep. If he assured me of his heart, and loved me again, all my pleasure should be found in his happiness. Great might be his profit, for he would become King of this realm, and little enough is it for his deserts, so courteous is he and wise. If he have nothing better than friendship to give me, I choose death before life, so deep is my distress."

When the princess had spoken what it pleased her to say, the chamberlain, whom she had bidden, gave her loyal counsel.

"Lady," said he, "since you have set your love upon this knight, send him now—if so it please you—some goodly gift-girdle or scarf or ring. If he receive the gift with delight, rejoicing in your favour, you may be assured that he loves you. There is no Emperor, under Heaven, if he were tendered your tenderness, but would go the more lightly for your grace."

The damsel hearkened to the counsel of her chamberlain, and made reply,

"If only I knew that he desired my love! Did ever maiden woo her knight before, by asking whether he loved or hated her? What if he make of me a mock and a jest in the ears of his friends! Ah, if the secrets of the heart were but written on the face! But get you ready, for go you must, at once."

"Lady," answered the chamberlain, "I am ready to do your bidding."

"You must greet the knight a hundred times in my name, and will place my girdle in his hand, and this my golden ring."

When the chamberlain had gone upon his errand, the maiden was so sick at heart, that for a little she would have bidden him return. Nevertheless, she let him go his way, and eased her shame with words.

"Alas, what has come upon me, that I should put my heart upon a stranger. I know nothing of his folk, whether they be mean or high; nor do I know whether he will part as swiftly as he came. I have done foolishly, and am worthy of blame, since I have bestowed my love very lightly. I spoke to him yesterday for the first time, and now I pray him for his love. Doubtless he will make me a song! Yet if he be the courteous gentleman I believe him, he will understand, and not deal hardly with me. At least the dice are cast, and if he may not love me, I shall know myself the most woeful of ladies, and never taste of joy all the days of my life." Whilst the maiden lamented in this fashion, the chamberlain hastened to the lodging of Eliduc. He came before the knight, and having saluted him in his lady's name, he gave to his hand the ring and the girdle. The knight thanked him earnestly for the gifts. He placed the ring upon his finger, and the girdle he girt about his body. He said no more to the chamberlain, nor asked him any questions; save only that he proffered him a gift. This the messenger might not have, and returned the way he came. The chamberlain entered in the palace and found the princess within her chamber. He greeted her on the part of the knight, and thanked her for her bounty.

"Diva, diva," cried the lady hastily, "hide nothing from me; does he love me, or does he not?"

"Lady," answered the chamberlain, "as I deem, he loves you, and truly. Eliduc is no cozener with words. I hold him for a discreet and prudent gentleman, who knows well how to hide what is in his heart. I gave him greeting in your name, and granted him your gifts. He set the ring upon his finger, and as to your girdle, he girt it upon him, and belted it tightly about his middle. I said no more to him, nor he to me; but if he received not your gifts in tenderness, I am the more deceived. Lady, I have told you his words: I cannot tell you his thoughts. Only, mark carefully what I am about to say. If Eliduc had not a richer gift to offer, he would not have taken your presents at my hand."

"It pleases you to jest," said the lady. "I know well that Eliduc does not altogether hate me. Since my only fault is to cherish him too fondly, should he hate me, he would indeed be blameworthy. Never again by you, or by any other, will I require him of aught, or look to him for comfort. He shall see that a maiden's love is no slight thing, lightly given, and lightly taken again—but, perchance, he will not dwell in the realm so long as to know of the matter."

"Lady, the knight has covenanted to serve the King, in all loyalty, for the space of a year. You have full leisure to tell, whatever you desire him to learn."

When the maiden heard that Eliduc remained in the country, she rejoiced very greatly. She was glad that the knight would sojourn awhile in her city, for she knew naught of the torment he endured, since first he looked upon her. He had neither peace nor delight, for he could not get her from his mind. He reproached himself bitterly. He called to remembrance the covenant he made with his wife, when he departed from his own land, that he would never be false to his oath. But his heart was a captive now, in a very strong prison. He desired greatly to be loyal and honest, but he could not deny his love for the maiden—Guillardun, so frank and so fair.

Eliduc strove to act as his honour required. He had speech and sight of the lady, and did not refuse her kiss and embrace. He never spoke of love, and was diligent to offend in nothing. He was careful in this, because he would keep faith with his wife, and would attempt no matter against his King. Very grievously he pained himself, but at the end he might do no more. Eliduc caused his horse to be saddled, and calling his companions about him, rode to the castle to get audience of the King. He considered, too, that he might see his lady, and learn what was in her heart. It was the hour of meat, and the King having risen from table, had entered in his daughter's chamber. The King was at chess, with a lord who had but come from over-sea. The lady sat near the board, to watch the movements of the game. When Eliduc came before the prince, he welcomed him gladly, bidding him to seat himself close at hand. Afterwards he turned to his daughter, and said, "Princess, it becomes you to have a closer friendship with this lord, and to treat him well and worshipfully. Amongst five hundred, there is no better knight than he."

When the maiden had listened demurely to her father's commandment, there was no gayer lady than she. She rose lightly to her feet, and taking the knight a little from the others, seated him at her side. They remained silent, because of the greatness of their love. She did not dare to speak the first, and to him the maid was more dreadful than a knight in mail. At the end Eliduc thanked her courteously for the gifts she had sent him; never was grace so precious and so kind. The maiden made answer to the knight, that very dear to her was the use he had found for her ring, and the girdle with which he had belted his body. She loved him so fondly that she wished him for her husband. If she might not have her wish, one thing she knew well, that she would take no living man, but would die unwed. She trusted he would not deny her hope.

"Lady," answered the knight, "I have great joy in your love, and thank you humbly for the goodwill you bear me. I ought indeed to be a happy man, since you deign to show me at what price you value our friendship. Have you remembered that I may not remain always in your realm? I covenanted with the King to serve him as his man for the space of one year. Perchance I may stay longer in his service, for I would not leave him till his quarrel be ended. Then I shall return to my own land; so, fair lady, you permit me to say farewell."

The maiden made answer to her knight,

"Fair friend, right sweetly I thank you for your courteous speech. So apt a clerk will know, without more words, that he may have of me just what he would. It becomes my love to give faith to all you say."

The two lovers spoke together no further; each was well assured of what was in the other's heart. Eliduc rode back to his lodging, right joyous and content. Often he had speech with his friend, and passing great was the love which grew between the twain.

Eliduc pressed on the war so fiercely that in the end he took captive the King who troubled his lord, and had delivered the land from its foes. He was greatly praised of all as a crafty captain in the field, and a hardy comrade with the spear. The poor and the minstrel counted him a generous knight. About this time that King, who had bidden Eliduc avoid his realm, sought diligently to find him. He had sent three messengers beyond the seas to seek his ancient Seneschal. A strong enemy had wrought him much grief and loss. All his castles were taken from him, and all his country was a spoil to the foe. Often and sorely he repented him of the evil counsel to which he had given ear. He mourned the absence of his mightiest knight, and drove from his councils those false lords who, for malice and envy, had defamed him. These he outlawed for ever from his realm. The King wrote letters to Eliduc, conjuring him by the loving friendship that was once between them, and summoning him as a vassal is required of his lord, to hasten to his aid, in that his bitter need. When Eliduc heard these tidings they pressed heavily upon him, by reason of the grievous love he bore the dame. She, too, loved him with a woman's whole heart. Between the two there was nothing but the purest love and tenderness. Never by word or deed had they spoiled their friendship. To speak a little closely together; to give some fond and foolish gift; this was the sum of their love. In her wish and hope the maiden trusted to hold the knight in her land, and to have him as her lord. Naught she deemed that he was wedded to a wife beyond the sea. "Alas," said Eliduc, "I have loitered too long in this country, and have gone astray. Here I have set my heart on a maiden, Guillardun, the daughter of the King, and she, on me. If, now, we part, there is no help that one, or both, of us, must die. Yet go I must. My lord requires me by letters, and by the oath of fealty that I have sworn. My own honour demands that I should return to my wife. I dare not stay; needs must I go. I cannot wed my lady, for not a priest in Christendom would make us man and wife. All things turn to blame. God, what a tearing asunder will our parting be! Yet there is one who will ever think me in the right, though I be held in scorn of all. I will be guided by her wishes, and what she counsels that will I do. The King, her sire, is troubled no longer by any war. First, I will go to him, praying that I may return to my own land, for a little, because of the need of my rightful lord. Then I will seek out the maiden, and show her the whole business. She will tell me her desire, and I shall act according to her wish."

The knight hesitated no longer as to the path he should follow. He went straight to the King, and craved leave to depart. He told him the story of his lord's distress, and read, and placed in the King's hands, the letters calling him back to his home. When the King had read the writing, and knew that Eliduc purposed to depart, he was passing sad and heavy. He offered the knight the third part of his kingdom, with all the treasure that he pleased to ask, if he would remain at his side. He offered these things to the knight—these, and the gratitude of all his days besides.

"Do not tempt me, sire," replied the knight. "My lord is in such deadly peril, and his letters have come so great a way to require me, that go I must to aid him in his need. When I have ended my task, I will return very gladly, if you care for my services, and with me a goodly company of knights to fight in your quarrels."

The King thanked Eliduc for his words, and granted him graciously the leave that he demanded. He gave him, moreover, all the goods of his house; gold and silver, hound and horses, silken cloths, both rich and fair, these he might have at his will. Eliduc took of them discreetly, according to his need. Then, very softly, he asked one other gift. If it pleased the King, right willingly would he say farewell to the princess, before he went. The King replied that it was his pleasure, too. He sent a page to open the door of the maiden's chamber, and to tell her the knight's request. When she saw him, she took him by the hand, and saluted him very sweetly. Eliduc was the more fain of counsel than of claspings. He seated himself by the maiden's side, and as shortly as he might, commenced to show her of the business. He had done no more than read her of his letters, than her face lost its fair colour, and near she came to swoon. When Eliduc saw her about to fall, he knew not what he did, for grief. He kissed her mouth, once and again, and wept above her, very tenderly. He took, and held her fast in his arms, till she had returned from her swoon.

"Fair dear friend," said he softly, "bear with me while I tell you that you are my life and my death, and in you is all my comfort. I have bidden farewell to your father, and purposed to go back to my own land, for reason of this bitter business of my lord. But my will is only in your pleasure, and whatever the future brings me, your counsel I will do."

"Since you cannot stay," said the maiden, "take me with you, wherever you go. If not, my life is so joyless without you, that I would wish to end it with my knife." Very sweetly made answer Sir Eliduc, for in honesty he loved honest maid,

"Fair friend, I have sworn faith to your father, and am his man. If I carried you with me, I should give the lie to my troth. Let this covenant be made between us. Should you give me leave to return to my own land I swear to you on my honour as a knight, that I will come again on any day that you shall name. My life is in your hands. Nothing on earth shall keep me from your side, so only that I have life and health."

Then she, who loved so fondly, granted her knight permission to depart, and fixed the term, and named the day for his return. Great was their sorrow that the hour had come to bid farewell. They gave rings of gold for remembrance, and sweetly kissed adieu. So they severed from each other's arms.

Eliduc sought the sea, and with a fair wind, crossed swiftly to the other side. His lord was greatly content to learn the tidings of his knight's return. His friends and his kinsfolk came to greet him, and the common folk welcomed him very gladly. But, amongst them all, none was so blithe at his home-coming as the fair and prudent lady who was his wife. Despite this show of friendship, Eliduc was ever sad, and deep in thought. He went heavily, till he might look upon his friend. He felt no happiness, nor made pretence of any, till he should meet with her again. His wife was sick at heart, because of the coldness of her husband. She took counsel with her soul, as to what she had done amiss. Often she asked him privily, if she had come short or offended in any measure, whilst he was without the realm. If she was accused by any, let him tell her the accusation, that she might purge herself of the offence.

"Wife," answered Eliduc, "neither I, nor any other, charge you with aught that is against your honour to do. The cause of my sorrow is in myself. I have pledged my faith to the King of that country, from whence I come, that I will return to help him in his need. When my lord the King has peace in his realm, within eight days I shall be once more upon the sea. Great travail I must endure, and many pains I shall suffer, in readiness for that hour. Return I must, and till then I have no mind for anything but toil; for I will not give the lie to my plighted word."

Eliduc put his fief once more in the hands of his dame. He sought his lord, and aided him to the best of his might. By the counsel and prowess of the knight, the King came again into his own. When the term appointed by his lady, and the day she named for his return drew near, Eliduc wrought in such fashion that peace was accorded between the foes. Then the knight made him ready for his journey, and took thought to the folk he should carry with him. His choice fell on two of his nephews, whom he loved very dearly, and on a certain chamberlain of his household. These were trusted servitors, who were of his inmost mind, and knew much of his counsel. Together with these went his squires, these only, for Eliduc had no care to take many. All these, nephew and squire and chamberlain, Eliduc made to promise, and confirm by an oath, that they would reveal nothing of his business.

The company put to sea without further tarrying, and, crossing quickly, came to that land where Eliduc so greatly desired to be. The knight sought a hostel some distance from the haven, for he would not be seen of any, nor have it bruited that Eliduc was returned. He called his chamberlain, and sent him to his friend, bearing letters that her knight had come, according to the covenant that had been made. At nightfall, before the gates were made fast, Eliduc issued forth from the city, and followed after his messenger. He had clothed himself in mean apparel, and rode at a footpace straight to the city, where dwelt the daughter of the King. The chamberlain arrived before the palace, and by dint of asking and prying, found himself within the lady's chamber. He saluted the maiden, and told her that her lover was near. When Guillardun heard these tidings she was astonied beyond measure, and for joy and pity wept right tenderly. She kissed the letters of her friend, and the messenger who brought such welcome tidings. The chamberlain prayed the lady to attire and make her ready to join her friend. The day was spent in preparing for the adventure, according to such plan as had been devised. When dark was come, and all was still, the damsel stole forth from the palace, and the chamberlain with her. For fear that any man should know her again, the maiden had hidden, beneath a riding cloak, her silken gown, embroidered with gold. About the space of a bow shot from the city gate, there was a coppice standing within a fair meadow. Near by this wood, Eliduc and his comrades awaited the coming of Guillardun. When Eliduc saw the lady, wrapped in her mantle, and his chamberlain leading her by the hand, he got from his horse, and kissed her right tenderly. Great joy had his companions at so fair a sight. He set her on the horse, and climbing before her, took bridle in glove, and returned to the haven, with all the speed he might. He entered forthwith in the ship, which put to sea, having on board none, save Eliduc, his men, and his lady, Guillardun. With a fair wind, and a quiet hour, the sailors thought that they would swiftly come to shore. But when their journey was near its end, a sudden tempest arose on the sea. A mighty wind drove them far from their harbourage, so that their rudder was broken, and their sail torn from the mast. Devoutly they cried on St. Nicholas, St. Clement, and Madame St. Mary, to aid them in this peril. They implored the Mother that she would approach her

Son, not to permit them to perish, but to bring them to the harbour where they would come. Without sail or oar, the ship drifted here and there, at the mercy of the storm. They were very close to death, when one of the company, with a loud voice began to cry,

"What need is there of prayers! Sir, you have with you, her, who brings us to our death. We shall never win to land, because you, who already have a faithful wife, seek to wed this foreign woman, against God and His law, against honour and your plighted troth. Grant us to cast her in the sea, and straightway the winds and the waves will be still."

When Eliduc heard these words he was like to come to harm for rage.

"Bad servant and felon traitor," he cried, "you should pay dearly for your speech, if I might leave my lady."

Eliduc held his friend fast in his arms, and cherished her as well as he was able. When the lady heard that her knight was already wedded in his own realm, she swooned where she lay. Her face became pale and discoloured; she neither breathed nor sighed, nor could any bring her any comfort. Those who carried her to a sheltered place, were persuaded that she was but dead, because of the fury of the storm. Eliduc was passing heavy. He rose to his feet, and hastening to his squire, smote him so grievously with an oar, that he fell senseless on the deck. He haled him by his legs to the side of the ship and flung the body in the sea, where it was swiftly swallowed by the waves. He went to the broken rudder, and governed the nave so skillfully, that it presently drew to land. So, having come to their fair haven, they cast anchor, and made fast their bridge to the shore. Dame Guillardun lay yet in her swoon, and seemed no other than if she were really dead. Eliduc's sorrow was all the more, since he deemed that he had slain her with his hand. He inquired of his companions in what near place they might lay the lady to her rest, "for I will not bid her farewell, till she is put in holy ground with such pomp and rite as befit the obsequies of the daughter of a King." His comrades answered him never a word, for they were all bemused by reason of what had befallen. Eliduc, therefore, considered within himself to what place he should carry the lady. His own home was so near the haven where he had come, that very easily they could ride there before evening. He called to mind that in his realm there was a certain great forest, both long and deep. Within this wood there was a little chapel, served by a holy hermit for forty years, with whom Eliduc had oftimes spoken.

"To this holy man," he said, "I will bear my lady. In his chapel he shall bury her sweet body. I will endow him so richly of my lands, that upon her chantry shall be founded a mighty abbey. There some convent of monks or nuns or canons shall ever hold her in remembrance, praying God to grant her mercy in His day."

Eliduc got to horse, but first took oath of his comrades that never, by them, should be discovered, that which they should see. He set his friend before him on the palfrey, and thus the living and the dead rode together, till they had entered the wood, and come before the chapel. The squires called and beat upon the door, but it remained fast, and none was found to give them any answer. Eliduc bade that one should climb through a window, and open the door from within. When they had come within the chapel they found a new made tomb, and writ thereon, that the holy hermit having finished his course, was made perfect, eight days before. Passing sad was Eliduc, and esmayed. His companions would have digged a second grave, and set therein, his friend; but the knight would in no wise consent, for—he said—he purposed to take counsel of the priests of his country, as to building some church or abbey above her tomb. "At this hour we will but lay her body before the altar, and commend her to God His holy keeping." He commanded them to bring their mantles and make a bed upon the altar-pace. Thereon they laid the maiden, and having wrapped her close in her lover's cloak, left her alone. When the moment came for Eliduc to take farewell of his lady, he deemed that his own last hour had come. He kissed her eyes and her face.

"Fair friend," said he, "if it be pleasing to God, never will I bear sword or lance again, or seek the pleasures of this mortal world. Fair friend, in an ill hour you saw me! Sweet lady, in a bitter hour you followed me to death! Fairest, now were you a queen, were it not for the pure and loyal love you set upon me? Passing sad of heart am I for you, my friend. The hour that I have seen you in your shroud, I will take the habit of some holy order, and every day, upon your tomb, I will tell over the chaplet of my sorrow."

Having taken farewell of the maiden, Eliduc came forth from the chapel, and closed the doors. He sent messages to his wife, that he was returning to his house, but weary and overborne. When the dame heard these tidings, she was happy in her heart, and made ready to greet him. She received her lord tenderly; but little joy came of her welcome, for she got neither smiles in answer, nor tender words in return. She dared not inquire the reason, during the two days Eliduc remained in the house. The knight heard Mass very early in the morning, and then set forth on the road leading to the chapel where the maiden lay. He found her as he had parted, for she had not come back from her swoon, and there was neither stir in her, nor breath. He marvelled greatly, for he saw her, vermeil and white, as he had known her in life. She had lost none of her sweet colour, save that she was a little blanched. He wept bitterly above her, and entreated for her soul. Having made his prayer, he went again to his house.

On a day when Eliduc went forth, his wife called to her a varlet of her household, commanding him to follow his lord afar off, and mark where he went, and on what business. She promised to give him harness and horses, if he did according to her will. The varlet hid himself in the wood, and followed so cunningly after his lord, that he was not perceived. He watched the knight enter the chapel, and heard the cry and lamentation that he made. When Eliduc came out, the varlet hastened to his mistress, and told her what he had seen, the tears and dolour, and all that befell his lord within the hermitage. The lady summoned all her courage.

"We will go together, as soon as we may, to this hermitage. My lord tells me that he rides presently to the Court to speak with the King. I knew that my husband loved this dead hermit very tenderly, but I little thought that his loss would make him mad with grief."

The next day the dame let her lord go forth in peace. When, about noon, Eliduc rode to the Court to greet his King, the lady rose quickly, and carrying the varlet with her, went swiftly to the hermitage. She entered the chapel, and saw the bed upon the altar-pace, and the maiden thereon, like a new sprung rose. Stooping down the lady removed the mantle. She marked the rigid body, the long arms, and the frail white hands, with their slender fingers, folded on the breast. Thus she learned the secret of the sorrow of her lord. She called the varlet within the chapel, and showed him this wonder.

"Seest thou," she said, "this woman, who for beauty shineth as a gem! This lady, in her life, was the lover of my lord. It was for her that all his days were spoiled by grief. By my faith I marvel little at his sorrow, since I, who am a woman too, will—for pity's sake or love—never know joy again, having seen so fair a lady in the dust."

So the wife wept above the body of the maiden. Whilst the lady sat weeping, a weasel came from under the altar, and ran across Guillardun's body. The varlet smote it with his staff, and killed it as it passed. He took the vermin and flung it away. The companion of this weasel presently came forth to seek him. She ran to the place where he lay, and finding that he would not get him on his feet, seemed as one distraught. She went forth from the chapel, and hastened to the wood, from whence she returned quickly, bearing a vermeil flower beneath her teeth. This red flower she placed within the mouth of that weasel the varlet had slain, and immediately he stood upon his feet. When the lady saw this, she cried to the varlet,

"Throw, man, throw, and gain the flower."

The servitor flung his staff, and the weasels fled away, leaving that fair flower upon the floor. The lady rose. She took the flower, and returned with it swiftly to the altar pace. Within the mouth of the maiden, she set a flower that was more vermeil still. For a short space the dame and the damsel were alike breathless. Then the maiden came to herself, with a sigh. She opened her eyes, and commenced to speak.

"Diva," she said, "have I slept so long, indeed!"

When the lady heard her voice she gave thanks to God. She inquired of the maiden as to her name and degree. The damsel made answer to her,

"Lady, I was born in Logres, and am daughter to the King of that realm. Greatly there I loved a knight, named Eliduc, the seneschal of my sire. We fled together from my home, to my own most grievous fault. He never told me that he was wedded to a wife in his own country, and he hid the matter so cunningly, that I knew naught thereof. When I heard tell of his dame, I swooned for pure sorrow. Now I find that this false lover, has, like a felon, betrayed me in a strange land. What will chance to a maiden in so foul a plight? Great is that woman's folly who puts her trust in man."

"Fair damsel," replied the lady, "there is nothing in the whole world that can give such joy to this felon, as to hear that you are yet alive. He deems that you are dead, and every day he beweeps your swoon in the chapel. I am his wife, and my heart is sick, just for looking on his sorrow. To learn the reason of his grief, I caused him to be followed, and that is why I have found you here. It is a great happiness for me to know that you live. You shall return with me to my home, and I will place you in the tenderness of your friend. Then I shall release him of his marriage troth, since it is my dearest hope to take the veil."

When the wife had comforted the maiden with such words, they went together to her own house. She called to her servitor, and bade him seek his lord. The varlet went here and there, till he lighted on Eliduc. He came before him, and showed him of all these things. Eliduc mounted straightway on his horse, and waiting neither for squire or companion, that same night came to his hall. When he found alive, her, who once was dead, Eliduc thanked his wife for so dear a gift. He rejoiced beyond measure, and of all his days, no day was more happy than this. He kissed the maiden often, and very sweetly she gave him again his kiss, for great was the joy between the twain. The dame looked on their happiness, and knew that her lord meetly had bestowed his love. She prayed him, therefore, that he would grant her leave to depart, since she would serve God as a cloistered nun. Of his wealth she craved such a portion as would permit her to found a convent. He would then be able to wed the maiden on whom his heart was set, for it was neither honest nor seemly that a man should maintain a wife with either hand.

Eliduc could do no otherwise than consent. He gave the permission she asked, and did all according to her will. He endowed the lady of his lands, near by that chapel and hermitage, within the wood. There he built a church with offices and refectory, fair to see. Much wealth he bestowed on the convent, in money and estate. When all was brought to a good end, the lady took the veil upon her head. Thirty other ladies entered in the house with her, and long she ruled them as their Abbess, right wisely and well.

Eliduc wedded with his friend, in great pomp, and passing rich was the marriage feast. They dwelt in unity together for many days, for ever between them was perfect love. They walked uprightly, and gave alms of their goods, till such a time as it became them to turn to God. After much thought, Eliduc built a great church close beside his castle. He endowed it with all his gold and silver, and with the rest of his land. He set priests there, and holy layfolk also, for the business of the house, and the fair services of religion. When all was builded and ordered, Eliduc offered himself, with them, that he—weak man—might serve the omnipotent God. He set with the Abbess Guildeluec—who once was his dame—that wife whom he loved so dearly well. The Abbess received her as a sister, and welcomed her right honourably. She admonished her in the offices of God, and taught her of the rules and practice of their holy Order. They prayed to God for their friend, that He would grant him mercy in His day. In turn, he entreated God for them. Messages came from convent and monastery as to how they fared, so that each might encourage the other in His way. Each strove painfully, for himself and his, to love God the more dearly, and to abide in His holy faith. Each made a good end, and the mercy of God was abundantly made clear to all.

Of the adventure of these three lovers, the courteous Bretons made this Lay for remembrance, since they deemed it a matter that men should not forget.

POEMS BY WALTHER VON DER VOGELWEIDE

By Walther von der Vogelweide

W alther von der Vogelweide (ca. 1170–ca. 1230) was the most famous Middle High German poet who already falls into the second generation after the rise of the "classical" Minnesang from ca. 1170 to ca. 1200. He originated perhaps from Austria, but he also might have been born in Bavaria or Tyrol. We only know for sure that he lived the last years of his life in Würzburg, in Franconia, or in northern Bavaria, and died there as well. His grave can still be visited today behind the cathedral, in the "Lusamgärtlein" (the delightful little garden). We also know that he served for some time at the court of Bishop Wolfger von Erlau in Passau, since there is an entry in the account books about a payment to Walther in 1203 of five shillings for a fur coat. According to the poet's own testimony, Emperor Frederick II granted him a small estate for his retirement by ca. 1220. Walther composed ca. 300 stanzas, which have been preserved in ca. 37 manuscripts, which demonstrates his enormous popularity throughout the centuries. He has never been forgotten and has always been remembered as the poet of the German empire. Walther was unique in being the first German poet to compose political and didactic stanzas (gnomic poems) in which he vehemently addressed problems in the imperial government and the conflicts between the state and the church, strongly taking the side of the former against the unfairly fighting clergy (as he saw it). In the poems selected here we hear strong opinions about ethical and social issues. Walther also developed deeply moving love poetry that strongly favors fulfilled and happy love, almost in a utopian fashion. The poet was very outspoken in his criticism of the traditional, highly esoteric, but not fulfilling concept of courtly love, and argued that a simple love affair irrespective of social status would be preferable over the usually pompous but empty stances by contemporary poets.

8,4. *Ich saz ûf eime steine.*

I sat upon a boulder,
crossed one leg over the other,
and set my elbow down thereon;
cradled, in this hand, my chin,
nestled one cheek snug into it,
and thought hard, in deep disquiet: 5
wherefore on earth ought one to live.
There was no counsel I could give,
how one could gain three things together
without one blighted or another.   10
The two are goods that go, and man's esteem,
which often do each other harm.
The third thing is God's gracious favor,
above those two, the greater treasure.
I'd want them in one chest, all three.   15
Yes! Alas, it cannot be
that wealth, and this world's honor,
and the grace of God moreover,
can come—all three together—into one heart,
paths and ways before them barred: 20
Betrayal, poised for ambush, hiding,
Violence on the roadway riding,
Peace and Justice wounded sore.
Those three shall not have safe passage till the two are whole once more.

9,16. *Ich sach mit mînen ougen.*

I saw—these eyes beheld them—
the secrets of men and women,
there I saw, there I heard
what each one did, what each one said.
In Rome I heard lying,   5
two kings they were betraying.
From that the greatest strife arose
that ever will be, ever was—
whence the split asunder
of priests and laymen: all begun there,   10
a great distress, the worst of all,
the body dead, dead the soul.

The priests fought, it was bitter,
but the laymen's force was greater;
the priests all put their swords down,
and snatched up the stole again.   15
They banished those they sought to,
not the one they had been right to;
then they disordered the houses of God.
In a hermit's cell far off I heard   20
lamentation, grieving.
There a hermit, weeping,
bewailed to God the pain in him:
"Alas! Alas! The Pope too young! Help, O Lord, Your Christendom!"

33,11. *Wir clagen alle und wizzen doch niht waz uns wirret.*

We all cry woe and do not know what things upset us:
that the Pope, our Holy Father there, has so misled us.
How like a father now he goes before us, at our head.
We follow after him, never straying one foot from his lead.
Take note, World, what in all this fills me with displeasure: 5
When he lusts for wealth, they all lust with their father;
when he lies, they go along with him and lie his lies;
and when he tries his tricks, they try the tricks he tries.
Now see who can twist this, take note who falsifies:
the new Judas and the old one yonder thus grow infamous together. 10

33,31· *Diu cristenheit gelepte nie sô gar nâch wâne.*

The Christian people never lived so darkly drifting.
Those who should teach them have no sense of the good, the uplifting.
An ignorant layman acting so—what an outrage that would be:
they sin, though, and have no fear; so God is their enemy.
They go their way to Hell pointing us toward Heaven.   5
Who follows just their words, they tell us laymen,
and not their works, that man is saved, no doubt about it, *there.*
Priests should be more chaste than simple laymen are.
From what scriptures have they managed to infer
they labor in great numbers, and are diligent, where they bring down a
handsome woman?   10

102,1. *Diu minne lât sich nennen dâ.*

Minne lets her name be said
where she herself will never come:
familiar in the mouths of fools, house-trained, couth—
and in their hearts a stranger.
Noble women, watch yourselves!   5
Keep your Yes from youngsters hid,
so it will be no child's game.
Born enemies, Minne and raw youth!
How often in a handsome figure
one sees *the person*—sadly, false.   10
You must first study why, how, when, where, *and on whom*—this most important—
you so bestow your loving *Yes!* that it is fitting there, and well accordant.
See, Minne, see who studies so: let *that* one be your child—
that man, that woman; out with everyone else.

81,7. *Wer sieht den lewen wer sieht den risen.*

Who slays the lion? Who slays the giant?
Who overcomes this one, that one?
Every man who rules himself has done this,
who brings his body under watch and all his members
out of wildness to the haven of staid discipline.   5
Borrowed breeding, shamefastness for strangers—
for some short while, perhaps, that glitters.
The gloss comes on quickly and quickly wears thin.

79,25. *Swer sich ze friunde gewinnen lât.*

Who lets himself be won as friend,
and has this strength: that he can stand,
without wavering, to be held on to—
one can cherish such a friend, one will want to.
So often I have chosen out as friend   5
a man, when he stood fast, so rounded,
seek as I might to hold him I'd befriended,
I had to lose him in the end.

30,29. *Swer sich des stæten friundes durch übermuot behêret.*

Whoever lords it over his true friend, like one superior,
whoever dishonors his own in order to honor a stranger,
would come to know, were he offended too by those established higher,
that fast, back-slapping friendship falls apart, fast, once tested:
when the new friend's called upon to put up life and fortune for his sake.   5
We've learned: those who have switched so on the make
were brought back by distress to their *born* friends, whose friendship lasted.
That shall happen often in the dispensation of the Lord.
And I have heard the folks affirm, agreeing with this word:
"In times of need a man shall know the faithful friend, the trusty sword."   10

26,13. *Die wîsen râtent swer ze himelrîche welle.*

The wise men counsel: whoever wants to enter Heaven
should set a watch upon, and guard with every weapon
the way, lest one who'd cast him back should rise up before him.
One enemy's called Death, who brings his grief to the way there;
and next to him rides one severely banished, Fire is his name;   5
then one they call Usury, who has brought scandal, shame,
upon this very path—and others who waylay you, many another:
Envy and Hate, they too have set themselves upon the way,
and Avarice beyond all bounds, who covets shamelessly.
And scores more, galloping ahead, whose names I did not get to say.   10

[trans. Frederick Goldin]

Under the Linden

By Walther von der Vogelweide

1. Under the linden tree
down at the meadow,
where there was both our bed,
there you can find,
beautifully arranged,
broken flowers and grass.
At the edge of the forest in a dale,
tandaradei
the nightingale sang beautifully.

2. I went down
to the meadow,
and my lover was there already.
I was welcomed by him
in such a manner,
my Lady (Virgin Mary?)!
that I will be filled with bliss forever.
Did he kiss me? More than thousand times,
tandaradei
see, how red my lips are.

3. He had arranged
so richly
a bed out of flowers.
If anyone passes by on that walkway
she or he will always chuckle
with deep sympathy.

Judging by the roses s/he may,
tandaradei,
recognize where my head was positioned.

4. If anyone were to know
that he was lying with me,
which God may forbid, I would be ashamed.
How he caressed me,
may this never, never
be found out; only he and I
and a little bird should know,
tandardei,
that will be loyal to us.

[trans. Albrecht Classen]

THE UNFORTUNATE LORD HEINRICH

By Hartmann von Aue

artmann von Aue (ca. 1160–1210) was one of the most famous medieval German poets of Arthurian romances and courtly love poetry. We know virtually nothing about his biography, except for what he relates in his literary works. But we can be certain that he hailed from Swabia in southwestern Germany and was a knight who had joined the Crusade of 1196–1197. In ca. 1210 Gottfried von Strassburg mentioned in his Tristan that Hartmann, his great model, was still alive. Hartmann "translated" Chrétien de Troyes' romance Erec (Erec, rather freely) and Yvain (Iwein, rather narrowly) into Middle High German. In the first, the protagonist runs into the problem that he is too dedicated to his wife, Enite, and abandons all of his social obligations, and has then to work very hard for the rest of the romance to regain his true status as a knight. In Iwein, the protagonist marries fairly early on the widow of a king whom he had killed in battle, but then returns to his knightly quests and forgets his wife Laudine. When she rejects him as her husband, he loses his mind and roams the forest, not wearing any clothes and eating raw flesh. After he has regained his human status, he strives for a long time to return to his previous status as knight and to earn his wife's respect and love once again. Hartmann also composed the religious narrative Gregorius, which is indirectly based on the ancient tale of Oedipus, with the protagonist, the product of incest, sleeping with his own mother and then retiring to a lonely island to do penance. Ultimately, God forgives him and calls him back to society to serve for the rest of his life as pope. The short verse narrative Lord Henry (ca. 1190) belongs to some of the best literary short stories of all times. Hartmann also composed eighteen courtly love poems.

There was a knight so learned
that he read in books
whatever he found written there.
His name was Hartmann and
he was a vassal of the House of Aue.
He began searching around
in various kinds of books,
looking through them to see
whether he might find something
with which he could make
oppressive hours more pleasant,
things of such a nature
which would do honor to God
and with which he could
endear himself to his fellow men.
Now he will begin to interpret for you
a tale which he found written.
It is for this reason that he has mentioned his name
so that he would not be
without reward for the work
which he has expended on it
and so that whoever might hear it recited or might read it
after his [Hartmann's] death
might pray
to God for the salvation of his soul.
One says that he is his own intercessor
and redeems himself thereby
who intercedes for the sins of another.

The story which he read tells of a lord living in Swabia in whom no quality was lacking that a knight in the flower of manhood should have to win full esteem. No one in all those lands was regarded so highly. He had at his disposal lineage as well as power and wealth. Also, he possessed capabilities in many areas. However sufficient his possessions were, however flawless his ancestry, which was doubtless comparable to that of princes, still he was not nearly so rich by reason of birth and possessions as he was because of his sense of dignity and noble attitude.

His name was very well known. He was called Lord Heinrich and was born of the House of Aue. His heart had foresworn duplicity and ill-breeding, and he kept this oath with constancy to the end of his days. His honor and conduct were without the slightest fault. That abundance of worldly honors one could rightly wish for had been lavished upon him. And he knew how to increase these honors through his many sterling qualities. He was a flower of young manhood, a mirror of the joy of the world, a diamond of constant loyalty, a full crown of courtly behavior. He was a refuge to those in need, a shield of protection for his kin. His generosity weighed the amount to be given against the need. Both excess and lack were foreign to him. He carried the wearisome burden of honors upon his back. He was a bridge stretching forth help and was well-versed in singing of courtly love. Thus he knew how to gain the honor and glory of the world. He embodied all the qualities of the courtly gentleman and showed mature wisdom.

When Lord Heinrich had thus attained the enjoyment of honor, possessions, a happy heart, and earthly joy—he was praised and esteemed as the first among his kinfolk—his lofty existence was turned into a life of utter humiliation. In his case, as also with Absalom was made clear, as Holy Scripture has told us, the empty crown of worldly sweetness falls from its place of highest esteem into dust under foot. There it says, *media vita in morte sumus*, which means we are hovering in the midst of death when we think we are living to the fullest.

The stability of this world, its constant and best wealth, power, and majesty can be mastered by no one. We can see a true picture of that happening with the candle which turns to ashes in the act of giving forth light. We are made of fragile stuff. Just look how our joy dissolves in tears. Life's sweetness is mixed with bitter gall. Our blossom must fall just when it seems to be thriving best. Heinrich's fate made very evident that he who lives on this earth in great esteem is despised in the sight of God. Through God's command he plunged from his esteemed position into a despicable state of misery: he fell victim to leprosy. When the grave chastisement became evident on his body, he was repulsive to everyone. However pleasant all the world found him before, now he was so repulsive that people avoided looking at him. The noble and wealthy Job met with this fate, too. In the midst of good fortune he piteously found himself on a dung heap.

When poor Heinrich first began to realize that the world found him repugnant, he behaved as most people in a similar situation do. His reaction to his bitterly felt anguish differed greatly from the patience of Job. The good man Job suffered with patient bearing all the afflictions that came his way so that his soul might find joy. The disease and tribulations which he suffered from the world were occasions for him to praise God and he was happy. Alas, poor Heinrich did not at all react in this manner. He was gloomy and dejected. His soaring heart sank, his buoyant joy went under. His self-esteem tumbled. Honey turned to gall. A sudden dark thunderclap shattered his noontime. A cloud, thick and sullen, enveloped the radiance of his sun. Many a sigh escaped him at the thought of having to leave such honor behind. Repeatedly he cursed and damned the day of his birth.

And yet a little joy was left to him. He still had one consolation. He had often heard that there were several different strains of the disease and some of them were curable. Hence his hopes and thoughts were quite mixed. He thought that he could perhaps be cured, and so he hurried off to Montpellier to seek medical advice. Here he quickly found nothing but the sad news that he would never recover. He received the news with disappointment and rode off toward Salerno and here also sought the skills of experienced doctors in the hope of being cured.

The best physician whom he found there immediately gave him a strange answer: he was curable and yet he would never be cured. "How can that be?" asked Heinrich. "What you are saying is quite impossible. If I am curable, then I'll recover. And whatever is imposed upon me in the way of a fee or however strenuous the treatment might be, I'm quite confident that I can accomplish it." "Give up your hopes," the doctor replied. "I'll tell you the nature of your sickness, although my explanation won't do you any good. For a cure a certain medicine is all that is necessary. Hence you are curable. However, no one is so wealthy or has such keen intellectual powers that he can attain it. Thus you will forever remain uncured, unless God wishes to be your physician."

"Why are you trying to discourage me?" asked poor Heinrich. "I have a great deal of wealth at my disposal. Unless you want to act contrary to your medical skills and medical ethics, not to mention that you would be turning down my silver and gold, I'll make you so favorably disposed toward me that you will quite readily heal me." "It's not my good will that is lacking," replied the doctor. "And if the medicine were of such a kind that one could find it for sale or that one could acquire it by any means, I would not let you languish. But that is unfortunately not the case. Hence you must of necessity remain without my help. You would have to find a virgin of marriageable age who would be willing to suffer death for your sake. Now it is not the usual state of affairs among people that someone freely takes such an act upon himself. Nothing else is necessary for a cure than the blood from the heart of such a girl. This would be a cure for your disease."

Now poor Heinrich saw clearly that it would be impossible for anyone to find a person who would willingly die for him. Thus the one consolation which had made him undertake the journey was taken from him. And from this time on, he had no hope left concerning his recovery. Because of this the pain of his heart was so great and strong that it infuriated him most of all that he should go on living. He journeyed home and began distributing his lands as well as his personal effects according to his own feelings and the judicious advice of others as to where it would do the most good. With discrimination he increased the means of his poor relatives and also gave material comfort to poor people who were strangers to him so that God might have mercy on his soul. Monasteries received the rest. Thus did he free himself from all his major possessions except for a farm on cleared land. Hither he fled from people. Heinrich was not the only one to bewail his tragic affliction. In all the lands where he was known and even in foreign lands where he was known only by reputation people grieved for him.

The man who had already been farming this land for a long time was a free peasant who never had any of the great troubles which other peasants had whose lords were worse and did not spare them taxation and other fees. Whatever this farmer did willingly seemed good enough to his lord. What is more, he protected him from any violence inflicted by outside parties. Because of this no one of his class in the whole land was as well off as he. To this peasant came his lord, poor Heinrich. Whatever Heinrich had spared him earlier, how that was now repaid! How handsomely he reaped the benefits of this! The farmer was not at all bothered by what he had to do for Heinrich's sake. Out of loyalty he was determined to endure willingly the burdensome task that was now his lot because of his lord. He spared no means to make Heinrich comfortable.

God had given the peasant a good life according to his class. He was capable of strenuous physical labor, and he had a hard-working wife. In addition, he had beautiful children who really bring joy to a man's life. One of the children, as one says, was a girl, a child eight years old. Her actions revealed her real goodness. She would never budge from her lord even a foot. To gain his favor and greeting she served him constantly in every way she could with her kind attention. She had such a pleasing way about her that she could have fittingly been the child of the emperor in her loveliness.

The others were smart enough to know how to avoid him without being too obvious. But she fled to him all the time and nowhere else. She alone made the time pass quickly for him. With the pure goodness of a child she had opened her heart to her lord so she could always be found at his feet. With pleasing eagerness she attended her lord. He, in turn, tried to please her in whatever way he could. Her lord gave her in abundance whatever fitted in with her childhood games. Also in his favor was the fact that children are so easy to win over. He got for her whatever he found for sale—a mirror, hair ribbons—whatever children find nice—a belt and a ring. By means of these attentions he brought things to the point that she became so close to him that he called her his bride. The dear child never let him remain alone. She thought of him as a completely healthy person. However strongly she was influenced by the gifts and playthings, still it was before all else a sweet disposition, a gift of God, which made this way of acting please her. Her devotion manifested great kindness.

Once, when the unfortunate Heinrich had already spent three years there and God had tormented him with great bodily suffering, the peasant, his wife, and the girl I have already mentioned were one day sitting together with him as they worked. They were lamenting over the sufferings of their lord, and they had every reason to be sad. For they feared that his death would work great harm for them in that they might lose their good standing and their property, and that a different lord would be much more severe with them. These thoughts kept running through their minds until the peasant thus began to inquire, saying, "My dear lord, I would like to ask a question, if I may do so with your favor. There are so many doctors of medicine in Salerno. Why is it that none of them was able to find help for you with his skill? Sir, that is what surprises me." Poor Heinrich emitted a sigh of bitter anguish from the bottom of his heart. Such was the sadness with which he spoke that sobs punctuated his speech: "I deserved this shameful humiliation at God's hands. For you saw very well how formerly my gate stood wide open to worldly joy and that no one among his family and relatives had his wish fulfilled better than I. This was impossible since I always had my way completely. During this time I took very little notice of Him who in His goodness had given me this life. My attitude was that of all fools of this world who are persuaded that they can have honor and possessions without God. Thus did my foolish notion deceive me. For I very seldom looked to Him from whose favor many honors and possessions came my way. When, then, the Heavenly Gatekeeper had enough of my arrogance, He closed the gates of happiness to me. Now I'll never enter there! My foolish attitude spoiled that for me. As punishment God imposed an infirmity upon me of such a nature that no one can free me of it. Now I have become repugnant to the common people. Those of prominence take no notice of me. However lowly the man who looks at me, I am still more lowly than he. He shows me his contempt by casting his eyes from me. Now the loyalty in you really becomes evident for the first time—that you let me stay with you in my wretched condition and that you do not in the least flee from me. But although you do not shun me, although I am loved by you, if by no one else, and however much you have me to thank for your prosperity, still you would easily resign yourself to my death. Who in the world was ever so worthless and so wretched? I used to be your lord, now I am your suppliant. Dear friend, by keeping me here in my sickness you are earning for yourself, your wife, and my bride life everlasting.

"I'll gladly tell you what you asked me. In Salerno I was not able to find a doctor who dared or wanted to take me into his charge. For the means by which I was to recover from my sickness was to be of such a kind that no one in the world is at all able to gain it. I was told nothing else but that I would have to find a virgin fully able to marry who would be willing to suffer death for my sake. Hence I must bear shameful misery till my death. May God send it to me quickly!"

The innocent girl heard what he told her father, for the dear child had the feet of her dear lord resting in her lap. One could easily compare her childlike attitude to the goodness of the angels. She understood what he said and forgot not a word. She kept thinking about it in her heart until she went to bed that night where she lay at the feet of her father and mother as she was accustomed to do. After they had both fallen asleep, she pressed many a deep sigh from her heart. Her sadness because of the sufferings of her lord became so great that the flood from her eyes poured over the feet of her sleeping parents. Thus did the dear child awaken them.

When they felt the tears, they awoke and asked her what was the matter with her and what kind of distress it could be that caused her to weep so quietly. At first she did not want to tell them anything. But when her father repeatedly begged and threatened her saying she had to tell them, she spoke: "You could well weep with me. What can cause us more trouble about our lord but that we shall lose him and with him give up our possessions and good standing? We shall never again get a lord so good that he would treat us the way he does." They said, "Daughter, you are right, but sorrowing and lamenting are not going to help us one bit. Dear child, don't talk about it. We are just as sorry as you are. Unfortunately, we are not able to help him in the least. God is the one who has taken him from us. If anyone else had done it, we would have to curse him."

Thus did they silence her. That night as well as the whole next day she remained dejected. Whatever anyone else did, these thoughts never left her heart. Then finally everybody went to bed the following night. When she had lain down on her usual place for sleeping, she again bathed everything with the tears from her eyes, for she bore hidden in her heart the greatest amount of goodness that I ever heard of in a child. What child had ever acted as she did? One thing she was completely resolved to do: if she was still alive the next day, she would in fact give her life for her lord.

This thought made her happy and light-hearted. She had not a care in the world except for one irritating fear: when she told her lord her intention, he might back down; and if she made her plans known to all three of them, she would not find any constancy in them and they would not let her go through with it. So greatly was she disturbed about this that her mother and father were awakened by it as in the previous night. They sat up facing her and said, "Look, what is the matter with you? It is very foolish for you to take this sad situation so completely to heart since no one can do anything about it anyway. Why don't you let us sleep?" Thus did they begin to take her to task: what good did her crying do since no one could prevent for make good the misfortune? And so for a second time they thought they had silenced the dear girl. But they little realized what she had resolved to do. The girl replied to them, "As my lord told us, he is quite able to be healed. And unless you want to keep me from it, I am suitable medicine for him. I am a virgin and have the right disposition. Before I see him go to ruin, I would rather die for him." When they heard this, both mother and father became sad and troubled. The father asked his daughter to put such thoughts out of her mind and to promise her lord only what she could really carry out, for her present plan was out of the question for her. "Daughter, you are just a child and your devotion in such matters is too great. You are not able to go through with it the way you have just proclaimed. You have no idea what death is like. When it comes to such a pass that there is no way out and that you must die, then you would much prefer to go on living if you could bring it about. For you have never entered into a more deplorable pit. So, shut your mouth. If you ever in the future talk about such things again, you'll get what's good for you!" And so he thought that by pleas and intimidation he had silenced her. But he was not able to do it.

His daughter answered him, "Dear father, however young and inexperienced I may be, I still have sense enough to understand from what I've heard the harsh fact that death of the body is violent and severe. But whoever lives a long life filled with trials and hardships doesn't have it very easy either. For after a person has struggled and made it to a ripe old age through much hard work, then he still has to suffer death anyway. If he then suffers the loss of his soul, it would be better for him never to have been born. I have the opportunity, and because of it I shall always praise God, of being able to give my young body in return for eternal life. Now, you should not try to make it hard for me. I want to do the best thing for you as well as for me. I alone am able to preserve us from suffering and harm, as I shall now explain to you. We have honor and possessions. These come from the favorable disposition of my lord. For he has never spoken a command to cause us suffering, and he never took away any of our possessions. As long as he remains alive, things will go well for us. If we let him die, we shall also go to ruin. I want to keep him alive for our sakes through a well thought-out plan so that things will go well for all of us. Now let me do it, for it has to be."

When the mother say how serious her daughter was, she began to cry and said, "Remember, dear child, how great the hardships were that I suffered for your sake, and let me receive a better reward than the words I hear you speaking. You are going to break my heart. Make your words a little more pleasant for me to hear. You are going to forfeit salvation by God by what you are doing to us. Don't you remember his commandment? He certainly commanded and asked that one show father and mother love and honor, and as a reward he promised that the soul would be saved and one would enjoy a long life on earth. You say you want to offer your life for the joy of both of us. But you will actually be filling our lives completely with suffering. Your father and I enjoy living because of you. What good to us are life, property, earthly well-being if we have to do without you? You should not cause us to worry. My dear daughter, you ought to be a joy for the both of us, our pleasure unmixed with suffering, a bright delight for us to look upon, the cheer of our life, a flower among your kin, a staff for our old age. And if through your own fault we have to stand at your graveside, you will be forever cut off from God's favor. That is what you will earn in regard to us! Daughter, if you wish to be good to us, then for the sake of our Lord's favor, change your attitude and forget these ideas I have heard from you."

"Mother," she replied, "I give you and father full credit for how well you have provided for me, as a mother and father should provide for their child. This attention I experience from your hands day after day. From your good favor I have a soul and a beautiful body. Everyone who sees me says in praise that I'm the most beautiful child he has seen in his whole life. To whom should I attribute this favor besides God, if not to the two of you. For this reason I shall always stand ready to obey your command. How great is my obligation in this!

"Mother, wonderful woman, since I have you to thank for both body and soul, let it be with your approval that I deliver both of them from the devil that I may give myself to God. Certainly the life of this world is nothing but loss to the soul. Besides, until now worldly desires have not touched me. I want to thank God now that he has granted me the insight, young though I am, to look with contempt upon this fragile life. I wish to deliver myself into God's dominion as pure as I am now. If I were to continue living, I'm afraid that the sweetness of the world would drag me down underfoot as it has done to many whom its sweetness has also deceived. Then I must even be kept from God. To Him we should bewail the fact that I must live even till tomorrow. I don't find the world a nice place at all. Its comfort is great hardship, its pleasure great suffering, its sweet reward bitter want, its long life a sudden death. Nothing is more certain than that today's joy will be followed by tomorrow's suffering. And finally at the end is always death. That is an anguish to make you weep. Neither noble birth, nor riches, nor beauty, nor strength, nor exhilaration can protect one. Virtue and honor help one in the face of death no more than lowliness and vice. Our life and our youthful vitality have no more substance than clouds or dust. Our stability trembles like a leaf. Whether man or woman, whoever likes to fill himself with smoke is a very misguided fool who doesn't know how to think things out rightly and who simply follows the world. For over the foul dung is spread for us a silk cloth. He whom this splendor leads astray is born for hell and has lost nothing less than both body and soul. Now call to mind, dear woman, the love you as a mother owe to me and temper the sorrow which you have because of me. Then father will think things over in similar fashion. I well know he doesn't begrudge me salvation. He is a man honest enough to recognize well that you could not long enjoy having me even if I remain alive. If I were to remain here with you unmarried for two or three years, then my lord is probably dead, and we shall very likely suffer such distress from poverty that you will not be able to give any suitor a sufficient dowry on my behalf, and I would have to lead such an impoverished existence that you would rather see me dead. But let us forget about this problem for a minute. Even if nothing were causing us distress and my dear lord were to be preserved for us and went on living until I were wed to a man who was well-off and respected—you would then think that everything had turned out for the best for me. My heart has told me otherwise. If it turns out that I love him, that would bring distress. If I find him repulsive, that is as bad as being dead. In either case my lot is one of suffering, a life filled with hardship and far from comfort with all sorts of things that cause women trouble and lead them astray from joy.

"Now put me in possession of that full abundance that never dwindles. A Free Yeoman seeks my hand to whom I give myself gladly. You should certainly give me to Him. Then my life is really well taken care of. His plow works very well for him, his farm is filled with all provisions. There neither horse nor cattle die. There on is not vexed by crying children. There it is neither too warm nor too cold. There no one grows old as the years pass: older people become younger. There one finds neither frost nor hunger. There suffering of any kind is absent. There one finds complete happiness without any hardship. To Him I wish to go and flee such fields that rain and hail destroy and floods wash away, fields with which one struggles and always has. What one is so tediously able to gain through toil in the course of a year is suddenly destroyed in half a day. These are the farm lands I wish to leave. Let them receive my curse. You love me. That is as it should be. Now I would gladly see that your love does not turn out to be the opposite. If you can come to see that I have the right understanding of the situation, and if you wish me to have possessions and honors, then let me go to our Lord Jesus Christ whose grace is so constant that it never fades, and who has as great a love for me, poor as I am, as for a queen. It is certainly His commandment that I be obedient to you, for I have my life from you. This I do without regret. But at the same time I must not be disloyal to myself. I have always heard people say that whoever makes someone else happy in such a way that he himself becomes unhappy and whoever treats someone else like a king and shows only contempt for himself—that this is too much devotion. I certainly want to be obedient to you by showing you devotion, but above all else I must be true to myself! If you want to keep me from my salvation, then I would rather let you weep a bit over me than not to be clear about what I owe to myself. I constantly long to go where I shall find complete happiness. Besides, you have other children. Let them be your joy and thus console yourselves over losing me. No one can keep me from saving my lord and myself! Mother, I heard you complain just now saying it would cause your heart great pain if you should have to stand at my grave. You will most certainly be spared this. You will not stand at my grave because no one will let you see where I shall die. This will take place in Salerno. There death shall free us four from every kind of misery. Through death we shall all be saved, I much more so than you."

When they saw the child so eager for death speaking so wisely and acting in contradiction to all human norms, they began to consider that no tongue in a child's mouth could manifest such wisdom and such insight. They were convinced the Holy Spirit must be the cause of these ideas, who also was active in St. Nicholas as he lay in the cradle and taught him wisdom so he turned his childlike goodness toward God. They considered in their hearts that they did not want to and should not at all prevent her from doing what she had taken upon herself to do. The idea must have come to her from God.

The peasant and his wife turned cold with grief. They sat there in bed and for love of their child so forgot their tongue and were so out of their senses that neither of them could then speak a single word. The mother was torn by a fit of weeping in her suffering. Thus they both sat sad and dejected until they realized what little good their grieving was doing them. Since nothing was able to change her mind, the only sensible thing for them to do was to grant her wish willingly because they could never lose her in a better way. If they showed opposition to her plan, it could get them into a lot of trouble with their lord and other than that they would accomplish nothing by it. With a show of agreement they then said they were happy with her plan.

This made the innocent girl happy. When it had barely become day she went to where her lord was sleeping. His bride called to him saying, "Lord, are you asleep?" "No, I'm not, my bride, but tell me, why are you up so early today?" "Lord, my grief over your illness forces me." He said, "My bride, you show very well in the way you treat me that you are sorry. May God repay you accordingly. But there is nothing that can be done about it." "Truly, my dear lord, there is help for you. Since you can be helped, I shall not let you wait another day. Lord, you told us that if you had a virgin who would willingly suffer death on your account, you would thereby be healed. I myself want to be that girl, so help me God. Your life is more useful than mine."

The lord thanked her very much for her intentions and in sorrow his eyes filled unnoticed with tears. He said, "My bride, death is by no means a pleasant affair as you perhaps picture it to yourself. You have made it very clear to me that you would help me if you could. That is enough for me from you. I know your affectionate heart. Your intentions are pure and good. I desire nothing more from you. You are not able to carry out for me what you have just said. May God reward you for the devotion you have shown toward me. Since I have already tried several remedies, I would be the laughingstock of the people here if this didn't do any good and my disease continued as before. My bride, you act like children do when they are impulsive. They act immediately on whatever comes to mind, whether it be good or bad, and regret it afterwards. My bride, you are acting that way, too. You are convinced of what you are saying now. If, however, someone were to take you up on it so that your intention would be carried out, you would very probably regret it." He asked her to think it over a little more. "Your mother and father," he said, "cannot easily do without you. I should not desire something that would cause suffering to people who have always been good to me. Whatever the both of them advise, dear bride, that you should do." In saying this he smiled broadly for he had no idea what would then take place. Thus did the noble man speak to her.

The mother and father said, "Dear lord, you have been very good to us and shown us great respect. The only fitting response for us is to repay you in kind. Our daughter desires to suffer death for your sake. We are quite happy to give her our blessing, so completely has she convinced us. It was not a quick decision on her part. For three days now she has been constantly urging us to give our blessing to her plan. This she has now achieved. May God let you be healed through her. We are willing to give her up for your sake."

His bride was offering to die in order to deliver him from his illness, and her determination was evident. This caused much joylessness and displays of sorrow. Quite different were the worries they had, the three of them on the one hand and the girl on the other. The father and mother began to weep bitterly, and they had every right to weep over the death of their very dear child. The lord also began to think about the devotion of the child, and such sadness took hold of him that he wept much and could not at all make up his mind whether it was better to go through with it or let things be. Because of fear the girl also cried. She was afraid he would become faint-hearted and not go through with it. Thus they were all dejected and sought no cheer. Finally their lord, poor Heinrich, pulled himself together and thanked all three of them for their loyalty and generous care. The girl was exuberant that he was willing to go along with her plan. He prepared himself as quickly as possible for the trip to Salerno. What was suitable for the girl was quickly ready. Beautiful horses and expensive clothes which she had never worn before: ermine, velvet, and the best sable one could find. These were the girl's clothes.

Now who could fully express the deep sorrow and lamenting, the bitter suffering of her mother and the misery of her father? The departure of their dear child would have been a torment for them as they sent her away healthy to her death never to be seen by them again, except that the pure goodness of God which gave the child's heart the determination to die willingly relieved their distress. It had come about without any help from them. Hence they were spared all self-incrimination and depression. For otherwise it would have been a miracle that their hearts did not break. Their sorrow turned to joy so that afterwards they suffered no distress about the child's death.

And so the girl rode off toward Salerno happily and willingly with her lord. What could now trouble her except that the journey was so long and her life was thus prolonged? And when he had finally brought her there as he had planned, he found his doctor and with great elation told him he had found the kind of girl he had told him to get. Then he let him have a look at her. This seemed unbelievable to the doctor. He said, "Child, did you reach this decision on your own or were you influenced in your plan by entreaties and threats from your lord?" The girl answered that these ideas came from her heart.

This surprised him greatly and he took her aside and begged her in all seriousness to tell him whether her lord had persuaded her by means of threats. He said, "Child, you must seriously consider the matter further and I'll tell you exactly why. If you were to die and you didn't do it willingly, then your young life would be at an end, but unfortunately it would not help us the least little bit. Now keep nothing concerning your decision from me. I'll tell you what is going to happen to you. I undress you. Then you stand there completely unclothed, and the shame that you certainly will fee as you stand there naked before me will be great indeed. Then I bind your arms and legs. If you have any regard for your physical well-being, then consider the suffering yet to come. I cut into you all the way to your heart and tear it still beating from you. Now, young lady, tell me how you feel about all this. Never has a child so suffered as you are going to suffer under my hands. That I should carry it out and witness it fills me with great trepidation. Consider how your body will be treated. And if you regret it the least little bit, then I have performed my work and you have lost your life in vain." Again he entreated her in all seriousness that unless she knew she had great determination, she should forget the whole idea.

The girl said cheerfully, for she well understood that on this day death would help her escape from worldly cares, "May God reward you, dear sir, that you have told me the complete truth. As a matter of fact, I am a little hesitant. A certain doubt has arisen in me. I want to tell you exactly what kind of doubt it is that has taken hold of me. I am afraid that our efforts will not be brought to completion because of your cowardice. You talk like a woman. You have about as much courage as a rabbit. Your qualms about my dying are excessive. It's certainly true that you are not taking care of things very well with your great skill. I am a woman and have the nerve. If you are not afraid to cut me open, I certainly have the courage to suffer it. The gruesome details of the operation which you have just explained to me—I was aware of all that apart from you. I certainly would not have come here if I didn't know that I am so firm of purpose I can easily endure it. I have lost all paleness, if you please, and the firmness of my resolve has so increased that I'm standing here about as fearful as if I were about to go dancing. For no bodily suffering that is over within one day is so great that I should think that this one day was too high a price to pay for eternal life which never passes away. Nothing should make you uneasy concerning me since my mind is made up. If you are confident you can give my lord his health again and give me eternal life, then for heaven's sake, do it soon. Show what kind of doctor you are. He in whose name it shall be done is urging me on, and I well know for whose sake I am doing it. He gives due recognition to service and lets nothing go unrewarded. I know well that He Himself says that whoever performs great service, such a person's reward will accordingly be the greatest. Hence I shall consider this way of dying a sweet affliction because of such certain reward. It would certainly be a foolish attitude if I were to turn my back on the heavenly crown. Then I would certainly be silly, for I am of humble origin."

Now he had heard that she was completely unshakeable and he led her out again to the sick man, her lord, and said to him, "Nothing can stop us. Your girl is completely suitable. Be happy, I shall soon make you healthy." Again he led her to his private room where her lord saw nothing and closed and bolted the door to him. He did not want to let him see how her end would come about. In the room that was well supplied with suitable medicines he ordered the girl to undress immediately. This made her happy and joyful. She tore the garments at the stays. Almost at once she stood there undressed and was naked and bare, but was not the least bit ashamed.

When the doctor looked at her, he realized in his heart that a creature more beautiful than she was rare in the whole world. He felt so completely sorry for her that his heart and mind almost made him hesitate. The generous girl saw a high table standing there. He commanded her to climb upon it. He tied her to it tightly and took in his hands a sharp knife that was lying there that he used for such operations. It was long and broad, but it did not at all cut as well as he would have wished. Since she was not to survive, her suffering saddened him and he wanted to make her death as pleasant as he could. Next to him a very good whetstone was lying. He took the knife and began stroking it across the stone very carefully, thereby sharpening the knife. Poor Heinrich, who was standing there in front of the door and who disturbed her joy, heard this and it saddened him greatly that he should never see her alive again. And so he began to look around and he searched until he found a hole going through the wall. Through the crack he caught a glimpse of her bound and naked. Her body was very lovely. Then he looked at her and at himself, and a whole new attitude took hold of him. What he had thought before no longer seemed good to him. And in an instant his former attitude was transformed to one of new goodness.

As he saw her in all her beauty, he said to himself, "You are really harboring a foolish thought in that you desire to live one day apart from His approval against whom no one can accomplish anything. Since you certainly have to die, you really don't know what you are doing in not bearing with great willingness this wretched existence God has given you. Besides, you do not really know whether the child's death will cure you. Whatever God has assigned for you, that you must always let happen. I will not witness the death of the child."

He made up his mind immediately and began pounding on the wall and asked to be let in. The doctor said, "I don't have the time to open up for you." "No, doctor, I must talk to you." "Sir, I can't. Wait until this is finished." "No, doctor, we must talk before that." "Well, tell me what you want through the wall." "It's really not that sort of thing." Immediately he let him in. Then poor Heinrich went to where he saw the girl bound. He said to the doctor, "This child is so lovely. I just cannot see her die. May God's will in my regard be done. We must let her up again. I shall give you the silver in accordance with our agreement, but you must let the girl live." This the doctor of Salerno was happy to hear and he obeyed, immediately untying the girl.

When the girl realized she was not going to die, she took it with a heavy heart. She acted not at all as she usually did nor in accordance with her upbringing. She had her fill of sorrow, beat her breast, tearing and pulling at herself. No one could have looked at her without crying, so dolefully did she behave. With great bitterness she shrieked, "Woe is me, poor me! What is going to happen to me now? Have I then lost the splendid heavenly crown? It was to be given to me as my reward for this ordeal. Now I am really dead. Alas, powerful Christ, what honor has been taken from us, my lord and me! We are both bereft of the honors which were predestined for us. If this had been completed, his body would have been restored to health and I would have been eternally blessed."

Thus did she again and again ask to die. But no matter how desperately she longed for it, her pleadings were in vain. Since no one did as she wanted, she began to scold, saying, "I have to suffer because of my lord's timidity. People didn't tell me the truth. That I've found out for myself. I always heard people say you were upright and good and had the steadfastness of a man. So help me God, they lied! The world has always been deceived in you. You always were and still are a great big coward. This is obvious to me through the fact that, even though I am brave enough to suffer, you don't have the courage to permit it. Lord, what caused you to become afraid when I was being bound? After all, there was a thick wall between you and me. My lord, don't you have enough backbone to be able to stand another person's death? I can promise you explicitly nobody is going to do anything to you. And the whole affair is to your advantage."

However much she pleaded and begged and even scolded, it did not help her a bit. She still had to go on living. However much she scolded, poor Heinrich accepted it calmly and with good grace, as an able knight should who never was lacking in refinement and good breeding. After the luckless visitor had dressed the girl again and had paid the doctor as he had agreed to do, he rode straight home again to his own country although he well knew that at home he would find nothing but ridicule and sarcasm from all sides. All this he put in God's hands.

In the meantime, the dear girl had scolded and cried herself almost to death. Then He, *Cordis Speculator*, for whom the gate of the heart is never locked, saw clearly her devotion and her distress. Since He in His sweet providence had thought it best to try them both just as completely as He had tried the wealthy Job, Holy Christ made manifest how dear devotion and compassion are to Him. He freed them both from all their miseries and at that very moment cleansed Heinrich and made him completely healthy. Good Lord Heinrich improved to the extent that while still on the journey he regained full health under the treatment of God our Lord and was just as he had been at the age of twenty. When they had thus been made happy, he had it announced at home in his own country to those who, he knew, would in their good will and sympathy rejoice in their hearts at his good fortune. Justly they would have to be joyful because of the favors God had shown him.

Those closest to him who knew he was coming rode out or went on foot three days toward him to welcome him. They would believe no one's word, only their own eyes. They saw the mysterious working of God manifested in the handsomeness of his body. Concerning the peasant and his wife, one can certainly presume, unless one wants to do them an injustice, that they did not remain at home. The joy they experienced can never be expressed in writing, for God provided them with a tasty feast for their eyes, namely, their daughter and their lord. Never did anyone experience joy equal to theirs when they saw both of them were healthy. They did not know how to act. Their greetings were a strange assortment of unusual ways of behaving. The happiness in their hearts was so great that a rain of tears from their eyes flooded their merriment. The report is certainly true that they kissed their daughter's lips well over three times.

The Swabians received him with a splendid gift, namely, a greeting filled with good will. God knows that an honest man, who has seen them at home, has to admit that no greater good will was ever shown than when they, his countrymen, welcomed him on his journey home. What happened afterwards? What more needs to be said? He was better off than before in material wealth and honor. All this he referred to God with great constancy and acted according to His commandment much more than he had previously. For this reason his honor rests on a solid foundation.

The peasant and his wife had well-earned possessions and honor for the way they had taken care of him. Nor was he so dishonest as to prevent them from having them. He gave them as their own on the spot the extensive farm, both the land and the people, where he had stayed while he was sick. His bride he treated as a courtly lady or even better, giving her all sorts of things and seeing to her pleasure. Justice demanded this of him.

At this time his counsellors began to advise him to marry and praised this institution. But their suggestions diverged. Then he told them what he planned to do. If it seemed good to them, he would send for those nearest him and bring the matter to a conclusion according to what they might advise him. He had invitations and summonses sent to whoever might be of help. When he had gotten them all there, both relatives and vassals, he explained his intentions to them. With one voice they said it was proper and opportune for him to marry. A lively dispute arose among them as they were giving their advice. One counselled in one direction, another in the opposite direction, as always happens when people are called upon to render advice. They could not agree at all.

Then Lord Heinrich spoke, "You all well know that a short time ago I was greatly repugnant and disgusting to people. Now no one shuns me. God's commandment has given me a sound body. Now tell me, in God's name, how can I repay the person whom I have to thank for the favor which God has bestowed on me; namely, that I have regained my health?" They said, "Promise that you and what you own shall ever be at this person's service."

His bride was standing nearby. He looked at her lovingly, and embracing her he said, "You have certainly all been told that I have this wonderful girl standing here by me to thank for having my health again. She is just as freeborn as I am. My every thought tells me to take her as my wife. May God grant that this seem fitting to you. Then I shall have her as my wife. Truly, if this cannot be, I will die without marrying, for I owe her my life and good standing. By God's grace I bid you all that this may find your favor."

All spoke at once that it would certainly be fitting. Priests were readily found who gave him to her in marriage. After a long and happy life they both gained possession of the eternal kingdom. May the same thing fall to the lot of us all at the end! May God help us to attain the reward which they received. Amen.

[trans. Frank Tobin]

DIVINA COMMEDIA: HELL

By Dante Alighieri

D ante Alighieri (1265–1321) is regarded as one of the most illustrious poets from the entire Middle Ages. His Divina Commedia (written between 1308 and his death in 1321) can be rightly identified as one of the most influential epic or allegorical poems ever written. It stands uniquely at the threshold of the Middle Ages, not yet being the harbinger of the early modern world, or the Renaissance, yet providing infinite inspiration for the next generations of Italian and European authors and poets. His Divina Commedia enjoys the same global reputation as Homer's Iliad and Odyssee and as Virgil's Aeneid. It is divided into three parts, Inferno, Purgatorio, and Paradiso, and in total consists of 33 cantos each, plus the introductory canto, for the perfect number of 100. Many if not most modern authors have studied Dante's work and prove to be deeply influenced by him in one way or another. In the early 1290s Dante published a collection of poems combined with autobiographical comments in his Vita Nuova. Here he already refers to his beloved Beatrice, who was later to become his spiritual guide in Paradiso, the third part of his Comedy, taking him into heaven. This major piece of world literature begins with Dante formulating thoughts about being lost in life, hence being a victim of, as we would say today, mid-life crisis. Upon entering Inferno, the ancient Roman poet Virgil meets him and functions as his guide down to the bottom and this first part deals with the many different sinners and sins that he had witnessed in his life. As much as the Divina Commedia was fictional, as much it also allowed Dante to get even with many of his real enemies, all of whom he placed down in hell. Nevertheless, the pilgrim Dante also comes across tragic lovers, such as Francesca and Paulo, whose suffering he grieves over deeply because they died over their adulterous love affair. Fundamentally, however, this allegorical romance represents the soul's journey through the three stages of human existence, from the depth of all being to the height in heaven.

CANTO I

Dante, astray in a wood, reaches the foot of a hill which he begins to ascend; he is hindered by three beasts; he turns back and is met by Virgil, who proposes to guide him into the eternal world.

Midway upon the journey of our life I found myself in a dark wood, where the right way was lost.[1] Ah! how hard a thing it is to tell what this wild and rough and difficult wood was, which in thought renews my fear! So bitter is it that death is little more. But in order to treat of the good that I found in it, I will tell of the other things that I saw there.

I cannot well report how I entered it, so full was I of slumber at that moment when I abandoned the true way. But after I had reached the foot of a hill, where that valley ended which had pierced my heart with fear, I looked upward, and saw its shoulders clothed already with the rays of the planet which leads man aright along every path. Then was the fear a little quieted which had lasted in the lake of my heart through the night that I had passed so piteously. And even as one who with spent breath, issued forth from the sea upon the shore, turns to the perilous water and gazes, so did my mind, which still was flying, turn back to look again upon the pass which never left person alive.

After I had rested a little my weary body, I again took my way along the desert slope, so that the firm foot was always the lower. And lo! almost at the beginning of the steep a she-leopard,[2] light and very nimble, which was covered with a spotted coat. And she did not withdraw from before my face, nay, hindered so my road that I often turned to go back.

The time was the beginning of the morning, and the Sun was mounting up with those stars that were with him when the Love Divine first set in motion those beautiful things;[3] so that the hour of the time and the sweet season were occasion to me of good hope concerning that wild beast with the dappled skin; but not so that the sight which appeared to me of a lion[4] did not give me fear. He appeared to be coming against me, with his head high and with ravening hunger, so that it appeared that the air was affrighted at him; and a she-wolf,[5] which in her leanness seemed laden with all cravings, and ere now had made many folk to live forlorn,—she brought on me so much heaviness, with the fear that came from the sight of her, that I lost hope of the height. And such as is he who gains willingly, and the time arrives which makes him lose, so that in all his thoughts he laments and is sad, such did the beast without peace make me, which, coming on against me, was pushing me back, little by little, thither where the Sun is silent.

While I was falling back to the low place, one who appeared faint-voiced through long silence presented himself before my eyes. When I saw him in the great desert, "Have pity on me!" I cried to him, "whatso thou be, whether shade or real man." He answered me: "Not man; man once I was, and my parents were Lombards, and both Mantuans by country. I was born *sub Julio,* though late,[6] and I lived at Rome under the good Augustus, at the time of the false and lying gods. I was a poet, and sang of that just son of Anchises who came from Troy, after proud Ilion had been burned. But thou, why dost thou return to such great annoy? Why dost thou not ascend the delectable mountain which is the source and cause of all joy?" "Art thou then that Virgil and that fount which pours forth so broad a stream of speech?" replied I with bashful front to him: "O honor and light of the other poets! may the long study avail me and the great love, which have made me search thy volume! Thou art my master and my author; thou alone art he from whom I took the fair style that has done me honour. Behold the beast because of which I turned; help me against her, famous sage, for she makes my veins and pulses tremble." "It behoves thee to hold another course," he replied, when he saw me weeping, "if thou wouldst escape from this savage place; for this beast, because of which thou criest out, lets not any one pass along her way, but so hinders him that she kills him; and she has a nature so malign and evil that she never sates her greedy will, and after food has more hunger than before. Many are the animals with which she wives, and there shall be more yet, until the hound shall come that will make her die of grief. He shall not feed on land or pelf, but wisdom and love and valor, and his birthplace shall be between Feltro and Feltro. Of that low Italy shall he be the salvation, for which the virgin Camilla died, and Euryalus, Turnus and Nisus of their wounds. He shall hunt her through every town till he shall have put her back again in Hell, there whence envy first sent her forth. Wherefore I think and deem it for thy best that thou follow me, and I will be thy guide, and will lead thee hence through the eternal place where thou shalt hear the despairing shrieks, shalt see the ancient spirits woeful who each proclaim the second death.[7] And then thou shalt see those who are contented in the fire, because they hope to come, whenever it may be, to the blessed folk; to whom if thou wouldst then ascend, there shall be a soul more worthy than I for that. With her I will leave thee at my departure; for that Emperor who reigns there above wills not, because I was rebellious[8] to His law, that through me any one should come into His city. In all parts He governs and there He reigns; there is His city and His lofty seat. O happy the man whom thereto He elects!" And I to him: "Poet, I beseech thee by that God whom thou didst not know, in order that I may escape this ill and worse, that thou lead me thither where thou now hast said, so that I may see the gate of St. Peter,[9] and those whom thou reportest so afflicted."

Then he moved on, and I held behind him.

CANTO II

Dante, doubtful of his own powers, is discouraged at the outset.—Virgil cheers him by telling him that he has been sent to his aid by a blessed Spirit from Heaven, who revealed herself as Beatrice.—Dante casts off fear, and the poets proceed.

The day was going, and the dusky air was taking the living things that are on earth from their fatigues, and I alone was preparing to sustain the war alike of the journey and of the woe, which my memory that errs not shall retrace.

O Muses, O lofty genius, now assist me! O memory that didst inscribe that which I saw, here shall thy nobility appear!

I began: —

"Poet, who guidest me, consider my power, if it be sufficient, before thou trust me to the deep pass. Thou sayest[1] that the parent of Silvius while still corruptible went to the immortal world and was there in the body; and truly if the Adversary of every ill was courteous to him, it seems not unmeet to the man of understanding, thinking on the high effect that should proceed from him, and on the who and the what; for in the empyrean heaven he was chosen for father of revered Rome and of her empire; both which (would one say truth) were ordained for the holy place where the successor of the greater Peter has his seat. Through this going, whereof thou givest him vaunt, he learned things which were the cause of his victory and of the papal mantle. Afterward the Chosen Vessel[2] went thither to bring thence comfort to that faith which is the beginning of the way of salvation. But I, why go I thither? or who concedes it? I am not Aeneas, I am not Paul; neither I nor others believe me worthy of this; wherefore if I yield myself to go, I fear lest the going may be mad. Thou art wise, thou understandest better than I speak."

And as is he who unwills what he willed, and by reason of new thoughts changes his purpose, so that he withdraws wholly from what he had begun, such I became on that dark hillside: because in my thought I abandoned the enterprise which had been so hasty in its beginning.

"If I have rightly understood thy speech," replied that shade of the magnanimous one, "thy soul is hurt by cowardice, which oftentimes encumbers a man so that it turns him back from honorable enterprise, as false seeing does a beast when it shies. In order that thou loose thee from this fear I will tell thee why I came, and what I heard at the first moment that I grieved for thee. I was among those who are suspended, and a Lady blessed and beautiful called me, such that I besought her to command. Her eyes were more shining than the star, and she began to say to me sweet and clear, with angelic voice, in her speech: 'O courteous Mantuan soul! of whom the fame yet lasts in the world, and shall last so long as motion continues, my friend, and not of fortune, is so hindered on his road upon the desert hillside that he has turned for fear, and I am afraid, through that which I have heard of him in heaven, lest he be already so astray that I may have risen late to his succor. Now do thou move, and with thy ornate speech and with whatever is needful for his deliverance, assist him so that I may be consoled thereby. I am Beatrice who make thee go. I come from a place whither I desire to return. Love moved me, that makes me speak. When I shall be before my Lord, I will often praise thee to Him.' Then she was silent, and thereon I began: 'O Lady of Virtue! through whom alone the human race excels all contained within that heaven which has the smallest circles,[3] thy command so pleases me that to obey it, were it already done, were slow to me. There is no need for thee further to open to me thy will; but tell me the reason why thou dost not beware of descending down here into this centre, from the ample place [4] whither thou burnest to return.[5] 'Since thou wishest to know so inwardly, I will tell thee briefly,' she replied to me, 'wherefore I fear not to come here within. One need be afraid only of those things that have power to do one harm, of others not, for they are not fearful. I am made by God, thanks be to Him, such that your misery touches me not, nor does the flame of this burning assail me. A gentle Lady [5] is in heaven who feels compassion for this hindrance whereto I send thee, so that she breaks stern judgment there above. She summoned Lucia [6] in her request, and said, "Thy faithful one now has need of thee, and I commend him to thee." Lucia, the foe of every cruel one, moved and came to the place where I was seated with the ancient Rachel.[7] She said, "Beatrice, true praise of God, why dost thou not succor him who so loved thee that for thee he came forth from the vulgar throng? Dost thou not hear the pity of his plaint? Dost thou not see the death that combats him on the stream where the sea has no vaunt?" Never were persons in the world swift to do their good, or to fly their harm, as I, after these words were uttered, came down here from my blessed seat, putting my trust in thy upright speech, which honors thee and them who have heard it.' After she had said this to me, weeping she turned her lucent eyes, whereby she made me more quick to come. And I came to thee thus as she willed. I withdrew thee from before that wild beast which took from thee the short way on the beautiful mountain. What is it then? Why, why dost thou hold back? why dost thou harbor

---

1. The action begins on the night before Good Friday, A.D. 1300. Dante was thirty-five years old.
2. The type of pleasures of sense.
3. It was a common belief that the spring was the season of the Creation and that on March 25, the vernal equinox, the Sun was created and placed in Aries, to begin his course.
4. Pride.
5. Avarice. Cf. Jeremiah 5:6. These three beasts correspond with the triple division of sins into those of in continence, of violence, and of fraud which Virgil makes in the eleventh canto, according to which the sinners in Hell are divided into three main classes.
6. Virgil was twenty-five years old at the time of Caesar's death, 44 B.C.

such cowardice in thy heart? why hast thou not daring and assurance, since three such blessed Ladies care for thee in the court of Heaven, and my speech pledges thee such good?"

As the flowerets, bent and closed by the chill of night, when the sun brightens them erect themselves all open on their stem, so I became with my drooping courage, and such good daring ran to my heart that I began like a person enfreed: O compassionate she who succored me, and courteous thou who didst speedily obey the true words that she addressed to thee! Thou by thy words hast so disposed my heart with desire of going, that I have returned to my first intent. Now go, for one sole will is in us both: thou leader, thou lord, and thou master." Thus I said to him; and when he moved on, I entered along the deep and savage road.

CANTO III

The gate of Hell.—Virgil leads Dante in.—The punishment of those who had lived without infamy and without praise,—Acheron, and the sinners on its ban.—Charon.—Earthquake.—Dante swoons.

"Through me is the way into the woeful city; through me is the way into the eternal woe; through me is the way among the lost people. Justice moved my lofty maker: the divine Power, the supreme Wisdom and the primal Love made me. Before me were no things created, save eternal, and I eternal last. Leave every hope, ye who enter!"

These words of obscure color I saw written at the top of a gate; whereat I: "Master, their meaning is dire to me."

And he to me, like a person well advised: "Here it behoves to leave every fear; it behoves that all cowardice should here be dead. We have come to the place where I have told thee that thou shalt see the woeful people, who have lost the good of the understanding."

And when he had put his hand on mine with a cheerful look, wherefrom I took courage, he brought me within to the secret things. Here sighs, laments, and deep wailings were resounding through the starless air; wherefore at first I wept thereat. Strange tongues, horrible utterances, words of woe, accents of anger, voices high and faint, and sounds of hands with them, were making a tumult which whirls always in that air forever dark, like the sand when the whirlwind breathes.

And I, who had my head girt with horror, said: "Master, what is that which I hear? and what folk is it that seems so overcome with its woe?"

And he to me: "The wretched souls of those who lived without infamy and without praise maintain this miserable mode. They are mingled with that caitiff choir of the angels, who were not rebels, nor were faithful to God, but were for themselves. The heavens chased them out in order to be not less beautiful, nor does the deep Hell receive them, for the damned would have some boast of them."

And I: "Master, what is so grievous to them, that makes them lament so bitterly?"

7. Cf. Revelation 20:10, 14.
8. Cf. *Hell,* Canto iv.
9. *Purgatory,* Canto ix.
1. *Aeneid vi.*

He answered: "I will tell thee very briefly. These have not hope of death; and their blind life is so debased, that they are envious of every other lot. Fame of them the world permits not to be; mercy and justice disdain them. Let us not speak of them, but do thou look and pass on."

And I, who was gazing, saw a banner, which, whirling, ran so swiftly that it seemed to me disdainful of any pause, and behind it came so long a train of folk, that I should never have believed death had undone so many. After I had recognized some among them, I saw and knew the shade of him who made, through cowardice, the great refusal.[1] At once I understood and was certain, that this was the sect of the caitiffs displeasing to God and to his enemies. These wretches, who never were alive, were naked, and much stung by gad-flies and by wasps that were there; these streaked their faces with blood, which, mingled with tears, was gathered at their feet by loathsome worms.

And when I gave myself to looking onward, I saw people on the bank of a great river; wherefore I said: "Master, now grant to me that I may know who these are, and what rule makes them appear so ready to pass over, as I discern through the faint light." And he to me: "The things will be clear to thee, when we shall stay our steps on the sad shore of Acheron." Then with eyes ashamed and downcast, fearing lest my speech might be troublesome to him, far as to the river I refrained from speaking.

And behold! coming toward us in a boat, an old man, white with ancient hair, crying: "Woe to you, wicked souls! hope not ever to see the Heavens! I come to carry you to the other bank, into the eternal darkness, into heat and into frost. And thou who art there, living soul, depart from these that are dead." But when he saw that I did not depart, he said: "By another way, by other ports thou shalt come to the shore, not here, for passage; a lighter bark must carry thee."[2]

And my Leader to him: "Charon, vex not thyself; it is thus willed there where is power for that which is willed; and ask no more." Thereon were quiet the fleecy jaws of the ferryman of the livid marsh, who round about his eyes had wheels of flame.

But those souls, who were weary and naked, changed color and gnashed their teeth, soon as they heard his cruel words. They blasphemed God and their parents, the human race, the place, the time and the seed of their sowing and of their birth. Then, all of them bitterly weeping, drew together to the evil bank, which awaits every man who fears not God. Charon the demon, with eyes of glowing coal, beckoning to them, collects them all; he beats with his oar whoever lingers.

As in autumn the leaves depart one after the other, until the bough sees all its spoils upon the earth, in like wise the evil seed of Adam throw themselves from that shore one by one, at signals, as the bird at his recall. Thus they go over the dusky wave, and before they have landed on the farther side, already on this a new throng is assembled.

"My son," said the courteous Master, "those who die in the wrath of God, all come together here from every land; and they are eager to pass over the stream, for the divine justice spurs them so that fear is turned to desire. A good soul never passes this way; and therefore if Charon fret at thee, well' mayest thou now know what his speech signifies."

2. St. Paul (Acts 9:15, and 2 Corinthians 12:1–4. See *The Vision of Paul,* above).
3. The heaven of the moon.
4. I.e., from the Empyrean to Limbo.
5. The Virgin Mary, never spoken of by name in Hell.

This ended, the gloomy plain trembled so mightily that the memory of the terror even now bathes me with sweat. The tearful land gave forth a wind that flashed a crimson light which vanquished all sensation in me, and I fell as a man whom slumber seizes.

CANTO IV

The further side of Acheron.—Virgil leads Dante into Umbo, the First Circle of Hell, containing the spirits of those who lived virtuously but without faith in Christ.—Greeting of Virgil by his fellow poets.—They enter a castle, where are the shades of ancient worthies.—After seeing them Virgil and Dante depart. [1]

A heavy thunder broke the deep sleep in my head, so that I started up like a person who is waked by force, and, risen erect, I moved my rested eye round about, and looked fixedly to distinguish the place where I was. True it is, that I found myself on the brink of the woeful valley of the abyss which collects a thunder of infinite wailings. It was so dark, deep, and cloudy, that, though I fixed my sight on the depth, I did not discern anything there.

"Now let us descend here below into the blind world," began the Poet all deadly pale, "I will be first, and thou shalt be second."

And I, who had observed his color, said: "How shall I come, if thou fearest, who art wont to be the comfort to my doubting?" And he to me: "The anguish of the folk who are here below paints on my face that pity which thou takest for fear. Let us go on, for the long way urges us."

Thus he placed himself,[1] and thus he made me enter into the first circle that girds the abyss. Here, as one listened, there was no lamentation but that of sighs which made the eternal air to tremble; this came of the woe without torments felt by the crowds, which were many and great, of infants and of women and of men.

The good Master to me: "Thou dost not ask what spirits are these that thou seest. Now I would have thee know, before thou goest farther, that these did not sin; and though they have merits it suffices not, because they did not have baptism, which is part of the faith that thou believest; and if they were before Christianity, they did not duly worship God: and of such as these am I myself. For such defects, and not for other guilt, are we lost, and only so far harmed that without hope we live in desire."

Great woe seized me at my heart when I heard him, because I knew that people of much worth were suspended in that limbo. "Tell me, my Master, tell me, Lord," I began, with wish to be assured of that faith which vanquishes every error, "did ever any one who afterwards was blessed go forth from here, either by his own or by another's merit?" And he, who understood my covert speech, answered: "I was new in this state [2] when I saw a Mighty One come hither crowned with sign of victory.[3] He drew out hence the shade of the first parent, of Abel his son, and that of Noah, of Moses the law-giver and obedient, Abraham the patriarch and David the King, Israel with his father and with his offspring, and with Rachel, for whom he did so much, and many others; and He made them blessed. And I would have thee know that before these, human spirits were not saved."

We ceased not going on because he spoke, but all the while were passing through the wood, the wood, I mean, of crowded spirits; nor yet had our way been long from the place of my slumber, when I saw a fire, which overcame a hemisphere of darkness. We were still a little distant from it, yet not so far but that I could in part discern that honorable folk possessed that place. "O thou who honorest both science and art, who are these,

6. Illuminating Grace.
7. The type of contemplative life.

who have such honor that it separates them from the manner of the others?" And he to me: "The honorable renown of them which sounds above in thy life wins grace in heaven which thus advances them." At this a voice was heard by me: "Honor the loftiest Poet! his shade returns which had departed." When the voice had stopped and was quiet, I saw four great shades coming to us; they had a semblance neither sad nor glad. The good Master began to say: "Look at him with that sword in hand who comes before the three, even as lord; he is Homer, the sovereign poet; the next who comes is Horace, the satirist; Ovid is the third, and the last is Lucan. Since each shares with me the name which the single voice sounded, they do me honor, and in that do well."

Thus I saw assembled the fair school of that Lord of the loftiest song who soars above the others like an eagle. After they had discoursed somewhat together, they turned to me with sign of salutation; and my Master smiled thereat. And far more of honor yet they did me, for they made me of their band, so that I was the sixth amid so much wisdom. Thus we went on as far as the light, speaking things concerning which silence is becoming, even as was speech there where I was.

We came to the foot of a noble castle,[4] seven times circled by high walls,[5] defended round about by a fair streamlet. This we passed as if hard ground; through seven gates[6] I entered with these sages; we came to a meadow of fresh verdure. People were there with slow and grave eyes, of great authority in their looks; they spoke seldom, and with soft voices. Thereon we withdrew ourselves upon one side, into an open, luminous, and high place, so that they all could be seen. There before me upon the green enamel were shown to me the great spirits, whom for having seen I inwardly exalt myself.

I saw Electra with many companions, among whom I recognized Hector and Aeneas, Caesar in armor, with his gerfalcon eyes; I saw Camilla and Penthesilea, on the other side I saw the King Latinus, who was sitting with Lavinia his daughter. I saw that Brutus who drove out Tarquin; Lucretia, Julia, Marcia, and Cornelia; and alone, apart, I saw the Saladin. When I raised my brows a little more, I saw the Master of those who know,[7] seated amid the philosophic family; all regard him, all do him honor. Here I saw Socrates and Plato, who in front of the others stand nearest to him; Democritus, who ascribes the world to chance; Diogenes, Anaxagoras, and Thales, Empedocles, Heraclitus, and Zeno; and I saw the good collector of the qualities, Dioscorides, I mean, and I saw Orpheus, Tully, and Linus, and moral Seneca, Euclid the geometer, and Ptolemy, Hippocrates, Avicenna, and Galen, and Averrhoes, who made the great comment. I cannot report of all in full, because the long theme so drives me that many times the speech comes short of the fact.

The company of six is reduced to two. By another way the wise guide leads me out from the quiet into the air that trembles, and I come into a region where is nothing that can give light.

1. Dante purposely refrains from naming anyone in this group and thereby immortalizing him. This soul is often identified with Pope Celestine V. Compare the Laodiceans in Revelations, and Kipling's *Tomlinson*.
2. I.e., the boat to Purgatory. Charon recognizes that Dante is not among the damned. Personages of heathen mythology were held by the Church to have been demons who had a real existence; they were adopted into the Christian mythology, and hence appear with entire propriety as characters in Hell.

CANTO V

The Second Circle, that of Carnal Sinners.—Minos.—Shades renowned of old.—Francesca da Rimini.

Thus I descended from the first circle down into the second, which girdles less space, and so much more woe that it goads to wailing. There stands Minos horribly, and snarls; he examines the transgressions at the entrance; he judges, and he sends according as he entwines himself. I mean, that when the ill born soul comes there before him, it confesses itself wholly, and that discerner of the sins sees what place of Hell is for it; he girds himself with his tail so many times as the grades he wills that it be sent down. Always many of them stand before him; they go, in turn, each to the judgment; they speak and hear, and then are whirled below.

"O thou that comest to the woeful inn," said Minos to me, when he saw me, leaving the act of so great an office, "beware how thou enterest, and to whom thou trustest thyself; let not the amplitude of the entrance deceive thee." And my Leader to him: "Wherefore dost thou too cry out? Hinder not his fated going; thus is it willed there where is power for that which is willed; and ask no more."

Now the notes of woe begin to make themselves heard by me; now I am come where much wailing smites me. I had come into a place mute of all light, that bellows as the sea does in a tempest, if it be combated by contrary winds. The infernal hurricane which never rests carries along the spirits with its rapine; whirling and smiting it molests them. When they arrive before its rush, here are the shrieks, the complaint, and the lamentation; here they blaspheme the divine power. I understood that to such torment are condemned the carnal sinners who subject the reason to the appetite. And as their wings bear along the starlings in the cold season in a large and full troop, so did that blast the evil spirits; hither, thither, down, up it carries them; no hope ever comforts them, neither of repose, nor of less pain.

And as the cranes go singing their lays, making in air a long line of themselves, so I saw come, uttering wails, shades borne along by the aforesaid strife. Wherefore I said: "Master, who are these folk whom the black air so castigates?" "The first of those of whom thou wishest to have knowledge," said he to me then, "was empress of many tongues. She was so abandoned to the vice of luxury that lust she made licit in her law, to take away the blame into which she had been brought. She is Semiramis, of whom it is read that she succeeded Ninus and had been his wife; she held the land which the Sultan rules. That other is she[1] who, for love, slew herself, and broke faith to the ashes of Sichaeus; next is Cleopatra, the luxurious. See Helen, for whom so long a time of ill revolved; and see the great Achilles, who fought to the end with love. See Paris, Tristan,—" and more than a thousand shades whom love had parted from our life he showed me, and, pointing to them, named to me.

After I had heard my Teacher name the dames of eld and the cavaliers, pity overcame me, and I was well nigh bewildered. I began: "Poet, willingly would I speak with those two that go together, and seem to be so light upon the wind."[2] And he to me: "Thou shalt see when they are nearer to us, and do thou then pray them by that love which leads them, and they will come." Soon as the wind sways them toward us, I lifted my voice: "O wearied souls, come to speak with us, if Another[3] deny it not."

1. In the lead, in front of Dante.
2. Virgil died in 19 b.c.
3. Christ's Harrowing of Hell.

As doves, called by desire, with wings open and steady, come through the air borne by their will to their sweet nest, these issued from the troop where Dido is, coming to us through the malign air, so strong was the compassionate cry.

"O living creature, gracious and benign, that goest through the black air visiting us who stained the world blood-red, if the King of the universe were a friend we would pray Him tor thy peace, since thou hast pity on our perverse ill. Of what it pleases thee to hear, and what to speak, we will hear and we will speak to you, while the wind, as now, is hushed for us. The city where I was born sits upon the seashore, where the Po, with his followers, descends to have peace. Love, which quickly lays hold on gentle heart, seized this one for the fair person that was taken from me, and the mode still hurts me. Love, which absolves no loved one from loving, seized me for the pleasing of him so strongly that, as thou seest, it does not even now abandon me. Love brought us to one death. Caina awaits him who quenched our life." These words were borne to us from them.

Soon as I had heard those injured souls I bowed my face, and held it down so long until the Poet said to me: "What art thou thinking?"

When I replied, I began: "Alas! how many sweet thoughts, how great desire, led these unto the woeful pass." Then I turned me again to them, and spoke, and began: "Francesca, thy torments make me sad and piteous to weeping. But tell me, at the time of the sweet sighs, by what and how did love concede to thee to know thy dubious desires?" And she to me: "There is no greater woe than the remembering in misery the happy time, and that thy Teacher knows.[4] But if thou hast so great desire to know the first root of our love, I will do like one who weeps and tells.

"We were reading one day, for delight, of Lancelot, how love constrained him. We were alone and without any suspicion. Many times that reading urged our eyes, and took the color from our faces, but only one point was it that overcame us. When we read of the longed-for smile being kissed by such a lover, this one, who never shall be divided from me, kissed my mouth all trembling. Gallehaut was the book, and he who wrote it.[5] That day we read no farther in it."

While the one spirit said this, the other was so weeping that through pity I swooned as if I had been dying, and fell as a dead body falls.

CANTO VI

The Third Circle, that of the Gluttonous.—Cerberus.—Ciacco.

CANTO VII

The Fourth Circle, that of the Avaricious and the Prodigal.—Pluto.—Fortune. The Styx.—The Fifth Circle, that of the Wrathful.

---

4. Philosophy.
5. The virtues.
6. The liberal arts.
7. Aristotle.

CANTO VIII

The Fifth Circle.—Phlegyas and his boat.—Passage of the Styx.—Filippo Argenti.—The City of Dis.—The demons refuse entrance to the poets.

CANTO IX

The City of Dis.—Erichtho.—The Three Furies.—The Heavenly Messenger.—The Sixth Circle: that of the Heresiarchs.

CANTO X

The Sixth Circle: Heresiarchs.—Farinata degli Uberti.—Cavalcante Cavalcanti.—Frederick II.

Now, along a solitary path between the wall of the city and the torments, my Master goes on, and I behind his shoulders.

"O virtue supreme," I began, "that through the impious circles dost turn me according to thy pleasure, speak to me and satisfy my desires. The folk that are lying in the sepulchres, might they be seen? all the lids are now lifted, and no one keeps guard." And he to me: "All will be locked in when they shall return here from Jehoshaphat with the bodies which they have left on earth.[1] Upon this side Epicurus with all his followers, who make the soul mortal with the body, have their burial place. Therefore as to the request that thou makest of me, thou shalt soon be satisfied here within; and also as to the desire of which thou art silent to me."[2] And I: "Good Leader, I hold not my heart hidden from thee except in order to speak little; and not only now hast thou disposed me to this.'

"O Tuscan, who goest thy way alive through the city of fire, speaking thus modestly, may it please thee to stop in this place. Thy mode of speech makes manifest that thou art native of that noble fatherland to which perchance I was too molestful." Suddenly this sound issued from one of the coffers, wherefore in fear I drew a little nearer to my Leader. And he said to me: "Turn thee: what art thou doing? See there Farinata who has risen erect; all from the girdle upwards wilt thou see him."[3]

I had already fixed my face on his and he was straightening himself up with breast and front as though he had Hell in great scorn. And the bold and ready hands of my Leader pushed me among the sepulchres to him, saying: "Let thy words be clear."

When I was at the foot of his tomb, he looked at me a little, and then, as though disdainful, asked me, "Who were thy ancestors?" I, who was desirous to obey, concealed it not from him, but disclosed it all to him; whereon he raised up his brows a little, then said:"They were fiercely adverse to me and to my forefathers and to my party, so that at two times I scattered them."[4] "If they were driven out, they returned from every side," replied I to him, "both the one and the other time, but yours have not learned well that art."[5]

Then there arose to sight alongside of this one, a shade uncovered far as to the chin: I think that it had risen on its knees. It looked round about me, as if it had desire to see if another were with me, but when its expectancy was quite spent, weeping it said: "If through this blind prison thou goest by reason of loftiness of genius, where

1. Dido.
2. Francesca da Rimini, daughter of Guido Vecchio da Polenta, lord of Ravenna; and her lover, Paolo, the brother of her husband, the son of Malatesta da Verrucchio, lord of Rimini. Their death, at the hands of her husband, took place about 1285.

is my son? and why is he not with thee?" And I to him: "I come not of myself; he who waits yonder is leading me through here, whom perchance your Guido had in disdain." [6]

His words and the mode of the punishment had already read to me the name of this one; wherefore my answer was so full.

Suddenly straightening up, he cried: "How didst thou say, 'he had'? lives he not still? does not the sweet light strike his eyes?" When he became aware of some delay that I made before answering, he fell again supine, and appeared no more outside.

But that other magnanimous one, at whose instance I had stayed, changed not aspect, nor moved his neck, nor bent his side. "And if," he said, continuing his first discourse, "they have ill learned that art, it torments me more than this bed. But the face of the Lady who rules here[7] will not be rekindled fifty times ere thou shalt know how much that art weighs. And, so mayest thou return to the sweet world, tell me wherefore is that people so pitiless against my party in its every law?" Thereon I to him: "The rout and the great carnage which colored the Arbia red cause such prayer to be made in our temple." After he had, sighing, shaken his head, "In that I was not alone," he said, "nor surely without cause would I have moved with the others; but I was alone there,[8] where it was agreed by every one to destroy Florence, he who defended her with open face." "Ah! so may your seed ever have repose," I prayed to him, "loose for me that knot, which has here entangled my judgment. It seems, if I hear rightly, that ye see in advance that which time is bringing with it, and as to the present have another way."[9] "We see," he said, "like him who has bad light, the things that are far from us, so much the supreme Ruler still shines on us; when they draw near, or are, our intelligence is wholly vain, and if another report not to us, we know nothing of your human state; wherefore thou canst comprehend that our knowledge will be utterly dead from that moment when the gate of the future shall be closed." Then, as compunctious for my fault, I said: "Now, then, you will tell to that fallen one that his son is still conjoined with the living, and if just now I was dumb to answer, make him know that I was so because I was already thinking in the error which you have solved for me."

And now my Master was recalling me, wherefore more hastily I prayed the spirit that he would tell me who was with him. He said to me: "Here I lie with more than a thousand; here within is the second Frederick[10] and the Cardinal,[11] and of the others I am silent."

Thereon he hid himself; and I turned my steps toward the ancient Poet, reflecting on that speech which seemed hostile to me. He moved on, and then, thus going, he said to me: "Why art thou so disturbed?" And I satisfied him as to his question. "Let thy memory preserve that which thou hast heard against thyself," that Sage bade me, "and now give heed here—" and he raised his finger: "When thou shalt be in presence of the sweet radiance of her whose beautiful eye sees everything, from her thou shalt learn the journey of thy life." Then to the left he turned his step.

We left the wall, and went toward the middle by a path that strikes into a valley which even up there was making its stench displeasing.

---

3. The name of God is never spoken by the spirits in Hell, save once, in blasphemous defiance, by Vanni Fucci; nor by Dante in addressing them.

4. Thy Teacher who lives sorrowfully in Limbo without hope, but with memory of the life lighted by the Sun.

5. In the romance, it was Gallehaut that prevailed on Guenever to give a kiss to Lancelot.

CANTO XI

The Sixth Circle: Heretics.—Tomb of Pope Anastasius.—Discourse of Virgil on the divisions of the lower Hell.

Upon the edge of a high bank which great rocks broken in a circle made, we came above a more cruel pen. And here, because of the horrible excess of the stench which the deep abyss throws out, we drew aside behind the lid of a great tomb, whereon I saw an inscription which said: "I hold Pope Anastasius, whom Photinus drew from the right way."

"It behoves that our descent be slow, so that the sense may first accustom itself a little to the dismal blast, and then it will be of no concern." Thus the Master, and I said to him: "Some compensation do thou find that the time pass not lost." And he: "Behold, I am thinking of that. My son, within these rocks," he began then to say, "are three lesser circles from grade to grade, like those which thou art leaving. All are full of accursed spirits; but, in order that hereafter the sight alone may suffice thee, hear how and wherefore they are in bonds.

"Of every wickedness that acquires hate in heaven injury is the end, and every such end afflicts others either by force or by fraud. But because fraud is an evil peculiar to man, it more displeases God; and therefore the fraudulent are the lower, and woe assails them more.

"The first circle[1] is wholly of the violent: but because violence is done to three persons it is divided and constructed in three rounds. To God, to one's self, to one's neighbor may violence be done; I say to them and to their belongings, as thou shalt hear with plain discourse. By violence, death and grievous wounds are inflicted on one's neighbor; and on his substance ruins, burnings, and harmful extortions. Wherefore the first round torments homicides, and every one who smites wrongfully, all despoilers and plunderers, in various troops.

"Man may lay violent hands upon himself and on his goods; and, therefore, in the second round it behoves that he repent without avail who deprives himself of your world, gambles away and dissipates his property, and laments there where he ought to be joyous.

"Violence may be done to the Deity, by denying and blaspheming Him in the heart, and by contemning nature and His bounty: and therefore the smallest round seals with its signet both Sodom and Cahors[2] and him who, contemning God, speaks from his heart.

"The fraud, by which every conscience is stung, man may practice on one that confides in him, or on one that has no stock of confidence. This latter mode seems to destroy only the bond of love which nature makes; wherefore in the second circle nest hypocrisy, flatteries, and he who bewitches, falsity, robbery, and simony, panders, barrators, and such like filth.

"By the other mode that love is forgotten which nature makes and that which is thereafter added, whereby special confidence is created. Hence, in the smallest circle, where is the point of the universe, upon which Dis sits, whoso betrays is consumed forever."

And I: "Master, full clearly thy discourse proceeds, and full well divides this pit, and the people that possess it; but, tell me, they of the fat marsh, and they whom the wind drives, and they whom the rain beats, and they who encounter with such rough tongues, why are they not punished within the ruddy city[3] if God be wroth with them? and if he be not so, why are they in such plight?"

---

1. Joel 3:12.
2. Probably the wish to see Farinata, concerning whom Dante had already asked.
3. Farinata degli Uberti was the head of the Ghibelline party in Tuscany for many years. He died not far from the time of Dante's birth.

And he said to me: "Why does thy wit so wander beyond its wont? or thy mind, where else is it gazing? Dost thou not remember those words with which thy Ethics treats in full of the three dispositions that Heaven abides not: incontinence, wickedness, and mad bestiality; and how incontinence less offends God, and incurs less blame?[4] If thou consider well this doctrine, and bring to mind who are those that up above suffer punishment outside, thou wilt see clearly why they are divided from these felons, and why less wroth the divine vengeance hammers them."

"O Sun that healest every troubled vision, thou dost content me so, when thou solvest, that doubt, not less than knowledge, pleases me; yet turn thee a little back," said I, "to where thou say est that usury offends the Divine Goodness, and loose the knot."

"Philosophy," he said to me, "points out to him who understands it, not only in one part alone, how Nature takes her course from the Divine Intellect and from Its art. And if thou note thy Physics,[5] well thou wilt find, after not many pages, that your art follows her so far as it can, as the disciple does the master, so that your art is as it were grandchild of God. From these two, if thou bring to mind Genesis at its beginning,[6] it behoves mankind to gam their life and to advance. But because the usurer holds another way, he contemns Nature in herself, and in her follower, since upon other thing he sets his hope. But follow me now, for to go on pleases me; for the Fishes are quivering on the horizon, and the Wain lies quite over Caurus,[7] and far onwards is the descent of the steep."

CANTO XII

The Seventh Circle, first round: those who do violence to others. The Minotaur.—The Centaurs.—Chiron. — Nessus. — The River of boiling blood, and the sinners in it.

CANTO XIII

The Seventh Circle, second round: those who have done violence to themselves and to their goods.—The Wood of Self-murderers. The Harpies.—Pier delle Vigne.—Lano of Siena and others.

---

3. In this lower Hell, within the walls of the city of Dis.

4. Aristotle *Ethics* vii. 1.

5. Aristotle *Physics* ii. 2.

6. "In the sweat of thy face shalt thou eat bread." Genesis 3:19.

7. The sign of the Fishes precedes that of the Ram, and, as the Sun was in the latter sign, the time indicated is about 4, or from 4 to 5 a.m.

4. Dante's ancestors were Guelfs; Farinata had dispersed the Guelfs in 1248 and 1260.

5. The Guelfs had returned to Florence in 1251 and 1266 and, regaining power, had finally expelled the Ghibellines permanently.

6. Guido Cavalcanti, Dante's first friend and Farinata's son-in-law. Guido died a few months after Dante's vision.

7. Proserpine, identified with the mystical Hecate, and hence with the Moon.

8. At Empoli, in 1260, after the terrible rout of the Florentine Guelfs at Montaperti on the Arbia.

9. That is, are ignorant of the present. Farinata foretells future events, but Cavalcante shows himself ignorant of present conditions.

10. The famous Frederick II, *"stupor mundi"* Emperor from 1212 to 1250.

11. Ottaviano degli Ubaldini, a fierce Ghibelline, who was reported as saying, "If there be a soul I have lost it for the Ghibellines." He died in 1273.

CANTO XIV

The Seventh Circle, third round: those who have done violence to God.—The Burning Sand.—Capaneus. —Figure of the Old Man in Crete.—The Rivers of Hell.

CANTO XV

Third round of the Seventh Circle: of those who have done violence to Nature.—Brunetto Latini.— Prophecies of misfortune to Dante.

CANTO XVI

The Seventh Circle, third round: those who have done violence to Nature.—Guido Guerra. Tegghiaio Aldobrandi and Jacopo Rusticucci.—The roar of Phlegethon as it pours downward.—The cord thrown into the abyss.

CANTO XVII

Third round of the Seventh Circle: of those who have done violence to Art.—Geryon.—The Usurers.— Descent to the Eighth Circle.

CANTO XVIII

Eighth Circle: the fraudulent; the first pouch: panders and seducers.—Venedico Caccianimico.—Jason.— Second Valley: false flatterers.—Alessio Interminei.—Thais.

CANTO XIX

Eighth Circle: third pouch: simonists.—Pope Nicholas lit

CANTO XX

Eighth Circle: fourth pouch: diviners, soothsayers, and magicians—Amphiaraus.—Tiresias.—Aruns.— Man to.—Eurypylus.—Michael Scott.—Asdente.

CANTO XXI

Eighth Circle: fifth pouch: barrators.—A magistrate of Lucca.—The Malebranche.—Parley with them.

---

1. The first circle below.
2. Cahors, a town in southern France, on the river Lot, noted in the Middle Ages for usury.

CANTO XXII

Eighth Circle: fifth pouch, continued: barrators.—Ciampolo of Navarre.—Fra Gomita.—Michael Zanche.—Fray of the Malebranche.

CANTO XXIII

Eighth Circle.—Escape from the fifth pouch.—The sixth pouch: hypocrites, in cloaks of gilded lead.—Jovial Friars.—Caiaphas.—Annas.—Frate Catalano.

CANTO XXIV

Eighth Circle. The poets climb from the sixth pouch.—Seventh pouch, filled with serpents, by which thieves are tormented.—Vanni Fucci.—Prophecy of calamity to Dante.

CANTO XXV

Eighth Circle: seventh pouch: fraudulent thieves.—Cacus.—Agnello Brunelleschi and others.

[trans. Charles Eliot Norton]

THE NATURE OF A TRUE PRINCE

By John of Salisbury

S ince the late eleventh century medieval Europe experienced a tremendous intellectual, cultural, and economic transformation, which has been commonly called "the Renaissance of the Twelfth Century." The Englishman John of Salisbury (ca. 1120–1180) was one of its most remarkable representatives. After early childhood studies in Salisbury, he became a student at cathedral schools, mostly in northern France (Paris and Chartres), attending lessons by some of the greatest masters of his time, Bernard of Chartres, Thierry of Chartres, Peter Abelard, and Gilbert of Poitiers (1138–ca. 1146). In 1148 he began his career as a civil servant, first in the church, but then also for the English king. Since 1153 he served as secretary to the Archbishop of Canterbury, first Theobald, then, from 1162, Thomas Beckett. In 1163 the English king, in a bitter conflict with Beckett, not only exiled the Archbishop, but also forced John to leave England, who subsequently lived with his friend Peter of Celle in Rheims for six years, during which time he composed his History of the Popes, the Historia pontificale. At the end of his life John became the bishop of Chartres (1176–1180). John of Salisbury is most famous for this Historia Pontificalis, as well as his Metalogicon, in which he discusses his own experiences at the schools, with some biting criticism of a group of opponents called "Cornificians" who allegedly had tried to undermine the values of scholarship. Most importantly, John was the author of the political treatise Policraticus sive de nugis curialium et de vestigiis philosophorum, in which he examines from many different perspectives the principles of politics of his time, addressing primarily the ideals of a good prince/king and the dangers of tyranny. He also discusses the principles of law and how a ruler and his people have to follow them. John's letters to his friends and teachers are regarded as masterpieces of medieval humanism. In his Polycraticus John proves to be a most foresightful writer whose political and ethical viewpoints have much to say, even, if not especially, to us today.

THE PRINCE AND THE LAW

Between a tyrant and a prince there is this single or chief difference, that the latter obeys the law and rules the people by its dictates, accounting himself as but their servant. It is by virtue of the law that he makes good his claim to the foremost and chief place in the management of the affairs of the commonwealth and in the bearing of its burdens; and his elevation over others consists in this, that whereas private men are held responsible only for their private affairs, on the prince fall the burdens of the whole community. Wherefore deservedly there is conferred on him, and gathered together in his hands, the power of all his subjects, to the end that he may be

John of Salisbury, "The Nature of a True Prince," *The Statesman's Book of John of Salisbury; Being the Fourth, Fifth, and Sixth Books, and Selections From the Seventh and Eighth Books, of the Policraticus*, trans. John Dickinson. Random House, Inc., 1927.

sufficient unto himself in seeking and bringing about the advantage of each individually, and of all; and to the end that the state of the human commonwealth may be ordered in the best possible manner, seeing that each and all are members one of another. Wherein we indeed but follow nature, the best guide of life; for nature has gathered together all the senses of her microcosm or little world, which is man, into the head, and has subjected all the members in obedience to it in such wise that they will all function properly so long as they follow the guidance of the head, and the head remains sane. Therefore the prince stands on a pinnacle which is exalted and made splendid with all the great and high privileges which he deems necessary for himself. And rightly so, because nothing is more advantageous to the people than that the needs of the prince should be fully satisfied; since it is impossible that his will should be found opposed to justice. Therefore, according to the usual definition, the prince is the public power, and a kind of likeness on earth of the divine majesty. Beyond doubt a large share of the divine power is shown to be in princes by the fact that at their nod men bow their necks and for the most part offer up their heads to the axe to be struck off, and, as by a divine impulse, the prince is feared by each of those over whom he is set as an object of fear. And this I do not think could be, except as a result of the will of God. For all power is from the Lord God, and has been with Him always, and is from everlasting. The power which the prince has is therefore from God, for the power of God is never lost, nor severed from Him, but He merely exercises it through a subordinate hand, making all things teach His mercy or justice. "Who, therefore, resists the ruling power, resists the ordinance of God," in whose hand is the authority of conferring that power, and when He so desires, of withdrawing it again, or diminishing it. For it is not the ruler's own act when his will is turned to cruelty against his subjects, but it is rather the dispensation of God for His good pleasure to punish or chasten them. …

Princes should not deem that it detracts from their princely dignity to believe that the enactments of their own justice are not to be preferred to the justice of God, whose justice is an everlasting justice, and His law is equity. Now equity, as the learned jurists define it, is a certain fitness of things which compares all things rationally, and seeks to apply like rules of right and wrong to like cases, being impartially disposed toward all persons, and allotting to each that which belongs to him. Of this equity the interpreter is the law, to which the will and intention of equity and justice are known. Therefore Crisippus asserted that the power of the law extends over all things, both divine and human, and that it accordingly presides over all goods and ills, and is the ruler and guide of material things as well as of human beings. To which Papinian, a man most learned in the law, and Demosthenes, the great orator, seem to assent, subjecting all men to its obedience because all law is, as it were, a discovery, and a gift from God, a precept of wise men, the corrector of excesses of the will, the bond which knits together the fabric of the state, and the banisher of crime; and it is therefore fitting that all men should live according to it who lead their lives in a corporate political body. All are accordingly bound by the necessity of keeping the law, unless perchance there is any who can be thought to have been given the licence of wrongdoing. However, it is said that the prince is absolved from the obligations of the law; but this is not true in the sense that it is lawful for him to do unjust acts, but only in the sense that his character should be such as to cause him to practise equity not through fear of the penalties of the law but through love of justice; and should also be such as to cause him from the same motive to promote the advantage of the commonwealth, and in all things to prefer the good of others before his private will. Who, indeed, in respect of public matters can properly speak of the will of the prince at all, since therein he may not lawfully have any will of his own apart from that which the law or equity enjoins, or the calculation of the common interest requires? For in these matters his will is to have the force of a judgment; and most properly that which pleases him therein has the force of law, because his decision may not be at variance with the intention of equity. "From thy countenance," says the Lord, 'let my judgment go forth, let thine eyes look upon equity"; for the uncorrupted judge is one whose decision, from assiduous contemplation of equity, is the very likeness thereof. The prince accordingly is the minister of the common interest and the bond-servant of equity, and he bears the public person in the sense that he punishes the wrongs and injuries of all, and all crimes, with even-handed equity. His rod and staff, also, administered with wise moderation, restore irregularities and false departures to the straight path of equity, so that deservedly may the Spirit congratulate the power of the prince with the words, "Thy rod and thy staff, they have comforted me." His shield, too, is strong, but it is a shield for the protection of the weak, and one which wards off powerfully the darts of the wicked from the innocent. Those who derive the greatest advantage from his performance of the duties of his office are those who can do least for themselves, and his power is chiefly exercised against those who desire to do harm. Therefore not without reason he bears a sword, wherewith he sheds blood blamelessly, without becoming thereby a man of blood, and frequently puts men to death without incurring the name or guilt of homicide. …

This sword, then, the prince receives from the hand of the Church, although she herself has no sword of blood at all. Nevertheless she has this sword, but she uses it by the hand of the prince, upon whom she confers the power of bodily coercion, retaining to herself authority over spiritual things in the person of the pontiffs. The prince is, then, as it were, a minister of the priestly power, and one who exercises that side of the sacred offices which seems unworthy of the hands of the priesthood. For every office existing under, and concerned with the execution of, the sacred laws is really a religious office, but that is inferior which consists in punishing crimes, and which therefore seems to be typified in the person of the hangman. Wherefore Constantine, most faithful emperor of the Romans, when he had convoked the council of priests at Nicaea, neither dared to take the chief place for himself nor even to sit among the presbyters, but chose the hindmost seat. Moreover, the decrees which he heard approved by them he reverenced as if he had seen them emanate from the judgment-seat of the divine majesty. Even the rolls of petitions containing accusations against priests which they brought to him in a steady stream he took and placed in his bosom without opening them. … But if one who has been appointed prince has performed duly and faithfully the ministry which he has undertaken, as great honour and reverence are to be shown to him as the head excels in honour all the members of the body. Now he performs his ministry faithfully when he is mindful of his true status, and remembers that he bears the person of the *universitas* of those subject to him; and when he is fully conscious that he owes his life not to himself and his own private ends, but to others, and allots it to them accordingly, with duly ordered charity and affection. Therefore he owes the whole of himself to God, most of himself to his country, much to his relatives and friends, very little to foreigners, but still somewhat. He has duties to the very wise and the very foolish, to little children and to the aged. Supervision over these classes of persons is common to all in authority, both those who have care over spiritual things and those who exercise temporal jurisdiction. … And so let him be both father and husband to his subjects, or, if he has known some affection more tender still, let him employ that; let him desire to be loved rather than feared, and show himself to them as such a man that they will out of devotion prefer his life to their own, and regard his preservation and safety as a kind of public life; and then all things will prosper well for him, and a small bodyguard will, in case of need, prevail by their loyalty against innumerable adversaries. For love is strong as death; and the wedge which is held together by strands of love is not easily broken. …

ON LIBERTY AND TYRANNY

Liberty means judging everything freely in accordance with one's individual judgment, and does not hesitate to reprove what it sees opposed to good morals. Nothing but virtue is more splendid than liberty, if indeed liberty can ever properly be severed from virtue. For to all right-thinking men it is clear that true liberty issues from no other source. Wherefore, since all agree that virtue is the highest good in life, and that it alone can strike off the heavy and hateful yoke of slavery, it has been the opinion of philosophers that men should die, if need arose, for the sake of virtue, which is the only reason for living. But virtue can never be fully attained without liberty, and the absence of liberty proves that virtue in its full perfection is wanting. Therefore a man is free in proportion to the measure of his virtues, and the extent to which he is free determines what his virtues can accomplish; while, on the other hand, it is the vices alone which bring about slavery, and subject a man to persons and things in unmeet obedience; and though slavery of the person may seem at times the more to be pitied, in reality slavery to the vices is ever far the more wretched. And so what is more lovely than liberty? And what more agreeable to a man who has any reverence for virtue? We read that it has been the impelling motive of all good princes; and that none ever trod liberty under foot save the open foes of virtue. The jurists know what good laws were introduced for the sake of liberty, and the testimony of historians has made famous the great deeds done for love of it. … If I wished to recall individual instances of this kind, time would run out before the examples were exhausted. The practice of liberty is a notable thing and displeasing only to those who have the character of slaves.

Things which are done or spoken freely avoid the fault of timidity on the one hand and of rashness on the other, and so long as the straight and narrow path is followed, merit praise and win affection. But when under the pretext of liberty rashness unleashes the violence of its spirit, it properly incurs reproach, although, as a thing more pleasing in the ears of the vulgar than convincing to the mind of the wise man, it often finds in the indulgence of others the safety which it does not owe to its own prudence. Nevertheless, it is the part of a good and wise man to give a free rein to the liberty of others and to accept with patience the words of free speaking, whatever they may be. Nor does he oppose himself to its works so long as these do not involve the casting away of virtue. For since each virtue shines by its own proper light, the merit of tolerance is resplendent with a very special glory. …

A tyrant, … as the philosophers have described him, is one who oppresses the people by rulership based upon force, while he who rules in accordance with the laws is a prince. Law is the gift of God, the model of equity, a standard of justice, a likeness of the divine will, the guardian of well-being, a bond of union and solidarity between peoples, a rule defining duties, a barrier against the vices and the destroyer thereof, a punishment of violence and all wrongdoing. The law is assailed by force or by fraud, and, as it were, either wrecked by the fury of the lion or undermined by the wiles of the serpent. In whatever way this comes to pass, it is plain that it is the grace of God which is being assailed, and that it is God Himself who in a sense is challenged to battle. The prince fights for the laws and the liberty of the people; the tyrant thinks nothing done unless he brings the laws to nought and reduces the people to slavery. Hence the prince is a kind of likeness of divinity; and the tyrant, on the contrary, a likeness of the boldness of the Adversary, even of the wickedness of Lucifer, imitating him that sought to build his throne to the north and make himself like unto the Most High, with the exception of His goodness. For had he desired to be like unto Him in goodness, he would never have striven to tear from Him the glory of His power and wisdom. What he more likely did aspire to was to be equal with him in authority to dispense rewards. The prince, as the likeness of the Deity, is to be loved, worshipped, and cherished; the tyrant, the likeness of wickedness, is generally to be even killed. The origin of tyranny is iniquity, and springing from a poisonous root, it is a tree which grows and sprouts into a baleful pestilent growth, and to which the axe must by all means be laid. For if iniquity and injustice, banishing charity, had not brought about tyranny, firm concord and perpetual peace would have possessed the peoples of the earth forever, and no one would think of enlarging his boundaries. Then kingdoms would be as friendly and peaceful, according to the authority of the great father Augustine, and would enjoy as undisturbed repose, as the separate families in a well-ordered state, or as different persons in the same family; or perhaps, which is even more credible, there would be no kingdoms at all, since it is clear from the ancient historians that in the beginning these were founded by iniquity as presumptuous encroachments against the Lord, or else were extorted from Him.

[From *Policraticus*, trans. J. Dickinson.]

THE PROBLEMS OF A
CHRISTIAN HUMANIST

By John of Salisbury

Consider the leading teachers of philosophy of our own day, those who are most loudly acclaimed, surrounded by a noisy throng of disciples. Mark them carefully; you will find them dwelling on one rule, or on two or three words, or else they have selected (as though it were an important matter) a small number of questions suitable for dispute, on which to exercise their talent and waste their life. They do not however succeed in solving them but hand down to posterity for solution by their disciples their problems, with all the ambiguity with which they have invested them.

In their lecture room they invite you to battle with them, become pressing, and demand the clash of wit. If you hesitate to engage, if you delay but for a moment, they are upon you. If you advance and, though unwillingly, engage them and press them hard, they take refuge in subterfuge; they change front; they torture words; with tricks of magic they transform themselves until you marvel at the reappearance of the slippery, changing Proteus. But he can be trapped more easily if you insist on understanding his meaning and intention despite his voluble and erratic language. He will finally be vanquished by his own meaning and be caught by the words of his mouth, if you can grasp their significance and hold it firmly.

The points of dispute of our modern Proteus however are as useless as they are trivial. If in disgust over time wasted on such trifles you press your attack he again has recourse to evasion. As if taking refuge in the bosom of Mother Earth like Antaeus, he strives to recover his strength in the element in which he was born and brought up. Such a roundabout way; so many detours! As though it were necessary to traverse a labyrinth to reach the common place! ...

If therefore you hoist them with their own petard you may well pity them their poverty in almost every capacity. Some seem to excel in details; others offer for sale all branches of philosophy, and yet in the details they are without the proper philosophic background. There are some who hope to attain perfection as the result of excellence in one branch; there are others who devote their energy to the whole field though they lack the knowledge of its parts. I find it hard to say which are in greater error, *since* perfection is not derived from one and no one has the power to devote himself faithfully to all. However he who seeks perfection in all from one is the more absurd, while he who claims proficiency in all is the more arrogant. It is the mark of the indolent to occupy himself with one thing to the exclusion of all else; of the dilettante to embrace them all.

At any rate he who makes a wide survey in order to select his specialty displays discretion and is the more devoted to his choice after having weighed the value of others. Perhaps that is the intention of the moralist who enjoins the reading of books. ...

All reading should be done in such a way that some of it when finished should be disregarded, some condemned, and some viewed *en passant*, that the subject matter be not entirely unknown; but above all careful attention should be given to those matters which lay the foundation of the life of the state, be it by the law of the state or else by ethical principles, or which have in view the health of body and soul. Since then the chief branch [grammar] among the liberal arts, without which no one can teach or be taught properly, is to be merely greeted *en passant* and as it were from the door, who can imagine that time should be devoted to other branches which being difficult to understand or impractical and harmful do not conduce to the betterment of man? For even those things that are required for man's use prove very harmful if they occupy his attention to the exclusion of all others.

Does anyone doubt the desirability of reading the historians, the orators, and the authorities on approved mathematics, since without a knowledge of them men cannot be, or at least usually are not, liberally educated? Indeed those who are ignorant of those writers are termed illiterate even if they can read and write. But when such writers lay claim to the mind as though it belonged exclusively to them, although they praise learning they do not teach; rather they hinder the cultivation of virtue. This is the reason that Cicero, when dealing with the poets, to make his remarks more effective, burst out, "The shout of approbation of the populace, as though it were some great and wise teacher qualified to recommend, puts the stamp of genius upon whom it wishes. But they who are so lauded, what darkness do they spread, what fears engender, and what passions inflame!" ... Elsewhere however Cicero highly commends writers. He says, "He alone who fears no contempt himself casts contempt upon poets and writers in other branches of artistic literature, as well as upon the historians. They know what virtue is and offer the material for philosophic study, for they brand vices; they do not teach them. Their works are attractive too on account of the help and pleasure they give to the reader. They make their way amid dangers which threaten character, with the intention of securing a foothold for virtue." ... I myself am of the opinion of those who believe that a man cannot be literate without a knowledge of the authors. Copious reading, however, by no means makes the philosopher, since it is grace alone that leads to wisdom. ... It may be assumed that all writings except those that have been disapproved should be read, since it is believed that all that has been written and all that has been done have been ordained for man's utility although at times he makes bad use of them. For the angels too were, so to speak, ordained on account of the soul, but the corporeal world, according to the statement of the fathers, for the use of the body. ... Just so in books there is something profitable for everybody provided, be it understood, the reading is done with discrimination and that only is selected which is edifying to faith and morals. There is matter which is of profit to stronger minds but is to be kept from the artless; there is that which an innately sound mind rejects; there is that which it digests for character-building or perfecting eloquence; there is that which hardens the soul and causes spiritual indigestion in matters of faith and good works. There is scarcely a piece of writing in which something is not found either in meaning or expression that the discriminating reader will not reject. The safe and cautious thing to do is to read only Catholic books. It is somewhat dangerous to expose the unsophisticated to pagan literature; but a training in both is very useful to those safe in the faith, for accurate reading on a wide range of subjects makes the scholar; careful selection of the better makes the saint. ...

Therefore let the pagan writers be read in a way that their authority be not prejudicial to reason; for the burning weed, as the rose is plucked, sometimes burns the hand of him who touches it.

Wisdom is as it were a spring from which rivers go out watering all the land, and its divine pages not only fill with delight the place of its birth but also make their way among the nations to such an extent that they are not entirely unknown even to the Ethiopians. It is from this source that the flowering, perfumed, fruitful works of the pagan world spring, and should perchance any artless reader enter their field let him keep in mind this quotation:

> Flee hence, O ye who gather flowers
> Or berries growing on the ground; the clammy
> Snake is hiding in the grass.
> [Virgil, *Eclogues*, III, 92–93]

It is no sluggard who carries off the apples of the Hesperides guarded by the ever-sleepless dragon, nor one who reads as though not awake but drowsing and dreaming as if eager to reach the end of his task. It is certain that the pious and wise reader who spends time lovingly over his books always rejects errors and comes close to life in all things.

[From *Policraticus*, book VII, trans. J. B. Pike, Frivolities of Courtiers and Footprints of Philosophers (Minneapolis, Minn.: University of Minnesota Press, 1938)]

A Philosophy of History

By Otto of Freising

*O*tto *of Freising (1114–1158) was a famous bishop and chronicler, son of high-ranking parents in the southern part of Germany. Through his mother he was half-brother of King Conrad III and uncle of Emperor Frederick Barbarossa. Otto studied in Paris and later joined the Cistercian order. He became abbot of the Cistercian monastery of Morimond in Burgundy (northeastern France) in ca. 1136, and soon afterwards was elected bishop of Freising, northeast of Munich. In 1147 he accompanied the German King Conrad III on a crusade, and he even reached Jerusalem, but the experience was disastrous. Drawing in many different ways on Saint Augustine's treatise* De civitate, *Otto composed his* Chronica sive Historia de duabus civitatibus *(Chronicle or History of the Two Cities) between 1143 and 1145, contrasting in metaphorical terms the heavenly and the earthly kingdoms. Otto is also highly reputed for his biography of Emperor Frederick I, his* Gesta Friderici imperatoris *(Deeds of Emperor Frederick), completed in 1156. Otto became famous as a most efficient reformer in the Church, in his order, and as a bishop.*

In pondering long and often in my heart upon the changes and vicissitudes of temporal affairs and their varied and irregular issues, even as I hold that a wise man ought by no means to cleave to the things of time, so I find that it is by the faculty of reason alone that one must escape and find release from them. For it is the part of a wise man not to be whirled about after the manner of a revolving wheel, but through the stability of his powers to be firmly fashioned as a thing foursquare. Accordingly, since things are changeable and can never be at rest, what man in his right mind will deny that the wise man ought, as I have said, to depart from them to that city which stays at rest and abides to all eternity? This, is the City of God, the heavenly Jerusalem, for which the children of God sigh while they are set in this land of sojourn, oppressed by the turmoil of the things of time as if they were oppressed by the Babylonian captivity. For, inasmuch as there are two cities—the one of time, the other of eternity; the one of the earth, earthy, the other of heaven, heavenly; the one of the devil, the other of Christ—ecclesiastical writers have declared that the former is Babylon, the latter Jerusalem.

But, whereas many of the Gentiles have written much regarding one of these cities, to hand down to posterity the great exploits of men of old (the many evidences of their merits, as they fancied), they have yet left to us the task of setting forth what, in the judgment of our writers, is rather the tale of human miseries. …

In those writings the discerning reader will be able to find not so much histories as pitiful tragedies made up of mortal woes. We believe that this has come to pass by what is surely a wise and proper dispensation of the

Creator, in order that, whereas men in their folly desire to cleave to earthly and transitory things, they may be frightened away from them by their own vicissitudes, if by nothing else, so as to be directed by the wretchedness of this fleeting life from the creature to a knowledge of the Creator. But we, set down as it were at the end of time, do not so much read of the miseries of mortals in the books of the writers named above as find them for ourselves in consequence of the experiences of our own time. For, to pass over other things, the empire of the Romans, which in Daniel is compared to iron on account of its sole lordship—monarchy, the Greeks call it—over the whole world, a world subdued by war, has in consequence of so many fluctuations and changes, particularly in our day, become, instead of the noblest and the foremost, almost the last. …

For being transferred from the City [Rome] to the Greeks, from the Greeks to the Franks, from the Franks to the Lombards, from the Lombards again to the German Franks, that empire not only became decrepit and senile through lapse of time, but also, like a once smooth pebble that has been rolled this way and that by the waters, contracted many a stain and developed many a defect. The world's misery is exhibited, therefore, even in the case of the chief power in the world, and Rome's fall foreshadows the dissolution of the whole structure.

But what wonder if human power is changeable, seeing that even mortal wisdom is prone to slip? We read that in Egypt there was so great wisdom that, as Plato states, the Egyptians called the philosophers of the Greeks childish and immature. … And yet Babylon the great, not only renowned for wisdom, but also "the glory of kingdoms, the beauty of the Chaldeans' pride," has become, in the words of the prophecy of Isaiah, without hope of restoration, a shrine of owls, a house of serpents and of ostriches, the lurking-place of creeping things. Egypt too is said to be in large measure uninhabitable and impassable. The careful student of history will find that learning was transferred from Egypt to the Greeks, then to the Romans, and finally to the Gauls and the Spaniards. And so it is to be observed that all human power or learning had its origin in the East, but is coming to an end in the West, that thereby the transitoriness and decay of all things human may be displayed. This, by God's grace, we shall show more fully in what follows.

Since, then, the changeable nature of the world is proved by this and like evidence, I thought it necessary, my dear brother Isingrim, in response to your request, to compose a history whereby through God's favour I might display the miseries of the citizens of Babylon and also the glory of the kingdom of Christ to which the citizens of Jerusalem are to look forward with hope, and of which they are to have a foretaste even in this life. I have undertaken therefore to bring down as far as our own time, according to the ability that God has given me, the record of the conflicts and miseries of the one city, Babylon; and furthermore, not to be silent concerning our hopes regarding that other city, so far as I can gather hints from the Scriptures, but to make mention also of its citizens who are now sojourning in the worldly city. In this work I follow most of all those illustrious lights of the Church, Augustine and Orosius, and have planned to draw from their fountains what is pertinent to my theme and my purpose. The one of these has discoursed most keenly and eloquently on the origin and the progress of the glorious City of God and its ordained limits, setting forth how it has ever spread among the citizens of the world, and showing which of its citizens or princes stood forth pre-eminent in the various epochs of the princes or citizens of the world. The other, in answer to those who, uttering vain babblings, preferred the former times to Christian times, has composed a very valuable history of the fluctuations and wretched issues of human greatness, the wars and the hazards of wars, and the shifting of thrones, from the foundation of the world down to his own time. Following in their steps I have undertaken to speak of the two cities in such a way that we shall not lose the thread of history, that the devout reader may observe what is to be avoided in mundane affairs by reason of the countless miseries wrought by their unstable character, and that the studious and painstaking investigator may find a record of past happenings free from all obscurity. …

For it is not because of indiscretion or frivolity, but out of devotion, which always knows how to excuse ignorance, that I, though I am without proper training, have ventured to undertake so arduous a task. Nor can anyone rightfully accuse me of falsehood in matters which—compared with the customs of the present time—will appear incredible, since down to the days still fresh in our memory I have recorded nothing save what I found in the writings of trustworthy men, and then only a few instances out of many. For I should never hold the view that these men are to be held in contempt if certain of them have preserved in their writings the apostolic simplicity, for, as overshrewd subtlety sometimes kindles error, so a devout rusticity is ever the friend of truth.

As we are about to speak, then, concerning the sorrow-burdened insecurity of the one city and the blessed permanence of the other, let us call upon God, who endures with patience the turbulence and confusion of this world, and by the vision of Himself augments and glorifies the joyous peace of that other city, to the end that by His aid we may be able to say the things which are pleasing to Him. ...

But when the Lord wished His city to spread abroad and to be extended from that people [the Jews] to all nations, He permitted the realm to be weakened under pressure of the people's sins, and the people itself to be led into captivity. But among the nations which He was to summon to faith in Himself, He established the sovereignty of the Romans to rule over the rest. When this had reached its fullest development and the pinnacle of power, He willed that His Son Christ should appear in the flesh. ... So then the Lord, transferring His city from that people to the Gentiles, willed that they should first be humbled, despised, and afflicted by many misfortunes—even as it is written, "He scourgeth every son whom He receiveth." But because scourgings, when they exceed due measure, break the spirit rather than heal it (as medicines taken to excess), at the proper time, as I have said before, He exalted His forsaken and humbled Church. That it might therefore become more tranquil with respect to the promised heavenly kingdom, He bestowed upon it the greatest temporal power possessed by any realm. And thus as I have said the City of God, increasing gradually, reached its pinnacle and undivided authority. And observe that before His incarnation His city was not honoured to the full, but that afterwards, when He had risen to the skies with the body He had assumed and had, so to say, accepted His throne, [then] according to the parable He exalted His kingdom, which is the Church, to the highest dignity—than which there is nothing loftier on earth—that hereby He might reveal Himself to the citizens of the world as not only the God of heaven but also as Lord of the earth, and that through the prosperity of this land of our sojourn He might teach His citizens that the delights of their own country were eagerly to be sought. ...

Furthermore, enough has been said above, I think regarding the two cities: how one made progress, first by remaining hidden in the other until the coming of Christ, after that by advancing gradually to the time of Constantin. But after Constantine, when troubles from without had finally ceased, it began to be grievously troubled at the instigation of the devil by internal strife even to the time of the Elder Theodosius; Arius was the author of this and the lords of the world, the Augusti, were his coadjutors. But from that time on, since not only all the people but also the emperors (except a few) were orthodox Catholics, I seem to myself to have composed a history not of two cities but virtually of one only, which I call the Church. For although the elect and the reprobate are in one household, yet I cannot call these cities two as I did above; I must call them properly but one—composite, however, as the grain is mixed with, the chaff. Wherefore in the books that follow let us pursue the course of history which we have begun. Since not only emperors of the Romans but also other kings (kings of renowned realms) became Christians, inasmuch as the sound of the word of God went out into all the earth and unto the ends of the world, the City of Earth was laid to rest and destined to be utterly exterminated in the end; hence our history is a history of the City of Christ, but that city, so long as it is in the land of sojourn, is "like unto a net, that was cast into the sea," containing the good and the bad. However, the faithless city of unbelieving Jews and Gentiles still remains, but, since nobler kingdoms have been won by our people, while these unbelieving Jews and Gentiles are insignificant not only in the sight of God but even in that of the world, hardly anything done by these unbelievers is found to be worthy of record or to be handed on to posterity.

[From *The Two Cities,* trans. C. C. Mierow (New York: Columbia University Press, 1928)]

THE VISION OF GOD

By Nicholas of Cusa

N icholas of Cusa, (1401–1464), who originated from the small town Bernkastel-Kues (which is the modern name) on the Moselle, near the French border, received his education by the Brothers of the Common Life at Deventer in Holland, before he joined the University of Heidelberg in 1416, and the University of Padua, Italy, in 1418 (canon law), completing his studies with a Ph.D. in 1423. In 1425, after a short stint in Rome, he returned to Germany to study theology at the University of Cologne for one year. He was both a mathematician and a theologian, an astronomer and a philosopher. Subsequently he found employment in the service of the Cardinal Giordano Orsini, who introduced him, among others, to the famous papal secretary and humanist Poggio Bracciolini. In 1437 he worked as an academic canon lawyer at the Council of Basel. While having supported the conciliary movement for a long time, in 1438 he turned his back on it and joined the papal party, representing the Pope in Germany and elsewhere. He even once went to Constantinople to convince the Greeks to join the Church council of Ferrara to over-come the split between these two huge groups. In his De concordantia Catholica (On the Catholic Concordance) from 1432–1433, Nicholas reflected on the need of the Church to find its way back to a universal unity under God from whom all grace flows to mankind. At the same time Nicholas embraced a certain degree of toleration (not yet tolerance!) even in religious terms and advocated the open dialogue among the various groups who all needed only to accept Christ, the Trinity, and the Church. This found its impressive manifestation in his famous De pace fidei, which reflects on religious pluralism. In his more scientific works, De li non aliud and De docta ignorantia, he discussed, among many other topics, the idea that the earth might move, that God is the sphere, the center of which is everywhere, while the circumference is nowhere. In many ways Nicholas was deeply influenced by the famous fourteenth-century German mystic and philosopher Meister Eckhart, happily embracing paradoxes in his intellectual and religious discourse.

In 1449 Nicholas was appointed as cardinal-priest, and in 1450 as Bishop of Brixen, South Tyrol. He was primar-ily concerned with the reform of convents all over Germany. He also preached a crusade against the Turks, but in his reformist zeal he ran into many political conflicts with Duke Sigmund of Tyrol, many members of monasteries, and their aristocratic family members.

Nicholas of Cusa, The Vision of God, trans. E. Gurney-Salter. Orion Publishing Group, 1928.

I will now show you, dearest brethren, as I promised you, an easy path unto mystical theology. For, knowing you to be led by zeal for God, I think you worthy of the opening up of this treasure, as assuredly very precious and most fruitful. And first I pray the Almighty to give me utterance, and the heavenly Word who alone can express Himself, that I may be able, as ye can receive it, to relate the marvels of revelation, which are beyond all sight of our eyes, our reason, and our understanding. I will endeavour by a very simple and commonplace method to lead you by experience into the divine darkness; wherein while ye abide ye shall perceive present with you the light inaccessible, and shall each endeavour, in the measure that God shall grant him, to draw ever nearer thereunto, and to partake here, by a sweetest foretaste, of that feast of everlasting bliss, whereunto we are called in the word of life, through the gospel of Christ, who is blessed for ever.

If I strive in human fashion to transport you to things divine, I must needs use a comparison of some kind. Now among men's works I have found no image better suited to our purpose than that of an image which is omnivoyant—its face, by the painter s cunning art, being made to appear as though looking on all around it. There are many excellent pictures of such faces—for example, that of the archeress in the market-place of Nuremberg; that by the eminent painter, Roger, in his priceless picture in the governors house at Brussels; the Veronica in my chapel at Coblenz, and, in the castle of Brixen, the angel holding the arms of the Church, and many others elsewhere. Yet, lest ye should fail in the exercise, which requireth a figure of this description to be looked upon, I send for your indulgence such a picture as I have been able to procure, setting forth the figure of an omnivoyant, and this I call the icon of God.

This picture, brethren, ye shall set up in some place, let us say, on a north wall, and shall stand round it, a little way off, and look upon it. And each of you shall find that, from whatsoever quarter he regardeth it, it looketh upon him as if it looked on none other. And it shall seem to a brother standing to eastward as if that face looketh toward the east, while one to southward shall think it looketh toward the south, and one to westward, toward the west. First, then, ye will marvel how it can be that the face should look on all and each at the same time. For the imagination of him standing to eastward cannot conceive the gaze of the icon to be turned unto any other quarter, such as west or south. Then let the brother who stood to eastward place himself to westward and he will find its gaze fastened on him in the west just as it was afore in the east. And, as he knoweth the icon to be fixed and unmoved, he will marvel at the motion of its immovable gaze. …

And while he observeth how that gaze never quitteth any, he seeth that it taketh such diligent care of each one who findeth himself observed as though it cared only for him, and for no other, and this to such a degree that one on whom it resteth cannot even conceive that it should take care of any other. He will also see that it taketh the same most diligent care of the least of creatures as of the greatest, and of the whole universe.

'Tis by means of this perceptible image that I purpose to uplift you, my most loving brethren, by a certain devotional exercise, unto mystical Theology, premising three things that be serviceable thereunto.

In the first place, I think, it should be presupposed that there is nothing which seemeth proper to the gaze of the icon of God which doth not more really exist in the veritable gaze of God Himself. For God, who is the very summit of all perfection, and greater than can be conceived, is called *Theos* from this very fact that He beholdeth all things. Wherefore, if the countenance portrayed in a picture can seem to look upon each and all at one and the same time, this faculty (since it is the perfection of seeing) must no less really pertain unto the reality than it doth apparently unto the icon or appearance. For if the sight of one man is keener than that of another among us, if one will with difficulty distinguish objects near him, while another can make out those at a distance, if one perceive an object slowly, the other more quickly—there is no doubt but that Absolute Sight, whence all sight springeth, surpasseth in keenness, in speed, and in strength the sight of all who actually see and who can become capable of sight. ...

Approach thee now, brother contemplative, unto the icon of God, and place thyself first to the east thereof, then to the south, and finally to the west. Then, because its glance regardeth thee alike in each position, and leaveth thee not whithersoever thou goest, a questioning will arise in thee and thou wilt stir it up, saying: Lord, in this image of Thee I now behold Thy providence by a certain experience of sense. For if Thou leavest not me, who am the vilest of men, never and to none wilt Thou be lacking. For Thou art present to all and to each, even as to those same, all and each, is present the Being without whom they cannot exist. For Thou, the Absolute Being of all, art as entirely present to all as though Thou hadst no care for any other. And this befalleth because there is none that doth not prefer its own being to all others, and its own mode of being to that of all others, and so defendeth its own being as that it would rather allow the being of all others to go to perdition than its own. Even so, Thou, Lord, dost regard every living thing in such wise that none of them can conceive that Thou hast any other care but that it alone should exist, in the best mode possible to it, and that each thinketh all other existing things exist for the sole purpose of serving this end, namely, the best state of him whom Thou beholdest.

Thou dost not, Lord, permit me to conceive by any imagining whatsoever that Thou, Lord, lovest anything else more than me; since Thy regard leaveth not me, me only. And, since where the eye is, there is love, I prove by experience that Thou lovest me because Thine eyes are so attentively upon me, Thy poor little servant. Lord, Thy glance is love. And just as Thy gaze beholdeth me so attentively that it never turneth aside from me, even so is it with Thy love. And since 'tis deathless, it abideth ever with me, and Thy love, Lord, is nothing else but Thy very Self, who lovest me. Hence Thou art ever with me, Lord; Thou desertest me not, Lord; on all sides Thou guardest me, for that Thou takest most diligent care for me. Thy Being, Lord, letteth not go of my being. I exist in that measure in which Thou art with me, and, since Thy look is Thy being, I am because Thou dost look at me, and if Thou didst turn Thy glance from me I should cease to be.

But I know that Thy glance is that supreme Goodness which cannot fail to communicate itself to all able to receive it. Thou, therefore, canst never let me go so long as I am able to receive Thee. Wherefore it behooveth me to make myself, in so far as I can, ever more able to receive Thee. But I know that the capacity which maketh union possible is nothing else save likeness. And incapacity springeth from lack of likeness. If, therefore, I have rendered myself by all possible means like unto Thy goodness, then, according to the degree of that likeness, I shall be capable of the truth.

Lord, Thou hast given me my being, of such a nature that it can make itself continuously more able to receive Thy grace and goodness. And this power, which I have of Thee, wherein I possess a living image of Thine almighty power, is free will. By this I can either enlarge or restrict my capacity for Thy grace. The enlarging is by conformity with Thee, when I strive to be good because Thou art good, to be just because Thou art just, to be merciful because Thou art merciful; when all my endeavour is turned toward Thee because all Thy endeavour is turned toward me; when I look unto Thee alone with all my attention, nor ever turn aside the eyes of my mind, because Thou dost enfold me with Thy constant regard; when I direct my love toward Thee alone because Thou, who art Love's self, hast turned Thee toward me alone. And what, Lord, is my life, save that embrace wherein Thy delightsome sweetness doth so lovingly enfold me? I love my life supremely because Thou art my life's sweetness.

Now I behold as in a mirror, in an icon, in a riddle, life eternal, for that is nothing other than that blessed regard wherewith Thou never ceasest most lovingly to behold me, yea, even the secret places of my soul With Thee, to behold is to give life; 'tis unceasingly to impart sweetest love of Thee; 'tis to inflame me to love of Thee by love's imparting, and to feed me by inflaming, and by feeding to kindle my yearnings, and by kindling to make me drink of the dew of gladness, and by drinking to infuse in me. a fountain of life, and by infusing to make it increase and endure. 'Tis to cause me to share Thine immortality, to endow me with the glory imperishable of Thy heavenly and most high and most mighty kingdom; 'tis to make me partaker of that inheritance which is only of Thy Son, to stablish me in possession of eternal bliss. There is the source of all delights that can be desired; not only can nothing better be thought out by men and angels, but nothing better can exist in any mode of being! For it is the absolute maximum of every rational desire, than which a greater cannot be.

[From *The Vision* of God, trans. E. Gurney-Salter (London: Deni, 1928)]

THE LIFE OF CHARLEMAGNE

By Einhard

EINHARD'S PREFACE

Since I have taken upon myself to narrate the public and private life, and no small part of the deeds, of my lord and foster-father, the most lent and most justly renowned King Charles, I have condensed the matter into as brief a form as possible. I have been careful not to omit any facts that could come to my knowledge, but at the same time not to offend by a prolix style those minds that despise everything modern, if one can possibly avoid offending by a new work men who seem to despise also the masterpieces of antiquity, the works of most learned and luminous writers. Very many of them, l have no doubt, are men devoted to a life of literary leisure, who feel that the affairs of the present generation ought not to be passed by, and who do not consider everything done today as unworthy of mention and deserving to be given over to silence and oblivion, but are nevertheless seduced by lust of immortality to celebrate the glorious deeds of other times by some sort of composition rather than to deprive posterity of the mention of their own names by not writing at all.

Be this as it may, I see no reason why I should refrain from entering upon a task of this kind, since no man can write with more accuracy than I of events that took place about me, and of facts concerning which I had personal knowledge, ocular demonstration as the saying goes, and I have no means of ascertaining whether or not any one else has the subject in hand.

In any event, I would rather commit my story to writing, and hand it down to posterity in partnership with others, so to speak, than to suffer the most glorious life of this most excellent king, the greatest of all the princes of his day, and his illustrious deeds, hard for men of later times to imitate, to be wrapped in the darkness of oblivion.

But there are still other reasons, neither unwarrantable nor insufficient, in my opinion, that urge me to write on this subject, namely, the care that King Charles bestowed upon me in my childhood, and my constant friendship with himself and his children after I took up my abode at court. In this way he strongly endeared me to himself, and made me greatly his debtor as well in death as in life, so that were I unmindful of the benefits conferred upon me, to keep silence concerning the most glorious and illustrious deeds of a man who claims so much at my hands, and suffer his life to lack due eulogy and written memorial, as if he had never lived, I should deservedly appear ungrateful, and be so considered, albeit my powers are feeble, scanty, next to nothing indeed, and not at all adapted to write and set forth a life that would tax the eloquence of a Tully [note: *Tully* is Marcus Tullius Cicero].

I submit the book. It contains the history of a very great and distinguished man; but there is nothing in it to wonder at besides his deeds, except the fact that I, who am a barbarian, and very little versed in the Roman language, seem to suppose myself capable of writing gracefully and respectably in Latin, and to carry my presumption so far as to disdain the sentiment that Cicero is said in the first book of the *Tusculan Disputations* to have expressed when speaking of the Latin authors. His words are: «It is an outrageous abuse both of time and literature for a man to commit his thoughts to writing without having the ability either to arrange them or elucidate them, or attract readers by some charm of style.» This dictum of the famous orator might have deterred me from writing if I had not made up my mind that it was better to risk the opinions of the world, and put my little talents for composition to the test, than to slight the memory of so great a man for the sake of sparing myself. …

CHAPTER 9: SPANISH EXPEDITION

In the midst of this vigorous and almost uninterrupted struggle with the Saxons, he covered the frontier by garrisons at the proper points, and marched over the Pyrenees into Spain at the head of all the forces that he could muster. All the towns and castles that he attacked surrendered. and up to the time of his homeward march he sustained no loss whatever; but on his return through the Pyrenees he had cause to rue the treachery of the Gascons. That region is well adapted for ambuscades by reason of the thick forests that cover it; and as the army was advancing in the long line of march necessitated by the narrowness of the road, the Gascons, who lay in ambush [778] on the top of a very high mountain, attacked the rear of the baggage train and the rear guard in charge of it, and hurled them down to the very bottom of the valley [at Roncevalles, later celebrated in the *Song of Roland*]. In the struggle that ensued they cut them off to a man; they then plundered the baggage, and dispersed with all speed in every direction under cover of approaching night. The lightness of their armor and the nature of the battle ground stood the Gascons in good stead on this occasion, whereas the Franks fought at a disadvantage in every respect, because of the weight of their armor and the unevenness of the ground. Eggihard, the King's steward; Anselm, Count Palatine; and Roland, Governor of the March of Brittany, with very many others, fell in this engagement. This ill turn could not be avenged for the nonce, because the enemy scattered so widely after carrying out their plan that not the least clue could be had to their whereabouts. …

CHAPTER 13: WAR WITH THE HUNS

The war against the Avars, or Huns, followed [791], and, except the Saxon war, was the greatest that he waged; he took it up with more spirit than any of his other wars, and made far greater preparations for it. He conducted one campaign in person in Pannonia, of which the Huns then had possession. He entrusted all subsequent operations to his son, Pepin, and the governors of the provinces, to counts even, and lieutenants. Although they most vigorously prosecuted the war, it only came to a conclusion after a seven years' struggle. The utter depopulation of Pannonia, and the site of the Khan's palace, now a desert, where not a trace of human habitation is visible bear witness how many battles were fought in those years, and how much blood was shed. The entire body of the Hun nobility perished in this contest, and all its glory with it. All the money and treasure that had been years amassing was seized, and no war in which the Franks have ever engaged within the memory of man brought them such riches and such booty. Up to that time the Huns had passed for, a poor people, but so much gold and silver was found in the Khan's palace, and so much valuable spoil taken in battle, that one may well think that the Franks took justly from the Huns what the Huns had formerly taken unjustly from other nations. Only two of the chief men of the Franks fell in this war—Eric, Duke of Friuli, who was killed in Tarsatch [799], a town on the coast of Liburnia by the treachery of the inhabitants; and Gerold, Governor of Bavaria, who met his death in Pannonia, slain [799], with two men that were accompanying him, by an unknown hand while he was marshaling his forces for battle against the Huns, and riding up and down the line encouraging his men. This war was otherwise almost a bloodless one so far as the Franks were concerned, and ended most satisfactorily, although by reason of its magnitude it was long protracted. …

CHAPTER 16: FOREIGN RELATIONS

He added to the glory of his reign by gaining the good will of several kings and nations; so close, indeed, was the alliance that he contracted with Alfonso [II 791-842] King of Galicia and Asturias, that the latter, when sending letters or ambassadors to Charles, invariably styled himself his man. His munificence won the kings of the Scots also to pay such deference to his wishes that they never gave him any other title than lord or themselves than subjects and slaves: there are letters from them extant in which these feelings in his regard are expressed. His relations with Aaron [ie Harun Al-Rashid, 786-809], King of the Persians, who ruled over almost the whole of the East, India excepted, were so friendly that this prince preferred his favor to that of all the kings and potentates of the earth, and considered that to him alone marks of honor and munificence were due. Accordingly, when the ambassadors sent by Charles to visit the most holy sepulcher and place of resurrection of our Lord and Savior presented themselves before him with gifts, and made known their master's wishes, he not only granted what was asked, but gave possession of that holy and blessed spot. When they returned, he dispatched his ambassadors with them, and sent magnificent gifts, besides stuffs, perfumes, and other rich products of the Eastern lands. A few years before this, Charles had asked him for an elephant, and he sent the only one that he had. The Emperors of Constantinople, Nicephorus [I 802-811], Michael [I, 811-813], and Leo [V, 813-820], made advances to Charles, and sought friendship and alliance with him by several embassies; and even when the Greeks suspected him of designing to wrest the empire from them, because of his assumption of the title Emperor, they made a close alliance with him, that he might have no cause of offense. In fact, the power of the Franks was always viewed by the Greeks and Romans with a jealous eye, whence the Greek proverb "Have the Frank for your friend, but not for your neighbor."

CHAPTER 17: PUBLIC WORKS

This King, who showed himself so great in extending his empire and subduing foreign nations, and was constantly occupied with plans to that end, undertook also very many works calculated to adorn and benefit his kingdom, and brought several of them to completion. Among these, the most deserving of mention are the basilica of the Holy Mother of God at Aix-la-Chapelle, built in the most admirable manner, and a bridge over the Rhine at Mayence, half a mile long, the breadth of the river at this point. This bridge was destroyed by fire

[May, 813] the year before Charles died, but, owing to his death so soon after, could not be repaired, although he had intended to rebuild it in stone. He began two palaces of beautiful workmanship—one near his manor called Ingelheim, not far from Mayence; the other at Nimeguen, on the Waal, the stream that washes the south side of the island of the Batavians. But, above all, sacred edifices were the object of his care throughout his whole kingdom; and whenever he found them falling to ruin from age, he commanded the priests and fathers who had charge of them to repair them, and made sure by commissioners that his instructions were obeyed. He also fitted out a fleet for the war with the Northmen; the vessels required for this purpose were built on the rivers that flow from Gaul and Germany into the Northern Ocean. Moreover, since the Northmen continually overran and laid waste the Gallic and German coasts, he caused watch and ward to be kept in all the harbors, and at the mouths of rivers large enough to admit the entrance of vessels, to prevent the enemy from disembarking; and in the South, in Narbonensis and Septimania, and along the whole coast of Italy as far as Rome, he took the same precautions against the Moors, who had recently begun their piratical practices. Hence, Italy suffered no great harm in his time at the hands of the Moors, nor Gaul and Germany from the Northmen, save that the Moors got possession of the Etruscan town of Civita Vecchia by treachery, and sacked it, and the Northmen harried some of the islands in Frisia off the German coast.

CHAPTER 18: PRIVATE LIFE

Thus did Charles defend and increase as well, as beautify his, kingdom, as is well known; and here let me express my admiration of his great qualities and his extraordinary constancy alike in good and evil fortune. I will now forthwith proceed to give the details of his private and family life.

After his father's death, while sharing the kingdom with his brother, he bore his unfriendliness and jealousy most patiently, and, to the wonder of all, could not be provoked to be angry with him. Later he married a daughter of Desiderius, King of the Lombards, at the instance of his mother; but he repudiated her at the end of a year for some reason unknown, and married Hildegard, a woman of high birth, of Suabian origin. He had three sons by her—Charles, Pepin and Louis—and as many daughters—Hruodrud, Bertha, and Gisela. He had three other daughters besides these—Theoderada, Hiltrud, and Ruodhaid—two by his third wife, Fastrada, a woman of East Frankish (that is to say, of German) origin, and the third by a concubine, whose name for the moment escapes me. At the death of Fastrada [794], he married Liutgard, an Alemannic woman, who bore him no children. After her death [Jun4 4, 800] he had three concubines—Gersuinda, a Saxon by whom he had Adaltrud; Regina, who was the mother of Drogo and Hugh; and Ethelind, by whom he had Theodoric. Charles' mother, Berthrada, passed her old age with him in great honor; he entertained the greatest veneration for her; and there was never any disagreement between them except when he divorced the daughter of King Desiderius, whom he had married to please her. She died soon after Hildegard, after living to three grandsons and as many granddaughters in her son's house, and he buried her with great pomp in the Basilica of St. Denis, where his father lay. He had an only sister, Gisela, who had consecrated herself to a religious life from girlhood, and he cherished as much affection for her as for his mother. She also died a few years before him in the nunnery where she passed her life....

CHAPTER 29: REFORMS

It was after he had received the imperial name that, finding the laws of his people very defective (the Franks have two sets of laws, very different in many particulars), he determined to add what was wanting, to reconcile the discrepancies, and to correct what was vicious and wrongly cited in them. However, he went no further in this matter than to supplement the laws by a few capitularies, and those imperfect ones; but he caused the unwritten laws of all the tribes that came under his rule to be compiled and reduced to writing. He also had the old rude songs that celebrate the deeds and wars of the ancient kings written out for transmission to posterity. He began a grammar of his native language. He gave the months names in his own tongue, in place of the Latin and barbarous names by which they were formerly known among the Franks. He likewise designated the winds by twelve appropriate names; there were hardly more than four distinctive ones in use before. He called January, Wintarmanoth; February, Hornung; March, Lentzinmanoth; April, Ostarmanoth; May, Winnemanoth; June, Brachmanoth; July, Heuvimanoth; August, Aranmanoth; September, Witumanoth; October, Windumemanoth; Novemher, Herbistmanoth; December, Heilagmanoth. He styled the winds as follows; Subsolanus, Ostroniwint; Eurus, Ostsundroni, Euroauster, Sundostroni; Auster, Sundroni; Austro-Africus, Sundwestroni; Africus, Westsundroni; Zephyrus, Westroni; Caurus, Westnordroni; Circius, Nordwestroni; Septentrio, Nordroni; Aquilo, Nordostroni; Vulturnus, Ostnordroni.

CHARLEMAGNE'S INCOME
FROM HIS FARMS

By Charlemagne

Charlemagne (ca. 742–814) was the most influential and powerful Germanic king since the fall of the Roman Empire at the end of the fifth century (the last Roman emperor, Romulus Augustulus, had been deposed by Odoacer in 476). He was king of the Franks from 768 and was crowned emperor in Rome in 800. His life was very rich and complex, and there is no need here to summarize in great detail what he accomplished altogether. It suffices to emphasize that Charlemagne was enormously successful in his constant military conquests, expanding the Frankish monarchy far and wide, at the end including (in modern terms) France, northern Spain, Germany, Austria, parts of Hungary, northern Italy, Saxony, and Frisia. Under his rule the Carolingian Renaissance emerged, which was a strong revival of education, especially conducted by Alcuin of York, a kind of master teacher whom Charlemagne had called from England. Charlemagne was constantly forced or wanted to go on military campaigns, either to defeat external enemies or to conquer new lands. This required a very careful logistic, which was based on the royal estates ("villae" or in dative plural "villis"), from which the military could draw its resources. At the same time, Charlemagne had a peripatetic rulership, constantly moving from one place to another since only his actual presence guaranteed the maintenance of his authority. His court hence stayed at those estates until the resources were depleted. The following text taken from his Capitulare de villis proves to be a major text reflecting the extensive administrative efforts made to maintain the huge Carolingian empire. Today, the Capitulare also provides much valuable information about the management of an early-medieval farm, about the types of fruit, wheat, animals, bees, etc., that could be found at every estate all over the empire, and about the existential need at that time to be on the guard for everything supporting everyday life, when famine was never far away.

We desire that each steward shall make an annual statement of all our income, giving an account of our lands cultivated by the oxen which our own plowmen drive and of our lands which the tenants of farms ought to plow; of the pigs, of the rents, of the obligations and fines; of the game taken in our forests without our permission; of the various compositions; of the mills, of the forest, of the fields, of the bridges and ships; of the free men and the districts under obligations to our treasury; of markets, vineyards, and those who owe wine to us; of the hay, firewood, torches, planks, and other kinds of lumber; of the waste lands; of the vegetables, millet, panic; of the wool, flax, and hemp; of the fruits of the trees; of the nut trees, larger and smaller; of the grafted trees of all kinds; of the gardens; of the turnips; of the fish ponds; of the hides, skins, and horns; of the honey and wax; of the fat, tallow, and soap; of the mulberry wine, cooked wine, mead, vinegar, beer, and wine, new and old; of the new grain and the old; of the hens and eggs; of the geese; of the number of fishermen, workers in metal, sword makers, and shoemakers; of the bins and boxes; of the turners and saddlers: or the forges and mines,—that is, of iron, lead, or other substances; of the colts and fillies. They shall make all these known to us, set forth separately and in order, at Christmas, so that we may know what and how much of each thing we have.

The greatest care must be taken that whatever is prepared or made with the hands,—that is, bacon, smoked meat, sausage,[1] partially salted meat, wine, vinegar, mulberry wine, cooked wine, garum,[2] mustard, cheese, butter, malt, beer, mead, honey, wax, flour,—all should be prepared and made with the greatest cleanliness.

Each steward on each of our domains shall always have, for the sake of ornament, peacocks, pheasants, ducks, pigeons, partridges, and turtle-doves.

In each of our estates the chambers shall be provided with counterpanes, cushions, pillows, bedclothes, coverings for the tables and benches; vessels of brass, lead, iron, and wood; andirons, chains, pothooks, adzes axes, augers, cutlasses, and all other kinds of tools, so that it shall never be necessary to go elsewhere for them, or to borrow them. And the weapons which are carried against the enemy shall be well cared for, so as to keep them in good condition; and when they are brought back they shall be placed in the chamber.

For our women's work they are to give at the proper time, as has been ordered, the materials,—that is, the linen, wool, woad, vermilion, madder, wool combs, teasels, soap, grease, vessels, and the other objects which are necessary.

Of the kinds of food not forbidden on fast days, two thirds shall be sent each year for our own use,—that is, of the vegetables, fish, cheese, butter, honey, mustard, vinegar, millet, panic, dried and green herbs, radishes, and, in addition, of the wax, soap, and other small products; and let it be reported to us, by a statement, how much is left, as we have said above; and this statement must not be omitted as in the past, because after those two thirds we wish to know how much remains.

Each steward shall have in his district good workmen, namely, blacksmiths, a goldsmith, a silversmith, shoemakers, turners, carpenters, sword makers, fishermen, foilers, soap makers, men who know how to make beer, cider, perry, or other kind of liquor good to drink, bakers to make pastry for our table, net makers who know how to make nets for hunting, fishing, and fowling, and other sorts of workmen too numerous to be designated.

[trans. Munro]

---

1   Some of the many names of products here given are of uncertain meaning.
2   A kind of drink made of salt fish.

ENGLAND IN THE MIDDLE AGES

By King Alfred, his Introduction to the Pastoral Charge by Gregory the Great

King Alfred (848/849–October 26, 899) was King of Wessex from 871 to 899 and is commonly identified as King Alfred the Great because of his successful defense against Viking attacks against England. He was the first to use the epithet "Anglo-Saxon" for his kingship. He is highly recognized for his major attempts to introduce a better education system, legal system, and an improved military organization. Very similar to Charlemagne, Alfred called in outstanding scholars to his court and charged them with the development of a sophisticated educational organization for his kingdom. Most amazingly, Alfred translated four major religious and philosophical works himself from Latin into Anglo-Saxon: Gregory the Great's Pastoral Care, *Boethius's* Consolation of Philosophy, *St. Augustine's* Soliloquies, *and the first fifty psalms of the Psalter. He also can be recognized for his translation of excerpts from the Vulgate book of* Exodus *(Old Testament) in his law code.*

I. KING ALFRED'S INTEREST IN LEARNING

King Alfred, in his introduction to the *Pastoral Charge,* by Gregory the Great, which he translated into Anglo-Saxon, gives a remarkable picture of the conditions of the time.

King Alfred bids greet Bishop Waerferth with loving words and with friendship; and I let it be known to thee that it has very often come into my mind what wise men there formerly were throughout England, both of sacred and secular orders; and what happy times there were then; and how the kings who had power over the nation in those days obeyed God and his ministers; how they preserved peace, morality, and order at home, and at the same time enlarged their territory abroad; and how they prospered both in war and in wisdom; and also the sacred orders, how zealous they were both in teaching and learning, and in all the services they owed to God; and how foreigners came to this land in search of wisdom and instruction, the which we should now have to get from abroad if we were to have them.

So general became the decay of learning in England that there were very few on this side of the Humber who could understand the rituals in English, or translate a letter from Latin into English; and I believe that there were not many beyond the Humber. There were so few, in fact, that I cannot remember a single person south of the Thames when I came to the throne. Thanks be to God Almighty that we now have some teachers among us. And therefore I command thee to disengage thyself, as I believe thou art willing, from worldly matters as often as thou art able, that thou mayest apply the wisdom which God has given thee wherever thou canst. Consider what punishments would come upon us if we neither loved wisdom ourselves nor suffered other men to obtain it: we should love the name only of Christian, and very few of the Christian virtues.

When I thought of all this I remembered also how I saw the country before it had been all ravaged and burned; how the churches throughout the whole of England stood filled with treasures and books. There was also a great multitude of God's servants, but they had very little knowledge of the books, for they could not understand anything of them because they were not written in their own language. As if they had said: "Our forefathers, who formerly held these places, loved wisdom, and through it they obtained wealth and bequeathed it to us. In this we can still see their traces, but we cannot follow them, and therefore we have lost both the wealth and the wisdom, because we would not incline our hearts after their example."

When I remembered all this, I wondered extremely that the good and wise men who were formerly all over England, and had learned perfectly all the books, did not wish to translate them into their own language. But again I soon answered myself and said, "Their own desire for learning was so great that they did not suppose that men would ever be so careless, and that learning would so decay; and they wished, moreover, that the wisdom in this land might increase with our knowledge of languages." Then I remembered how the law was first known in Hebrew, and when the Greeks had learned it how they translated the whole of it into their own language, and all other books besides. And again the Romans, when they had learned it, translated the whole of it, through learned interpreters, into, their own language. And also all other Christian nations translated a part of it into their own language.

Therefore it seems better to me, if you agree, for us also to translate some of the books which are most needful for all men to know into the language which we can all understand; and for you to see to it, as can easily be done if we have tranquillity enough, that all the free-born youth now in England, who are rich enough to be able to devote themselves to it, be set to learn as long as they are not fit for any other occupation, until that they are well able to read English writing; and let those afterwards be taught more in the Latin language who are to continue learning, and be promoted to a higher rank.

When I remembered how the knowledge of Latin had decayed throughout England, and yet that many could read English writing, I began, among other various and manifold troubles of this kingdom, to translate into English the book which is called in Latin *Pastoralis*, and in English *Shepherd's Book*, sometimes word by word, and sometimes according to the sense, as I had learned it from Plegmund, my archbishop, and Asser, my bishop, and Grimbold, my mass-priest, and John, my mass-priest. And when I had learned it as I could best understand it and most clearly interpret it, I translated it into English.

I will send a copy of this to every bishopric in my kingdom; and on each copy there shall be a clasp worth fifty mancuses. And I command, in God's name, that no man take the clasp from the book, or the book from the minster. It is uncertain how long there may be such learned bishops, as thanks be to God there now are nearly everywhere; therefore I wish these copies always to remain in their places, unless the bishop wish to take them with him, or they be lent out anywhere, or any one wish to make a copy of them.

[trans. King Alfred]

Bruno, the Ideal of a Scholar in the Tenth Century

By Ruotger

There was a marked revival of interest in learning in Germany under Otto the Great. We can form some idea of its character from Ruotger's Life of Bruno, Otto's scholarly brother, which is one of the most interesting biographies of the earlier Middle Ages.

When [in 928] the noble child of kings was four years old he was sent to Utrecht, to be instructed by the venerable Bishop Baldric in liberal studies. ... Of his progress we have heard from the bishop's own lips, for he was wont to tell of it often to the glory of Godo. So we know that when the boy had acquired the first rudiments of grammar he began to read, under his teacher's guidance, the poet Prudentius. This poet is Catholic in faith and in aspiration, excellent in eloquence and in truth, pleasing in meter, rich in meaning. His verses delighted the boy's heart. He mastered the words and the inner meaning, and, if I may say so, drank the purest nectar of the spirit like one athirst. As time went on, his eager mind grasped all sorts of liberal studies within the range of Greek and Latin eloquence. ... He would not allow books which he had studied or had before him to be carelessly torn or creased, or handled heedlessly in any way. ...

Bruno had given himself to God when he was very young; but when his brother Otto came to the throne, he recalled Bruno from the retirement of the schools to the palace, and gave him an honorable post, as was fitting. Yet he never ceased to seek learning. He was not satisfied to gather in the treasury of his mind lore easy to mine. Nay, he collected from far and near riddles and philosophical problems foreign to the human understanding and gave them room in his heart The seven liberal arts had been long forgotten: he brought them again to light. Whatever historians, orators, poets, philosophers had to tell that was novel or great he closely investigated, aided by teachers of the language in which the books were written.

His Latin style was well-nigh perfect, and his influence made the style of others polished and clear. He was in no wise haughty, but was dignified, courteous, affable, charming. After meals most men, even, so we understand, eminent ones, are given to rest awhile. Bruno, on the contrary, busied himself tirelessly with reading and thinking. He would not give up the morning hours at any price and never yielded to drowsiness. Jests and buffoonery which make everybody shake with laughter when put into the mouths of various persons in tragedy and comedy, he read through gravely and seriously. He thought their meaning was worthless; he estimated the style as the main thing. He took his library everywhere with him. When he followed the king he had, wherever the royal tents were pitched, the source and the materials for his studies,—the source in the sacred books, the materials in secular ones. ... Even when he traveled he was not idle; and in a crowd he was as if alone, We could not say this of many men. ...

He allowed himself no luxuries. He refused over and over again in the king's palace to wear the fine and soft clothing in which he had been nurtured. Among servants clad in purple and soldiers gleaming with gold he wore the mean garb and the sheepskins of a rustic. He especially spurned the comforts of the couch. He rarely frequented the bath with those who wished to make their skin white and shining. This is the more wonderful because he had been used from the cradle to the greatest daintiness and to royal splendor.

Always and everywhere, in public and in private, he bore himself as one who would avoid human praise; yet he served as an example to his inferiors. Many men profited by his words and yet more by his example.

[From *Readings in European History*, ed. James Harvey Robinson]

TALES ILLUSTRATING THE MIRACULOUS POWER OF THE SACRAMENTS

By Caesarius of Heisterbach, Jacques de Vitry, Stephen of Bourbon

C aesarius of Heisterbach (ca. 1180–ca. 1240) was the prior of the former Cistercian abbey of Heisterbach near Bonn, Germany since 1199. After he had joined his convent, he was appointed master of novices, that is, of young aspirants who applied to join the convent, that is, mostly younger students who were supposed to embrace the spirit of austere asceticism characteristic of that order. In this role Caesarius resorted to storytelling about miraculous events in the lives of people that regularly motivate them to abandon their secular existence and to enter a monastery. These miracle tales became so famous that he was asked by his Abbot Henry to record these accounts, which became the basis for his most famous collection, the Dialogus magnus visionum ac miraculorum (ca. 1219–1223). Here a teacher and his student examine specific cases of miraculous events through which the listener can learn ethical, moral, and religious lessons. In 1228 Caesarius was appointed prior of his monastery and had to accompany his abbot on many travels through Germany and Friesland. He continued to write many other treatises and narratives, as listed in his Epistola Catalogica from 1238, containing thirty-six items. But his Dialogus (ca. 1219–1223) was the most popular one for a long time to come and deserves our full attention because it provides an excellent mirror of contemporary culture and the history of mentality during the thirteenth century. The text has survived in more than 100 manuscripts and was first printed in 1471 in Cologne, thus proving to be a true 'bestseller' throughout the entire Middle Ages.

There were many tales current in the twelfth and thirteenth centuries which were used by preachers and writers to show the wondrous workings of the sacraments and the timely intervention in human affairs of the Virgin and the saints. Three collections of these anecdotes are especially well known: (1) The *Dialogues concerning Miracles*, brought together by a devout Cistercian monk, Caesar of Heisterbach (d. *ca.* 1240), early in the thirteenth century; (2) the sermon stories of Jacques de Vitry (d. 1240), a bishop and cardinal, famous for his preaching; (3) the anecdotes or apologues of Stephen of Bourbon, a Dominican inquisitor (d. 1261), a man of wide experience and much sagacity.

In Hemmenrode a certain aged priest, Henry by name, died a few years ago. He was a holy and just man, and had been for many years sacristan in that monastery. When he was celebrating the mass one day at the altar of St. John the Baptist, in the choir of the lay brethren, a certain one of the lay brethren standing near saw, in the hands of the priest, the Saviour in the form of a man. Nevertheless the priest himself did not see it. One of the elders of that convent related this to me.

I have heard that a certain rustic, wishing to become wealthy and having many hives of bees, asked certain evil men how he could get rich and increase the number of his bees. He was told by some one that if he retained the sacred host on Easter and placed it in some one of his hives, he would entice away all of his neighbor's bees, which, leaving their own hives, would come to the place where the body of our Lord was and there would make honey. So he did this.

Then all the bees came to the hive where the body of Christ was, and just as if they felt sorrow for the irreverence done to it, by their labor they began to construct a little church and to erect foundations, and bases, and columns, and an altar; then with the greatest reverence they placed the body of our Lord upon the altar. And within their little beehive they formed the little church with wonderful and most beautiful workmanship. The bees, of the vicinity, leaving their hives, came to that one; and over that work they sang in their own manner certain wonderful melodies like hymns.

The rustic, hearing this, marveled. But waiting until the fitting time for collecting the honey, he found nothing in his hives. Finding himself impoverished through the means by which he had expected to be enriched, he went to the hive where he had placed the host, and where he saw the bees had come together. But when he approached, just as if they wished to vindicate the insult to our Saviour, the bees rushed upon the rustic and stung him so severely that he escaped with difficulty and in great agony. Going to the priest, he related all that he had done, and what the bees had done.

The priest, by the advice of the bishop, collected his parishioners and made a procession to that place. Then the bees, leaving the hive, rose in the air, making sweet melody. Raising the hive, they found inside the noble structure of that little church and the body of our Lord placed upon the altar. Then, returning thanks, they bore to their own church that little church of the bees, constructed with such skill and elegance, and placed it on the altar.

By this deed those who do not reverence, but offer insult instead, to the sacred body of Christ, or the sacred place where it is, ought to be put to great confusion.

Also it is related that once when a certain holy father was engaged with the brethren in some work, he forgot to recite the *nones* at the right time, on account of his occupation. Afterwards he saw the devil passing before him, bearing on his shoulders a very large book, in the shape of a roll, which looked as large as a tower; and he adjured the devil in the name of the Lord to drop the book. When the monk unrolled the book, he found written on one page that he himself had not said the *nones* on the day and at the hour when he ought Whereupon, prostrating himself at once at the feet of his companions, he confessed his negligence, and immediately looking again in the devil's roll, he found that what had been written there was erased, and thereby he knew the efficacy of confession.

A certain very religious man told me that this happened in a place where he had been staying. A virtuous and pious matron came frequently to the church and served God most devoutly day and night. There also came a certain monk, the guardian and treasurer of the monastery, who had a great reputation for piety, and truly devout he was. When, however, the two frequently conversed together in the church concerning religious matters, the devil, envying their virtue and reputation, tempted them very sorely, so that the spiritual love was changed to carnal Accordingly they fixed upon a night when the monk was to leave his monastery, taking the treasures of the church, and the matron her home, with a sum of money which she should steal from her husband.

After they had fled, the monks, on rising in the morning, saw that the chests had been broken open and the treasures of the church stolen; and not finding the monk, they quickly pursued him; likewise the husband his wife. Overtaking the monk and the woman with the treasure and money, they brought them back and threw them into prison. So great was the scandal throughout the whole country, and so much were all religious persons reviled, that the harm from the infamy and scandal was far greater than from the sin itself.

Then the monk, restored to his senses, began with many tears to pray to the blessed Virgin, whom from infancy he had always served, and never before had any such misfortune happened to him. Likewise the said matron began urgently to implore the aid of the blessed Virgin, whom regularly, day and night, she had been accustomed to salute and kneel in prayer before her image. At length the blessed Virgin, very angry, appeared, and after she had sorely upbraided them, she said: "I can obtain the remission of your sins from my Son, but what can I do about such a dreadful scandal? For you have so befouled the name of religious persons before all the people, that in the future no one will trust them. The harm you have done is almost irremediable."

Nevertheless the merciful Virgin, overcome by their prayers, summoned the demons who had caused the deed and enjoined upon them that, as they had caused the scandal to religion, they must bring it to an end. As they were not able to resist her commands, after much anxiety and various conferences, they found a way to remove the infamy. In the night they placed the monk in his church, and, repairing the broken receptacle as it was before, they placed the treasure in it. Also after replacing the money in it they closed and locked the chest which the matron had opened. And they set the woman in her room and in the place where she was accustomed to pray by night.

When the monks found the treasure of their monastery, and their brother praying to God just as he had been accustomed to do, and as the husband saw his wife, and the money was found just as it had been before, they became stupefied and wondered. Rushing to the prison, they saw the monk and the woman in fetters just as they had left them; for one of the demons was seen by them transformed into the likeness of a monk and another into the likeness of a woman. When everybody in the whole city had come together to see the miracle, the demons said in the hearing of all, "Let us go, for sufficiently have we deluded these people by causing them to think evil of religious persons." And, saying this, they suddenly disappeared. Then all threw themselves at the feet of the monk and of the woman and demanded pardon.

Behold how great infamy and scandal and what inestimable damage the devil would have wrought against religious persons, if the blessed Virgin had not aided them.

[trans. Munro]

Tales Illustrating the Medieval Attitude Toward Heretics

By Caesarius of Heisterbach

From the lips of the same brother Elias, a venerable man, I learned that when certain heretics were scattering the virulent seeds of error in parts of Burgundy, both the Preaching Friars and the Minorites drew the two-edged sword of God's word against these same heretics, opposing them valiantly, until they were finally taken by the magistrate of the district. He sent them to the stake, as they merited, in order that these workers of iniquity should perish in their wickedness as a wholesome lesson to others.

Quantities of wood having been supplied in plenty to feed the flames, suddenly a toad of wonderful size appeared, and without being driven, betook itself of its own accord into the midst of the flames. One of the heretics, who was reported to be their bishop, had fallen on his back in the fire. The toad took his place on this man's face and in the sight of all ate out the heretic's tongue.

By the next day his whole body, except his bones, had been turned into disgusting toads, which could not be counted for their great number. The inhabitants, seeing the miracle, glorified God and praised him in his servants, the Preaching Friars, because the Lord had, in his mercy, delivered them from the horror of such pollution.

God omnipotent surely wished to show through the most unseemly and filthiest of animals, how foul and infamous are the teachings of heretics, so that all might thereafter carefully shun the heretic as they would the poisonous toad. Just as among four-footed creatures the toad is held the foulest, so the teachings of the heretic are more debased and filthy than those of any other religious sect. The blindness of heresy justifies the perfidy of the Jews. Its pollution makes the madness of the Mohammedans a pure thing in contrast The licentiousness of the heretics would leave Sodom and Gomorrah stainless. What is held most enormous in crime becomes most holy when compared with the shame and ignominy of heresy. Therefore, dear Christian, flee this unspeakable evil, in comparison with which all other crimes are as trifles.

Two men, simply clad but not without guile, not sheep but ravening wolves, came to Besançon, feigning the greatest piety. Moreover they were pale and thin, they went about barefooted and fasted daily, they did not miss a single morning the matins in the cathedral, nor did they accept anything from any one except a little food. When by this hypocrisy they had attracted the attention of every one, they began to vomit forth their hidden. poison and to preach to the ignorant new and unheard-of heresies. In order, moreover, that the people might believe their teachings, they ordered meal to be sifted on the sidewalk and walked on it without leaving a trace of a footprint Likewise, walking upon the water, they did not sink; also they had little huts burned over their heads, and after the huts had been burned to ashes, they came out uninjured. After this they said to the people, "If you do not believe our words, believe our miracles."

The bishop and the clergy, hearing of this, were greatly disturbed. And when they wished to resist the men, affirming that they were heretics and deceivers and ministers of the devil, they escaped with difficulty from being stoned by the people. Now that bishop was a good and learned man and a native of our province. Our aged monk, Conrad, who told me these facts and who was in that city at the time, knew him well.

The bishop, seeing that his words were of no avail and that the people intrusted to his charge were being seduced from the faith by the devil's agents, summoned a certain clerk that he knew, who was very well versed in necromancy, and said: "Certain men in my city are doing so and so. I ask you to find out from the devil, by your art, who they are, whence they come, and by what means they work so many and such wonderful miracles. For it is impossible that they should do wonders through divine inspiration when their teaching is so contrary to that of God." The clerk said, "My lord, I have long ago renounced that art." The bishop replied: "You see clearly in what straits I am. I must either acquiesce in their teachings or be stoned by the people. Therefore I enjoin upon you, for the remission of your sins, that you obey me in this matter."

The clerk, obeying the bishop, summoned the devil, and, when asked why he had called him, responded: "I am sorry that I have deserted you. And because I desire to be more obedient to you in the future than in the past, I ask you to tell me who these men are, what they teach, and by what means they work so great miracles." The devil replied, "They are mine and sent by me, and they preach what I have placed in their mouths." The clerk responded, "How is it that they cannot be injured, or sunk in the water, or burned by fire?" The demon replied again, "They have under their armpits, sewed between the skin and the flesh, my compacts, in which the homage done by them to me is written; and it is by virtue of these that they work such miracles and cannot be injured by any one." Then the clerk said, "What if those should be taken away from them?" The devil replied, "Then they would be weak, just like other men." The clerk, having heard this, thanked the demon, saying, "Now go, and when you are summoned by me, return."

He then went to the bishop and related these things to him in due order. The latter, filled with great joy, summoned all the people of the city to a suitable place and said: "I am your shepherd, ye are my sheep. If those men, as you say, confirm their teaching by signs, I will follow them with you. If not, it is fitting that they should be punished and that you should penitently return to the faith of your fathers with me." The people replied, "We have seen many signs from them." The bishop said, "But I have not seen them."

Why prolong my tale? The plan pleased the people. The heretics were summoned. The bishop was present. A fire was kindled in the midst of the city. However, before the heretics entered it, they were secretly summoned to the bishop. He said to them, "I want to see if you have anything evil about you." Hearing this, they stripped quickly and said with great confidence, "Search our bodies and our garments carefully." The soldiers, however, following the instructions of the bishop, raised the men's arms, and noticing under the armpits some scars that were healed up, cut them open with their knives and extracted from them little scrolls which had been sewed in.

Having received these, the bishop went forth with the heretics to the people and, having commanded silence, cried out in a loud voice, "Now shall your prophets enter the fire, and if they are not injured I will believe in them." The wretched men trembled and said, "We are not able to enter now." Then the bishop told the people of the evil which had been detected, and showed the compacts. Then all were furious and hurled the devil's ministers into the fire which had been prepared, to be tortured with the devil in eternal flames. And thus, through the grace of God and the zeal of the bishop, the growing heresy was extinguished, and the people who had been seduced and corrupted were cleansed by penance.

[trans. Munro]

THE EUCHARIST
AS A CHARM
FROM DIALOGUS MIRACULORUM

By Caesarius of Heisterbach

*A*dapted from Coulton Introduction, p. 58. *Caesarius of Heisterbach was possibly born and certainly educated in Cologne. After some inward struggle he became a Cistercian monk at the monastery of Heisterbach, where he eventually became prior and Teacher of the Novices. It was for the novices that he wrote his* Dialogus Miraculorum, *one of the most intimate documents of the Middle Ages. This, some biographical and chronological treatises and some homelies were all apparently written between 1220 and 1235. The Dialogue was printed five times between 1475 and 1605. His faults are those of his time, but his earnestness and vividness are apparent also. Modern commentators have note, however, his credulousness. The citation here are to the volume and page numbers of Joseph Strange's critical edition (Cologne: 1851).*

THE EUCHARIST AS A CHARM

(Caes. Heist. vol. II, p. 170-)

MONK: I THINK it is less than two years now since a certain priest who doubted of the Sacrament of Christ's Body celebrated mass in the town of Wildenburg. As he was reciting the canon of the mass, with some hesitation concerning so marvelous a conversion of bread into Christ's Body, the Lord showed him raw flesh in the host. This was seen also by Widekind, a noble standing behind his back, who drew the priest aside after mass and enquired diligently what he had done or thought during the canon; he, therefore, terrified both by the vision and by the question, confessed and denied not how at that hour he had doubted of the sacrament. And each told the other how he had seen raw flesh in the host. This same Widekind had to wife the daughter of Siegfried of Runkel, a niece of the abbess of Rheindorf, who told me this vision last year. Would you also know what the Lord shows to priests of evil life, for that He is crucified by them? … A certain lecherous priest wooed a woman; and, unable to obtain her consent, he kept the most pure Body of the Lord in his mouth after mass, hoping that, if he thus kissed her, her will would be bent to his desire by the force of the Sacrament. But the Lord, (who complains through the mouth of the Prophet Zachariah, sayin "You crucify me daily, even the whole nation of you" [a misquote of Zach. 3:9] thus hindered his evildoing. When he would fain have gone forth from the church door, he seemed to himself to grow so huge that he struck his head against the ceiling of the sacred building. The wretched man was so startled that he drew the host from his mouth, and buried it, not knowing what he did, in a corner of the church [note: churches were commonly unpaved at this date]. But, fearing the swift vengeance of God, he confessed the sacrilege to a priest his familiar friend. So they went together to the place and threw back the dust, where they found not the appearance of bread, but the shape, though small, of a man hanging on the cross, fleshy and blood-stained. What was afterwards done with it or what the priest did, I forget, for it is long since this told me by Hermann our Cantor, to whom the story was well-known.

NOVICE. If all priests heard such stories, and believed in them, I think that they would honor Divine Sacraments more than they do now.

MONK: It is somewhat pitiful that we men, for whose salvation this sacrament was instituted, should be so lukewarm about it; while brute beasts, worms, and reptiles recognize in it their Creator. … A certain woman kept many bees, which throve not but died in great numbers; and, as she sought everywhere for a remedy, it was told her that if she placed the Lord>s Body among them, this plague would soon cease. She therefore went to church and, making as though she would communicate, took the Lord>s Body, which she took from her mouth as soon as the priest had departed, and laid it in one of her hives. Mark the marvelous power of God! These little worms, recognizing the might of their Creator, built their sweetest Guest, out of their sweetest honeycombs, a chapel of marvelous workmanship, wherein they set up a tiny altar of the same material and laid thereon this most holy Body: and God blessed their labors. In process of time the woman opened this hive, and was aware of the aforesaid chapel whereupon she hastened and confessed to the priest all that she had done and seen. Then he took with him his parishioners and came to the hive, where they drove away the bees that hovered round and buzzed in Praise of their creator; and, marveling at the little chapel with its walls and windows, roof and tower, door and altar, they brought back the Lord's Body with praise and glory to the church. For though God be marvelous in the saints, yet these His smallest creatures preached Him yet more marvelously. Yet, lest any presume to do this again, I will tell you of a terrible thing which the mistress [of novices] at Sankt Nicolas Insel [a convent of nuns on an island in the river Moselle] told me last year. There was in that island a demoniac girl, a laywoman, whom I also have seen there. A certain priest inquired of the devil that was in her, why Hartdyfa of Cochem had been so cruelly tormented for so long a time; and the demon answered through the girl's mouth, "Why? she has well and abundantly deserved it; for she sowed the most High on her cabbage beds." The priest understood not this saying, nor would n it further; he therefore sought out the woman Hartdyfa and told her of the devil's words, warning her not to deny if she understood them. She confessed her fault forthwith, saying, " I understand only too well; but I have never yet told it to any man. When I was young, and had got me a garden-plot to till, I took in a wandering woman one night as my guest: to whom when I complained of the ravage of my garden, telling how my cabbages were eaten up with caterpillars, she replied, 'I will teach thee a good remedy. Take thou the Lord's Body and crumble it up and sprinkle the crumbs over thy cabbages; so shall that plague cease forthwith.' I, wretched woman, caring more for my garden than for the Sacrament, having received the Lord's Body at Easter, took it from my mouth and used it as she had taught me, which did indeed turn to the comfort of my cabbages, but to mine own torment, as the devil has said."

NOVICE:. That woman was more cruel than Pilate's minions, who spared the dead Jesus and would not break His bones.

MONK:. Wherefore even to this day she is punished for that enormous fault, and her tortures are unheard-of. Let those who turn God's sacraments to temporal profit -or, more abominable still, to witchcraft-mark well this chastisement, even though they fear not the guilt.

CONFESSION, ORDEAL
AND MIRACLE
FROM DIALOGUS MIRACULORUM

By Caesarius of Heisterbach

A dapted from Coulton Introduction, p. 58. *Caesarius of Heisterbach was possibly born and certainly educated in Cologne. After some inward struggle he became a Cistercian monk at the monastery of Heisterbach, where he eventually became prior and Teacher of the Novices. It was for the novices that he wrote his* Dialogus Miraculorum, *one of the most intimate documents of the Middle Ages. This, some biographical and chronological treatises and some homelies were all apparently written between 1220 and 1235. The Dialogue was printed five times between 1475 and 1605. His faults are those of his time, but his earnestness and vividness are apparent also. Modern commentators have note, however, his credulousness. The citation here are to the volume and page numbers of Joseph Strange's critical edition (Cologne: 1851).*

CONFESSION, ORDEAL AND MIRACLE

From Caesarius of Heisterbach, vol. II, p. 243.

DOM BERNARD of Lippe, who was once an abbot and is now a bishop in Livonia, is wont to tell a miracle contrary to this last. "I knew, (he said,) a fisher in the bishopric of Utrecht who had long lived incontinently with a certain woman; and, because his sin was too notorious, fearing one day to be accused at the synod then impending, he said within himself: 'What will you now do, poor wretch? If you are accused of incontinence in this synod and must confess, you will forthwith be compelled to take her to wife; or if you deny it you will be convicted by the ordeal of white-hot iron and be still more confounded." So, coming forthwith to a priest (rather, as the event showed, from fear of punishment than from love of righteousness), he confessed his sin, asked from counsel and found it-. 'If,' said the priest, 'you have a firm purpose never to sin again with her, then you may carry the white-hot iron without further care and deny your sin; for I hope that the virtue of confession will free you." And this did, to the amazement of all who well knew his incontinence. Lo! here by God's power, as in former examples, the fire restrained its force against its own nature; and, as you will hear later, it grew hot even more marvelously against nature. To be brief, the man was absolved. Many days afterwards, as he rowed with another fisher at his work on the river, and the house of the aforesaid woman came in sight, then the other said unto him: 'I marvel greatly, and many marvel with me, why the iron did not burn you at the synod, though thy sin was so notorious.' He, boasting unworthily of the grace that had been conferred on him (for he had already conceived the purpose of sinning again), smote the river water with his hand and said: 'The fire hurt me no more than this water!' Mark the marvelous justice of God! who had guarded the penitent in His mercy, punished now by a just and strange miracle the same man when he relapsed: for no sooner had he touched the water than it was to him as white-hot iron. He drew back his hand suddenly cried aloud; but he left his skin in the water. Then, in tardy repentance, he told his comrade all that had befallen him."

Our fellow-monk Lambert was wont to tell a like miracle to this. A countryman who had a feud against another gave money to a certain wicked man of the Order of wandering Religious, (of whom there are many,) that he might burn the other's house; which this man, entering under the cloak of religion, set afire at a convenient time. Again this abandoned wretch, forgetful of the hospitality he had-received, set fire to the same house for the same bribe, after that it had been rebuilt. The, master, troubled at this double loss, accused all of whom he had any suspicion, but they purged themselves by the ordeal of white-hot iron. Again the burned house was rebuilt; and this iron which had been used for the ordeal was thrown into one corner of it. To be brief, that false religious vagrant came again, corrupted by his former covetousness, and was received with all kindness. He marked the aforesaid iron and asked what purpose it served: to which his host answered: "I know not who has twice set fire to my house; and, though I had suspicion of certain men, they have borne that iron at white-heat and yet were not burned" Then said the other: "The iron might be turned to some use": and lifting it up (as God would have it) he was so burned in the hand that he cried aloud and cast it down. When the master of the house saw this, he caught the incendiary by the cloak and cried: "Thou art the true culprit!" The e man was taken before the judge, confessed his crime unwillingly, and was condemned to be broken upon the wheel.

ADMONITIONS OF THE BLESSED FATHER
ST. FRANCIS TO HIS BRETHREN

By St. Francis of Assisi

St. Francis, or Giovanni di Pietro di Bernardone, nicknamed Francesco, was born ca. 1181/1182 as the son of a wealthy silk merchant in the Tuscan city of Assisi, Pietro di Bernardone. In 1204, when the young man was on his way to war in Puglia, he had a mystical vision, returned home and from then on dedicated his whole life to poverty in the service of God. Although he underwent severe conflicts with his father, who was strictly opposed to Francesco's religious conversion, the latter soon founded an order of preaching monks which was recognized by Pope Innocent III in 1215 as the Franciscans. St. Francis also established a parallel order for women, the Order of Poor Clares, all of whom, male and female, relied entirely on begging for alms. In contrast to the Benedictines, the Franciscans lived in cities where they could reach out to the people and preach. In 1219 Francis accompanied the Fifth Crusade to Egypt where he tried to convert the Sultan to Christianity. Although he failed in his intentions, he seems to have impressed the Muslim court. In 1224 Francis received his stigmata, physical signs of him having been accepted by Christ as his follower. He died on Oct. 3, 1226, and on July 16, 1228, Pope Gregory IX pronounced him a saint. The Franciscans grew to an international order and continue to exist all over the world until today. On March 13, 2013, the newly elected pope, Cardinal Jorge Mario Bergoglio of Argentina, a Jesuit, chose Francis as his papal name in honor of the founder of the Franciscans.

I. OUR LORD said to His Disciples: 'I am the way, and the truth, and the life. No man cometh to the Father but by Me. If you had known ME you would surely have known My Father also; and from henceforth you shall know Him and have seen Him. Philip saith to Him, Lord, show us the Father, and it is enough for us. Jesus saith to him, Have I been so long a time with you, and have you not known Me? Philip, he that seeth Me seeth the Father also.'

The Father dwells in light inaccessible. God is a Spirit, and no one ever saw God; therefore it is only by the spirit we can see Him, for the spirit giveth life, the flesh profiteth nothing. For neither can the Son, inasmuch as He is equal to the Father, be seen, as the Father and the Holy Ghost cannot be seen; therefore all those who saw Our Lord Jesus Christ according to His Humanity, but did not see and believe according to the spirit and the Divinity that He was the Son of God, were condemned.

II. In like manner, all those who behold the Sacrament, which is sanctified by the Word of God upon the Altar in the hands of the priest, under the appearances of bread and wine, but who do not see and believe according to the Spirit and the Divinity that It is really the most holy Body and Blood of Our Lord Jesus Christ, are condemned. He, the Most High, has declared it, when He said: 'This is My Body, and the Blood of the New Testament;' and 'They who eat My Flesh and drink My Blood shall have eternal life.' He who has the Spirit of God, Who dwells in His faithful servants—he it is who receives the most holy Body and Blood of the Lord; but all others who presume to receive Him not having this spirit, eat and drink judgment to themselves. Wherefore, 'O ye sons of men, how long will you be dull of heart? why do you love vanity and seek after lying?' Why will you not know the truth, and believe in the Son of God? Behold, every day He humbles Himself as when He descended from His royal throne in heaven into the womb of the Virgin Mary; every day He comes to us with like humility; every day He descends from the Bosom of His Heavenly Father upon the Altar in the hands of the priest. And as He appeared in true flesh to His holy Apostles, so now He shows Himself to us under the form of bread. And as they with the eyes of their body saw only His flesh, but contemplating Him with their spiritual eyes, believed Him to be their Lord and their God; so we, who see only bread and wine with our bodily eyes, believe most firmly that It is His most holy Body and true and living Blood. And in this way Our Lord is always present with His faithful servants, as He said: 'Behold, I am with you all days, even to the consummation of the world.'

III. God said to Adam: 'Of every tree in paradise thou mayest eat; but of the tree of knowledge of good and evil thou shalt not eat.' Adam might eat of every tree in paradise, because as long as he was obedient he did not sin. That man eats of the tree of knowledge of good and evil, who acts according to his own will, and prides himself upon the good which the Lord has given him and works in him ; and thus through the suggestion of the devil and his own transgression, this good becomes to him as the apple of the knowledge of evil. Therefore it is necessary that he should suffer punishment.

IV. Our Lord said in the Gospel: 'He who does not renounce all he possesses, cannot be My disciple,' and 'He that will save his life shall lose it.' That man renounces all he has, and loses his life, who places himself by obedience entirely in the hands of his Superiors, and always does and says those things that are agreeable to their wishes (provided that the things he does are good). This is true obedience. And if a subject thinks that something would be better and more profitable to his soul than what his Superiors command, let him sacrifice his will to God, and endeavour to accomplish the work enjoined him. This is charitable obedience, which causes him to sacrifice himself for God and his neighbour. If, however, a prelate orders a subject to do anything that would be injurious to his soul, he may refuse to obey, but he must not on that account leave his Superior. And if, for this cause, he suffer persecution from Superiors, he should love them the more in the Lord. Now he who would rather suffer persecution than separate himself from his Brethren, practises perfect obedience, for he gives his life for his Brethren. There are many religious who, under pretence of doing a greater good than what is commanded by their Superiors, look back, and return to the vomit of their own will. These are murderers, for they cause the loss of many souls through their fault.

V. Our Lord says: 'I did not come to be ministered unto, but to minister.' Those who are appointed to be over others, should glory in this office only as much as if they had been chosen to wash the feet of their Brethren; and if they are more disturbed at the loss of their dignity, than they would be at the loss of that lowly office, they may be sure their soul is in danger, and in proportion to the disturbance they feel is the greatness of their peril. Think, O man, how great is the excellence God has bestowed on you, for He created and formed you to the image of His beloved Son according to the body, and to His own likeness according to the spirit. And all creatures under heaven, according to their nature, know, serve, and obey their Creator better than you; the devils did not crucify Him, but you, incited by them, have crucified Him, and still crucify Him when you delight in vice and sin. Of what then can you glory? For if you were so wise and clever that you knew all things, and could interpret all languages, and penetrate all heavenly mysteries with the greatest clearness, you could not glory in all this, for one demon knows more of heavenly, and even of earthly things, than all men put together, although some have been endowed with special wisdom by God. Again, if you were richer and more beautiful than all others, nay, even if you could work miracles and put the devils to flight, still all these things are contrary to your nature, and in no way belong to you. In all this you cannot glory, but in one thing we may glory, that is in our infirmities, and in bearing daily the holy Cross of Our Lord Jesus Christ. Let us all, my Brethren, consider the Good Shepherd, Who bore the suffering of the Cross to save His sheep. The sheep of the Lord followed Him in tribulation and persecution, in shame and hunger, in infirmity and temptations, and other sufferings, and for this they have received eternal life from the Lord. Therefore it is a great shame to the servants of God, that the Saints should do the works, and that we should expect glory and honour for preaching and reciting the works they have performed.

VI. The Apostle has said: 'The letter killeth; the Spirit giveth life.' Those are killed by the letter who desire to know the words only that they may be reputed more learned than others, and that they may acquire great riches to bestow on their relations and friends. Those religious are killed by the letter, who will not follow the spirit of the Divine teaching, but only care to know the words and to interpret them to others. And they are enlivened by the spirit of the Divine teaching, who offer all their knowledge, and all they wish to know, to the great God, from Whom is all good, for they do not live by the body only, but by the words and examples of the Holy Scriptures.

VII. The Apostle says: 'No one can say, the Lord Jesus, except by the Holy Ghost,' and 'There is none that doeth good, no, not one.' Therefore, whoever envies his Brother for the good which God says or does in him, commits a sin like unto blasphemy, for he envies the Most High Himself, Who is the Author of all good words and works.

VIII. The Lord says in the Gospel: 'Love your enemies, do good to them who hate you, and pray for those who persecute you,' etc. They really love their enemies who do not grieve for the injury done to themselves, but for the sin committed, on account of the love they bear to God, and who show this love by their works.

IX. There are many who, if they commit sin, or suffer any injury, immediately blame their neighbour or their enemy. But this is not just, for each one has his enemy in his power, namely, his body, by which he sinned. Therefore blessed is the man who having this enemy in his power always keeps it chained, and wisely defends himself from it, for if he do this, no other visible enemy can hurt him.

X. Nothing but sin should be displeasing to the servant of God. And no matter in what way a person sins, if the servant of God is disturbed and angry at it (unless it be for the love of God,) he commits a fault and deserves punishment. The true servant of God is not troubled or angry about anything; he lives justly and seeks not himself. Blessed is he who keeps nothing back, but who renders 'to Caesar the things that are Caesar's, and to God the things that are God's.'

XI. The servant of God may know whether he has the spirit of God, if, when the Lord works some good through him, he is not puffed up in body or mind, knowing that in himself he is contrary to all good, but rather appears viler in his own eyes, and esteems himself more miserable than other men.

XII. It cannot be known how much humility or patience a servant of God has, when he has everything according to his wishes or necessity. But when the time comes that those who ought to befriend him turn against him, then he has as much humility and patience as he shows, and no more.

XIII. 'Blessed are the poor in spirit, for theirs is the kingdom of heaven.' There are many who recite long offices and prayers, who afflict their bodies with abstinences and penances, but who are scandalised and disturbed by a single word, or by any injury done; to them, or by the loss of anything belonging to them. These are not truly poor in spirit, for he who is truly poor in spirit hates himself and loves others, even if they strike him on the cheek.

XIV. 'Blessed are the peace-makers, for they shall be called the children of God.' Those are truly peace-makers who in all the sufferings of this life keep their body and soul in peace for the love of our Lord Jesus Christ.

XV. 'Blessed are the clean of heart, for they shall see God.' Those are truly clean of heart who despise the things of earth and aspire to those of heaven, and who never desist from adoring and contemplating the living God with a pure heart and mind.

XVI. Blessed is that servant who is not more exalted on account of the good God says and works by him, than for that which He says and works by others. That man sins who wishes to receive more from others than he is himself willing to give to the Lord his God. Blessed is the man who bears with the weakness of his neighbour, as he would wish others to bear with him in like case.

XVII. Blessed is the servant who gives and attributes all good to the Lord God, for he who retains anything for himself hides the money of the Lord his God, and all that he seems to have shall be taken from him. Blessed is that servant who does not think himself better when he is praised and exalted by men, than when he is despised and considered simple and good-for-nothing, for what a man is in the sight of God, that he is and no more. Woe to that religious who is placed in a high position by others, and is net willing to descend from it. And blessed is that servant who is elevated by others against his will, and who always desires to be under the feet of all.

XVIII. Blessed is the: religious who takes pleasure only in holy words and works of God, and who thus leads men to the love of God, with joy, happiness, and exultation. But woe to that religious who delights in vain and idle words, and by these tempts men to laughter. Blessed is that servant who does not speak for the hope of reward, who does not manifest all his thoughts, nor speak with eagerness, but who wisely considers what he should say and answer. Woe to that religious who does not keep secret the good which God does in him, manifesting it to others only by his works ; but who, for the hope of the reward, is more anxious to speak of it to men than to show it to God ; he may indeed receive the recompense he seeks, but those who hear him will derive but little benefit.

XIX. Blessed is that servant who bears discipline, accusations, and reprehensions from others as patiently as from himself. Blessed is the servant who mildly yields to reproof, obeys with modesty, humbly confesses his fault, and willingly makes satisfaction. Blessed is the servant who is not quick in excusing himself, and who humbly bears the shame and reprehension for sin when he has committed no fault. Blessed is that servant who is as humble among his Brethren and inferiors as among his Superiors and Prelates. Blessed is the servant who always remains under the rod of correction. He is a faithful and prudent servant who in all his offences does not delay to punish himself interiorly by contrition, and exteriorly by confession and works of satisfaction.

XX. Blessed is the servant who loves his Brother as much when he is ill and cannot do anything for him, as when he is well and can be of use to him. And blessed is he who loves his Brother as much when he is at a distance from him as when he is near, and who would say nothing about him behind his back, that he could not with charity say before his face. Blessed is that servant who trusts in the priests who live justly, according to the rules of the holy Roman Church, and woe to those who despise them; for even if they were sinners, still no one ought to judge them, for God reserves to Himself alone the right of doing so. For as their charge is greater than that of any others, namely, the administration of the most holy Body and Blood of Our Lord Jesus Christ, which they receive, and which they alone can give to others, so the, sin of those who offend against them is greater than against anyone else in the world.

XXI. Where charity and wisdom are, there is neither fear nor ignorance. Where patience and humility are, there is neither anger nor perturbation of mind. Where joyful poverty is found, there is neither cupidity nor avarice. Where there are quietness and meditation, there is neither solicitude nor dissipation. Where the fear of God guards the house, the enemy can find no entrance. Where mercy and discretion are, there is neither superfluity nor parsimony.

XXII. Blessed is the man who treasures up for heaven the good things which the Lord shows . him, and who does not desire to manifest them to men through the hope of reward, for the Most High will Himself make manifest his works to whom He pleases. Blessed is the servant who keeps the secrets of his Lord in his heart. These are the words of life and salvation, and whoever chooses them and fulfils them, shall find life and receive salvation from the Lord. Amen.

* * * *

The Praises of Wisdom, Simplicity, Poverty, Humility, Charity and Obedience.

O QUEENLY Wisdom, the Lord save thee with thy Sister, pure and holy Simplicity. O Lady holy Poverty, the Lord save thee with thy Sister holy Humility. O Lady holy Charity, the Lord save thee with thy Sister holy Obedience. O all ye holy virtues, may the Lord, from Whom you proceed, save you ! There is absolutely no man in the whole world who can possess one of you unless he first die to himself. He who possesses one virtue, and does not offend against the others possesses all ; and he who offends against one, possesses none, and offends against all and confounds altogether vices and sins. Holy Wisdom confounds Satan and all his malice. Pure and holy Simplicity confounds all the wisdom of this world and the prudence of the flesh. Holy Poverty confounds cupidity and avarice and all worldly cares. Holy Humility confounds pride, and all men and all things that are in the world. Holy Charity confounds all carnal and diabolical temptations and all earthly fears. Holy Obedience confounds the carnal and natural will, and keeps the body under subjection to the spirit and to Superiors ; it is submissive and docile to all men, and not to men only, but even to wild beasts, who may do with it whatever they will, according to the power God gives them from above. Thanks be to God. Amen.

* * * *

Of Perfect Joy—that the most Precious Gift which we can receive from the Holy Ghost, is Strength to conquer Self, and to bear Reproaches patiently for the Love of God.

ALTHOUGH the Friar Minor should give good example of great sanctity and edification throughout the whole world, still that is not perfect joy. And even if the Friar Minor should give sight to the blind, cure the paralysed, cast out devils, cause the deaf to hear, the lame to walk, the dumb to speak, and what is still greater, restore to life one who has been dead four days, still this is not perfect joy. And if the Friar Minor should know all kinds of languages, and all sciences, and the Scriptures, so that he could prophesy and reveal not only things future, but even the secrets of consciences, this would not be perfect joy. If the Friar Minor were to speak with the tongues of angels, if he knew the courses of the stars and the virtues of herbs, if all the hidden treasures of the earth were revealed to him, and if he understood the virtues and properties of all birds, fishes, animals, men, roots, stones, trees and water, this would not be perfect joy. And if the Friar Minor were to preach so eloquently as to convert all infidels to the faith, even this would not be perfect joy.

But if when we come to Our Lady of Angels, all drenched with rain and frozen with cold, covered with mud and exhausted with hunger, we should knock at the door, and the porter coming should say angrily: 'Who are you?' and when we answer: 'We are two of your Brethren,' he should reply: 'Nay, rather you are two impostors, who go about the world stealing the alms of the poor;' and if he should not let us in, but make us stand in the snow and rain, cold and almost starved to death; then, if we should bear patiently all these insults and injuries without disturbance of mind or murmuring, and if we should think humbly and charitably that the porter knew us truly, and that God inspired him to act in this way, write that this is perfect joy. And if we persevere in knocking, and the same porter should come out and treat us as importunate beggars, striking us violently and saying: 'Depart hence, you vile poltroons! Go to the hospital. Who are you? you shall not eat here;' and if we bear this patiently, and forgive these injuries with our whole heart, write that this is perfect joy. And if we, being overpowered with hunger, frozen with cold, and finding night approaching, knock at the door, and crying and weeping implore to be admitted, and the porter enraged exclaim, 'These are most impudent and obstinate men; I will pacify them;' and coming out with a thick and knotted stick, he take us by the cowl, and throwing us on the ground, beat us so severely as to cover us with wounds: if we bear all these injuries, all these evils and blows with joy, considering that we ought to share in the sufferings of Christ the Blessed, write and note most diligently, that this is perfect joy.

And now listen to the conclusion. Of all the gifts of the Holy Spirit which Christ has ever granted or will grant to His servants, the principal is the grace to conquer self, and willingly to suffer injuries for the love of God. 'What hast thou that thou hast not received? And if thou hast received it, why dost thou glory as if thou hadst not received it?' But in the Cross of afflictions and tribulations we may glory, for this in our own. And therefore the Apostle says: 'Far be it from me to glory, save in the Cross of Our Lord Jesus Christ.'

* * * *

CONFERENCE XV

Of those who Apply themselves to Learning

Those Brothers who study from curiosity will find their hands empty in the days of tribulation. Therefore I would rather they should be strengthened in virtue, that when the day of trial comes, they may have the Lord with them in their anguish; but I desire them to be grounded in holy Humility and pure Simplicity, in holy

Prayer, and my Lady Poverty. This is the only secure way to our own salvation, and the edification of others; for Christ, Whom the Brethren are bound to imitate, has taught us only this way, both by His Word and example. Many Brethren, under pretence of edifying others, will turn aside from their vocation, which is holy Humility, pure Simplicity, Prayer and Devotion, and our Lady holy Poverty. And it will happen to them that, while they imagine they are full of devotion, inflamed with love, and illuminated with the knowledge of God through their understanding the Holy Scriptures, they will, on this very account, remain cold and vain; and thus they will not be able to return to their first vocation, because they have lost the time of living as they ought, in vain and false study.

CONFERENCE XVI

Of Vain and Conceited Preachers

THERE are many, my Brethren, who devote themselves entirely to acquiring knowledge, losing their holy vocation by leaving the road of humility and prayer, and becoming dissipated in body and mind—who, if they find anyone converted and moved to penance by their sermons, become proud and puffed up by their work, and another's gains, when they have rather preached only to their own prejudice and condemnation, and have in reality worked nothing, except as the instruments of those by whom the Lord has truly acquired this fruit For while they believe that sinners are moved and converted by their knowledge and preaching, it is really by the prayers and tears of some poor, humble and simple Brothers that God works these conversions, although these holy Brothers are generally unconscious of it. God wills it to be so, lest they should become proud thereof. These, my Brethren, are 'knights of the round table,' who hide in deserts and lonely places, that they may more diligently give themselves up to prayer and meditation, weeping for their own sins and those of others, living simply and conversing humbly, whose sanctity is known to God, but hidden from their Brethren and from all men. But when the angels present their souls to God, then the Lord will show them the fruit and reward of their labours; namely, many souls that have been saved through their prayers, tears, and example. And He will say to them: 'Behold, My beloved children, such and such souls that have been saved by your prayers, tears, and example, and, "because you have been faithful in a few things, I will place you over many things." Others have preached and laboured with words of wisdom and knowledge, and I, on account of your merits, have rendered their words fruitful; receive, therefore, the reward of their labours, and the fruit of your merits, that is, the eternal kingdom which you have taken by violence with your humility and simplicity, your prayers and tears.' These, therefore, carrying their sheaves, namely, the fruit and merit of their holy Humility and Simplicity, shall enter rejoicing and exulting into the joy of their Lord ; while those, on the contrary, who have thought of nothing but knowing and pointing out the way of salvation to others, without walking therein themselves, will stand naked and empty-handed before the tribunal of Christ, bearing only the sheaves of shame, confusion, and sorrow. Thus the truth of holy Humility and Simplicity, of holy Prayer and Poverty, which is our vocation, will be exalted, glorified, and magnified; which truth those who are puffed up by the vain love of science contradict by their life and idle words, calling the truth falsehood, and persecuting those who walk in this truth. Then the errors and false opinions which they have held—which they have declared to be the truth—and by which they have plunged many into an abyss of blindness, will end in sorrow, shame, and confusion; and on account of the darkness of their minds, they will be cast into the exterior darkness, with the spirits of darkness.

CONFERENCE XVII

Of the Marks and Praise of a Good Preacher

I WISH, my beloved Brethren, the ministers of the Word of God to be such, that, devoting themselves to spiritual studies, they should not be hindered by undertaking any other duties. For they are chosen by the great King to proclaim to the people the laws which proceed from His mouth. The preacher ought first to imbibe in secret prayer what he afterwards brings forth in holy words; he ought to be inflamed interiorly before he speaks exteriorly. This office is certainly worthy of honour, and those who fulfil it ought to be reverenced by all, for they are the life of the body, the adversaries of the devils, the light of the world. Those preachers are to be commended who sometimes examine and try themselves; but those know badly how to act who devote themselves entirely to preaching and not at all to devotion. Others, again, are to be pitied, who often sell what they do for the oil of empty praise. The office of preaching, my Brethren, is more acceptable to the Father of mercies than any sacrifice, especially if it be undertaken with the fervour of charity, so that the preacher labours more by his example than by his words—more by tears of devotion than by loquacious speaking. Therefore that preacher is to be pitied as devoid of true piety, who in his sermons seeks not the salvation of souls, but his own praise; or who destroys by the wickedness of his life, what he builds up by the truth of his doctrine. A Brother, simple and slow of speech, who by his good example excites others to good, is much to be preferred to such an one. 'The barren has borne many children,' says the Prophet, 'and she that had many sons has become weak.' The barren is the poor little Brother who has not the office of bringing forth sons in the Church. In the day of judgment he will bear many, because those whom he now converts to Christ by his hidden prayers will then be called his, for his glory by the Judge. He who had many sons shall be made weak, because the vain and loquacious preacher, who rejoices now because he thinks he has gained many by his own strength, shall know then that they do not in anywise belong to him.

CONFERENCE XVIII

Of Murmuring and Detraction

THE vice of detraction, my Brethren, is an enemy to the very source of piety and grace, and is abominable to the most merciful God; because the detractor feeds on the blood of the souls he has murdered with the sword of his tongue. The impiety of the detractor is far greater than that of the thief, because the law of Christ (which is fulfilled by showing mercy) commands us to desire more ardently the salvation of the soul, than the safety of the body. The Religious who murmurs against his Brethren, or his Superiors, what does he do but drench his Mother, holy Religion, with the gall of bitterness and insults? Detractors are of the generation of Cham, who ridiculed the shame of his father instead of hiding it; thus these make known and exaggerate the faults of their Superiors and their Order, and they consequently deserve to be cursed by God. These, like swine, wallow in mire; for, after the manner of these unclean animals (being themselves far more unclean in their consciences), they feed and gorge themselves on the defects and weaknesses which they curiously seek for, and often falsely affirm they see and find in others; like mad dogs, they grumble at religious discipline and correction; they bark against their Order and their Superiors; and when they can, they bite. This is what the detractor says: 'My life is most imperfect, I have no particular grace or merit, therefore I cannot find favour either with God or man. I know what I will do. I will discover the defects of my Brethren, and thus I shall obtain favour with my Superiors. I know they are men like unto myself, and in this way I may also get into office, because, when the cedars are fallen, the branches only will remain in the way.'

Alas! miserable man, feed thyself upon human flesh, and, unable to live otherwise, gnaw the entrails of my Brethren.

Detractors wish to appear good without being so, to declaim against vice, but not to give up practising it; they praise only those in authority, whose favour they wish to gain; and they never praise anyone unless they think he will hear of it. They make themselves pale with fasting for the sake of praise, that they may be considered spiritual; they can judge all things, and may not be judged by any. They glory in the good opinion of men, not in good works; in having the name of angels, but not the virtues.

CONFERENCE XIX

The Brethren are not to be called Masters

Do not, my Brethren, seek to be called Master; for the name of Master belongs only to Christ, Who has created all things. I would willingly know how to do all things, but I would never willingly be looked upon as a Master, nor honoured with the title of Master, lest I should seem to act in opposition to the words of Christ in the Gospel; for it is better to be humble, with very little knowledge, than (were that possible) to know how to do all great and wonderful works, and oppose the lowly teaching of our glorious Master. For the name of Master belongs only to Our Lord Jesus Christ, Whose works are perfect, and Who has commanded that no one on earth should be called by this title; for this only befits Him, Who is the One, True, and Perfect Master in heaven, the Blessed Christ, Who is God and Man, the Life, the Creator of the world, worthy of praise and glory for ever and ever. Amen.

* * * *

MAXIMS OF THE HOLY FATHER ST. FRANCIS

I. MAN'S greatest enemy is his body. The body does not think over past evils to deplore them, nor does it look forward to future ones in order to fear them; its only care is to enjoy the present. But what is still worse, it usurps all good, transfers it all to its own glory, and impudently arrogates to itself what is given to the soul. It seizes for itself all the praise due to virtue, the esteem shown to fasts and vigils; it seeks even the reward due to tears, leaving nothing to the soul.

II. It is a noble prodigality to offer the love of God in exchange for alms, and those who think less of this love than of money are to be considered most foolish; for the love of God is of such inestimable worth that with it we may purchase the kingdom of heaven, and the love of Him Who has loved us so much should be much valued.

III. A Religious should earnestly desire the grace of prayer, for without it he will never advance in the service of God, nor obtain anything from Him.

IV. The blessed treasure of Poverty is so excellent and divine, that we are unworthy to possess it in our vile vessels. By this virtue all earthly and transitory things are trampled under foot, all stumbling-blocks are removed from among us, and the human mind is most closely united to the Eternal Good. This it is which causes the soul on earth to converse with the Angels in heaven. This it is which unites us to Christ on the Cross, which hides us with Christ in the tomb; by it we rise with Christ from the sepulchre, and accompany Him to heaven. This it is which, when guarded by true humility and charity, gives to souls who love it, even in this world, the gift of agility, by which they fly to the highest heavens.

V. The Son of God descends from the bosom of the Father to the depths of our lowliness, that, as Our Lord and Master, He may teach us humility both by word and example. It is therefore foolish to be puffed up with human favour, or to be proud of earthly honour. For what is great before men, is abominable before God; and what a man is in the sight of God, that he is and no more.

VI. Superiors ought never to neglect holy and devout prayer, on account of the business of their office, or through solicitude in preaching. They must also sometimes go to beg for alms, work with their hands, and exercise themselves in other lowly offices like the other Friars, to give good example, and for the profit of many souls. For by this example of the Ministers and great preachers, the Brethren and the people will be edified, they will willingly give themselves to prayer, and will embrace the practice of humble and useful works. But if Superiors will not do these actions themselves, they cannot, without much shame, disadvantage and condemnation of themselves, urge others to do them. For after the example of Christ they must first do and then teach, or rather both together, do and teach.

VII. A man has as much knowledge as he shows by his works, and no more; and a Religious is a good preacher only inasmuch as he acts upon his preaching, for a tree is known by its fruits.

VIII. Our Lord and the Saints will be more honoured on their Festivals by the practice of poverty and mortification through which they entered heaven, than by superfluity and indulgence which keep souls back from heaven.

IX. Generosity is one of the attributes of God, Who causes the sun to shine, and the rain to fall upon all, whether just or unjust, and ministers to all most lovingly the necessaries of life. Generosity is the sister of charity, the destroyer of hatred, and the preserver of love.

X. It is not lawful to take the things of others to give to the poor. It is a sin worthy of punishment, not an act deserving a reward, to give away what belongs to others.

XI. It is a shame for anyone to be distracted with vain follies, when in the time of prayer he is speaking to the great King.

XII. The knowledge of himself will easily lead to the knowledge of God that man who, in studying the Holy Scripture, searches into the mysteries of God with humility, and not with presumption.

XIII. When a servant of God is troubled about anything, he ought immediately to have recourse to prayer, and persevere in it before his Heavenly Father, until salutary joy is restored to his soul. For if he remains long in sadness, there will grow in him that confusion of heart which if not purged by tears will produce a grievous rust therein.

XIV. The price we pay for fame is the lessening of the secrets of the conscience. It is far more hurtful and dangerous to abuse virtues than to be without them; neither is it a greater virtue to seek for good, than to preserve it when acquired.

XV. What a Superior grants to an inferior through condescension, and because he has asked for it, is called a permission. But what the Superior commands without the inferior asking for it may be considered holy obedience. Therefore I consider obedience better and safer than a permission, for in the latter something of self-will is found, whereas in the former the precept of the Superior alone is accomplished. The highest obedience is when one vessel draws another, when the will of the Superior governs the will of the inferior, and flesh and blood have nothing to do with it. But it may be considered the highest and most perfect obedience, when leave is obtained to go and preach to the Infidels out of zeal for the salvation of souls and the desire of martyrdom, provided this desire comes from a Divine inspiration, for then one vessel draws another, the Divine Will draws the human will; therefore, to ask this is acceptable to God, and has all the merit of perfect obedience.

XVI. If we endeavour to be at rest when we take the food of the body, which will itself soon be the food of worms, with what peace and tranquillity should not the soul take the food of life, which is God, Who converses familiarly with us in prayer, and when we perform the duty of reciting the Divine Office!

XVII. Idleness is the sink of all bad thoughts; let all, therefore, labour and exercise themselves in work, lest through idleness their heart or their tongue should go astray.

XVIII. When the servant of God receives Divine consolations in prayer, he should say, 'O Lord, Thou hast sent this consolation to me, who am a sinner, and most unworthy, and I confide it to Thy keeping, for I feel I am one who robs Thee of Thy treasure.' And when he returns from prayer, he should think himself as poor and sinful as if he had received no such grace.

XIX. Superiors should rarely command through Obedience; they should not at first hurl the thunderbolt, which should be the last resort; nor should they too quickly lay their hand upon the sword. But if anyone does not fear the sword, if the subject delays to fulfil the precept of Obedience, then he fears not God and has no reverence for authority, unless there be some good cause for the delay. The Superior, therefore, must not be rash in commanding, for what is authority in the hands of a rash man but a sword in the hands of a madman? But what more desperate than the case of a man who neglects and despises Obedience?

XX. I consider holy Obedience so fruitful in merit, that they who submit their necks to this yoke cannot pass any time without profit, nor even spend a single hour without merit.

XXI. No one should take a foolish pride in what a sinner can do. A sinner can fast, pray, weep, and macerate his body; this only he cannot do, remain faithful to his God. In this, therefore, we may glory, in returning to God all His glory, in serving Him faithfully, and in ascribing to Him whatever He gives us.

XXII. All reverence and honour should be shown to the priests of God, who are superior to all other men in dignity. They are the spiritual Fathers of Christians, and the spirit and life of the world. As for me, if I were to meet a priest and an Angel in the road, I would immediately kiss the priest's hand, and I would say to the Angel: 'Wait for me, O Angel, for this hand has touched the Word of life, and has something supernatural about it.'

XXIII. I rejoice more over the kingdom of France than does the king of France himself, because I rejoice in the joy the king has in his kingdom. But I have this advantage over the king in the joy which I feel, for the king has all the labour and expense of his kingdom, while I rejoice without labour and without expense.

XXIV. Religious Superiors should take great care not to change the customs, except to improve them; not to seek for favours, not to exercise power; but to fulfil their office.

XXV. The highest wisdom consists in doing good works, keeping a guard over oneself, and meditating on the judgments of God.

XXVI. True Poverty is the root of obedience, the mother of self-denial, the destroyer of self-complacency, the extirpator of vanity and avarice.

XXVII. Obedience is the work of faith, the test of true hope, the proof of charity, the mother of humility, the author of the peace of God, which exceeds all understanding.

XXVIII. In books the Brethren should seek the word of God, not value nor beauty. They should have but few books, and those in common, and let these be such as are suitable for poor Religious.

XXIX. A poor man may be more generous than a rich one; for if a rich man gives away all that he has, he will fall from his state in life, to his own confusion; and if he does not give of the things he has, although he would be willing to do so if he would not lose his position thereby, his will is good, but it cannot be taken for the deed, because he still possesses goods. But the poor man who has nothing, who would like to give to the poor, but has nothing to give, who would like to build hospitals, but has not wherewith to do so—in him the will is taken for the deed.

XXX. To him who tastes God, all the sweetness of the world will be but bitterness. Taste, therefore, and see how sweet the Lord is, and thou wilt never weary of enjoying Him. It is quite otherwise with the love of the world, for bitterness is always hidden in it; the i love of worldly things produces many fruits of sorrow; thus, if thou lovest wife, children, possessions, houses, or honours, when these die or perish they procure for thee as much sorrow as thou hast had affection and love for them.

* * * *

FAVORITE SENTENCES OF THE HOLY FATHER ST. FRANCIS[1]

I. THESE are the weapons by which the chaste soul is overcome: looks, speeches, touches, embraces.

II. He who retires into the desert avoids three combats: seeing, hearing, and detraction.

III. Beloved, in this vale of misery may you possess nothing so fair and so delightful that your soul would be entirely occupied with it.

IV. Fly from creatures, if thou desirest to possess creatures.

V. Fly from the world, if thou wilt be pure. If thou art pure, the world does not delight thee.[2]

VI. Fly, keep silence, and be quiet.

VII. If thou excusest thyself, God will accuse thee; and if thou accusest thyself, God will excuse thee.

VIII. He is not perfectly good who cannot be good among the wicked.

IX. Temptation, when it is not consented to, is matter for the exercise of virtue.

X. Love makes all heavy things light, and all bitter things sweet.

XI. The love of God is never idle.

XII. Rich clothing and sumptuous dwellings, eating, drinking, sleep, and idleness, enervate men, and foster luxury.

XIII. When I say 'Hail Mary,' the heavens smile, the angels rejoice, the world exults, hell trembles, the devils fly.

XIV. As wax melts before the heat of the fire, and dust is scattered by the wind, so the whole army of the evil spirits is dispersed by the invocation of the holy Name of Mary.

XV. Let every creature become more despicable to the heart, that the Creator may become more sweet.

---

1   These *Sentences* were frequently used by St. Francis in instructing his Brethren. Some are his own, others are taken from the holy Fathers of the Church, or composed according to their doctrine.

2   The play upon the words is lost in the translation. ' Fuge *mundum,* si vis esse *mundus.* Si tu es *mundus,* jam non delectat te *mundus.'*

FAMILIAR COLLOQUIES OF THE BLESSED FATHER ST. FRANCIS.

COLLOQUY I

That Meekness and Patience will Soften the hardest Hearts.

When the blessed Father came once to the city of Imola, he went to the Bishop and humbly asked him to allow him to assemble the people to hear the Word of God; but the Bishop answered him harshly: 'It is sufficient, Brother, that I preach to my people myself.' The truly humble man bowed his head and went away; but after a short time he again presented himself before the Bishop, who demanded rather angrily what more he had to ask him. The Saint replied with a humble heart and manner: 'My lord, if a father turns away his son by one door, he must return by another.' The Bishop, overcome by this humility, embraced him joyfully, saying: 'Henceforth I give thee and thy Brothers a general leave to preach in my diocese, for thy humility deserves this reward.'

COLLOQUY II

The Friars Minor ought not to Reserve for themselves any of the Goods of the Novices.

When there was such great poverty at St. Mary of the Angels that they could not provide for the necessities of the guests who came, the Vicar went to the man of God, and representing to him the extreme want of the Brethren, begged him to allow them to reserve some of the goods of novices who entered, as a fund to which they might have recourse in time of need. To which the Saint, enlightened from above, replied: 'Far be it from us, dearest Brother, to act contrary to our Rule for the sake of any man. I would rather strip the altar of the glorious Virgin if necessity required it, than allow the least thing against our vow of Poverty, and the regular observance of our evangelical profession. For it would be more pleasing to the Blessed Virgin that we should observe the holy Gospel perfectly, and leave her altar unadorned, than that we should decorate her altar, and fail in fulfilling the evangelical counsel which we have promised to her Son.'

COLLOQUY III

That the Friars Minor should not Erect superfluous Buildings

The same Vicar of the holy Father, Brother Peter of Catania, caused a small building to be erected for the greater convenience of performing the Divine Office, and to procure for the Friars who came as guests every day in great numbers more quiet and tranquillity. At this the blessed Father was a little displeased, and said: 'Brother, this place is the model and example for the whole Order. I would rather that the Religious of this house should suffer some troubles and inconveniences for the love of God, so that others who come here should see a good example of poverty, than that they should have more buildings, lest the guests when they return to their own Monasteries should begin to build spacious houses, saying: "At St. Mary of the Angels, which is the first and principal house of the Order, they have many buildings; there cannot therefore be any fault against holy Poverty if we construct the same."'

COLLOQUY IV

That the Praise of all that is Good is to be Referred to God

The holy Father once preached to the people at Terni in presence of the Bishop, who, surprised at the eloquence and learning of the humble preacher, when he had come down from the pulpit, rose, and said to his flock: 'Give great praise to God, Who by the mouth of this insignificant poor man has taught you so much good, has revealed to you His mysteries, and has placed before you the reward of virtue and the punishment of vice. Therefore avoid sin, doing what God has taught you to-day through this poor man.' On this the blessed Francis threw himself at the Bishop's feet, exclaiming: 'I tell you truly, my Lord Bishop, no one has ever shown me so much honour as you have done to-day. Others call me holy and blessed for my works, giving the praise and glory to me, and not to God; but you in your wisdom have truly honoured me, giving to the Lord the praise and honour which are His, separating the precious from the vile, and attributing to God wisdom and power, and to me foolishness and weakness.'

COLLOQUY V

Those who are Fools for God's Sake are stronger than the Wise of this World

Moved by the suggestions of some lax Brethren who desired an easier life, the Cardinal Ugolino of Ostia begged the holy Father to follow the counsels of the most prudent and learned men of the Order, and consent to mitigate the severity of his Rule, or to choose one of the old Rules of St. Augustine, St. Basil, or St. Benedict, to be observed by himself and his Brethren. The zealous lover of evangelical perfection did not answer the suggestion at once, but having called the Brethren to Chapter, he thus spoke to them before the Cardinal with great fervour of spirit: 'My Brethren, my Brethren, God has called me to walk in the way of simplicity and humility, and He has shown me that this is His will both for myself and for those who will follow and adhere to me. I will not therefore have the Rule of St. Benedict, or St. Basil, or any other proposed to me, except that which has been given and shown me by the Divine Mercy. Our Lord has Himself told me that He wishes me to be His poor little fool in this world, and I will not follow, nor allow those who belong to me to follow, any other road to heaven than this one, which although it may appear folly to the world, is true wisdom in the sight of God. I fear that your wisdom and your knowledge will end for you in ignorance and confusion.' These words filled the Cardinal and the Brethren with great fear, and throwing themselves at the feet of the Saint they humbly implored his pardon.

COLLOQUY VI

The Poor of Christ should Prefer Living on Alms to Feasting with the Rich

St. Francis once consented to dine with the same Cardinal Ugolino, but while the tables were being prepared, he went out secretly and begged some crusts of bread in the street. When he returned and was seated at table with the Cardinal, he produced these, and divided them among the guests and attendants, as if he were presenting them with some dainty morsel, while he himself eat of them more willingly than of the richest dishes. The noble Cardinal was confused and ashamed at this conduct, but remained silent on account of his guests. But after dinner, taking the holy man aside, he gently reproved him in private, not having ventured to do so in public.' Why,' said he, 'O beloved friend, hast thou done this? Thou hast offered me a great insult by bringing these morsels of bread to the feast to which I invited thee, and covered me with shame before all present.' The blessed Father answered him: 'Nay, rather, my lord, I did thee a great honour, while I was honouring a still greater Lord. I must be a model and example to my Brethren, and the more so because I know for certain that in the Order there are and will be many true Friars Minor both in name and deed, who for the love of the Lord our God, and by the grace of the Holy Spirit Who will teach them, will humble themselves in all things, and serve their Brethren in all lowliness and subjection. But on the contrary, there are and will be others who, out of human respect or evil custom, will disdain to humble themselves, and will refuse to beg alms and to do such like servile works. Therefore I must teach all who shall enter this Order, so that both in this world and the next they may be without excuse before God. When, then, I am invited by you, or by any other great lord, I will never blush to go and seek alms; but on the contrary, I consider it a true nobility, and a royal dignity and honour to imitate Him Who, although He was the Lord of all, and possessed all things in His glorious Majesty, was despised and in want of all things when He took upon Him our humanity. I desire, therefore, that all the Brethren, both present and future, should understand clearly that I feel the greatest consolation, both for soul and body, when I am seated at the table of the poor, and I rejoice much more when I see before me the poor food received in alms for the love of God, than when, either at your or others' tables, I sit down to rich and dainty dishes, of which I eat unwillingly. The bread of alms is holy and blessed bread, sanctified by the praise and love of the Omnipotent. For when a Brother begs, he first says: "Praised and blessed be the Lord our God !" and then he adds: "Give me an alms for the love of God." Thus praise sanctifies the bread, and the love of God blesses it' When he heard these words, the Cardinal shed tears of devotion, and exclaimed: 'My Son, do what is good in thine eyes, for I see that God is with thee, and thou art with Him.'

COLLOQUY VII

The Friars Minor should remain in their Humble Vocation

The same Cardinal once asked the blessed Father whether or not he was willing that the Friars Minor should be promoted to ecclesiastical dignities, asserting that the universal Church would derive great benefit from being governed by men of such sanctity and virtue. 'My lord,' replied the man of God; my Brethren are called less than others,[3] in order that they may not presume to become greater. If you wish them to bear fruit in the Church of God, keep them in the state to which they are called, and do not make them ascend to ecclesiastical dignities.'

COLLOQUY VIII

That it is not becoming for Superiors to indulge their Appetite, or make use of Delicate Meats

ONE of his companions asked St. Francis why he did not deal more mildly with himself, and why he afflicted his tender body, half dead with penance, with such rigorous abstinence; begging him that for the future he would allow better food to be prepared for him. This true model of penitents and Superiors replied: 'I know well, Brother, that many things are necessary for my body, and that I do not always give it what it really requires; but I remember that I am placed by God as a model and example to many, and therefore I will not use more delicate nor better dressed food, but poor food, poorly cooked; and in all things that are needful for this life, I rejoice and delight only in those which savour of holy Poverty, and all that are sumptuous and delicate I utterly abhor.'

* * * *

COLLOQUY XIV

The Religious should Win the Minds of the People more by their own Humility than by the Sufferance of the Bishops, and that by Examples of Holiness they will Profit the Church more than by Privileges and Exemptions

After the general Chapter of Assisi, at which more than five thousand Brethren were assembled from every Province, the holy Father sent them two and two to preach the Word of God in all countries. Many of them returned to him complaining sorrowfully that some Bishops were opposed to them, and would not allow them to preach in their dioceses. 'Father,' said they,' we went to the places thou didst assign to us, we obeyed thy commands, but we could not fulfil our desires, nor those of the people; for many Bishops expelled us from their dioceses, and, as often happens to the poor, being unknown and suspected, we had to endure many insults. We beg of you, therefore, Father, to obtain for us from the Sovereign Pontiff permission and privilege to preach all over the world, without the consent of the Bishops.' At which the blessed Father, filled with holy indignation, exclaimed: 'O my Brethren, you know not the will of God, and you seek by your foolishness to rob me of the conquest of the world. For our Lord Jesus Christ wishes that I should overcome the world by the most profound subjection and humility, and that I should perform the great work of drawing souls to Him by the example of my lowliness. My Brethren, you will convert all by your words if you humble yourselves before all by your actions. Those who cruelly persecute you will be converted to Christ by the example of your patience, and will desire to kiss the very ground on which you walk. I ought not so much to wish for liberty under pretence of the salvation of others, as I should wish to have that profound humility which becomes my state, and by which I shall both

---

3   Minores—majores.

advance in virtue myself, and shall strengthen others in virtue. You must first by holy humility, and the reverence the people have for you, gain over the Bishops, that they may see and love your holy lives, and be satisfied with the respect you show to them. Then they will themselves ask you to preach to their people, and will command all to be present at your sermons. Humility will obtain more for you than privileges. If the Prelates of the Church see you truly humble, and entirely free from avarice, and that you exhort the people to pay what is due to their own Churches, they will beg of you to labour for the salvation of their flocks, and to hear the confessions of all, although I do not desire you to burden yourselves much with this ministry; for those who are converted to God, and deplore their sins, will find many priests to hear their confessions. In this way you will easily conciliate Bishops and Prelates.'

COLLOQUY XV

What they ought to be who Devote themselves to Study

Some of his companions, hearing that many doctors in Paris, and others in Germany, Italy and France had joined his Order, asked the blessed Father if he were willing that his children should devote themselves to the study of the Holy Scriptures. He replied: 'I am willing, provided that, after the example of Christ, of Whom we read that He prayed more than He read, they never omit the practice of prayer. And let them not study only that they may know how to speak, but that they may practise what they learn, and that when they have done this they may propose it for the practice of others. I wish my Brethren to be disciples of the Gospel, and so to advance in the knowledge of truth, as at the same time to increase in holy simplicity, that thus they may not separate the prudence of the serpent from the simplicity of the dove, which the greatest of Masters with His blessed lips has commanded us to unite.'

COLLOQUY XXXIX

Religious and Learned Men ought to Preach to the People by the Example of a Holy Life

Being once asked by a Doctor of Theology of the Order of Friars Preachers how these words of the Prophet Ezechiel were to be understood: 'If thou dost not warn the wicked man, that he may be converted from his wicked way and live, the same wicked man shall die in his iniquity, but I will require his blood at thy hand,' the Saint replied: 'If these words are to be understood in a general way, I believe them to mean that the servant of God ought so to burn and shine by his life and conduct, that by the light of his example, and the tongue of his holy conversation, he may reprove all the wicked, and make known to them their iniquity. But if, on the contrary, he becomes a cause of scandal to the people or his neighbour, he will not escape the vengeance of God.'

COLLOQUY XL

True Obedience is like Death

THE holy Father once commanded a disobedient Religious to be stripped of his garments, placed in a deep pit, and covered with earth. When the Brethren were fulfilling this order, and only the head of the offender remained uncovered, the compassionate Father drew near, and said: 'Art thou dead, Brother? art thou dead ?' The disobedient Friar, now penitent, replied: 'Yes, Father, I am now indeed dead.' 'Rise, then,' said the Saint, 'if thou art truly dead, and henceforth obey the command of thy Superior, as thou oughtest, and show no repugnance to anything he enjoins, any more than a corpse would do. I wish my followers to be dead, not living.'

COLLOQUY XLI

What a precious Treasure is Poverty

THE holy man once entered a certain church with Brother Masseo, and began to beseech God to inspire him and his followers with the love of holy Poverty, and he prayed with such fervour that his face shone like fire. Then, all inflamed with this divine ardour, he approached Brother Masseo with open arms, and called him to him. The Brother, filled with wonder and admiration, threw himself into the arms of his blessed Father, and so great was the fire which burnt in the heart of Francis, that solely by the breath which came from his mouth, Masseo was raised many cubits above the earth. The Brother afterwards said, that while he was thus lifted up, he was filled with such sweetness that he had never in his life experienced anything like it. Then Francis said: 'Let us go to Rome, to beseech the holy Apostles Peter and Paul, that they would teach us how we may rightly and fruitfully possess this precious treasure of holy Poverty, for it is so divine and glorious, and we are so vile and abject, that we are unworthy to contain it in such vessels. It is indeed a heavenly grace, which so teaches and penetrates us, that henceforth we may trample under foot all earthly things, and may cast away from us all impediments which could hinder the soul from being most freely and speedily united to its God.'

SOME PROPHECIES OF THE HOLY FATHER ST. FRANCIS[4]

I.

He Prophesies that he will found a Religious Order, and take it for his Spouse

While St. Francis was still living in the world, he was invited by his friends to a sumptuous banquet. But he withdrew into a corner, and appeared as if rapt in thought. His companions asked him of what he was thinking,

---

4   'The spirit of prophecy,' says St. Bonaventure, 'was so resplendent in St. Francis that he foresaw the future, and penetrated the secrets of hearths, beholding things absent as if they were present.' Those given above are but a few out of the many prophecies uttered by the Saint.

and whether he were considering about taking a wife. ' Yes,' he replied, 'and one so beautiful that you have never seen her equal meaning the holy Order, which by the inspiration of God he was about to found.

* * * *

PARABLES AND SIMILITUDES OF THE HOLY FATHER ST. FRANCIS

PARABLE I

The Providence of God will never Fail the Poor in Spirit

The holy Father proposed the following parable to Pope Innocent III., who considered the Rule of the Friars Minor too hard and impracticable on account of the great poverty it enjoined:

'A poor but most beautiful virgin lived in a solitary and desert place, when the king of that country, captivated by her loveliness, took her for his spouse. He dwelt with her some years in that desert, and she bore him children who had the beauty of their mother, and the features of the king their father. The monarch having returned to his court and royal throne, the tender mother brought up her children carefully; and when they were grown up, she sent them to the king, saying: "You are the children of a great king who dwells in his royal palace. I cannot, and will not, leave this desert; but do you go to your father and declare to him who you are. He will give you all that is necessary and becoming your high rank." The children obeyed; and when the king saw them, he recognised in them his own likeness, and the wondrous beauty of their mother. He therefore said graciously to them: "I acknowledge you to be my children, and I will treat you as princes; for if I feed and clothe my servants and strangers, how much more shall I cherish my own offspring, in whom I see the beauty and grace of their mother, whom I so ardently love? All the children she has borne me shall sit at my table, and dwell at my court." Most Holy Father, this King is Christ Our Lord, the Monarch of heaven and earth; and this beautiful virgin is Poverty, who dwelt alone in the desert of this world, scorned and rejected by men. The King of kings, Christ the Lord, was enamoured of her beauty; and as soon as He entered into this world, He espoused her to Himself in the Crib. She, in this desert, has borne Him many children—apostles, anchorets, monks, and others who have embraced voluntary Poverty; and these, who bear the royal marks of Christ—namely, poverty, humility, and obedience—she has sent to the heavenly King, who receives them lovingly, and promises to nourish them, saying: "I, Who make my sun to rise upon the just and the unjust—I, Who feed, clothe, and preserve the infidel Moors and Pagans, who are strangers to the faith—will much more willingly give to you, my beloved children, and to all who are bora of my beloved spouse, Poverty, all that is necessary for you." Most holy Father, this Lady and Queen, holy Poverty, has sent us, her children, to the heavenly- King; we are not worse than those who went before us; we have not degenerated from the beauty of our Father and Mother, since we profess the most high and perfect poverty. Do not fear, therefore, lest the children and heirs of the Eternal King should perish with hunger, for we are born in the likeness of the Lord Christ, and by the virtue of the Holy Spirit, of a poor Mother, and by the spirit of poverty, we shall be abundantly nourished in the Order of Poverty. For if the King of Heaven has promised His eternal kingdom to those who imitate Him, how much more will He give us those things which He bestows indifferently on the good and bad!'

When the Vicar of Christ had attentively considered this parable, he marvelled greatly; and seeing evidently that God spoke by the mouth of the holy man, he approved the Rule.

PARABLE II

Of the Custody and Mortification of the Eyes

THE holy Father used frequently to exhort his Brethren to guard and mortify their senses with the utmost care. He especially taught them the custody of the eyes, proposing to them the following parable:

'A certain pious king sent two messengers successively to the queen with a communication from himself, The first messenger returned and brought an answer from the queen, which he delivered exactly; but of the queen herself he said nothing, because he always kept his eyes modestly cast down, and had not raised them to look at her. The second messenger also returned; but after delivering in a few words the answer of the queen, he began to speak warmly of her beauty. "Truly, my lord," he said, "the queen is the most fair and lovely woman, and thou art indeed happy and blessed to have her for thy spouse." At this the king was angry, and said: "Thou wicked servant, didst thou dare to cast thine eyes upon my royal spouse? I believe thou dost covet what thou hast so curiously gazed upon." Then he commanded the other messenger to be recalled, and said to him: "What dost thou think of the queen?" He replied: "She listened very willingly and humbly to the message of the king, and replied most prudently." But the monarch again asked him: "What dost thou think of her countenance? Did she not seem to thee very fair and beautiful, more so than any other woman?" The servant replied: "My lord, I know nothing of the queen's beauty. Whether she be fair or not, it is for thee alone to know and judge. My duty was only to convey thy message to her." "Thou hast answered well and wisely," rejoined the king; "thou who hast such chaste and modest eyes shall be my chamberlain. From the purity of thine eyes I see the chastity of thy soul; thou art worthy to have the care of the royal apartments confided to thee. But thou, who hast such immortified eyes, depart from the palace; thou shalt not remain in my house, for I have no confidence in thy virtue."

'My Brethren, you have heard this parable, and you understand the meaning of it. If you have gazed on any female, do penance, and guard your eyes in future. Death lurks in such glances, and enters by the windows of the eyes. The heavenly King forbids you to look upon His spouses. Now, every Christian woman is His spouse, and who would not fear to look upon the spouse of Christ? Beware of the jealous anger of the King!'

SIMILITUDE I

Of true and perfect Obedience

A CERTAIN person once inquired of St. Francis whom he considered to be truly obedient, and the holy man proposed to him as an example a dead body. 'Take,' he said, 'a dead body, and place it where thou wilt. It will not refuse to be moved; it will not complain of its position ; it will not expostulate if it be abandoned. If it be placed in an elevated seat, it still looks down, not up; if it be clothed in purple, it appears paler. This is like a truly obedient man, who does not inquire why he is moved, does not care where he is placed, does not beg to be changed; being raised to dignities, he preserves his wonted humility, and the more he is honoured, the more unworthy does he consider himself to be.'

SIMILITUDE II

Of the same

'I have often,' said the holy Father on another occasion, seen a blind man, who had no one to guide him on his way but a little dog. Wherever the dog led him, he followed. He did not ask his guide why he conducted him this way or that; if he led him over rough stones, he still followed; if through the streets and squares, it was the same; if he took him to a church, he prayed; if he entered a house, the blind man asked an alms. Thus he followed wherever the dog chose to lead him, and never went anywhere without him. Such ought to be the truly and perfectly obedient man. He should be blind in obeying: having his eyes, as it were, closed before the commands of his Superiors, and neither wish nor seek to understand them, except that he may promptly and humbly fulfil them. Wherever the wish or command of his Superior leads him, he must follow; if it be through rough and stony paths, he must cheerfully bear it; if through smooth ways, he must proceed in virtue of holy Obedience. The truly obedient man should in all things consider, not the difficulty of the command, but the authority of the one who commands, and the merit of Obedience.

SIMILITUDE III

Of the Cares and Solicitudes of Married Persons

St. Francis being once assailed by a violent temptation of the flesh, and the enemy suggesting to him that he should take a wife, he first chastised his body by a severe discipline, and then going half-naked into the garden, which was covered with snow, he proposed to himself the following lively and apposite example of the cares and anxieties of married persons about their families, so different from the quietude of monastic life. Plunging into the snow, he made seven heaps of it, and thus spoke to himself:' Behold, the largest of these is thy wife, the other four are thy two sons and two daughters, and the remaining two are a manservant and a maidservant whom thou must have to serve thee. Make haste, therefore, to clothe them all, for they are perishing with cold. But if thou findest so many anxieties too troublesome for thee, be careful to serve God alone with much earnestness.' By this example the tempter, being overcome, left him, and the holy man remained the conqueror in this perilous conflict.

SIMILITUDE IV

Of the great Multitude who should Join the Order

When the Saint had as yet only four companions, he foretold the increase of his family to Blessed Egidius, his companion, under this similitude:

'Our Order is like a fisherman who lets down his nets into the sea, and taking a great multitude of fishes, he picks out the largest and keeps them, but lets the small ones go. Our net is let down into the sea of the world, and gathers into itself men of great sanctity and religious virtue; but those who have little fervour, and are tepid in the service of God, it lets go; or having received them, casts them out again. So great will be the multitude of fishes, that I fear lest the net should be broken by their number.'

SIMILITUDE V

That the Servant of God should Refer all Praise and Honour to Him

The holy Father was daily much honoured by the people, who, out of devotion and reverence for his sanctity, would kiss his hands, his habit, his feet, and even his footprints as he passed. As he never forbade their doing this, one of his disciples, doubting his humility, and somewhat scandalised at his allowing so much honour to be paid him, said to him: 'Brother, dost thou not see and remark what these people are doing? How canst thou permit it? Men honour thee, and reverence thee exceedingly as a Saint, and thou dost not prevent nor repulse them; on the contrary, it seems as if thou didst take pleasure in this homage. How is this?' The blessed Father replied: 'So far am I, Brother, from refusing these honours, that they seem to me very little. On the contrary, the people certainly should reverence me much more.' His companion, still more troubled, replied: 'I do not understand, Brother, how thou canst be considered a Saint, when thou desirest the praise and honour of men.' Then the blessed Father replied: 'Listen, Brother, and understand. I do not ascribe or appropriate any of this honour to myself; I give it all to God, and I keep myself in the depths of my lowliness. I know my own vileness, and I acknowledge the Majesty of God. But these men gain no little merit by these signs of respect, for they recognise and honour God, and reverence Him in His creatures. They who acknowledge the graces of God in His creatures, cannot be ignorant of God Himself. Creatures do not lose their humility because the Majesty of God is honoured in them. Just as statues of Our Lord or His Mother are honoured, and yet the statue of wood or stone does not become puffed up or exalted, so the servant of God, who is His true and living image, and in whom God is venerated and worshipped on account of the many graces which shine forth in him, does not think more of himself, but becomes the more firmly established in his humility; he attributes all to God, nothing to himself; he looks upon himself as wood or stone, or rather as pure nothingness in respect to God, to Whom he refers all honour and glory, but to himself misery, shame, and confusion.'

ATTITUDE OF THE CIVIL GOVERNMENT TOWARD HERETICS

Law Issued by Emperor Frederick II (for Sicily, ca. 1235)

F rederick II (1194–1250) was probably the most powerful of German emperors, although he regularly ruled from Southern Italy and Sicily instead of north of the Alps. However, shortly after his death the entire dynasty of the Hohenstaufen collapsed, which soon led to a period of lackluster kings and then an interregnum, deeply weakening Germany in its basic foundations. Frederick spoke six languages more or less fluently—Latin, Sicilian, German, French, Greek, and Arabic—and he was famous not only for his political leadership, but also for his great interest in the sciences, in linguistics (inquiry about the original human language), and, above all, in the art of falconry. His book on hunting with falcons, De arte venandi cum avibus, written in the 1240s, continues to be the best study on birds of prey and on how to tame and train them for hunting.

The following document is a good example of the cordial manner in which the temporal rulers cooperated with the Church in the detection and punishment of heresy, which was universally regarded as the most horrible of crime. It is taken from the laws of the enlightened Frederick II of Hohenstaufen.[1]

The heretics endeavor to rend the seamless garment of our Lord, and in accordance with their vicious name, which means division, they would destroy the unity of that same indivisible faith. They would withdraw the sheep from Peter's guardianship, to which they were intrusted by the Good Shepherd. They are ravening wolves within, but feign a love for the flock, until they shall have crept into the Lord's fold. They are bad angels, sons of perversity, appointed by the father of lies and deception to mislead the simple-minded. They are serpents who deceive the doves. Like serpents they creep stealthily abroad; with honeyed sweetness they vomit forth their virus. While they pretend to offer life-giving food they strike with their tail, and prepare a deadly draught, as with some dire poison.

These sects do not assume the old names lest they should be recognized, but, what is perhaps more heinous, not content like the Arians, who took their name from Arius, or the Nestorians, from Nestorius, and others of

---

1. Extracts from the laws in France and Germany relating to heretics will be found in *Translations and Reprints*, Vol. Ill, No. 6.

the same class, they must imitate the example of the martyrs who suffered death for the Catholic faith. They call themselves Patarins, as if they, too, were sufferers.[2]

These same wretched Patarins, who refuse to accept the holy belief in the eternal Trinity, combine three offenses in their wickedness. They offend God, their neighbor, and themselves,—God, since they refuse to place their faith in him or recognize his Son; their fellow-men, since they deceive them by offering them the seductions of a perverse heresy under the form of spiritual nurture. Against themselves they rage even more fiercely, for, prodigal of life and careless of death, in addition, to the sacrifice of their souls, they involve their bodies in the toils of a horrible end, which they might avoid by acknowledging the truth and adhering to the true faith. What is worst of all, the survivors are not terrified by such examples.

Against these, who offend alike against God, themselves, and their fellow-men, we cannot restrain ourselves, and must draw forth the sword of merited retribution. We pursue them the more closely inasmuch as they are known, to the obvious prejudice of the Christian faith, to extend the crimes of their superstition toward the Roman church, which is regarded as the head of all other churches. Thus from the confines of Italy, especially from parts of Lombardy, where we are convinced that their wickedness is widespread, we now find rivulets of their perfidy reaching even to our kingdom of Sicily.

Feeling this most acutely, we decree, in the first place, that the crime of heresy and of reprehensible teaching, of whatever kind, by whatever name its adherents may be known, shall, as provided by the older laws, be included among the recognized crimes. (For should not what is recognized to be an offense against the Divine Majesty be judged more terrible than the crime of leze majesty directed against ourself, although in the eyes of the law one is not graver than the other?) As the crime of treason deprives the guilty of life and property, and even blackens the memory of the dead, so in the aforesaid crimes of which the Patarins are guilty, we wish the same rules to be observed in all respects.

And in order that the wickedness of those who walk in darkness, since they do not follow God, should be thoroughly exterminated, we desire that those who practice this class of crimes should, like other malefactors, be diligently sought for and hunted out by our officers. If such be discovered, even if there be only the slightest suspicion of their guilt, we command that they shall be examined by churchmen and prelates. If they shall be found by these to have deviated from the Catholic faith, even in a single respect, and if, when admonished by such churchmen in their function of pastors, they refuse by leaving the wiles of the devil to recognize the God of light, and stubbornly adhere to their error, we command, by this our present edict, that such condemned Patarins shall suffer the death they court; that, condemned to the sentence of the flames, they shall be burned alive in the sight of the people. Nor are we loath to satisfy their cravings in this respect, for they only suffer the penalty of their crime and reap no further gain. No one shall dare to intercede with, us for any such, and should any one presume to do this, we shall properly direct the darts of our indignation against him, too. ...

All who shall receive, trust, aid, or abet the Patarins in any way, seeking to shield others from a penalty which they rashly do not fear for themselves, shall be deprived of all their goods and banished forever. Their sons shall thereafter be excluded from all honors whatsoever and shall be branded with perpetual disgrace. They shall not be permitted to act as witnesses in any case, but shall be rejected as infamous.

---

2   The name Patarin, which seems here to be derived from the Latin word *patior*, to suffer, appears to have been given to the Cathari of Milan because they lived among the ragpickers (*patari*).

But if any one of the sons of such harborers or fautors shall point out a Patarin, whose guilt shall be thus proven, he shall, by the imperial clemency, be freed from the opprobrium and restored to his full rights, in view of the good faith which he has shown.

[From *Readings in European History*, ed. James Harvey Robinson]

MEDIEVAL IDEAS OF
THE EARTH AND STARS

By Anonymous

A little Anglo-Saxon manual of the tenth century thus describes the heavenly bodies.

On the second day God made the heaven, which is called the firmament, which is visible and corporeal; and yet we may never see it, on account of its great elevation and the thickness of the clouds, and on account of the weakness of our eyes. The heaven incloses in its bosom all the world, and it ever turns about us, swifter than any mill-wheel, all as deep under this earth as it is above. It is all round and entire and studded with stars.[1]

Truly the sun goes by God's command between heaven and earth, by day above and by night under the earth. She is ever running about the earth, and so light shines under the earth by night as it does above our heads by day. ... The sun is very great: as broad she is, from what books say, as the whole compass of the earth; but she appears to us very small, because she is very far from our sight. Everything, the further it is, the less it seems. ... The moon and all the stars receive light from the great sun. The sun is typical of our Saviour, Christ, who is the sun of righteousness, as the bright stars are typical of the believers in God's congregation, who shine in good converse. ... No one of us has any light of goodness except by the grace of Christ, who is called the sun of true righteousness. ...

Truly the moon's orb is always whole and perfect, although it does not always shine quite equally. Every day the moon's light is waxing or waning four points through the sun's light. ... We speak of new moon according to the custom of men, but the moon is always the same, though its light often varies. ... It happens sometimes when the moon runs on the same track that the sun runs, that its orb intercepts the sun's, so that the sun is all darkened and the stars appear as by night. This happens seldom, and never but at new moons. By this it is clear that the moon is very large, since it thus darkens the sun.

Some men say stars fall from heaven, but it is not stars that fall, but it is fire from the sky, which flies down from the heavenly bodies as sparks do from fire. Certainly there are still as many stars in the heavens as there

---

1   Educated persons realized all through the Middle Ages that the earth was a sphere. Bede—of whose work, *On The Nature of Things*, the present treatise is an abridgment—says (Chapter XLVI): "We speak of the globe of the earth, not that it is perfectly round, owing to the inequalities of mountains and plains, but because, if all its lines be considered, it has the perfect form of a sphere." He adds that stars far to the south are not visible to northern peoples, owing to the convexity of the earth.

were at the beginning, when God made them. They are almost all fixed in the firmament, and will not fall thence while this world endures. The sun, and the moon, and the evening star, and morning star, and three other stars are not fast in the firmament, but they have their own course severally. These seven stars are called planets.

Those stars are called comets which appear suddenly and unusually, and which are rayed so that the ray goes from them like a sunbeam. They are not seen for any long time, and as oft as they appear they foreshadow something new toward the people over whom they shine.

A few examples of mediaeval zoology and of the edifying habits of beasts and birds may be added.

The pelican is a bird of such fashion as is the crane, and it is found in Egypt. … Its nature is such that when, it comes to its little ones, and they are large and beautiful, it wishes to fondle them, and to cover them with its wings. But the little ones are fierce; they seize him to peck him, and wish to devour him and pick out his two eyes. Then he takes them and pecks them, and slays them with torment, and thereupon leaves them,—leaves them lying dead. On the third day he returns, and is grieved to find them dead, and makes sore lamentations when he sees his little ones dead; with his beak he strikes his body so that the blood gushes forth: the blood goes dropping down and falls upon his birdlings: the blood has such virtue that by it they come to life. …

This bird signifies the son of Mary, and we are the young birds in fashion of men. We are so raised and restored from death by the precious blood which God shed for us, as the birdlings are which were three days dead. Now hear by science what that signifies,—why the birdlings peck at the father's eye, and why the father is angry when he kills them thus: he who denies truth will put out the eye of God, and God will take vengeance upon that people. Have in remembrance that this is the meaning.

Satyrs be somewhat like men, and have crooked noses, and horns in the forehead, and are like to goats in their feet St. Anthony saw such an one in the wilderness, as it is said, and he asked what he was, and he answered Anthony, and said, "I am deadly, and one of them that dwelleth in the wilderness." These wonderful beasts be divers; for some of them be called Cynophali, for they have heads as hounds, and seem, by the working, beasts rather than men; and some be called Cyclops, and have that name because each of them hath but one eye, and that in the middle of the forehead; and some be all headless and noseless and their eyes be in the shoulders; and some have plain faces without nostrils, and the nether lips of them stretch so that they hele therewith their faces when they be in the heat of the sun; and some of them have closed mouths, in their breasts, only one hole, and breathe and suck, as it were, with pipes and veins, and these be accounted tongueless, and use signs and becks instead of speaking; also in Scythia be some with so great and large ears, that they spread their ears and cover all their bodies with them, and these be called Panchios. …

And others there be in Ethiopia, and each of them have only one foot, so great and so large that they be-shadow themselves with the foot when they lie gaping on the ground in strong heat of the sun; and yet they be so swift that they be likened to hounds in swiftness of running, and therefore among the Greeks they be called Cynopodes. Also some have the soles of their feet turned backward behind the legs, and in each foot eight toes and such go about and stare in the desert of Lybia.

The cat is a full lecherous beast in youth, swift, pliant, and merry, and leapeth and runneth on everything that is to fore him: and is led by a straw, and playeth therewith: and is a right heavy beast in age and full sleepy, and lieth slyly in wait for mice: and is aware where they be, more by smell than by sight, and hunteth and runneth on them in privy places; and when he taketh a mouse, he playeth therewith, and eateth him after the play. In time of love is hard fighting for wives, and one scratcheth and rendeth the other grievously with biting and with claws.

And he maketh a ruthful noise and ghastful, when one proffereth to fight with another: nor is he hurt when he is thrown down off an high place. And when he hath a fair skin, he is, as it were, proud thereof, and goeth fast about; and when his skin is burnt, then he bideth at home; and he is oft, for his fair skin, taken of the skinner, and slain and flayed.

QUESTIONS IN ABELARD'S *YEA AND NAY*

By Peter Abelard

Peter Abelard (1079–1142) was born "Pierre le Pallet," in the little village of Le Pallet, about 10 miles east of Nantes, in Brittany, which is due south of Rennes, in the southwestern corner of that region. He demonstrated a high degree of intelligence and soon gained a solid education that allowed him to study at various schools of higher learning in Paris and elsewhere, which were later to become the University of Paris, the Sorbonne. Abelard's particular focus was dialectic, a type of intellectual rumination on the contrastive sides of things, as originally taught by Aristotle. His great teaching skills attracted many students to him, which aroused the anger and jealousy of the other teachers. At that time Peter changed his name to "Abelard" and founded his own schools in the vicinity of Paris. Next he turned to theology and immediately proved his brilliance, which gave him the chair of a canon at Nôtre Dame in Paris. As innovative as his biblical interpretations were, they met much opposition and criticism of such luminaries as Bernard of Clairvaux. Most famously, Abelard composed his Sic et Non *(Yea and Nay) in order to illustrate the many contradictions even in the most authoritative texts, such as the Bible. He also wrote the highly respected treatise* Scito te ipsum *(Know Thyself), in which he explores the value of intentions, which make an action good or bad. Ultimately, God would be the one to decide the ethical nature of a deed because only He can look into people's hearts. Wherever Abelard went, and whatever he wrote, he created deep controversies and profoundly provoked his contemporaries, which finally led to his condemnation by the Church, though he died just before matters became really dangerous for him. Today he is commonly known for his highly problematic relationship with Heloise (see page 209).*

A belard supplies one hundred and fifty-eight problems, carefully balancing the authorities pro and con, and leaves the student to solve each problem as best he may. This doubtless shocked many of his contemporaries. Later scholastic lecturers did not hesitate to muster all possible objections to a particular position, but they always had a solution of their own to propose and defend.

The following will serve as examples of the questions Abelard raised in the *Yea and Nay*:

Should human faith be based upon reason, or no?
Is God one, or no?
Is God a substance, or no?
Does the first Psalm refer to Christ or no?
Is sin pleasing to God, or no?
Is God the author of evil, or no?
Is God all-powerful, or no?
Can God be resisted, or no?
Has God free will, or no?
Was the first man persuaded to sin by the devil, or no?
Was Adam saved, or no?
Did all the apostles have wives except John, or no?
Are the flesh and blood of Christ in very truth and essence present in the sacrament of the altar, or no?
Do we sometimes sin unwillingly, or no?
Does God punish the same sin both here and in the future, or no?
Is it worse to sin openly than secretly, or no?

[From *Readings in European History*, ed. James Harvey Robinson]

PROLOGUE TO *SIC ET NON*

By Peter Abelard

P *eter Abelard (1079–1142) was one of the great intellectuals of the 12th century, with especial importance in the field of logic. His tendency to disputation is perhaps best demonstrated by his book Sic et Non, a list of 158 philosophical and theological questions about which there were divided opinions. This dialectical method of intellectual reflection—also seen in Gratian's approach to canon law—was to become an important feature of western education and distinguishes it sharply from other world cultures such as Islam and the Confucian world. Abelard's mistake was to leave the questions open for discussion and so he was repeatedly charged with heresy. For a long period all his works were included in the later Index of Forbidden Books.*

H ere begins Peter Abelard's prologue to *Sic et Non*:

(1–11) When, in such a quantity of words, some of the writings of the saints seem not only to differ from, but even to contradict, each other, one should not rashly pass judgement concerning those by whom the world itself is to be judged, as it is written: "*The saints shall judge nations*" (cf. Wisdom 3: 7–8), and again "*You also shall sit as judging*" (cf. Matthew 19:28). Let us not presume to declare them liars or condemn them as mistaken—those people of whom the Lord said "*He who hears you, hears me; and he who rejects you, rejects me*" (Luke 10:16). Thus with our weakness in mind, let us believe that we lack felicity in understanding rather than that they lack felicity in writing—those of whom the Truth Himself said: "*For it is not you who are speaking, but the Spirit of your Father who speaks through you*" (Matthew 10:20). So, since the Spirit through which these things were written and spoken and revealed to the writers is itself absent from us, why should it be surprising if we should also lack an understanding of these same things?

(54–85) We also ought to pay close attention so that, when some of the writings of the saints are presented to us as if they were contradictory or other than the truth, we are not misled by false attributions of authorship or corruptions in the text itself. For many apocryphal works are inscribed with the names of saints in order that they might obtain authority, and even some places in the text of the Holy Testament itself have been corrupted by **scribal error**. Whence that most trustworthy author and truest translator, Jerome, warned us in his letter to Laeta concerning the education of her daughter, when he said (Epist. 107, 12), "Let her be wary of all apocrypha; and if she ever wishes to read such works not for the truth of dogma, but for the miracles contained in them, let her know that they do not belong to those men whose names are indicated in the inscription and that it requires great wisdom to seek gold amid the mud." The same man has this to say about the 77th Psalm (Tractatus sive Homil. in Ps. LXXVII), concerning the attribution in its title (which is like this: 'recognized as Asaph's'), "It is written according to Matthew (cf. 13:34–35), *"when the Lord had spoken in parables and they did not understand, etc ..."* he said these things happened so that what had been written by the prophet Isaiah might be fulfilled (Psalm 77:2): *"I will open my mouth in parables".* The Gospel has this wording even up to today. However, Isaiah does not say this, but Asaph." And further: "Therefore let us say plainly that, as it is written in Matthew and John that the Lord was crucified at the sixth hour, and in Mark that it was the third hour—this was a scribal error and 'the sixth hour' had been written in Mark, but many scribes thought it was a gamma instead of the Greek episemon [i.e. a symbol for 'six'; it resembles gamma, which can be used as a symbol for 'three'], just as the error was scribal when they wrote 'Isaiah' instead of 'Asaph'. For we know that many churches were made up of uneducated Gentiles. Therefore, when they read in the Gospel "... that it might be fulfilled as it was written by the prophet Asaph", the first one to copy the Gospel began to say, 'Who is this prophet Asaph? He is not known among the people.' And what did this scribe do? In attempting to correct an error he committed one. We may say something similar about another place in Matthew; he says *'then he brought back the thirty pieces of silver, the price of him who was priced, as it was written in the prophet Jeremiah'* (cf. Matthew 27:9). We are not able to find this in Jeremiah, but in Zachariah (cf. Zacharias 11:13). Therefore you see that this is also an error just like the other." And if in the Gospels some things were corrupted due to scribal ignorance, what is so surprising if it should also happen sometimes in the writings of the Church Fathers who came later, and possessed far less authority? So if something in the writings of the saints should seem perhaps to be deviating from the truth, it is honest and in accordance with humility and appropriate to charity (which 'believes all things, hopes all things, endures all things' (1 Corinthians 13:7) and does not readily suspect errors from those whom she embraces) that either we believe that this place in the text may have been corrupted or not translated faithfully, or that we acknowledge that we do not understand it.

(86–148) Nor is it any less a matter for consideration whether such statements are ones taken from the writings of the saints that either were retracted elsewhere by these same saints and corrected when the truth was afterwards recognized—as St. Augustine often did—or whether they spoke reflecting the opinion of others rather than according to their own judgment ...

(176–187) What is so amazing, then, if some things are proposed or even written by the Holy Fathers sometimes based on opinion rather than on the truth? When conflicting things are said about the same topic, one must carefully distinguish that which is offered with the stricture of a command, that which is offered with the lenience of indulgence and that which is offered with exhortation to perfection, so that we might seek a remedy for the apparent conflict in accordance with this variety of intents. If indeed it is a command, we must distinguish whether it is general or specific, that is, directed toward everyone in general or toward certain people in particular. The times and causes of dispensation ought also to be distinguished, because what is permitted at one time is found to be prohibited at another, and what is often commanded with rigor may sometimes be tempered with dispensation. It is very necessary to distinguish these things in the statutes of the Church decrees or canons. Moreover, an easy solution for many controversies may be found as long as we are able to be on our guard for the same words being used with conflicting meanings by different authors.

(188–194) The reader who is eager to resolve conflicts in the writings of the holy ones will be attentive to all the methods described above. If the conflict is obviously such that it cannot be resolved by logic, then the authorities must be compared together, and whatever has stronger witnesses and greater confirmation should be retained above all. Whence also these words of Isidore to the bishop of Massio (Epist. 4, 13): "I have thought that this should be added at the end of the letter, that whenever a discordant opinion is found in the acts of councils, the judgement of that person possessing greater or more ancient authority is preferred."

(195–208) Indeed it is established that the prophets themselves at one time or another have lacked the gift of prophecy and offered from their habit of prophecy some false statements, derived from their own spirit, while believing that they were in possession of the Spirit of prophecy; and this was permitted to happen to them so as to preserve their humility, so that in this way they might recognize more truly what sorts of things come from the Spirit of God and what sorts from their own spirit, and recognize that when they possessed the Spirit of prophecy they had it as a gift from the Spirit Who cannot lie or be mistaken. For when this Spirit is possessed, just as it does not confer all its gifts on one person, so does it not illuminate the mind of the inspired one concerning all things, but reveals now this and now that, and when it makes one thing apparent it conceals another. Indeed, St. Gregory declares this with clear examples in his first homily on Ezekiel. And it did not shame even the very chief of the apostles, who shone so greatly with miracles and with the gifts of divine grace after that special effusion of the Holy Spirit promised by God, who taught his students the entire truth—it did not shame him to abandon a harmful untruth, when up to that point he had fallen into a not insignificant error concerning circumcision and the observance of certain ancient rites, and when he had been earnestly, wholesomely and publicly corrected by his fellow apostle Paul.

(209–249) When it is clear that even the prophets and apostles themselves were not complete strangers to error, what is so surprising, then, if among such manifold writings of the Holy Fathers some things seem to be handed down or written erroneously, for the reason given above? But just as these holy 'defendants' should not be charged with lying if at one time or another, not from duplicity but from ignorance, they make some statements other than what the real truth would have them think; so in the same way something that is said for love while giving some instruction should not be imputed to presumption or sin, since it is well known that all things are distinguished by God according to intention, just as it is written (Matthew 6:22), "*If thy eye be sound, thy whole body will be full of light.*" ...

(249–291) If God on occasion does allow this to happen even to the holy ones themselves, as we have said, in those situations that would cause no damage to the faith, it does not happen unproductively to those by whom everything is undertaken for the good. Even the ecclesiastical teachers themselves, diligently attentive and believing some things in their works needed correction, grant to posterity the license to emend or not to follow them; if somehow these teachers were not able to retract or correct in their works. ... However, so that the room for this freedom is not excluded, and that very healthy task of treating difficult questions and translating their language and style is not denied to later authors, the excellence of the canonical authority of the Old and New Testaments has been distinguished from that of the works of later authors. If there should be something in the Old or New Testament that seems as if it were absurd, you may not say that the author of this work did not possess the truth, but that the manuscript is corrupt, or the translator has made a mistake, or that you do not understand. But in works of later witness, contained in innumerable volumes, if perhaps some things are thought to deviate from the truth because they are not understood as they have been expressed, in these works the reader or listener has the freedom of judgement to approve what seems good or disapprove of what offends, and therefore when it comes to things of this type, unless they are supported either by sure reasoning or canonical authority, so that what is either argued or narrated there may be shown either to be entirely so or to be potentially so, if it does not seem good to someone or they do not wish to believe it, they are not reproached."

(292–304) And thus he [Augustine] calls the canonical Scriptures of the Old and New Testaments documents about which it is heretical to say that something in them contradicts the truth. Indeed, concerning Holy Scripture … he writes (Epist. 28, iii, 3): "it seems to me a most dangerous thing to allow that anything in the sacred books may be a lie, that is, that those men who preserved and wrote the Scriptures for us should have lied about anything in their books. For if a single white lie is admitted anywhere in so lofty an authority, then no particle of these books will remain which will not be explained as the idea or practice of the author's mind, using this most dangerous example whenever anyone finds something difficult to practice or hard to believe." …

(330–350) With these prefatory words, it seems right, as we have undertaken to collect the diverse sayings of the Holy Fathers, which stand out in our memory to some extent due to their apparent disagreement as they focus on an issue; this may lure the weaker readers to the greatest exercise of seeking the truth, and may render them sharper readers because of the investigation. Indeed this first key of wisdom is defined, of course, as assiduous or frequent questioning. Aristotle, the most clear-sighted philosopher of all, advised his students, in his preface 'Ad Aliquid', to embrace this questioning with complete willingness, saying (cited by Boethius, In Categorias Aristotelis, ii): "Perhaps it is difficult to clarify things of this type with confidence unless they are dealt with often and in detail. However, it would not be useless to have some doubts concerning individual points." **And indeed, through doubting we come to questioning and through questions we perceive the truth**. … And when some passages of Scripture are brought before us, the more the authority of the Scripture itself is commended, the more fully they excite the reader and tempt him to seek the truth.

ON THE FAME OF ABELARD

By Heloise

Heloise (ca. 1101–1164) is known to us above all as the mistress and later wife of the famous French philosopher Abelard (1079–1142). She met him when he entered the house of her uncle, the canon Fulbert, where she lived after the death of her parents. Abelard was asked to tutor her, but in the course of their studies they fell in love. The situation soon became very dangerous, especially because she was pregnant with his child, which she delivered secretly in Abelard's home country, the Bretagne (the son was called Astrolabe; we do not know anything about his future life). Abelard subsequently agreed to wed Heloise, but both tried hard to keep their marriage private because it was an embarrassment for a member of the teaching staff at the cathedral school, being a cleric (member of the Church). Celibacy was only really required of members of the higher orders of the clergy, so technically the couple could have taken their marital vows, and yet Abelard tried to find a cunning alternative, keeping it all hidden from public view. When Fulbert realized this, he hired a gang of criminals who broke into Abelard's apartment and castrated him, to the horror of all of Paris. Later Abelard forced Heloise to take the veil and provided her and her fellow-sisters with a place to start a convent, Paraclete, where she assumed the role of abbess. When, years later, Heloise got hold of Abelard's autobiographical writing Historia calamitatium, she began to correspond with him. These letters have survived until today, although many scholars continue to doubt their authenticity because the high level of learning, the extraordinary literary skills, and her rhetorical power seem to be impossible for a woman, who actually argues vehemently against the institution of marriage, at least in her case. Much evidence, however, supports the claim that she was, indeed, the author, and that she was equally educated and intelligent as Abelard.

A letter of consolation you had written to a friend, my dearest Abelard, was lately as by chance put into my hands. The superscription in a moment told me from whom it came, and the sentiments I felt for the writer compelled me to read it more eagerly. I had lost the reality; I hoped therefore from his words, a faint image of himself, to draw some comfort. But alas! for I well remember it, almost every line was marked with gall and wormwood. It related the lamentable story of our conversion, and the long list of your own unabated sufferings.

Indeed, you amply fulfilled the promises you there made to your friend, that, in comparison of your own, his misfortunes should appear as nothing, or as light as air. Having exposed the persecutions you had suffered from your masters, and the cruel deed of my uncle, you were naturally led to a recital of the hateful and invidious conduct of Albericus of Reims, and Lotulphus of Lombardy. By their suggestions, your admirable work on the

Trinity was condemned to the flames, and yourself were thrown into confinement. This you did not omit to mention. The machinations of the abbot of St. Denys and of your false brethren are there brought forward; but chiefly—for from them you had most to suffer—the calumnious aspersions of those false apostles, Norbert and Bernard, whom envy had roused against you.

It was even, you say, imputed as a crime to you to have given the name of Paraclete, contrary to the common practice, to the oratory you had erected. In time, the incessant persecutions of that cruel tyrant of St. Gildas, and of those execrable monks, whom yet you call your children and to which at this moment you are exposed, close the melancholy tale of a life of sorrow.

Who do you think could read or hear these things and not be moved to tears? What then must be my situation? The singular precision with which each event is stated could but more strongly renew my sorrows. I was doubly agitated, because I perceived the tide of danger was still rising against you. Are we then to despair of your life? And must our breasts, trembling at every sound, be hourly alarmed by the rumours of that terrible event?

For Christ's sake, my Abelard—and He, I trust, as yet protects you—do inform us, and that repeatedly, of each circumstance of your present dangers. I and my sisters are the sole remains of all your friends. Let us, at least, partake of your joys and sorrows. The condolence of others is used to bring some relief to the sufferer, and a load laid on many shoulders is more easily supported. But should the storm subside a little, then be even more solicitous to inform us, for your letters will be messengers of joy. In short, whatever be their contents, to us they must always bring comfort; because this at least they will tell us, that we are remembered by you. …

My Abelard, you well know how much I lost in losing you; and that infamous act of treachery which, by a cruelty before unheard-of, deprived me of you, even tore me from myself. The loss was great, indeed, but the manner of it was doubly excruciating. When the cause of grief is most pungent, then should consolation apply her strongest medicines. But it is you only can administer relief: by you I was wounded, and by you I must be healed. It is in your power alone to give me pain, to give me joy, and to give me comfort. And it is you only that are obliged to do it. I have obeyed the last title of your commands; and so far was I unable to oppose them, that, to comply with your wishes, I could bear to sacrifice myself. One thing remains which is still greater, and will hardly be credited; my love for you had risen to such a degree of frenzy, that to please you, it even deprived itself of what alone in the universe it valued, and that forever. No sooner did I receive your commands than I quitted at once the habit of the world, and with it all the reluctance of my nature. I meant that you should be the sole possessor of whatever I had once a right to call my own.

Heaven knows! in all my love it was you, and you only I sought for. I looked for no dowry, no alliances of marriage. I was even insensible to my own pleasures; nor had I a will to gratify. All was absorbed in you. I call Abelard to witness. In the name of wife there may be something more holy, more imposing; but the name of mistress was ever to me a more charming sound. The more I humbled myself before you, the greater right I thought I should have to your favour; and thus also I hoped the less to injure the splendid reputation you had acquired.

This circumstance, on your own account, you did not quite forget to mention in the letter to your friend. You related also some of the arguments I then urged to deter you from that fatal marriage; but you suppressed the greater part, by which I was induced to prefer love to matrimony and liberty to chains. I call Heaven to witness! Should Augustus, master of the world, offer me his hand in marriage, and secure to me the uninterrupted command of the universe, I should deem it at once more eligible and more honourable to be called the mistress of Abelard than the wife of Caesar. The source of merit is not in riches or in power; these are the gifts of fortune; but virtue only gives worth and excellence. …

But that happiness which in others is sometimes the effect of fancy, in me was the child of evidence. They might think their husbands perfect, and were happy in the idea, but I knew that you were such, and the universe knew the same. Thus, the more my affection was secured from all possible error, the more steady became its flame. Where was found the king or the philosopher that had emulated your reputation? Was there a village, a city, a kingdom, that did not ardently wish even to see you? When you appeared in public, who did not run to behold you? And when you withdrew, every neck was stretched, every eye sprang forward to pursue you. The married and the unmarried women, when Abelard was away, longed for his company; and when he was present, every bosom was on fire. No lady of distinction, no princess, that did not envy Heloise the possession of her Abelard.

You possessed, indeed, two qualifications—a tone of voice and a grace in singing—which gave you the control over every female heart. These powers were peculiarly yours; for I do not know that they ever fell to the share of any other philosopher. To soften, by playful amusement, the stern labours of philosophy, you composed several sonnets on love and on similar subjects. These you were often heard to sing, when the harmony of your voice gave new charms to the expression. In all circles nothing was talked of but Abelard; even the most ignorant, who could not judge of composition, were enchanted by the melody of your voice. Female hearts were unable to resist the impression. Thus was my name soon carried to distant nations; for the loves of Heloise and Abelard were the constant theme of all your songs. What wonder if I became the subject of general envy?

You possessed, besides, every endowment of mind and body. But, alas! if my happiness then raised the envy of others, will they not now be compelled to pity me? And surely even she who was then my enemy will now drop a tear at my sad reverse of fortune.

You know. Abelard. I was the great cause of your misfortunes; but yet I was not guilty. It is the motive with which we act, and not the event of things, that makes us criminal. Equity weighs the intention, and not the mere actions we may have done. What, at all times, were my dispositions in your regard, you, who knew them, can only judge. To you I refer all my actions, and on your decision I rest my cause. I call no other witness. ...

By that God, then, to whom your life is consecrated, I conjure you, give me so much of yourself as is at your disposal; that is, send me some lines of consolation. Do it with this design, at least; that, my mind being more at ease, I may serve God with more alacrity. When formerly the love of pleasure was your pursuit, how often did I hear from you? In your songs the name of Heloise was made familiar to every tongue: it was heard in every street; the walls of every house repeated it. With how much greater propriety might you now call me to God, than you did then to pleasure? Weigh your obligations; think on my petition.

I have written you a long letter, but the conclusion shall be short: My only friend, farewell.

[From *Abelard and Heloise*, trans. A. S. Richardson (Boston: James R. Osgood & Co., 1884)]

ROGER BACON AND THE BEGINNING OF MODERN EXPERIMENTAL SCIENCE

By Roger Bacon

T*he following passage makes clear Bacon's attitude toward investigation, and also shows that he was not the only one who was turning his attention to experiment, which was to prove so fruitful in the following centuries.*

One man I know, and one only, who can be praised for his achievements in experimental science.[1] Of discourses and battles of words he takes no heed: he pursues the works of wisdom and in them finds satisfaction. What others strive to see dimly and blindly, like bats blinking at the sun in the twilight, he gazes at in the full light of day, because he is a master of experiment. Through experiment he gains knowledge of natural things, medical, chemical, indeed of everything in the heavens and on earth.

He is ashamed that things should be known to laymen, old women, soldiers, plowmen, of which he is ignorant. Therefore he has looked closely into the doings of those who melt metals and who work in gold and silver and other metals and in minerals of all sorts; he knows everything relating to the art of war, the making of weapons, and the chase; he has looked carefully into agriculture, mensuration, and farming work; he has even taken note of remedies, lot casting, and charms used by old women and by wizards and magicians, and of the devices and deceptions of conjurers, so that nothing which deserves investigation should escape him, and in order that he might be able to expose the impostures of the magicians.

If philosophy is to be carried to its perfection and is to be handled with certainty and advantage, his aid is indispensable. As for reward, he neither receives it nor looks for it. If he frequented the courts of kings and princes he would easily find those who would bestow upon him both honor and wealth. Or if he would show the results of his researches in Paris the whole world would follow him. But since either of these courses would hinder him from pursuing the great experiments in which he takes delight, he puts honor and wealth aside, knowing well that his knowledge would secure him wealth whenever he chose. For the last three years he has been working at the invention of a mirror which should produce combustion at a fixed distance, and he will, with God's aid, soon reach his end.

---

1   Of Peter of Maricourt, to whom Bacon refers, very little is known.

Roger Bacon, "Roger Bacon and the Beginning of Modern Experimental Science," *Readings in European History*, vol. 1, ed. James Harvey Robinson, pp. 460–461. Ginn and Company, Ltd, 1904. Copyright in the Public Domain.

In a curious letter "On the hidden workings of nature and art and the emptyness of magic," Bacon forecasts the wonderful achievements which he believed would come with the progress of applied science.

I will now enumerate the marvelous results of art and nature which will make all kinds of magic appear trivial and unworthy. Instruments for navigation can be made which will do away with the necessity of rowers, so that great vessels, both in rivers and on the sea, shall be borne about with only a single man to guide them and with greater speed than if they were full of men. And carriages can be constructed to move without animals to draw them, and with incredible velocity. Machines for flying can be made in which a man sits and turns an ingenious device by which skillfully contrived wings are made to strike the air in the manner of a flying bird. Then arrangements can be devised, compact in themselves, for raising and lowering weights indefinitely great. … Bridges can be constructed ingeniously so as to span rivers without any supports.

Some other hopes expressed elsewhere in this letter seem a bit fantastic, even to us, habituated as we are to the most incredible achievements. We may, however, yet learn to make gold and to prolong human life almost indefinitely, as Bacon believed would be possible.

EXPERIMENTAL SCIENCE CONT.

By Roger Bacon

One of the most inquisitive minds of his time, Roger Bacon, (ca. 1210/1220–1294), had a deep influence on medieval theology, philosophy, and science, but we have to be careful in our easily too-enthusiastic assessment of his mind set since he was, despite his many amazingly forward-looking ideas, clearly still a medieval man and a devout Christian. He was born in England sometime between 1210 and 1220 near Ilchester in Somerset, or perhaps in Bisley in Gloucestershire, as the son of a wealthy family. Throughout his life he spent an enormous amount of money on books and his experiments. Around 1227 Bacon began with his studies at the University of Oxford under Adam of Marsh and Thomas of Wales, focusing on Aristotelian philosophy and mathematics. He probably received his Magister Artium at Oxford, but possibly not until he went to Paris in 1245 where he completed his studies under William of Auvergne, Alexander of Hales, and Albert the Great. Subsequently he lectured on Aristotle at the University of Paris, and earned his doctoral degree in theology. As early as ca. 1240 Bacon had written the medical treatise De retardatione accidentium senectutis (The Cure of Old Age) in which he emphasizes the use of diet and hygiene, closely following the medical principles already established by the ancient Greek scholar Galen and further developed by the Persian philosopher and physician Ibn Sinna (Avicenna, 980–1037), that is, the concept of the four humours in the human body that have to be well balanced for man to enjoy good health. But Bacon relied the most on the Arabic physicians Haly ben Rodwân (ca. 980–1060) and Damascenus (ninth century) and created a remarkable compilation of their statements. In other words, his book was a learned treatise and not based on his own experiences, as he states himself ("absque experientia, dicam"). In ca. 1247 or 1250 Bacon returned to Oxford, where he composed his De mirabile potestate artis et naturae (On the Marvelous Power of Magic and Nature), which is an extensive letter addressed to William of Auvergne or John of Basingstoke. In this treatise Bacon draws the important distinction between magic that works by suggestion versus natural science. De mirabile potestate also contains a fairly vague formula for gunpowder. Next followed his commentary on Aristotle's De sensu et sensato and his very popular treatise De multiplicatione specierum (On the Multiplication of Species, twenty-four manuscripts) in which he attributed all natural causation to this process. In 1257 Bacon joined the Franciscan Order, but he continued with his scientific writings, such as his Communia naturalium (General Principals of Natural Philosophy), Communia mathematica (General Principles of Mathematical Science), Computus naturalium (On the Calendar), and De speculis comburentibus (On Burning Mirrors). Bacon always pursued scientific research highly innovative for his time, deeply influenced by the newly introduced Arabic-Aristotelian natural philosophy, but he never neglected to subordinate all his findings under the quest for God.

He published his Opus Maius *(Major Work), truly encyclopedic in its scope, in 1266 or 1267 and dispatched it to Pope Clement IV who had originally commissioned him to write it for his own illumination. Here Bacon deals with a wide range of topics, including philosophy, mathematics, astrology, astronomy, the calendar, music, optics, experimental science, and natural and moral philosophy. In the first part he examines the causes of human errors, which he identifies as excessive submission under any kind of authority, foolish habit, popular prejudice, and false concepts of knowledge. In the second part Bacon discusses the close relationship between philosophy and theology, before he turns to the significance of studying foreign languages in the third part. Not only does Bacon strongly admonish his readers to study the ancient languages, he also recommends them to be wary about too-literal translations since they would destroy both the meaning and the aesthetics of the original text. According to Bacon, foreign languages are extremely important because most philosophical treatises up to his time were almost all written in a foreign tongue, that is, not in Latin. Subsequently, Bacon presents the Hebrew and Greek alphabets, explains some grammatical aspects, and justifies the study of these old languages by emphasizing that the Holy Scripture in its Latin version (Vulgate) has been the object of severe corruptions through false translations and erroneous interpretations. Furthermore, Bacon argues for acquiring the knowledge of a foreign language, aside from Latin, because it promotes international commerce, justice, peace, and facilitates, as to be expected, Christian proselytizing. We do not know whether Bacon ever studied Arabic, although he makes some fleeting references to it in his* Opus Tertium. *But his rudimentary knowledge of Greek, documented in his* Compendium Studii Philosophiae, *already proves to be highly exceptional within all of medieval Europe. Foreshadowing both Martin Luther's and Erasmus of Rotterdam's major contributions, among other sixteenth-century Humanists, Bacon hoped to establish an improved translation of the original biblical text and asked for a better translation of Aristotle's works.*

Having laid down the main points of the wisdom of the Latins as regards **language**, **mathematics** and **optics**, I wish now to review the principles of wisdom from the point of view of **experimental science**, because without experiment it is impossible to know anything thoroughly.

There are two ways of acquiring knowledge, one through **reason**, the other by **experiment**. **Argument** reaches a conclusion and compels us to admit it, but it neither makes us certain nor so annihilates doubt that the mind rests calm in the intuition of truth, unless it finds this certitude by way of **experience**. Thus many have arguments toward attainable facts, but because they have not experienced them, they overlook them and neither avoid a harmful nor follow a beneficial course. Even if a man that has never seen fire, proves by good reasoning that fire burns, and devours and destroys things, nevertheless the mind of one hearing his arguments would never be convinced, nor would he avoid fire until he puts his hand or some combustible thing into it in order to prove by experiment what the argument taught. But after the fact of combustion is experienced, the mind is satisfied and lies calm in the **certainty of truth**. Hence argument is not enough, but experience is.

This is evident even in mathematics, where demonstration is the surest. The mind of a man that receives that clearest of demonstrations concerning the equilateral triangle without experiment will never stick to the conclusion nor act upon it till confirmed by experiment by means of the intersection of two circles from either section of which two lines are drawn to the ends of a given line. Then one receives the conclusion without doubt. What **Aristotle** says of the demonstration by the **syllogism** being able to give knowledge, can be understood if it is accompanied by **experience**, but not of the bare demonstration. What he says in the first book of the Metaphysics, that those knowing the reason and cause are wiser than the experienced, he speaks concerning the experienced who know the bare fact only without the cause. But I speak here of the **experienced that know the**

reason and cause through their experience. And such are perfect in their knowledge, as Aristotle wishes to be in the sixth book of the Ethics, whose simple statements are to be believed as if they carried demonstration, as he says in that very place.

Whoever wishes without proof to revel in the truths of things need only know how to neglect experience. This is evident from examples. Authors write many things and the people cling to them through arguments which they make without experiment, that are utterly false. It is commonly believed among all classes that one can break **adamant only with the blood of a goat**, and philosophers and theologians strengthen this **myth**. But it is not yet proved by adamant being broken by blood of this kind, as much as it is argued to this conclusion. And yet, even without the blood it can be broken with ease. I have seen this with my eyes; and this must needs be because gems cannot be cut out save by the breaking of the stone. Similarly it is commonly believed that the secretions of the beaver that the doctors use are the testicles of the male, but this is not so, as the beaver has this secretion beneath its breast and even the male as well as the female produces a secretion of this kind. In addition also to this secretion the male has its testicles in the natural place and thus again it is a horrible lie that, since hunters chase the beaver for this secretion, the beaver knowing what they are after, tears out his testicles with his teeth and throws them away. Again it is popularly said that cold water in a vase freezes more quickly than hot; and the argument for this is that contrary is excited by the contrary, like enemies running together. They even impute this to Aristotle in the second book of Meteorology, but he certainly did not say this, but says something like it by which they have been deceived, that if both cold and hot water are poured into a cold place as on ice, the cold freezes quicker (which is true), but if they are placed in two vases, the hot will freeze quicker. It is necessary, then, to prove everything by experience.

Experience is of two kinds. One is through the **external senses**: such are the experiments that are made upon the heaven through instruments in regard to facts there, and the facts on earth that we prove in various ways to be certain in our own sight. And facts that are not true in places where we are, we know through other wise men that have experienced them. Thus Aristotle with the authority of Alexander, sent 2,000 men throughout various parts of the earth in order to learn at first hand everything on the surface of the world, as Pliny says in his Natural History. And this experience is human and philosophical just as far as a man is able to make use of the beneficent grace given to him, but such experience is not enough for man, because it does not give full certainty as regards corporeal things because of their complexity and touches the spiritual not at all. Hence man's intellect must be aided in another way, and thus the patriarchs and prophets who first gave science to the world secured **inner light** and did not rest entirely on the senses. So also many of the faithful since Christ. For **grace** makes many things clear to the faithful, and there is **divine inspiration** not alone concerning spiritual but even about corporeal things. In accordance with which Ptolemy says in the Centilogium that there is a double way of coming to the knowledge of things, one through the experiments of science, the other through **divine inspiration**, which latter is far the better as he says.

Of this inner experience there are seven degrees, one through **spiritual illumination** in regard to scientific things. The second grade consists of **virtue**, for evil is ignorance as Aristotle says in the second book of the Ethics. And Algazel says in the logic that the mind is disturbed by faults, just as a rusty mirror in which the images of things cannot be clearly seen, but the mind is prepared by virtue like a well polished mirror in which the images of things show clearly. On account of this, true philosophers have accomplished more in ethics in proportion to the soundness of their virtue, denying to one another that they can discover the cause of things unless they have minds free from faults. Augustine relates this fact concerning Socrates in Book VIII, chapter

III, of the City of God: to the same purpose Scripture says, to an evil mind, etc., for it is impossible that the mind should lie calm in the sunlight of truth while it is spotted with evil, but like a parrot or magpie it will repeat words foreign to it which it has learned through long practice. And this is our experience, because a **known truth draws men into its light for love of it, but the proof of this love is the sight of the result**. And indeed he that is busy against truth must necessarily ignore this, that it is permitted him to know how to fashion many high sounding words and to write sentences not his own, just as the brute that imitates the human voice or an ape that attempts to carry out the works of men, although he does not understand their purpose. **Virtue, then, clears the mind** so that one can better understand not only ethical, but even scientific things. I have carefully proved this in the case of many pure youths who, on account of their innocent minds, have gone further in knowledge than I dare to say, because they have had correct teaching in religious doctrine, to which class the bearer of this treatise belongs, to whose knowledge of principles but few of the Latins rise. Since he is so young (about twenty years old) and poor besides, not able to have masters nor the length of any one year to learn all the great things he knows, and since he neither has great genius or a wonderful memory, there can be no other cause, save the **grace of God**, which, on account of the clearness of his mind, has granted to him these things which it has refused to almost all students, for a pure man, he has received pure things from me. Nor have I been able to find in him any kind of a mortal fault, although I have searched diligently, and he has a mind so clear and far-seeing that he receives less from instruction than can be supposed. And I have tried to lend my aid to the purpose that these two youths may be useful implements for the Church of God, inasmuch as they have with the Grace of God examined the whole learning of the Latins.

The third degree of spiritual experience is the **gift of the Holy Spirit**, which Isaiah describes. The fourth lies in the **beatitudes** which our Lord enumerates in the Gospels. The fifth is the **spiritual sensibility**. The sixth is in such fruits as the **peace of God**, which passes all understanding. The seventh lies in **states of rapture** and in the methods of those also, various ones of whom receive it in various ways, that they may see many things which it is not permitted to speak of to man. And whoever is thoroughly practiced in these experiences or in many of them, is able to assure himself and others, not only concerning spiritual things, but all human knowledge. And indeed, since all speculative thought proceeds through arguments which either proceed through a proposition by authority or through other propositions of argument, in accordance with this which I am now investigating, there is a science that is necessary to us, which is called **experimental**. I wish to explain this, not only as useful to philosophy, but to the knowledge of God and the understanding of the whole world: as in a former book I followed language and science to their end, which is the **Divine wisdom** by which all things are ordered.

And because this experimental science is a study entirely unknown by the common people, I cannot convince them of its utility, unless its **virtue and characteristics** are shown. This alone enables us to find out surely what can be done through nature, what through the application of art, what through fraud, what is the purport and what is mere dream in chance, conjuration, invocations, imprecations, magical sacrifices and what there is in them; so that all falsity may be lifted and the truths we alone of the art retained. This alone teaches us to examine all the insane ideas of the **magicians** in order not to confirm but to avoid them, just as logic criticizes the art of **sophistry**. This science has three great purposes in regard to the other sciences: the first is that one may (1) **criticize by experiment** the noble conclusions of all the other sciences, for the other sciences know that their principles come from experiment, but the conclusions through arguments drawn from the principles discovered, if they care to have the result of their conclusions precise and complete. It is necessary that they have this through the aid of this noble science. It is true that mathematics reaches conclusions in accordance with universal experience about figures and numbers, which indeed apply to all sciences and to this experience, because **no science can be known without mathematics**. If we would attain to experiments precise, complete and made certain in accordance with the proper method, it is necessary to undertake an examination of the science itself, which is called experimental on our authority. I find an example in the rainbow and in like phenomena, of which nature are the circles about the sun and stars, also the halo beginning from the side of the sun or of a star which seems to be visible in straight lines and is called by Aristotle in the third book of the Meteorology a perpendicular, but by Seneca a halo, and is also called a circular corona, which have many of the colors of the rainbow. Now the natural philosopher discusses these things, and in regard to perspective has many facts to add which are concerned with the operation of seeing which is pertinent in this place. But neither Aristotle or Avicenna have given us knowledge of these things in their books upon Nature, nor Seneca, who wrote a special book concerning them. But **experimental science** analyzes such things.

(2: Comparison:) The experimenter considers whether among visible things, he can find colors formed and arranged as given in the rainbow. He finds that there are hexagonal crystals from Ireland or India which are called rainbow-hued in Solinus *Concerning the Wonders of the World* and he holds these in a ray of sunlight falling through the window, and finds all the colors of the rainbow, arranged as in it in the shaded part next the ray. Moreover, the same experimenter places himself in a somewhat shady place and puts the stone up to his eye when it is almost closed, and beholds the colors of the rainbow clearly arranged, as in the bow. And because many persons making use of these stones think that it is on account of some special property of the stones and because of their hexagonal shape the investigator proceeds further and finds this in a crystal, properly shaped, and in other transparent stones. And not only are these Irish crystals in white, but also black, so that the phenomenon occurs in smoky crystal and also in all stones of similar transparency. Moreover, in stones not shaped hexagonally, provided the surfaces are rough, the same as those of the Irish crystals, not entirely smooth and yet not rougher than those—the surfaces have the same quality as nature has given the Irish crystals, for the difference of roughness makes the difference of color. He watches, also, rowers and in the drops falling from the raised oars he finds the same colors, whenever the rays of the sun penetrate the drops.

The case is the same with water falling from the paddles of a water-wheel. And when the investigator looks in a summer morning at the drops of dew clinging to the grass in the field or plane, he sees the same colors. And, likewise, when it rains, if he stands in a shady place and the sun's rays beyond him shine through the falling drops, then in some rather dark place the same colors appear, and they can often be seen at night about a candle. In the summer time, as soon as he rises from sleep while his eyes are not yet fully opened, if he suddenly looks at a window through which the light of the sun is streaming, he will see the colors. Again, sitting outside of the sunlight, if he holds his head covering beyond his eyes, or, likewise, if he closes his eyes, the same thing happens in the shade at the edges, and it also takes place through a glass vase filled with water, sitting in the sunlight. Similarly, if any one holding water in his mouth suddenly sprinkles the water in jets and stands at the side of them; or if through a lamp of oil hanging in the air the rays shine in the proper way, or the light shines upon the surface of the oil, the colors again appear. Thus, in an infinite number of ways, natural as well as artificial, colors of this kind are to be seen, if only the diligent investigator knows how to find them.

Experimental science is also that which alone, as the mistress of the speculative sciences, can discover magnificent truths in the fields of the other sciences, to which these other sciences can in no way attain. And these truths are not of the nature of former truths, but they may be even outside of them, in the fields of things where there are neither as yet conclusions or principles, and good examples may be given of this, but in everything which follows it is not necessary for the inexperienced to seek a reason in order to understand at the beginning, but rather he will never have a reason before he has tried the experiment. Whence in the first place there should be **credulity** until **experiment** follows, in order that the reason may be found. If one who has never seen that a magnet draws iron nor heard from others that it attracts, seeks the reason before experimenting, he will never find it. Indeed, in the first place, he ought to believe those who have experimented or who have it from investigators, nor ought he to doubt the truth of it because he himself is ignorant of it and because he has no reason for it.

The **third value** of this science is this—it is on account of the prerogatives through which it looks, not only to the other sciences, but by its own power investigates the secrets of nature, and this takes place in two ways—in the knowledge of future and present events, and in those wonderful works by which it surpasses astronomy commonly so-called in the power of its **conclusions**. For Ptolemy in the introduction of the *Almagest*, says that there is another and surer way than the ordinary astronomy; that is, the experimental method which follows after the course of nature, to which many faithful philosophers, such as Aristotle and a vast crowd of the authors of predictions from the stars, are favorable, as he himself says, and we ourselves know through our own experience, which cannot be denied. This wisdom has been found as a natural remedy for human ignorance or imprudence; for it is difficult to have astronomical implements sufficiently exact and more difficult to have tables absolutely verified, especially when the motion of the planets is involved in them. The use of these tables is difficult, but the use of the instruments more so.

This science has found definitions and ways through which it quickly comes to the answer of a whole question, as far as the nature of a single science can do so, and through which it shows us the outlines of the virtues of the skies and the influence of the sky upon this earth, without the difficulty of astronomy. This part so-called has four principal laws as the secret of the science, and some bear witness that a use of this science, which illustrates its nature, is in the change of a region in order that the customs of the people may be changed. In connection with which Aristotle, the most learned of philosophers, when Alexander asked of him concerning some tribes that he had found, whether he should kill them on account of their barbarity or let them live, responded in the Book of Secrets if you can change their air let them live; if not, kill them. He wished that their air could be altered usefully, so that the complexion of their bodies could be changed, and finally the mind aroused through the complexion should absorb good customs from the liberty of their environment; this is one use of this science.

MARSIGLIO OF PADUA AND HIS "DEFENDER OF PEACE"

By Marsiglio of Padua

M arsiglio (Marsilio) of Padua (ca. 1275–ca. 1342) was professor of philosophy and rector of the University of Paris in 1313, and he also served as priest, physician, and diplomat. One of his most famous friends late in life was William of Ockham. Similar to Dante, Marsiglio attacked the Papacy as one of the major sources of discontent and internecine strife within medieval Christendom. For him, the solution was to have the secular states, or kingdoms, rule over the Church, not the other way around. He had studied Aristotelian philosophy at the University of Padua in northeastern Italy near Venice. Marsiglio completed his masterpiece, the Defensor pacis (The Defender of Peace), in 1324, but his authorship was not revealed until 1326. Rightly afraid of being persecuted by the pope for his heretical views, Marsiglio sought refuge at the court of the German Emperor, Louis of Bavaria, for the rest of his life. In his famous treatise he argues, on the one hand, that civil governments should control their local churches, and on the other that the state should administer any organized Church, hence the papacy. Marsiglio was deeply influenced by Aristotelian thinking and insisted, accordingly, on man's general need to enjoy life here on earth to the best of his abilities. This would be possible by living within a community that was created by the free will of its members. Although Marsiglio was certainly not a harbinger of modern democracy, especially because he assigned central power still to the intellectual and hereditary elite and to a singular ruler with absolute power, he still insisted on the supremacy of the law as set up by the people who would retain the right to remove that ruler from his office.

Only peace can furnish the necessary conditions for progress, for peace is the mother of all the higher arts. The evils of discord and strife have nearly all been described by Aristotle; but one great and important cause of trouble naturally escaped him,—a potent, hidden influence which interferes with the welfare not only of the empire but of all the governments of Europe. [Marsiglio cleverly refrains from revealing this modern cause of discord until he has described the proper nature and organization of the state.]

The power of making the laws should belong to the whole body of citizens, for there is no lawgiver among men superior to the people themselves. The argument that there are an infinite number of fools in the world may be met by pointing out that "foolish" is a relative term, and that the people know their own needs best and will not legislate against their own interests. Any particular class of people is, however, likely to be self-seeking, as is shown by the decrees of the popes and the clergy, where the self-interest of the lawmaker is only too apparent

The actual administration must, nevertheless, be in the hands of a single person or group of persons.[11] Perhaps a king is the best head for the state, but the monarch should be elected and not hold his office hereditarily, and should be deposed if he exceed his powers.[22]

[At the end of Part I the time comes to take up the chief cause of trouble which has grown up since Aristotle's time,—namely, the papacy and the clergy.] The bishops of Rome have extended their jurisdiction not only over the clergy but, since the Donation of Constantine, over secular rulers as well. This is illustrated by the acts of the popes of the time (including the famous bull *Unam Sanctam*) and of the existing bishop of Rome, John XXII, who claims, both in Italy and Germany, to have supreme jurisdiction over the emperor and over the lesser princes and communities, even in purely temporal and feudal matters.

In its original meaning the "church" meant all believers in Christ,—all those for whom he shed his blood. "Churchmen" *(viri ecclesiastici)* then include all the faithful, whether they be priests or not The assumed supremacy of the bishop of Rome is without foundation. Even if Peter was ever in Rome,—which is doubtful,—there is no reason to suppose that he handed down any exceptional power to the succeeding bishops.

The third part of the *Defensor Pacis* contains a brief summary of the main arguments of the book. It is possible that this résumé was not prepared by Marsiglio himself, but it furnishes a clear analysis of the whole treatise. It opens as follows:

In our preceding pages we have found that civil discord and dissension in the various kingdoms and communities is due, above all, to a cause which, unless it be obviated, will continue to be a source of future calamity, —namely, the claims, aspirations, and enterprises of the Roman bishop and of his band of ecclesiastics, bent upon gaining secular power and superfluous worldly possessions. The bishop of Rome is wont to support his claim to supreme authority over others by the assertion that the plenitude of power was delegated to him by Christ through the person of St. Peter, as we showed at the end of Part I, and in several chapters of Part II. But in reality no princely authority, nor any coercive jurisdiction in this world—to say nothing of *supreme* authority—belongs to him or to any other bishop, priest, or clerk, whether jointly or severally. This we have proved by sound human arguments in Part I, chapters xii, xiii, and xv. We have, in Part II, chapters vi and vii, further supported our conclusions by the testimony of eternal truth and by the discussions of the saints and learned men who have interpreted this truth.

---

1 All this is strikingly similar to the teachings of Rousseau in his *Social Contract*. See *History of Western Europe,* § 214.
2 Rather singularly Marsiglio appears to have no enthusiasm for a universal monarchy or empire.

Then in the sixth and seventh chapters we established from the Scriptures and by sound reasoning what was the character and extent of the legitimate authority of the priests and bishops. We demonstrated that the plenitude of power to which the clergy, especially the Roman bishop, lays claim belongs neither to the clergy as a whole nor to any of its members. In this way the foundations of the bishop of Rome's malign assumptions would seem to be completely undermined.

Now, in order that this plague which has scattered the seeds of discord and strife in kingdoms and communities, nor has ceased to provoke dissension, may be the more speedily checked and prevented from further increase, we add a third and last part to the preceding two. This is nothing more than a collection of the clear and inevitable deductions from the statements and demonstrations given above. If these conclusions be duly attended to and acted upon this plague and its sophistical source will be easily abolished, now and hereafter, from the various kingdoms and other states.

Of Marsiglio's conclusions the most interesting are the following:

It is necessary to accept as true and essential to salvation *only* the holy and canonical Scriptures, together with their clear implications as interpreted by a general council of the faithful. This is assuredly true and may be assumed.

Doubtful points in the Christian belief are to be determined by a general council,—in no case by a single person, whoever he may be.

No one, according to the gospel, may be forced to observe the divine law by a temporal penalty or any punishment of this world.

The human lawgiver can only be the whole body of citizens or a majority of them.

No one may be compelled by temporal penalties to obey the decretals or ordinances of the bishops of Rome, or of any other bishop, unless the decrees are issued with the sanction of the human lawgiver [namely, the people].

No bishop or priest, as such, has any coercive authority or jurisdiction over any clerk or layman, even over a heretic.

No bishop or priest, or assembly of bishops or priests, may excommunicate any person, or interdict the performance of divine services, except with the authority of the lawgiver [namely, the people].

All bishops have equal authority immediately from Christ, nor, according to divine law, can it be shown that any one of them is superior to, or subordinate to, another, either in divine or temporal matters.

With the consent of the human legislator, other bishops may, together or separately, excommunicate the Roman bishop and exercise other forms of authority over him.

The determination of the number of churches and of priests, deacons, and other officials necessary to administer them, belongs to the rulers who shall conform to the laws of the faithful people.

The temporal possessions of the Church, except such as are necessary for the support of the priests and other ministers of the gospel and for the maintenance of divine services and the relief of the helpless poor, may properly, and according to divine law, be devoted, in whole or in part, by the human law, to public needs and the public defense.

Marsiglio's modern independence of thought and methods of criticism may be illustrated by the following passage, in which he questions a universally accepted belief of the Middle Ages.

Since, then, it is evident from the Scriptures that Paul spent two years in Rome, there received all the gentiles who were converted, and preached there, it is clear that he was in a special sense bishop of Rome, since he fulfilled the duties of pastor there, having his authority immediately from Christ through revelation and, by the consent of the other apostles, through election.

As for St. Peter, on the other hand, I maintain that it cannot be proved by Holy Scripture that he was bishop of Rome, or, what is more, that he ever was in Rome. It is true that, according to a certain popular ecclesiastical legend of the saints, St. Peter reached Rome before St. Paul preached the word there, and was later arrested; moreover it is related that St. Paul, on his arrival at Rome, engaged with St. Peter in many conflicts with Simon. Magus, and at the same time stoutly withstood emperors and their ministers in the cause of the faith. Finally, according to the same story, both were decapitated at the same time for confessing Christ, and slept in the Lord, thus consecrating the Roman Church in Christ.

It is most astonishing, however, that neither St. Luke, who wrote the Acts of the Apostles, nor St. Paul, makes any mention of St. Peter. Moreover the last chapter of Acts makes it very probable that St. Peter had not arrived in Rome before them. For when Paul addressed the Jews upon his arrival, in explaining the reason for his coming to Rome, he said, among other things, "But when the Jews spoke against it [his liberation] I was constrained to appeal unto Caesar." And they said unto him, " We neither received letters out of Jerusalem concerning thee, neither any of the brethren that came shewed or spoke any harm of thee. But we desire to hear of thee what thou thinkest: for as concerning this sect [of the Christians] we know that every where it is spoken against."

I would that any one anxious for the truth, and not bent upon mere discussion, should tell me if it be probable that St. Peter had preceded Paul in Rome and yet had made no proclamation of Christ's faith, which the Jews, in speaking to Paul, call a "sect." Moreover would not Paul, in reproving them for their incredulity, have spoken of Peter had he been there preaching, and have called as a witness one who, according to the third chapter of Acts, beheld Christ's resurrection? Then, from what has been said, who could suppose that Paul could spend two years in Rome and still have no intercourse or communication with St. Peter? And if he had, why did the author of Acts make absolutely no mention of the fact? In other less important towns, when Paul came upon Peter he makes mention of him and associated with him, for example, in Corinth (I Cor. iii), and in Antioch (Gal. ii), and so in other places. Why does he say nothing of Peter if he found him in Rome, the most celebrated of all cities, where, according to the story mentioned above, Peter was conspicuous as bishop?

Such a state of affairs is well-nigh incredible, so that the story or legend ought not to be regarded as probable in reference to the matter in hand, and should be reckoned as apocryphal. We must, however, following Holy Scripture, hold that St. Paul was bishop of Rome, and if any one else was there with him, Paul was nevertheless in charge, and in a special sense bishop of Rome, as is shown by the reasons adduced. Peter would seem to have been bishop of Antioch, as appears in the second chapter of Galatians. I do not deny that Peter was ever in Rome, but hold it as probable that he did not precede Paul, but rather the contrary.

THE DECAMERON

By Giovanni Boccaccio

G iovanni Boccaccio (1313-1375) is regarded as one of the most influential early Renaissance writers of Italy. In many respects, however, he was still steeped in the Middle Ages, which makes it difficult for us to situate him correctly between both periods. Nevertheless, his interest in classical learning and classical Latin, as well as his new world views, ultimately characterize him as a new personality, the harbinger of the Renaissance. He was the illegitimate son of a Florentine merchant, who acknowledged him only around 1320 and took him into his house and family. In 1327 he accompanied his father, who was a councillor and chamberlain in the court of King Robert of Anjou, to Naples. This helped young Boccaccio to learn much about traditional courtly culture and literature. He studied at the university in Naples from 1331 to 1336. In 1334 Boccaccio began writing poetry, first his allegorical work Caccia di Diana (ca. 1334), then Filocolo (ca. 1336), the first prose romance in Italian, and shortly before 1341 Il Filostrato. These were then followed by a stream of other poetic but also philological works. Most famously, around 1350 Boccaccio, reflecting on the devastating consequences of the Black Death, composed his collection of Decameron, in which a group of three men and seven ladies retire to their estates outside of Florence to escape the certain grip of death. In order to pass the time, they tell each other ten stories every day for ten days. With his Decameron, Boccaccio became one of the most influential writers and exerted a tremendous influence all over Europe far into the modern age. Around 1350, Boccaccio struck a friendship with the other famous Renaissance poet, Petrarch (d. 1374), through whose influence he turned increasingly to humanism and scholarly endeavors. Between 1355 and 1360 he composed De casibus virorum illustrium and, most importantly, De claris mulieribus, praising glorious women in the past. Around 1350 and 1365 Boccaccio finally penned his Genealogia deorum gentilium, dealing with classical mythology.

Beginneth here the book called Decameron, otherwise Prince Galeotto, wherein are contained one hundred novels told in ten days by seven ladies and three young men.

PROEM

Voice: Author

'Tis humane to have compassion on the afflicted; and as it shews well in all, so it is especially demanded of those who have had need of comfort and have found it in others: among whom, if any had ever need thereof or found it precious or delectable, I may be numbered; seeing that from my early youth even to the present I was beyond measure aflame with a most aspiring and noble love more perhaps than, were I to enlarge upon it, would seem to accord with my lowly condition. Whereby, among people of discernment to whose knowledge it had come, I had much praise and high esteem, but nevertheless extreme discomfort and suffering, not indeed by reason of cruelty on the part of the beloved lady, but through superabundant ardour engendered in the soul by ill-bridled desire; the which, as it allowed me no reasonable period of quiescence, frequently occasioned me an inordinate distress. In which distress so much relief was afforded me by the delectable discourse of a friend and his commendable consolations, that I entertain a very solid conviction that to them I owe it that I am not dead. But, as it pleased Him, who, being infinite, has assigned by immutable law an end to all things mundane, my love, beyond all other fervent, and neither to be broken nor bent by any force of determination, or counsel of prudence, or fear of manifest shame or ensuing danger, did nevertheless in course of time abate of its own accord, in such wise that it has now left nought of itself in my mind but that pleasure which it is wont to afford to him who does not adventure too far out in navigating its deep seas; so that, whereas it was used to be grievous, now, all discomfort being done away, I find that which remains to be delightful. But the cessation of the pain has not banished the memory of the kind offices done me by those who shared by sympathy the burden of my griefs; nor will it ever, I believe, pass from me except by death. And as among the virtues gratitude is in my judgment most especially to be commended, and ingratitude in equal measure to be censured, therefore, that I show myself not ungrateful, I have resolved, now that I may call myself free, to endeavour, in return for what I have received, to afford, so far as in me lies, some solace, if not to those who succoured me, and who, perchance, by reason of their good sense or good fortune, need it not, at least to such as may be apt to receive it.

Voice: Author

And though my support or comfort, so to say, may be of little avail to the needy, nevertheless it seems to me meet to offer it most readily where the need is most apparent, because it will there be most serviceable and also most kindly received. Who will deny, that it should be given, for all that it may be worth, to gentle ladies much rather than to men? Within their soft bosoms, betwixt fear and shame, they harbour secret fires of love, and how much of strength concealment adds to those fires, they know who have proved it. Moreover, restrained by the will, the caprice, the commandment of fathers, mothers, brothers, and husbands, confined most part of their time within the narrow compass of their chambers, they live, so to say, a life of vacant ease, and, yearning and renouncing in the same moment, meditate divers matters which cannot all be cheerful. If thereby a melancholy bred of amorous desire make entrance into their minds, it is like to tarry there to their sore distress, unless it be dispelled by a change of ideas. Besides which they have much less power to support such a weight than men. For, when men are enamoured, their case is very different, as we may readily perceive. They, if they are afflicted by a melancholy and heaviness of mood, have many ways of relief and diversion; they may go where they will, may hear and see many things, may hawk, hunt, fish, ride, play or traffic. By which means all are able to compose their minds, either in whole or in part, and repair the ravage wrought by the dumpish mood, at least for some space of time; and shortly after, by one way or another, either solace ensues, or the dumps become less grievous. Wherefore, in some measure to compensate the injustice of Fortune, which to those whose strength is least, as we see it to be in the delicate frames of ladies, has been most niggard of support, I, for the succour and diversion of such of them as love (for others may find sufficient solace in the needle and the spindle and the reel), do intend to recount one hundred Novels or Fables or Parables or Stories, as we may please to call them, which were recounted in ten days by an honourable company of seven ladies and three young men in the time of the late mortal pestilence, as also some canzonets sung by the said ladies for their delectation. In which pleasant novels will be found some passages of love rudely crossed, with other courses of events of which the issues are felicitous, in times as well modern as ancient: from which stories the said ladies, who shall read them, may derive both pleasure from the entertaining matters set forth therein, and also good counsel, in that they may learn what to shun, and likewise what to pursue. Which cannot, I believe, come to pass, unless the dumps be banished by diversion of mind. And if it so happen (as God grant it may) let them give thanks to Love, who, liberating me from his fetters, has given me the power to devote myself to their gratification.

FIRST DAY—NOVEL II

Voice: Neifile

Abraham, a Jew, at the instance of Jehannot de Chevigny, goes to the court of Rome, and having marked the evil life of the clergy, returns to Paris, and becomes a Christian.

Voice: Author

Pamfilo's story elicited the mirth of some of the ladies and the hearty commendation of all, who listened to it with close attention until the end. Whereupon the queen bade Neifile, who sat next her, to tell a story, that the commencement thus made of their diversions might have its sequel. Neifile, whose graces of mind matched the beauty of her person, consented with a gladsome goodwill, and thus began:

Voice: Neifile

Pamfilo has shewn by his story that the goodness of God spares to regard our errors when they result from unavoidable ignorance; and in mine I mean to shew you how the same goodness, bearing patiently with the shortcomings of those who should be its faithful witness in deed and word, draws from them contrariwise evidence of His infallible truth; to the end that what we believe we may with more assured conviction follow.

In Paris, gracious ladies, as I have heard tell, there was once a great merchant, a large dealer in drapery, a good man, most loyal and righteous, his name Jehannot de Chevigny, between whom and a Jew, Abraham by name, also a merchant, and a man of great wealth, as also most loyal and righteous, there subsisted a very close friendship. Now Jehannot, observing Abraham's loyalty and rectitude, began to be sorely vexed in spirit that the soul of one so worthy and wise and good should perish for want of faith. Wherefore he began in a friendly manner to plead with him, that he should leave the errors of the Jewish faith and turn to the Christian verity, which, being sound and holy, he might see daily prospering and gaining ground, whereas, on the contrary, his own religion was dwindling and was almost come to nothing. The Jew replied that he believed that there was no faith sound and holy except the Jewish faith, in which he was born, and in which he meant to live and die; nor would anything ever turn him therefrom. Nothing daunted, however, Jehannot some days afterwards began again to ply Abraham with similar arguments, explaining to him in such crude fashion as merchants use the reasons why our faith is better than the Jewish. And though the Jew was a great master in the Jewish law, yet, whether it was by reason of his friendship for Jehannot, or that the Holy Spirit dictated the words that the simple merchant used, at any rate the Jew began to be much interested in Jehannot's arguments, though still too staunch in his faith to suffer himself to be converted. But Jehannot was no less assiduous in plying him with argument than he was obstinate in adhering to his law, insomuch that at length the Jew, overcome by such incessant appeals, said: "Well, well, Jehannot, thou wouldst have me become a Christian, and I am disposed to do so, provided I first go to Rome and there see him whom thou callest God's vicar on earth, and observe what manner of life he leads and his brother cardinals with him; and if such it be that thereby, in conjunction with thy words, I may understand that thy faith is better than mine, as thou hast sought to shew me, I will do as I have said: otherwise, I will remain as I am a Jew." When Jehannot heard this, he was greatly distressed, saying to himself: "I thought to have converted him; but now I see that the pains which I took for so excellent a purpose are all in vain; for, if he goes to the court of Rome and sees the iniquitous and foul life which the clergy lead there, so far from turning Christian, had he been converted already, he would without doubt relapse into Judaism." Then turning to Abraham he said: "Nay, but, my friend, why wouldst thou be at all this labour and great expense of travelling from here to Rome? to say nothing of the risks both by sea and by land which a rich man like thee must needs run. Thinkest thou not to find here one that can give thee baptism? And as for any doubts that thou mayst have touching the faith to which I point thee, where wilt thou find greater masters and sages therein than here, to resolve thee of any question thou mayst put to them? Wherefore in my opinion this journey of thine is superfluous. Think that the prelates there are such as thou mayst have seen here, nay, as much better as they are nearer to the Chief Pastor. And so, by my advice thou wilt spare thy pains until some time of indulgence, when I, perhaps, may be able to bear thee company." The Jew replied: "Jehannot, I doubt not that so it is as thou sayst; but once and for all I tell thee that I am minded to go there, and will never otherwise do that which thou wouldst have me and hast so earnestly besought me to do." "Go then," said Jehannot, seeing that his mind was made up, "and good luck go with thee;" and so he gave up the contest because nothing would be lost, though he felt sure that he would never become a Christian after seeing the court of Rome. The Jew took horse, and posted with all possible speed to Rome; where on his arrival he was honourably received by his fellow Jews. He said nothing to any one of the purpose for which he had come; but began circumspectly to acquaint himself with the ways of the Pope and the cardinals and the other prelates and all the courtiers; and from what he saw for himself, being a man of great intelligence, or learned from others, he discovered that without distinction of rank they were all sunk in the most disgraceful lewdness, sinning not only in the way of nature but after the manner of the men of Sodom, without any restraint of remorse or shame, in such sort that, when any great favour was to be procured, the influence of the courtesans and boys was of no small moment. Moreover he found them one and all gluttonous, wine-bibbers, drunkards, and next after lewdness, most addicted to the shameless service of the belly, like brute beasts. And, as he probed the matter still further, he perceived that they were all so greedy and avaricious that human, nay Christian blood, and things sacred of what kind soever, spiritualities no less than temporalities, they bought and sold for money; which traffic was greater and employed more brokers than the drapery trade and all the other trades of Paris put together; open simony and gluttonous excess being glosed under such specious terms as "arrangement" and "moderate use of creature comforts," as if God could not penetrate the thoughts of even the most corrupt hearts, to say nothing of the signification of words, and would suffer Himself to be misled after the manner of men by the names of things. Which matters, with many others which are not to be mentioned, our modest and sober-minded Jew found by no means to his liking, so that, his curiosity being fully satisfied, he was minded to return to Paris; which accordingly he did. There, on his arrival, he was met by Jehannot; and the two made great cheer together. Jehannot expected Abraham's conversion least of all things, and allowed him some days of rest before he asked what he thought of the Holy Father and the cardinals and the other courtiers. To which the Jew forthwith replied: "I think God owes them all an evil recompense: I tell thee, so far as I was able to carry my investigations, holiness, devotion, good works or exemplary living in any kind was nowhere to be found in any clerk; but only lewdness, avarice, gluttony, and the like, and worse, if worse may be, appeared to be held in such honour of all, that (to my thinking) the place is a centre of diabolical rather than of divine activities. To the best of my judgment, your Pastor, and by consequence all that are about him devote all their zeal and ingenuity and subtlety to devise how best and most speedily they may bring the Christian religion to nought and banish it from the world. And because I see that what they so zealously endeavour does not come to pass, but that on the contrary your religion continually grows, and shines more and more clear, therein I seem to discern a very evident token that it, rather than any other, as being more true and holy than any other, has the Holy Spirit for its foundation and support. For which cause, whereas I met your exhortations in a harsh and obdurate temper, and would not become a Christian, now I frankly tell you that I would on no account omit to become such. Go we then to the church, and there according to the traditional rite of your holy faith let me receive baptism." Jehannot, who had anticipated a diametrically opposite conclusion, as soon as he heard him so speak, was the best pleased man that ever was in the world. So taking Abraham with him to Notre Dame he prayed the clergy there to baptise him. When they heard that it was his own wish, they forthwith did so, and Jehannot raised him from the sacred font, and named him Jean; and afterwards he caused teachers of great eminence thoroughly to instruct him in our faith, which he readily learned, and afterwards practised in a good, a virtuous, nay, a holy life.

FIRST DAY—NOVEL III

Voice: Filomena

Melchisedech, a Jew, by a story of three rings averts a great danger with which he was menaced by Saladin.

Voice: Author

When Neifile had brought her story to a close amid the commendations of all the company, Filomena, at the queen's behest, thus began:

Voice: Filomena

The story told by Neifile brings to my mind another in which also a Jew appears, but this time as the hero of a perilous adventure; and as enough has been said of God and of the truth of our faith, it will not now be inopportune if we descend to mundane events and the actions of men. Wherefore I propose to tell you a story, which will perhaps dispose you to be more circumspect than you have been wont to be in answering questions addressed to you. Well ye know, or should know, loving gossips, that, as it often happens that folk by their own folly forfeit a happy estate and are plunged in most grievous misery, so good sense will extricate the wise from extremity of peril, and establish them in complete and assured peace. Of the change from good to evil fortune, which folly may effect, instances abound; indeed, occurring as they do by the thousand day by day, they are so conspicuous that their recital would be beside our present purpose. But that good sense may be our succour in misfortune, I will now, as I promised, make plain to you within the narrow compass of a little story.

Voice: Filomena

Saladin, who by his great valour had from small beginnings made himself Soldan of Egypt, and gained many victories over kings both Christian and Saracen, having in divers wars and by divers lavish displays of magnificence spent all his treasure, and in order to meet a certain emergency being in need of a large sum of money, and being at a loss to raise it with a celerity adequate to his necessity, bethought him of a wealthy Jew, Melchisedech by name, who lent at usance in Alexandria, and who, were he but willing, was, as he believed, able to accommodate him, but was so miserly that he would never do so of his own accord, nor was Saladin disposed to constrain him thereto. So great, however, was his necessity that, after pondering every method whereby the Jew might be induced to be compliant, at last he determined to devise a colourably reasonable pretext for extorting the money from him. So he sent for him, received him affably, seated him by his side, and presently said to him: "My good man, I have heard from many people that thou art very wise, and of great discernment in divine things; wherefore I would gladly know of thee, which of the three laws thou reputest the true law, the law of the Jews, the law of the Saracens, or the law of the Christians?" The Jew, who was indeed a wise man, saw plainly enough that Saladin meant to entangle him in his speech, that he might have occasion to harass him, and bethought him that he could not praise any of the three laws above another without furnishing Saladin with the pretext which he sought. So, concentrating all the force of his mind to shape such an answer as might avoid the snare, he presently lit on what he sought, saying: "My lord, a pretty question indeed is this which you propound, and fain would I answer it; to which end it is apposite that I tell you a story, which, if you will hearken, is as follows: If I mistake not, I remember to have often heard tell of a great and rich man of old time, who among other most precious jewels had in his treasury a ring of extraordinary beauty and value, which by reason of its value and beauty he was minded to leave to his heirs for ever; for which cause he ordained, that, whichever of his sons was found in possession of the ring as by his bequest, should thereby be designate his heir, and be entitled to receive from the rest the honour and homage due to a superior. The son, to whom he bequeathed the ring, left it in like manner to his descendants, making the like ordinance as his predecessor. In short the ring passed from hand to hand for many generations; and in the end came to the hands of one who had three sons, goodly and virtuous all, and very obedient to their father, so that he loved them all indifferently. The rule touching the descent of the ring was known to the young men, and each aspiring to hold the place of honour among them did all he could to persuade his father, who was now old, to leave the ring to him at his death. The worthy man, who loved them all equally, and knew not how to choose from among them a sole legatee, promised the ring to each in turn, and in order to satisfy all three, caused a cunning artificer secretly to make other two rings, so like the first, that the maker himself could hardly tell which was the true ring. So, before he died, he disposed of the rings, giving one privily to each of his sons; whereby it came to pass, that after his decease each of the sons claimed the inheritance and the place of honour, and, his claim being disputed by his brothers, produced his ring in witness of right. And the rings being found so like one to another that it was impossible to distinguish the true one, the suit to determine the true heir remained pendent, and still so remains. And so, my lord, to your question, touching the three laws given to the three peoples by God the Father, I answer: Each of these peoples deems itself to have the true inheritance, the true law, the true commandments of God; but which of them is justified in so believing, is a question which, like that of the rings, remains pendent." The excellent adroitness with which the Jew had contrived to evade the snare which he had laid for his feet was not lost upon Saladin. He therefore determined to let the Jew know his need, and did so, telling him at the same time what he had intended to do, in the event of his answering less circumspectly than he had done.

Voice: *Filomena*

Thereupon the Jew gave the Soldan all the accommodation that he required, which the Soldan afterwards repaid him in full. He also gave him most munificent gifts with his lifelong amity and a great and honourable position near his person.

SECOND DAY—NOVEL VII

Voice: *Panfilo*

The Soldan of Babylon sends one of his daughters overseas, designing to marry her to the King of Algarve. By divers adventures she comes in the space of four years into the hands of nine men in divers places. At last she is restored to her father, whom she quits again in the guise of a virgin, and, as was at first intended, is married to the King of Algarve.

Voice: Author

Had Emilia's story but lasted a little longer, the young ladies would perhaps have been moved to tears, so great was the sympathy which they felt for Madam Beritola in her various fortunes. But now that it was ended, the Queen bade Pamfilo follow suit; and he, than whom none was more obedient, thus began:

Voice: Panfilo

Hardly, gracious ladies, is it given to us to know that which makes for our good; insomuch that, as has been observable in a multitude of instances, many, deeming that the acquisition of great riches would ensure them an easy and tranquil existence, have not only besought them of God in prayer, but have sought them with such ardour that they have spared no pains and shrunk from no danger in the quest, and have attained their end only to lose, at the hands of some one covetous of their vast inheritance, a life with which before the days of their prosperity they were well content. Others, whose course, perilous with a thousand battles, stained with the blood of their brothers and their friends, has raised them from base to regal estate, have found in place of the felicity they expected an infinity of cares and fears, and have proved by experience that a chalice may be poisoned, though it be of gold, and set on the table of a king. Many have most ardently desired beauty and strength and other advantages of person, and have only been taught their error by the death or dolorous life which these very advantages entailed upon them. And so, not to instance each particular human desire, I say, in sum, that there is none of them that men may indulge in full confidence as exempt from the chances and changes of fortune; wherefore, if we would act rightly, we ought to school ourselves to take and be content with that which He gives us, who alone knows and can afford us that of which we have need. But, divers as are the aberrations of desire to which men are prone, so, gracious ladies, there is one to which you are especially liable, in that you are unduly solicitous of beauty, insomuch, that, not content with the charms which nature has allotted you, you endeavour to enhance them with wondrous ingenuity of art; wherefore I am minded to make you acquainted with the coil of misadventures in which her beauty involved a fair Saracen, who in the course of, perhaps, four years was wedded nine several times.

Voice: Panfilo

There was of yore a Soldan of Babylon, by name of Beminedab, who in his day had cause enough to be well content with his luck. Many children male and female had he, and among them a daughter, Alatiel by name, who by common consent of all that saw her was the most beautiful woman then to be found in the world. Now the Soldan, having been signally aided by the King of Algarve in inflicting a great defeat upon a host of Arabs that had attacked him, had at his instance and by way of special favour given Alatiel to the King to wife; wherefore, with an honourable escort of gentlemen and ladies most nobly and richly equipped, he placed her aboard a well-armed, well-furnished ship, and, commending her to God, sped her on her journey. The mariners, as soon as the weather was favourable, hoisted sail, and for some days after their departure from Alexandria had a prosperous voyage; but when they had passed Sardinia, and were beginning to think that they were nearing their journey's end, they were caught one day between divers cross winds, each blowing with extreme fury, whereby the ship laboured so sorely that not only the lady but the seamen from time to time gave themselves up for lost. But still, most manfully and skilfully they struggled might and main with the tempest, which, ever waxing rather than waning, buffeted them for two days with immense unintermittent surges; and being not far from the island of Majorca, as the third night began to close in, wrapt in clouds and mist and thick darkness, so that they saw neither the sky nor aught else, nor by any nautical skill might conjecture where they were, they felt the ship's timbers part. Wherefore, seeing no way to save the ship, each thought only how best to save himself, and, a boat being thrown out, the masters first, and then the men, one by one, though the first-comers sought with knives in their hands to bar the passage of the rest, all, rather than remain in the leaky ship, crowded into it, and there found the death which they hoped to escape. For the boat, being in such stress of weather and with such a burden quite unmanageable, went under, and all aboard her perished; whereas the ship, leaky though she was, and all but full of water, yet, driven by the fury of the tempest, was hurled with prodigious velocity upon the shore of the island of Majorca, and struck it with such force as to embed herself in the sand, perhaps a stone's throw from terra firma, where she remained all night beaten and washed by the sea, but no more to be moved by the utmost violence of the gale. None had remained aboard her but the lady and her women, whom the malice of the elements and their fears had brought to the verge of death. When it was broad day and the storm was somewhat abated, the lady, half dead, raised her head, and in faltering accents began to call first one and then another of her servants. She called in vain, however; for those whom she called were too far off to hear. Great indeed was her wonder and fear to find herself thus without sight of human face or sound of other voice than her own; but, struggling to her feet as best she might, she looked about her, and saw the ladies that were of her escort, and the other women, all prostrate on the deck; so, after calling them one by one, she began at length to touch them, and finding few that shewed sign of life, for indeed, between grievous sea-sickness and fear, they had little life left, she grew more terrified than before. However, being in sore need of counsel, all alone as she was, and without knowledge or means of learning where she was, she at last induced such as had life in them to get upon their feet, with whom, as none knew where the men were gone, and the ship was now full of water and visibly breaking up, she abandoned herself to piteous lamentations.

Voice: *Panfilo*

It was already none before they descried any one on the shore or elsewhere to whom they could make appeal for help; but shortly after none it so chanced that a gentleman, Pericone da Visalgo by name, being on his return from one of his estates, passed that way with some mounted servants. Catching sight of the ship, he apprehended the circumstances at a glance, and bade one of his servants try to get aboard her, and let him know the result. The servant with some difficulty succeeded in boarding the vessel, and found the gentle lady with her few companions ensconced under shelter of the prow, and shrinking timidly from observation. At the first sight of him they wept, and again and again implored him to have pity on them; but finding that he did not understand them, nor they him, they sought by gestures to make him apprehend their forlorn condition.

With these tidings the servant, after making such survey of the ship as he could, returned to Pericone, who forthwith caused the ladies, and all articles of value which were in the ship and could be removed, to be brought off her, and took them with him to one of his castles. The ladies' powers were soon in a measure restored by food and rest, and by the honour which was paid to Alatiel, and Alatiel alone by all the rest, as well as by the richness of her dress, Pericone perceived that she must be some great lady. Nor, though she was still pale, and her person bore evident marks of the sea's rough usage, did he fail to note that it was cast in a mould of extraordinary beauty. Wherefore his mind was soon made up that, if she lacked a husband, he would take her to wife, and that, if he could not have her to wife, then he would make her his mistress. So this ardent lover, who was a man of powerful frame and haughty mien, devoted himself for several days to the service of the lady with excellent effect, for the lady completely recovered her strength and spirits, so that her beauty far exceeded Pericone's most sanguine conjectures. Great therefore beyond measure was his sorrow that he understood not her speech, nor she his, so that neither could know who the other was; but being inordinately enamoured of her beauty, he sought by such mute blandishments as he could devise to declare his love, and bring her of her own accord to gratify his desire. All in vain, however; she repulsed his advances point blank; whereby his passion only grew the stronger. So some days passed; and the lady perceiving Pericone's constancy, and bethinking her that sooner or later she must yield either to force or to love, and gratify his passion, and judging by what she observed of the customs of the people that she was amongst Christians, and in a part where, were she able to speak their language, she would gain little by making herself known, determined with a lofty courage to stand firm and immovable in this extremity of her misfortunes. Wherefore she bade the three women, who were all that were left to her, on no account to let any know who they were, unless they were so circumstanced that they might safely count on assistance in effecting their escape: she also exhorted them most earnestly to preserve their chastity, averring that she was firmly resolved that none but her husband should enjoy her. The women heartily assented, and promised that her injunctions should be obeyed to the utmost of their power.

Day by day Pericone's passion waxed more ardent, being fomented by the proximity and contrariety of its object. Wherefore seeing that blandishment availed nothing, he was minded to have recourse to wiles and stratagems, and in the last resort to force. The lady, debarred by her law from the use of wine, found it, perhaps, on that account all the more palatable; which Pericone observing determined to enlist Bacchus in the service of Venus. So, ignoring her coyness, he provided one evening a supper, which was ordered with all possible pomp and beauty, and graced by the presence of the lady. No lack was there of incentives to hilarity; and Pericone directed the servant who waited on Alatiel to ply her with divers sorts of blended wines; which command the man faithfully executed. She, suspecting nothing, and seduced by the delicious flavour of the liquor, drank somewhat more freely than was seemly, and forgetting her past woes, became frolicsome, and incited by some women who trod some measures in the Majorcan style, she shewed the company how they footed it in Alexandria. This novel demeanour was by no means lost on Pericone, who saw in it a good omen of his speedy success; so, with profuse relays of food and wine he prolonged the supper far into the night.

Voice: *Panfilo*

When the guests were at length gone, he attended the lady alone to her chamber, where, the heat of the wine overpowering the cold counsels of modesty, she made no more account of Pericone's presence than if he had been one of her women, and forthwith undressed and went to bed. Pericone was not slow to follow her, and as soon as the light was out lay down by her side, and taking her in his arms, without the least demur on her part, began to solace himself with her after the manner of lovers; which experience--she knew not till then with what horn men butt--caused her to repent that she had not yielded to his blandishments; nor did she thereafter wait to be invited to such nights of delight, but many a time declared her readiness, not by words, for she had none to convey her meaning, but by gestures.

Voice: *Panfilo*

But this great felicity which she now shared with Pericone was not to last: for not content with making her, instead of the consort of a king, the mistress of a castellan, Fortune had now in store for her a harsher experience, though of an amorous character. Pericone had a brother, twenty-five years of age, fair and fresh as a rose, his name Marato. On sight of Alatiel Marato had been mightily taken with her; he inferred from her bearing that he stood high in her good graces; he believed that nothing stood between him and the gratification of his passion but the jealous vigilance with which Pericone guarded her. So musing, he hit upon a ruthless expedient, which had effect in action as hasty as heinous.

Voice: *Panfilo*

It so chanced that there then lay in the port of the city a ship, commanded by two Genoese, bound with a cargo of merchandise for Klarenza in the Morea: her sails were already hoist; and she tarried only for a favourable breeze. Marato approached the masters and arranged with them to take himself and the lady aboard on the following night. This done he concerted further action with some of his most trusty friends, who readily lent him their aid to carry his design into execution. So on the following evening towards nightfall, the conspirators stole unobserved into Pericone's house, which was entirely unguarded, and there hid themselves, as pre-arranged. Then, as the night wore on, Marato shewed them where Pericone and the lady slept, and they entered the room, and slew Pericone. The lady thus rudely roused wept; but silencing her by menaces of death they carried her off with the best part of Pericone's treasure, and hied them unobserved to the coast, where Marato parted from his companions, and forthwith took the lady aboard the ship. The wind was now fair and fresh, the mariners spread the canvas, and the vessel sped on her course.

Voice: *Panfilo*

This new misadventure, following so hard upon the former, caused the lady no small chagrin; but Marato, with the aid of the good St. Crescent-in-hand that God has given us, found means to afford her such consolation that she was already grown so familiar with him as entirely to forget Pericone, when Fortune, not content with her former caprices, added a new dispensation of woe; for what with the beauty of her person, which, as we have often said, was extraordinary, and the exquisite charm of her manners, the two young men, who commanded the ship, fell so desperately in love with her that they thought of nothing but how they might best serve and please her, so only that Marato should not discover the reason of their assiduous attentions. And neither being ignorant of the other's love, they held secret counsel together, and resolved to make conquest of the lady on joint account: as if love admitted of being held in partnership like merchandise or money. Which design being thwarted by the jealousy with which Alatiel was guarded by Marato, they chose a day and hour, when the ship was speeding amain under canvas, and Marato was on the poop looking out over the sea and quite off his guard; and going stealthily up behind him, they suddenly laid hands on him, and threw him into the sea, and were already more than a mile on their course before any perceived that Marato was overboard. Which when the lady learned, and knew that he was irretrievably lost, she relapsed into her former plaintive mood. But the twain were forthwith by her side with soft speeches and profuse promises, which, however ill she understood them, were not altogether inapt to allay a grief which had in it more of concern for her own hapless self than of sorrow for her lost lover. So, in course of time, the lady beginning visibly to recover heart, they began privily to debate which of them should first take her to bed with him; and neither being willing to give way to the other, and no compromise being discoverable, high words passed between them, and the dispute grew so hot, that they both waxed very wroth, drew their knives, and rushed madly at one another, and before they could be parted by their men, several stabs had been given and received on either side, whereby the one fell dead on the spot, and the other was severely wounded in divers parts of the body. The lady was much disconcerted to find herself thus alone with none to afford her either succour or counsel, and was mightily afraid lest the wrath of the kinsfolk and friends of the twain should vent itself upon her. From this mortal peril she was, however, delivered by the intercessions of the wounded man and their speedy arrival at Klarenza.

Voice: Panfilo

As there she tarried at the same inn with her wounded lover, the fame of her great beauty was speedily bruited abroad, and reached the ears of the Prince of the Morea, who was then staying there. The Prince was curious to see her, and having so done, pronounced her even more beautiful than rumour had reported her; nay, he fell in love with her in such a degree that he could think of nought else; and having heard in what guise she had come thither, he deemed that he might have her. While he was casting about how to compass his end, the kinsfolk of the wounded man, being apprised of the fact, forthwith sent her to him to the boundless delight, as well of the lady, who saw therein her deliverance from a great peril, as of the Prince. The royal bearing, which enhanced the lady's charms, did not escape the Prince, who, being unable to discover her true rank, set her down as at any rate of noble lineage; wherefore he loved her as much again as before, and shewed her no small honour, treating her not as his mistress but as his wife. So the lady, contrasting her present happy estate with her past woes, was comforted; and, as her gaiety revived, her beauty waxed in such a degree that all the Morea talked of it and of little else: insomuch that the Prince's friend and kinsman, the young, handsome and gallant Duke of Athens, was smitten with a desire to see her, and taking occasion to pay the Prince a visit, as he was now and again wont to do, came to Klarenza with a goodly company of honourable gentlemen. The Prince received him with all distinction and made him heartily welcome, but did not at first shew him the lady. By and by, however, their conversation began to turn upon her and her charms, and the Duke asked if she were really so marvellous a creature as folk said. The Prince replied: "Nay, but even more so; and thereof thou shalt have better assurance than my words, to wit, the witness of thine own eyes." So, without delay, for the Duke was now all impatience, they waited on the lady, who was prepared for their visit, and received them very courteously and graciously. They seated her between them, and being debarred from the pleasure of conversing with her, for of their speech she understood little or nothing, they both, and especially the Duke, who was scarce able to believe that she was of mortal mould, gazed upon her in mute admiration; whereby the Duke, cheating himself with the idea that he was but gratifying his curiosity, drank with his eyes, unawares, deep draughts of the poisoned chalice of love, and, to his own lamentable hurt, fell a prey to a most ardent passion. His first thought, when they had left her, and he had time for reflection, was that the Prince was the luckiest man in the world to have a creature so fair to solace him; and swayed by his passion, his mind soon inclined to divers other and less honourable meditations, whereof the issue was that, come what might, he would despoil the Prince of his felicity, and, if possible, make it his own. This resolution was no sooner taken than, being of a hasty temperament, he cast to the winds all considerations of honour and justice, and studied only how to compass his end by craft. So, one day, as the first step towards the accomplishment of his evil purpose, he arranged with the Prince's most trusted chamberlain, one Ciuriaci, that his horses and all other his personal effects should, with the utmost secrecy, be got ready against a possible sudden departure: and then at nightfall, attended by a single comrade (both carrying arms), he was privily admitted by Ciuriaci into the Prince's chamber. It was a hot night, and the Prince had risen without disturbing the lady, and was standing bare to the skin at an open window fronting the sea, to enjoy a light breeze that blew thence. So, by preconcert with his comrade, the Duke stole up to the window, and in a trice ran the Prince through the body, and caught him up, and threw him out of the window. The palace was close by the sea, but at a considerable altitude above it, and the window, through which the Prince's body was thrown, looked over some houses, which, being sapped by the sea, had become ruinous, and were rarely or never visited by a soul; whereby, as the Duke had foreseen, the fall of the Prince's body passed, as indeed it could not but pass, unobserved. Thereupon the Duke's accomplice whipped out a halter, which he had brought with him for the purpose, and, making as if he were but in play, threw it round Ciuriaci's neck, drew it so tight that he could not utter a sound, and then, with the Duke's aid, strangled him, and sent him after his master. All this was accomplished, as the Duke knew full well, without awakening any in the palace, not even the lady, whom he now approached with a light, and holding it over the bed gently uncovered her person, as she lay fast asleep, and surveyed her from head to foot to his no small satisfaction; for fair as she had seemed to him dressed, he found her unadorned charms incomparably greater. As he gazed, his passion waxed beyond measure, and, reckless of his recent crime, and of the blood which still stained his hands, he got forthwith into the bed; and she, being too sound asleep to distinguish between him and the Prince, suffered him to lie with her.

Voice: Panfilo

But, boundless as was his delight, it brooked no long continuance; so, rising, he called to him some of his comrades, by whom he had the lady secured in such manner that she could utter no sound, and borne out of the palace by the same secret door by which he had gained entrance; he then set her on horseback and in dead silence put his troop in motion, taking the road to Athens. He did not, however, venture to take the lady to Athens, where she would have encountered his Duchess--for he was married--but lodged her in a very beautiful villa which he had hard by the city overlooking the sea, where, most forlorn of ladies, she lived secluded, but with no lack of meet and respectful service.

On the following morning the Prince's courtiers awaited his rising until none, but perceiving no sign of it, opened the doors, which had not been secured, and entered his bedroom. Finding it vacant, they supposed that the Prince was gone off privily somewhere to have a few days of unbroken delight with his fair lady; and so they gave themselves no further trouble. But the next day it so chanced that an idiot, roaming about the ruins where lay the corpses of the Prince and Ciuriaci, drew the latter out by the halter and went off dragging it after him. The corpse was soon recognised by not a few, who, at first struck dumb with amazement, soon recovered sense enough to cajole the idiot into retracing his steps and shewing them the spot where he had found it; and having thus, to the immeasurable grief of all the citizens, discovered the Prince's body, they buried it with all honour. Needless to say that no pains were spared to trace the perpetrators of so heinous a crime, and that the absence and evidently furtive departure of the Duke of Athens caused him to be suspected both of the murder and of the abduction of the lady. So the citizens were instant with one accord that the Prince's brother, whom they chose as his successor, should exact the debt of vengeance; and he, having satisfied himself by further investigation that their suspicion was well founded, summoned to his aid his kinsfolk, friends and divers vassals, and speedily gathered a large, powerful and well-equipped army, with intent to make war upon the Duke of Athens. The Duke, being informed of his movements, made ready likewise to defend himself with all his power; nor had he any lack of allies, among whom the Emperor of Constantinople sent his son, Constantine, and his nephew, Manuel, with a great and goodly force. The two young men were honourably received by the Duke, and still more so by the Duchess, who was Constantine's sister.

Day by day war grew more imminent; and at last the Duchess took occasion to call Constantine and Manuel into her private chamber, and with many tears told them the whole story at large, explaining the casus belli, dilating on the indignity which she suffered at the hands of the Duke, if, as was believed, he really kept a mistress in secret, and beseeching them in most piteous accents to do the best they could to devise some expedient whereby the Duke's honour might be cleared, and her own peace of mind assured. The young men knew exactly how matters stood; and so, without wearying the Duchess with many questions, they did their best to console her, and succeeded in raising her hopes. Before taking their leave they learned from her where the lady was, whose marvellous beauty they had heard lauded so often; and being eager to see her, they besought the Duke to afford them an opportunity. Forgetful of what a like complaisance had cost the Prince, he consented, and next morning brought them to the villa where the lady lived, and with her and a few of his boon companions regaled them with a lordly breakfast, which was served in a most lovely garden. Constantine had no sooner seated himself and surveyed the lady, than he was lost in admiration, inly affirming that he had never seen so beautiful a creature, and that for such a prize the Duke, or any other man, might well be pardoned treachery or any other crime: he scanned her again and again, and ever with more and more admiration; whereby it fared with him even as it had fared with the Duke. He went away hotly in love with her, and dismissing all thought of the war, cast about for some method by which, without betraying his passion to any, he might devise some means of wresting the lady from the Duke.

As he thus burned and brooded, the Prince drew dangerously near the Duke's dominions; wherefore order was given for an advance, and the Duke, with Constantine and the rest, marshalled his forces and led them forth from Athens to bar the Prince's passage of the frontier at certain points. Some days thus passed, during which Constantine, whose mind and soul were entirely absorbed by his passion for the lady, bethought him, that, as the Duke was no longer in her neighbourhood, he might readily compass his end. He therefore feigned to be seriously unwell, and, having by this pretext obtained the Duke's leave, he ceded his command to Manuel, and returned to his sister at Athens. He had not been there many days before the Duchess recurred to the dishonour which the Duke did her by keeping the lady; whereupon he said that of that, if she approved, he would certainly relieve her by seeing that the lady was removed from the villa to some distant place. The Duchess, supposing that Constantine was prompted not by jealousy of the Duke but by jealousy for her honour, gave her hearty consent to his plan, provided he so contrived that the Duke should never know that she had been privy to it; on which point Constantine gave her ample assurance. So, being authorised by the Duchess to act as he might deem best, he secretly equipped a light bark and manned her with some of his men, to whom he confided his plan, bidding them lie to off the garden of the lady's villa; and so, having sent the bark forward, he hied him with other of his men to the villa. He gained ready admission of the servants, and was made heartily welcome by the lady, who, at his desire, attended by some of her servants, walked with him and some of his comrades in the garden. By and by, feigning that he had a message for her from the Duke, he drew her aside towards a gate that led down to the sea, and which one of his confederates had already opened. A concerted signal brought the bark alongside, and to seize the lady and set her aboard the bark was but the work of an instant. Her retinue hung back as they heard Constantine menace with death whoso but stirred or spoke, and suffered him, protesting that what he did was done not to wrong the Duke but solely to vindicate his sister's honour, to embark with his men. The lady wept, of course, but Constantine was at her side, the rowers gave way, and the bark, speeding like a thing of life over the waves, made Egina shortly after dawn. There Constantine and the lady landed, she still lamenting her fatal beauty, and took a little rest and pleasure. Then, re-embarking, they continued their voyage, and in the course of a few days reached Chios, which Constantine, fearing paternal censure, and that he might be deprived of his fair booty, deemed a safe place of sojourn. So, after some days of repose the lady ceased to bewail her harsh destiny, and suffering Constantine to console her as his predecessors had done, began once more to enjoy the good gifts which Fortune sent her.

Voice: Panfilo

Now while they thus dallied, Osbech, King of the Turks, who was perennially at war with the Emperor, came by chance to Smyrna; and there learning that Constantine was wantoning in careless ease at Chios with a lady of whom he had made prize, he made a descent by night upon the island with an armed flotilla. Landing his men in dead silence, he made captives of not a few of the Chians whom he surprised in their beds; others, who took the alarm and rushed to arms, he slew; and having wasted the whole island with fire, he shipped the booty and the prisoners, and sailed back to Smyrna. As there he overhauled the booty, he lit upon the fair lady, and knew her for the same that had been taken in bed and fast asleep with Constantine: whereat, being a young man, he was delighted beyond measure, and made her his wife out of hand with all due form and ceremony. And so for several months he enjoyed her.

Voice: *Panfilo*

Now there had been for some time and still was a treaty pending between the Emperor and Basano, King of Cappadocia, whereby Basano with his forces was to fall on Osbech on one side while the Emperor attacked him on the other. Some demands made by Basano, which the Emperor deemed unreasonable, had so far retarded the conclusion of the treaty; but no sooner had the Emperor learned the fate of his son than, distraught with grief, he forthwith conceded the King of Cappadocia's demands, and was instant with him to fall at once upon Osbech while he made ready to attack him on the other side. Getting wind of the Emperor's design, Osbech collected his forces, and, lest he should be caught and crushed between the convergent armies of two most mighty potentates, advanced against the King of Cappadocia. The fair lady he left at Smyrna in the care of a faithful dependant and friend, and after a while joined battle with the King of Cappadocia, in which battle he was slain, and his army defeated and dispersed. Wherefore Basano with his victorious host advanced, carrying everything before him, upon Smyrna, and receiving everywhere the submission due to a conqueror.

Voice: *Panfilo*

Meanwhile Osbech's dependant, by name Antioco, who had charge of the fair lady, was so smitten with her charms that, albeit he was somewhat advanced in years, he broke faith with his friend and lord, and allowed himself to become enamoured of her. He had the advantage of knowing her language, which counted for much with one who for some years had been, as it were, compelled to live the life of a deaf mute, finding none whom she could understand or by whom she might be understood; and goaded by passion, he in the course of a few days established such a degree of intimacy with her that in no long time it passed from friendship into love, so that their lord, far away amid the clash of arms and the tumult of the battle, was forgotten, and marvellous pleasure had they of one another between the sheets.

Voice: *Panfilo*

However, news came at last of Osbech's defeat and death, and the victorious and unchecked advance of Basano, whose advent they were by no means minded to await. Wherefore, taking with them the best part of the treasure that Osbech had left there, they hied them with all possible secrecy to Rhodes. There they had not along abode before Antioco fell ill of a mortal disease. He had then with him a Cypriote merchant, an intimate and very dear friend, to whom, as he felt his end approach, he resolved to leave all that he possessed, including his dear lady. So, when he felt death imminent, he called them to him and said: "'Tis now quite evident to me that my life is fast ebbing away; and sorely do I regret it, for never had I so much pleasure of life as now. Well content indeed I am in one respect, in that, as die I must, I at least die in the arms of the two persons whom I love more than any other in the world, to wit, in thine arms, dearest friend, and those of this lady, whom, since I have known her, I have loved more than myself. But yet 'tis grievous to me to know that I must leave her here in a strange land with none to afford her either protection or counsel; and but that I leave her with thee, who, I doubt not, wilt have for my sake no less care of her than thou wouldst have had of me, 'twould grieve me still more; wherefore with all my heart and soul I pray thee, that, if I die, thou take her with all else that belongs to me into thy charge, and so acquit thyself of thy trust as thou mayst deem conducive to the peace of my soul. And of thee, dearest lady, I entreat one favour, that I be not forgotten of thee, after my death, so that there whither I go it may still be my boast to be beloved here of the most beautiful lady that nature ever formed. Let me but die with these two hopes assured, and without doubt I shall depart in peace."

Voice: Panfilo

Both the merchant and the lady wept to hear him thus speak, and, when he had done, comforted him, and promised faithfully, in the event of his death, to do even as he besought them. He died almost immediately afterwards, and was honourably buried by them. A few days sufficed the merchant to wind up all his affairs in Rhodes; and being minded to return to Cyprus aboard a Catalan boat that was there, he asked the fair lady what she purposed to do if he went back to Cyprus. The lady answered, that, if it were agreeable to him, she would gladly accompany him, hoping that for love of Antioco he would treat and regard her as his sister. The merchant replied that it would afford him all the pleasure in the world; and, to protect her from insult until their arrival in Cyprus, he gave her out as his wife, and, suiting action to word, slept with her on the boat in an alcove in a little cabin in the poop. Whereby that happened which on neither side was intended when they left Rhodes, to wit, that the darkness and the comfort and the warmth of the bed, forces of no mean efficacy, did so prevail with them that dead Antioco was forgotten alike as lover and as friend, and by a common impulse they began to wanton together, insomuch that before they were arrived at Baffa, where the Cypriote resided, they were indeed man and wife. At Baffa the lady tarried with the merchant a good while, during which it so befell that a gentleman, Antigono by name, a man of ripe age and riper wisdom but no great wealth, being one that had had vast and various experience of affairs in the service of the King of Cyprus but had found fortune adverse to him, came to Baffa on business; and passing one day by the house where the fair lady was then living by herself, for the Cypriote merchant was gone to Armenia with some of his wares, he chanced to catch sight of the lady at one of the windows, and, being struck by her extraordinary beauty, regarded her attentively, and began to have some vague recollection of having seen her before, but could by no means remember where. The fair lady, however, so long the sport of Fortune, but now nearing the term of her woes, no sooner saw Antigono than she remembered to have seen him in her father's service, and in no mean capacity, at Alexandria. Wherefore she forthwith sent for him, hoping that by his counsel she might elude her merchant and be reinstated in her true character and dignity of princess. When he presented himself, she asked him with some embarrassment whether he were, as she took him to be, Antigono of Famagosta. He answered in the affirmative, adding: "And of you, madam, I have a sort of recollection, though I cannot say where I have seen you; wherefore, so it irk you not, bring, I pray you, yourself to my remembrance." Satisfied that it was Antigono himself, the lady in a flood of tears threw herself upon him to his no small amazement, and embraced his neck: then, after a little while, she asked him whether he had never seen her in Alexandria. The question awakened Antigono's memory; he at once recognised Alatiel, the Soldan's daughter, whom he had thought to have been drowned at sea, and would have paid her due homage; but she would not suffer it, and bade him be seated with her for a while. Being seated, he respectfully asked her, how, and when and whence she had come thither, seeing that all Egypt believed for certain that she had been drowned at sea some years before. "And would that so it had been," said the lady, "rather than I should have led the life that I have led; and so doubtless will my father say, if he shall ever come to know of it." And so saying, she burst into such a flood of tears that 'twas a wonder to see. Wherefore Antigono said to her: "Nay but, madam, be not distressed before the occasion arises. I pray you, tell me the story of your adventures, and what has been the tenor of your life; perchance 'twill prove to be no such matter but, God helping us, we may set it all straight." "Antigono," said the fair lady, "when I saw thee, 'twas as if I saw my father, and 'twas the tender love by which I am holden to him that prompted me to make myself known to thee, though I might have kept my secret; and few indeed there are, whom to have met would have afforded me such pleasure as this which I have in meeting and recognising thee before all others; wherefore I will now make known to thee as to a father that which in my evil fortune I have ever kept close. If, when thou hast heard my story, thou seest any means whereby I may be reinstated in my former honour, I pray thee use it. If not, disclose to none that thou hast seen me or heard aught of me."

Voice: Panfilo

Then, weeping between every word, she told him her whole story from the day of the shipwreck at Majorca to that hour. Antigono wept in sympathy, and then said: "Madam, as throughout this train of misfortunes you have happily escaped recognition, I undertake to restore you to your father in such sort that you shall be dearer to him than ever before, and be afterwards married to the King of Algarve." "How?" she asked. Whereupon he explained to her in detail how he meant to proceed; and, lest delay should give occasion to another to interfere, he went back at once to Famagosta, and having obtained audience of the King, thus he spoke: "Sire, so please you, you have it in your power at little cost to yourself to do a thing, which will at once redound most signally to your honour and confer a great boon on me, who have grown poor in your service." "How?" asked the King. Then said Antigono: "At Baffa is of late arrived a fair damsel, daughter of the Soldan, long thought to be drowned, who to preserve her chastity has suffered long and severe hardship. She is now reduced to poverty, and is desirous of returning to her father. If you should be pleased to send her back to him under my escort, your honour and my interest would be served in high and equal measure; nor do I think that such a service would ever be forgotten by the Soldan."

Voice: Panfilo

With true royal generosity the King forthwith signified his approval, and had Alatiel brought under honourable escort to Famagosta, where, attended by his Queen, he received her with every circumstance of festal pomp and courtly magnificence. Schooled by Antigono, she gave the King and Queen such a version of her adventures as satisfied their inquiries in every particular. So, after a few days, the King sent her back to the Soldan under escort of Antigono, attended by a goodly company of honourable men and women; and of the cheer which the Soldan made her, and not her only but Antigono and all his company, it boots not to ask. When she was somewhat rested, the Soldan inquired how it was that she was yet alive, and where she had been so long without letting him know how it fared with her. Whereupon the lady, who had got Antigono's lesson by heart, answered thus: "My father, 'twas perhaps the twentieth night after my departure from you when our ship parted her timbers in a terrible storm and went ashore nigh a place called Aguamorta, away there in the West: what was the fate of the men that were aboard our ship I know not, nor knew I ever; I remember only, that, when day came, and I returned, as it were, from death to life, the wreck, having been sighted, was boarded by folk from all the countryside, intent on plunder; and I and two of my women were taken ashore, where the women were forthwith parted from me by the young men, nor did I ever learn their fate. Now hear my own. Struggling might and main, I was seized by two young men, who dragged me, weeping bitterly, by the hair of the head, towards a great forest; but, on sight of four men who were then passing that way on horseback, they forthwith loosed me and took to flight. Whereupon the four men, who struck me as persons of great authority, ran up to me; and much they questioned me, and much I said to them; but neither did they understand me, nor I them. So, after long time conferring together, they set me on one of their horses and brought me to a house, where dwelt a community of ladies, religious according to their law; and what the men may have said I know not, but there I was kindly received and ever honourably entreated by all; and with them I did afterwards most reverentially pay my devotions to St. Crescent-in-Hollow, who is held in great honour by the women of that country. When I had been some time with them, and had learned something of their language, they asked me who and whence I was: whereto I, knowing that I was in a convent, and fearing to be cast out as a foe to their law if I told the truth, answered that I was the daughter of a great gentleman of Cyprus, who had intended to marry me to a gentleman of Crete; but that on the voyage we had been driven out of our course and wrecked at Aguamorta. And so I continued, as occasion required, observing their usages with much assiduity, lest worse should befall me; but being one day asked by their superior, whom they call abbess, whether I was minded to go back to Cyprus, I answered that there was nought that I desired so much. However, so solicitous for my honour was the abbess, that there was none going to Cyprus to whom she would entrust me, until, two months or so ago, there arrived some worthy men from France, of whom one was a kinsman of the abbess, with their wives. They were on their way to visit the sepulchre where He whom they hold to be God was buried after He had suffered death at the hands of the Jews; and the abbess, learning their destination, prayed them to take charge of me, and restore me to my father in Cyprus. With what cheer, with what honour, these gentlemen and their wives entertained me, 'twere long to tell. But, in brief, we embarked, and in the course of a few days arrived at Baffa, where it was so ordered by the providence of God, who perchance took pity on me, that in the very hour of our disembarkation I, not knowing a soul and being at a loss how to answer the gentlemen, who would fain have discharged the trust laid upon them by the reverend abbess and restored me to my father, fell in, on the shore, with Antigono, whom I forthwith called, and in our language, that I might be understood neither of the gentlemen nor of their wives, bade him acknowledge me as his daughter. He understood my case at once, made much of me, and to the utmost of his slender power honourably requited the gentlemen. He then brought me to the King of Cyprus, who accorded me welcome there and conduct hither so honourable as words of mine can never describe. It aught remains to tell, you may best learn it from the lips of Antigono, who has often heard my story."

Voice: *Panfilo*

Then Antigono, addressing the Soldan, said: "Sire, what she has told you accords with what she has often told me, and with what I have learned from the gentlemen and ladies who accompanied her. One thing, however, she has omitted, because, I suppose, it hardly becomes her to tell it; to wit, all that the gentlemen and ladies, who accompanied her, said of the virtuous and gracious and noble life which she led with the devout ladies, and of the tears and wailings of both the ladies and the gentlemen, when they parted with her to me. But were I to essay to repeat all that they said to me, the day that now is, and the night that is to follow, were all too short: suffice it to say so much as this, that, by what I gathered from their words and have been able to see for myself, you may make it your boast, that among all the daughters of all your peers that wear the crown none can be matched with yours for virtue and true worth."

By all which the Soldan was so overjoyed that 'twas a wonder to see. Again and again he made supplication to God, that of His grace power might be vouchsafed him adequately to recompense all who had done honour to his daughter, and most especially the King of Cyprus, for the honourable escort under which he had sent her thither; for Antigono he provided a magnificent guerdon, and some days later gave him his congè to return to Cyprus, at the same time by a special ambassage conveying to the King his grateful acknowledgments of the manner in which he had treated his daughter. Then, being minded that his first intent, to wit, that his daughter should be the bride of the King of Algarve, should not be frustrate, he wrote to the King, telling him all, and adding that, if he were still minded to have her, he might send for her. The King was overjoyed by these tidings, and having sent for her with great pomp, gave her on her arrival a hearty welcome. So she, who had lain with eight men, in all, perhaps, ten thousand times, was bedded with him as a virgin, and made him believe that a virgin she was, and lived long and happily with him as his queen: wherefore 'twas said: "Mouth, for kisses, was never the worse: like as the moon reneweth her course."

FIFTH DAY—NOVEL IX

Voice: Dioneo

Federigo degli Alberighi loves and is not loved in return: he wastes his substance by lavishness until nought is left but a single falcon, which, his lady being come to see him at his house, he gives her to eat: she, knowing his case, changes her mind, takes him to husband and makes him rich.

Voice: Author

So ended Filomena; and the queen, being ware that besides herself only Dioneo (by virtue of his privilege) was left to speak, said with gladsome mien:

Voice: Dioneo

'Tis now for me to take up my parable; which, dearest ladies, I will do with a story like in some degree to the foregoing, and that, not only that you may know how potent are your charms to sway the gentle heart, but that you may also learn how upon fitting occasions to make bestowal of your guerdons of your own accord, instead of always waiting for the guidance of Fortune, which most times, not wisely, but without rule or measure, scatters her gifts.

Voice: Dioneo

You are then to know, that Coppo di Borghese Domenichi, a man that in our day was, and perchance still is, had in respect and great reverence in our city, being not only by reason of his noble lineage, but, and yet more, for manners and merit most illustrious and worthy of eternal renown, was in his old age not seldom wont to amuse himself by discoursing of things past with his neighbours and other folk; wherein he had not his match for accuracy and compass of memory and concinnity of speech. Among other good stories, he would tell, how that there was of yore in Florence a gallant named Federigo di Messer Filippo Alberighi, who for feats of arms and courtesy had not his peer in Tuscany; who, as is the common lot of gentlemen, became enamoured of a lady named Monna Giovanna, who in her day held rank among the fairest and most elegant ladies of Florence; to gain whose love he jousted, tilted, gave entertainments, scattered largess, and in short set no bounds to his expenditure. However the lady, no less virtuous than fair, cared not a jot for what he did for her sake, nor yet for him.

Voice: Dioneo

Spending thus greatly beyond his means, and making nothing, Federigo could hardly fail to come to lack, and was at length reduced to such poverty that he had nothing left but a little estate, on the rents of which he lived very straitly, and a single falcon, the best in the world. The estate was at Campi, and thither, deeming it no longer possible for him to live in the city as he desired, he repaired, more in love than ever before; and there, in complete seclusion, diverting himself with hawking, he bore his poverty as patiently as he might.

Voice: Dioneo

Now, Federigo being thus reduced to extreme poverty, it so happened that one day Monna Giovanna's husband, who was very rich, fell ill, and, seeing that he was nearing his end, made his will, whereby he left his estate to his son, who was now growing up, and in the event of his death without lawful heir named Monna Giovanna, whom he dearly loved, heir in his stead; and having made these dispositions he died.

Voice: Dioneo

Monna Giovanna, being thus left a widow, did as our ladies are wont, and repaired in the summer to one of her estates in the country which lay very near to that of Federigo. And so it befell that the urchin began to make friends with Federigo, and to shew a fondness for hawks and dogs, and having seen Federigo's falcon fly not a few times, took a singular fancy to him, and greatly longed to have him for his own, but still did not dare to ask him of Federigo, knowing that Federigo prized him so much. So the matter stood when by chance the boy fell sick; whereby the mother was sore distressed, for he was her only son, and she loved him as much as might be, insomuch that all day long she was beside him, and ceased not to comfort him, and again and again asked him if there were aught that he wished for, imploring him to say the word, and, if it might by any means be had, she would assuredly do her utmost to procure it for him. Thus repeatedly exhorted, the boy said: "Mother mine, do but get me Federigo's falcon, and I doubt not I shall soon be well." Whereupon the lady was silent a while, bethinking her what she should do. She knew that Federigo had long loved her, and had never had so much as a single kind look from her: wherefore she said to herself: How can I send or go to beg of him this falcon, which by what I hear is the best that ever flew, and moreover is his sole comfort? And how could I be so unfeeling as to seek to deprive a gentleman of the one solace that is now left him? And so, albeit she very well knew that she might have the falcon for the asking, she was perplexed, and knew not what to say, and gave her son no answer. At length, however, the love she bore the boy carried the day, and she made up her mind, for his contentment, come what might, not to send, but to go herself and fetch him the falcon. So: "Be of good cheer, my son," she said, "and doubt not thou wilt soon be well; for I promise thee that the very first thing that I shall do tomorrow morning will be to go and fetch thee the falcon." Whereat the child was so pleased that he began to mend that very day.

Voice: Dioneo

On the morrow the lady, as if for pleasure, hied her with another lady to Federigo's little house, and asked to see him. 'Twas still, as for some days past, no weather for hawking, and Federigo was in his garden, busy about some small matters which needed to be set right there. When he heard that Monna Giovanna was at the door, asking to see him, he was not a little surprised and pleased, and hied him to her with all speed. As soon as she saw him, she came forward to meet him with womanly grace, and having received his respectful salutation, said to him: "Good morrow, Federigo," and continued: "I am come to requite thee for what thou hast lost by loving me more than thou shouldst: which compensation is this, that I and this lady that accompanies me will breakfast with thee without ceremony this morning." "Madam," Federigo replied with all humility, "I mind not ever to have lost aught by loving you, but rather to have been so much profited that, if I ever deserved well in aught, 'twas to your merit that I owed it, and to the love that I bore you. And of a surety had I still as much to spend as I have spent in the past, I should not prize it so much as this visit you so frankly pay me, come as you are to one who can afford you but a sorry sort of hospitality." Which said, with some confusion, he bade her welcome to his house, and then led her into his garden, where, having none else to present to her by way of companion, he said: "Madam, as there is none other here, this good woman, wife of this husbandman, will bear you company, while I go to have the table set." Now, albeit his poverty was extreme, yet he had not known as yet how sore was the need to which his extravagance had reduced him; but this morning 'twas brought home to him, for that he could find nought wherewith to do honour to the lady, for love of whom he had done the honours of his house to men without number: wherefore, distressed beyond measure, and inwardly cursing his evil fortune, he sped hither and thither like one beside himself, but never a coin found he, nor yet aught to pledge. Meanwhile it grew late, and sorely he longed that the lady might not leave his house altogether unhonoured, and yet to crave help of his own husbandman was more than his pride could brook. In these desperate straits his glance happened to fall on his brave falcon on his perch in his little parlour. And so, as a last resource, he took him, and finding him plump, deemed that he would make a dish meet for such a lady. Wherefore, without thinking twice about it, he wrung the bird's neck, and caused his maid forthwith pluck him and set him on a spit, and roast him carefully; and having still some spotless table-linen, he had the table laid therewith, and with a cheerful countenance hied him back to his lady in the garden, and told her that such breakfast as he could give her was ready. So the lady and her companion rose and came to table, and there, with Federigo, who waited on them most faithfully, ate the brave falcon, knowing not what they ate.

Voice: Dioneo

When they were risen from table, and had dallied a while in gay converse with him, the lady deemed it time to tell the reason of her visit: wherefore, graciously addressing Federigo, thus began she: "Federigo, by what thou rememberest of thy past life and my virtue, which, perchance, thou hast deemed harshness and cruelty, I doubt not thou must marvel at my presumption, when thou hearest the main purpose of my visit; but if thou hadst sons, or hadst had them, so that thou mightest know the full force of the love that is borne them, I should make no doubt that thou wouldst hold me in part excused. Nor, having a son, may I, for that thou hast none, claim exemption from the laws to which all other mothers are subject, and, being thus bound to own their sway, I must, though fain were I not, and though 'tis neither meet nor right, crave of thee that which I know thou dost of all things and with justice prize most highly, seeing that this extremity of thy adverse fortune has left thee nought else wherewith to delight, divert and console thee; which gift is no other than thy falcon, on which my boy has so set his heart that, if I bring him it not, I fear lest he grow so much worse of the malady that he has, that thereby it may come to pass that I lose him. And so, not for the love which thou dost bear me, and which may nowise bind thee, but for that nobleness of temper, whereof in courtesy more conspicuously than in aught else thou hast given proof, I implore thee that thou be pleased to give me the bird, that thereby I may say that I have kept my son alive, and thus made him for aye thy debtor."

Voice: *Dioneo*

No sooner had Federigo apprehended what the lady wanted, than, for grief that 'twas not in his power to serve her, because he had given her the falcon to eat, he fell a weeping in her presence, before he could so much as utter a word. At first the lady supposed that 'twas only because he was loath to part with the brave falcon that he wept, and as good as made up her mind that he would refuse her: however, she awaited with patience Federigo's answer, which was on this wise: "Madam, since it pleased God that I should set my affections upon you there have been matters not a few, in which to my sorrow I have deemed Fortune adverse to me; but they have all been trifles in comparison of the trick that she now plays me: the which I shall never forgive her, seeing that you are come here to my poor house, where, while I was rich, you deigned not to come, and ask a trifling favour of me, which she has put it out of my power to grant: how 'tis so, I will briefly tell you. When I learned that you, of your grace, were minded to breakfast with me, having respect to your high dignity and desert, I deemed it due and seemly that in your honour I should regale you, to the best of my power, with fare of a more excellent quality than is commonly set before others; and, calling to mind the falcon which you now ask of me, and his excellence, I judged him meet food for you, and so you have had him roasted on the trencher this morning; and well indeed I thought I had bestowed him; but, as now I see that you would fain have had him in another guise, so mortified am I that I am not able to serve you, that I doubt I shall never know peace of mind more." In witness whereof he had the feathers and feet and beak of the bird brought in and laid before her.

Voice: *Dioneo*

The first thing the lady did, when she had heard Federigo's story, and seen the relics of the bird, was to chide him that he had killed so fine a falcon to furnish a woman with a breakfast; after which the magnanimity of her host, which poverty had been and was powerless to impair, elicited no small share of inward commendation. Then, frustrate of her hope of possessing the falcon, and doubting of her son's recovery, she took her leave with the heaviest of hearts, and hied her back to the boy: who, whether for fretting, that he might not have the falcon, or by the unaided energy of his disorder, departed this life not many days after, to the exceeding great grief of his mother. For a while she would do nought but weep and bitterly bewail herself; but being still young, and left very wealthy, she was often urged by her brothers to marry again, and though she would rather have not done so, yet being importuned, and remembering Federigo's high desert, and the magnificent generosity with which he had finally killed his falcon to do her honour, she said to her brothers: "Gladly, with your consent, would I remain a widow, but if you will not be satisfied except I take a husband, rest assured that none other will I ever take save Federigo degli Alberighi." Whereupon her brothers derided her, saying: "Foolish woman, what is't thou sayst? How shouldst thou want Federigo, who has not a thing in the world?" To whom she answered: "My brothers, well wot I that 'tis as you say; but I had rather have a man without wealth than wealth without a man." The brothers, perceiving that her mind was made up, and knowing Federigo for a good man and true, poor though he was, gave her to him with all her wealth. And so Federigo, being mated with such a wife, and one that he had so much loved, and being very wealthy to boot, lived happily, keeping more exact accounts, to the end of his days.

Sir Gawain and the Green Knight

By Anonymous

After the siege and the assault of Troy, when that burg was destroyed and burnt to ashes, and the traitor tried for his treason, the noble Æneas and his kin sailed forth to become princes and patrons of well-nigh all the Western Isles. Thus Romulus built Rome (and gave to the city his own name, which it bears even to this day); and Ticius turned him to Tuscany; and Langobard raised him up dwellings in Lombardy; and Felix Brutus sailed far over the French flood, and founded the kingdom of Britain, wherein have been war and waste and wonder, and bliss and bale, ofttimes since.

And in that kingdom of Britain have been wrought more gallant deeds than in any other; but of all British kings Arthur was the most valiant, as I have heard tell, therefore will I set forth a wondrous adventure that fell out in his time. And if ye will listen to me, but for a little while, I will tell it even as it stands in story stiff and strong, fixed in the letter, as it hath long been known in the land.

****

King Arthur lay at Camelot upon a Christmas-tide, with many a gallant lord and lovely lady, and all the noble brotherhood of the Round Table. There they held rich revels with gay talk and jest; one while they would ride forth to joust and tourney, and again back to the court to make carols;[1] for there was the feast holden fifteen days with all the mirth that men could devise, song and glee, glorious to hear, in the daytime, and dancing at night. Halls and chambers were crowded with noble guests, the bravest of knights and the loveliest of ladies, and Arthur himself was the comeliest king that ever held a court. For all this fair folk were in their youth, the fairest and most fortunate under heaven, and the king himself of such fame that it were hard now to name so valiant a hero.

---

1   Dance accompanied by song. Often mentioned in old romances.

Now the New Year had but newly come in, and on that day a double portion was served on the high table to all the noble guests, and thither came the king with all his knights, when the service in the chapel had been sung to an end. And they greeted each other for the New Year, and gave rich gifts, the one to the other (and they that received them were not wroth, that may ye well believe!), and the maidens laughed and made mirth till it was time to get them to meat. Then they washed and sat them down to the feast in fitting rank and order, and Guinevere the queen, gaily clad, sat on the high daïs. Silken was her seat, with a fair canopy over her head, of rich tapestries of Tars, embroidered, and studded with costly gems; fair she was to look upon, with her shining grey eyes, a fairer woman might no man boast himself of having seen.

But Arthur would not eat till all were served, so full of joy and gladness was he, even as a child; he liked not either to lie long, or to sit long at meat, so worked upon him his young blood and his wild brain. And another custom he had also, that came of his nobility, that he would never eat upon an high day till he had been advised of some knightly deed, or some strange and marvellous tale, of his ancestors, or of arms, or of other ventures. Or till some stranger knight should seek of him leave to joust with one of the Round Table, that they might set their lives in jeopardy, one against another, as fortune might favour them. Such was the king's custom when he sat in hall at each high feast with his noble knights, therefore on that New Year tide, he abode, fair of face, on the throne, and made much mirth withal.

Thus the king sat before the high tables, and spake of many things; and there good Sir Gawain was seated by Guinevere the queen, and on her other side sat Agravain, *à la dure main*;[2] both were the king's sister's sons and full gallant knights. And at the end of the table was Bishop Bawdewyn, and Ywain, King Urien's son, sat at the other side alone. These were worthily served on the daïs, and at the lower tables sat many valiant knights. Then they bare the first course with the blast of trumpets and waving of banners, with the sound of drums and pipes, of song and lute, that many a heart was uplifted at the melody. Many were the dainties, and rare the meats, so great was the plenty they might scarce find room on the board to set on the dishes. Each helped himself as he liked best, and to each two were twelve dishes, with great plenty of beer and wine.

Now I will say no more of the service, but that ye may know there was no lack, for there drew near a venture that the folk might well have left their labour to gaze upon. As the sound of the music ceased, and the first course had been fitly served, there came in at the hall door one terrible to behold, of stature greater than any on earth; from neck to loin so strong and thickly made, and with limbs so long and so great that he seemed even as a giant. And yet he was but a man, only the mightiest that might mount a steed; broad of chest and shoulders and slender of waist, and all his features of like fashion; but men marvelled much at his colour, for he rode even as a knight, yet was green all over.

For he was clad all in green, with a straight coat, and a mantle above; all decked and lined with fur was the cloth and the hood that was thrown back from his locks and lay on his shoulders. Hose had he of the same green, and spurs of bright gold with silken fastenings richly worked; and all his vesture was verily green. Around his waist and his saddle were bands with fair stones set upon silken work, 'twere too long to tell of all the trifles that were embroidered thereon—birds and insects in gay gauds of green and gold. All the trappings of his steed were of metal of like enamel, even the stirrups that he stood in stained of the same, and stirrups and saddle-bow alike

---

2 *Agravain, "à la dure main."* This characterisation of Gawain's brother seems to indicate that there was a French source at the root of this story. The author distinctly tells us more than once that the tale, as he tells it, was written *in a book*, M. Gaston Paris thinks that the direct source was an Anglo-Norman poem, now lost.

gleamed and shone with green stones. Even the steed on which he rode was of the same hue, a green horse, great and strong, and hard to hold, with broidered bridle, meet for the rider.

The knight was thus gaily dressed in green, his hair falling around his shoulders; on his breast hung a beard, as thick and green as a bush, and the beard and the hair of his head were clipped all round above his elbows. The lower part of his sleeves were fastened with clasps in the same wise as a king's mantle. The horse's mane was crisp and plaited with many a knot folded in with gold thread about the fair green, here a twist of the hair, here another of gold. The tail was twined in like manner, and both were bound about with a band of bright green set with many a precious stone; then they were tied aloft in a cunning knot, whereon rang many bells of burnished gold. Such a steed might no other ride, nor had such ever been looked upon in that hall ere that time; and all who saw that knight spake and said that a man might scarce abide his stroke.

The knight bore no helm nor hauberk, neither gorget nor breast-plate, neither shaft nor buckler to smite nor to shield, but in one hand he had a holly-bough, that is greenest when the groves are bare, and in his other an axe, huge and uncomely, a cruel weapon in fashion, if one would picture it. The head was an ell-yard long, the metal all of green steel and gold, the blade burnished bright, with a broad edge, as well shapen to shear as a sharp razor. The steel was set into a strong staff, all bound round with iron, even to the end, and engraved with green in cunning work. A lace was twined about it, that looped at the head, and all adown the handle it was clasped with tassels on buttons of bright green richly broidered.

The knight rideth through the entrance of the hall, driving straight to the high daïs, and greeted no man, but looked ever upwards; and the first words he spake were, "Where is the ruler of this folk? I would gladly look upon that hero, and have speech with him." He cast his eyes on the knights, and mustered them up and down, striving ever to see who of them was of most renown.

Then was there great gazing to behold that chief, for each man marvelled what it might mean that a knight and his steed should have even such a hue as the green grass; and that seemed even greener than green enamel on bright gold. All looked on him as he stood, and drew near unto him wondering greatly what he might be; for many marvels had they seen, but none such as this, and phantasm and faërie did the folk deem it. Therefore were the gallant knights slow to answer, and gazed astounded, and sat stone still in a deep silence through that goodly hall, as if a slumber were fallen upon them. I deem it was not all for doubt, but some for courtesy that they might give ear unto his errand.

Then Arthur beheld this adventurer before his high daïs, and knightly he greeted him, for fearful was he never. "Sir," he said, "thou art welcome to this place—lord of this hall am I, and men call me Arthur. Light thee down, and tarry awhile, and what thy will is, that shall we learn after."

"Nay," quoth the stranger, "so help me He that sitteth on high, 'twas not mine errand to tarry any while in this dwelling; but the praise of this thy folk and thy city is lifted up on high, and thy warriors are holden for the best and the most valiant of those who ride mail-clad to the fight. The wisest and the worthiest of this world are they, and well proven in all knightly sports. And here, as I have heard tell, is fairest courtesy, therefore have I come hither as at this time. Ye may be sure by the branch that I bear here that I come in peace, seeking no strife. For had I willed to journey in warlike guise I have at home both hauberk and helm, shield and shining spear, and other weapons to mine hand, but since I seek no war my raiment is that of peace. But if thou be as bold as all men tell thou wilt freely grant me the boon I ask."

And Arthur answered, "Sir Knight, if thou cravest battle here thou shalt not fail for lack of a foe."

And the knight answered, "Nay, I ask no fight, in faith here on the benches are but beardless children, were I clad in armour on my steed there is no man here might match me. Therefore I ask in this court but a Christmas jest, for that it is Yule-tide, and New Year, and there are here many fain for sport. If any one in this hall holds himself so hardy,[3] so bold both of blood and brain, as to dare strike me one stroke for another, I will give him as a gift this axe, which is heavy enough, in sooth, to handle as he may list, and I will abide the first blow, unarmed as I sit. If any knight be so bold as to prove my words let him come swiftly to me here, and take this weapon, I quit claim to it, he may keep it as his own, and I will abide his stroke, firm on the floor. Then shalt thou give me the right to deal him another, the respite of a year and a day shall he have. Now haste, and let see whether any here dare say aught."

Now if the knights had been astounded at the first, yet stiller were they all, high and low, when they had heard his words. The knight on his steed straightened himself in the saddle, and rolled his eyes fiercely round the hall, red they gleamed under his green and bushy brows. He frowned and twisted his beard, waiting to see who should rise, and when none answered he cried aloud in mockery, "What, is this Arthur's hall, and these the knights whose renown hath run through many realms? Where are now your pride and your conquests, your wrath, and anger, and mighty words? Now are the praise and the renown of the Round Table overthrown by one man's speech, since all keep silence for dread ere ever they have seen a blow!"

With that he laughed so loudly that the blood rushed to the king's fair face for very shame; he waxed wroth, as did all his knights, and sprang to his feet, and drew near to the stranger and said, "Now by heaven foolish is thy asking, and thy folly shall find its fitting answer. I know no man aghast at thy great words. Give me here thine axe and I shall grant thee the boon thou hast asked." Lightly he sprang to him and caught at his hand, and the knight, fierce of aspect, lighted down from his charger.

Then Arthur took the axe and gripped the haft, and swung it round, ready to strike. And the knight stood before him, taller by the head than any in the hall; he stood, and stroked his beard, and drew down his coat, no more dismayed for the king's threats than if one had brought him a drink of wine.

Then Gawain, who sat by the queen, leaned forward to the king and spake, "I beseech ye, my lord, let this venture be mine. Would ye but bid me rise from this seat, and stand by your side, so that my liege lady thought it not ill, then would I come to your counsel before this goodly court. For I think it not seemly when such challenges be made in your hall that ye yourself should undertake it, while there are many bold knights who sit beside ye, none are there, methinks, of readier will under heaven, or more valiant in open field. I am the weakest, I wot, and the feeblest of wit, and it will be the less loss of my life if ye seek sooth. For save that ye are mine uncle naught is there in me to praise, no virtue is there in my body save your blood, and since this challenge is such folly that it beseems ye not to take it, and I have asked it from ye first, let it fall to me, and if I bear myself ungallantly then let all this court blame me."

Then they all spake with one voice that the king should leave this venture and grant it to Gawain.

Then Arthur commanded the knight to rise, and he rose up quickly and knelt down before the king, and caught hold of the weapon; and the king loosed his hold of it, and lifted up his hand, and gave him his

---

3   *If any in this hall holds himself so hardy.* This, the main incident of the tale, is apparently of very early date. The oldest version we possess is that found in the Irish tale of the *Fled Bricrend* (Bricriu's feast) [edited and translated by the Rev. G. Henderson, M.A., Irish Texts Society, vol. ii.], where the hero of the tale is the Irish champion, Cuchulinn. Two mediæval romances, the *Mule sans Frein* (French) and *Diu Krône* (German), again attribute it to Gawain; while the continuator of Chrétien de Troye's *Conte del Graal* gives as hero a certain Carados, whom he represents as Arthur's nephew; and the prose *Perceval* has Lancelot. So far as the mediæval versions are concerned, the original hero is undoubtedly Gawain; and our poem gives the fullest and most complete form of the story we possess. In the Irish version the magician is a *giant*, and the abnormal size and stature of the Green Knight is, in all probability, the survival of a primitive feature. His curious *colour* is a trait found nowhere else. In *Diu Krône* we are told that the challenger changes shapes in a terrifying manner, but no details are given.

blessing, and bade him be strong both of heart and hand. "Keep thee well, nephew," quoth Arthur, "that thou give him but the one blow, and if thou redest him rightly I trow thou shalt well abide the stroke he may give thee after."

Gawain stepped to the stranger, axe in hand, and he, never fearing, awaited his coming. Then the Green Knight spake to Sir Gawain, "Make we our covenant ere we go further. First, I ask thee, knight, what is thy name? Tell me truly, that I may know thee."

"In faith," quoth the good knight, "Gawain am I, who give thee this buffet, let what may come of it; and at this time twelvemonth will I take another at thine hand with whatsoever weapon thou wilt, and none other."

Then the other answered again, "Sir Gawain, so may I thrive as I am fain to take this buffet at thine hand," and he quoth further, "Sir Gawain, it liketh me well that I shall take at thy fist that which I have asked here, and thou hast readily and truly rehearsed all the covenant that I asked of the king, save that thou shalt swear me, by thy troth, to seek me thyself wherever thou hopest that I may be found, and win thee such reward as thou dealest me to-day, before this folk."

"Where shall I seek thee?" quoth Gawain. "Where is thy place? By Him that made me, I wot never where thou dwellest, nor know I thee, knight, thy court, nor thy name. But teach me truly all that pertaineth thereto, and tell me thy name, and I shall use all my wit to win my way thither, and that I swear thee for sooth, and by my sure troth."

"That is enough in the New Year, it needs no more," quoth the Green Knight to the gallant Gawain, "if I tell thee truly when I have taken the blow, and thou hast smitten me; then will I teach thee of my house and home, and mine own name, then mayest thou ask thy road and keep covenant. And if I waste no words then farest thou the better, for thou canst dwell in thy land, and seek no further. But take now thy toll, and let see how thy strikest."

"Gladly will I," quoth Gawain, handling his axe.

Then the Green Knight swiftly made him ready, he bowed down his head, and laid his long locks on the crown that his bare neck might be seen. Gawain gripped his axe and raised it on high, the left foot he set forward on the floor, and let the blow fall lightly on the bare neck. The sharp edge of the blade sundered the bones, smote through the neck, and clave it in two, so that the edge of the steel bit on the ground, and the fair head fell to the earth that many struck it with their feet as it rolled forth. The blood spurted forth, and glistened on the green raiment, but the knight neither faltered nor fell; he started forward with out-stretched hand, and caught the head, and lifted it up; then he turned to his steed, and took hold of the bride, set his foot in the stirrup, and mounted. His head he held by the hair, in his hand. Then he seated himself in his saddle as if naught ailed him, and he were not headless. He turned his steed about, the grim corpse bleeding freely the while, and they who looked upon him doubted them much for the covenant.

For he held up the head in his hand, and turned the face towards them that sat on the high daïs, and it lifted up the eyelids and looked upon them and spake as ye shall hear. "Look, Gawain, that thou art ready to go as thou hast promised, and seek leally till thou find me, even as thou hast sworn in this hall in the hearing of these knights. Come thou, I charge thee, to the Green Chapel, such a stroke as thou hast dealt thou hast deserved, and it shall be promptly paid thee on New Year's morn. Many men know me as the knight of the Green Chapel, and if thou askest, thou shalt not fail to find me. Therefore it behoves thee to come, or to yield thee as recreant."

With that he turned his bridle, and galloped out at the hall door, his head in his hands, so that the sparks flew from beneath his horse's hoofs. Whither he went none knew, no more than they wist whence he had come; and the king and Gawain they gazed and laughed, for in sooth this had proved a greater marvel than any they had known aforetime.

Though Arthur the king was astonished at his heart, yet he let no sign of it be seen, but spake in courteous wise to the fair queen: "Dear lady, be not dismayed, such craft is well suited to Christmas-tide when we seek jesting, laughter and song, and fair carols of knights and ladies. But now I may well get me to meat, for I have seen a marvel I may not forget." Then he looked on Sir Gawain, and said gaily, "Now, fair nephew, hang up thine axe, since it has hewn enough," and they hung it on the dossal above the daïs, where all men might look on it for a marvel, and by its true token tell of the wonder. Then the twain sat them down together, the king and the good knight, and men served them with a double portion, as was the share of the noblest, with all manner of meat and of minstrelsy. And they spent that day in gladness, but Sir Gawain must well bethink him of the heavy venture to which he had set his hand.

****

This beginning of adventures had Arthur at the New Year; for he yearned to hear gallant tales, though his words were few when he sat at the feast. But now had they stern work on hand. Gawain was glad to begin the jest in the hall, but ye need have no marvel if the end be heavy. For though a man be merry in mind when he has well drunk, yet a year runs full swiftly, and the beginning but rarely matches the end.

For Yule was now over-past[4], and the year after, each season in its turn following the other. For after Christmas comes crabbed Lent, that will have fish for flesh and simpler cheer. But then the weather of the world chides with winter; the cold withdraws itself, the clouds uplift, and the rain falls in warm showers on the fair plains. Then the flowers come forth, meadows and grove are clad in green, the birds make ready to build, and sing sweetly for solace of the soft summer that follows thereafter. The blossoms bud and blow in the hedgerows rich and rank, and noble notes enough are heard in the fair woods.

After the season of summer, with the soft winds, when zephyr breathes lightly on seeds and herbs, joyous indeed is the growth that waxes thereout when the dew drips from the leaves beneath the blissful glance of the bright sun. But then comes harvest and hardens the grain, warning it to wax ripe ere the winter. The drought drives the dust on high, flying over the face of the land; the angry wind of the welkin wrestles with the sun; the leaves fall from the trees and light upon the ground, and all brown are the groves that but now were green, and ripe is the fruit that once was flower. So the year passes into many yesterdays, and winter comes again, as it needs no sage to tell us.

When the Michaelmas moon was come in with warnings of winter, Sir Gawain bethought him full oft of his perilous journey. Yet till All Hallows Day he lingered with Arthur, and on that day they made a great feast for the hero's sake, with much revel and richness of the Round Table. Courteous knights and comely ladies, all were in sorrow for the love of that knight, and though they spake no word of it, many were joyless for his sake.

---

4   *For Yule was over-past.* This passage, descriptive of the flight of the year, should be especially noticed. Combined with the other passages—the description of Gawain's journey, the early morning hunts, the dawning of New Year's Day, and the ride to the Green Chapel—they indicate a knowledge of Nature, and an observant eye for her moods, uncommon among mediæval poets. It is usual enough to find graceful and charming descriptions of spring and early summer—an appreciation of *May* in especial, when the summer courts were held, is part of the stock-in-trade of mediæval romancers—but a sympathy with the year in all its changes is far rarer, and certainly deserves to be specially reckoned to the credit of this nameless writer.

And after meat, sadly Sir Gawain turned to his uncle, and spake of his journey, and said, "Liege lord of my life, leave from you I crave. Ye know well how the matter stands without more words, to-morrow am I bound to set forth in search of the Green Knight."

Then came together all the noblest knights, Ywain and Erec, and many another. Sir Dodinel le Sauvage, the Duke of Clarence, Launcelot and Lionel, and Lucan the Good, Sir Bors and Sir Bedivere, valiant knights both, and many another hero, with Sir Mador de la Porte, and they all drew near, heavy at heart, to take counsel with Sir Gawain. Much sorrow and weeping was there in the hall to think that so worthy a knight as Gawain should wend his way to seek a deadly blow, and should no more wield his sword in fight. But the knight made ever good cheer, and said, "Nay, wherefore should I shrink? What may a man do but prove his fate?"

He dwelt there all that day, and on the morn he arose and asked betimes for his armour; and they brought it unto him on this wise: first, a rich carpet was stretched on the floor[5] (and brightly did the gold gear glitter upon it), then the knight stepped on to it, and handled the steel; clad he was in a doublet of silk, with a close hood, lined fairly throughout. Then they set the steel shoes upon his feet, and wrapped his legs with greaves, with polished knee-caps, fastened with knots of gold. Then they cased his thighs in cuisses closed with thongs, and brought him the byrny of bright steel rings sewn upon a fair stuff. Well burnished braces they set on each arm with good elbow-pieces, and gloves of mail, and all the goodly gear that should shield him in his need. And they cast over all a rich surcoat, and set the golden spurs on his heels, and girt him with a trusty sword fastened with a silken bawdrick. When he was thus clad his harness was costly, for the least loop or latchet gleamed with gold. So armed as he was he hearkened Mass and made his offering at the high altar. Then he came to the king, and the knights of his court, and courteously took leave of lords and ladies, and they kissed him, and commended him to Christ.

With that was Gringalet ready, girt with a saddle that gleamed gaily with many golden fringes, enriched and decked anew for the venture. The bridle was all barred about with bright gold buttons, and all the covertures and trappings of the steed, the crupper and the rich skirts, accorded with the saddle; spread fair with the rich red gold that glittered and gleamed in the rays of the sun.

Then the knight called for his helmet, which was well lined throughout, and set it high on his head, and hasped it behind. He wore a light kerchief over the vintail, that was broidered and studded with fair gems on a broad silken ribbon, with birds of gay colour, and many a turtle and true-lover's knot interlaced thickly, even as many a maiden had wrought diligently for seven winter long. But the circlet which crowned his helmet was yet more precious, being adorned with a device in diamonds. Then they brought him his shield, which was of bright red, with the pentangle painted thereon in gleaming gold.[6] And why that noble prince bare the pentangle I am minded to tell you, though my tale tarry thereby. It is a sign that Solomon set ere-while, as betokening truth; for it is a figure with five points and each line overlaps the other, and nowhere hath it beginning or end, so that in English it is called "the endless knot." And therefore was it well suiting to this knight and to his arms, since Gawain was faithful in five and five-fold, for pure was he as gold, void of all villainy and endowed with all virtues. Therefore he bare the pentangle on shield and surcoat as truest of heroes and gentlest of knights.

---

5   *First a rich carpet was stretched on the floor.* The description of the arming of Gawain is rather more detailed in the original, but some of the minor points are not easy to understand, the identification of sundry of the pieces of armour being doubtful.

6   *The pentangle painted thereupon in gleaming gold.* I do not remember that the pentangle is elsewhere attributed to Gawain. He often bears a red shield; but the blazon varies. Indeed, the heraldic devices borne by Arthur's knights are distractingly chaotic–their legends are older than the science of heraldry, and no one has done for them the good office that the compiler of the Thidrek Saga has rendered to his Teutonic heroes.

For first he was faultless in his five senses; and his five fingers never failed him; and all his trust upon earth was in the five wounds that Christ bare on the cross, as the Creed tells. And wherever this knight found himself in stress of battle he deemed well that he drew his strength from the five joys which the Queen of Heaven had of her Child. And for this cause did he bear an image of Our Lady on the one half of his shield, that whenever he looked upon it he might not lack for aid. And the fifth five that the hero used were frankness and fellowship above all, purity and courtesy that never failed him, and compassion that surpasses all; and in these five virtues was that hero wrapped and clothed. And all these, five-fold, were linked one in the other, so that they had no end, and were fixed on five points that never failed, neither at any side were they joined or sundered, nor could ye find beginning or end. And therefore on his shield was the knot shapen, red-gold upon red, which is the pure pentangle. Now was Sir Gawain ready, and he took his lance in hand, and bade them all Farewell, he deemed it had been for ever.

Then he smote the steed with his spurs, and sprang on his way, so that sparks flew from the stones after him. All that saw him were grieved at heart, and said one to the other, "By Christ, 'tis great pity that one of such noble life should be lost! I'faith, 'twere not easy to find his equal upon earth. The king had done better to have wrought more warily. Yonder knight should have been made a duke; a gallant leader of men is he, and such a fate had beseemed him better than to be hewn in pieces at the will of an elfish man, for mere pride. Who ever knew a king to take such counsel as to risk his knights on a Christmas jest?" Many were the tears that flowed from their eyes when that goodly knight rode from the hall. He made no delaying, but went his way swiftly, and rode many a wild road, as I heard say in the book.

So rode Sir Gawain through the realm of Logres, on an errand that he held for no jest. Often he lay companionless at night, and must lack the fare that he liked. No comrade had he save his steed, and none save God with whom to take counsel. At length he drew nigh to North Wales, and left the isles of Anglesey on his left hand, crossing over the fords by the foreland over at Holyhead, till he came into the wilderness of Wirral[7], where but few dwell who love God and man of true heart. And ever he asked, as he fared, of all whom he met, if they had heard any tidings of a Green Knight in the country thereabout, or of a Green Chapel? And all answered him, Nay, never in their lives had they seen any man of such a hue. And the knight wended his way by many a strange road and many a rugged path, and the fashion of his countenance changed full often ere he saw the Green Chapel.

Many a cliff did he climb in that unknown land, where afar from his friends he rode as a stranger. Never did he come to a stream or a ford but he found a foe before him, and that one so marvellous, so foul and fell, that it behoved him to fight. So many wonders did that knight behold, that it were too long to tell the tenth part of them. Sometimes he fought with dragons and wolves; sometimes with wild men that dwelt in the rocks; another while with bulls, and bears, and wild boars, or with giants of the high moorland that drew near to him. Had he not been a doughty knight, enduring, and of well-proved valour, and a servant of God, doubtless he had been slain, for he was oft in danger of death. Yet he cared not so much for the strife, what he deemed worse was when the cold clear water was shed from the clouds, and froze ere it fell on the fallow ground. More nights than enough he slept in his harness on the bare rocks, near slain with the sleet, while the stream leapt bubbling from the crest of the hills, and hung in hard icicles over his head.

---

7   *The Wilderness of Wirral.* This is in Cheshire. Sir F. Madden suggests that the forest which forms the final stage of Gawain's journey is that of Inglewood, in Cumberland. The geography here is far clearer than is often the case in such descriptions.

Thus in peril and pain, and many a hardship, the knight rode alone till Christmas Eve, and in that tide he made his prayer to the Blessed Virgin that she would guide his steps and lead him to some dwelling. On that morning he rode by a hill, and came into a thick forest, wild and drear; on each side were high hills, and thick woods below them of great hoar oaks, a hundred together, of hazel and hawthorn with their trailing boughs intertwined, and rough ragged moss spreading everywhere. On the bare twigs the birds chirped piteously, for pain of the cold. The knight upon Gringalet rode lonely beneath them, through marsh and mire, much troubled at heart lest he should fail to see the service of the Lord, who on that self-same night was born of a maiden for the cure of our grief; and therefore he said, sighing, "I beseech Thee, Lord, and Mary Thy gentle Mother, for some shelter where I may hear Mass, and Thy mattins at morn. This I ask meekly, and thereto I pray my Paternoster, Ave, and Credo." Thus he rode praying, and lamenting his misdeeds, and he crossed himself, and said, "May the Cross of Christ speed me."

Now that knight had crossed himself but thrice ere he was aware in the wood of a dwelling within a moat, above a lawn, on a mound surrounded by many mighty trees that stood round the moat. 'Twas the fairest castle that ever a knight owned[8]; built in a meadow with a park all about it, and a spiked palisade, closely driven, that enclosed the trees for more than two miles. The knight was ware of the hold from the side, as it shone through the oaks. Then he lifted off his helmet, and thanked Christ and S. Julian that they had courteously granted his prayer, and hearkened to his cry. "Now," quoth the knight, "I beseech ye, grant me fair hostel." Then he pricked Gringalet with his golden spurs, and rode gaily towards the great gate, and came swiftly to the bridge end.

The bridge was drawn up and the gates close shut; the walls were strong and thick, so that they might fear no tempest. The knight on his charger abode on the bank of the deep double ditch that surrounded the castle. The walls were set deep in the water, and rose aloft to a wondrous height; they were of hard hewn stone up to the corbels, which were adorned beneath the battlements with fair carvings, and turrets set in between with many a loophole; a better barbican Sir Gawain had never looked upon. And within he beheld the high hall, with its tower and many windows with carven cornices, and chalk-white chimneys on the turreted roofs that shone fair in the sun. And everywhere, thickly scattered on the castle battlements, were pinnacles, so many that it seemed as if it were all wrought out of paper, so white was it.

The knight on his steed deemed it fair enough, if he might come to be sheltered within it to lodge there while that the Holy-day lasted. He called aloud, and soon there came a porter of kindly countenance, who stood on the wall and greeted this knight and asked his errand.

"Good sir," quoth Gawain, "wilt thou go mine errand to the high lord of the castle, and crave for me lodging?"

"Yea, by S. Peter," quoth the porter. "In sooth I trow that ye be welcome to dwell here so long as it may like ye."

Then he went, and came again swiftly, and many folk with him to receive the knight. They let down the great drawbridge, and came forth and knelt on their knees on the cold earth to give him worthy welcome. They held wide open the great gates, and courteously he bid them rise, and rode over the bridge. Then men came to him and held his stirrup while he dismounted, and took and stabled his steed. There came down knights and squires to bring the guest with joy to the hall. When he raised his helmet there were many to take it from his hand, fain to serve him, and they took from him sword and shield.

---

8 *'Twas the fairest castle that ever a knight owned.* Here, again, I have omitted some of the details of the original, the architectural terms lacking identification.

Sir Gawain gave good greeting to the noble and the mighty men who came to do him honour. Clad in his shining armour they led him to the hall, where a great fire burnt brightly on the floor; and the lord of the household came forth from his chamber to meet the hero fitly. He spake to the knight, and said: "Ye are welcome to do here as it likes ye. All that is here is your own to have at your will and disposal."

"Gramercy!" quote Gawain, "may Christ requite ye."

As friends that were fain each embraced the other; and Gawain looked on the knight who greeted him so kindly, and thought 'twas a bold warrior that owned that burg.

Of mighty stature he was, and of high age; broad and flowing was his beard, and of a bright hue. He was stalwart of limb, and strong in his stride, his face fiery red, and his speech free: in sooth he seemed one well fitted to be a leader of valiant men.

Then the lord led Sir Gawain to a chamber, and commanded folk to wait upon him, and at his bidding there came men enough who brought the guest to a fair bower. The bedding was noble, with curtains of pure silk wrought with gold, and wondrous coverings of fair cloth all embroidered. The curtains ran on ropes with rings of red gold, and the walls were hung with carpets of Orient, and the same spread on the floor. There with mirthful speeches they took from the guest his byrny and all his shining armour, and brought him rich robes of the choicest in its stead. They were long and flowing, and became him well, and when he was clad in them all who looked on the hero thought that surely God had never made a fairer knight: he seemed as if he might be a prince without peer in the field where men strive in battle.

Then before the hearth-place, whereon the fire burned, they made ready a chair for Gawain, hung about with cloth and fair cushions; and there they cast around him a mantle of brown samite, richly embroidered and furred within with costly skins of ermine, with a hood of the same, and he seated himself in that rich seat, and warmed himself at the fire, and was cheered at heart. And while he sat thus the serving men set up a table on trestles, and covered it with a fair white cloth, and set thereon salt-cellar, and napkin, and silver spoons; and the knight washed at his will, and set him down to meat.

The folk served him courteously with many dishes seasoned of the best, a double portion. All kinds of fish were there, some baked in bread, some broiled on the embers, some sodden, some stewed and savoured with spices, with all sorts of cunning devices to his taste. And often he called it a feast, when they spake gaily to him all together, and said, "Now take ye this penance, and it shall be for your amendment." Much mirth thereof did Sir Gawain make.

Then they questioned that prince courteously of whence he came; and he told them that he was of the court of Arthur, who is the rich royal King of the Round Table, and that it was Gawain himself who was within their walls, and would keep Christmas with them, as the chance had fallen out. And when the lord of the castle heard those tidings he laughed aloud for gladness, and all men in that keep were joyful that they should be in the company of him to whom belonged all fame, and valour, and courtesy, and whose honour was praised above that of all men on earth. Each said softly to his fellow, "Now shall we see courteous bearing, and the manner of speech befitting courts. What charm lieth in gentle speech shall we learn without asking, since here we have welcomed the fine father of courtesy. God has surely shewn us His grace since He sends us such a guest as Gawain! When men shall sit and sing, blithe for Christ's birth, this knight shall bring us to the knowledge of fair manners, and it may be that hearing him we may learn the cunning speech of love."

By the time the knight had risen from dinner it was near nightfall. Then chaplains took their way to the chapel, and rang loudly, even as they should, for the solemn evensong of the high feast. Thither went the lord, and the lady also, and entered with her maidens into a comely closet, and thither also went Gawain. Then the lord took him by the sleeve and led him to a seat, and called him by his name, and told him he was of all men in the world the most welcome. And Sir Gawain thanked him truly, and each kissed the other, and they sat gravely together throughout the service.

Then was the lady fain to look upon that knight; and she came forth from her closet with many fair maidens. The fairest of ladies was she in face, and figure, and colouring, fairer even than Guinevere, so the knight thought. She came through the chancel to greet the hero, another lady held her by the left hand, older than she, and seemingly of high estate, with many nobles about her. But unlike to look upon were those ladies, for if the younger were fair, the elder was yellow. Rich red were the cheeks of the one, rough and wrinkled those of the other; the kerchiefs of the one were broidered with many glistening pearls, her throat and neck bare, and whiter than the snow that lies on the hills; the neck of the other was swathed in a gorget, with a white wimple over her black chin. Her forehead was wrapped in silk with many folds, worked with knots, so that naught of her was seen save her black brows, her eyes, her nose and her lips, and those were bleared, and ill to look upon. A worshipful lady in sooth one might call her! In figure was she short and broad, and thickly made—far fairer to behold was she whom she led by the hand.

When Gawain beheld that fair lady, who looked at him graciously, with leave of the lord he went towards them, and, bowing low, he greeted the elder, but the younger and fairer he took lightly in his arms, and kissed her courteously, and greeted her in knightly wise. Then she hailed him as friend, and he quickly prayed to be counted as her servant, if she so willed. Then they took him between them, and talking, led him to the chamber, to the hearth, and bade them bring spices, and they brought them in plenty with the good wine that was wont to be drunk at such seasons. Then the lord sprang to his feet and bade them make merry, and took off his hood, and hung it on a spear, and bade him win the worship thereof who should make most mirth that Christmas-tide. "And I shall try, by my faith, to fool it with the best, by the help of my friends, ere I lose my raiment." Thus with gay words the lord made trial to gladden Gawain with jests that night, till it was time to bid them light the tapers, and Sir Gawain took leave of them and gat him to rest.

In the morn when all men call to mind how Christ our Lord was born on earth to die for us, there is joy, for His sake, in all dwellings of the world; and so was there here on that day. For high feast was held, with many dainties and cunningly cooked messes. On the daïs sat gallant men, clad in their best. The ancient dame sat on the high seat, with the lord of the castle beside her. Gawain and the fair lady sat together, even in the midst of the board, when the feast was served; and so throughout all the hall each sat in his degree, and was served in order. There was meat, there was mirth, there was much joy, so that to tell thereof would take me too long, though peradventure I might strive to declare it. But Gawain and that fair lady had much joy of each other's company through her sweet words and courteous converse. And there was music made before each prince, trumpets and drums, and merry piping; each man hearkened his minstrel, and they too hearkened theirs.

So they held high feast that day and the next, and the third day thereafter, and the joy on S. John's Day was fair to hearken, for 'twas the last of the feast and the guests would depart in the grey of the morning. Therefore they awoke early, and drank wine, and danced fair carols, and at last, when it was late, each man took his leave to wend early on his way. Gawain would bid his host farewell, but the lord took him by the hand, and led him to his own chamber beside the hearth, and there he thanked him for the favour he had shown him in honouring his dwelling at that high season, and gladdening his castle with his fair countenance. "I wis, sir, that while I live I shall be held the worthier that Gawain has been my guest at God's own feast."

"Gramercy, sir," quoth Gawain, "in good faith, all the honour is yours, may the High King give it you, and I am but at your will to work your behest, inasmuch as I am beholden to you in great and small by rights."

Then the lord did his best to persuade the knight to tarry with him, but Gawain answered that he might in no wise do so. Then the host asked him courteously what stern behest had driven him at the holy season from the king's court, to fare all alone, ere yet the feast was ended?

"Forsooth," quoth the knight, "ye say but the truth: 'tis a high quest and a pressing that hath brought me afield, for I am summoned myself to a certain place, and I know not whither in the world I may wend to find it; so help me Christ, I would give all the kingdom of Logres an I might find it by New Year's morn. Therefore, sir, I make request of you that ye tell me truly if ye ever heard word of the Green Chapel, where it may be found, and the Green Knight that keeps it. For I am pledged by solemn compact sworn between us to meet that knight at the New Year if so I were on life; and of that same New Year it wants but little—I'faith, I would look on that hero more joyfully than on any other fair sight! Therefore, by your will, it behoves me to leave you, for I have but barely three days, and I would as fain fall dead as fail of mine errand."

Then the lord quoth, laughing, "Now must ye needs stay, for I will show you your goal, the Green Chapel, ere your term be at an end, have ye no fear! But ye can take your ease, friend, in your bed, till the fourth day, and go forth on the first of the year and come to that place at mid-morn to do as ye will. Dwell here till New Year's Day, and then rise and set forth, and ye shall be set in the way; 'tis not two miles hence."

Then was Gawain glad, and he laughed gaily. "Now I thank you for this above all else. Now my quest is achieved I will dwell here at your will, and otherwise do as ye shall ask."

Then the lord took him, and set him beside him, and bade the ladies be fetched for their greater pleasure, tho' between themselves they had solace. The lord, for gladness, made merry jest, even as one who wist not what to do for joy; and he cried aloud to the knight, "Ye have promised to do the thing I bid ye: will ye hold to this behest, here, at once?"

"Yea, forsooth," said that true knight, "while I abide in your burg I am bound by your behest."

"Ye have travelled from far," said the host, "and since then ye have waked with me, ye are not well refreshed by rest and sleep, as I know. Ye shall therefore abide in your chamber, and lie at your ease tomorrow at Mass-tide, and go to meat when ye will with my wife, who shall sit with you, and comfort you with her company till I return; and I shall rise early and go forth to the chase." And Gawain agreed to all this courteously.

"Sir knight," quoth the host, "we shall make a covenant. Whatsoever I win in the wood shall be yours, and whatever may fall to your share, that shall ye exchange for it. Let us swear, friend, to make this exchange, however our hap may be, for worse or for better."

"I grant ye your will," quoth Gawain the good; "if ye list so to do, it liketh me well."

"Bring hither the wine-cup, the bargain is made," so said the lord of that castle. They laughed each one, and drank of the wine, and made merry, these lords and ladies, as it pleased them. Then with gay talk and merry jest they arose, and stood, and spoke softly, and kissed courteously, and took leave of each other. With burning torches, and many a serving-man, was each led to his couch; yet ere they gat them to bed the old lord oft repeated their covenant, for he knew well how to make sport.

****

Full early, ere daylight, the folk rose up; the guests who would depart called their grooms, and they made them ready, and saddled the steeds, tightened up the girths, and trussed up their mails. The knights, all arrayed for riding, leapt up lightly, and took their bridles, and each rode his way as pleased him best.

The lord of the land was not the last. Ready for the chase, with many of his men, he ate a sop hastily when he had heard Mass, and then with blast of the bugle fared forth to the field.[9] He and his nobles were to horse ere daylight glimmered upon the earth.

Then the huntsmen coupled their hounds, unclosed the kennel door, and called them out. They blew three blasts gaily on the bugles, the hounds bayed fiercely, and they that would go a-hunting checked and chastised them. A hundred hunters there were of the best, so I have heard tell. Then the trackers gat them to the trysting-place and uncoupled the hounds, and forest rang again with their gay blasts.

At the first sound of the hunt the game quaked for fear, and fled, trembling, along the vale. They betook them to the heights, but the liers in wait turned them back with loud cries; the harts they let pass them, and the stags with their spreading antlers, for the lord had forbidden that they should be slain, but the hinds and the does they turned back, and drave down into the valleys. Then might ye see much shooting of arrows. As the deer fled under the boughs a broad whistling shaft smote and wounded each sorely, so that, wounded and bleeding, they fell dying on the banks. The hounds followed swiftly on their tracks, and hunters, blowing the horn, sped after them with ringing shouts as if the cliffs burst asunder. What game escaped those that shot was run down at the outer ring. Thus were they driven on the hills, and harassed at the waters, so well did the men know their work, and the greyhounds were so great and swift that they ran them down as fast as the hunters could slay them. Thus the lord passed the day in mirth and joyfulness, even to nightfall.

So the lord roamed the woods, and Gawain, that good night, lay ever a-bed, curtained about, under the costly coverlet, while the daylight gleamed on the walls. And as he lay half slumbering, he heard a little sound at the door, and he raised his head, and caught back a corner of the curtain, and waited to see what it might be. It was the lovely lady, the lord's wife; she shut the door softly behind her, and turned towards the bed; and Gawain was shamed, laid him down softly and made as if he slept. And she came lightly to the bedside, within the curtain, and sat herself down beside him, to wait till he wakened. The knight lay there awhile, and marvelled within himself what her coming might betoken; and he said to himself, "'Twere more seemly if I asked her what hath brought her hither." Then he made feint to waken, and turned towards her, and opened his eyes as one astonished, and crossed himself; and she looked on him laughing, with her cheeks red and white, lovely to behold, and small smiling lips.

"Good morrow, Sir Gawain," said that fair lady; "ye are but a careless sleeper, since one can enter thus. Now are ye taken unawares, and lest ye escape me I shall bind you in your bed; of that be ye assured!" Laughing, she spake these words.

"Good morrow, fair lady," quoth Gawain blithely. "I will do your will, as it likes me well. For I yield me readily, and pray your grace, and that is best, by my faith, since I needs must do so." Thus he jested again, laughing. "But an ye would, fair lady, grant me this grace that ye pray your prisoner to rise. I would get me from bed, and array me better, then could I talk with ye in more comfort."

"Nay, forsooth, fair sir," quoth the lady, "ye shall not rise, I will rede ye better. I shall keep ye here, since ye can do no other, and talk with my knight whom I have captured. For I know well that ye are Sir Gawain, whom

---

9 *With blast of the bugle fared forth to the field.* The account of each day's hunting contains a number of obsolete terms and details of woodcraft, not given in full. The meaning of some has been lost, and the minute descriptions of skinning and dismembering the game would be distinctly repulsive to the general reader. They are valuable for a student of the history of the English sport, but interfere with the progress of the story. The fact that the author devotes so much space to them seems to indicate that he lived in the country and was keenly interested in field sports. (Gottfried von Strassbourg's *Tristan* contains a similar and almost more detailed description.)

all the world worships, wheresoever ye may ride. Your honour and your courtesy are praised by lords and ladies, by all who live. Now ye are here and we are alone, my lord and his men are afield; the serving men in their beds, and my maidens also, and the door shut upon us. And since in this hour I have him that all men love, I shall use my time well with speech, while it lasts. Ye are welcome to my company, for it behoves me in sooth to be your servant."

"In good faith," quoth Gawain, "I think me that I am not him of whom ye speak, for unworthy am I of such service as ye here proffer. In sooth, I were glad if I might set myself by word or service to your pleasure; a pure joy would it be to me!"

"In good faith, Sir Gawain," quoth the gay lady, "the praise and the prowess that pleases all ladies I lack them not, nor hold them light; yet are there ladies enough who would liever now have the knight in their hold, as I have ye here, to dally with your courteous words, to bring them comfort and to ease their cares, than much of the treasure and the gold that are theirs. And now, through the grace of Him who upholds the heavens, I have wholly in my power that which they all desire!"

Thus the lady, fair to look upon, made him great cheer, and Sir Gawain, with modest words, answered her again: "Madam," he quoth, "may Mary requite ye, for in good faith I have found in ye a noble frankness. Much courtesy have other folk shown me, but the honour they have done me is naught to the worship of yourself, who knoweth but good."

"By Mary," quoth the lady, "I think otherwise; for were I worth all the women alive, and had I the wealth of the world in my hand, and might choose me a lord to my liking, then, for all that I have seen in ye, Sir Knight, of beauty and courtesy and blithe semblance, and for all that I have hearkened and hold for true, there should be no knight on earth to be chosen before ye!"

"Well I wot," quoth Sir Gawain, "that ye have chosen a better; but I am proud that ye should so prize me, and as your servant do I hold ye my sovereign, and your knight am I, and may Christ reward ye."

So they talked of many matters till mid-morn was past, and ever the lady made as though she loved him, and the knight turned her speech aside. For though she were the brightest of maidens, yet had he forborne to shew her love for the danger that awaited him, and the blow that must be given without delay.

Then the lady prayed her leave from him, and he granted it readily. And she gave [the text reads "have"] him good-day, with laughing glance, but he must needs marvel at her words:

"Now He that speeds fair speech reward ye this disport; but that ye be Gawain my mind misdoubts me greatly."

"Wherefore?" quoth the knight quickly, fearing lest he had lacked in some courtesy.

And the lady spake: "So true a knight as Gawain is holden, and one so perfect in courtesy, would never have tarried so long with a lady but he would of his courtesy have craved a kiss at parting."

Then quoth Gawain, "I wot I will do even as it may please ye, and kiss at your commandment, as a true knight should who forbears to ask for fear of displeasure."

At that she came near and bent down and kissed the knight, and each commended the other to Christ, and she went forth from the chamber softly.

Then Sir Gawain arose and called his chamberlain and chose his garments, and when he was ready he gat him forth to Mass, and then went to meat, and made merry all day till the rising of the moon, and never had a knight fairer lodging than had he with those two noble ladies, the elder and the younger.

And even the lord of the land chased the hinds through holt and heath till eventide, and then with much blowing of bugles and baying of hounds they bore the game homeward; and by the time daylight was done all the folk had returned to that fair castle. And when the lord and Sir Gawain met together, then were they both well pleased. The lord commanded them all to assemble in the great hall, and the ladies to descend with their maidens, and there, before them all, he bade the men fetch in the spoil of the day's hunting, and he called unto Gawain, and counted the tale of the beasts, and showed them unto him, and said, "What think ye of this game, Sir Knight? Have I deserved of ye thanks for my woodcraft?"

"Yea, I wis," quoth the other, "here is the fairest spoil I have seen this seven year in the winter season."

"And all this do I give ye, Gawain," quoth the host, "for by accord of covenant ye may claim it as your own."

"That is sooth," quoth the other, "I grant you that same; and I have fairly won this within walls, and with as good will do I yield it to ye." With that he clasped his hands round the lord's neck and kissed him as courteously as he might. "Take ye here my spoils, no more have I won; ye should have it freely, though it were greater than this."

"'Tis good," said the host, "gramercy thereof. Yet were I fain to know where ye won this same favour, and if it were by your own wit?"

"Nay," answered Gawain, "that was not in the bond. Ask me no more: ye have taken what was yours by right, be content with that."

They laughed and jested together, and sat them down to supper, where they were served with many dainties; and after supper they sat by the hearth, and wine was served out to them; and oft in their jesting they promised to observe on the morrow the same covenant that they had made before, and whatever chance might betide to exchange their spoil, be it much or little, when they met at night. Thus they renewed their bargain before the whole court, and then the night-drink was served, and each courteously took leave of the other and gat him to bed.

By the time the cock had crowed thrice the lord of the castle had left his bed; Mass was sung and meat fitly served. The folk were forth to the wood ere the day broke, with hound and horn they rode over the plain, and uncoupled their dogs among the thorns. Soon they struck on the scent, and the hunt cheered on the hounds who were first to seize it, urging them with shouts. The others hastened to the cry, forty at once, and there rose such a clamour from the pack that the rocks rang again. The huntsmen spurred them on with shouting and blasts of the horn; and the hounds drew together to a thicket betwixt the water and a high crag in the cliff beneath the hillside. There where the rough rock fell ruggedly they, the huntsmen, fared to the finding, and cast about round the hill and the thicket behind them. The knights wist well what beast was within, and would drive him forth with the bloodhounds. And as they beat the bushes, suddenly over the beaters there rushed forth a wondrous great and fierce boar, long since had he left the herd to roam by himself. Grunting, he cast many to the ground, and fled forth at his best speed, without more mischief. The men hallooed loudly and cried, "Hay! Hay!" and blew the horns to urge on the hounds, and rode swiftly after the boar. Many a time did he turn to bay and tare the hounds, and they yelped, and howled shrilly. Then the men made ready their arrows and shot at him, but the points were turned on his thick hide, and the barbs would not bite upon him, for the shafts shivered in pieces, and the head but leapt again wherever it hit.

But when the boar felt the stroke of the arrows he waxed mad with rage, and turned on the hunters and tare many, so that, affrighted, they fled before him. But the lord on a swift steed pursued him, blowing his bugle; as a gallant knight he rode through the woodland chasing the boar till the sun grew low.

So did the hunters this day, while Sir Gawain lay in his bed lapped in rich gear; and the lady forgat not to salute him, for early was she at his side, to cheer his mood.

She came to the bedside and looked on the knight, and Gawain gave her fit greeting, and she greeted him again with ready words, and sat her by his side and laughed, and with a sweet look she spoke to him:

"Sir, if ye be Gawain, I think it a wonder that ye be so stern and cold, and care not for the courtesies of friendship, but if one teach ye to know them ye cast the lesson out of your mind. Ye have soon forgotten what I taught ye yesterday, by all the truest tokens that I knew!"

"What is that?" quoth the knight. "I trow I know not. If it be sooth that ye say, then is the blame mine own."

"But I taught ye of kissing, " quoth the fair lady. "Wherever a fair countenance is shown him, it behoves a courteous knight quickly to claim a kiss."

"Nay, my dear," said Sir Gawain, "cease that speech; that durst I not do lest I were denied, for if I were forbidden I wot I were wrong did I further entreat."

"I' faith," quoth the lady merrily, "ye may not be forbid, ye are strong enough to constrain by strength an ye will, were any so discourteous as to give ye denial."

"Yea, by Heaven," said Gawain, "ye speak well; but threats profit little in the land where I dwell, and so with a gift that is given not of good will! I am at your commandment to kiss when ye like, to take or to leave as ye list."

Then the lady bent her down and kissed him courteously.

And as they spake together she said, "I would learn somewhat from ye, an ye would not be wroth, for young ye bare and fair, and so courteous and knightly as ye are known to be, the head of all chivalry, and versed in all wisdom of love and war—'tis ever told of true knights how they adventured their lives for their true love, and endured hardships for her favours, and avenged her with valour, and eased her sorrows, and brought joy to her bower; and ye are the fairest knight of your time, and your fame and your honour are everywhere, yet I have sat by ye here twice, and never a word have I heard of love! Ye who are so courteous and skilled in such love ought surely to teach one so young and unskilled some little craft of true love! Why are ye so unlearned who art otherwise so famous? Or is it that ye deemed me unworthy to hearken to your teaching? For shame, Sir Knight! I come hither alone and sit at your side to learn of ye some skill; teach me of your wit, while my lord is from home."

"In good faith," quoth Gawain, "great is my joy and my profit that so fair a lady as ye are should deign to come hither, and trouble ye with so poor a man, and make sport with your knight with kindly countenance, it pleaseth me much. But that I, in my turn, should take it upon me to tell of love and such like matters to ye who know more by half, or a hundred fold, of such craft than I do, or ever shall in all my lifetime, by my troth 'twere folly indeed! I will work your will to the best of my might as I am bounden, and evermore will I be your servant, so help me Christ!"

Then often with guile she questioned that knight that she might win him to woo her, but he defended himself so fairly that none might in any wise blame him, and naught but bliss and harmless jesting was there between them. They laughed and talked together till at last she kissed him, and craved her leave of him, and went her way.

Then the knight arose and went forth to Mass, and afterward dinner was served and he sat and spake with the ladies all day. But the lord of the castle rode ever over the land chasing the wild boar, that fled through the thickets, slaying the best of his hounds and breaking their backs in sunder; till at last he was so weary he might run no longer, but made for a hole in a mound by a rock. He got the mound at his back and faced the hounds, whetting his white tusks and foaming at the mouth. The huntsmen stood aloof, fearing to draw nigh him; so many of them had been already wounded that they were loth to be torn with his tusks, so fierce he was and mad with rage. At length the lord himself came up, and saw the beast at bay, and the men standing aloof. Then quickly he sprang to the ground and drew out a bright blade, and waded through the stream to the boar.

When the beast was aware of the knight with weapon in hand, he set up his bristles and snorted loudly, and many feared for their lord lest he should be slain. Then the boar leapt upon the knight so that beast and man were one atop of the other in the water; but the boar had the worst of it, for the man had marked, even as he sprang, and set the point of his brand to the beast's chest, and drove it up to the hilt, so that the heart was split in twain, and the boar fell snarling, and was swept down by the water to where a hundred hounds seized on him, and the men drew him to shore for the dogs to slay.

Then was there loud blowing of horns and baying of hounds, the huntsmen smote off the boar's head, and hung the carcase by the four feet to a stout pole, and so went on their way homewards. The head they bore before the lord himself, who had slain the beast at the ford by force of his strong hand.

It seemed him o'er long ere he saw Sir Gawain in the hall, and he called, and the guest came to take that which fell to his share. And when he saw Gawain the lord laughed aloud, and bade them call the ladies and the household together, and he showed them the game, and told them the tale, how they hunted the wild boar through the woods, and of his length and breadth and height; and Sir Gawain commended his deeds and praised him for his valour, well proven, for so mighty a beast had he never seen before.

Then they handled the huge head, and the lord said aloud, "Now, Gawain, this game is your own by sure covenant, as ye right well know."

"'Tis sooth," quoth the knight, "and as truly will I give ye all I have gained." He took the host round the neck, and kissed him courteously twice. "Now are we quits," he said, "this eventide, of all the covenants that we made since I came hither."

And the lord answered, "By S. Giles, ye are the best I know; ye will be rich in a short space if ye drive such bargains!"

Then they set up the tables on trestles, and covered them with fair cloths, and lit waxen tapers on the walls. The knights sat and were served in the hall, and much game and glee was there round the hearth, with many songs, both at supper and after; song of Christmas, and new carols, with all the mirth one may think of. And ever that lovely lady sat by the knight, and with still stolen looks made such feint of pleasing him, that Gawain marvelled much, and was wroth with himself, but he could not for his courtesy return her fair glances, but dealt with her cunningly, however she might strive to wrest the thing.

When they had tarried in the hall so long as it seemed them good, they turned to the inner chamber and the wide hearthplace, and there they drank wine, and the host proffered to renew the covenant for New Year's Eve; but the knight craved leave to depart on the morrow, for it was nigh to the term when he must fulfil his pledge. But the lord would withhold him from so doing, and prayed him to tarry, and said,

"As I am a true knight I swear my troth that ye shall come to the Green Chapel to achieve your task on New Year's morn, long before prime. Therefore abide ye in your bed, and I will hunt in this wood, and hold ye to the covenant to exchange with me against all the spoil I may bring hither. For twice have I tried ye, and found ye true, and the morrow shall be the third time and the best. Make we merry now while we may, and think on joy, for misfortune may take a man whensoever it wills."

Then Gawain granted his request, and they brought them drink, and they gat them with lights to bed.

Sir Gawain lay and slept softly, but the lord, who was keen on woodcraft, was afoot early. After Mass he and his men ate a morsel, and he asked for his steed; all the knights who should ride with him were already mounted before the hall gates.

'Twas a fair frosty morning, for the sun rose red in ruddy vapour, and the welkin was clear of clouds. The hunters scattered them by a forest side, and the rocks rang again with the blast of their horns. Some came on the scent of a fox, and a hound gave tongue; the huntsmen shouted, and the pack followed in a crowd on the trail. The fox ran before them, and when they saw him they pursued him with noise and much shouting, and he wound and turned through many a thick grove, often cowering and hearkening in a hedge. At last by a little ditch he leapt out of a spinney, stole away slily by a copse path, and so out of the wood and away from the hounds. But he went, ere he wist, to a chosen tryst, and three started forth on him at once, so he must needs double back, and betake him to the wood again.

Then was it joyful to hearken to the hounds; when all the pack had met together and had sight of their game they made as loud a din as if all the lofty cliffs had fallen clattering together. The huntsmen shouted and threatened, and followed close upon him so that he might scarce escape, but Reynard was wily, and he turned and doubled upon them, and led the lord and his men over the hills, now on the slopes, now in the vales, while the knight at home slept through the cold morning beneath his costly curtains.

But the fair lady of the castle rose betimes, and clad herself in a rich mantle that reached even to the ground, left her throat and her fair neck bare, and was bordered and lined with costly furs. On her head she wore no golden circlet, but a network of precious stones, that gleamed and shone through her tresses in clusters of twenty together. Thus she came into the chamber, closed the door after her, and set open a window, and called to him gaily, "Sir Knight, how may ye sleep? The morning is so fair."

Sir Gawain was deep in slumber, and in his dream he vexed him much for the destiny that should befall him on the morrow, when he should meet the knight at the Green Chapel, and abide his blow; but when the lady spake he heard her, and came to himself, and roused from his dream and answered swiftly. The lady came laughing, and kissed him courteously, and he welcomed her fittingly with a cheerful countenance. He saw her so glorious and gaily dressed, so faultless of features and complexion, that it warmed his heart to look upon her.

They spake to each other smiling, and all was bliss and good cheer between them. They exchanged fair words, and much happiness was therein, yet was there a gulf between them, and she might win no more of her knight, for that gallant prince watched well his words—he would neither take her love, nor frankly refuse it. He cared for his courtesy, lest he be deemed churlish, and yet more for his honour lest he be traitor to his host. "God forbid," quoth he to himself, "that it should so befall." Thus with courteous words did he set aside all the special speeches that came from her lips.

Then spake the lady to the knight, "Ye deserve blame if ye hold not that lady who sits beside ye above all else in the world, if ye have not already a love whom ye hold dearer, and like better, and have sworn such firm faith to that lady that ye care not to loose it—and that am I now fain to believe. And now I pray ye straitly that ye tell me that in truth, and hide it not."

And the knight answered, "By S. John" (and he smiled as he spake) "no such love have I, nor do I think to have yet awhile."

"That is the worst word I may hear," quoth the lady, "but in sooth I have mine answer; kiss me now courteously, and I will go hence; I can but mourn as a maiden that loves much."

Sighing, she stooped down and kissed him, and then she rose up and spake as she stood, "Now, dear, at our parting do me this grace: give me some gift, if it were but thy glove, that I may bethink me of my knight, and lessen my mourning."

"Now, I wis," quoth the knight, "I would that I had here the most precious thing that I possess on earth that I might leave ye as love-token, great or small, for ye have deserved forsooth more reward than I might give ye. But it is not to your honour to have at this time a glove for reward as gift from Gawain, and I am here on a strange errand, and have no man with me, nor mails with goodly things—that mislikes me much, lady, at this time; but each man must fare as he is taken, if for sorrow and ill."

"Nay, knight highly honoured," quoth that lovesome lady, "though I have naught of yours, yet shall ye have somewhat of mine." With that she reached him a ring of red gold with a sparkling stone therein, that shone even as the sun (wit ye well, it was worth many marks); but the knight refused it, and spake readily,

"I will take no gift, lady, at this time. I have none to give, and none will I take."

She prayed him to take it, but he refused her prayer, and sware in sooth that he would not have it.

The lady was sorely vexed, and said, "If ye refuse my ring as too costly, that ye will not be so highly beholden to me, I will give you my girdle[10] as a lesser gift." With that she loosened a lace that was fastened at her side, knit upon her kirtle under her mantle. It was wrought of green silk, and gold, only braided by the fingers, and that she offered to the knight, and besought him though it were of little worth that he would take it, and he said nay, he would touch neither gold nor gear ere God give him grace to achieve the adventure for which he had come hither. "And therefore, I pray ye, displease ye not, and ask me no longer, for I may not grant it. I am dearly beholden to ye for the favour ye have shown me, and ever, in heat and cold, will I be your true servant."

"Now," said the lady, "ye refuse this silk, for it is simple in itself, and so it seems, indeed; lo, it is small to look upon and less in cost, but whoso knew the virtue that is knit therein he would, peradventure, value it more highly. For whatever knight is girded with this green lace, while he bears it knotted about him there is no man under heaven can overcome him, for he may not be slain for any magic on earth."

Then Gawain bethought him, and it came into his heart that this were a jewel for the jeopardy that awaited him when he came to the Green Chapel to seek the return blow—could he so order it that he should escape unslain, 'twere a craft worth trying. Then he bare with her chiding, and let her say her say, and she pressed the girdle on him and prayed him to take it, and he granted her prayer, and she gave it him with good will, and besought him for her sake never to reveal it but to hide it loyally from her lord; and the knight agreed that never should any man know it, save they two alone. He thanked her often and heartily, and she kissed him for the third time.

Then she took her leave of him, and when she was gone Sir Gawain arose, and clad him in rich attire, and took the girdle, and knotted it round him, and hid it beneath his robes. Then he took his way to the chapel, and sought out a priest privily and prayed him to teach him better how his soul might be saved when he should

---

10   *I will give [you] my girdle.* This magic girdle, which confers invulnerability on its owner, is a noticeable feature of our story. It is found nowhere else in this connection, yet in other romances we find that Gawain possesses a girdle with similar powers (cf., my *Legend of Sir Gawain*, Chap. IX.). Such a talisman was also owned by Cuchulinn, the Irish hero, who has many points of contact with Gawain. It seems not improbable that this was also an old feature of the story. I have commented, in the Introduction, on the lady's persistent wooing of Gawain, and need not repeat the remarks here. The Celtic *Lay of the Great Fool* (*Amadan Mor*) presents some curious points of contact with our story, which may, however, well be noted here. In the *Lay* the hero is mysteriously deprived of his legs, through the draught from a cup proffered by a *Gruagach* or magician. He comes to a castle, the lord of which goes out hunting, leaving his wife in the care of the Great Fool, who is to allow no man to enter. He falls asleep, and a young knight arrives and kisses the host's wife. The Great Fool, awaking, refuses to allow the intruder to depart; and, in spite of threats and blandishments, insists on detaining him till the husband returns. Finally, the stranger reveals himself as the host in another shape; he is also the *Gruagach*, who deprived the hero of his limbs, and the Great Fool's brother. He has only intended to test the *Amadon Mor's* fidelity. A curious point in connection with this story is that it possesses a prose opening which shows a marked affinity with the "Perceval" *enfances*. That the Perceval and Gawain stories early became connected is certain, but what is the precise connection between them and the Celtic *Lay* is not clear. *In its present form* the latter is certainly posterior to the Grail romances, but it is quite possible that the matter with which it deals represents a tradition older than the Arthurian story.

go hence; and there he shrived him, and showed his misdeeds, both great and small, and besought mercy and craved absolution; and the priest assoiled him, and set him as clean as if Doomsday had been on the morrow. And afterwards Sir Gawain made him merry with the ladies, with carols, and all kinds of joy, as never he did but that one day, even to nightfall; and all the men marvelled at him, and said that never since he came thither had he been so merry.

Meanwhile the lord of the castle was abroad chasing the fox; awhile he lost him, and as he rode through a spinny he heard the hounds near at hand, and Reynard came creeping through a thick grove, with all the pack at his heels. Then the lord drew out his shining brand, and cast it at the beast, and the fox swerved aside for the sharp edge, and would have doubled back, but a hound was on him ere he might turn, and right before the horse's feet they all fell on him, and worried him fiercely, snarling the while.

Then the lord leapt from his saddle, and caught the fox from the jaws, and held it aloft over his head, and hallooed loudly, and many brave hounds bayed as they beheld it; and the hunters hied them thither, blowing their horns; all that bare bugles blew them at once, and all the others shouted. 'Twas the merriest meeting that ever men heard, the clamour that was raised at the death of the fox. They rewarded the hounds, stroking them and rubbing their heads, and took Reynard and stripped him of his coat; then blowing their horns, they turned them homewards, for it was nigh nightfall.

The lord was gladsome at his return, and found a bright fire on the hearth, and the knight beside it, the good Sir Gawain, who was in joyous mood for the pleasure he had had with the ladies. He wore a robe of blue, that reached even to the ground, and a surcoat richly furred, that became him well. A hood like to the surcoat fell on his shoulders, and all alike were done about with fur. He met the host in the midst of the floor, and jesting, he greeted him, and said, "Now shall I be first to fulfil our covenant which we made together when there was no lack of wine." Then he embraced the knight, and kissed him thrice, as solemnly as he might.

"Of a sooth," quoth the other, "ye have good luck in the matter of this covenant, if ye made a good exchange!"

"Yea, it matters naught of the exchange," quoth Gawain, "since what I owe is swiftly paid."

"Marry," said the other, "mine is behind, for I have hunted all this day, and naught have I got but this foul fox-skin, and that is but poor payment for three such kisses as ye have here given me."

"Enough," quoth Sir Gawain, "I thank ye, by the Rood."

Then the lord told them of his hunting, and how the fox had been slain.

With mirth and minstrelsy, and dainties at their will, they made them as merry as a folk well might till 'twas time for them to sever, for at last they must needs betake them to their beds. Then the knight took his leave of the lord, and thanked him fairly.

"For the fair sojourn that I have had here at this high feast may the High King give ye honour. I give ye myself, as one of your servants, if ye so like; for I must needs, as you know, go hence with the morn, and ye will give me, as ye promised, a guide to show me the way to the Green Chapel, an God will suffer me on New Year's Day to deal the doom of my weird."

"By my faith," quoth the host, "all that ever I promised, that shall I keep with good will." Then he gave him a servant to set him in the way, and lead him by the downs, that he should have no need to ford the stream, and should fare by the shortest road through the groves; and Gawain thanked the lord for the honour done him. Then he would take leave of the ladies, and courteously he kissed them, and spake, praying them to receive his thanks, and they made like reply; then with many sighs they commended him to Christ, and he departed courteously from that folk. Each man that he met he thanked him for his service and his solace, and the pains he had been at to do his will; and each found it as hard to part from the knight as if he had ever dwelt with him.

Then they led him with torches to his chamber, and brought him to his bed to rest. That he slept soundly I may not say, for the morrow gave him much to think on. Let him rest awhile, for he was near that which he sought, and if ye will but listen to me I will tell ye how it fared with him thereafter.

****

Now the New Year drew nigh, and the night passed, and the day chased the darkness, as is God's will; but wild weather wakened therewith. The clouds cast the cold to the earth, with enough of the north to slay them that lacked clothing. The snow drave smartly, and the whistling wind blew from the heights, and made great drifts in the valleys. The knight, lying in his bed, listened, for though his eyes were shut, he might sleep but little, and hearkened every cock that crew.

He arose ere the day broke, by the light of a lamp that burned in his chamber, and called to his chamberlain, bidding him bring his armour and saddle his steed. The other gat him up, and fetched his garments, and robed Sir Gawain.

First he clad him in his clothes to keep off the cold, and then in his harness, which was well and fairly kept. Both hauberk and plates were well burnished, the rings of the rich byrny freed from rust, and all as fresh as at first, so that the knight was fain to thank them. Then he did on each piece, and bade them bring his steed, while he put the fairest raiment on himself; his coat with its fair cognizance, adorned with precious stones upon velvet, with broidered seams, and all furred within with costly skins. And he left not the lace, the lady's gift, that Gawain forgot not, for his own good. When he had girded on his sword he wrapped the gift twice about him, swathed around his waist. The girdle of green silk set gaily and well upon the royal red cloth, rich to behold, but the knight ware it not for pride of the pendants, polished though they were with fair gold that gleamed brightly on the ends, but to save himself from sword and knife, when it behoved him to abide his hurt without question. With that the hero went forth, and thanked that kindly folk full often.

Then was Gringalet ready, that was great and strong, and had been well cared for and tended in every wise; in fair condition was that proud steed, and fit for a journey. Then Gawain went to him, and looked on his coat, and said by his sooth, "There is a folk in this place that thinketh on honour; much joy may they have, and the lord who maintains them, and may all good betide that lovely lady all her life long. Since they for charity cherish a guest, and hold honour in their hands, may He who holds the heaven on high requite them, and also ye all. And if I might live anywhere on earth, I would give ye full reward, readily, if so I might." Then he set foot in the stirrup and bestrode his steed, and his squire gave him his shield, which he laid on his shoulder. Then he smote Gringalet with his golden spurs, and the steed pranced on the stones and would stand no longer.

By that his man was mounted, who bare his spear and lance, and Gawain quoth, "I commend this castle to Christ, may He give it ever good fortune." Then the drawbridge was let down, and the broad gates unbarred and opened on both sides; the knight crossed himself, and passed through the gateway, and praised the porter, who knelt before the prince, and gave him good-day, and commended him to God. Thus the knight went on his way with the one man who should guide him to that dread place where he should receive rueful payment.

The two went by hedges where the boughs were bare, and climbed the cliffs where the cold clings. Naught fell from the heavens, but 'twas ill beneath them; mist brooded over the moor and hung on the mountains; each hill had a cap, a great cloak, of mist. The streams foamed and bubbled between their banks, dashing sparkling on the shores where they shelved downwards. Rugged and dangerous was the way through the woods, till it was time for the sun-rising. Then were they on a high hill; the snow lay white beside them, and the man who rode with Gawain drew rein by his master.

"Sir," he said, "I have brought ye hither, and now ye are not far from the place that ye have sought so specially. But I will tell ye for sooth, since I know ye well, and ye are such a knight as I well love, would ye follow my counsel ye would fare the better. The place whither ye go is accounted full perilous, for he who liveth in that waste is the worst on earth, for he is strong and fierce, and loveth to deal mighty blows; taller is he than any man on earth, and greater of frame than any four in Arthur's court, or in any other. And this is his custom at the Green Chapel; there may no man pass by that place, however proud his arms, but he does him to death by force of his hand, for he is a discourteous knight, and shews no mercy. Be he churl or chaplain who rides by that chapel, monk or mass priest, or any man else, he thinks it as pleasant to slay them as to pass alive himself. Therefore, I tell ye, as sooth as ye sit in saddle, if ye come there and that knight know it, ye shall be slain, though ye had twenty lives; trow me that truly! He has dwelt here full long and seen many a combat; ye may not defend ye against his blows. Therefore, good Sir Gawain, let the man be, and get ye away some other road; for God's sake seek ye another land, and there may Christ speed ye! And I will hie me home again, and I promise ye further that I will swear by God and the saints, or any other oath ye please, that I will keep counsel faithfully, and never let any wit the tale that ye fled for fear of any man."

"Gramercy," quoth Gawain, but ill-pleased. "Good fortune be his who wishes me good, and that thou wouldst keep faith with me I will believe; but didst thou keep it never so truly, an I passed here and fled for fear as thou sayest, then were I a coward knight, and might not be held guiltless. So I will to the chapel let chance what may, and talk with that man, even as I may list, whether for weal or for woe as fate may have it. Fierce though he may be in fight, yet God knoweth well how to save His servants."

"Well," quoth the other, "now that ye have said so much that ye will take your own harm on yourself, and ye be pleased to lose your life, I will neither let nor keep ye. Have here your helm and the spear in your hand, and ride down this same road beside the rock till ye come to the bottom of the valley, and there look a little to the left hand, and ye shall see in that vale the chapel, and the grim man who keeps it. Now fare ye well, noble Gawain; for all the gold on earth I would not go with ye nor bear ye fellowship one step further." With that the man turned his bridle into the wood, smote the horse with his spurs as hard as he could, and galloped off, leaving the knight alone.

Quoth Gawain, "I will neither greet nor groan, but commend myself to God, and yield me to His will."

Then the knight spurred Gringalet, and rode adown the path close in by a bank beside a grove. So he rode through the rough thicket, right into the dale, and there he halted, for it seemed him wild enough. No sign of a chapel could he see, but high and burnt banks on either side and rough rugged crags with great stones above. An ill-looking place he thought it.

Then he drew in his horse and looked around to seek the chapel, but he saw none and thought it strange. Then he saw as it were a mound on a level space of land by a bank beside the stream where it ran swiftly, the water bubbled within as if boiling. The knight turned his steed to the mound, and lighted down and tied the rein to the branch of a linden; and he turned to the mound and walked round it, questioning with himself what it might be. It had a hole at the end and at either side, and was overgrown with clumps of grass, and it was hollow within as an old cave or the crevice of a crag; he knew not what it might be.

"Ah," quoth Gawain, "can this be the Green Chapel? Here might the devil say his mattins at midnight! Now I wis there is wizardry here. 'Tis an ugly oratory, all overgrown with grass, and 'twould well beseem that fellow in green to say his devotions on devil's wise. Now feel I in five wits, 'tis the foul fiend himself who hath set me this tryst, to destroy me here! This is a chapel of mischance: ill-luck betide it, 'tis the cursedest kirk that ever I came in!"

Helmet on head and lance in hand, he came up to the rough dwelling, when he heard over the high hill beyond the brook, as it were in a bank, a wondrous fierce noise, that rang in the cliff as if it would cleave asunder. 'Twas as if one ground a scythe on a grindstone, it whirred and whetted like water on a mill-wheel and rushed and rang, terrible to hear.

"By God," quoth Gawain, "I trow that gear is preparing for the knight who will meet me here. Alas! naught may help me, yet should my life be forfeit, I fear not a jot!" With that he called aloud. "Who waiteth in this place to give me tryst? Now is Gawain come hither: if any man will aught of him let him hasten hither now or never."

"Stay," quoth one on the bank above his head, "and ye shall speedily have that which I promised ye." Yet for a while the noise of whetting went on ere he appeared, and then he came forth from a cave in the crag with a fell weapon, a Danish axe newly dight, wherewith to deal the blow. An evil head it had, four feet large, no less, sharply ground, and bound to the handle by the lace that gleamed brightly. And the knight himself was all green as before, face and foot, locks and beard, but now he was afoot. When he came to the water he would not wade it, but sprang over with the pole of his axe, and strode boldly over the brent that was white with snow.

Sir Gawain went to meet him, but he made no low bow. The other said, "Now, fair sir, one may trust thee to keep tryst. Thou art welcome, Gawain, to my place. Thou hast timed thy coming as befits a true man. Thou knowest the covenant set between us: at this time twelve months agone thou didst take that which fell to thee, and I at this New Year will readily requite thee. We are in this valley, verily alone, here are no knights to sever us, do what we will. Have off thy helm from thine head, and have here thy pay; make me no more talking than I did then when thou didst strike off my head with one blow."

"Nay," quoth Gawain, "by God that gave me life, I shall make no moan whatever befall me, but make thou ready for the blow and I shall stand still and say never a word to thee, do as thou wilt."

With that he bent his head and shewed his neck all bare, and made as if he had no fear, for he would not be thought a-dread.

Then the Green Knight made him ready, and grasped his grim weapon to smite Gawain. With all his force he bore it aloft with a mighty feint of slaying him: had it fallen as straight as he aimed he who was ever doughty of deed had been slain by the blow. But Gawain swerved aside as the axe came gliding down to slay him as he stood, and shrank a little with the shoulders, for the sharp iron. The other heaved up the blade and rebuked the prince with many proud words:

"Thou art not Gawain," he said, "who is held so valiant, that never feared he man by hill or vale, but thou shrinkest for fear ere thou feelest hurt. Such cowardice did I never hear of Gawain! Neither did I flinch from thy blow, or make strife in King Arthur's hall. My head fell to my feet, and yet I fled not; but thou didst wax faint of heart ere any harm befell. Wherefore must I be deemed the braver knight."

Quoth Gawain, "I shrank once, but so will I no more, though an my head fall on the stones I cannot replace it. But haste, Sir Knight, by thy faith, and bring me to the point, deal me my destiny, and do it out of hand, for I will stand thee a stroke and move no more till thine axe have hit me—my troth on it."

"Have at thee, then," quoth the other, and heaved aloft the axe with fierce mien, as if he were mad. He struck at him fiercely but wounded him not, withholding his hand ere it might strike him.

Gawain abode the stroke, and flinched in no limb, but stood still as a stone or the stump of a tree that is fast rooted in the rocky ground with a hundred roots.

Then spake gaily the man in green, "So now thou hast thine heart whole it behoves me to smite. Hold aside thy hood that Arthur gave thee, and keep thy neck thus bent lest it cover it again."

Then Gawain said angrily, "Why talk on thus? Thou dost threaten too long. I hope thy heart misgives thee."

"For sooth," quoth the other, "so fiercely thou speakest I will no longer let thine errand wait its reward." Then he braced himself to strike, frowning with lips and brow, 'twas no marvel that it pleased but ill him who hoped for no rescue. He lifted the axe lightly and let it fall with the edge of the blade on the bare neck. Though he struck swiftly it hurt him no more than on the one side where it severed the skin. The sharp blade cut into the flesh so that the blood ran over his shoulder to the ground. And when the knight saw the blood staining the snow, he sprang forth, swift-foot, more than a spear's length, seized his helmet and set it on his head, cast his shield over his shoulder, drew out his bright sword, and spake boldly (never since he was born was he half so blithe), "Stop, Sir Knight, bid me no more blows. I have stood a stroke here without flinching, and if thou give me another, I shall requite thee, and give thee as good again. By the covenant made betwixt us in Arthur's hall but one blow falls to me here. Halt, therefore."

Then the Green Knight drew off from him and leaned on his axe, setting the shaft on the ground, and looked on Gawain as he stood all armed and faced him fearlessly—at heart it pleased him well. Then he spake merrily in a loud voice, and said to the knight, "Bold sir, be not so fierce, no man here hath done thee wrong, nor will do, save by covenant, as we made at Arthur's court. I promised thee a blow and thou hast it—hold thyself well paid! I release thee of all other claims. If I had been so minded I might perchance have given thee a rougher buffet. First I menaced thee with a feigned one, and hurt thee not for the covenant that we made in the first night, and which thou didst hold truly. All the gain didst thou give me as a true man should. The other feint I proffered thee for the morrow: my fair wife kissed thee, and thou didst give me her kisses—for both those days I gave thee two blows without scathe—true man, true return. But the third time thou didst fail, and therefore hadst thou that blow. For 'tis my weed thou wearest, that same woven girdle, my own wife wrought it, that do I wot for sooth. Now know I well thy kisses, and thy conversation, and the wooing of my wife, for 'twas mine own doing. I sent her to try thee, and in sooth I think thou art the most faultless knight that ever trode earth. As a pearl among white peas is of more worth than they, so is Gawain, i' faith, by other knights. But thou didst lack a little, Sir Knight, and wast wanting in loyalty, yet that was for no evil work, nor for wooing neither, but because thou lovedst thy life—therefore I blame thee the less."

Then the other stood a great while, still sorely angered and vexed within himself; all the blood flew to his face, and he shrank for shame as the Green Knight spake; and the first words he said were, "Cursed be ye, cowardice and covetousness, for in ye is the destruction of virtue." Then he loosed the girdle, and gave it to the knight. "Lo, take there the falsity, may foul befall it! For fear of thy blow cowardice bade me make friends with covetousness and forsake the customs of largess and loyalty, which befit all knights. Now am I faulty and false and have been afeared: from treachery and untruth come sorrow and care. I avow to thee, Sir Knight, that I have ill done; do then thy will. I shall be more wary hereafter."

Then the other laughed and said gaily, "I wot I am whole of the hurt I had, and thou hast made such free confession of thy misdeeds, and hast so borne the penance of mine axe edge, that I hold thee absolved from that sin, and purged as clean as if thou hadst never sinned since thou wast born. And this girdle that is wrought with gold and green, like my raiment, do I give thee, Sir Gawain, that thou mayest think upon this chance when thou goest forth among princes of renown, and keep this for a token of the adventure of the Green Chapel, as it chanced between chivalrous knights. And thou shalt come again with me to my dwelling and pass the rest of this feast in gladness." Then the lord laid hold of him, and said, "I wot we shall soon make peace with my wife, who was thy bitter enemy."

"Nay, forsooth," said Sir Gawain, and seized his helmet and took it off swiftly, and thanked the knight: "I have fared ill, may bliss betide thee, and may He who rules all things reward thee swiftly. Commend me to that courteous lady, thy fair wife, and to the other my honoured ladies, who have beguiled their knight with skilful craft. But 'tis no marvel if one be made a fool and brought to sorrow by women's wiles, for so was Adam beguiled by one, and Solomon by many, and Samson all too soon, for Delilah dealt him his doom; and David thereafter was wedded with Bathsheba, which brought him much sorrow—if one might love a woman and believe her not, 'twere great gain! And since all they were beguiled by women, methinks 'tis the less blame to me that I was misled! But as for thy girdle, that will I take with good will, not for gain of the gold, nor for samite, nor silk, nor the costly pendants, neither for weal nor for worship, but in sign of my frailty. I shall look upon it when I ride in renown and remind myself of the fault and faintness of the flesh; and so when pride uplifts me for prowess of arms, the sight of this lace shall humble my heart. But one thing would I pray, if it displease thee not: since thou art lord of yonder land wherein I have dwelt, tell me what thy rightful name may be, and I will ask no more."

"That will I truly," quoth the other. "Bernlak de Hautdesert am I called in this land. Morgain le Fay dwelleth in mine house[11], and through knowledge of clerkly craft hath she taken many. For long time was she the mistress of Merlin, who knew well all you knights of the court. Morgain the goddess is she called therefore, and there is none so haughty but she can bring him low. She sent me in this guise to yon fair hall to test the truth of the renown that is spread abroad of the valour of the Round Table. She taught me this marvel to betray your wits, to vex Guinevere and fright her to death by the man who spake with his head in his hand at the high table. That is she who is at home, that ancient lady, she is even thine aunt, Arthur's half-sister, the daughter of the Duchess of Tintagel, who afterward married King Uther. Therefore I bid thee, knight, come to thine aunt, and make merry in thine house; my folk love thee, and I wish thee as well as any man on earth, by my faith, for thy true dealing."

But Sir Gawain said nay, he would in no wise do so; so they embraced and kissed, and commended each other to the Prince of Paradise, and parted right there, on the cold ground. Gawain on his steed rode swiftly to the king's hall, and the Green Knight got him whithersoever he would.

Sir Gawain who had thus won grace of his life, rode through wild ways on Gringalet; oft he lodged in a house, and oft without, and many adventures did he have and came off victor full often, as at this time I cannot relate in tale. The hurt that he had in his neck was healed, he bare the shining girdle as a baldric bound by his side, and made fast with a knot 'neath his left arm, in token that he was taken in a fault—and thus he came in safety again to the court.

---

11   *Morgain le Fay, who dwelleth in my house.* The enmity between Morgain le Fay and Guinevere, which is here stated to have been the *motif* of the enchantment, is no invention of the author, but is found in the *Merlin*, probably the earliest of the Arthurian *prose* romances. In a later version of our story, a poem, written in ballad form, and contained in the "Percy" MS., Morgain does not appear; her place is taken by an old witch, mother to the lady, but the enchantment is still due to her spells. In this later form the knight bears the curious name of *Sir Bredbeddle.* That given in our romance, *Bernlak de Hautdesert,,* seems to point to the original French source of the story. (It is curious that Morgain should here be represented as extremely old, while Arthur is still in his first youth. There is evidently a discrepancy or misunderstanding of the source here.)

Then joy awakened in that dwelling when the king knew that the good Sir Gawain was come, for he deemed it gain. King Arthur kissed the knight, and the queen also, and many valiant knights sought to embrace him. They asked him how he had fared, and he told them all that had chanced to him—the adventure of the chapel, the fashion of the knight, the love of the lady—at last of the lace. He showed them the wound in the neck which he won for his disloyalty at the hand of the knight, the blood flew to his face for shame as he told the tale.

"Lo, lady," he quoth, and handled the lace, "this is the bond of the blame that I bear in my neck, this is the harm and the loss I have suffered, the cowardice and covetousness in which I was caught, the token of my covenant in which I was taken. And I must needs wear it so long as I live, for none may hide his harm, but undone it may not be, for if it hath clung to thee once, it may never be severed."

Then the king comforted the knight, and the court laughed loudly at the tale, and all made accord that the lords and the ladies who belonged to the Round Table, each hero among them, should wear bound about him a baldric of bright green for the sake of Sir Gawain.[12] And to this was agreed all the honour of the Round Table, and he who ware it was honoured the more thereafter, as it is testified in the best book of romance. That in Arthur's days this adventure befell, the book of Brutus bears witness. For since that bold knight came hither first, and the siege and the assault were ceased at Troy, I wis

Many a venture herebefore
Hath fallen such as this:
May He that bare the crown of thorn
Bring us unto His bliss.
Amen.

---

12   *A baldric of bright green, for sake of Sir Gawain.* The later version connects this *lace* with that worn by the knights of the Bath; but this latter was *white,* not *green.* The knights wore it on the left shoulder till they had done some gallant deed, or till some noble lady took it off for them.

Some Lyric Poems of
Christine de Pizan

By Christine de Pizan

In about 1402, Christine de Pizan became involved in one of the probably most famous literary and intellectual debates of the entire Middle Ages and beyond, a public debate concerning the position of women and their presentation by poets and writers. Whether Christine can be truly called a "feminist" in modern terms, as many scholars have suggested—perhaps in a bit overdramatized fashion—seems questionable since she never argued for a fundamental change of her society and the power structure upon which it was based. She did not write a fiery manifesto demanding equality of men and women both in political and economic terms; and she also did not protest against the strict rules by the Catholic Church that women had to be quiet and simply listen to men's teachings according to St. Paul's rulings in 1 Corinthians 14: 34–38 and 1 Timothy 2: 11–15.[1] Nevertheless, both her personal experiences as a widow and her exacerbation over numerous comments by male writers about women incited her to actions. Christine protested, above all, against the heavy use of Ovid's Ars amatoria (2 C.E.; Art of Love) in the schools of her time and the contemporary literature,[2] and the second part of the Roman de la rose (Romance of the Rose) by Jean de Meun (1269–1278), containing what she construed as strongly misogynist comments.

The royal secretary and Provost of Lille, Jean de Montreuil, had read the Roman in the Spring of 1401 and had commented on it in a highly positive treatise, which is lost today. Christine learned about his essay and responded critically against it. This was followed by a flurry of letters involving two other royal secretaries, Pierre and Gontier Col, defending their colleague. At the same time, the chancellor of the university of Paris, Jean Gerson, announced his support of Christine's case against the Roman, especially because Pierre apparently made such blatant and vitriolic claims that Gerson even threatened him with a heresy trial. Gerson preached against his opponent and even published a poem in the form of a vision in May of 1402. Already in February of the same year Christine had presented copies of the letters exchanged to one of her major patrons, the Queen of France, Isabeau of Bavaria, hoping that she would take up that cause in defense of women. Christine also appealed to the Provost of Paris, Guillaume de Tignonville and composed an allegorical poem, Le Dit de la Rose, in which she outlined her resolve to combat evil attacks by ill-minded

---

1   For a good collection of the relevant quotes by St. Paul, see http://en.wikipedia.org/wiki/Paul_the_Apostle_and_women (last accessed on July 27, 2013).

2   http://en.wikipedia.org/wiki/Ars_Amatoria.

men against women.[3] The central figure Loyalty appears to Christine and charges her to publicize the new Order of the Rose "with its ideal of loyalty between lovers. Then, as the goddess disappears, she leaves behind her on the pillow the charter of the new order, written in blue letters on golden parchment."[4]

The public conflict came to an end in the winter of 1402 to 1403 when Gerson sent a highly critical letter to Pierre Col and then offered a number of public sermons during Spring of 1403, calumniating the lack of moral standards in the Roman de la rose and its corrupting influence. Since then Christine went to work to produce two of the most important treatises on women's lives, first The Book of the City of Ladies and The Treasury of the City of Ladies (alternatively: The Book of the Three Virtues). The first was obviously influenced by Boccaccio's De Claris Mulieribus (On Famous Women), which had been recently translated into French and which contained a long list of virtuous and outstanding women from the past. Christine followed his model, but added biblical heroines, saints, and some contemporary women. While Boccaccio had grouped his women figures simply chronologically, Christine presented her figures according to thematic aspects, having them interacting with the three allegorical figures of Reason, Rectitude, and Justice, who instruct the narrator to erect a city in defense of women. But we would have to careful in our evaluation here, because it is not a city defending women against men in a gender war. Instead, as the allegorical framework indicates, the poet outlines ways how women can, if they hold together, maintain their value system and pursue reason, rectitude, and justice, all fundamental ideals of timeless importance.

Subsequently, Christine composed many other treatises and a variety of texts in other genres, such as a courtly romance, religious poetry, and a mirror for princes.

***

Christine de Pizan was born* in Venice, Italy. Her family moved to France where her father was appointed royal astrologer. After being married for ten happy years to a royal notary, Christine was suddenly left a widow at age 25 with three children and many debts when her husband was stricken with the plague. Thanks to her father's education of her, she was able to earn her living first as a scribe and then as a lyric poet, historian and political activist for various noble patrons. Thus becoming one of the first professional women writers, she championed the cause of women and of her adopted country, France, at a time of deep political turmoil and bloodshed, the Hundred Years' War. Most of the following poems—whether *ballades, rondeaux,* or *virelais*—contain some the earliest evidence of the *woman's* joy and suffering in love and life, since lyric poetry had almost always been written by men. Another (no. 6) displays her ability at political poetry, an even more exclusively masculine province; while no. 2 is somewhat in between political and poetic lament.

(*Born: Venice, Italy 1364/5; Died: Poissy, France 1430?)

[These were composed ca. 1395–1402, unless otherwise noted below]

1. (*One Hundred Ballades*, XI)—Her best-known poem

---

3   For an excellent new edition of all texts pertinent to that debate, see Christine de Pizan, *Le Livre des epistres du debat sus le Rommant de la Rose,* ed. Andrea Valentini. Textes Littéraires du Moyen Âge, 29 (Paris: Classiques Garnier, 2014); see also my review in Mediaevistik, forthcoming.

4   *The Writings of Christine de Pizan.* Selected and ed. by Charity Cannon Willard (New York: Persea Books, 1994), 140-41.

ALONE AM I AND ALONE I WISH TO BE

[Seulete suy et seulete vueil estre…]

Alone am I and alone I wish to be,
All alone my sweet love has left me,
Alone am I, without partner or lord,
Alone am I, all grieving and angry,   4
Alone am I, in arduous languor,
Alone am I, more lost than all others,
Alone am I, without my love I remain.

Alone am I, in the doorway or window,   8
Alone am I, ensconced in a corner,
Alone am I, nourished only by tears,
Alone am I, whether suffering or appeased,
Alone am I, nothing suits me better,   12
Alone am I, enclosed in my room,
Alone am I, without my love I remain.

Alone am I, in all places and beings,
Alone am I, wherever I go or stay,   16
Alone am I, more than anything on earth,
Alone am I, abandoned by everyone,
Alone am I, so harshly cast down,
Alone am I, often weeping aloud,   20
Alone am I, without my love I remain.

Prince, now my sorrow has begun:
Alone am I, fraught with every woe,
Alone am I, more darkened than black,   24
Alone am I, without my love I remain.

2. (*One Hundred Ballades*, LVIII)—An ironic encomium to an unknown ignoble noble who loves poetry (possibly Louis, Duke of Orléans)

SIR KNIGHT, YOU LOVE PRETTY POEMS

[**Dant chevalier, vous amez moult beaulx diz …**]

Sir Knight, you love pretty poems;
But I beg you to prize good deeds even more.
You'd be starting a bit late in the game,
But still worth it: better late than never.   4
By dishing out only ballades,
You're serving only light desserts;
It's the main course, the great deed, that you'll never do.
Oh Gods, oh Gods, what a valiant knight!   8

You're a good and courageous knight,
But you love peacetime ease a bit too much;
And you've the right, for it's cowards
Who can't bear the wartime weight of arms.   12
Curses and defeat upon such a knight
Who fears striving for honor!
But then you've earned a restful life.
Oh Gods, oh Gods, what a valiant knight!   16

And there's worse, by God in Heaven,
The awful truth is, you can do more:
For the slander, liar-poet, full of calumny,
You are known to commit—but I'll be quiet now—   20
For this, throughout court and palace,
Many are saying: he might be banished.
What good is he? For writing virelays?
Oh Gods, oh Gods, what a valiant knight!   24

Leave the slandering of others in peace,
Sir Knight! For it's a thousand times worse
That clerics and laymen say of you:
Oh Gods, oh Gods, what a valiant knight!   28

3. (*One Hundred Ballades*, LXXVIII)—Against jealous old husbands

WHAT SHALL WE DO WITH THIS JEALOUS HUSBAND?
[**Que ferons nous de ce mary jaloux?**]

What shall we do with this jealous husband?
I pray to God he be flayed alive.
He keeps us under such close watch
That we can't even approach each other.   4
May they tie him up with a rough rope,
The dirty old villain, prone to faking gout,
Who causes us so much pain and bother!

May his body be ravaged by wolves!   8
Of what use is he but to hinder?
What good is this old man full of coughs,
Except for quarreling, snarling and spitting?
May the Devil love him and hold him dear,   12
But I hate him so, the foul, vile, villainous slob
Who causes us so much pain and bother!

Hah! He surely deserves to be made a cuckold,
The baboon, who does nothing but snoop   16
Around his house. Hah! What can we do about him?
Give him a chill so he'll go to bed;
Or make him go downstairs, without walking—
Down goes the villain full of suspicion,   20
Who causes us so much pain and bother!

4. (*Rondeaux*, I)—Another widow's lament

LIKE THE MOURNING DOVE, WITHOUT A MATE, I'M ALL ALONE
[**Com turtre suis, sans per, toute seulete…**]

Like the mourning dove, without a mate, I'm all alone;
Like a sheep without a shepherd gone astray;
For by death I was separated long ago
From my dear mate, whom I ceaselessly mourn.   4

It's been seven years since I lost him, poor me;

SOME LYRIC POEMS OF CHRISTINE DE PIZAN ❦ 323

Better I'd been buried right then!
Like the mourning dove, without a mate, I'm all alone:

For since then I've lived in grief and suffering   8
And in grievous tribulation,
Nor do I have any hope that, for as long as I shall live,
I shall ever find solace to make me happy;
Like the mourning dove, without a mate, I'm all alone.   12

5. (*Other Ballades*, XXVI, composed 1404–10)—Christine's wedding-night poem

A SWEET THING IS MARRIAGE

[Doulce chose est que mariage …]

A sweet thing is marriage,
I can prove it well from my own example,
Indeed, as one who has a good and wise husband,
Like the one God enabled me to find.   4
Praise be to Him who wished to save
Him for me; for his many fine qualities
I can certainly vouch for.
And surely, the dear man loves me well.   8

On our wedding night
Right then, I could experience
His goodness, for he never did me any offense
To cause me harm or pain.   12
But by the time we were to waken,
He had kissed me a hundred times, I swear,
Without base or lewd demands,
And surely, the dear man loves me well.   16

And he said in the sweetest terms:
"God made me come to you,
Sweet beloved, and for your use
I believe he nurtured me."   20
And thus he kept on dreaming
All night in this manner.
Without otherwise changing his mind,
And surely, the dear man loves me well.   24

Prince, he drives me senseless
When he says he is all mine;
He'll make me die of love's sweetness,
And surely, the dear man loves me well. 28

6. (*Other Ballades* XLII, composed 1404–10)—On the death of the duke of Burgundy, Philip the Bold, April 17, 1404. (Philip, whose duchy was more powerful than most kingdoms, was arguably the patron who truly launched Christine's career as a serious author. Because of his admiration for the Book of Fortune's Transformation, he commissioned her to write the biography of his late brother, King Charles V, which she had completed by January 1404.)

WEEP, PEOPLE OF FRANCE, FOR OUR COMMON GRIEF
[Plourez, François! Tous d'un commun vouloir]

Weep, people of France, for our common grief,
Great and small, weep for this great loss!
Weep, good King!*—well you might grieve—   *Charles VI of France, Philip's nephew
Weep you must, in sorrow for all to see.   4
Weep for the death of him whom deservedly
You should love, and by right of lineage,
Your loyal, noble uncle, most wise,
Prince of the Burgundians and excellent Duke: 8
For I say to you that in many a great trial,
You will still utter loudly with heavy heart,
"Would that we had the good duke of Burgundy here."

Weep, duke of Berry*! And weep, all his heirs,   12 *John, another important patron.
For you have good reason! Death caused this in you.
Duke of Orléans,** this should trouble you greatly,
For by his good sense he covered your many errors.
Duke of Brittany,* weep as well! For I am certain   16 *John VI, mentored by Philip.
You'll miss his influence at your young age.
Weep, Flemings*, for his noble leadership!   *Flanders was then part of Burgundy.
All you of noble blood, go to mourn in sorrow!
Weep, you subjects! For joy has left you,   20
Of which you'll often say with deep regret,
"Would that we had the good duke of Burgundy here."

Weep, queen of France*! And drape black your heart   *Isabel of Bavaria, wife of Charles VI.
For him through whom you were granted your throne.*   *Philip helped negotiate Isabel's   24
Weep, ladies, you'll remain without joy!   marriage to Richard II.
France, weep! You've lost a rook,

From which you'll receive check;
Watch out for checkmate when Death, outrageously   28
Has taken such a knight from you—it's too bad.
Weep, commoners, without delay!
For you're losing much and each shall attest it,
Of which you'll speak often, downcast and sad: 32
"Would that we had the good duke of Burgundy here."

Royal Prince, pray with all your might
For the good duke! For without much delay
In your councils you'll be inclined to say: 36
"Would that we had the good duke of Burgundy here."

_____

** *Louis, Duke of Orléans was a high-ranking, brilliant but troublesome lord; a patron whom Christine often sought to warn and reform. See poem 2 above. He fathered the renowned, more prudent later-15C poet Charles d'Orléans.*

7. (Virelays I)

I SING FROM BEHIND A VEIL

[Je chante par couverture …]

I sing from behind a veil;
However much my eyes may brim with tears,
No one will know the tribulation
My poor heart endures.   4

For this I hide my suffering,
Since I find no pity in others;
The more there is cause to weep,
The less one finds sympathy.   8

For this I neither complain nor murmur
From within my piteous grief;
Thus I laugh when I wish to cry,
And without rhyme or measure   12
I sing from behind a veil.

There's little of value
In parading one's misery;
Those of happy hearts   16

Only construe it as madness.

So I've no concern to show
My true feelings and desires;
Rather, as I'm accustomed,
To conceal my secret sorrow,   20
I sing from behind a veil.

8. (*Rondeaux* XVIII)

LAUGHING GREEN EYES, WHICH HAVE CAPTURED MY HEART
[Rians vairs yeux, qui mon cuer avez pris]

Laughing green eyes, which have captured my heart
In the web of your amorous gaze,
I surrender to you, and happily yield
As I'm taken by love's sweet surprise.

Assigning true value could never be done
In assessing your charms and your virtues,
Laughing green eyes, which have captured my heart.

So gentle are you, so kind and refined,
That no man exists who exceeds you
In soothing all pain with just a mere glance,
Laughing green eyes, which have captured my heart.

9. (*Rondeaux* LXII)

A FOUNT OF TEARS, A STREAM OF SORROW
[Source de plour, riviere de tristesse]

A fount of tears, a stream of sorrow,
A river of pain, then sea of bitterness
Engulf and submerge in boundless pain
My poor heart, reeling in distress.

So I plunge myself into grief's rugged depths;
For within me surges, stronger than the Seine,
A fount of tears, a stream of sorrow.

Ebbing and flowing with all their might,
As Fortune's winds command them,
All overwhelm me as I lie low—so low
That I hardly rise again; so gravely weigh
A fount of tears, a stream of sorrow.

[trans. Nadia Margolis]

Mutacion de Fortune (Book of Fortune's Transformation)

By Christine de Pizan

From de Pizan's *Mutacion de Fortune* (*Book of Fortune's Transformation*), 1403:

Comment sera ce possible	However is it possible
A moy simple et pou sensible	That I of wit just passable,
De proprement exprimer	Shall properly relate
4 Ce qu'on ne peut extimer	What we cannot estimate
Bonnement, ne bien comprendre,	Nor understand well. No—
Non, tant ait homs sceu apprendre,	For all that we try to know
Qu'entierement peust descrire,	We can never conceive it all
8 Ce que bien voulsisse escripre	In spite of the Muse's call,
Tant sont les diversitez	Such are the diversities,
Grandes des adversitez	So great are the adversities,
Particulieres et fais	Complex details, great events
12 Compris es tres pesans faiz,	To comprehend in any sense
Que l'influence müable	That, in mutably holding sway,
De Fortune decevable	Deceitful Fortune's way
Fait, par la refleccion	Caused, by her reflection
16 De sa grant repleccion	Huge beyond perception
Qui droite abisme est, sanz faille.	Truly, 'tis a deep abyss.
Si ne peut que je ne faille	So how can I claim not to miss
D'emprendre si grant ouvrage …	Undertaking so great a task

[…]

1159	Ovid recounts these miracles,
1160	But it behooves me to tell you
	Of my transmutation,
	In which, by the visitation
	Of Fortune, I was reformed,
1164	From woman to man transformed:
	I was living at Hymeneus's house
	And attended to his daily tasks,
	Happily spending my life there.
1168	But I believe Dame Fortune was
	Envious of my quietude,
	And decided to send me questing;
	Now I had to leave off resting
1172	For I could not disobey her.
	A well-equipped, large and rapid ship
	Hymeneus thus prepared,
	And commended it to my captain,
1176	With whom, and my household, he had me go
	On board, and then, by his leave,
	We set off without further thought.
	We reached the high seas in little time,
1180	Without ever encountering
	Adverse winds or any storms—
	Or, whenever we did, so wise
	Was my captain that he could steer
1184	Our ship through all winds, straight and clear.
	For several days of ocean breeze,
	He thus could navigate the seas,
	This skilled helmsman, who knew well the ways
1188	Of the Star of the Sea, and how
	A ship's sails should turn—such was his trade—
	To keep a straight and steady course,
	Without our suffering harm or grief;
1192	Thus we continued on our way.
	Alas! Now 'tis time for me to tell
	Of the sorrow that overcame my joy,
	Which at this point overtook me,
1196	So that I can never forget it:
	As we were sailing along
	Pursuing our course,
	I noticed the weather darkening

1200	And the clouds thickening so
	That we could barely see a thing.
	The captain, who saw me looking doubtful
	And afraid that damage might be done us
1204	By a sudden gale or storm,
	Climbed atop the stern and assessed
	From whence the wind was coming.
	He summoned the ship's crew and ordered them about,
1208	Some he had climb to the crow's nest
	To see if we were nearing land,
	And there escape the swelling sea, if one could,
1212	Lest the great storm unleash itself.
	To one he'd shout orders, of another he'd ask questions,
	And others he'd instruct and command
	That ropes be tightened and sails hoisted,
1216	According to the winds overtaking us,
	Or that topsails be raised or lowered,
	Loosen or tighten as need be,
	According to how his judgment perceived
1220	The best course of action to take
	Against the storm that was gathering
	And now headed straight for us.

1224 Oh God, I know not how to tell
Of the pain which henceforth became my lot
(For tears and sighs trouble
My heart and visage, and my sorrow doubles
As these words recall to mind
1228 This incident that would grieve me so),
Which would better be kept tucked away.

As our captain was looking straight ahead
From atop the stern of the ship,
1232 Shouting that all must turn
Toward the nearest stretch of land,
A sudden, violent wind
Arose; moving like a scythe
1236 This tornado twisted 'round
Came upon and struck the ship,
And snatched our good captain
With such force that it carried him out to sea
1240 So far; then how I wished I were dead!

For there was no chance of saving him.
Our ship turned about on its own
Such that I feared it would plunge

1244   Beneath the sea, but then death no longer appealed
To me, when I heard the cry
Of the sailors, who mightily
Screamed when they saw plunged into the sea

1248   The man who had guided, day and night,
Their ship through any peril or plight.
Once I knew it for a fact—for I'd been in doubt—

1252   From under the stern, where I was,
I rose up like a woman enraged,
I climbed atop the stern and into the sea,
I would have plunged were it not

1256   For someone restraining me: I would have dove in.
Not even Alcyone jumped
So soon into the sea, when she lost
Ceyx, whom she loved so much,

1260   As I would have fallen into the sea,
Had they let me, but I was held back
By my servants and family, who came
In great haste calling out to me,

1264   But my heart was ready to faint.
From the cries, screams, and bitter grief,
Laments, complaints and clamor
By me and my household altogether,

1268   You'd say the entire atmosphere was trembling.
Alas! With good reason we mourned
The one by whose hand we were guided,
Who had been a good leader

1272   Preventing others from perishing
And was such a loyal friend to me
That never will there be a friend
Equal to him, nor like him, in any way,

1276   And so, to see him die this way
At sea, it was no wonder
My pain was unparalleled.
For I believe there would have been no way

1280   That the ship ever would have returned
To safe harbor and, without doubt,
Many times all would have been lost [were it not for him],
Such as I saw in that storm.

1284	But great anger took away the fear
	I had because of him,
	My heart grieved over nothing else;
	There I lay, fully extended,
1288	Wishing for death; and while awaiting it
	I cried out with such force
	That you'd think at that moment
	That my voice, which I did not silence,
1292	Pierced right through the clouds and heaven,
	No comfort proved to any avail,
	For the loss pained me so.
	In this state I remained a long time,
1296	In which I refused all pleasure,
	Without hope of ever having
	Solace or joy, to tell the truth,
	And our discomfited vessel
1300	Was tossed here and there,
	Every wind threatened it,
	For there was no one on board experienced enough
	To know how to steer it on course.
1304	I believed that I could never return
	From this sea, which separates
	Grief from joy; here I thought I'd be
1308	All the rest of my life, passing on the left side
	Of Happiness, who had taken a dislike to me,
	Because of which I lay transfixed.
	But matters would not remain this way;
1312	I've taken many a step on earth since then,
	To speak briefly, such was my sorrow,
	Grief and so much did my eyes weep,
	That even Fortune took pity
1316	On my troubles, and my friendship
	Sought to gain, like a good governess/teacher …

[trans. Nadia Margolis]

Eventually, however, the ship is crushed, and Christine continues with her lament:

"My crying was so pitiable that Lady Fortune came and was moved, trying to help me in my widowhood. I was amazed about her succor. I was very frightened, but too fatigued to do anything. I fell asleep, and when I woke up again, Lady Fortune approached me, but instead of causing more harm to me, the opposite happened. She touched my body everywhere and felt each limb carefully, massaging it thoroughly. Then she left me again and I remained behind on the beach, with the waves rising and falling again. Then the ship finally hit the rocks and was smashed. This made me awake fully, and I felt a strange change of my whole body. I sensed a complete transformation everywhere. I was no longer weak and submissive, instead there was a new-found strength. I felt no more need to cry, and did no longer just want to lie there, miserably. I was amazed about this radical change in me, from terrible loneliness and sense of forlornness, fear and fright to a sense of masculinity, feeling a man's muscles on my body. My voice gained assurance, and my body gained strength. The wedding ring had fallen off my finger, a gift of the God Hymeneus [God of Marriage]. Nevertheless, I still loved the soul of my deceased husband, although I was turned into a man. … I raised my eyes, I saw the tattered ship, both sail and mast ruined, the ropes ripped, the hull destroyed, taking in water, imbibing the drink of Neptune. When I witnessed this complete shipwreck, I turned to the repair, with a hammer in my hand, and with mortar and nails I fixed the planks, gathered moss and filled the gaps with it. I made the hull watertight again. I drained the bilge and made the ship float anew. Very soon I could sail with it once more because I had learned to steer it and to overcome the challenges of the ocean.

[**trans. Albrecht Classen**]

ON THE PEACE OF FAITH

(DE PACE FIDEI)

By Nicholas of Cusa

CHAPTER ONE

1. After the brutal deeds recently committed by the Turkish ruler at Constantinople were reported to a certain man, who had once seen the sites of those regions, he was inflamed by a zeal for God; with many sighs he implored the Creator of all things that in his mercy he restrain the persecution, raging more than ever because of different religious rites. It happened that after several days—perhaps because of long continued meditation—a vision was revealed to this zealous man. From it he concluded that of a few wise men familiar from their own experience with all such differences which are observed in religions throughout the world, a single easy harmony could be found and through it a lasting peace established by appropriate and true means. And so in order for this vision eventually to come to the notice of those who have the decisive word in these great matters, he has written down his vision plainly below, as far as his memory recalled it.

2. For he was caught up to a certain intellectual height, where, as if among those who had departed from life, an examination of this question was thus held in a council of the highest with the Almighty presiding. The King of heaven and earth stated that the sad news of the groans of the oppressed had been brought to him from this world's realm: because of religion many take up arms against each other and by their power either force men to renounce their long practiced tradition or inflict death on them. There were many bearers of these lamentations from all the earth, and the King ordered that they be present in the full assembly of the saints. Now all of them, as if known to the inhabitants of heaven, seemed to have been established from the beginning by the King of the universe over the individual provinces and traditions; to be sure, their condition was not that of men but of intellectual powers.

Nicholas of Cusa, "On the Peace of Faith," http://www.appstate.edu/~bondhl/bondpeac.htm, trans. H. Lawrence Bond. H. Lawrence Bond, 2000.

3. Then one leader, in the name of all these envoys, delivered the following speech: *"O Lord, King of the universe, what does every creature have that you have not given it? It pleased you to inspire the body of man, formed out of the mire of the earth, with a rational spirit so that in him the image of your ineffable power may shine forth. From one individual was multiplied the many people who inhabit the earth's surface. And even if that intellectual spirit, sown in earth and swallowed up in shadow, does not see the light and the source of his beginning, nevertheless, you created along with him everything through which he, kindled by wonder at those things which he contacts by the senses, can sometimes lift the eyes of his mind to you, the Creator of all, and can be reunited to you in highest love and so can finally return to his source with joy.*

4. *But you know, O Lord, that a great multitude cannot exist without considerable diversity and that almost everyone is forced to lead a life burdened with sorrows and full of miseries and to live in servile submission under the subjection of the rulers who reign over them. Therefore, only a few have enough leisure that they can proceed to a knowledge of themselves using their own free choice. For they are distracted by many bodily cares and duties; and so they are not able to seek you who are a hidden God. Therefore, you appointed for your people different kings and seers who are called prophets; in carrying out the responsibility of your mission many of them have instituted worship and laws in your name and taught the unlettered people. They accepted these laws as if you, the King of kings, had spoken to them face to face, and they believed they heard not them but you in them. You sent the different nations different prophets and teachers, some at one time and others at another. However, it is a characteristic of the earthly human condition that a long-standing custom which is taken as having become nature is defended as truth. Thus not insignificant dissensions occur when each community prefers its faith to another.*

5. *Therefore, come to our aid you who alone are able. For this rivalry exists for sake of you, whom alone they revere in everything that all seem to worship. For each one desires in all that he seems to desire only the good which you are; no one is seeking with all his intellectual searching for anything else than the truth which you are. For what does the living seek except to live? What does the existing seek except to exist? Therefore, it is you, the giver of life and being, who seem to be sought in the different rites by different ways and are named with different names, because as you are you remain unknown and ineffable to all. For you who are infinite power are none of those things which you have created, nor can a creature grasp the concept of your infinity since there is no proportion between the finite and the infinite. But you, almighty God, who are invisible to every mind, are able to show yourself as visible to whom you will and in the way in which you can be grasped. Therefore, do not hide yourself any longer, O Lord; be merciful and show your face, and all peoples will be saved who are no longer able to forsake the source of life and its sweetness when they have had even a little foretaste of them. For no one withdraws from you unless he does not know you.*

6. *If thus you would deign to do this, the sword and the bilious spite of hatred and all evil sufferings will cease; and all will know that there is only one religion in the variety of rites. But if perhaps this difference of rites cannot be removed or if it is not expedient to do so in order that the diversity may contribute to devotion,*

as when any region expends a more attentive effort in performing its ceremonies as if they would become the more pleasing to you, the King: at any rate, just as you are one, there should be one religion and one veneration of worship. Therefore, may you be appeased, O Lord, for your wrath is compassion and your justice mercy: spare your weak creature. So we, your deputies, whom you have placed as keepers for your people and whom you see here, humbly beseech your majesty by every means of entreaty possible to us."

CHAPTER TWO

7. In response to the archangel's supplication, when all the heavenly citizens together bowed to the highest King, he who was seated on the throne said that he had left man to his own choice and had created him capable in his choice for fellowship with God. But the animal and earthly man is held in ignorance under the Prince of Darkness and walks in accordance with the conditions of the sensible life which is from nowhere else but the world of the Prince of Darkness and not in accordance with the intellectual inner man whose life is from the realm of his origin. Hence, he said that with much care and diligence he had recalled man from his wrong way through various prophets who, by comparison with others, were seers. And finally when all the prophets themselves could not sufficiently overcome the Prince of Darkness, he sent his Word, through which he had also created the world. This Word he clothed with humanity so that at least in this way he might illuminate the docile man having a most free choice and so that he might see that he should walk not according to the outward man but according to the inner man, if he hoped to return one day to the sweetness of eternal life. And since his Word put on the mortal man and with its blood bore witness to this truth: man is capable of eternal life for the attainment of which the animal and sensible life is to be regarded as nothing, and eternal life itself is nothing except the ultimate desire of the inner man, namely, the truth which alone is desired and which, as it is eternal, nourishes the intellect eternally. The truth which nourishes the intellect is nothing but the Word itself; in it all things are enfolded and through it all things are unfolded, and it has put on human nature so that no man may doubt that according to the election of his free choice he can attain the immortal nourishment of the truth in his own human nature, in that man who is also the Word. The Highest added: "And since these things have been done, what is it that could have been done and was not done?"

CHAPTER THREE

8. To this question of the King of kings, the incarnate Word, holding the chief position among all the heavenlies, replied on behalf of all: *"Father of Mercies, even though your works are most perfect and nothing has to be added for their completion, nevertheless, since from the beginning you decreed that man stay a being of free choice and since in the sensible world nothing remains stable and because of time opinions and conjectures as well as languages and interpretations vary as things transitory, human nature needs frequent*

visitation so that the erroneous notions of which there are a great many concerning your Word might be rooted out and truth might continuously shine forth. Since truth is one and since it is not possible that it not be understood by every free intellect, all diversity of religions will be led to one orthodox faith."

9. The King agreed. And after the angels who are set over the nations and languages were called forth, he instructed each angel to lead one who is quite knowledgeable to the incarnate Word. And at once there appeared before the Word the more eminent men of this world, as if caught up into ecstasy. The Word of God addressed them thus: "The Lord, King of heaven and earth, has heard the groans of the slain and the bound and of those reduced to servitude who suffer because of the diversity of religions. And since all those who either cause this persecution or suffer it are led only by the belief that in this way it is expedient to be saved and pleasing to their Creator, therefore, the Lord has had mercy on his people and has decided that by the common consent of all men all diversity of religions be brought peacefully to one religion to remain inviolable from now on. He commits this responsibility of ministry to you as the elected men and from his court gives you as assistants the ministering angelic spirits who are supposed to guard and direct you, and he deems Jerusalem as the place best suited for this."

CHAPTER FOUR

10. One who was older than the others and apparently a Greek first made adoration and then replied: "We give praises to our God whose mercy is above all his works; he alone is able to cause so great a diversity of religions to be brought into one concordant peace. His command we his creation are not able not to obey. Therefore, we beseech you now to instruct us how this unity of religion could be introduced by us. For we are persuaded a nation will accept with difficulty another faith different from that which up to now each nation has defended even by its blood."

The Word answered: "You will find that not another faith but the one and the same faith is presupposed everywhere. For you who are now present are called 'wise' among those who share your own language, or at least 'philosophers,' i.e. 'lovers of wisdom.'"

"This is so," said the Greek.

"If, therefore, all of you love wisdom, do you not presuppose that there is this wisdom?"

All shouted together that no one doubts that there is.

11. The Word added: "There can be only one wisdom. For if it were possible for there to be plural wisdoms, they would have to derive from one wisdom, for before all plurality is unity."

The Greek: "None of us doubts that it is one wisdom which we all love and because of which we are called philosophers. Through participation in it there are many wise men, although this wisdom remains in itself simple and undivided."

The Word: "Therefore, you all agree that the simplest wisdom is one and that its power is ineffable. And each experiences this ineffable and infinite power in the unfolding of its strength. For whenever sight turns itself to those things which are visible and whatever it sees it considers to have come forth from the power of wisdom—and the same is true of hearing and the individual things which sense perceives—it affirms that invisible wisdom exceeds all things.

12. The Greek: "We who have made this profession of philosophy love the sweetness of wisdom by no other way than a foretaste in wonder at the things which are subject to sense. For who would not die for the sake of reaching such wisdom from which all beauty, all sweetness of life and everything desirable emanate? What a power of wisdom shines forth in the creation of man, in his limbs, in their order, in the life infused, in the harmony of the organs, in movement, and especially in the rational spirit, which is capable of wonderful arts and is, so to speak, a sign of wisdom in which the eternal wisdom shines forth above all things in a close image, as truth in a close likeness! And what is more wonderful above all else: this reflection of wisdom comes nearer and nearer to truth by means of a vigorous conversion of the spirit until from the shadow of image the living reflection itself continually becomes truer and more like true wisdom, although absolute wisdom itself, as it is, is never attainable in anything else; thus eternal, inexhaustible wisdom itself is the perpetual and unfailing intellectual food."

The Word: "You are proceeding rightly toward the purpose to which we strive. Therefore, even though you were called from the different religions, all of you presuppose in all such diversity the one thing which you call wisdom. But tell me, does not one wisdom encompass all that can be said?"

CHAPTER FIVE

13. The Italian answered: "Certainly the Word is not apart from wisdom. For the Word of the Supremely Wise is in wisdom, and wisdom is in the Word, nor is anything outside wisdom. For infinite wisdom encompasses everything."

The Word: "If, therefore, anyone should say that all things have been created in wisdom and another that all have been created in the Word, would they say the same thing or something different?"

The Italian: "Even if a difference in the manner of speech appears, nevertheless, it is the same thing in meaning. For the Word of the Creator in which he has created all things can be nothing other than his wisdom."

14. The Word: "What, therefore, does this seem to you: is this wisdom God or creature?"

The Italian: "Since God the Creator creates all things in wisdom, he is necessarily the wisdom of created wisdom. For before every creature is the wisdom through which every created thing is that which it is."

The Word: "So wisdom is eternal, since it is before everything begun [initiatum] and created."

The Italian: "No one can deny that what is understood to be before everything created [principiatum] is eternal."

The Word: "Therefore, it is the beginning [principium]."

The Italian: "This is true."

The Word: "Therefore, it is the most simple. For every composed thing is derived from a beginning [principiatum]; for the things which compose cannot exist subsequent to that which has been composed."

The Italian: "I admit this."

15. The Word: "Therefore, wisdom is eternity."

The Italian: "This also cannot be otherwise."

The Word: "But it is not possible for there to be more than one eternity, since unity is before all plurality."

The Italian: "No one denies this."

The Word: "Therefore, wisdom is the one, simple and eternal God, the beginning [principium] of all things."

The Italian: "This is necessarily so."

The Word: "See how you, the philosophers of the various traditions, agree in the religion of one God whom you all presuppose, in that which as lovers of wisdom you profess."

CHAPTER SIX

16. Here the Arab rose and answered: "Nothing clearer or truer can be said."

The Word: "But just as you, since you are lovers of wisdom, profess absolute wisdom, do you suppose that there are men vigorous in intellect who do not love wisdom?"

The Arab: "I certainly think that all men by nature desire wisdom, since wisdom is the life of the intellect, which cannot be preserved in its life by any other nourishment than the truth and the word of life or its intellectual bread, which is wisdom. For just as every existing thing desires all without which it cannot exist, so the intellectual life desires wisdom."

The Word: "Therefore, all human beings profess with you that there is one absolute wisdom whom they presuppose, and this is the one God."

The Arab: "This is so, and no one who is understanding can establish otherwise."

The Word: "Therefore, for all who are vigorous in intellect there is one religion and worship, which is presupposed in all the diversity of rites."

17. The Arab: "You are wisdom because you are the Word of God. However, I ask those who worship more than one god how they concur with the philosophers in the concept of one God? For at no time were the philosophers found to have felt other than the impossibility of there being several gods unless one superexalted God stood over them. He alone is the beginning from which the others have what they have in a much more exalted way than a monad is for numbers."

The Word: "All who have ever worshiped more than one god presupposed there is divinity. For this they worship in all the gods as participating in it. For just as without whiteness existing there are no white things, so without divinity existing there are no gods. Therefore, the worship of gods acknowledges divinity. And whoever says there are many gods is saying that there is antecedently one source [principium] of all of them; just as whoever declares there are many saints admits that there is one saint of saints through whose participation all the others are saints. Never was there a people so dull as to believe in plural gods each of which would have been the first cause, source, or creator of the universe."

The Arab: "So I believe. That there is more than one source is a contradiction. For since the source [principium] cannot be caused [principiatum], for it would have been caused of itself and would have been before it was, which reason does not grasp, therefore, the source is eternal. And it is not possible for there to be more than one eternal, for before all plurality is unity. So the source and cause [principium et causa] of the universe necessarily will be one. Consequently, I have not found any nation which has turned aside from the path of truth in this."

18. The Word: "Therefore, the strife would be ended if all who worship more than one god would look at what they presuppose, namely, the Deity which is the cause of all things, and would, as reason itself dictates, take that deity as manifest into their religion, just as they worship it implicitly in all whom they call gods."

The Arab: "Perhaps this will not be difficult, but to remove the worship of gods would be a grave matter. For people certainly believe that help is given to them from worship and are inclined to these divine powers for their salvation."

The Word: "If people were informed about salvation in just the manner stated, they would seek salvation in him who gave being and is himself Savior and infinite salvation, rather than in those who of themselves have nothing except what is given by the Savior himself. Whenever people would take refuge with the gods (whom, because they lived in a godlike manner the opinion of all has held as holy) as if with an acceptable intercessor in some infirmity or other necessity of theirs, or if they would respectfully worship such an intercessor with the reverence [dulia] of veneration or keep his memory reverently because he is a friend of God and his life is to be imitated, then, provided doing either would give to the one and only God all the worship of divine adoration [latriae], it would not contradict the one religion and the people would be easily quieted."

CHAPTER SEVEN

19. At this time the Indian asked: "What then of statues and images?"

The Word: "Images which bring to awareness what is allowed in the true worship of the one God are not condemned. But when they lead one away from the worship of adoration [a cultu latriae] of the one God, as if something of divinity were in the stones and were bound up in the statue, then because they deceive and turn away from the truth, they rightly should be broken into pieces."

The Indian: "It is difficult to turn a people from a long established idolatry because of the oracles that are given."

The Word: "Rarely are these oracles made up otherwise than by priests who assert that the divinity has answered thus. For once a question has been proposed, they invent a response whether by some art, which they bring to observation from the disposition of the sky, or by lot, which they ascribe to the divinity, as if heaven or Apollo or the sun ordered them to answer. Consequently, it happens that for the most part their answers are either ambiguous, so that they would not be convicted of lying openly, or completely false; and if sometimes the answers are true, they are true by chance. And when a priest is a good conjecturer, he divines better, and the responses are truer."

20. The Indian: "It has been ascertained that often some spirit bound in the statue has publicly given answers."

The Word: "Not the soul of a man or of Apollo or of Asclepius or of another who is worshiped as a god, but the evil spirit, the enemy of human salvation from the beginning, pretended that sometimes, but rarely, he was bound to a statue and was forced to answer, by faith through man, in order to deceive in this way, but after the falsehood was discovered it ceased. So today 'they have a mouth and do not speak.' When through experience this falsehood of the seducer was discovered in many regions, idolatry was condemned in almost all places where wise men live. And similarly in the East it will not be difficult to expose the falsehood of idolatry in order to call on the one God, so that thus those nations might conform to the other nations of the world."

The Indian: "Now that the obvious errors have been discovered and, in consequence, the very prudent Romans, and the Greeks and the Arabs also, have destroyed idols, it is to be hoped in every way that the Indians, as idolaters, will act similarly, especially since they are wise and do not doubt the necessity of religion consisting in the worship of one God. For even if alongside this they would venerate idols in their own way, and these idols would pertain to the worship of the one God, they will thus reach a peaceful conclusion. But it will be very difficult for a concord to be accepted everywhere about the triune God; for it will seem to all that the trinity cannot be conceived without three things, that if there is threeness in the divinity, there will also be plurality in the deity. But it has already been stated, and in truth it is necessary, that there is only one absolute deity. Therefore, there is no plurality in absolute deity but in those who participate, who are not God absolutely, but gods by participation."

21. The Word: "As creator, God is three and one; as infinite, he is neither three nor one nor any of the things which can be spoken. For the names which are attributed to God are taken from creatures, since he in himself is ineffable and beyond everything that can be named or spoken. Since those who worship God should adore him as the beginning of the universe, yet in this one universe one finds a multiplicity of parts, inequality and separation (for the multiplicity of stars, trees, human beings, rocks is obvious to sense), nevertheless, the beginning of all multiplicity is unity; therefore, the beginning of multiplicity is eternal unity. An inequality of parts is found in the one universe, since none is similar to another; but inequality descends from the equality of unity; therefore, before all inequality there is eternal equality. A distinction or separation of parts is found in the one universe; but before all distinction there is a connection of unity and equality, and from this connection separation or distinction descends; the connection therefore is eternal. But there cannot be more than one eternal. Therefore, in one eternity there is found unity, the equality of unity, and the union or connection of unity and equality. So the most simple beginning [principium] of the universe is unitrine, since in the beginning that which has been derived [principiatum] must be enfolded, but everything that has been derived declares thus that it is enfolded in its beginning, and in every thing that has been derived such a threefold distinction is found in the unity of essence. Therefore, the most simple beginning of all things will be threefold and one."

CHAPTER EIGHT

22. The Chaldean: "Even if the wise could somewhat grasp these things, nevertheless, they would exceed the common people. For, as I understand, it is not true that there are three gods, but there is one God, who is one and threefold. Do you want to say that this one God is threefold in power?"

The Word: "God is the absolute power of all powers, because he is omnipotent. Therefore, since there is only one absolute power, which is the divine essence, to say that this power is threefold is to assert only that God is threefold. But you should not thus understand power as distinguished from reality, since in God power is reality itself; so too with absolute potency, which is also power. For it would not seem absurd to anyone if it should be said that divine omnipotence, which is God, has in itself unity, which is being, equality and connection. Thus the potency of unity unites or gives essence to everything that has being—a thing exists insofar as it is one; one and being are interchangeable. And the potency of equality gives equality or forms every existing thing—for as a thing is neither more nor less than it is, it is equal; for if it were greater or less, it would not exist; therefore, it cannot exist apart from equality. So the potency of connection unites or joins. Hence omnipotence in the power of unity summons from non-being, so that what was not becomes capable of being; and in the power of equality it forms; and in the power of connection it joins, as in the essence of love you see how loving joins the lover to the loveable. Therefore, when the human being is summoned by omnipotence from non-being, unity comes first in order, then equality, and finally their nexus. For nothing can exist unless it is one; therefore, one exists antecedently. And since the human being is summoned from non-being, the unity of the human being comes first in order and then the equality of that unity or being, for equality is the unfolding of form in the unity so that the unity of a human being is summoned forth and not that of a lion or of some other thing. But equality cannot exist unless it arises from unity, for unity or identity, not otherness, produces equality. And finally love or the nexus proceeds from unity and equality. For unity and equality are not separable from each other. Therefore, the nexus or love is so constituted that when unity is posited, equality is posited, and when unity and equality are posited, love or the nexus is posited.

23. Therefore, if no equality is found unless it is the equality of unity, and no nexus is found unless it is the nexus of unity and equality in such a way that the nexus is in the unity and the equality, and the equality is in the unity and the unity in the equality, and both the unity and the equality are in the nexus: it is clear that there is no essential distinction in the trinity. For things that are essentially different are so constituted that one can exist without the existence of the other. But since trinity is so constituted that when unity is posited, the equality of unity is posited and conversely, and when unity and equality are posited, the nexus is posited and conversely, hence it is not in essence but in relation that it appears that unity is one thing, equality a different thing and connection another. Numerical distinction, however, is essential distinction. For the number two differs from three essentially; when two is posited, three is not posited, and three does not follow in consequence of the being of two. Therefore, the trinity in God is not composite or plural or numerical, but it is simplest unity. Those, therefore, who believe in God as one will not deny that he is threefold when they understand that this trinity is not different from simplest unity but is simplest unity in such a way that if this trinity were not in unity, it would not be the omnipotent beginning for the creation of the universe and of individual things. The more united a power is the stronger it is; but the more united it is the simpler it is. Therefore, the more powerful or the stronger it is, the simpler it is. So because the divine essence is omnipotent, it is most simple and threefold. For without trinity it would not be the simplest, strongest and omnipotent beginning."

The Chaldean: "I believe that no one can disagree with this understanding. But that God has a son and a participant in deity the Arabs and also many others repudiate."

24. The Word: "Some call the unity 'Father,' the equality 'Son,' and the nexus 'Holy Spirit,' since these terms, although not proper terms, nevertheless, appropriately signify the Trinity. For from the Father is the Son and from the unity and equality of the Son is the love or Spirit. For the nature of the Father passes over into an equality in the Son. Therefore, the love, and nexus, originates from the unity and the equality. And if simpler terms could be found, they would be more suitable, such as, 'unity,' 'that-ness' and 'identity.' For these terms seem to unfold more the most fruitful simplicity of the essence. Consider also that since in the essence of the rational soul there is a certain fruitfulness, namely, the mind, wisdom and love or will, because the mind projects from itself understanding or wisdom, from which comes will or love, and this trinity in the unity of the essence of the soul is the fruitfulness which it has in the likeness of the most fruitful uncreated Trinity: so every created thing bears the image of the creative power and in its own way has a fruitfulness in a close or distant likeness to the most fruitful Trinity, which is the creator of all things. Thus the creature not only has being from the divine being but has a fruitful being, in its own way threefold, from the most fruitful three and one being; without this fruitful being neither could the world exist nor would the creature exist in the best way it could."

CHAPTER NINE

25. Then the Jew answered: "The supremely blest Trinity, which cannot be denied, has been excellently explained. For a prophet disclosing this to us as briefly as possible declared that God had asked how he who gave others the fruitfulness of generation could himself be sterile. And although the Jews shun the Trinity because they consider it a plurality, nevertheless, once it is understood that the Trinity is the most simple fruitfulness, they will very willingly agree."

26. The Word: "Also the Arabs and all wise philosophers will easily understand from these things that to deny the Trinity is to deny the divine fruitfulness and creative power and that to accept the Trinity is to deny a plurality and consociality of gods. For this fruitfulness, which is also a trinity, makes it unnecessary that there be many gods to concur in the creation of all things, since one infinite fruitfulness is sufficient to create everything creatable. The Arabs will be able to grasp the truth much better in this way rather than in the way in which they say that God has an essence and a soul and add that God has a word and a spirit. For if God is said to have a soul, this soul can be understood only as reason or the Word which is God; for reason is not other than the Word. And what then is the Holy Spirit of God except the love which is God? For nothing is verified of the most simple God that he is not himself. If it is true that God has a Word, it is true that the Word is God; if it is true that God has a Spirit, it is true that the Spirit is God. For having improperly suits God, because he is all things

in such a way that in God to have is to be. Hence the Arab does not deny that God is mind and that from this mind, word or wisdom is begotten, and from them spirit or love proceeds. And this is that 'trinity' which has been explained above and has been set forth by the Arabs, although most of them do not notice that they are acknowledging the Trinity. So also in your prophets you Jews discover that the heavens were formed by the Word of God and by his Spirit. But in the way in which the Arabs and Jews deny a trinity, certainly it is to be denied by all; but in the way in which the truth of the Trinity is explained above, it must be embraced by all."

CHAPTER TEN

27. Then the Scythian: "There can be no doubt regarding the adoration of the most simple Trinity, which all who venerate gods today also worship. For the wise say that God is the creator of both sexes and that he is love, wishing through this to explain the most fruitful Trinity of the Creator to the extent that they can. Others assert that the superexalted God projects from himself intellect or reason; and this they call 'God from God,' and they call him 'God the Creator,' for every created thing has a cause and reason why it is this and not that. Therefore, the one infinite reason of all things is God. But reason, which is the Logos or Word, emanates from that which speaks it so that when the Omnipotent speaks the Word, those things which are enfolded in the Word are made in reality, so that if Omnipotence should say 'Let there be light,' then the light enfolded in the Word thus actually exists. Therefore, this Word of God is intellectual, so that according as a thing has been conceived in the intellect so that it should be, thus it would exist in reality. They say further that the spirit of connection proceeds in third order; it connects all to one, so that there is unity as the unity of the universe. For they posited a world soul or spirit which connects all things, and through it each creature has participation in the order so that each is part of the universe. Therefore, it is necessary that this spirit in the beginning is itself the beginning. Now love joins. Hence love, or charity, which is God, can be called this spirit whose power is diffused throughout the universe; in this way the nexus by which the parts are connected to one, or the whole, and without which there would be no perfection has God as its beginning. So it is clearly seen that all the wise have touched on something of the trinity in unity. And, consequently, when they hear the explanation we have heard they will rejoice and give praise."

28. The Frenchman answers: "Once I heard this argument brought forward among the learned: eternity is either unbegotten or begotten or neither unbegotten nor begotten. I see that the unbegotten is reasonably called the 'omnipotent Father' the begotten the 'Word' or 'Son,' the neither unbegotten nor begotten 'love' or the 'Holy Spirit,' for it proceeds from both and is neither unbegotten since it is not the Father nor begotten since it is not the Son, but it proceeds from both. Eternity, therefore, is one, and it is threefold and most simple; the one deity is threefold, the one essence is threefold, the one life is threefold, the one potency is threefold, the one power is threefold. In this 'school' I have

now made progress so that what was obscure is visible more clearly than light, as far as it is now given. And since in the world a very great contradiction remains, as some assert that the Word was made flesh for the redemption of all but others hold different opinions, we have to be informed how to reach concord in this difficult matter."

The Word: "The Apostle Peter has undertaken the explanation of this part. Hear him; for he will sufficiently teach everything that is hidden to you."

And when Peter appeared in their midst, he thus began:

CHAPTER ELEVEN

29. Peter: "Every disagreement about the incarnate Word seems to have these different forms. First, some say that the Word of God is not God; and this part has already been sufficiently explained, for the Word of God can be only God. Now this Word is reason; for in Greek logos signifies 'word,' which is reason. That God, who is the creator of all rational souls and spirits, possesses reason is beyond doubt. But this reason of God is only God, as has already been explained; for in God having coincides with being. For he from whom all things are embraces all things in himself and is all in all, for he is the former of all; therefore, he is the form of forms. Now the form of forms enfolds in himself all formable forms. Therefore, the Word, or Reason, the infinite cause and measure of all that can be made, is God. So those who admit that the Word of God has become flesh or man must confess that that man whom they call the Word of God is also God."

30. Then the Persian said: "Peter, the Word of God is God. How could God, who is immutable, become not God but a man, and the creator a creature? Except for a few in Europe, almost all of us deny this. And if there are some among us who are called Christians, they agree with us about the impossibility of the infinite being finite and the eternal temporal."

Peter: "I firmly deny with you that the eternal is temporal. But since all of you who hold to the law of the Arabs say that Christ is the Word of God, and you say well, you must also acknowledge that he is God."

The Persian: "We acknowledge that he is the Word and Spirit of God, as though among all who are or were no one had that excellence of the Word and Spirit of God; however, we do not admit therefore that he was God, who has no sharer. So lest we fall into a plurality of gods, we deny that he is God, although we do profess him to be nearest to God."

31. Peter: "Do you believe in a human nature in Christ?"

The Persian: "We do, and we affirm both that it was true in him and that it remained."

Peter: "Very good. This nature, because it was human, was not divine. And so in everything that you have seen in Christ according to this human nature, by which he was similar to other men, you have not apprehended Christ as God but as man."

The Persian: "That is so."

Peter: "No one differs with you on this point. For human nature was most perfect in Christ; by it he was a true and mortal man like other men; but in accordance with that nature he was not the Word of God. Therefore, tell me: when you acknowledge him to be the Word of God, what do you mean?"

32. The Persian: "Not nature but grace, namely, that he obtained the sublime grace that God placed his Word in him."

Peter: "Did not God similarly place his Word in other prophets? For all have spoken through the Word of the Lord and were heralds of the Word of God."

The Persian: "This is so. But of all prophets Christ was the greatest; therefore, it befits him more properly than the other prophets to be called the Word of God. For several missives could contain a word of the king for particular matters and individual provinces, but there is only one which contains the word of the king by which the whole kingdom is ruled, namely, the missive which contains the law and precept which all are bound to obey."

Peter: "You seem to have provided a good likeness to this end, namely, that the word of the king written on different sheets does not change the sheets into other natures; for after the writing down of the word their nature still remains as it was before. In this way you say that the human nature remained in Christ."

The Persian: "We do."

33. Peter: "Good. But notice what a difference there is between missives and the heir of the kingdom. The word of the king is properly living, free and unlimited in the heir of the kingdom but not at all in the missives."

The Persian: "I admit that; if a king sends his heir into the kingdom, the heir carries the word of the father living and unlimited."

Peter: "Is not the heir properly the word and not the messenger or envoy, or the letter or missive? And are not all the words of messengers and letters enfolded in the word of the heir? And even if the heir of the kingdom is not the father but the son, he is not different from the king's nature, and because of this equality he is the heir."

34. The Persian: "I understand that well. But this stands in the way: the king and the son are two; therefore, we do not admit that God has a son. For the son would be a different god from the Father, just as the son of the king would be a different man from the father."

Peter: "You oppose this likeness, because it does not properly apply if you consider the subjects [supposita]. But if you remove the numerical distinction of the subjects and look at the power which is in the royal dignity of the Father and of the Son, his heir, then you see how that royal power is one in the Father and in the Son; in the Father as in the unbegotten, in the Son as in the begotten or living Word of the Father."

The Persian: "Continue."

Peter: "Suppose, therefore, that there is such an absolute unbegotten and begotten royal power and that such an unbegotten power calls one who is by nature an alien to join with him in the begotten connatural succession so that a different nature in union with his own nature possesses the kingdom at the same time and undividedly. Do not the natural succession and the gracious or adoptive succession concur in one inheritance?"

The Persian: "This is clear."

35. Peter: "So also sonship and adoption are united in the one succession of one kingdom; but the succession of adoption is not supposited [suppositatur] in itself but in the succession of sonship. For if adoption, which does not succeed from its own nature, is to succeed when there is sonship, it is necessary that adoption not be supposited in itself but in sonship, as he who succeeds by nature. If, therefore, adoption, so that it succeeds with sonship in obtaining the simplest and indivisible inheritance, does not acquire succession from itself but from sonship, the adoptive successor will not be one person and the natural successor another, although the nature of adoption is different from the nature of the natural successor. For if the adopted successor were separate and were not of the same hypostasis with the natural successor, how would he concur in the succession of indivisible inheritance? Therefore, it must be held that in Christ the human nature is so united with the Word or the divine nature that the human nature does not pass into the divine but clings in such an indissoluble way that it is not a person separately in itself but in the divine nature; the end then is that the human nature, called to the succession of eternal life with the divine, can obtain immortality in the divine nature."

CHAPTER TWELVE

36. The Persian: "I understand this adequately; but clarify what you have said with another understandable example."

Peter: "Precise similitudes are not possible; but consider wisdom in itself. Is it accident or substance?"

The Persian: "Substance as it is in itself; but accident as it befalls another."

Peter: "But all wisdom in all the wise is from that which is wisdom per se, because it is God."

The Persian: "These things have been shown."

Peter: "Is not one man wiser than another?"

The Persian: "Certainly."

Peter: "Therefore, he who is wiser is closer to wisdom per se, which is absolutely maximum; and he who is less wise is farther from it."

The Persian: "I agree."

Peter: "But in accordance with human nature never is anyone so wise that he could not be wiser. For between contracted wisdom, i.e., human wisdom, and wisdom per se, which is divine and maximum and infinite, there always remains an infinite distance."

The Persian: "And this is evident also."

37. Peter: "So it is with absolute mastery and contracted mastery; for in absolute mastery there is an infinite art, in contracted mastery a finite art. Therefore, suppose that someone's intellect had such mastery and such wisdom that it would not be possible to have a greater wisdom or greater mastery; then his intellect has been most greatly united with wisdom per se or mastery per se, so much that this union could not be greater. Has not this intellect in the power of the united greatest wisdom and of the united greatest mastery, to whom it is united, obtained divine power? And would not the human intellectual nature in a man who has such an intellect be most immediately united to divine nature or eternal wisdom, to the Word or omnipotent art?"

The Persian: "I admit all this, but this union would still be one of grace."

38. Peter: "If the union of the lower nature with the divine would be so great that it could not be greater, then the lower would be united with the divine also in personal union. For as long as the lower nature is not elevated to personal and hypostatic union with the higher nature, it could be greater. Therefore,

if the union is posited as the greatest, the lower exists in the higher by adhering; and this occurs not by nature but by grace. However, this greatest grace, which cannot be greater, is not separate from nature but is united with it. Hence, even though it is by grace that human nature is united with the divine, nevertheless, this grace, since it cannot be greater, most immediately terminates in nature."

The Persian: "However you will have stated it, because human nature can be elevated by grace to union with the divine in any man, the man Christ should no more be said to be God than any other saint, even though he is the holiest of men."

39. Peter: "If you consider the loftiest height which cannot be greater and the greatest grace which cannot be greater, and the greatest holiness, and so on, to be in Christ alone; then if you consider it impossible for there to be more than one greatest height which cannot be greater, and the same for grace and holiness; and next if you see all height of every prophet, whatever degree he may have reached, to be improportionally distant from that height which cannot be greater so that given any degree of height, between it and the only highest there can occur an infinite number higher than the given and lower than the highest (so too with grace, holiness, prudence, wisdom, mastery, etc.): then you would see clearly that there can be only the one Christ, in whom human nature is united with the divine nature in supposited unity. And even the Arabs admit this, although many do not consider this thoroughly. For the Arabs say that Christ alone is the loftiest in this world and the next and is the Word of God. Nor do those who say that Christ is God and man say anything other than that Christ alone is the loftiest man and the Word of God."

The Persian: "It seems that when that union which is necessary in the highest is considered well, the Arabs can be brought to accept this belief, since through it the unity of God, which they most greatly strive to protect, is not violated but preserved. But tell me how can it be grasped that human nature is not supposited in itself but by adhering to the divine?"

40. Peter: "Take this example, although it is a remote one: a magnet draws iron upward, and by adhering to the magnetic ore the nature of the iron does not subsist in its own weighty nature, otherwise it would not hang in the air, but in accordance with its nature it would fall toward the center of the earth. Yet in the power of the magnet's nature the iron, by adhering to the magnet, subsists in the air and not by the power of its own nature according to which it could not be there. Now the iron's nature is inclined in this way to the magnet's nature because the iron has in itself a likeness to the magnet's nature, from which it is said to have taken its origin. So if the intellectual human nature should adhere in the closest way to divine intellectual nature, from which it has received its being, it would adhere to it as inseparably as to the font of its life."

The Persian: "I understand."

41. Peter: "Further, the sect of Arabs, which is large, also admits that Christ raised the dead and created birds from clay and many other things which they expressly confess Jesus Christ to have done as one having power; from this belief they can easily be led, since it cannot be denied that he himself did

these things in the power of the divine nature to which the human was hypostatically [suppositaliter] united. For the power of Christ by which he ordered those things to be done which the Arabs confess were done by him could not have been according to human nature unless the human would have been assumed in union with the divine, whose power it is to order in such a way."

The Persian: "These things and more the Arabs affirm about Christ, and they are written in the Qur'an. Nevertheless, it will be more difficult to bring the Jews than others to this belief for they admit nothing expressly about Christ."

Peter: "They have all these things in their scriptures about Christ; but following the literal sense they do not want to understand. Nevertheless, this resistance of the Jews will not impede concord. For they are few and will not be able by arms to disturb the whole world."

CHAPTER THIRTEEN

42. The Syrian responded: "Peter, earlier I heard that concord can be found in every tradition; explain how this can be verified in this point."

Peter: "I will, but first tell me: is not God alone eternal and immortal?"

The Syrian: "So I believe, for everything except God has a beginning. Therefore, since it has a beginning, it will, in accordance with its nature, also have an end."

Peter: "Does not almost every religion—of the Jews, Christians, Arabs and most other men—hold that the human mortal nature of every man will arise after temporal death to everlasting life."

Syrian: "So it believes."

Peter: "Therefore, all these acknowledge that human nature ought to be united with divine and immortal nature. For otherwise how would human nature pass on to immortality if it did not adhere to the divine in inseparable union?"

The Syrian: "Faith of the resurrection necessarily presupposes this."

43. Peter: "Therefore, if faith holds this, then the human nature is antecedently united with the divine nature in some man, namely, in him who is the face of all peoples and the highest Messiah and Christ, as the Arabs and Jews call Christ. For he who is, according to all, the closest to God will be that one in whom the nature of all men is antecedently united in God. For this reason he is the savior and mediator of all; in him human nature, which is one and through which all men are men, is united with the divine and immortal nature so that in this way all men, being of the same nature, obtain resurrection from the dead."

The Syrian: "I understand that you want to say that faith of the resurrection of the dead presupposes union of the human nature with the divine without which this faith would be impossible; and you assert that this union is in Christ; consequently, this faith presupposes him."

44. Peter: "You understand correctly. Therefore, accept that all the promises which are found to have been given to the Jews are confirmed in the faith in the Messiah or mediator, by whom alone the promises regarding eternal life could and can be fulfilled."

The Syrian: "What of the other traditions?"

Peter: "The same. For all men desire and expect only eternal life in their human nature, and for this they instituted ceremonies for the purification of souls and sacrifices [sacra] in order better to fit themselves for eternal life in their nature. Men do not desire happiness, which is eternal life, in any other nature than their own; man does not wish to be anything else but man, not an angel or any other nature; but he wants to be a happy man who would obtain final happiness. Now this happiness is nothing else but the fruition or union of the human life with its source, from which life itself flows, that is, with the divine immortal life. But how would this be possible for man unless it is conceded that the common nature of all men is elevated to such a union in some person through whom as mediator all men could acquire the ultimate goal of their desires? And this person is the way because he is the man through whom every man has access to God, who is the goal of desires. It is Christ, therefore, who is presupposed by all who hope to obtain final happiness."

45. The Syrian: "I like what you say very much. For if human intellect believes that it can obtain union with wisdom in which it acquires an eternal nourishment for its life, it presupposes that the intellect of some highest man has acquired the union in the highest way and has obtained this highest mastery through which it hopes similarly at some time to attain that wisdom. For if it did not believe it possible even in some highest of all men, it would hope in vain. The hope of all men is that they can sometime obtain happiness, for this is the end of all religion. And there is no deception in this, for this hope, common to all, is from an innate longing, and to such hope religion, thus likewise innate in all, seeks to attain. Therefore, I see that this master and mediator, who holds the highest perfection and the highest rank in human nature, is presupposed by all. But the Jews say perhaps this prince of nature, in whom all the deficiencies of all men are made full, has not yet been born but will be born one day."

Peter: "It is enough that Arabs as well as Christians and others who have borne testimony in their own blood testify—through what the prophets have said about him and through what he did beyond human possibility when he was in the world—that he has come."

CHAPTER FOURTEEN

46. The Spaniard: "There will perhaps be another difficulty about the Messiah, whom the greater part of the world admits has come, and this is the question of his birth, for Christians and Arabs assert that he was born of the Virgin Mary and others maintain that this is impossible."

Peter: "All who believe that Christ has come acknowledge that he was born of the Virgin. For since he is the finality of perfection of nature and alone most high, of which father should he be the son? For every father who begets in the perfection of nature differs from the finality of perfection in such a way that he cannot communicate the final perfection beyond which there can be no higher and which is not possible except for one man. Only that father who is the creator of nature can do this. Therefore, the most high has as father only him from whom is all fatherhood. So the most high is conceived by divine power in the womb of a virgin, and in this virgin the highest fruitfulness concurred with virginity. Hence Christ was born to us in such a way that he is joined to all men most intimately. For he has as father him from whom every father of man has his fatherhood; and he has her as mother who was united carnally with no man; thus through a most close conjoining each one may find in Christ his own nature in final perfection."

47. The Turk: "Not a small difference still remains, for Christians assert that Christ was crucified by the Jews but others deny it."

Peter: "Because some are ignorant of the mystery of death they deny that Christ was crucified and say that he still lives and will come at the time of the Antichrist. And since he will come as they assert, they believe that he will come in mortal flesh, as if otherwise he could not subdue the Antichrist. And they deny that Christ was crucified by the Jews apparently out of reverence for Christ, as if such men would have had no power over Christ. But notice that one rightly ought to believe the accounts, which are many, and the preaching of the Apostles, who died for the truth, namely, that Christ so died. For thus the prophets foretold that he had to be condemned to the most shameful death, which was the death of the cross. And this is the reason: for Christ came having been sent by God the Father in order to proclaim the Kingdom of Heaven, and of that Kingdom he said things that could not be better proved by him than by the testimony of his blood. Hence that he might be most obedient to God the Father and might furnish all certainty for the truth which he announced, he died, and he died a most shameful death so that no man should refuse to receive this truth, as a testimony for which all would know that Christ voluntarily accepted death. For he preached the Kingdom of Heaven by proclaiming how man, capable of that kingdom, could reach it. In comparison with that kingdom the life of this world, which is loved so persistently by all, is to be regarded as nothing. And in order that it may be known that this life of the Kingdom of Heaven is truth, he gave up the life of this world for truth. Thus he might most perfectly proclaim the Kingdom of Heaven and liberate the world from ignorance, by which the world prefers this life to the life of the future, and might give himself up in sacrifice for many; so that thus lifted up on the cross in the sight of all, he might draw all to believe and glorify the Gospel and strengthen the fainthearted and freely give himself up for the redemption of many, and do everything in the best possible way so that men might obtain the faith of salvation, the hope of acquiring it and love by fulfilling the commandments of God.

48. Therefore, if the Arabs would consider the fruit of Christ's death and that it was up to him as one sent by God to sacrifice himself in order to fulfill the desire of his Father and that there was nothing more glorious for Christ than to die for the sake of truth and obedience, even the most shameful death: they would not remove from Christ this glory of the cross, by which he merited to be the most high and to be superexalted in the glory of the Father. Finally, if Christ preached that in the resurrection men will attain immortality after death, how could the world be better assured of this than that he willingly died and was resurrected and appeared alive? For the world then was made certain by a final attestation when, from the testimony of many, who saw him alive and died so that they might be faithful witnesses of his resurrection, it heard that the man Christ had died openly on the cross and had publicly risen from the dead and was alive. Therefore, this was the most perfect proclamation of the Gospel, which Christ made known in himself, and which could not be more perfect; and without death and resurrection it could always have been more perfect. Therefore, whoever believes that Christ most perfectly fulfilled the will of God the Father must confess all these things without which the proclamation would not have been most perfect.

49. Notice, further, that the Kingdom of Heaven was hidden to all until Christ. For this is the gospel of Christ to announce the kingdom which is unknown to all. Therefore, there was no faith or hope of obtaining the Kingdom of Heaven, nor could it have been loved by anyone since it was completely unknown. Nor was it possible that any man would have attained that kingdom, since human nature had not yet been elevated to that exaltation so that it would become partaker of the divine nature. Therefore, Christ opened the Kingdom of Heaven in every way of opening. But no one can enter the Kingdom of Heaven unless he lay aside the kingdom of this world through death. For it is necessary that the mortal lay aside mortality, that is, the potentiality of dying; and this may be done only through death. Then can the mortal put on immortality. Now if Christ as mortal man had not yet died, he would not yet have laid aside mortality; this would mean he did not enter the Kingdom of Heaven in which no mortal can be. Therefore, if he who is the firstfruits and first-born of all men did not open the heavenly realms, our nature united with God has not yet been introduced into the kingdom. Thus no man could have been in the Kingdom of Heaven if human nature united with God had not yet been introduced. All men who believe in the Kingdom of Heaven assert the contrary; for all confess that some holy ones in their tradition have obtained happiness. Therefore, the faith of all who confess that their holy ones are in eternal glory presupposes that Christ died and ascended into heaven."

CHAPTER FIFTEEN

50. The German: "All this is excellent, but I perceive not a few discrepancies regarding happiness. For it is said that only temporal things, which consist of sensible goods, have been promised to the Jews in their law. And one reads that only carnal things, though everlasting, have been promised to the Arabs in their law, which is written in the Qur'an. But the Gospel promises the form of angels, namely, that men will be similar to angels, who have nothing of carnality in them."

Peter: "What in this world can be conceived the desire for which does not diminish but continually increases?"

The German: "All temporal things diminish, only intellectual things never do; even if eating, drinking, living to excess and the like are sometimes pleasing, at other times they are unpleasant and inconsistent. But knowing, understanding, and contemplating truth with the mind's eye are always pleasing. And the older a man becomes the more these things please him, and the more he acquires of these the more his desire for having them is increased."

51. Peter: "Therefore, if the desire is to be continuous and the nourishment everlasting, it will be neither temporal nor sensible but the food of intellectual life. And although the promise of a Paradise where there are rivers of wine and honey and a multitude of young women is found in the law of the Qur'an … it is necessary that these things be understood figuratively. For elsewhere the Qur'an forbids lying together and all other carnal pleasures in churches and synagogues or mosques. It ought not be believed that mosques are holier than Paradise. Therefore, how would these things be prohibited here in mosques which will be permitted there in Paradise? Elsewhere it says that all these things are found there because it is necessary that in Paradise there occurs the fulfillment of all the things which are desired there. In this it reveals well enough when it wants to say that such things are found there. For since these things would be so desired in this world, from the presupposition that there would be an equal desire in the next world, then they should be found there exquisitely and abundantly. For otherwise it could declare that that life is the fulfillment of desires only by this similitude. It did not want to state to an uneducated populace other more hidden things but only those things which seem happier according to the senses, lest the populace, which does not relish the things of the spirit, would disparage the promises.

52. Hence the whole concern of him who wrote that law appears chiefly to have been to turn the people away from idolatry; and to that end he made such promises and set forth all these things. But he did not condemn the Gospel; on the contrary, he praised it giving to understand that the happiness promised in the Gospel is not less than that corporeal happiness. And the understanding and the wise among them know this to be true. And Avicenna incomparably prefers the intellectual happiness of the vision or fruition of God and of the truth to the happiness described in the law of the Arabs,

although he was an adherent of that law; so it is with other wise men. Therefore, in this matter there will be no difficulty in reconciling all traditions. For it is said that that happiness is above everything that can be written or spoken for it is the completion of every desire and the attainment of the good in its source and of life in immortality."

53. The German: "What then of the Jews who do not grasp the promise of the Kingdom of Heaven but only the promise of temporal things?"

Peter: "The Jews often surrender themselves to death for the sake of the observance of the law and its holiness. Hence if they did not believe that thus they would obtain happiness after death, for they prefer zeal for the law to life, they would not die. Therefore, it is not the belief of the Jews that there is no eternal life or that they could not obtain it; otherwise none of all these would die for the law. But the happiness they expect they do not expect from the works of the law—because those laws do not promise it—but from the faith which presupposes Christ, as was stated before."

CHAPTER SIXTEEN

54. The Tartar: "I have heard many things here previously unknown to me. The Tartars, who are many and simple, for the most part believing in one God, marvel at the variety of rites of others who also worship the same God with them. For assuredly they laugh at the fact that some Christians and all the Arabs and Jews are circumcised, that some have their faces branded, and others are baptized. Finally, regarding marriage there is much diversity, for one has only one wife, another has only one that is truly married to him but many concubines, yet another has many legitimate wives. And concerning sacrifices the rite is so diverse that it cannot be recited. Among these varieties the sacrifice of the Christians in which they offer bread and wine and say that these are the body and blood of Christ, which they eat and drink after the oblation, seems especially abominable: they devour whom they worship. I do not grasp how there could be a oneness in these things which vary also according to place and time; and unless it occurs, persecution will not end. For diversity gives birth to division and to hostility, hatred and war."

55. Then by commission of the Word, Paul, teacher to the gentiles, rose and said:

Paul: "It is necessary that it be shown that salvation of the soul is not granted from works but from faith. For Abraham, father of the faith of all believers, whether Christians or Arabs or Jews, believed in God, and this was credited to him as righteousness: the soul of the just will inherit eternal life. When this is acknowledged these varieties of rites will not be a cause of disturbance. For they have been instituted and received as sensible signs of the truth of faith. But signs are subject to change, not however that which is signified."

The Tartar: "Explain how faith saves."

Paul: "If God has promised something from his sheer generosity and grace, should he who is able to give all things and is truthful not be believed?"

The Tartar: "Certainly. No one believing him can be deceived; and whoever does not believe him would be unworthy of obtaining any grace."

Paul: "Therefore, what justifies him who obtains righteousness?"

The Tartar: "Not merits; otherwise it would not be grace but obligation."

Paul: "Excellent. But because no living being is justified in the sight of God through works but through grace, the Omnipotent gives to whom he will what he will. Then if anyone should be worthy to obtain the promise which has been made out of pure grace, he must believe God. In believing, therefore, he is justified, since from faith alone he obtains the promise, for he believes God and expects God's word to be done."

56. The Tartar: "After God has promised, it is just that the promises be kept. Therefore, whoever believes God is justified through the promise rather than through faith."

Paul: "God, who promised to Abraham a seed in whom all would be blessed, justified Abraham that he might obtain the promise. But if Abraham had not believed God, he would have obtained neither justification nor the promise."

The Tartar: "This is true."

Paul: "Therefore, in Abraham faith had such effect that the fulfillment of the promise—that promise which otherwise would not have been just or fulfilled—was just."

57. The Tartar: "What, therefore, did God promise?"

Paul: "God promised Abraham that in Isaac he would give him a seed in which all peoples would be blessed. And this promise was given when according to the ordinary course of nature it was impossible for Sarah, his wife, to conceive from him and to give birth; but because he believed, he acquired a son Isaac. Later God tested Abraham that he should offer up and slay the boy Isaac in whom the promise of the seed was made. And Abraham obeyed God, yet he believed no less that the promise would also be fulfilled even from the dead son after his having to be raised from the dead. Hence God found such great faith in Abraham; thereupon Abraham was justified, and the promise was fulfilled in the one seed, which descended from him through Isaac."

The Tartar: "What is this seed?"

Paul: "Christ. For all peoples obtain divine blessing in him."
The Tartar: "What is this blessing?"

Paul: "The divine blessing is the final goal of desires or the happiness which is called eternal life, about which you have already heard sufficiently."

The Tartar: "Therefore, do you mean to say that God promised us the blessing of eternal happiness in Christ?"

Paul: "This is what I mean. Consequently, it is necessary to believe God as Abraham believed, so that whoever so believes is justified, along with the faithful Abraham, in order to obtain the promise in the one seed of Abraham, Christ Jesus; this promise is the divine blessing enfolding every good in itself."

58. The Tartar: "Therefore, do you mean to say that this faith alone justifies so that we may receive eternal life?"

Paul: "Yes."

The Tartar: "How will you give to the simple Tartars understanding of this so that they may grasp that it is Christ in whom they can obtain happiness?"

Paul: "You have heard that not only Christians but also Arabs acknowledge that Christ is the highest of all who have been or will be in this age or the next and that he is the face of all peoples. If, therefore, the blessing of all is in one seed, this can only be Christ."

The Tartar: "What kind of sign do you bring for this?"

Paul: "I bring forward the testimony of the Arabs as well as of the Christians that the spirit making the dead to live is the spirit of Christ. If, therefore, the spirit of life is in Christ, who is able to give life to those he will, then he is the spirit without whom no dead can be revived and no spirit can live eternally. For the fullness of divinity and grace indwell the spirit of Christ, and from this fullness all who are to be saved receive the grace of salvation."

The Tartar: "It is pleasing to have heard this thing from you, Teacher of the Gentiles, for along with the things that I heard earlier they are sufficient for our purpose. I see also that this faith is necessary for salvation; without faith no one will be saved. But I ask, does faith suffice?"

Paul: "Without faith it is impossible for anyone to please God. But it must be a formed faith; for without works it is dead."

59.   The Tartar: "Which works are these?"

Paul: "If you believe God, you keep his commandments. For how do you believe God to be God if you do not strive to fulfill what he commands?"

The Tartar: "It is fitting that God's commandments be kept. But the Jews say they have his commandments through Moses, the Arabs through Mohammed, the Christians through Jesus, and the other nations perhaps venerate their own prophets by whose hands they claim to have received the divine commandments. How, therefore, would we come to agreement?"

Paul: "The divine commandments are very brief and well known to all and are common to all nations. Indeed, the light showing them to us was created simultaneously with the rational soul. For God speaks in us that we should love him from whom we have received being and that we should do to another only what we want done to us. Therefore, love is the fulfillment of the law of God, and all laws are brought back to this."

60.   The Tartar: "I do not doubt that both the faith and the law of love of which you spoke will be grasped by the Tartars. But I have much hesitation about rites; for I do not know how they will accept circumcision, which they scorn."

Paul: "Accepting circumcision has no bearing on the truth of salvation. For circumcision does not save, and there is salvation without it. Yet whoever does not believe circumcision to be necessary for obtaining salvation but allows it to be done on him in order to be in this also more like Abraham and his followers is not condemned because of circumcision if he has the faith which was just described. Thus Christ was circumcised, and many among the Christians after him, as still today with the Ethiopian Jacobites and others who are circumcised but not as if this rite were a sacrament necessary for salvation. But how peace could be preserved among the faithful if some are circumcised and others not is a major question. Hence because the larger part of the world is without circumcision and in view of the fact that circumcision is not necessary, I consider it fitting that in order to preserve peace the smaller part thus conform to the larger part, with whom they are united in faith. But if because of peace the larger part should conform to the smaller part and accept circumcision, it ought to be done voluntarily so that peace thus might be established by mutual interchanges. For if in the cause of peace other nations accept faith from Christians and the Christians circumcision from them, peace would be better made and strengthened. Yet I think that the practice of this would be difficult. Therefore, it should suffice that peace be established in faith and in the law of love and that rite thus be mutually tolerated."

CHAPTER SEVENTEEN

61. The Armenian: "What do you think should be done about baptism since Christians consider it a necessary sacrament?"

Paul: "Baptism is a sacrament of faith. For whoever believes that it is possible to obtain a justification in Jesus Christ believes that there is a taking away of sins through him. Each of the faithful will show this cleansing signified in the baptismal washing. For baptism is nothing but the confession of this faith in the sacramental sign. He would not be one of the faithful who would not acknowledge his faith in speech and in signs which Christ instituted for this purpose. Both the Hebrews and the Arabs perform baptismal washings for the sake of religious devotion, and they will not find it difficult to accept the washing instituted by Christ for the profession of faith."

62. The Armenian: "It seems necessary to accept this sacrament since it is necessary for salvation."

Paul: "Faith is a necessity for adults, who can be saved without the sacrament when they cannot receive it. But when they can, they cannot be called the faithful who do not wish to show themselves as such through the sacrament of regeneration."

The Armenian: "What about little children?"

Paul: "The Hebrews and the Arabs more readily agree that little children be baptized. Since for the sake of religion they let males be circumcised on the eighth day, commutation of this circumcision to baptism will be agreeable, and the option of whether they wish to be content with baptism will be given."

CHAPTER EIGHTEEN

63. The Bohemian: "In everything that has already been set forth it should be possible to find agreement, but it will be very difficult with sacrifices. For we know that Christians cannot give up the offering of bread and wine for the sacrament of the Eucharist in order to please others, since this sacrifice was instituted by Christ. But it is not easy to believe that other nations which do not have the custom of sacrificing in this way will accept this manner, especially since they say that it is insanity to believe in a conversion of the bread into Christ's flesh and of the wine into his blood and then to consume the sacraments."

Paul: "This sacrament of the Eucharist represents nothing else but that from the grace in Christ Jesus we will obtain the refreshment of eternal life, just as in this world we are refreshed by bread and wine. Therefore, when we believe that Christ is the food of the mind, then we take him under visible forms which feed the body. And since it is necessary that we agree in the belief that we obtain the food of the life of the spirit in Christ, why should we not show that we believe this in the sacrament of the Eucharist? It is to be hoped that in general all the faithful want to enjoy in this world, by faith, the food which will in truth be the food of our life in the other world."

64. The Bohemian: "How will you persuade all peoples that in the sacrament of the Eucharist the substance of the bread is changed into the body of Christ?"

Paul: "The believer knows that the Word of God in Christ Jesus will lead us from the misery of this world to the sonship of God and to the possession of eternal life, for with God nothing is impossible. Therefore, if we believe this and hope, then we do not doubt that according to Christ's ordinance the Word of God can change bread into flesh. If nature does this in animals, how should the Word, through whom God also made the worlds, not do this? Therefore, the necessity of faith demands that we believe it. For if it is possible that we the sons of Adam, who are from the earth, are transformed in Christ Jesus by the Word of God into sons of the immortal God and if we believe this and hope it to come and if it is possible that we will then as Jesus be the Word of God the Father: it is necessary that we likewise believe in the transubstantiation of the bread into flesh and of the wine into blood through the same Word, by whom bread is bread and wine is wine, and flesh is flesh and blood is blood, and through whom nature converts food into him who is fed."

65. The Bohemian: "This conversion of the substance of the bread is difficult to grasp."

Paul: "It is very easy through faith. For this is attainable only by the mind, which alone looks on the 'that' of substance, not its 'what'; for substance precedes every accident. And so since substance is neither a quality nor a quantity and only the substance is changed so that it is no longer the substance of bread but the substance of flesh, this conversion is only spiritual, for it is most distantly removed from everything that can be grasped by sense. Therefore, there is no increase of the quantity of flesh from this conversion, nor is it multiplied in number. Consequently, there is only one substance of flesh into which the substance of bread has been changed, even if the bread is offered in different places and many breads are placed in sacrifice." The Bohemian: "I grasp your teaching, which is very agreeable to me, that this sacrament is the sacrament of the food of eternal life through which we obtain the inheritance of the sons of God in Christ Jesus, the Son of God; that there is a likeness of this in the sacrament of the Eucharist; and that it is attained only by the mind and is tasted and received through faith. What if these secrets are not received? For the uneducated will perhaps shudder not only at believing this but at taking such great sacraments."

66. Paul: "If faith is present, this sacrament, as it is in sensible signs, is not thus of such a necessity that without it there is no salvation; for it is sufficient for salvation to believe and in this way to eat the bread of life. And so regarding its distribution, whether and to whom and how often it should be given to the people, no law of necessity has been set down. Therefore, if anyone having faith considers himself unworthy to approach the table of the highest King, this is a humility rather to be praised. Thus, as to the question of its use and rite, that which is seen by Church leaders to be more expedient for the time in any religion—always with faith preserved—could be ordered in such a way that by means of a common law the peace of faith might not persevere less intact because of a diversity of rites."

CHAPTER NINETEEN

67. The Englishman: "What will be done about the other sacraments, that is, marriage, orders, confirmation, and extreme unction?"

Paul: "It is very often necessary to condescend to human weakness if it does not offend against eternal salvation. For to seek exact conformity in all things is rather to disturb the peace. It is to be hoped, however, that agreement may be found in marriage and in orders. For it seems that in all nations marriage was introduced, as it were, through natural law so that one man has one true wife. So, likewise, priesthood is also found in every religion. Therefore, agreement will be easier in these common things, and also in the judgment of all the others the Christian religion will be proved to observe a more praiseworthy purity in both sacraments."

The Englishman: "What about fastings, ecclesiastical duties [officiis ecclesiasticis], abstinence from food and drink, forms of prayers, etc.?"

Paul: "Where no conformity in manner can be found, nations should be permitted their own devotional practices and ceremonials, provided faith and peace are preserved. A certain diversity will perhaps even increase devotion when each nation will strive to make its own rite more splendid through zeal and diligence in order thus to surpass another and so to obtain greater merit with God and praise in the world."

68. After these things were thus discussed with the wise of the nations, very many books of those who wrote on the observances of the ancients were produced, and indeed excellent ones in every language, for example, among the Latins Marcus Varro, among the Greeks Eusebius, who collected information about the diversity of religions, and very many other authors. After these were examined it was discovered that all the diversity consisted in rites rather than in the worship of one God;

from all the writings collected into one it was found that all from the beginning always presupposed and worshiped the one God in all practice of worship, although people in their simplicity, seduced by the adverse power of the Prince of Darkness, often did not consider what they were doing.

Therefore, in the way it has been set forth, a concord of religions was concluded in the heaven of reason. And it was commanded by the King of Kings that the wise return and lead the nations to the unity of true worship, that ministering spirits lead them and assist them and, finally, that with the full power of all they come together in Jerusalem as to a common center and accept one faith in the name of all and thereupon establish an everlasting peace so that in peace the Creator of all, blessed forever, will be praised. Amen.

[trans. H. Lawrence Bond]

THE PLOWMAN AND DEATH

By Johann Tepl

J ohann of Tepl (ca. 1350–ca. 1414) (also known as Johann of Saaz) grew up in western Bohemia, near Prague, at a time when the German Emperor Charles IV of the house of Luxemburg ruled in Prague. Charles had a very open mind and was highly educated, so he laid the foundation for far-reaching contacts with Italian Renaissance poets, such as Petrarch. Johann of Tepl had close contacts with the imperial chancellery in Prague and was thus influenced by Renaissance ideas, as his allegorical dialogue poem The Plowman and Death from ca. 1401 indicates, at least in the second half after chapter twenty-four when the Plowman embarks on a glorious defense of human life against the devastating force of death. In 1383 Johann is documented as a notary public in Saaz and as the headmaster of the local Latin school. In 1411 he was appointed city clerk of the Prague New City (Prager Neustadt). The Plowman dialogue narrative, one of the first prose texts, is the only known work by Johann, but it stands out as a major literary representative of the so-called Bohemian Renaissance, reflecting many influences from Italian Renaissance thinkers. The dialogue enjoyed tremendous popularity, as documented by eighteen manuscript copies, although those that must have existed in Bohemia (today Czech Republic) were all destroyed during the Hussite Wars from ca. 1419 to ca. 1434 in which the Bohemian/Czech Hussites ferociously and most successfully fought against the German empire in revenge for the burning at the stake of their spiritual and religious leader John Hus in 1415 in Constance. The Plowman was first printed in 1462/1463, and was reprinted seventeen times until 1547. While the Plowman at first argues bitterly and in desperation against Death who had taken his wife away from him, soon enough the debate turns to more global questions regarding the meaning of life and the value of human existence in face of death. Undoubtedly, this prose narrative belongs to the masterpieces of fifteenth-century German literature and carries timeless messages relevant for people of all cultures and periods.

THE PLOWMAN. CHAPTER ONE

Ferocious effacer of every being, terrible outlaw of all creation, hideous butcher of every human, Death, you take my curse! God, your Creator, detest you, increasing disaster reside with you, misfortune violently visit you: be wholly dishonoured for ever! Fretting affliction and misery never leave you, wherever you wander; grief, distress and sorrow accompany you all over; fatiguing enmity, disgraceful aversion, shameful disdain beset you with vengeance at every step; sky, earth, sun, moon, stars, river, mountain, field, valley, mead, the abyss of Hell and all that has life and breath be rancorous and resentful toward you and curse you until the end of Time! Founder in malice, vanish in calamitous woe, and continue in the severe, irrevocable proscription of God, of all mankind, and the whole of Creation for all future days! Shameless villain, your evil remembrance live and persist without end; fear and terror never part from you, live wherever you will! I and all humanity wring our hands and scream the hue and cry after you!

DEATH. CHAPTER TWO

Hark, hark, hark at the latest marvel! We are challenged by appalling and incredible complaints. Whence they have come is, in truth, unknown to Us. But threats, curses, screams of hue and cry, hand-wringing, and every kind of attack have never yet done Us any harm. However, son, whoever you are, announce yourself, and make known what grief has befallen you through Us to lead you to treat Us so unbecomingly, as We are quite unaccustomed to, although We have sent many knowledgeable, noble, beautiful, mighty and strong-standing people to graze over the edge—a cause of sufficient grief to widows and orphans and lands of the living!

You act like a man in earnest, as if oppressed by grave affliction. Your plaint lacks rhyme, from which we conclude that you will not unrail from your meaning for the sake of rhyme. But if you are raging, ranting, misty-minded or otherwise apart from your senses, then calm down, refrain, do not be so hasty to utter such terrible curses, so you be not burdened with future remorse. Do not imagine that you could ever weaken Our immense and magnificent power. But name yourself, and do not withhold those matters in which We have met you with such dreadful violence. We wish to be right and just before you; right and just are Our proceedings. We do not know what crime you are, so wantonly, laying to Our name.

THE PLOWMAN. CHAPTER THREE

I am a Plowman by name, my plough is of bird's-clothing*, and I live in the land of Bohemia. I will always be spiteful, inimical, adversarial to you: for horribly you have torn my 12th letter*, my hoard of joys, out of my alphabet; deplorably you have weeded the bright summer flower of my delights from the meadow of my heart; maliciously you have sundered me from the prop of my happiness, my chosen turtle-dove: you have committed irretrievable robbery on me!

Consider for yourself, if I rage, storm and cast charges at you with justice: through you I am robbed of a joyous existence, disinherited from the days of a good life, and divested of all bliss-bringing gain. I used to be bright and merry at every hour; all my days and nights were short and joyful, the one as full of delight, as full of bliss, as the other; my every year was a year of grace. Now I am told: Croak! Remain with dismal thoughts on a withered bough, in darkness and wilting, and howl incessantly! The wind drives me so, I am swimming the surge of the wild sea, the waves have won the upper hand, my anchor holds fast nowhere. Therefore I shall scream without ending: Death, you take my curse!

DEATH. CHAPTER FOUR

We are seized with wonder at such an outrageous challenge, the like of which We have never encountered. If you are a Plowman, living in the land of Bohemia, then it seems to Us that you do Us a heavy injustice, for We have done no conclusive work in that land for a long time—recently, only in a solid, handsome town, securely situated on a mountain; four letters of the alphabet—the 18th, the 1st, the 3rd and the 23rd—weave its name. We performed our act of grace on a respectable, blessed young lady there; her letter was the twelfth. She was virtuous and free from blemish; for We were present at her birth. At that time, Lady Honour sent her a gusseted mantle and garland, in the hands of Lady Fortune. She took the mantle and garland with her, whole, untorn, and untarnished, to the grave. Our witness, and hers, is He who knows all hearts. She was pure of conscience, assiduous, faithful, honest, and supremely gracious to one and all.—Verily, so gentle and constant a nature has seldom come into Our hands. Perhaps this is the one you mean; We know of no other.

THE PLOWMAN. CHAPTER FIVE

Yes, sir, I was her loving spouse, and she my sweetheart. You took her away, the joy-filled feast for my eyes: she is gone, my peaceful shield from hardship; my soothsaying, divining rod is away. She is gone, gone! Here I stand, poor Plowman, alone: the shining star has disappeared from my sky; the sun of my weal is descended to rest: never again will she rise! My radiant morning star will never rise again, her light has faded away, I have no sorrow-banisher more: black night is everywhere before my eyes. I do not believe ought exists that could ever bring me back to true happiness, for the proud banner of my joys has sunk, to my sorrow, to the dust.

Murder! To arms! be yelled from the depths of the heart, for the blanched year, for the disastrous day, and for the onerous hour when my constant, solid diamond was shattered, when my loding staff was mercilessly ripped out my hands, when the road to my weal-renewing fountain of youth was barred me. Dole without ending, woe without respite, miserable sinking, felled plunging, eternal fall be given to you, Death, to you and yours! Die besmirched with vice, greedy with disgrace and gnashing your teeth, and perish in the stink of Hell! God deprive you of your power and reduce you to dust! Lead a diabolical existence for ever!

DEATH. CHAPTER SIX

A fox struck a sleeping lion on the cheek, wherefore his hide was torn to shreds; a hare pinched a wolf, wherefore he has, to this day, no tail; a cat clawed a dog who was wanting to sleep, and so she must bear his enmity everlastingly. In this way will you chafe yourself against Us. For we believe: the servant shall serve, the Master shall rule. We will prove that We weigh justly, judge justly, and act justly in the world: We spare none for the title, take no heed of great knowledge, pay no regard to any form of beauty, and do not blink at the sight of talent, love, sorrow, age, youth or other qualities. We do as the sun, who shines over good and evil: We take good and evil into Our power. All those masters who can compel spirits must commit and relinquish their spirit to Us; the necromancers and magicians cannot withstand Us, and their riding on sticks, their riding on goats, helps them nought. The doctors who lengthen the lives of men must come to our shared shore: roots, herbs, ointments, and manifold apothecatical powders cannot help them. If we made account to even the butterflies and the grasshoppers for their species, they would not be satisfied. And if we let people live for the sake of friendship or enmity, of love or sorrow, the whole world would now stretch as Our Empire; every King would have placed his crown on Our head and presented his sceptre to Our hand; the Papal See and the three-crowned mitre would now be in Our power. Leave be with your curses; do not bring new tales from the prattling-rock; do not hew above you, or shavings will rain into your eyes!

THE PLOWMAN. CHAPTER SEVEN

Could I curse, could I rail, could I revile you to cause you the worst of evils, then that would be no more than you have despicably deserved of me. For bitter plaints must follow bitter grief: it would be inhuman of me not to weep for so virtuous a gift from God, which none but God alone can give. Truly, I shall mourn for ever: my honourable falcon has flown away, my virtuous wife. I am justified in my plaints, for she was of noble birth, rich in honours, beautiful, sprightly, and of a figure that towered over her boon companions; truthful and modest in words, chaste of body, good and cheerful in company—I am silent, for I am too weak to tell of all her honour and virtue, which God Himself granted her: Master Death, you know this yourself. I am right to arraign you for such intense heartache. Truly, were there any good in you, you yourself would feel pity. I will turn away from you, speak no good of you, I will oppose you for ever with all my power: all God's Creation shall assist me in my strivings against you; all that is in Heaven, on Earth and in Hell, hate you and feud with you!

DEATH. CHAPTER EIGHT

God has given Heaven's Throne to the good spirits, the Abyss of Hell to the evil, and the terrestrial lands to Our portion. In Heaven, peace and reward for virtue; in Hell, torment and punishment for sin; this sphere of Earth with its flowing rivers and all they contain was commended Us by the mighty Duke of all Worlds, with the order that We uproot and weed out all superfluity. If you imagine, foolish man, if you consider, and chisel into your reason with a burin, then you will find: if We had not eradicated, since the time when the first man was worked from clay, the growth and increase of humans on Earth, of beasts and worms in the barren wastes and wild woods, of scale-bearing, slippery fishes in the waters—then no one would now exist for gnats, no one would venture out for wolves, each man would guzzle another, each beast another, each living creature another, for they would lack food, and the Earth would be too narrow for them. He is foolish who weeps for mortals. Desist! The living to the living, the dead to the dead, as hitherto. Consider your cause more deeply, you fool, before you begin to complain!

THE PLOWMAN. CHAPTER NINE

I have irretrievably lost my highest treasure—should I not mourn? I must linger in misery to my final days, robbed of every delight. Gentle God, the mighty Lord, avenge me on you, wicked sorrowbringer! You have dispossessed me of every joy, deprived my life of pleasant days, disaccustomed me from great honour. Great honour was mine when the good, the pure, the sublime angel played with her children, born in a pure nest. The hen is dead who brought up such chicks. Oh God, mighty Lord, with what pride did I look before me when she walked with such modest steps, mindful of decorum, that people gave her loving looks, and said: "May the gentle soul be praised, honoured and thanked; God grant her and her nestlings a world of good!" If I knew how to properly thank God for this, in truth, I would do as was meet. What other poor man had he endowed so richly, so soon? Let others say what they will: when God gifts a man a pure, chaste and beautiful wife, this is a real gift, one that is higher than every earthly, material gift. Oh mightiest Lord of Heaven, what a boon you have conferred on the man you have wedded to a pure and spotless spouse! Delight, honest man, in a pure wife; delight, pure woman, in an honest plow: God give joy to you both! What does the fool know of this, who has never drunk from this fountain of youth? And crushing heartache may have befallen me, yet I thank God sincerely, for that I have known the flawless lady. You, evil Death, enemy of all mankind, be eternally hateful to God!

DEATH. CHAPTER TEN

You have not drunk from the fountain of wisdom; I mark that from your words. You have not seen the working of nature; you have not peered into the mixture of worldly events; you have not beheld the transformation of flesh: you are an ignorant whelp. Mark how the delightful roses, the strong-scented lilies in the garden, how the virtuous herbs and the joy-giving flowers in the meadows, how the firm-standing stones and the high-grown trees in the rugged fields, how the puissant bears and the strength-wielding lions in the eerie wilderness, how the strong, tall-grown warriors, how the nimble, exceptional, erudite and omniproficient people, and how all earthly creatures, however intelligent, and charming, and strong they may be, however long they preserve themselves, however long they continue—one and all must come to nought. Now, when all human generations who have been or are yet to be must pass from being to non-being, how may the Extolled One you mourn enjoy the advantage that she not be done to as all others, and all others not be done to as she? You yourself will not escape Us, although this may be far from your thoughts at present. "Everyone to follow!" each one of you must say. Your plaint is invalid; it helps you nought; it proceeds from a torpid mind.

THE PLOWMAN. CHAPTER ELEVEN

I have every faith in God, who has power over me and you, that He will shield me from you, and take severe revenge on you for the aforesaid outrage you have done me. You declaim like a trickster; you mix truth with falsehoods, intending to beat my enormous soul-sorrow, my mind-grief and heartache, out of sight, out of mind, out of senses. You will not succeed, for I am pained by my weighty, agonising loss, the which I can never replace. My curative medicine for all woe and hardship, God's servant, the nurse of my will, my body's attendant, the guardian of my honour and hers all day and all night, she was indefatigable. Whatever was entrusted to her was returned entire, intact and pure, often with increase. Honour, propriety, chastity, generosity, fidelity, moderation, care and modesty always inhabited her house; shamefacedness always bore the mirror of honour before her eyes; God was her gracious protector. He was also gracious and merciful to me for her sake; health, happiness and fortune were mine. This pure domestic bliss she had earned and deserved of God. Give her her reward and wages of grace, lenient meed-giver, expender to all faithful souls, richest of lords! Show her more grace than I could wish for her! Oh, oh, oh! brazen murderer, Master Death, vicious brat! the torturer be your judge and tie you with the words "Forgive me!" to the rack!*

DEATH. CHAPTER TWELVE

Could you measure, weigh, count and judge correctly, you would not discharge such words from a hollow head. You curse and demand vengeance without understanding and without need. What use is such asininity? We have already said: all that is rich in thought, noble, honourable, upright, and everything living, must perish by Our hand. Yet you yap and say that all your felicity lies in your pure, honest wife. If you take the view that felicity lies in wives, then We shall advise you to remain in felicity. But take heed that it turn not to disaster!

Tell Us: when you took your laudable wife, did you find her, or did you make her, virtuous? If you found her in virtue, then seek sensibly: you will find many more virtuous, pure women on Earth, one of whom may become your spouse; if, however, you made her virtuous, then rejoice: you are the living master, who can create and educate a wife in virtue.

But I shall tell you something else: the more love that fell your way, the more sorrow will befall you; if you had abstained from love, you would now be relieved of sorrow; the greater the love you enjoy, the greater the sorrow of life without love. Wife, child, wealth and all earthly goods must bring some measure of joy at first, and a greater of sorrow at last; all earthly love must turn to sorrow; sorrow is love's end, the end of joy is grief, sadness must follow pleasure, the enjoyment of one's will must end in disaffection—to such an end all living things must run. Learn a little more, if you wish to cackle with wisdom!

THE PLOWMAN. CHAPTER THIRTEEN

After injury comes insult; those in distress feel this all too well. And in this wise am I, an injured man, served by you. You have unbedded me from love and wedded me to sorrow; so long as God wills, must I suffer this at your hands. However dull-witted I may be, however little wisdom I may have acquired from sagacious masters, I am still well aware that you are the robber of my honour, the thief of my joys, the stealer of my good days, the devastator of my delights, and the destroyer of all that procured and guaranteed me a blissful life. Wherefore shall I now rejoice? Where shall I seek solace? Where shall I have refuge? Where shall I find a place of healing? Where shall I take good counsel? Gone is gone! All my delight is gone! She has disappeared from me before her time; she has flown away from me too soon; you have torn her from me all too hastily, the faithful one rich in love, thus making without mercy a widower of me and orphans of my children. Miserable, alone, overwhelmed by grief, I remain without your compensation; you have not yet been able to make me amends for your great misdemeanour. What of you, Master Death, universal marriage-breaker? No one may gain any good from you; you will give no one satisfaction for criminal deeds; you will make no one amends for evil. I see it: compassion does not live with you; curses are your daily fare; you are merciless in all places. Such benefaction as you confer on man, such favour as man receives from you, such reward as you give man, such an end as you bring man, may He who has power over life and death send you! Prince of the Heavenly Host, make good to me my tremendous loss, my great afflication, my wretched sorrow and pitiful call to arms! So avenge me on the arch-rogue, on Death, God, avenger of atrocity!

DEATH. CHAPTER FOURTEEN

Idle words; as much said as silence. For foolish words must lead to discord, discord to enmity, enmity to conflict, conflict to injury, injury to sorrow, and sorrow to repentance, for every confused man. You announce discord to Us. You complain that We have caused your sorrow through your so very dear wife. Yet she has been served with kindness and mercy: We have taken her into Our grace in joyful youth, with a proud body, in the best days of her life, with the highest esteem, at the best time, with honour inviolate. The prophets extolled this, they craved this, when they said: "It is best to die when it is best to live." He did not die well who desired death; he has lived too long who calls on Us for death; woe and hardship to him who is overloaded with the burden of age: in the midst of wealth he is poor!

In the year of the Ascension, on the Feast Day of Heaven's Gatekeeper's Chains, when 6,599 years were counted since the beginning of the World*, at the birth of a child, We bid the blessed martyress leave this short spell of shining misery, with the intention that she come full of grace, after good services, to the eternal joy, everlasting life, and unending peace, of God's inheritance. However spiteful you may be toward Us, We shall wish without grudges that your soul abide with hers in the celestial dwelling up there, and your body with hers in the terrestrial vault down here. We would stand surety to you that you will enjoy her beneficence. Be silent, cease! As little as you can deprive the sun of its light, the moon of its coldness, fire of its heat, and water of its wetness, so little can you rob Us of Our power.

THE PLOWMAN. CHAPTER FIFTEEN

A guilty man needs to colour his words. As you are doing. It is your custom to show yourself sweet and sour, gentle and harsh, kind and severe, to those you intend to deceive: so much is clear from my experience. However much gloss you give yourself, I know that I must live grief-stricken without the woman of nobility and grace for the sake of your vehement disfavour. I also know that no one has command of such power except you and God. But I am not tormented so by God: for if I had trespassed against God, which has, alas, ofttimes happened, He would have taken revenge on me, or the flawless lady would have atoned for me.

The malefactor is you. And so I would like to know who you are, what you are, where you are, whence you are, and what good you do, for you to possess so much power and to have challenged me so evilly without warning, desolated my bliss-covered meadow, undermined and brought down my tower of strength.

Ah God, Consoler of all afflicted hearts, console and compensate me, this poor, grieving, miserable, lone-sitting man! Send, Lord, plagues; undertake retaliation; shackle and eradicate abominable Death, Your enemy, and enemy to all! Truly, Lord, there is nothing in Your creation more heinous, nothing more hideous, nothing more cruel, nothing more unjust, than Death! He distresses and destroys Your entire earthly realm; he takes the upright away before the dishonest; the harmful, the old, the infirm, the useless, he often leaves here; the good and the useful, he carries all of them off. Pass judgment, Lord, just judgment on the false judge!

DEATH. CHAPTER SIXTEEN

Senseless people name evil good, call good evil. As you are doing. You accuse Us of passing false judgment: you do Us injustice. We shall prove this to you. You ask who We are: We are God's handle, Master Death, a truly effective reaper. Our scythe works its way. It cuts down white, black, red, brown, green, blue, grey, yellow, and all kinds of lustrous flowers in its path, irrespective of their splendour, their strength, their virtue. And the violet's beautiful colour, rich perfume, and palatable sap, avail it nought. See: that is justice. Our justification was acknowledged by the Romans and the poets, for they knew Us better than you do.

You ask what We are: We are nothing, and yet something. Nothing, because We have neither life, nor being, nor form, and We are no spirit, not visible, not tangible; something, because We are the end of life, the end of existence, the beginning of nullity, a cross between the two. We are a happening that fells all people. Huge giants must fall before Us; all living beings must be transformed by Us.

You ask where We are: We are not ascertainable. But Our form was found in a temple in Rome*, painted on a wall, as a hoodwinked man sitting on an ox; this man wielded a hatchet in his right hand and a shovel in his left hand, with which he was beating the ox. A great crowd of all kinds of people was hitting him, fighting him, and making casts at him, each one with the tools of his trade: even the nun with her psalter was there. They struck and made casts at the man on the ox, he who signified Us; yet Death contested and buried them all. Pythagoras likens Us to a man's form with the eyes of a basilisk: they wandered to the ends of the Earth, and every living creature had to die at their glance.

You ask where We are: We are from the Earthly Paradise. God created Us there and gave Us Our true name, when he said: "The day that ye bite of this fruit, ye shall die the death." And for that reason We call ourself: "We, Death, mighty ruler and master on Earth, in the air, and in the rivers of the sea."

You ask what good We do: you have already heard that We bring the world more advantage than harm. Now cease, rest content, and thank Us for the kindness we have done you!

THE PLOWMAN. CHAPTER SEVENTEEN

Old men can tell new tales; learned men unknown tales; far-travelled men, whom no one dares contradict, may freely venture to tell fictitious tales, for they speak of unknown matters and are thus exempt from punishment. Now, if you are one of those old men, you may well be fabricating. Although you fell into the worldly paradise as a reaper who strives after justice, your scythe hews unevenly: it uproots the flowers with violence, and leaves thistles standing; the weeds remain, the good herbs must perish. You claim that your scythe cuts straight ahead. How is it, then, that it leaves unscathed more thistles than flowers, more caraway than camomile, more evil people than good? Tell me, show me with your finger: where are the upright, worthy people of past days? I maintain: you have taken them away. My beloved is away with you; only the ashes remain. Where have they gone, they who lived on Earth and talked with God, who won grace and favour and mercy from His hands? Where have they gone, they who had their seat on Earth, who walked beneath the stars and determined the planets? Where have they gone, the profound, the masterly, the righteous, the sprightly men, about whom the chronicles have so much to say? All of them, and my gentle one, you have murdered; the base people are still here. Who bears the guilt for that? If you dared admit the truth, Master Death, you would name yourself. You insist that you judge fairly, spare no one, and the strokes of your scythe fell them one after the other. I stood there and saw with my own eyes two immense hosts—each numbering over three thousand men—fighting one another on a green heath; they were wading up to the ankles in blood. And among them there was you, buzzing and whirring with great diligence all around. You killed quite a few of the army; you left quite a few standing. I saw more lords than servants lying dead. You would pick one from the rest like so many soft pears. Is that how to reap justly? Is that how to judge justly? Is that your scythe cutting straight ahead? Come here, dear children, come here! Let us ride toward, let us sing the praises of, let us offer honour to Death, who judges so justly! God's judgment is hardly so just.

DEATH. CHAPTER EIGHTEEN

Who understands nothing of the matter, he can say nothing of the matter. And this has happened to Us. We did not know that you were so splendid a man. We have known you for a long time; but We had forgotten you.

We were there when the Sibyll informed you with wisdom; when Solomon, on his death-bed, bequeathed his wisdom to you; when God granted you all the power He had conferred on Moses in the land of Egypt; when you grabbed a lion by the legs and beat it against the wall.* We saw you count the stars, calculate the number of grains of sand, and of fishes in the sea, and measure raindrops. In Babylon, We saw you proffering food and drink with great honour and dignity to the Sultan. When you carried the banner before King Alexander under which he defeated Darius, We watched you and willingly allowed you the honour. When, in Academia and in Athens, you debated with distinguished, knowledgeable masters, who spoke so expertly about divinity, yet you so wisely prevailed over them, then We were especially delighted. When you instructed Nero to exercise righteousness and be patient, We heard you with a willing ear. We were surprised when you bore the Emperor Julius over the raging sea in a ship of reeds, defying the stormy gales. We saw you in your workshop, weaving a noble garment out of rainbows; angels, birds, animals, and all kinds of fish were fashioned in it; and the Owl and the Ape were woven in the woof. We laughed especially hard and extolled you when, in Paris, you sat on the Wheel of Fortune, danced on an ox's hide, worked in the Black Arts and exorcised the Devil into a peculiar glass. When God called you to His council, to speak about the Fall of Lady Eve, then, for the first time, We became cognisant of your great wisdom.

If We had realised who you were, We would have done as you command; We would have allowed your wife and all mankind to live for ever. And We would have done this to honour you alone: for you are, in truth, an intelligent ass!

THE PLOWMAN. CHAPTER NINETEEN

Men must often endure mockery and ill-treatment for the sake of the truth. And this is happening to me. You extol me for impossible things, for effecting unheard-of works. You exercise far too much force; you have treated me wickedly; and I am sorely grieved. Yet when I speak of this, you are spiteful to me and full of rage. Whoever commits evil and will not submit to accept punishment and suffer, but arrogantly resists, let him keep a close watch that he be not met with enmity!

Take me as an example! Whether you have proceeded too peremptorily, or too irremediably, unkindly or unjustly with me, I show tolerance and do not take vengeance, as I should by rights. And today I shall go further: if my manner toward you has been unreasonable or unseemly in any way, then tell me: I shall gladly and willingly make this good. But if this be not the case, then recompense me for my loss or instruct me what compensation I can draw for my great heartache. Truly, never before did such a reduction befall man. In spite of everything, you shall witness my moderation. Either you redress the malicious wrong you have committed against my sorrow-averter, against me and my children, or you come with me to God, who is the righteous judge of me, and you, and all the world. You may well request that I leave the matter in your hands; I trusted you to see your unjustness for yourself and afterwards give me satisfaction for your grievous undeed. Follow your reason! Otherwise the hammer must striketh anvil, force against force, come what may!

DEATH. CHAPTER TWENTY

People are pacified by good words, reason holds people to moderation, patience brings people to honour, and an angry man cannot decide what is truth. Had you spoken amicably to Us earlier, We would have amicably instructed you that you may not, in all propriety, lament and weep for the death of your wife. Do you know nothing of the sage who wished to die in the bath, have you not read in his books that no one should lament a mortal's death? If you know it not, then know it now: as soon as a human is born, so soon does he drink to clinch the deal of death. The end is brother to the beginning. He who is sent out is obliged to return. No one may resist what must come to pass. No individual may gainsay that which all humans must suffer. A man shall return what he has borrowed. All humans are strangers on this Earth. They must pass from something to nothing. Every man's life runs along on fast feet: this moment, living; in the turning of a hand, dead.

To briefly conclude: every human owes the debt of death and has inherited death. If you weep for your wife's youth, you are wrong to do so; as soon as a human has life, so soon is he old enough to die. Perhaps you think that age is a precious treasure? No, it is infirm, laborious, misshapen, cold, and ill-pleasing to all people; it avails nought and is suited to nothing: early apples fall gladly into manure; over-ripe pears fall gladly into a puddle.

If you lament her beauty, then that is childish of you: every single human's beauty must be destroyed by either age or death. All rosy little mouths must ashen; all red little cheeks must pale; all shining little eyes must darken. Have you not read where Hermes, the sage, teaches that a man should beware of beautiful women, saying: "What is beautiful is difficult to keep, even with daily care, for it is coveted by all; what is ugly is easy to keep, for it is displeasing to all." Let go! Do not lament a loss you cannot retrieve.

THE PLOWMAN. CHAPTER TWENTY-ONE

"Accept good punishment with good grace: that is the act of a wise man!" I hear sage voices proclaim. Your punishment is also bearable. Now, if a good punisher is supposed to be a good instructor, then advise me, teach me how I am to excavate, eradicate and expel such unspeakable sorrow, such deplorable grief, such sadness beyond measure from my heart, from my mind and from my senses. By God, it was unspeakable heartache that befell me when my chaste, true and constant household honour was so hastily torn away from me—she is dead, I am a widower, and my children are become orphans.

Oh Master Death, all the world complains of you, and so do I. But since there was never a man so evil that he was not good for something: advise me, help me, show me how I may cast such heavy sorrow from my heart, and how so pure a mother may be replaced for my children! Otherwise I must be disgruntled, and she sad, always. And you should not take this ill of me; for I see that, among the unreasoning beasts, an inner compulsion drives one spouse to mourn the other's death.

You owe me help, advice, and compensation; you did me the harm. If this does not happen, then even if God in His omnipotence had no vengeance, it would still have to be avenged, should shovel and hoe be exerted once more.

DEATH. CHAPTER TWENTY-TWO

Gack, gack, gack, gabbles the goose; howl, howl, says the wolf; one may preach whatever one wishes. And such is the yarn that you spin. We have already explained to you that Death shall be beyond the impeachment of mortals. The reason being that We are a tax-collector, to whom humankind must declare and pay the toll of their lives. So why do you resist? Truly: he who will deceive Us deceives himself.

Now listen, and make sure that this sinks in: life is created for the sake of Death. If life were not, We would not be, and Our business were nought; nor would the world order exist. Either you are filled too deeply with sorrow, or unreason is housing inside you. If you are from your reason, then beseech God to grant you rationality! If you are filled with sorrow, however, then stop, let go, and take this on board: man's life on Earth is but a breath of wind!

You ask for advice on how to put the grief from your heart. Aristotle once taught you that joy, sorrow, hope, and fear, these four emotions, encumber all the world, especially those who cannot guard themselves against them. Joy and fear shorten, hope and sorrow lengthen, the duration of time. Whoever does not banish these four from his mind must live with anxiety at all times. After joy sorrow, after love grief: such is the way of this Earth. Joy and grief must always be bound together. The end of one is where the other begins. Grief and joy are nothing other than a man grasping a thought and refusing to release it; likewise, the undemanding are never poor, and the demanding never know wealth: for sufficiency and insufficiency are not relative to possessions, or to external things, but only to the mind. Whoever will not drive all love from his heart must bear the presence of grief at all times. Drive the remembrance of love from your heart, from your senses, from your mind, and at once you will be relieved from sorrow! The moment you have lost something you cannot regain, make as if it had never been yours! And your sorrow will instantly leave.

If you will not do this, then further grief awaits you. For heartache will beset you after the death of each child, and heartache to all of them after your death; to you and to them, when the time comes to part from one another. You want their mother to be replaced. If you can bring back past years, spoken words and lost maidenhood, then bring your children their mother. I have counselled you enough. Can you understand, blunt-wit?

THE PLOWMAN. CHAPTER TWENTY-THREE

Time brings man to an awareness of this truth: the more learned, the more able. Your pronouncements are sweet and lively, as I am now beginning to perceive. But if joy, love, delight and diversion should be banished from the world, then the world would be in a bad way. Let us consider the Romans. They taught their children to follow their example and hold joy in honour, to tourney, joust, race, leap, and pursue all kinds of virtuous courtly arts in their leisure-time, to the intent that this would keep them out of the reach of evil. For the thoughts of man's mind cannot be idle: it must be working good or evil at all times; not even in sleep may it rest. If good thoughts were taken from the mind, evil ones would enter. Good out, evil in; evil out, good in; and this exchange must endure until the end of the world. Ever since joy, breeding, modesty, and other courtly virtues have been expelled from the world, have malice, disgrace, faithlessness, mockery and betrayal filled it to overflowing; as you may see everyday.

Now, if I were to beat the memory of my dearly beloved from my mind, an evil memory would return to my head: all the more reason for keeping my dearly beloved in constant remembrance. When great, heartfelt love is transformed into great, heartfelt sorrow, who can forget this so soon? That is what evil people do. Good friends think always of one another; distant roads, long years, do not part dear friends. She may be dead to me in body; she is ever living in my mind. Sir Death, you must advise more truly, if your counsel is to bring benefit; or else you must, Sir Bat, even more than the sparrowhawk, bear the enmity of birds!

DEATH. CHAPTER TWENTY-FOUR

No joy too great, no sorrow too deep, should affect the wise man during profit or loss. It affects you. He who asks for advice then will not follow the counsel given is not to be advised. Our wise words are lost on you. Now whether you like it or loathe it, We shall bring you the truth to light: listen who will.

Your short understanding, your clipped mind, your hollow heart, will make more of mankind than it has the power to become. Make of a man what you will, yet he cannot be more than this I say to you, with the leave of all pure women: a human is conceived in sin, nourished with impure, unspeakable feculence in the maternal body, born naked and smeared like a beehive; a mass of refuse, a churn of filth, a dish for worms, a stinkhouse, a repulsive washtub, a rancid carcass, a mildewed crate, a bottomless sack, a perforated pocket, a bellows, a rapacious maw, a reeking flagon of urine, a malodorous pail, a deceptive marionette-show, a loamy robber's den, an insatiably slaking trough, a painted delusion. Let recognise who will: every human created to completion has nine holes in his body; out of all these there flows such repellent filth that nothing could be more impure. You would never see human beauty, if you had the eyes of a lynx, and your gaze could penetrate to the innards; you would shudder at the sight. Strip the dressmaker's colouring from the loveliest of ladies, and you will see a shameful puppet, a hastily withering flower, a sparkle of little durance and a soon decomposing clod of earth! Show me a handful of beauty of all the belles who lived a hundred years ago, excluding those painted on the wall, and you shall have the Kaiser's crown! Let love flow away, let grief flow away! Let the Rhine run its course like other waters, you wise lad from Assville!

THE PLOWMAN. CHAPTER TWENTY-FIVE

Pah to you, you evil sack of shame! How you destroy, maltreat, and dishonour noble mankind, God's dearest creation, thereby reviling divinity! Now, for the first time, I see that you are mendacious and not created in Paradise as you claimed. Had you been in Paradise, you would know that God created man and all things, and created them wonderfully well; He set man above them all, conferred on him dominion over them all, and made them subservient to his feet, so that man should rule over the beasts of the earth, the birds of the air, the fish in the sea, and all fruits of the soil; and man does. Now if man were as despicable, evil and impure as you say, then truly, God would have worked an unclean and futile act. Had God's omnipotent Hand created so impure and ordurous a work of man as you say, He were a shameful Creator. And it would not be true that God had created all things, and man over them all, wonderfully well.

Sir Death, cease your pointless yapping! You sully God's most splendid creation. Angels, devils, imps, and birds of death, all these are spirits under the government of God; man is the most noble, the most skilled, and the most free of all God's works. God formed him in His image, as He Himself proclaimed at the Creation of the World.

Where has a workman ever effected so skilled and rich, so masterly and small, a sphere as the human head? Inside it there are artful, wondrous powers, incomprehensible to all spirits. In the eyeball there is the face, the most reliable of witnesses, masterfully worked in the way of a mirror; it reaches the clarity of the heavens. In the ears is the far-reaching sense of hearing, perfectly grated with a thin membrane for the perception and differentiation of a host of sweet sounds. In the nose is the sense of smell, entering and leaving through two holes, purposefully carpentered for the ease and convenience of all sweet and delightful scents. In the mouth are teeth, which grind the body's nourishment every day; also the tongue's thin leaf to pass thoughts between humans; and it holds the pleasurable sense of gustation for every kind of food. And then, in the head, there are thoughts coming from the depths of the heart, with which mankind rapidly reaches as far as he wills; with his thoughts, man clambers toward, and even above, the divine. Only man is in possession of reason, the noble treasure. He alone is the delightful form, whose like none but God is able to shape, and in which all skilled works, all art and mastery, are woven with wisdom. Let go, Sir Death! you are the enemy of man: that is why you speak him ill.

DEATH. CHAPTER TWENTY-SIX

Rebukes, curses, and wishes, no matter how many, can fill no sack, no matter how small. Furthermore: there is no contending with words against garrulous people. Now let Us accept your opinion that man has been endowed with every knowledge, beauty and dignity: he must, notwithstanding, fall into Our net; he must be drawn into Our snare. Grammar, the foundation of all eloquent speech, will not help him with her precise and finely-turned locutions. Rhetoric, the blossoming ground of honeyed words, will not help him with her ornate and richly-coloured expressions. Logic, the insightful demarcator of truth and untruth will not help him with her sly concealment, with the crooked ways that mislead truth. Geometry, the ascertainer, assessor, and measurer of the Earth, will not help him with her unerring measurement, or with her accurate weighing. Arithmetic, skilled marshal of numbers, will not help him with counting and calculations, or with her dexterous digits. Astronomy, Master of the Heavenly Bodies, will not help him with her astral power, the influence of the planets. Music, the organising handmaid of song, will not help him with her sweet melodies, with her harmonious voices. Philosophy, field of wisdom, tilled and sown, and grown to perfection, in knowledge of Nature and God and in the production of ethical living; Physic, with her draughts that help many; Geomancy, skilful respondent to all kinds of questions posed on Earth; Hydromancy, unveiler of the future by dint of the workings of water; Astrology, interpreter of sublunar events through the course of the Heavens; Chiromancy, smart soothsayer from the hand and the lines of the palm; Necromancy, mighty compeller of spirits through the sacrifice of dead men's fingers and secret signs; the musical art, with her select prayers and her strong incantations; the augur, versed in the language of birds and so the true prophet of future events; the haruspex, indicating the future in the smoke of the altar-victim; Paedomancy, conjuror with children's intestines, and ornithomancy, with grouse's guts; the jurist, the Christian without conscience: will not help him by twisting right and wrong and passing crooked judgments. These arts, and all those related, avail nought: every man must be felled by Us, scoured in Our fulling-tub and cleaned in Our rolling-press. Take my word, you riotous ploughhand!

THE PLOWMAN. CHAPTER TWENTY-SEVEN

One should not meet evil with evil; man should practise patience, and have the teachings of virtue at his command. I shall tread this path; perhaps this will exhaust your impatience.

I gather from your speech: you believe that you have advised me truly. Now if trueness dwells in you, advise me in good faith, as though after a sworn oath: what direction shall my life take now? Previously I lived in dear and happy wedlock; where should I turn to now? To the secular or the spiritual state? Both stand open to me. My mind formed images of man's many existences, then scrupulously weighed and appraised them: I found them all to be lacking, fragile and in sin. I am uncertain whither I should turn: every human station is tainted with affliction. Sir Death, advise! Advice is of the essence! In my thoughts I find, imagine and believe, in truth, that a home and being so pure, so pleasing to God, will never return. Upon my soul I say: if I knew that I would thrive in marriage as I have formerly done, I would live in that state for as long as my life continued. Blissful, joyful, merry and cheerful is the man with a worthy wife, wherever he may wander. It is a pleasure for such a man to strain for food and strive after honour. It is also a pleasure for him to meet honour with honour, fidelity with fidelity, and good with good. He does not need to watch her; a chaste wife is her own best guard. He who cannot believe and trust his wife must live in perpetual anxiety.

Lord of the Upper Regions, Prince of the Manifold Blessings, happy the man you endow with so spotless a bed-companion! He should look to Heaven and thank you with upraised hands every day.

Do what is best, Sir Death, multipotent Lord!

DEATH. CHAPTER TWENTY-EIGHT

To praise without end, to revile without purpose, at all times and places, is the custom of many. Praise and abuse should be meet and measured, that they be ready at hand when the need for one arises.

You praise married life beyond moderation. But We shall instruct you in the conjugal state, all pure women notwithstanding: as soon as men take a wife, so soon do they enter Our prison, two by two. From that moment on a man has an obligation, a dependent, a hand-drawn sledge, a yoke, a horse-collar, a burden, a pressing load, a devil from Purgatory, a daily grating rust-file, which he cannot rightly rid himself of until We grant him Our grace. A wedded man has thunder and hailstorms, foxes and snakes, in his house every day. A wife strives all her days to become the man; if he pulls up, she pulls down; if he wants this, she wants that; if he wants to go here, she wants to go there—he shall have his fill of such sports and defeat every day. She can deceive, outwit, flatter, concoct, caress, grouch, laugh and weep in the blink of an eye; she was born that way. Sick for work, but healthy for lust; and tame or wild, as suits her purpose. She needs no advisor to find an argument. All the time she strains not to do that which she is bidden, and to do what is forbidden. This is too sweet for her, and that is too sour; this is too much, and that is too little; now it is too early, now it is too late—everything is met with a reproach. If she ever praises anything, her words are turned to shame on a lathe; the praise is thickly mixed with mockery. No means can help a man living in wedlock: if he is too kind, if he is too harsh, he is punished; being kind and severe, half and half, is also no way: it will always incur harm or punition. Every day new presumption or bickering; every week alienating noncompliance or sulking; every month new atrocities or terrors; every year new clothes or daily squabbling: such is the lot of a wedded man, let him behave however he will. We shall keep silence over the aggravations of night, for shame for Our age. If We did not wish to spare the virtuous women, we could sing and say much more about the ones lacking in virtue. So recognise what you are praising: you cannot tell gold from lead!

THE PLOWMAN. CHAPTER TWENTY-NINE

"Those who dishonour women dishonour themselves" say the masters of truth. What is happening to you now, Sir Death? Your irrational vituperation against women, although it is made with their leave, is truly disgraceful for you and ignominious for them. In the writings of many wise masters one finds that, without a woman at the helm, no man may be steered to happiness; having a wife and child is not the slightest part of earthly joy. With such truth did Philosophy, the wise Mistress, bring peace to the mind of Boethius, the Roman rich in consolation. Every exceptional and thoughtful man is my witness: no man can keep his discipline if there be not a woman to take him in hand. Let anyone say who wishes: a modest, beautiful, chaste wife of untouched honour is above all earthly delights. I never yet saw a man, no matter how manly and spirited, who was not guided by a woman's words. Where nobility gathers, one sees every day: in all places, at every court, at every tournament, with every army on the march, women bring out what is best. Whoever is in a lady's service must abstain from misdemeanour. Women hold the power of terrestrial delight; they effect that all courtly deeds and pastimes on Earth be performed to their honour. A pure lady's warning finger punishes and disciplines a valiant man more than any weapon. Without glosing, and in few words: noble ladies are the support, the fortification, and the increase of the whole world.

Now, there must be lead among gold, corncockles among wheat, counterfeits among coins, and she-devils among women: but do not make the good pay for the bad. Believe me, Captain of Mountains!*

DEATH. CHAPTER THIRTY

A fool takes a cob for a gold nugget, a piece of horn for topaz, a pebble for a ruby; the idiot calls a barn a mountain, the Danube the Sea, a buzzard a falcon. And so do you praise what feasts the eyes; you pay no thought to causes. For you do not know that everything of this world is either desire of the flesh, or desire of the eyes, or pride in life. Desire of the flesh aims at lust; desire of the eyes at possessions or estate; and pride in life at honour. Possessions bring greed, lust causes lewdness and lechery, and honour brings arrogance and boastfulness. Possessions will lead to desire and fear, lust to malice and sin, and honour to vanity. Could you comprehend this, you would find vanity walking the whole of the world; and if joy or sorrow then befell you, you would endure it in patience and leave Us unreproached.

As well as an ass plucks the lyre, with such skill do you grasp the truth. That is why We are so sorely concerned for you. When We parted the youth Pyramus from the maiden Thisbe, who were one heart and one soul; when we dispossessed King Alexander of world dominion; when we annihilated Trojan Paris and Greek Helen: we were not upbraided so severely as we are now by you. We did not meet with such vexation for Kaiser Karl, Markgrave Willehalm, Dietrich von Bern, Boppe the Strong of Arm, or horn-skinned Siegfried.* Many still lament Aristotle and Avicenna; yet We remained unimpeached. When David, the mighty King, and Solomon, the Shrine of Wisdom, died, We were given more thanks than curses. Those who were in days of yore have all gone; you and everyone, who is now or is yet to be, must follow. For We, Death, remain Master here!

THE PLOWMAN. CHAPTER THIRTY-ONE

A man is often condemned by his own words, especially one who speaks now this, now that. You said earlier that you were something and yet nothing, not even a spirit, but you were the end of life and all of Earth's people were commended to your cure. Now you say that we must all hence and you, Sir Death, remain Master here. Two contradictory statements cannot both be true. If we all depart this life, and all earthly beings have an end, and you are, as you say, life's ending, then I reason: where life is not, there can never be dying and death—So where are you, Sir Death? Heaven is no home for you: it is given only to good spirits, and you are, after your own words, no spirit. Now when you have nothing more to manage on Earth, and Earth is gone for ever, then you must straight to Hell; where you must groan without end. Then shall both the living and the dead be avenged on you. No one can set a course by your changing words.

Are all sublunary beings really so evil, wretched and vicious in creation and form? That would be to speak against God, an accusation never levelled against the eternal Creator since the dawn of the world. Hitherto, God has loved virtue, hated evil, and overlooked or punished sin. And I believe that, henceforth, He will do exactly the same. Ever since my youth, I have heard, read and learnt that God created all earthly things. You say that all earthly life and being must have an end. Yet Plato and other messengers of wisdom say that: all events involve the decay of one and the birth of another; recurrence is the universal foundation; and everything in the revolving earth and heavens is an effect eternally transforming between the two. With your swaying words on which no one may build, you intend to deter me from my complaint. So I refer myself and you to God, my Saviour. Sir Death, my undoer, God give you a dire Amen!

DEATH. CHAPTER THIRTY-TWO

Often a man, having launched into speech, cannot cease, unless he is interrupted. And you are stamped with this mark. We have said and We say—and this by way of conclusion—: the Earth, and all it contains, is founded on temporality. In this age, she is become prone to change, for all things are reversed: back has moved to front, and front is back; depths have shifted to mountains, and heights to valleys; evil is made justice, and justice evil: all through the agency of the mass of mankind. I have thrusted the whole human race into fire's steady flame. The chance of finding a good, true, constant friend is almost as great on this Earth as that of grasping a light-beam. All humans are inclined more to evil than good. When someone does do good nowadays, he is acting from fear of Us. All people, and all their activity, are full of vanity. Your body, your wife, your children, your honour, your belongings, and all you possess, all flees away; it disappears in a moment; it drifts away in the wind, neither shine nor shadow can remain. Look, see, observe and note, the intentions of souls on this Earth: how they burrow through hill and vale, wood and field, Alps and deserts, the depths of the sea, the bowels of the Earth, for the sake of earthly goods; how they drive shafts, tunnels and mines down into the earth, boring through Earth's veins, to seek glittering stones, which they love before all things on account of their rarity; how they fell trees, paste together walls, barns and houses like swallows, plant and graft orchards, till the fields, lay down vineyards, build mills, raise the rent, practise fishery, hunting and gaming, drive large herds of cattle together, own numerous serving-lads and maids, ride high on horse, have chests and houses full of gold, silver, precious stones, costly garments and other wares, foster pleasure and lust, which they pursue and strive after night and day—what is the sum of this? All is vanity, a sickness of the soul, as transitory as the day that passed yestereve. They gain this through war and rapine; the greater the possessions, the greater the robbery. They bequeath it to discord and conflict. Oh, mortal man is always in fear, in affliction, in sorrow, in care, in dread, in terror, in days of pain, in days of sickness, in sadness, in mourning, in misery, in grief and in multeity of irritations; and the more worldly wealth a man has, the more annoyances he encounters. And this is the greatest of all, that a human cannot know when, where and how We shall suddenly overfall him and drive him the way of all flesh. This burden must be shouldered by master and servant, husband and wife, rich and poor, good and evil, young and old. O mournful prospect, and so little regarded by the witless! When it is too late, they would all be virtuous. All this is vanity over vanity and sinking of the soul.

So leave your complaining! Enter whichever rank you wish, you will step into affliction and vanity! Now depart from evil, and do good; seek peace, and hold on to it with constancy*; love a pure and clean conscience above all earthly things! And as we have advised you correctly, We shall accompany you to God, the Great, the Mighty, the Eternal.

THE JUDGMENT OF GOD. CHAPTER THIRTY-THREE

Springtide, summer, autumn and winter, the four invigorators and upholders of the year, fell into disaccord and fiery dispute. Every one of them boasted of their beneficence in rain, winds, thunder, showers, and in all kinds of storms; and every one would be the best in his working.

Spring said that he revives all fruit into lush profusion. Summer said that he ripens and readies all fruit for harvest. Autumn said that he brings all fruit to collection in barns, cellars and houses. Winter said that he consumes and expends all fruit and expels all poisonous vermin. They boasted and quarrelled violently. But they had forgotten that they were boasting of powers granted them by God.

As you both are now doing. The plaintiff laments his loss, as though it were his estate; he does not pause to reflect that it was loaned by Us. Death boasts of his mighty powers, which he only received in fief from Us. This one laments what is not his; that one boasts of a power that is not immanent. However, the quarrel is not entirely unfounded. You have both contested well: the one is forced by his sorrow to lament, the other by the plaintiff's attack to tell the truth. So plaintiff, yours is the honour! And Death, yours is the victory! Every man is obliged to give his life to Death, his body to the earth, and his soul to Us.

CHAPTER THIRTY-FOUR. THE PLOWMAN'S PRAYER FOR THE SOUL OF HIS WIFE

Ever-vigilant Watcher over all the world, God of gods, wonder-working Lord above all lords, almighty Spirit of spirits, Prince of all Princedoms, fountainhead of the flow of goodness, Holy of Holies, Crowner and Crown, Rewarder and Reward, Elector in whose curacy lies the cure of all souls: fortune has befallen the man who has entered Thy service! Joy and delight of angels, Moulder of the highest forms, Greyhead and Fresh-Faced Youth: hearken to me!

O Light, that receives none other light; Light, that outshines and darkens all outward light; Radiance, by which all other radiance is occulted; Radiance, in the face of which all lights are darkness, in which every shadow shines bright; Light, which spoke in the Beginning: "Let there be light!"; Fire forever burning, that knows no extinguishment; Beginning and End: hearken to me!

Grace and Salvation over all salvation; Path without pitfalls to life everlasting; Superior with no superior; Life, in which all is living; Truth of all truths; Wisdom circumflowing all wisdom; Holder of all strength; Guard over just and unjust hands; Healer of affliction and error; Plenisher of the needy, Refresher of the sick; Seal of the highest Majesty; Preserver of the harmony of Heaven; sole Perceiver of all human thoughts, Creator rich in invention of all human countenances; powerful Planet of planets; omnifacient Influence over all heavenly bodies; mighty and blissful Steward of the Celestial Court; Law, through which all heavenly rules may never unhinge from their eternal fixing; resplendent Sun: hearken to me!

Eternal Lamp, eternal Permalight; right-faring Sailor, whose cog never sinks; Standard-bearer, beneath whose banner no one walks without victory; Founder of Hell, Architect of Earth; Dammer of the surging sea, Compounder of the inconstant breezes; Strength of fire's heat; Creator of all elements; Sole Herdmaster of thunder, lightning, mist, shower, snow, rain, rainbow, dew, wind, frost, and all their effects; mighty Duke of the entire celestial army; irrefusable Kaiser; mildest, strongest, most merciful Creator: take pity and hearken to me!

Treasure, from which all treasures issue forth; Source, from which all pure springs flow; Guide, who leads none astray; Saviour for every ailment, to whom all things hive and hold, like bees to their queen; Cause of all things: hearken to me!

Cure-bringing Doctor for all epidemics; Master of Masters; unique Father of Creation; ever-present Beholder of all roads and ways; self-empowered Guide from the mother's womb into the Earth's vault; Creator of every form; fast Foundation of all good works; Lover of purity, Hater of crudity, Rewarder of all good deeds; only just Judge; the One, whose Beginning all things never escape in eternity: hearken to me!

Saviour in anxiety; tight Knot, which none can loosen; perfect Being, in command of all perfection; true Perceiver of all secret, universally unbeknown matters; Afforder of eternal joys, Destroyer of earthly delights; Host, Servant, and Household Member of all good people; Hunter, to whom no spoor remains hidden; choice Decanter of all senses; right and concentering Medium of all spheres; grace-conferring Auditor to all who cry to You: hearken to me!

Close support to the needy; Sorrow-averter for all who hope in You; Plenisher of the hungry; sole Effector with the power to make something from nothing and nothing from something; omnipotent Invigorator, Preserver and Annihilator of all ephemerae, time-dependants, and eternals, whose Being, that which You are in Yourself, no one can grasp, gather, depict or convey; highest Good of goods; worthy Lord Jesus: receive unto grace the spirit, receive in mercy the soul of my beloved wife! Give her eternal repose, bathe her with the dew of Your favour, preserve her in the shadow of Your wings! Take her, Lord, into complete sufficiency, where the slightest find the fulfillment of the greatest! Let her, Lord whence she is come, live in Your kingdom with the eternally blessed!

I ache for Margaretha, my chosen wife. Grant her, Lord rich in grace, that she see, behold, and take delight in herself in the mirror of Your Almighty, Eternal Divinity, the Light of all angelic choirs!

All that has its home beneath the Eternal Standard-Bearer's banner, whatever creature it be, help me in saying with blissful intensity, from the depths of my heart: Amen!

[trans. Frank Tobin]

9 781516 510917